The Yellow Jersey Companion to the

TOUR DE FRANCE

Les Woodland is the doyen of British cycling authors. In more than 40 years in the sport he has written 18 books on the subject, published in five countries and three different languages. His first, *Cycle Racing: Training to Win*, stayed in print for more than 20 years.

His other books are as varied as a manual of sound-recording and a guide to the public lavatories of Norfolk.

He lives near Toulouse in south-west France.

The Yellow Jersey Companion to the

TOUR DE FRANCE

Edited by Les Woodland

TED SMART

This edition produced for The Book People Ltd,
Hall Wood Avenue, Haydock, St Helens, WA11 9UL

Published by Yellow Jersey Press 2003

2 4 6 8 10 9 7 5 3 1

Copyright © Yellow Jersey Press 2003

First published in Great Britain in 2003 by
Yellow Jersey Press

Yellow Jersey Press
Random House, 20 Vauxhall Bridge Road,
London SW1V 2SA

Random House Australia (Pty) Limited
20 Alfred Street, Milsons Point, Sydney,
New South Wales 2061, Australia

Random House New Zealand Limited
18 Poland Road, Glenfield, Auckland 10,
New Zealand

Random House (Pty) Limited
Endulini, 5A Jubilee Road, Parktown 2193,
South Africa

The Random House Group Limited Reg. No. 954009
www.randomhouse.co.uk

A CIP catalogue record for this book
is available from the British Library

ISBN 0 224 063189

Papers used by Random House are natural, recyclable
products made from wood grown in sustainable forests.
The manufacturing processes conform to the environmental
regulations of the country of origin

Design & make-up by Roger Walker

Printed and bound in Great Britain by
Mackays of Chatham Ltd, Chatham, Kent

The Tour de France has the major fault of dividing the country, right down to the smallest hamlet, even families, into two rival camps. I know a man who grabbed his wife and held her on the grill of a heated stove, seated and with her skirt held up, for favouring Jacques Anquetil when he preferred Raymond Poulidor. The following year, the woman became a Poulidor-iste. But it was too late. The husband had switched his allegiance to Gimondi. The last I heard they were digging their heels in and the neighbours were complaining.

PIERRE CHANY

Foreword

The Métro map of Paris could be clearer but it should be easy enough to find Line 9. Run your finger along to Montmartre station and you're at the stop you want.

When you surface, you will be standing between two of the most important sites in cycling. To one side is a garish music bar called TGI Friday's, formerly the Taverne Zimmer. Turning in the other direction you will see the rue du Faubourg Montmartre. Walk down its gentle slope and on the right, opposite the Théâtre du Nord-Ouest, you'll see a video shop at number 10. The two floors above this belonged, until the end of the second world war, to a newspaper called *L'AUTO*, edited by HENRI DESGRANGE.

At first *L'Auto* wasn't a success, since Desgrange was neither an experienced editor nor an original thinker. His backers began to get restless at stagnant sales and the continuing success of a rival paper, *Le Vélo*, which they had hoped to kill off. The pressure was on Desgrange to think of an idea, and he couldn't.

There was a boardroom on those upper floors, with a stone staircase from the financial offices below. It was at a crisis meeting in that room, behind the street windows, that a 26-year-old rugby writer and AMATEUR cyclist called GÉO LEFÈVRE hesitatingly came up with an answer. He had been poached from *Le Vélo* for his brightness, and this was the moment he showed it. Lefèvre suggested a publicity stunt so outrageous that nobody could top it: a bike race that would go right round the country.

Desgrange, unconvinced, said, 'If I understand you right, *petit Géo*, you're proposing a Tour de France.' He hesitated, looked at his watch, and took Lefèvre to the Taverne Zimmer in the Boulevard Montmartre. This, as we have seen, is now TGI Friday's, and there's a small display, including an old bike, in one corner to commemorate the episode. The two men had lunch and Lefèvre ran through the idea over coffee. Desgrange said no more than that it was 'interesting' and that he'd mention it to Victor Goddet, the head of the paper's financial side. Goddet would dismiss the idea, he thought, thus saving further decision. But Goddet agreed, and so in a single column on January 19 1903 *L'Auto* announced the greatest bike race in the world.

It began, then, as a stunt. Newspapers liked long races because travel for most people in those days went little further than they could walk, and to ride a bicycle huge distances caught their imagination. Furthermore, a race would sell papers in every village it passed through. There was no other way to find out who had won.

That first Tour de France started hesitantly with riders not showing much interest; but it took off when the prizes were increased, pocket money promised, and distances cut. The second race, in 1904, raised such passions that crowds pushed and towed riders they favoured, and beat up those they didn't. At one point the authorities had to use gunfire to disperse mobs assembled in the darkness outside St-Étienne.

Worse, so many riders were disqualified for cheating in that Tour – including all the leaders – that Desgrange insisted that the 1904 Tour would be the last (*see* THE 1904 AFFAIR). It had been killed by the 'blind' emotions it had aroused, he said. But luckily for us, for whom the Tour is not only a race but the sport itself, the Tour de France went on. It has produced many more scandals. In fact just as you think it has reached some sort of middle-aged respectability, it turns up another incident to show that whatever it lacks, it's not bad taste, excess or scandal.

Desgrange's Tours – the word means 'circuit' rather than 'sightseeing trip' of English usage – were true tours of France. Stages covered vast distances, sometimes starting one evening to finish the next. Nothing could limit Desgrange. The sport had few rules in general, and none at all for a race of this length. If Desgrange needed more regulations, he made them up. Often he would announce a rider's disqualification in his own paper, *L'Auto*, for he was a tyrant who acted as organiser, judge, journalist and court of appeal. When national officials disqualified riders in 1904, what upset Desgrange more than the crookery was the fact that others had dared to interfere with his fiefdom.

Eventually things went too far. It was all very well for Desgrange to demand that the riders should race more than 500km in a day, but nobody could do it. No doubt they could manage the distance, even on foul roads and with heavy BIKES. They could cope with Desgrange's high-handed insistence that they were not to use GEARS, nor to share the pace in the most elementary of tactics, nor even to remove a jersey as the sun came up. But what they couldn't do was *race*. So they trudged through the day in a spectacle that excited nobody and exhausted everyone, and finally Desgrange learned his lesson.

His response was to trim the daily distance but make the race a month long. Speeds increased, but still the route shadowed the Belgian border and then the coast before ploughing through both the Alps and the Pyrénées before returning to Paris. The result was the same except that instead of trudging round France, riders began DOPING themselves to do it at speed.

So it was that JEAN MALLÉJAC collapsed at the foot of MONT VENTOUX, his legs still turning phantom pedals. TOM SIMPSON died at the top, drugged into exhaustion. FERDY KÜBLER ran foaming at the mouth into a café on the way down and shouted, 'Watch out – Ferdy's going to explode.' CHARLY GAUL rode with fleck-edged lips, like Kübler, and went on to become a recluse and lose his memory. And there were many more like them.

The Tour doctor, PIERRE DUMAS, spoke of riders swallowing substances or injecting themselves without consideration for health or hygiene. The French MANAGER, MARCEL BIDOT, said 'Three-quarters of the riders are doped. I visit their rooms each evening; I always leave frightened.' Simpson's death in 1967, by which time JACQUES GODDET (Victor Goddet's son) had taken over, forced international officials to intervene. They limited distances and days, and insisted on rest. In time they insisted, too, on more convincing dope controls.

Goddet and his colleague FÉLIX LÉVITAN brought the Tour into its modern era, although still insisting that 'excess is necessary'. They were the bridge between Desgrange with his desire to make men suffer like mules and the modern wish for a race of excitement. The Tour is still fiercely commercial, and it's no less of a business than it was when Desgrange started it. But it's also a true sporting event, glamorous, colourful and tense.

Riders have changed, too. No doubt, a university education is still not a requirement. In the 1980s LAURENT FIGNON was called 'the Professor' not only for his scholarly looks but because he'd been to university. ERWAN MENTHÉOUR and the American rider George Mount were both considered exotically academic because they read books. But gone are the men who, like old boxers, relied on brawn to overcome the absence of brain, for whom the alternative to riding was long hours down the mine or in the fields. Racing cyclists don't earn as much as tennis players, and get less per hour than soccer players. But they are well paid, earning a living wage at one end of the scale, and becoming millionaires at the other.

There's a tale that so many people turn out to watch the riders go past that the French economy dips 10 per cent during the Tour. It's a nice story and it may be true. But July is a holiday month in France, and those people by the roadside or in front of their televisions probably wouldn't be at work anyway. But even so, the Tour claims one hundred million television viewers across the world, the third largest audience after the summer Olympics and soccer's World Cup. And even if all worldwide TV figures are suspect, it's undeniable that pictures go out to 160 countries. Which isn't far short of all of them.

You only have to watch the Tour on TV to realise how different it is from other cycling events. It's a rare moment when riders don't have an audience, and it's an audience that goes to enormous trouble to watch. When the stage to SESTRIERE was cancelled in 1996 because a gale, sweeping snow and thickening ice made the MOUNTAINS unrideable, there were still spectators up there disappointed and resentful to see the riders go by in heated buses.

Races like the Giro in ITALY and the Vuelta in SPAIN can only dream of such loyalty, or the national importance of an event that can close the centre of Paris and bring in presidents and politicians merely so that advertisement-plastered cyclists can ride around for the benefit of loan companies, washing machine makers and freesheet newspapers. The commercial reality of the Tour is in blunt contrast to its conclusion in the Champs Elysées, with the Marseillaise booming out and speeches being made about the glory of the Republic, as opposed to the shabbiness of men selling their bodies in order to boost sales of fly spray.

But that is the essence of the Tour: back-breaking slog, muscle-tearing speed and sheer bad taste. It's no wonder it caught on. It's lasted 100 years and there's no sign it won't get better yet.

LES WOODLAND
St-Maurin, France

Note to the reader

Names are difficult. I have tried to spell them as the riders spelled them. That means a small *V* in Dutch names such as van Steenbergen and a small *D* in French names such as de Gaulle (although not in Dutch and Flemish-Belgian names). When, as with Roger De Vlaeminck, he has publicly said he doesn't much care if it's spelled De Vlaeminck or Devlaeminck, I have chosen the more popular option.

Towns and cities are trickier. I have tried to use the English equivalent where one exists – Dunkirk rather than Dunkerque, The Hague rather than Den Haag. Where there are alternative spellings but no English convention, as in Kortrijk and Courtrai, I have used the local name (in this case Kortrijk). A few places are in transition; Marseille seems to be losing the final S given it in English. I have used the local version.

In results, I have referred to race leaders throughout as yellow jerseys; this is inaccurate for the first years when there was no yellow jersey, but it seemed simpler. The jerseys for mountains and points are more recent, though, and the results list riders as 'leaders.'

Many races are called by different names in different countries. I have tried to use the same convention as with towns and cities. So it's 'Tour of Flanders' rather than 'Ronde van Vlaanderen', but 'Critérium des As' rather than 'Criterium of the Aces'. It's hard to be consistent because many races outside France are nevertheless better known by their French name, such as the 'Bicyclette Basque' in Spain.

To save space, small linking words are omitted in results: 'Tour Lombardy' rather than 'Tour *of* Lombardy', for instance.

The Companion

DJAMOLIDINE ABDOUJAPAROV
b. Tashkent, USSR, Feb 28 1964

Djamolidine Abdoujaparov was the Tour's leading sprinter of the early 1990s, winning the green JERSEY in 1991, 1993 and 1994. All sprinters take chances, bump shoulders and push through seemingly impossible gaps, but Abdoujaparov was so brave or foolish that he earned the NICKNAME of 'the Tashkent Terror', Tashkent being the area of the former Soviet Union where he was born.

In 1991, the year in which his homeland fell to bits with the end of the Cold War, Abdoujaparov did the same in the Tour. With only 60m to go of a 3,914km race, he crashed on the CHAMPS ELYSÉES while sprinting head-down for the line. Hitting the barrier at the side of the road, he flew over the handlebars.

The Australian PHIL ANDERSON said, 'We were both going full out and he just put his head down and ran into the wall.' Abdoujaparov – who was points leader and had won stages at Lyon and Reims – broke his collarbone and lay unconscious in the road. He eventually got to his feet and was helped across the line on foot. An ambulance took him to hospital, where he stayed for two days.

Abdoujaparov's role in the Tour was as brief as it was entertaining. He won his last stage in 1996, at Tulle, the year that ERIK ZABEL took over as the Tour's best SPRINTER. Abdoujaparov rode only one more Tour, in 1997,

before retiring – a decision prompted by a two-year ban following positive DOPING controls that year, including one in the Tour. He had already tested positive in 1989.

Abdoujaparov's memory lives on outside cycling. In October 1998, the year after the ban, Les Carter, the cycling fan and former Carter USM guitarist, formed a rock band with his name. The band has toured BRITAIN, GERMANY, Australia and AMERICA.

Djamolidine Abdoujaparov's name is pronounced *jah-mohl-ih-*DEEN *ahb-doo-ja-*PAHR-*awf.*

Winner

| 1991 | Ghent-Wevelgem, Tour Piedmont |

Tour de France

1990	145th	
1991	85th	Stage wins Lyon—Lyon, Dijon-Reims, and Points winner
1992	DNF	
1993	76th	Stage wins Vannes—Dinard, Orthez—Bordeaux, Viry—Chatillon—Paris, and Points winner
1994	57th	Stage wins Lille—Armentières, Morzine—Lac de Saint-Point, and Points winner
1995	56th	Stage win Sainte Geneviève des Bois—Paris
1996	78th	Stage win Besse—Tulle
1997	DNF	

VITTORIO ADORNI

b. San Lazzaro di Parma, Italy, Nov 14 1937

ITALY looked for many years for a successor to GINO BARTALI, who had retired in 1954, and FAUSTO COPPI, who died of malaria in 1960 after a racing and hunting trip in what is now Burkina Faso, Africa. For a while it looked as though it had found such a successor in Vittorio Adorni.

Adorni began cycling for pleasure in 1955, won a few minor competitions and then began racing seriously. He became Italian pursuit champion in 1958 and won 30 races as an AMATEUR. He turned professional after the Rome Olympics in 1960, for which he was picked only as a reserve even though he was national pursuit champion, and won 89 races in a career that lasted until 1970.

His talent and tactical ability won him the world championship in 1968 and the Giro d'Italia – then still mainly an Italian race with few foreign riders – in 1965. But he was too poor a SPRINTER and too tall and heavy – 1.82m and 76kg – to ride well in the MOUNTAINS. His Tour performances were therefore disappointing. He started three times, 1962, 1964 and 1965, but finished only in 1964, and never won a stage or a JERSEY.

Adorni set out to win selected races rather than ride well all year. 'You don't have to win lots of races each year to keep your market value high,' he said. 'It is the big wins that count.'

What Italy wanted, though, was a Coppi or Bartali who could win anywhere, and ride the best off their wheels. They grew tired of Adorni and viewed him as a classy dilettante, good for what they perceived as second-class stage races like the Tour of BELGIUM but not where it counted.

In 1970 he became a team MANAGER, helping MARINO BASSO and FELICE GIMONDI to win world championships in 1972 and 1973. From 1974 he became involved in ski and other sporting promotions, particularly the winter Olympics at Innsbruck in 1976 and the Montreal Games of 1976. In 1976 he opened an insurance business, which he still runs.

Winner

1964	Tour Sardinia
1965	Giro d'Italia, Tour Romandie
1966	GP Lugano, Tour Belgium
1967	Tour Romandie
1968	World championship
1969	Tour Reggio Calabria, Tour Switzerland, National championship

Tour de France

1962	DNF
1964	10th
1965	DNF

JAN ADRIAENSSENS

b. Willebroek, Belgium, Jun 6 1932

Some riders are made for stage races but rarely reach the headlines, and Jean 'Jan' Adriaenssens was one. He rode eight Tours and finished six times in the first ten, including third in 1956 and 1960, and fourth in 1958, and wore the yellow JERSEY in 1956 and 1960. Never once did he win a stage but that didn't matter to his SPONSORS and team-mates. Adriaenssens was a perfect team man, constantly supporting his leaders but still talented enough to make his mark.

His luckiest move came in 1960 on the stage to Lorient. The Tour was at that time still between NATIONAL TEAMS and Adriaenssens was riding for BELGIUM. The favourites were FRANCE but the French, as so often, were riven by rivalries and personality clashes. In the French team were the world-class pursuiter ROGER RIVIÈRE and HENRY ANGLADE, a small and difficult man whom Robert Chapatte (*see* BROADCASTING) had nicknamed 'Napoléon'. (*See* NICKNAMES for other riders.) Anglade's unpopularity was so widespread that it stuck.

Anglade and Rivière particularly disliked each other. The previous year Rivière had contrived to stop Anglade winning the Tour by helping FEDERICO BAHAMONTES of Spain to get up to the leaders, and combining with other French riders to keep him there. (*See* HENRY ANGLADE for more details.)

In 1960 Rivière won the first TIME TRIAL but Anglade had taken the yellow jersey by stage six. Rivière's grudge grew. Far from supporting Anglade, he attacked so hard on the Lorient stage that he beat him by 14 minutes in 112km. Adriaenssens stayed with him, along with Gastone Nencini and HANS JUNKERMANN. Adriaenssens gained enough time to move into the yellow jersey. He lost the lead in the Pyrenees but still finished third to Nencini and another Italian, Graziano Battistini, in Paris.

(And see GASTONE NENCINI for why the break led to Rivière's death; see PIERRE BEUFFEUIL for how General de Gaulle aided an unknown rider's victory in that year's Tour.)

Winner

1953	Circuit 6 Provinces
1955	Tour Morocco
1956	Tour Brabant, Four-days Dunkirk
1958	Circuit Ouest

Tour de France

1953	43rd	
1955	28th	
1956	3rd	Yellow Jersey
1957	9th	
1958	4th	
1959	6th	
1960	3rd	Yellow Jersey
1961	10th	

JAN AERTS
b. Laeken, Belgium, Sep 8 1907, d. Bruges, Belgium, Jun 15 1992

BELGIUM's Jan Aerts won three consecutive stages in 1933 to add to the three he'd won earlier in the race, despite opposition from that year's great French team, which included ANDRÉ LEDUCQ, ANTONIN MAGNE, GEORGES SPEICHER and MAURICE ARCHAMBAUD. They were known as 'the team of chums' because of their closeness, according to the writer Albert Baker d'Isy.

Against them Aerts had a team of eight including Georges Ronsse, national champion Georges Lemaire (the first French-speaker in Belgium's NATIONAL TEAM, who died two months later after colliding with a car during the Belgian club championship), and GASTON REBRY. In a reference to Baker d'Isy's name for the French, a Belgian journalist dismissed Belgium's team as 'a fine collection of talents but certainly not a team of chums.' (*See* BENONI BEHEYT for more on disagreement in Belgian teams.)

Aerts won stage four, from Metz to Belfort, won again on the approach to the Pyrenees at Ax-les-Thermes and then at Tarbes, and then on three successive days at BORDEAUX, La Rochelle and Rennes. But these wins came too near the end to make an impression. Aerts had lost time in the Alps (this was the first Tour since 1913 to run clockwise, taking the Alps first) and finished the Tour ninth, 42:53 behind Speicher. (*See* GEORGES SPEICHER for how he was hauled from a nightclub to win the world championship.)

Aerts was first man to win both the world AMATEUR (1927) and professional (1935) road championship. Professionals and amateurs rode together at the Nurburgring in GERMANY in 1927, and although Aerts finished fifth he won his title by being best amateur. The amateur and professional categories rode separately in August 1935, when Aerts won in front of a home crowd at Floreffe, beating Luciano Montero of SPAIN and another Belgian, Staf Danneels, in a race where 26 riders started and only 12 finished. Small fields were normal in early professional championships; in 1936 Antonin Magne was the best of just nine finishers from the 39 who started.

Aerts also won Paris-Brussels in 1931 and came third in Paris-Roubaix in 1935. He was a good SPRINTER, winning 12 Tour stages, but was handicapped by lack of ability in the mountains.

Jan Aerts *(continued)*

Winner

1931	Paris-Brussels
1933	Tour Belgium
1935	World championship
1936	National championship

Tour de France

1929	DNF	
1930	DNF	Stage win Les Sables—Bordeaux
1932	13th	Stage win Paris—Caen and Yellow Jersey
1933	9th	Stage wins Metz—Belfort, Perpignan—Ax-les-Thermes, Luchon—Tarbes, Pau—Bordeaux, Bordeaux—La Rochelle, La Rochelle—Rennes
1935	29th	Stage wins Metz—Belfort, Grenoble—Gap, Digne—Nice, La Roche-sur-Yon—Nantes

AGENTS

Riders know their price – those at the top, anyway – but rarely have time to negotiate. Some arrange their team contracts but CRITERIUM contracts and other deals are settled through agents.

Agents or other forms of intermediary have probably existed since the start of organised cycling. They were at their peak after the second world war, when Jean van Buggenhout of BELGIUM and Daniel Dousset of FRANCE had much of Europe tied up between them.

Van Buggenhout, a former TRACK rider, saw a way to exploit the explosion of criteriums in the 1940s and 50s. Cynics said many business-men backed the wrong side in dealing with German occupiers during the war, and money that felt uncomfortable in their pockets flooded into sport to alleviate consciences. Certainly the growth of money and opportunity opened the way for agents.

Van Buggenhout signed up Belgian riders and became the manipulator of first the country's criteriums and then its SPONSORS, since few riders could race anywhere or ride for anyone without his involvement.

Daniel Dousset, who died aged 80 in October 1997, was a track rider in the 1930s and 1940s, particularly in six-day races. He turned to management and took on the five-time Tour winner JACQUES ANQUETIL, the 1962 world champion JEAN STABLINSKI, the 1966 Tour winner LUCIEN AIMAR, the leading British rider TOM SIMPSON, and the hour record holder ROGER RIVIÈRE. As with van Buggenhout, that dominance led to his handling deals for lesser riders as well.

The writer William Fotheringham said, 'It was a cartel. If a cyclist was not on one of the agents' books he had no appearance MONEY: nothing to live off other than prize money and whatever his team might pay him [and many professional riders had no retainers at all]. As a result, the agent-rider relationship was one of dependence on the riders' side, exploitation on that of the manager.... Dousset or Piel [Roger Piel, another French agent] could always find new riders; the riders had nowhere else to turn. It was effectively a form of tied labour.'

In time the main agents retired, Dousset to a villa in the south of France. But by then the system had changed. GREG LEMOND and others are credited with pushing up riders' salaries and reducing the need to ride daily criteriums and other small races. The events still exist, but most are smaller, and agents have become as much business advisers as bookers. The most prominent criterium booker in France is Jean-Claude Ducasse. His equivalent in HOLLAND is Gerry van Gerwen. They and others call at Tour riders' hotels on the rest days to do their deals.

The number of agents has increased and there are also 1,900 professionals in Europe, a lot more than 50 years ago. Some have personal agents: LANCE ARMSTRONG uses a lawyer, Bill Stapleton, from his home town of Austin, Texas. Others use international sports management companies such as IMG. Many British riders have contract advice from the London law company Athletes 1. DAVID MILLAR's agent is his sister, Francis; GREG LEMOND's was his father, Bob.

On the track, the biggest agent is PATRICK SERCU, says the former six-day rider and world pursuit champion Tony Doyle, who deals with both road and track riders on behalf of Nike. 'He took over from the old Dutch world sprint champion, Jan Derksen, who was always known as Mr 10 Per Cent, but he [Derksen] has recently retired.'

An agent normally takes 10 per cent of fees he negotiates, although the proportion can vary. 'The deal will vary with the agent's relationship with the rider,' says Doyle. 'It could be 10 to 20 per cent, but typically it would be 10 per cent of what the agent has negotiated and then 20 per cent of whatever extra he gets, such as a TV ad.'

It is in the nature of agents not to understate their value, but one modern agent, Raimondo Scimone, has explained their importance in straightforward terms. Most riders, he says, 'are brashly confident about making their own career decisions and their ability to understand contracts. Shortly afterwards they realise their confidence was misplaced and get drawn into ugly disputes because they were too proud to use an agent.' The other benefit agents can offer to riders comes from negotiable extras. Frank Quinn said in 1990 that SEAN KELLY, whom he represented, would ask '£10,000 and the rest' to wear a brand of shoes. It was, he added drily, 'a year's wages for fellas in some parts.'

(*See* MONEY for more on how much riders earn; *see* RAYMOND POULIDOR for deals done.)

AGES

HENRI CORNET, the 1904 winner and the only rider to have won because the leader (MAURICE GARIN) had been disqualified, remains the youngest winner at 19 years and 11 months. He and LUCIEN PETIT-BRETON, incidentally, are the only riders to have won under false names. (*See* HIPPOLYTE AUCOUTURIER for details of other riders competing under false names.)

The oldest winner, FIRMIN LAMBOT of BELGIUM, was 36 when he won in 1922. The youngest post-war winner was FELICE GIMONDI, who was 22 in 1965, and the oldest was GINO BARTALI at 34 in 1948.

The commonest age is 29, which has produced 13 winners, and the best range is 26 to 29 with 31 wins. Only 21 winners have been more than 30. The oldest rider was JULES BANINO, who was 51 when he rode for the second and last time in 1924.

RIDERS' AGES AND DATES WON

Age (Years Months Days)	Date	Winner	Born
19 11 20	1904	Henri Cornet	Aug 4 1884
21 11 18	1935	Romain Maes	Aug 10 1913
22 6 6	1909	François Faber	Jan 26 1887
22 9 11	1910	Octave Lapize	Oct 20 1887
22 9 15	1965	Felice Gimondi	Sep 29 1942
22 9 19	1913	Philippe Thys	Oct 8 1890
22 11 12	1983	Laurent Fignon	Aug 12 1960
23 6 12	1957	Jacques Anquetil	Jan 8 1934
23 7 25	1997	Jan Ullrich	Dec 2 1973
23 9 9	1978	Bernard Hinault	Oct 14 1954
23 9 18	1914	Philippe Thys	Oct 8 1890
23 11 10	1984	Laurent Fignon	Aug 12 1960
24 0 13	1938	Gino Bartali	Jul 18 1914
24 0 14	1912	Odile Defraye	Jul 14 1888
24 1 1	1905	Louis Trousselier	Jun 29 1881
24 1 3	1969	Eddy Merckx	Jun 17 1945

Age (Years Months Days)	Date	Winner	Born
24 9 8	1979	Bernard Hinault	Oct 14 1954
24 9 17	1907	Lucien Petit-Breton	Oct 18 1882
25 1 1	1986	Greg LeMond	Jun 26 1961
25 1 2	1970	Eddy Merckx	Jun 17 1945
25 2 16	1966	Lucien Aimar	Apr 28 1941
25 7 11	1958	Charly Gaul	Dec 8 1932
25 9 22	1908	Lucien Petit-Breton	Oct 18 1882
26 1 1	1971	Eddy Merckx	Jun 17 1945
26 1 10	1947	Jean Robic	Jun 10 1921
26 1 15	1933	Georges Speicher	Jun 8 1907
26 4 8	1951	Hugo Koblet	Mar 21 1925
26 5 0	1930	André Leducq	Feb 27 1904
26 6 9	1937	Roger Lapébie	Jan 16 1911
26 9 5	1981	Bernard Hinault	Oct 14 1954
26 10 6	1911	Gustave Garrigou	Sep 24 1884
26 10 25	1967	Roger Pingeon	Aug 28 1940
26 11 6	1936	Sylvère Maes	Aug 27 1909
27 0 12	1991	Miguel Indurain	Jul 16 1964
27 1 6	1972	Eddy Merckx	Jun 17 1945
27 1 24	1906	René Pottier	Jun 5 1879
27 5 11	1931	Antonin Magne	Feb 15 1904
27 6 8	1961	Jacques Anquetil	Jan 8 1934
27 6 10	1975	Bernard Thévenet	Jan 10 1948
27 7 28	1987	Stephen Roche	Nov 28 1959
27 8 13	1927	Nicolas Frantz	Nov 4 1899
27 9 11	1982	Bernard Hinault	Oct 14 1954
27 10 7	1999	Lance Armstrong	Sep 18 1971
28 0 10	1992	Miguel Indurain	Jul 16 1964
28 0 27	1989	Greg LeMond	Jun 26 1961
28 1 13	1973	Luis Ocaña	Jun 9 1945
28 2 2	1968	Jan Janssen	May 19 1940
28 3 9	1988	Pedro Delgado	Apr 15 1960
28 4 14	1953	Louison Bobet	Mar 12 1925
28 5 4	1932	André Leducq	Feb 27 1904
28 6 7	1962	Jacques Anquetil	Jan 8 1934
28 6 20	1998	Marco Pantani	Jan 13 1970
28 8 11	1928	Nicolas Frantz	Nov 4 1899
28 10 5	2000	Lance Armstrong	Sep 18 1971
29 0 9	1993	Miguel Indurain	Jul 16 1964
29 0 26	1990	Greg LeMond	Jun 26 1961
29 1 4	1974	Eddy Merckx	Jun 17 1945
29 4 19	1954	Louison Bobet	Mar 12 1925
29 4 26	1956	Roger Walkowiak	Mar 2 1927
29 6 6	1963	Jacques Anquetil	Jan 8 1934
29 6 14	1977	Bernard Thévenet	Jan 10 1948

Age (Years Months Days)	Date	Winner	Born
29 8 29	1976	Lucien van Impe	Oct 20 1946
29 9 17	1920	Philippe Thys	Oct 8 1890
29 10 9	1949	Fausto Coppi	Sep 15 1919
29 10 14	2001	Lance Armstrong	Sep 18 1971
29 11 3	1939	Sylvère Maes	Aug 27 1909
29 11 20	1924	Ottavio Bottecchia	Aug 1 1894
30 0 8	1994	Miguel Indurain	Jul 16 1964
30 4 16	1960	Gastone Nencini	Mar 1 1930
30 4 18	1955	Louison Bobet	Mar 12 1925
30 5 14	1934	Antonin Magne	Feb 15 1904
30 6 6	1964	Jacques Anquetil	Jan 8 1934
30 9 7	1985	Bernard Hinault	Oct 14 1954
30 10 10	2002	Lance Armstrong	Sep 18 1971
30 11 18	1925	Ottavio Bottecchia	Aug 1 1894
31 0 7	1995	Miguel Indurain	Jul 16 1964
31 0 9	1959	Federico Bahamontes	Jul 9 1928
31 0 14	1950	Ferdy Kübler	Jul 24 1919
32 3 18	1996	Bjarne Riis	Apr 3 1964
32 3 26	1903	Maurice Garin	Mar 23 1871
32 7 1	1929	Maurice Dewaele	Dec 27 1896
32 10 4	1952	Fausto Coppi	Sep 15 1919
33 4 5	1921	Léon Scieur	Mar 19 1888
33 4 13	1919	Firmin Lambot	Mar 14 1886
33 7 18	1980	Joop Zoetemelk	Dec 3 1946
33 10 7	1926	Lucien Buysse	Sep 11 1892
34 0 7	1948	Gino Bartali	Jul 18 1914
34 6 0	1923	Henri Pélissier	Jan 22 1889
36 4 9	1922	Firmin Lambot	Mar 14 1886

JOAQUIM AGOSTINHO

b. Silveira do Concelho-Torrès Vedra, Portugal, Apr 7 1942, d. Quintera, Portugal, May 10 1984

Joaquim Agostinho was a delightful man, seemingly without enemies. He looked like a SPRINTER but couldn't win with five blocks' start. Instead he was a superb CLIMBER and an aggressive time-trialist, winning the Trofeo Baracchi in ITALY with HERMAN VAN SPRINGEL in 1969. Of the 13 Tours he started, he failed to finish only one and twice got a place on the podium.

Agostinho raced infrequently once he had raised enough to buy a farm 40km from Lisbon. He once left the Tour de l'Indre-et-Loire when he heard that thieves had stolen 20 of his cows. RAPHAËL GÉMINIANI said,

'Agostinho never knew his strength; he was a ball of muscles, like a steelworker. He came to cycling fairly late and that made it hard for him to get into it properly. It was a shame that he could never dedicate himself totally. Riding in the bunch scared him and he often crashed. 'Tinho' wasn't aggressive enough to impose himself totally. He was a wonderfully gentle man and his only ambition was to be his soft, likeable self. If he'd been more ambitious he could have won the Tour.'

Agostinho was in fact the best rider that Portugal has produced, and to have won just four stages in 11 completed Tours understates his talent, as Géminiani said. He could be a ceaseless and even senseless attacker, and then he could ride unnoticed for days only to return with such a startling performance that EDDY MERCKX himself named him as his greatest rival when the two made their debuts in 1969.

Agostinho won on ALPE D'HUEZ and finished third overall in 1979 when he was 36, and he promised to race until he was 50. Many think he would have done, if only as an AMATEUR, but his life was cut short when a dog ran into the road during the Tour of the Algarve in 1984, when he was about 42 (Agostinho's age was always uncertain and never confirmed). There are two ironies. The first is that Agostinho had retired the previous year and had come back only to take the chance to lead an all-Portuguese team in the race. The second is that he had spent three years with the Portuguese army in Angola, expecting to be killed any night, only to be dispatched by a dog in the Algarve. Such was Agostinho's popularity that police had to hold back crowds who came to see him lying in an open coffin.

Winner

1968	National championship
1969	Trofeo Baracchi, National championship
1970	Tour Portugal, National championship
1971	Tour Portugal, National championship
1972	Tour Portugal, National championship
1973	Tour Portugal, National championship

Tour de France

1969	8th	Stage wins Nancy—Mulhouse, La Grande-Motte—Revel
1970	14th	
1971	5th	
1972	8th	
1973	8th	Stage win Bordeaux—Bordeaux
1974	6th	
1975	15th	
1978	3rd	
1979	3rd	Stage win Les Menuires—Alpe d'Huez
1980	5th	
1981	DNF	
1983	11th	

LUCIEN AIMAR
b. Hyères, France, Apr 28 1941

Lucien Aimar was one of the 'more forgettable' Tour winners, according to the British journalist Geoffrey Nicholson. In 10 Tours he won only one stage, and the only Tour that he won, in 1966, owed more to the retirement of JACQUES ANQUETIL than to his own talent. He won no big races other than the Four-Days of Dunkirk in 1967 and the Trophée des Grimpeurs in 1970.

Aimar rode his first race at 14 and moved from southern France to Paris after military service in Algiers. He made good progress as an AMATEUR, winning Paris-Briare and the Route de France, and in 1964 he would have won the TOUR DE L'AVENIR (Tour of the Future) had he not been docked a minute for a flare of temper with the Belgian, JOS SPRUYT. The victory went instead to FELICE GIMONDI by 42 seconds.

He was still largely unknown, or at least unvalued, when he turned professional in 1964. At first he was a DOMESTIQUE to Anquetil, riding well for him but always in his shadow. But his time came when Anquetil abandoned the 1966 Tour on the road from Chamonix to St-Étienne, never to return. Aimar took over as leader and began experimenting on the flat with a 55x13 gear, then considered outrageously high, and showing his strength in the MOUNTAINS.

Nobody paid him much attention, however. The assumption was that RAYMOND POULIDOR would at last win the Tour with Anquetil out of the way, and all eyes turned to him. Aimar took advantage of his obscurity and won the race without taking a single stage. The victory was poorly received. FRANCE, and above all French journalists, had wanted Poulidor to win – that would have sold more papers. RAPHAËL GÉMINIANI confirms that the organisers, JACQUES GODDET and FÉLIX LÉVITAN, were openly disappointed that a lesser light, a pro of just two years' standing, had won, and thereby reduced the importance of their race.

Aimar rode his last Tour in 1973 and then boycotted it for a quarter of a century, accusing Lévitan of asking RUDI ALTIG to make a point of stopping Aimar from winning. He returned only in 1998. In a strange twist, Lévitan also boycotted the race after being fired as organiser. (See Lévitan entry for details.)

Aimar's return coincided with police drug raids in the FESTINA SCANDAL. Ironically, it had been for DOPING that Aimar had been stripped of his second place in the 1966 Flèche Wallonne – and then, in the confusion of drugs law at the time, given it back.

In the 1967 Tour Aimar was fined the equivalent of about £50 a day for refusing to wear the JERSEY of national champion, which he had been awarded when Desiré Letort, the apparent winner, had been disqualified for doping. Aimar had finished the race in second place, and was therefore named the new champion. The French federation sent him a tricolour jersey so he could wear it in the next race, the Tour de l'Oise, but Aimar refused, claiming he hadn't won it legitimately. 'Letort beat me fair and square,' he said.

Aimar retired at the end of 1973 and became organiser of the Tour of the Mediterranean.

(See LANCE ARMSTRONG for Aimar's comments on his success after illness.)

Winner

1966 Tour de France
1967 Four-days Dunkirk, National championship
1968 National championship
1970 Trophée Grimpeurs

Tour de France

1965	DNF	
1966	1st	Yellow Jersey
1967	6th	Stage win Strasbourg—Ballon d'Alsace
1968	7th	
1969	30th	
1970	17th	
1971	9th	
1972	17th	
1973	17th	

HENRI ALAVOINE
b. Paris, France, Mar 6 1890, d. Western Front, Jul 19 1916

Life was rarely easy in the early days and no one had it much tougher than Henri Alavoine of FRANCE. In 1909, during a race already made appalling by persistent snow, hail, freezing rain and roads flooded to hub height, he was forced after a crash to carry his bike on his shoulder for 10km to the FINISH of the last stage.

Organiser HENRI DESGRANGE believed that in the Tour he had created men should be supreme. Their bikes were mere tools and if they broke down then that was the rider's responsibility. The rule was applied so strictly that riders had to show any damage to race officials before they could change their bike or wheel. If the damage happened where there was no official, it was a rider's job to find one. Desgrange made sure MANAGERS didn't offer help from cars by insisting they were accompanied by officials of rival teams so that each would keep an eye on the other.

For many years Desgrange refused to let riders change their bikes or wheels at all, and they had to carry out their own repairs at blacksmiths' forges. (See EUGÈNE CHRISTOPHE for more details. And see CHEATS for details of how Alavoine turned Desgrange's passion for rules to his own advantage.)

Alavoine's brother, Jean, was also a talented Tourman as well as riding Milan – San Remo, Bordeaux-Paris and the Six-days of New York and Paris. He rode the Tour in 1909 (coming 3rd and winning two stages), 1912 (5th and three stages), 1913 (19th), 1914 (3rd and one stage), 1919 (2nd and five stages), 1920 and 1921 (both DNF), 1922 (2nd and three stages), 1923 (DNF but three stages), 1924 (14th) and 1925 (13th).

(*See* BROTHERS for more on siblings in the peloton. And *See* CRASHES, MECHANICS, LÉON SCIEUR.)

Tour de France

1909	30th
1910	DNF
1911	DNF
1912	38th
1913	25th
1914	52nd

RAUL ALCALA
b. Mexico, Mar 3 1964

Raul Alcala was the first of only two Mexicans to have ridden the Tour. The other Mexican was Miguel Arroyo, who rode in 1994 (48th), 1995 (61st) and 1997 (76th). The only South Americans before them had been from COLOMBIA, the result of FÉLIX LÉVITAN's plans to make his race more global (*see* AMATEURS).

A wide-faced man with high cheekbones, Alcala was the best YOUNG RIDER in his second Tour, 1987, when he finished ninth (in his first in 1986 he had finished 114th). His talented climbing suggested he might soon win the MOUNTAINS competition. He improved his 1987 ride by finishing eighth in both 1989 and 1990, the only years in which he won a stage. The stage win in 1989, from Luxembourg to Francorchamps, was Mexico's first. But he was never happy in Europe and sought a home from home by living in an area of Switzerland favoured by Mexican immigrants. His heart was always more in AMERICA, where his follow-ing was greater than in Europe, and he spent a lot of time racing there. He won the leading US stage race of the era, the Coors Classic, in 1987 and the Tour DuPont in 1993.

Alcala's Tour de France career ended in 1994 with 70th place, and he had no important wins after that.

(*See* PDM AFFAIR for how Alcala was involved in a mysterious mass 'food poisoning' in the 1991 Tour.)

Winner

1987	Coors Classic
1989	Tour Mexico
1990	Tour Asturias, Tour Mexico, Tour Trump
1992	San Sebastian Classic
1993	Tour DuPont
1994	Tour Mexico

Tour de France

1986	114th	
1987	9th	Young Rider winner
1988	20th	
1989	8th	Stage win Luxembourg— Francorchamps
1990	8th	Stage win Vittel—Epinal
1991	DNF	
1992	21st	
1993	27th	
1994	70th	

ALCYON

The firm Cycles Alcyon, one of FRANCE's BIKE-makers involved from the start in sponsoring riders, was founded in 1902 at Neuilly-sur-Seine by the engineer Edmond Gentil. He sold 3,000 bikes in 1902 and a staggering 40,000 in 1909. Production outgrew the original factory, and in 1909 Alcyon moved to a factory of 20,000 sq metres at Courbevoie. In 1910 Gentil began making cars as well as bikes and motor-bikes, although he gave up cars and returned to just two-wheelers after the first world war.

Until 1954 and the introduction of sponsors from outside the cycle industry – the so-called *extra-sportifs* (*see* FIORENZO MAGNI for more) – all but a handful of small teams in the Tour were sponsored by bike- and accessory-makers. (*See* SPONSORS for more details).

Alcyon was quick to spot the benefit of sponsorship in terms of publicity, and its bikes carried its team's riders to victory in 14 Tours, 12 editions of Paris-Roubaix, 13 of Bordeaux-Paris, and many TRACK and road championships.

Alcyon is French for kingfisher and its team riders wore pale kingfisher-blue jerseys. The first managers were Alphonse Baugé and then a former medical student and track rider, 'Père Ludo' Feuillet (see PHILIPPE THYS for Baugé's role in the creation of a yellow JERSEY.)

Feuillet's control was so tight that on at least one occasion he used his car to jam one of his own riders against a hedge so a more popular one could win. Rivals who envied the team's success – it was best team from 1909 to 1912 – but trembled at Alcyon's ruthless discipline called the team la taule, which means clink or jail. (See RALEIGH for why that team was called 'the firing squad'.)

The dominance achieved through Feuillet's leadership – Alcyon riders FRANÇOIS FABER, GUSTAVE GARRIGOU, OCTAVE LAPIZE and MAURICE DEWAELE all won the Tour – was a factor in HENRI DESGRANGE's decision to introduce NATIONAL TEAMS in 1930. Desgrange suspected, not without reason, that Feuillet had persuaded his riders to break Desgrange's rules against collaboration and to ride as a team rather than as individuals. In 1929, when the Alcyon team combined to help Dewaele win the Tour even when he was reduced by illness, Desgrange raged, 'My race has been won by a corpse.'

Alcyon developed a mythical stature in pre-war French racing. The Franco-American journalist RENÉ DE LATOUR recalled how older colleagues would tell of hanging about the firm's workshops to pick up inside stories. 'Famous men used to collect their bikes bright and shining on a Friday and Saturday,' he said, 'and take them back on Mondays covered with dust or mud [from a race]. The Alcyon service des courses was a happy hunting ground for cycling journalists.'

There is some confusion about when Alcyon finally went out of business. Many reports say the firm abandoned car-making in 1928 and that the bike factory closed soon after the second world war. But bikes of the same name were still around in the 1960s.

(And see LA FRANÇAISE.)

ALPE D'HUEZ

Alpe d'Huez, a wriggling route ending in a cul-de-sac, is situated on the edge of the Alps near Bourg d'Oisans, south-east of Grenoble. It is a critical point in any Tour. Like the PUY-DE-DOME, another dead-end at the top of a MOUNTAIN, Alpe d'Huez is feared because the ascent is so sudden and cruel. And with no descent on which to make up time, what goes wrong on its 21 ascending hairpins can't be put right.

JAN ULLRICH found that out in 2001 when LANCE ARMSTRONG bluffed him all day that he was suffering and vulnerable. In his efforts to dislodge Armstrong from the race leadership the German wore out both himself and his team, only for the American to come to life on the Alpe and ride away.

At the time of its inclusion in the Tour in 1952, Alpe d'Huez was no more than a primitive ski resort of three hotels at the top of a pot-holed road. The race organisers had always been unsure about mountain-top finishes, and so they were doubtful when hotel-owner Georges Rajon and two other businessmen offered the equivalent of about £2,100 to take the race up there. (The tradition that the publicity bestowed by a Tour FINISH was worth paying for began early in the race's life, and is now routine.)

Unpromising though Alpe d'Huez seemed, the post-war years were an exceptional period with more star riders than ever before, so the Tour was looking for an exceptionally hard race, 'une épreuve pour champions d'élite' as PIERRE CHANY put it. The organisers had already considered the Puy-de-Dôme and Montgenèvre, both of which they eventually included, as well as lengthy TIME TRIALS. The latter were subsequently shortened because HUGO KOBLET had been too good at them the previous year and they could influence the result too strongly. But in the event Koblet

Alpe d'Huez (continued)

FIRST TO THE TOP

1952	Fausto Coppi
1976	Joop Zoetemelk
1977	Hennie Kuiper
1978	Hennie Kuiper
1979	Joop Zoetemelk
1979	Joaquim Agostinho
1981	Peter Winnen
1982	Beat Breu
1983	Peter Winnen
1984	Luis Herrera
1986	Bernard Hinault
1987	Federico Echave
1988	Steven Rooks
1989	Gert-Jan Theunisse
1990	Gianni Bugno
1991	Gianni Bugno
1992	Andy Hampsten
1994	Roberto Conti
1995	Marco Pantani
1997	Marco Pantani
1999	Beppe Guerini
2001	Lance Armstrong

didn't ride anyway, victim of a mysterious ailment which ended his career. (*See* Koblet entry for details.)

Intrigued at the approach by Rajon and his colleagues from the Alpe d'Huez, organiser JACQUES GODDET sent the assistant commissaire, Elie Wermelinger, to have a look at the place. He arrived in the winter of 1952 when the area was snowbound, and needed tyre chains to get further than Bourg d'Oisans, grinding slowly up the hill with the guide sent to meet him. At the top of an unbordered, half-made road covered with gravel he found a primitive resort with no chalets or ski lift. It was a bleak place.

Wermelinger was either a visionary or Rajon and his supporters were very persuasive, because the commissaire brought back a favourable report. When FAUSTO COPPI saw the new course, he recognised immediately that it was his chance to make up for his defeat the previous year. He was in good form, had ridden an exciting Paris-Roubaix, and had just won the Giro for the fourth time. He allowed JEAN ROBIC to make the first move on this new mountain stage, and then overtook him in a single move and cruised to the top. It won him the yellow JERSEY and a full 1: 20 passed before Robic followed him across the line.

Despite this dramatic activity, the Tour showed no interest in a quick return to the Alpe d'Huez, and it didn't happen until Rajon approached Goddet's colleague, FÉLIX LÉVITAN, in 1975, and paid again for another FINISH. The Tour returned in 1976 and once more the Alpe supplied another exciting climax. Since then it has been a regular fixture.

In 1976, however, instead of a lone win like Coppi's, there was a two-man battle between LUCIEN VAN IMPE and JOOP ZOETEMELK. Both were Dutch-speakers, and the mountain quickly became the favourite place for Dutch SPECTATORS, especially after HENNIE KUIPER won there in 1977 and 1978. Out of a crowd estimated at 300,000, one in three is said to be Dutch – 'thousands of blond heads and red bodies' as one writer put it. Some camp for

three days to be sure of their place. The 15th hairpin – with a 14 per cent gradient – and the seventh are the most popular. The bends are about 700m apart and numbered from 20 in descending order. For some reason the first isn't numbered.

In 1978 there was further sensation at the Alpe d'Huez when MICHEL POLLENTIER of BELGIUM won alone to take the yellow jersey, only to be caught while trying to avoid the DOPING check. (*See* MICHEL POLLENTIER for his disgrace on the mountain.)

In 1986 the Frenchman BERNARD HINAULT and American GREG LEMOND finished almost hand-in-hand, seemingly friends but really quite the reverse. LeMond had understood that Hinault would help him win, but instead the Frenchman gave him a hard ride all race 'as an education'. The tension between them made the race one of the most exciting for years and the individual stage the best for decades. (*See* GREG LEMOND and BERNARD HINAULT.)

On Bastille Day 1999 Beppe Guerini of ITALY won after being knocked off by a 19-year-old spectator known only as 'Eric', who stepped into the road for a photograph. Riders assume fans will get out of the way but the view through the lens persuaded Richard that Guerini was further away and the two collided. The Italian got back on and won . . . and the snapper disappeared. Later that night he went to Guerini's hotel to apologise.

In 2001 Lance Armstrong produced the coup of the race – underhand or clever, according to how you feel about Armstrong – to beat Ullrich (*see* page 12).

The fastest climb of the Alpe d'Huez was 37:35 by MARCO PANTANI in 1997. Armstrong took 38 minutes in 2001, 10 minutes less than Hinault and LeMond in 1986, 4:15 less than LAURENT FIGNON in 1989, and 1:45 less than MIGUEL INDURAIN'S 39:45 in 1991.

RUDI ALTIG
b. Mannheim, Germany, Mar 18 1937

Rudi Altig was a consistent star of the 1960s. A giant, square-built German (1.80m and 80kg), he was a dangerous opponent anywhere, even in the MOUNTAINS. In an extraordinary few months in 1962 he took the Tour points competition, won the Tour of SPAIN and in November literally pushed Jacques Anquetil for 15km in the Trofeo Baracchi two-man TIME TRIAL and still won. 'Jacques didn't like it but I was stronger than he was and I was determined we were going to win,' he said; Anquetil was so weak that he lost control and crashed into a barrier at the FINISH.

Altig was GERMANY's most gifted rider until JAN ULLRICH arrived on the scene, wearing the yellow JERSEY for 18 days in four Tours and winning 18 stages in the three major stage races. Even when he helped Anquetil win the Tour in 1962, he did it while himself winning three stages and taking the yellow jersey. (*See* JACQUES ANQUETIL for how Altig's strength and tactical inexperience gave the Frenchman problems.)

Altig was unusual in being a TRACK specialist who also got to the top in road racing. He was born near Mannheim in 1937 and started racing in 1955, following his brother Willi to compete on the tracks at Schopp, Mannheim, Freisenheim, Hassloch, Saarbrucken and Darmstadt. The two quickly established themselves as one of Germany's best teams in madisons (the relay race that forms the basis of six-day events). In 1956 Altig rode at Herne Hill track in London, paired with a Berliner called Hans Jaroszewicz (Willi Altig had fallen ill). The promoter, Jim Wallace, recalled, 'They just about slaughtered a top-class field of international riders, with all our best home lads.'

Altig became German sprint champion in 1957 and held on to the title for another year before switching to pursuiting when the great coach Karly Ziegler joined his club, Endspurt Mannheim. He won the AMATEUR world pursuit championship in Amsterdam in 1959 and became well known for his practice of entertaining spectators with his ritual yoga routine, which involved standing on his head in the track centre. (Later, as a professional, Altig once walked out of a restaurant in La Rochelle on his hands; others who were with him – including TOM SIMPSON – tried to copy him but collapsed and had to scrabble about for the coins that fell from their pockets.)

Altig turned pro in 1960 and two years later RAPHAËL GÉMINIANI persuaded him his future was on the road. Altig didn't need much persuading. Success on the road would bring greater public recognition and make his name more bankable on the track. To be a star on both road and track would bring him lucrative six-day victories and bigger appearance fees.

Success followed immediately, with the yellow jersey in his first Tour. He came second in the 1965 world championship in a two-man sprint with Simpson and then won the following year on the Nurburgring with help from his commercial team-mate, Gianni Motta. World championship riders are supposed to ride for their country, in Motta's case ITALY, but Motta and Altig normally rode for Molteni, an Italian food company, and collusion was inevitable.

There was controversy over the result when the leading riders refused to give urine samples and were disqualified and suspended. In fact they were protesting at uncertainties and irregularities then surrounding DOPING checks, and also at restrictions on their race preparations. 'We are professionals, not sportsmen,' said Altig, who had also refused to take drugs tests in BELGIUM earlier that year. It was a situation the world cycling authorities had never faced, and 10 days later the sport's governing body, the UCI (Union Cycliste Internationale) relented and let the result stand.

Altig never gave up riding the track. When the road season finished he went straight to the winter six-day circuit. 'I rode the track because I could win MONEY there,' he said. 'If I hadn't been able to win money, I'd never have gone round the world's tracks riding six-days. These days riders are better paid but then we did anything we could to win money. The current era is different; there is no comparison but I don't regret how things were for me.'

Altig became MANAGER of the Puch-Wolber team when he retired, and spent five years as national coach. He is still a regular feature at stage finishes of the Tour de France when he walks between the crowds to meet the public-address commentator, DANIEL MANGEAS, for his daily interview. These days however he wears a hearing aid and complains that feedback from Mangeas' amplified delivery and the Frenchman's non-stop routine make it howl in his ear.

Winner

1962 Tour Spain, Trofeo Baracchi, Manx Premier, Critérium As
1963 Paris-Luxembourg
1964 Tour Flanders, National championship, Ruta Sol
1966 World championship, Tour Piedmont, Tour Tuscany
1968 Milan-San Remo

1969 GP Lugano
1970 GP Frankfurt, National championship

Tour de France

1962	31st	Stage wins Nancy—Spa, Brussels—Amiens, Aix-en-Provence—Antibes, and Points winner and Yellow Jersey
1964	15th	Stage win Forest—Metz, and Yellow Jersey
1966	12th	Stage wins Nancy—Charleville, Luchon—Revel, Rambouillet—Paris, and Yellow Jersey
1969	DNF	Stage win Roubaix—Roubaix, and Yellow Jersey

AMATEURS

Amateurs, in Britain at least, are people who do something for nothing, for love. But the birth of cycling as a professional sport has always made the definition of an amateur hazy. While most sports began as unpaid games and only later became sufficiently prosperous for the best to become professionals, cycling started the other way round, as an advertising venture for newspapers wanting to sell more copies. The longer the race, the greater the interest. But the longer the race, the more competitors had to be enticed, and so money became a feature early on.

The word 'amateur' is French. It means a devotee, an enthusiast, someone 'in love with something. In French, it meant someone riding for fun rather than as a job, but it didn't exclude being paid MONEY. In Britain and other English-speaking countries the word specifically meant someone who would refuse money if offered. While FRANCE and other Continental nations assumed the natural state of affairs to be professional, Britain regarded sport as the province of gentlemen.

Britain, though, was powerful in world cycling in the nineteenth century and strong enough in May 1891 to force France to run Bordeaux-Paris only for riders that Britain considered genuine amateurs. Seven thousand Frenchmen turned out to see not only victory by the Englishman George Mills but also to see British riders taking all the leading places.

You'd think it would be a cause of celebration for Britain and its administrators. Instead, they considered disqualifying Mills because he was works manager at a bike factory and they suspected his employer may have paid his fare to Bordeaux. An even worse fate awaited the American August Zimmerman, the first world amateur road champion. When he accepted an invitation to race in Britain in 1893, everybody in England enthusiastically greeted him, wrote the American cycling historian Peter Nye, 'except English cycling officials [who] accused Zimmerman of violating amateur laws by writing his book [*Points for Cyclists with Training*] and being featured in RALEIGH advertisements.' They banned him from racing in England.

When HENRI DESGRANGE set up the Tour in 1903, riders were employed and paid by bicycle companies such as ALCYON. Desgrange wanted them to ride as individuals, seeing his race as a competition between men and not combines. He lost patience in 1930 and did away with sponsored teams and restricted his race to riders representing their countries. The idea, though flawed (*see* NATIONAL TEAMS), was continued by his successors, JACQUES GODDET and FÉLIX LÉVITAN, until 1961.

In 1961, the Tour started a 'development' race, the TOUR DE L'AVENIR (Tour of the Future). It was for national teams which included amateurs and a semi-professional class called INDEPENDENTS, who could ride against professionals as well. But in 1966 the sport's governing body, the UCI (Union Cycliste Internationale), abandoned the independent class because too few riders used it as the step to professionalism that it was intended to be.

That left just amateurs and professionals, and in 1983 Lévitan saw a way of expanding the Tour's interests into cycling's developing nations while also restricting the power of professional sponsors. Opening the Tour not only to European professionals (at that time almost

all Tour riders were European) but also to amateurs from elsewhere could add interest and potential sources of money.

In 1983 he announced a race of 18 teams, half of them professional and the rest made up of amateurs older than 23. The age restriction was to avoid a clash with the Olympic Games; amateurs who had ridden against professionals wouldn't qualify for the Games, and Lévitan assumed that any amateur who hadn't made the Olympics by 23 would never get to the Games.

The idea impressed journalists but caused immediate alarm among sponsors. From 1930 till 1961 sponsors had been blocked from the Tour completely; now they were being threatened by cut-price rivals, amateur teams getting the same publicity for much less expenditure. They asked what the point was of backing a team for a whole season if the Tour was going to run up bargain-basement opposition to undermine them. If that was the case, they might as well stay away from the Tour.

The row was still going on when lack of interest by the most attractive amateur nations took the heat out of it. Both Czechoslovakia and East Germany said they wouldn't ride. Politics made them strong on amateurism and uncomfortable with capitalist sponsorship. Only COLOMBIA was interested (*see* entry for why), producing a new star in LUIS HERRERA. Lévitan was forced to compromise by accepting a 'limited' number of amateurs – 'limited', that is, by the amateurs' own reluctance – and by deciding on the possibility of an 'open' Tour every four years. But the idea died when the UCI did away with distinctions between amateurs and professionals at the turn of the millennium.

Lévitan's venture revealed lack of agreement and personal animosity between the two Tour organisers. Goddet's view was that professional racing was too much at the heart of cycling to threaten it. Why bite the hand that fed it? Prepared to disagree with his partner in public, he wrote, 'It's this fundamental observation that leads me to worry that the permanent formula [of amateurs every year] suggested by my colleague Félix Lévitan would dangerously weaken the framework of traditional cycling which, until now, has fed the Tour. Just 10 professional teams of only eight or nine men each would eliminate a considerable number of professional riders and result in general unemployment.'

He asked too if 'the new cycling nations' – the amateurs – were up to a 4,000km race. Better, he said, to keep things as they were and encourage the professional racing that already existed in Colombia and would soon, he said, start in AMERICA.

AMERICA

American SPRINTERS were among the world's best on the track in the 19th century. The country had 600 professionals in 1899, which the cycling historian Peter Nye points out was 'nearly the same number as on today's major league baseball rosters in the regular season; racing cyclists were so popular that children collected trading cards of them the way youngsters collect baseball cards today.'

Marshall 'Major' Taylor became world sprint champion at the age of 19 in 1899 and earned $10,000 in a three-month tour of Europe in 1901. His life turned sour when he retired, and he died penniless in Chicago in 1932 and was buried in a pauper's grave. It was symbolic of American racing. Insularity, the rise of the car, and the death of six-day racing – so important in America that Madison Square Garden gave the sport the two-man tag race still called a 'madison' in English and 'l'américaine' in French – meant cycling all but vanished between the wars.

The one notable American rider between the wars was Joseph Magnani. He came from a family of poor farmers in Illinois, south of Chicago. His family had come originally from FRANCE, so that was where he went to race in 1932 when he started showing talent on a bike. He turned pro in 1935 and raced until 1948, coming ninth in Paris-Nice in 1938 and seventh in the 1947 world championship. He rode the first Giro after the war which, says Nye,

probably makes him the only American to have raced with FAUSTO COPPI and GINO BARTALI. Magnani returned to Chicago in 1948 and worked as a designer for the Schwinn Bicycle Company. He died in 1975 after developing Parkinson's disease.

The fitness boom of the 1970s revived the sport in the US and races returned. In one, in the Sierra mountains, two riders – George Mount and John Howard – had turned the event into a two-man tussle. A certain Bob LeMond and his family happened to be driving on the same road when they came across Mount and Howard, and followed them over Mount Rose and down the descent. LeMond alternately jabbed the accelerator and stood on the brakes trying to keep up with them. He couldn't. In the back was his son, GREG LEMOND, for whom it was 'the coolest thing in the world' that his father couldn't keep up with guys on bicycles. A love affair was born.

Mount and another rider, Mike Neel, pioneered the way for post-war Americans in Europe. Neel turned pro after crashing in the Montreal Olympics in 1976 and moved to ITALY. There he got Mount a place in a club team, and Mount also turned pro after America boycotted the Moscow Olympics in 1980 because of the Soviet Union's involvement in Afghanistan. Mount rode the Giro twice and finished two world championships.

The first American to make a real mark, though, was JONATHAN BOYER, a quiet and introspective vegetarian, 'slightly dandified' as the writer Geoffrey Nicholson put it. He came fifth to BERNARD HINAULT in the 1980 world championship, and in 1981 became the first American to ride the Tour, finishing 32nd.

The American breakthrough became complete after a Polish political refugee, Edward Borysewicz (or Eddie B), took the job of national coach and promised to put American riders back on the Olympic rostrum for the first time since 1912. In 1984 America won nine medals at the Los Angeles Olympics.

Greg LeMond, the excited boy in the car, was an Eddie B prodigy. (*See* Greg LeMond entry for career details.) He inspired a generation of American riders, including ANDY HAMPSTEN,

DAVIS PHINNEY and Ron Keifel. Speaking English, and particularly American English, became common in the bunch and RADIO TOUR added it to its announcements.

Better than LeMond, though, is LANCE ARMSTRONG, whose dominance of world cycling at the turn of the century has won him admirers if not always friends (*see* Lance Armstrong entry for details.) George Mount says he admires him but that 'it's a shame he has no concept of the tremendous history there is to cycling, because he came to it from triathlon, and I'm sure that influences the way he sees the sport.'

The US is still hampered by being some distance from the heart of professional racing. There have been attempts to mount a major stage race there, but one such attempt proved the undoing of Tour de France organiser FÉLIX LÉVITAN in March 1987. Several big races have started up, only to collapse a few seasons later. America does have a domestic programme and championship, but its main teams are still based in Europe and only partly staffed by Americans.

(*See* RAUL ALCALA, STEVE BAUER, ROBERT CAPA, FALSE NAMES, GEORGE HINCAPIE, BOBBY JULICH, FREDDY MAERTENS, JEFF PIERCE, TRANSFERS.)

ANC-HALFORDS – *See* Hercules.

KIM ANDERSEN
b. Malling, Denmark, Feb 10 1958

DENMARK has produced more good riders than its size justifies, among whom BJARNE RIIS (winner in 1996) has been the most outstanding. But his compatriot Kim Andersen also performed well, riding the Tour six times between 1981 and 1987, and collecting two yellow JERSEYS, the first in 1983 when he won his only stage. Andersen rode in yellow for 12 days. Following his retirement he become a team MANAGER in 2000.

(*See* ARNE JONSSON, ROLF SORENSEN and JESPER SKIBBY for other Danes; and *see* BJARNE RIIS for his role in producing a Tour winner.)

Winner

1983	Tour Denmark, Trophée Grimpeurs
1984	Tour Denmark, Flèche Wallonne, Tour Limousin, GP Isbergues
1987	Tour Denmark, National championship
1990	GP Cholet
1991	GP Rennes, Tour Poitou Charentes

Tour de France

1981	DNF	
1982	17th	
1983	28th	Stage win Fleurance—Roquefort, and Yellow Jersey
1984	50th	
1985	47th	Yellow Jersey
1988	62nd	

PHIL ANDERSON
b. London, England, Mar 12 1958

Said to be the owner of cycling's most magnificent set of teeth, Phil Anderson is Australian by nationality and upbringing but was adopted by BRITAIN because he was born in London of a British father and an Australian mother. He is 'Skippy' to the French because of a TV kangaroo . . . and won a yellow JERSEY at his first attempt.

Anderson won the Commonwealth Games road race at Edmonton, Canada, in 1978 when he was 19. He moved to Paris the next year and the ACBB club in the suburb of Boulogne-Billancourt which had created many English-speaking professionals. He turned professional for PEUGEOT when he was 21 and moved to Lokeren in BELGIUM to ride CRITERIUMS. He rode his first Tour in 1981, an impudent apprentice who alone had the nerve or ability to cling to BERNARD HINAULT's wheel when he attacked in the Pyrenees. Anderson tagged on to Hinault all the way up the Pla d'Adet and gained enough time to become Australia's first *maillot jaune*. Hinault, of course, also made up time and the gap between them wasn't enough for Anderson to hold the lead in the next day's TIME TRIAL, which was Hinault's strength, so to nobody's surprise the Australian lost his jersey.

Many riders have tagged on to a star and profited from it only to return to obscurity. But next year Anderson won the stage from Basle to Nancy and wore the yellow jersey for nine days, coming fifth overall and finishing as best young rider. He never again did as well in the Tour – in 1985 he matched his fifth place but with neither a stage nor a jersey to his credit. All the same, 1985 was his best year, when he won the Tour of the Mediterranean, Tour of Catalonia, Dauphiné Libéré and the Tour of Switzerland, as well as coming second to Eric Vanderaerden in the Tour of Flanders and Ghent-Wevelgem. He might have done still better had he been more impressive as a CLIMBER or more consistent in time trials. He made up for his shortcomings – and made himself popular with fans in the process – by attempting lone breaks, often in the closing kilometres when he hoped to get clear of SPRINTERS.

Anderson continued to ride the Tour – finishing 39th in 1986, 27th in 1987 and 38th in 1989 – but his form became erratic, and was not helped by the onset of an arthritic disorder after 1985. At the end of 1990 he signed for the American Motorola team and had a brief renaissance, winning the Tour of the Mediterranean, followed by the Nissan Classic in Ireland and two Tours of Britain. He rode his last Tour in 1994.

Anderson was, to that point, the best of a long line of Australians who have been trying their luck in continental European racing far longer than either Americans or Britons. Two Aussies, DON KIRKHAM and Ivor Munro, rode the Tour as long ago as 1914, finishing 17th and 20th. HUBERT OPPERMAN rode the Tour of 1928 when 15 stages were run as team time trials. RUSSELL MOCKRIDGE made up numbers in the LUXEMBOURG team in 1955, finishing 64th. Bill Lawrie rode for the British team in 1967 but didn't finish.

Since Anderson really put them on the map Australians have become even more familiar in the Tour.

(*See* EARPIECES for Anderson's pioneering role in race communications.)

Winner

1983	Amstel Gold
1984	Championship Zurich, GP Frankfurt, Catalan Week
1985	Tour Mediterranean, Tour Switzerland, Dauphiné Libéré, GP Harelbeke, GP Frankfurt
1986	Paris-Tours
1987	Milan-Turin
1988	Tour Denmark
1989	Tour Romandie
1991	Tour Mediterranean, Tour Britain, Sicilian Week
1992	Nissan Classic, GP Isbergues
1993	Tour Britain, Tour Sweden

Tour de France

1981	10th	Yellow Jersey
1982	5th	Stage win Basle—Nancy, Yellow Jersey, Best Young Rider
1983	9th	
1984	10th	
1985	5th	
1986	39th	
1987	27th	
1989	38th	
1990	71st	
1991	45th	Stage win Rennes—Quimper
1992	81st	
1993	84th	
1994	69th	

HENRY ANGLADE
b. Thionville, France, Jul 9 1933

Henry Anglade was the Frenchman whom other Frenchmen contrived to keep from winning the Tour.

In 1959 he finished second in the Tour of Switzerland and won the Super Prestige Pernod, forerunner of the season-long World Cup, as well as being national champion. But he came second rather than first in that year's Tour de France because he got tangled up in French politics. And because other riders didn't like him.

Anglade was a short and bossy man, which in 1962 earned him the NICKNAME *Napoléon*

from the broadcaster Robert Chapatte. The name stuck – his bossiness didn't make him the most popular of riders – but Anglade felt flattered. 'Napoléon liked to win,' he said, 'hated being ridiculed or dismissed by others.'

A national champion would normally expect to be in the NATIONAL TEAM, but there were so many good French riders in 1959 that it was strategically possible to keep out a rider whom the others disliked. So Anglade rode instead for the Centre-Midi REGIONAL TEAM. That may have hurt his feelings, but it produced an advantage. He realised that a national team with rivals such as JACQUES ANQUETIL, LOUISON BOBET, RAPHAËL GÉMINIANI and ROGER RIVIÈRE was never likely to be stable. These cyclists normally rode for their own sponsors and thus saw little advantage in helping one of the others win. (See DOMESTIQUES for more on binding riders together.) In 1953 the French MANAGER, MARCEL BIDOT, had succeeded in getting his divided team to sign a contract of cooperation, but rivalries still sprang up every summer.

Anglade watched out for where rivalries and splits appeared, and took advantage of them. Thus he won the 13th stage at Aurillac and moved into second place overall behind Jos Hoevenaars.

CHARLY GAUL, the LUXEMBOURG CLIMBER and favourite, had lost time in the hot weather, which he hated. The weather changed on the stage to Grenoble, though, and Gaul went off on a spectacular attack in the MOUNTAINS with the other star climber, FEDERICO BAHA-MONTES. Gaul was too far down to affect the race but Bahamontes made up so much time that he took the yellow JERSEY.

Anglade thought his chance was over. He would never beat Bahamontes in the mountains. But then came a surprise. The Col du Petit St-Bernard was wrapped in cold, icy mist, and Bahamontes was in trouble and struggling behind the leaders. Anglade saw his moment, gave his all, and got up to the second group. In it was Rivière, who soon punctured.

Anglade said, 'I made the most of the situation to attack, knowing that Bahamontes was way behind. There were four of us and we got up to the two leaders.' He began to think he was going to win the Tour. But odd things had already been happening in the French team, and they were about to happen again. The rivalry between Rivière and Anquetil was so great that Rivière was determined his leader wouldn't beat him on the stage or overall. Delayed by waiting for a wheel, he set off again just as Bahamontes reached him.

Rivière, while not a star climber, was a world-class pursuiter. Bahamontes couldn't believe his luck and sat on his wheel. They didn't get to the FINISH until a minute after Anglade but it was enough to deny him victory. With Bahamontes back as probable winner, the French team contrived to keep it that way. This was legitimate to the extent that Anglade was in a rival team and didn't have to be helped, but the main reason was that Bahamontes was a hopeless CRITERIUM rider who never felt happy on fast corners; if he won the Tour he would do less harm to their post-Tour fees than a French winner would. (See CRITERIUM entry for more on riders' fees.)

'I don't have any regrets,' Anglade says now. 'The race was a long time ago and I have a principle to live without regrets.' Anquetil was jeered and whistled at when he reached the PARC DES PRINCES and he didn't forget it. That year he bought a boat and called it 'the Whistles of 59'. (See JAN ADRIAENSSENS for more on plots against Anglade.)

Anglade's pride is shown in one of his favourite stories. He couldn't bear GASTONE NENCINI's reputation as the world's fastest descender, so on a stage in the Giro so bitter that 57 abandoned, he bet Nencini a drink that he could get down the Dolomites faster. Nencini accepted, summoning the BLACK-BOARD MAN to witness the race. (See CHARLY GAUL for how the stage won him the Giro that year.)

'The road was just compacted earth,' Anglade recalled, 'and we started racing down the descent.' He started by following Nencini to see how he took corners, then passed him to win by 32 seconds. 'I just rode down as if I was by myself and I turned round and saw the gap chalked on the blackboard. I was relaxing in my hotel after the stage when I saw Nencini come in; he had come to pay for the aperitifs.'

In retirement Anglade learned how to make stained glass windows. One of his creations is in the back wall of the Nôtre Dame de Cyclistes, a rural chapel near Mont-de-Marsan in south-west France which has become a museum of old bikes and jerseys from the world's greatest cyclists. 'I am extremely proud of it and it gives me pleasure every time I see it,' he says.

Anglade followed the 2002 Tour as an employee of the SOCIÉTÉ DU TOUR DE FRANCE. (*See* MEMORIALS for other tributes to riders. *See* PIERRE BEUFFEUIL for how Anglade halted the race at the foot of General de Gaulle's garden, and how a rider scored his only stage win as a result.)

Winner

1959	Dauphiné Libéré, National
	championship
1963	Tour Var
1965	National championship
1966	Tour Hérault

Tour de France

1957	28th	
1958	17th	
1959	2nd	Stage win Albi—Aurillac
1960	8th	Yellow Jersey
1961	18th	
1962	12th	
1963	11th	
1964	4th	
1965	4th	
1967	DNF	

JACQUES ANQUETIL

b. Mont-St-Aignan, France, Jan 8 1934, d. Rouen, France, Nov 18 1987

Jacques Anquetil was an enigma, polite but distant, a man who won the Tour five times but in almost a languid style. He read races like a computer, knew the exact placings and abilities of his rivals but could name few of the rest of the field. Those closest to him speak of a man generous in relaxation and punctilious in business, but to everybody else he seemed cold and in a world of his own.

'He had an almost bizarre calmness,' said his friend ANDRÉ DARRIGADE. 'I had to say to him, "If you don't get going, you'll lose the Tour." I had to give him a kick up the backside every so often.'

Anquetil was accused of racing with no more effort than he calculated was needed. It was often said that although he could drop nobody, nobody could drop him. He was just always there, waiting for the TIME TRIALS at which he was close to unbeatable. He won, crouched like an egg, toes down, spraying sweat but body motionless except for legs turning a huge gear with immaculate smoothness.

The journalist Jean-Paul Rey said, 'If the key to a *coureur* [racing cyclist] is his style, Anquetil was unequalled. There has never been anyone who could ride so fast and so aesthetically.' JEAN-PAUL OLLIVIER, the French TV commentator, wrote, 'He was the world's most beautiful pedalling machine.' (*See* JACQUES AUGENDRE for further comments.)

Anquetil grew up outside Rouen in a single-storey building with beamed ceilings – 'The sort of house that tourists find pretty but those who live in them find uncomfortable,' he remembered. His father was a mason who refused to work for the Germans during the Occupation and was forced out, leaving his home to join his brothers on their strawberry smallholding. The family moved to the hamlet of Bourguet, near Quincampoix, to the north. The smallholding was a kilometre and a half from the house, and young Jacques rode, or rather raced, from one to the other four times a day.

At school his strongest subject was arithmetic. 'It's served me well,' he said with an eye on his reputation as a calculator. At home, his father was the absolute master, he said, putting him to work from the age of six.

The work and the regular cycling 'improved the gifts I was given', and Anquetil became a talented rider. He joined the AC Sottevillais in Sotteville, the suburb where he was studying metalwork. There he came under the influence of a bike-shop owner and coach called André Boucher, who entered him for his first race. Anquetil was 18. He won, decided not to be a cross-country runner after all (his other sport), and left college to become a bike-rider.

He made fast progress, not always winning but making enough of a mark to get into the French time trial team for the Helsinki Olympics in 1952, where he won a bronze medal for FRANCE behind BELGIUM and ITALY. His progress at the Olympics and back in France was being followed by the local representative of the La Perle bike company who, in the summer of 1953, sent the newspaper cuttings he had collected on this unusual young rider to the company's team manager, Francis Pélissier. (*See* also CHARLES PÉLISSIER and HENRI PÉLISSIER for how Henri was murdered.)

Francis Pélissier was looking for someone to challenge LOUISON BOBET in the Grand Prix des Nations. This 140km time trial near Paris had the status of unofficial world championship, and Bobet had won the previous year. Pélissier called Anquetil, who was surprised and flattered to hear from him. A month later, on September 29 1953, Anquetil won the Nations in a La Perle jersey while still just an INDEPENDENT or semi-professional. Bobet, who hadn't recognised the youngster as the unknown who'd beat him in a pursuit race the previous week, was one of the first to congratulate him.

Still unaccustomed to fuss, Anquetil was ill at ease with the reporters who surrounded him. He would rarely ever feel comfortable with them. 'It was no better than Paris-Normandy,' he said, referring to a race he'd won by nine minutes earlier in the year after riding the last 120km at 40km/h. Whether or not it was 'no better', he went on to win the Grand Prix des Nations six times in a row, from 1953 to 1958, and then again in 1961, 1965 and 1966. He was never beaten and his record has never been bettered.

Anquetil's ability against the clock was so great that the only way to beat him was in the MOUNTAINS. He was a competent CLIMBER but not a star, and there was a chance he could be caught on an off day. His biggest rival was RAYMOND POULIDOR, a man as warm and humble as Anquetil appeared cold and haughty. (*See* Raymond Poulidor entry for more on relations between them, and why many French enthusiasts liked Poulidor better.) Poulidor was the stronger climber but weaker against the clock, as well as in both his tactics and self-confidence.

The greatest clash between them, and for many people the greatest ever moment of the Tour, came on the PUY-DE-DOME on July 12 1964. Anquetil was in yellow but Poulidor, who had never won the Tour (and never would), was close to beating him. Neither was going well and, Poulidor recalled, 'Anquetil was letting breaks get away so that even if I beat him on the Puy I wouldn't get the BONUS that could win me the Tour.' In such ways was Anquetil's reputation as a strategist founded.

Millions were watching on TV and beside the road. JULIO JIMENEZ won the stage ahead of FEDERICO BAHAMONTES, but they seemed incidental. The interest was in the Poulidor-Anquetil clash as they turned on to the private road coiling up the old volcano. The pair rode side by side, barely looking at each other. Only one had to break. Poulidor could hear from Anquetil's breathing that he was in trouble, and rode half a length ahead. Anquetil, haggard and staring, bluffed and countered to suggest he was strong. At one stage they banged elbows and both fought for their balance.

Then Anquetil cracked in the final kilometre and Poulidor, now as exhausted as Anquetil, at least had the consolation that he might now finally take the yellow JERSEY. Poulidor took 42 seconds out of his rival and stood, gasping, at the summit. The last section was on a bend and he couldn't see what had happened to Anquetil. Another rider then came in and for a moment Poulidor and his supporters thought Anquetil had pulled up. But then, more haggard than ever, he struggled over the line, still in yellow by 14 seconds. 'If Poulidor had taken my jersey, I'd have gone home that night,' he said later.

The last chance for Poulidor to make up the gap and win the Tour was the 27.5km time trial from Versailles to the PARC DES PRINCES in Paris. But there was little chance that Poulidor could win unless Anquetil had mechanical trouble. It was Bastille Day, the national holiday, and the roads were lined with spectators. Anquetil, as leader, was the last to start, Poulidor the last but one. Rivalry between the two had split the nation, and each camp cheered on its man.

The fairy story didn't happen. Anquetil won by 21 seconds and got another 20 in bonus time. Poulidor was second. The crowd simply felt more sorry for Poulidor and turned on Anquetil in the stadium, whistling and jeering at him. (See HENRI ANGLADE).

Anquetil could never understand the way he was treated. 'He [Poulidor] always comes second, usually behind me,' he said. 'And still they shout more for him than for me. If he loses, he doesn't have to find excuses. But if I come second or third, then I've failed. They call me a calculator, a strategist, even if a miscalculation has just made me lose.' But the ill-feeling between them was overstated, although there was a time when they spoke only through their wives.

What finally made France despair of him was the way Anquetil spoke out for the right to take DRUGS. It had become common knowledge that most riders used them, but this was just starting to be seen as reprehensible. Anquetil tried to apply logic, and asked why an office worker could make his work easier but not a cyclist. He called it hypocrisy, but that wasn't an argument most people could or would follow.

In 1966 Anquetil led a STRIKE at BORDEAUX after testers descended on riders' hotels for urine samples. In September 1967 he was denied the world hour record after refusing to give a sample in the middle of the Vigorelli TRACK in Rome. Anquetil said a champion should be accorded dignity and not be asked to urinate in a tent in front of a crowd, and had a point, but only two months had passed since TOM SIMPSON had died on MONT VENTOUX and reactions were mixed. (*See* FERDI BRACKE

Trivia note: Anquetil was interested in the British love of time trialing and wanted to ride a 50-mile event. Tom Simpson told him courses were flat, and Alan Gayfer, the editor of *Cycling*, asked Anquetil how long he'd take. Gayfer recalled, 'He said 46 minutes. The existing record was 54:23. With no guidance, he estimated he'd take eight minutes off the record.' A London timber merchant called Vic Jenner said he would put up the money for Anquetil to ride on the Southend road, the fastest course in Britain. But Jenner died before anything could be done and it never happened.

for how the record was broken and for Anquetil's reaction.)

PIERRE CHANY said, 'Jacques had the strength – for which he was always criticised – to say out loud what others would only whisper. So, when I asked him, "What have you taken?" he didn't drop his eyes before replying. He had the strength of conviction.'

After Anquetil won the Dauphiné Libéré and then the 556km Bordeaux-Paris in 1965 without a night's sleep between them, Chany said, 'You can't be a champion like that just by taking a pill from a bottle.' (*See* ERCOLE BALDINI for Anquetil's experiment in riding a time trial without amphetamine.)

In contrast to the public Anquetil, who did little more than smile and walk away when he won, there was the private Anquetil who was fascinated by astronomy (he met Yuri Gagarin), and by card games (which he played badly, with the same caution he used in races), and was prepared to ride his bike into the swimming pool at a family party. He also had a half-justified reputation as a playboy, enhanced when he told an inquiring schoolboy that the best way to prepare for a race was 'with a good woman and a bottle of champagne'.

Anquetil was a complex man, and his complexity was reflected in the hot-and-cold way the French reacted to him. RAPHAËL GÉMINIANI said, 'Jacques was unique on his good days. You could ask everything of him and he'd do it, and then even more when things got hard. In all my life I've never come across a rider so brave, of a courage that exceeds imagination; but this quality often passed unnoticed because his riding style remained more or less perfect [and he made it look so easy].'

Anquetil retired on December 27 1969, and died in November 1987 after being afflicted with stomach cancer. His wife, Jeanine Boéda, said he had a constant fear of dying, and was convinced he wouldn't live as long as his father. He didn't. The father died at 56, the son at 53. He was buried at Quincampoix, where a large black marble marker recording his victories stands at the entrance to the village. The village sports centre is named after him.

Perhaps in death he was finally recognised for what he had done: he had brought France as many Tour victories – five – as any man had ever won. Eight thousand people came to his funeral service in Rouen cathedral. The Tour stopped to pay homage the following year. In 1997, a memorial service drew Poulidor and the other five-time winners, MIGUEL INDURAIN, BERNARD HINAULT and EDDY MERCKX. With an irony the master of time would have enjoyed, many of the guests arrived late after getting stuck in traffic.

Winner

1953 GP Nations, GP Lugano
1954 GP Nations, GP Lugano
1955 GP Nations, GP Martini
1956 GP Nations, GP Martini, World hour record
1957 GP Nations, Tour de France, Paris-Nice, GP Martini
1958 GP Nations, Four-days Dunkirk, GP Martini, GP Lugano
1959 Critérium As, Four-days Dunkirk, GP Martini, GP Lugano
1960 Giro d'Italia, Critérium As, GP Lugano
1961 Tour de France, Critérium International, Paris-Nice, GP Lugano, GP Nations
1962 Tour de France, Baracchi Trophy

Winner (continued)

1963 Tour de France, Tour Spain, Dauphiné Libéré, Critérium International, Critérium As, Paris-Nice
1964 Tour de France, Giro d'Italia, Ghent-Wevelgem
1965 Bordeaux-Paris, Manx Premier, Dauphiné Libéré, Critérium International, Critérium As, Paris-Nice, GP Lugano, GP Nations, Baracchi Trophy
1966 Liège-Bastogne-Liège, Paris-Nice, GP Nations
1967 Tour Catalonia, Critérium International
1968 Baracchi Trophy
1969 Tour Basque Country

Tour de France

1957	1st	Stage wins Rouen—Rouen, Besançon—Thonon, Barcelona—Barcelona, Bordeaux—Libourne, and Yellow Jersey
1958	DNF	
1959	3rd	
1961	1st	Stage wins Versailles—Versailles, Bergerac—Périgueux, and Yellow Jersey
1962	1st	Stage wins Luçon—La Rochelle, Bourgoin—Lyon, and Yellow Jersey
1963	1st	Stage wins Angers—Angers, Pau—Bagnères-de-Bigorre, Val d'Isère—Chamonix, Arbois—Besançon, and Yellow Jersey
1964	1st	Stage wins Briançon—Monaco, Hyères—Toulon, Peyrehorade — Bayonne, Versailles — Paris, and Yellow Jersey
1966	DNF	

MAURICE ARCHAMBAUD

b. Paris, France, Aug 30 1906, d. Raincy, France,
Dec 3 1955

Maurice Archambaud, a plump but talented
French rider, came, like Tour winners ANDRÉ
LEDUCQ (1930, 1932) and GEORGES SPEICHER
(1933), from the leading training stable of the
time, the VC de Levallois run by Paul Ruinart.
(*See* PAUL DUBOC for Ruinart's involvement in
a Tour poisoning.)

Archambaud was a world-class performer
against the watch, both on the road and on the
TRACK. In 1932 he won the first Grand Prix des
Nations TIME TRIAL, riding the 142km in
3:49:28. Like ROGER RIVIÈRE after him, he was
an hour-record holder (45.840km at Milan in
November 1937) who could also ride hard
stage races.

He rode his first Tour in 1932 and came 16th.
In 1933 he won the first stage and kept the
yellow JERSEY until the ninth stage before going
to pieces on the Col d'Allos and losing it. In
1936 he wore yellow again as far as Grenoble,
only to lose it again in the MOUNTAINS. Riders
strong enough to ride fast against the clock are
usually too heavy to star in the mountains, and
Archambaud was never a lean man anyway.

The Tour archivist JACQUES AUGENDRE
described Archambaud as 'having the air of an
old British lord' because of his quiet, introverted personality.

Winner

1932 GP Nations
1936 Paris-Nice
1937 World hour record
1939 Paris-Nice

Tour de France

1932 16th
1933 5th Stage wins Paris—Lille, Nice—
           Cannes, and Yellow Jersey
1934 DNF
1935 7th Stage wins Belfort—Geneva,
           Narbonne—Perpignan
1936 DNF Stage win Metz—Belfort, and
           Yellow Jersey

Tour de France (continued)

1937 DNF Stage win Lille—Charleville
1939 14th Stage win Narbonne—Béziers,
            Béziers—Montpellier, St
            Raphaël— Monaco, Dôle —
            Dijon

MORENO ARGENTIN

b. San Dona di Piave, Italy, Dec 17 1960

Hardly a great Tourman – three rides and just
one finish and two stage wins – Moreno
Argentin was a talented single-day rider.
Unusually among Italians, who ride in the cold
only reluctantly, he made his name in BEL-
GIUM, where he took a hat trick of wins in
Liège-Bastogne-Liège, which he won in 1985,
1986 and 1987, as well as in 1991.

The best story about Argentin is from the
Tour of the Mediterranean in February 1993,
when a bunch of 150 was bumping and boring
to the line. Moreno Argentin, the former
WORLD CHAMPION (1986), discovered the
unknown 21-year-old LANCE ARMSTRONG
alongside him. He looked at him in surprise
and said, 'What do you want, then, Bishop?'

Armstrong was upset at being mistaken for
another American, Andy Bishop, and
responded in kind, 'Fuck you, CHIAPPUCCI
[one of Argentin's compatriots], my name's
Lance Armstrong and by the end of the race
you'll know that.'

The race went into its last few hundred
metres. For a while Armstrong moved ahead as
the race charged for the line. Argentin caught
and passed him and then, five metres from the
line, jammed on his brakes. The result was that
the Italian finished fourth but kept Armstrong
behind him, which he preferred to having to
stand on the podium with a rider he considered
needlessly offensive. He had, he insisted, simply
not recognised Armstrong. Argentin, an established star, world champion and classics
winner, clearly felt he ought not to be sworn at
by an unknown.

Argentin rode away alone at the FINISH and
the row continued later when he began shouting insults at Armstrong and his team-mates.

For a while the two were enemies but they have since laughed about the incident and become friends.

(*See* Lance Armstrong entry for how the American mastered his anger.)

LANCE ARMSTRONG

b. Plano, USA, Sep 18 1971

Lance Armstrong was the fairy tale of the end of the 20th century, a man who came back from testicular cancer which had spread to his brain, threatening to kill him, yet went on to win the Tour de France four years in a row (1999–2002).

Armstrong is a driven man. He grew up in a broken home, son of a 17-year-old mother and an absent father whom he has never forgiven for leaving them. It was cycling, he says, that stopped him going wrong in life. His background, though, left him edgy, and his early career was marked by spats with rivals and team-mates, rows he now admits starting and regrets.

Jeremy Whittle, editor of *Procycling*, says of their first meeting in 1993, 'Brash is an adjective

that fitted him well. Back then, a raw and slightly brittle 21-year-old, there wasn't much time for doubt or uncertainty and even less patience for those who got in his way.' (*See* MORENO ARGENTIN for an example.)

Armstrong started out as a triathlete and became national junior champion before dropping the swimming and running to concentrate on cycling. He came to world attention when he won a rain-soaked world championship in Oslo in 1993. But his personality ensured that he met with less than total acclaim from European colleagues.

Three years later, on October 2 1996, he went to hospital in Austin, Texas, with a painful groin. He was 25. Doctors diagnosed testicular cancer that had already spread to his stomach and lungs, and was beginning to threaten his brain. He was given a less than 50-50 chance of survival. His hair fell out and he looked like a ghost as operations and drugs took their toll. The story varies but, according to Armstrong himself, his SPONSOR, the French moneylender Cofidis, sent an official, Alain Bondue, to his bedside to renegotiate his contract before eventually dispensing with him.

Astonishingly Armstrong recovered enough to ride a bike again. But finding a team was a different matter. 'All the teams in Europe that had offered me contracts before my cancer turned me down after I had recovered,' Armstrong said. He recalled, as he put it, his AGENT's fax machine overflowing with rejection letters in French, Dutch, Spanish and Italian. 'They said I was damaged goods.'

The man who came to his rescue was Thom Weisel, president of the new team being set up by the US Postal Service. Weisel personally guaranteed Armstrong's salary. It was less than what he had received before, but offers weren't flowing in and Weisel's plan was to top up the retainer with performance bonuses.

Armstrong was still weak, though. His coach, Chris Carmichael, was himself a former rider in Europe in the 1980s and had been American national coach. Medical treatment had left Armstrong in a poor state, Carmichael said. 'He couldn't eat much and he had lost weight, including muscle mass. That meant he couldn't push big gears the way he used to. We broke the workload down by having him pedal a smaller gear but more rapidly.' Armstrong's climbing style to this day is still to pedal fast, as quickly as 120rpm instead of the 70 to 90 of most riders. A benefit was that fast pedalling gave him the acceleration of a classic CLIMBER, dispensing with opposition like JAN ULLRICH, who preferred a high gear but constant speed, by using the sudden accelerations of mountain men like MARCO PANTANI.

He came back to racing in 1998 but it was too early and he had to abandon Paris-Nice. Armstrong holed up first in Nice and then in Texas without answering calls. And before long the calls stopped coming anyway. Armstrong returned mid-season with a win at the Tour of Luxembourg then showed his potential in September by finishing fourth at the Tour of Spain.

The following season Armstrong showed his dominance of the Tour de France by winning alone at SESTRIERE after a stage that covered six major summits. Wins followed in the 2000 and 2001 Tours. The 2002 Tour gave him one more than AMERICA's only other Tour winner, GREG LEMOND.

All athletes have a strong sense of competition, of rivalry, or they wouldn't succeed and it was probably more important to Armstrong to beat LeMond than it was disappointing for LeMond to be beaten. The two had already clashed over Armstrong's treatment by a controversial Italian doctor, Michele Ferrari, who was at the centre of DOPING inquiries in 2001 (*See* below.).

In 2000, Armstrong clashed with another rider involved in Italian doping inquiries, Marco Pantani. Pantani received an 8-month ban for insulin possession following the drug police raids on the 2001 Giro. After a series of appeals and counter-appeals Pantani served a six-month ban and returned to racing in March 2003. But while the spat between Armstrong and Pantini upset both men, it provided entertainment for everyone else. The background was MONT VENTOUX, one of the

Tour's most feared climbs and one on which reputations are won or wrecked.

Armstrong and Pantani duelled all the way up, each attacking the leading group until they arrived at the summit together. There Armstrong appeared to ease up to let the Italian win. At first Pantani looked happy but his mood changed when he began to suspect Armstrong had patronised him, 'letting' him win.

Armstrong said he wanted Pantani to win because he was a great climber and deserved it, but that just made things worse. Pantani now presumed that Armstrong thought him unable to win without help, and he took everything Armstrong said as an insult. That in turn offended Armstrong, and he made the row still more colourful by referring to Pantani at a press conference as '*Elefantino*', a nickname the jug-eared Pantani merited but not surprisingly disliked. The now wound-up Italian said he didn't like Armstrong's 'American ways' and that he'd 'teach him a lesson.' (*See* BERNARD HINAULT for more on 'American ways'.)

Before long Pantani was too occupied with never-ending inquiries into his medical preparation to have time for Armstrong. But the American, too, was no stranger to criticism and investigation. In 1999 the heavyweight French paper *Le Monde* reported that Armstrong had been found positive for steroids in a doping test. He answered that it was the accidental effect of a skin treatment and the row passed.

Many people wanted to know just what drugs Armstrong had been given during his cancer treatment, and the former winner LUCIEN AIMAR asked, 'Is it now necessary for Tour winners to have been invalids if they want to succeed?' The question may have stayed in the background had a French television crew not filmed the occupants of an unmarked car dumping bags of drug boxes, used medical pads and other items which the TV crew linked to Armstrong's team. The main drug was Actovegin, a drug said to enhance the the the oxygen-carrying limits of an athlete's blood.

A state inquiry opened but got nowhere. Actovegin wasn't one of the banned drugs on the list of the sport's governing body, the UCI

(Union Cycliste Internationale), although it was added afterwards. The US Postal team's MANAGER, JOHAN BRUYNEEL, said nothing had been brought into France without permission and nothing used that was banned. (*See* PEDRO DELGADO for a similar incident.) Months passed and the national drug-testing centre confirmed that it had found no evidence in the team's urine of a more popular blood-boosting drug, EPO. The inquiry was closed in 2002 and the US Postal team was cleared of any wrong-doing.

Armstrong said after the skin-treatment findings that 'people are against me', and it's a view he has stuck to. More criticism followed when he agreed, prior to the 2001 Tour and just hours before a London newspaper was to break the story, that he had had repeated contact with the controversial doctor Michele Ferrari. The doctor himself said he had been in daily contact with Armstrong during the racing season. But, as the American has often pointed out, he has repeatedly been tested for drugs and has always been found clear. However, the link with Ferrari proved embarrassing. Italian police had raided Ferrari's home a number of times since August 1998 but nothing at the time of going to press has been found and the investigation is ongoing.

Armstrong is selective about what races he rides outside the Tour, and makes no attempt to deny that the Tour is his only objective of the season and that all other races lead to it. Teammates are employed precisely to help him win it. Because of that his *palmarès* of wins outside the Tour is surprisingly thin, although in 2002 he won both the Midi-Libre and Dauphiné Libéré.

In 2001, before winning his third Tour, Armstrong announced he was a changed man. He regretted the rows in which he'd been involved and which, he said, he had sometimes started needlessly. He said he needed anger to win and conceded that it burst out at the wrong time. But he had come to terms with that and with himself, he said, so he could focus it only onto his racing. The man who once snubbed Tour organiser JEAN-MARIE LEBLANC by saying his job was to win bike races, not popularity contests (Leblanc had suggested the French might warm to Armstrong if he took more trouble to learn their language) even began talking French in television interviews. The fact that it was such bad French merely made him seem more human, more vulnerable, and France began to like as well as to admire him.

Armstrong's popularity in America has never been in doubt. His fairy-tale recovery from cancer overcame American indifference to cycle racing and also did a lot to raise awareness of testicular cancer, something Armstrong accelerated by founding an organisation to promote knowledge and research. His book *It's Not About the Bike* sold in huge numbers round the world.

In the August following his third Tour win, Armstrong was a guest of the American president at the White House. George W. Bush said Armstrong was 'a vivid reminder that the great achievements of life are often won or lost in the mountains, when the climb is the steepest, when the heart is tested.... He's done more than survive – he has triumphed.' Bush called him on his mobile phone after the 2002 race to congratulate him on his fourth consecutive victory.

Winner

1993	World championship, National championship
1995	San Sebastian Classic, Tour DuPont
1996	Flèche Wallonne, Tour DuPont
1998	Tour Luxembourg
1999	Tour de France
2000	Tour de France, GP Merckx, GP Nations
2001	Tour de France, Tour Switzerland
2002	Tour de France, Dauphiné Libéré, Midi-Libre

Tour de France

1993	DNF	Stage win Chalons-sur-Marne—Verdun
1994	DNF	
1995	36th	Stage win Montpon-Monesterol—Limoges
1996	DNF	
1999	1st	Stage wins Le Puy-de-Fou—Le Puy-de-Fou, Metz—Metz, Le Grand Bornand—Sestriere, Futuroscope—Futuroscope, and Yellow Jersey and Points leader
2000	1st	Stage win Freiburg—Mulhouse, and Yellow Jersey
2001	1st	Stage wins Aix-les-Bains—Alpe d'Huez, Grenoble—Chamrousse, Foix—St-Lary-Soulan, Montluçon—St-Armand-Montrond, and Yellow Jersey
2002	1st	Stage wins Luxembourg—Luxembourg, Pau—La Mongie, Lannemazan—Plateau de Beille, Regnié Durette—Macon, and Yellow Jersey

AUBISQUE

The Aubisque, often shrouded in mist, is the Pyrenean climb that most strongly conjures up the Tour's *grande époque*, when riders struggled night and day against seemingly impossible odds. It was first climbed on July 21 1910, when FRANÇOIS LAFOURCADE reached the summit too exhausted to speak to officials waiting for him. The next up, OCTAVE LAPIZE, was more vocal and accused them of being 'assassins'.

The col is 1,709m high and links the Ossau and Arrens valleys near Pau. From the Argelès side the road goes first over the smaller Col de Soulor, which is an eight per cent gradient for the first six kilometres and then almost flat for the next six. Then the road rises again in Arrens, twisting round hairpins of up to 11 per cent. Wandering mountain cattle stray onto the road when the Tour isn't passing. From the top

of the Soulor the road goes briefly down and then back up through two tunnels, one dark and curved so that one end isn't visible from the other.

The climb to the Aubisque itself is not demanding, with a gradient of eight per cent at the top. But the road is narrow and often precarious as it clings to the mountainside. The 17km drop from the café and souvenir shop at the top averages seven per cent and occasionally reaches 13 per cent and has frequent hairpins.

Most of the road now has a protective barrier, but there was nothing there when the Dutchman WIM VAN EST fell over the edge in 1951 when he was leading the race. He had to be pulled back up to the road with a tow rope made by knotting together all his team's spare tyres. But these stretched so much that they no longer fitted the rims and the Dutch team had to go home.

There was drama on the Aubisque in 1911, too, when Paul Duboc collapsed and lay retching after being poisoned. Supporters suspected GUSTAVE GARRIGOU, and became so threatening that he had to be disguised to ride safely through a lynch mob in Rouen. (*See* PAUL DUBOC for details.)

(And *see* MOUNTAINS for details of how the Tour paid 20,000 francs for repairs to the Aubisque so the race could pass in 1910; *see* BRIGADE ORANGE for how the tradition continues.)

HIPPOLYTE AUCOUTURIER
b. Commentry, France, Oct 17 1876, d. Paris, France, Apr 22 1944

Hippolyte Aucouturier (ladies' tailor) possessed the strangest name in Tour history apart from Samson, which was actually the made-up name of Julien Lootens of BELGIUM (who finished sixth in 1903).

Made-up names were common at the end of the 19th century, and in November 1869 riders in Paris-Rouen, the first long place-to-place race, included a British woman calling herself Miss America. The riders did it just for the fun of it, or to avoid the scandal still associated with riding a bike. (*See* HENRI CORNET and LUCIEN PETIT-BRETON for other riders who competed under false names; *see* NICKNAMES for riders given names by other people.)

Hippolyte ('the Terrible') Aucouturier was MAURICE GARIN's biggest rival in the pioneering Tour of 1903. He was a giant of a man with a moustache wider than his face, but his apparent indestructibility didn't stop him from pulling out on the first stage. He was reputed to drink too much during races, upsetting his stomach. In fact he had had typhoid fever the previous season and may not have recovered.

The RULES allowed riders to abandon one stage and start the next to compete for that day's prizes, although not for overall positions. Aucouturier did just that, and won the next two stages. He rode again the following year but was one of several riders disqualified for *violation des règlements* (breaking the rules) in THE 1904 AFFAIR. Undeterred, he tried again in 1905 and finished second, this time with three stage wins.

The oddest Aucouturier story comes from his win in the Paris-Roubaix race in 1903. He and two other riders, Claude Chapperon and Louis Trousselier, had been away for much of the race and were approaching the TRACK on which the race finished. The tradition for races with finishes on vélodromes (race tracks) was that riders would change to fixed-gear and brakeless track BIKES at the entrance. In Paris-Roubaix they had to ride three laps of the track and then sprint to decide the placings.

Each man had helpers at the stadium entrance, but confusion reigned and Chapperon grabbed Trousselier's bike in error. The two men began tugging at it and Aucouturier rode away from both and won by 90 metres. He won again in 1904, getting to Roubaix so early that only 20 SPECTATORS were in the track. (*See* LOUIS TROUSSELIER for how he gambled away his whole Tour winnings in a night.)

Winner

1903	Bordeaux-Paris, Paris-Roubaix
1904	Paris-Roubaix
1905	Bordeaux-Paris

Tour de France

1903	DNF	Stage wins Lyon—Marseille, Marseille—Toulouse
1904	DNF	
1905	2nd	Stage wins Nancy—Besançon, Grenoble—Toulon, Bordeaux—La Rochelle
1906	DNF	
1908	DNF	

JACQUES AUGENDRE

The French journalist Jacques Augendre is the only man to have followed 50 Tours, a feat he achieved in 2001. He works as the Tour's archivist at its office in Issy-les-Moulineaux in western Paris, where his neighbours at L'ÉQUIPE call him 'the Memory of the Tour de France'. (*See* JEAN-PAUL OLLIVIER and PIERRE CHANY for other journalists with extraordinary memories of the race.)

Augendre was working for *L'Équipe* during the 1947 and 1948 Tours but stayed in the office to edit other people's reports. He followed his first Tour in 1949, and since then has missed only 1952, 1954 and 1959, again because he was back in the office. He rates 1953 as his most enjoyable race, when LOUISON BOBET won after finishing fourth in 1948 and third in 1950. The win did much to restore post-war confidence in French cycling. For him the greatest rider is EDDY MERCKX and the most talented BERNARD HINAULT – 'a gifted rider who could win without training.' JACQUES ANQUETIL, says Augendre, was the most stylish, 'quite simply the perfect aesthetic representation of a cyclist.'

MAGNUS BACKSTEDT
b. Linköping, Sweden, Jan 30 1975

Magnus Backstedt – 1.93m tall and 90kg, and a professional since 1996 – was the first Swede to win a stage of the Tour, beating three others at Autun in 1998. This pleased Sweden but did little to excite anyone else. The race was having one of its lethargic days and the stars were content to let unimportant riders have their head. Backstedt's break had gained 11 minutes within two hours and 16 minutes at the end.

More significant to the Tour was Backstedt's role in the so-called Pisspot Rebellion that lost LAURENT JALABERT his yellow JERSEY in 2000. On July 6 the race set off gently from Vitré. Backstedt, remembering his glory two years earlier, attacked after 10km. He was in 30th place and calculated that the others wouldn't chase if they wanted an easy time two days before the big climbs. Even if they didn't, he could stay away for a couple of hours and gain publicity for his SPONSOR.

Unfortunately for him and also for Jalabert, the Frenchman had decided at that moment to attend to what the French call *besoins physiologiques*. To attack at such a moment was hardly polite, and there is a pecking order in professional cycling which lays down that riders who show disrespect to stars are rarely forgiven.

Backstedt insists he didn't know what was happening at the back of the race. Jalabert says he must have, and others may have known too because they were reluctant to chase. But then JACKY DURAND reacted. Durand was not only a specialist in long breakaways but dangerous enough to oblige the others to follow suit. Jalabert and the whole ONCE team, which he led and which had stopped with him, were obliged to chase for 13 minutes before giving up. Better, they reasoned, to lose the *maillot jaune* than leave the team exhausted two days before the Pyrenees.

Jalabert finished 7:49 down and slid from first to 10th. The stage was won by Leon van Bon of HOLLAND with Durand ninth. Backstedt, who'd started it, didn't figure. The yellow jersey went to Alberto Elli of ITALY, who kept it until LANCE ARMSTRONG took it in appalling weather on stage 10 from Dax to HAUTACAM.

Jalabert never recovered, suffered badly in the MOUNTAINS and finished the Tour 54th, his worst place. He still speaks of 'lack of respect' and denies he made a strategic error. It's unlikely Backstedt has been forgiven. Jalabert and his team may have attacked a similarly disadvantaged Alex Zülle at 50km/h after the CRASH on the Passage du Gois in 1999 but he and Zülle were equals. (*See* EARPIECES for more on how it happened.) But in 2000 when Jalabert was attending to his *besoins physiologiques* the Frenchman was a prince of the sport and Backstedt was a frog.

(*See* JEROEN BLIJLEVENS for how Backstedt was at the root of a fight in the CHAMPS

ELYSÉES; *see* GOSTA PETTERSSON for other prominent Swedes.)

BAGGAGE

Riders may not wear much when they're riding their bikes but their luggage is formidable. The Australian Stephen Hodge (83rd in 1989, 34th in 1990, 67th in 1991, 93rd in 1992, 83rd in 1994 and 64th in 1995) listed his travelling kit as: a warm tracksuit, light tracksuit, three short-sleeved team shirts, three racing singlets, three short-sleeved jerseys, a long-sleeved jersey, a thermal top and a thermal T-shirt, dress shorts, sports shoes, sandals, packet of team photos, briefcase with family pictures, tickets and note paper, programme of races for the season, airline timetables, six pairs of racing socks, two pairs of sports socks, two pairs of underpants, two pairs of boxer shorts, a pair of overshoes, three pairs of mitts, three pairs of shorts, leg and arm warmers, vitamins and other medicines, washing gear, short-wave radio to hear the BBC's World Service, shoe polish, heart-rate monitor, clothes-washing soap, marker pens and ball-points, scissors, team stickers, sunburn cream, safety pins, matches, moisturising cream, Tour bible, magazines, helmet, three pairs of sunglasses, towel, gloves and caps.

(*See* NORBERT CALLENS for details of a *maillot jaune* who forgot his yellow jersey.)

FEDERICO BAHAMONTES
b. Santo Domingo-Caudilla, Spain, Jul 9 1928

SPAIN has a record of providing good CLIMBERS – something which observers attribute to mountainous countryside and the advantage of a generally light Mediterranean physique – but none has been better than Federico Bahamontes. He finished on the podium three times in 10 rides but won just once, in 1959. Often he had no greater ambition than to beat his rival Jesus Loroño in the MOUNTAINS competition. Loroño won it in 1953, the year before Baha's first ride, and finished fifth overall in 1957. By contrast, Bahamontes won the mountains title six times. When LUCIEN VAN IMPE had a chance to win a seventh mountains title, he declined rather than beat his idol's record.

Bahamontes, the son of a Cuban immigrant, was a nervous man with a long face, curly hair and long, thin legs on which he pulled his shorts up high. His nervousness extended to his riding style, with his legs turning quickly, his knees out, his back straight, his hands repeatedly changing position, and his eyes in a fixed stare. Bahamontes' morale was fragile, and he was as likely to abandon a stage as win it.

He won his first race, in Andalucia, on July 18 1946, 13 years to the day before his Tour de France triumph. He won wearing a basketball shirt, being short of money because he earned only a small wage as a delivery boy. Successes followed quickly, especially in hilly races. In 1953 he won the first stage and the climbers' competition against a largely professional field in a race in Asturias, turned pro the next year and got his first selection for the Tour de France, which was then organised around NATIONAL TEAMS.

Bahamontes was then still unknown outside Spain, so winning the climbers' competition and finishing 25th in his first Tour was sensational. Still more startling was his behaviour on the GALIBIER. For all his talent uphill, he was a dreadful descender, sometimes dragging a foot speedway style round corners. Reaching the top of the Galibier alone, he remembered how he had once crashed in Spain and ended up against a cactus. Worried that he might again fall without being seen as he went down, he stopped, dismounted, and sat on a wall eating an ice cream provided by an astonished SPEC-TATOR, waiting for the race to catch him. Mechanics pretended to work on a non-existent fault to his bike, but Bahamontes himself never disguised the real reason.

That nervousness emerged again in 1956 when he had enough on the Col de Luitel and threw his bike into a ravine. Team officials had to drag it back out and plead with him to continue. So he did, and finished fourth overall. The following year was even more dramatic. While team-mates waved their fists and his MANAGER, Luis Puig, shouted at him to change his mind, Bahamontes waited for the VOITURE BALAI, the pickup van for those who drop out, and tugged off his shoes so that he couldn't be made to continue. His reason was that his team-mate MIGUEL POBLET had left the race, and Bahamontes considered he had too little support for it to be worth continuing.

'But you are a giant, you can do it without Poblet,' Puig argued.

'No.'

'But Federico, you must. For your mother, your dear mother.'

Bahamontes shook his head.

'Please Federico – for your mother.'

'No.'

'For Spain, for beloved Spain, then?'

'No.'

'For Franco.'

'*No, no, no!*'

Only in 1959 was he persuaded that he could win, and at the start at Mulhouse he said so – quite something for a man with such lack of confidence. The climax came on stage 10, when Bahamontes' battle with CHARLY GAUL produced a gap of 14 minutes on the rest across the Pyrenees. Gaul cracked when they clashed again in the Massif Central. Bahamontes became Spain's first winner, although with helpful collusion from a divided French team who wanted him and not Henry Anglade to win. (*See* HENRY ANGLADE, JAN ADRIAENSSENS and ROGER RIVIÈRE for details.)

Success brought an interview with Spain's *caudillo* and dictator, Francisco Franco. It was predictably awkward. 'He asked about tennis and football,' Bahamontes said, 'but I couldn't really help him because he supported Real Madrid and I was a Barcelona supporter. At the end of our interview he thanked me for what I'd done for the country.'

In 1960 he abandoned after only three days with nothing higher than a small hill behind him, upset by a knee injury and a succession of flat days. A photo of him sitting miserably on a suitcase as he waited for a train is one of the classic pictures of the Tour.

Bahamontes had won in 1959 with the help of FRANCE, so there is an irony to his complaint that he came second rather than first in 1963 because the organisers wanted the French favourite, JACQUES ANQUETIL, to win.

'They gave him an extra second at the end of stage 17,' he said, 'where he'd got all the peloton to work for him, and a motorbike had given him a hand as well. I had the yellow JERSEY but there was no point in continuing to fight even with just four days to go. There was a TIME TRIAL the following day [in which Anquetil was usually unbeatable] and I knew the whole thing had been set up against me.' (And *see* LUCIEN AIMAR for other complaints against the race organisers.)

Bahamontes rode just twice more, coming third in 1964 before suffering a sharp decline in 1965. On the stage to Bagnères-Bigorre in the Pyrenees, where he used to dominate, he suffered badly on the TOURMALET and AUBISQUE and only just scraped inside the time limit, 40 minutes back on JULIO JIMENEZ. Next day he attacked foolishly on the banks of the Garonne, got part way up the Portet d'Aspet, swung his leg over the saddle and left the Tour and the sport for good. JOCK WADLEY wrote, 'The Eagle [of Toledo, his NICKNAME] has had his last little flutter in the mountains before saying farewell to the Tour which he has enlivened with his pedals and his personality for 11 years.'

Bahamontes used to wander the streets at night and didn't discover the value of massages or a controlled diet until well into his career. His manager at Margnat, sponsored by a wine-maker, was Raoul Rémy. He said '[Baha-montes] never had a strategy in the mountains. He just didn't want anyone on his wheel.' Bahamontes himself said, 'I always did best on the really hot days because then my opponents couldn't take as much dope as they would have liked. [Amphetamine exaggerates thirst, already at near dangerous levels in an era when riders believed that drinking during a race slowed digestion.] . . . But I didn't use the stuff myself because I was always too nervous.'

Bahamontes will be remembered for his twitchy, staring style, and also for such extraordinary acceleration in the hills that in just 12.5km of the PUY-DE-DOME in 1959 he forced four riders onto the wrong side of the time limit and out of the race. 'His attacks were spectacular and decisive,' said RAPHAËL GÉMINIANI.

Bahamontes retired after his last Tour ride and now sells BIKES and motorbikes at his shop in Toledo. He also owns land outside the city. He goes on celebrity tours with Julio Jimenez and almost 40 years after his retirement still receives daily letters addressed simply to 'F. Bahamontes, Spain', or 'Federico Bahamontes' and a sketch of an eagle.

Winner

1955	Tour Asturias
1957	Tour Asturias
1958	National championship
1959	Tour de France
1965	Montjuich, Tour Sud-Est

Tour de France

1954	25th	Mountains winner
1956	4th	
1957	DNF	
1958	8th	Stage wins Pau—Luchon, Gap—Briançon, and Mountains winner
1959	1st	Stage win Clermont-Ferrand—Puy-de-Dôme, Mountains winner and Yellow Jersey
1960	DNF	
1962	14th	Stage win Luchon—Superbagnères, and Mountains winner

Tour de France (continued)

1963	2nd	Stage win St-Étienne—Grenoble, and Yellow Jersey and Mountains winner
1964	3rd	Stage wins Thonon—Briançon, Luchon—Pau, and Mountains winner
1965	DNF	

ERCOLE BALDINI
b. Villanova de Forli, Italy, Jan 26 1933

Ercole Baldini was a man of colossal early talent who disappointed because he only reluctantly took on the areas of the sport which could have turned ability into popularity.

A hefty Italian (1.78m and 80kg) on the scale of GERMANY's RUDI ALTIG, he beat the world hour record twice as an amateur, riding 44.870km in 1954 and 46.393km in 1956. On the second occasion he beat the professional record held by JACQUES ANQUETIL. His career included the Olympic and world pursuit titles in 1956, the Giro d'Italia in 1958, the Grand Prix des Nations in 1960, and two national road championships (1957 and 1958).

Baldini turned professional when he was 24, by which time critics said he had too many miles on the clock to be a superb pro. He could ride stage races, as his Giro victory showed, and he was a good CLIMBER despite his build. But he preferred to ride against the clock in TIME TRIALS.

RAPHAËL GÉMINIANI says, 'He was shy and reserved, a great rider. But he stayed a little too amateurish in attitude and the way he acted, which didn't appeal to the media and therefore the fans, who would have preferred more rivalry. He was most concerned with his rivalry with Jacques Anquetil, and he really rose to the occasion when they rode against each other in time trials. He didn't often beat him because they were Anquetil's speciality, but that didn't matter to him so much as the pleasure he got from them, which explains his lack of interest in the classics and the Tour de France.'

The French journalist PIERRE CHANY, a confidante of Anquetil's, was with the two of them before the Grand Prix de Forli, the classic time trial which both were to ride. Chany's anecdote doesn't give the date (although Baldini won in 1958 and 1959). Chany wrote, 'I can't remember which of them said it but one turned to the other and said, "You know what? We both know we're the favourites and that one or the other of us is going to win. Let's not bother with *l'am-phèt* [amphetamine]. Tomorrow, just to see, let's ride on just mineral water."

'The other agreed and they went off to bed. The next day, because they were both men of their word, they rode on mineral water. They certainly took the first two places, but they suffered like the damned to get an average speed that was a kilometre and a half slower than they would normally have ridden. "Never again!" they told me as they got off their bikes.' (*See* Anquetil entry for more on his views on DOPING.)

Baldini's career coincided with the big-spending habits of his Ignis team. (*See* SPONSORS for details.) Ignis paid Baldini the equivalent of £40,000 in advance for a year's contract — and that was in the 1960s. As a result, Baldini could pick and choose what races he rode even more. He deliberately priced himself out of the market for CRITERIUMS. But unfortunately he had a tendency to fat, and not racing made it worse.

The journalist Olivier Dazat said, 'The papers called GINO BARTALI 'the pious', but they just called Baldini 'the Fat'. Some occasional success in time trials or a duel with Jacques Anquetil ... didn't change anything. He was no longer progressing; he was getting fat.'

Baldini rode the Tour four times, coming sixth in 1959 and eighth in 1962. He retired to run his farms near Forli.

(*See* HENNIE KUIPER, MONEY.)

Winner

1956	World hour record
1957	National championship, Tour Lazio, Tour Romagna, GP Lugano, Baracchi Trophy
1958	World championship, Giro d'Italia, National championship, Baracchi Trophy
1959	Tour Emilia, Baracchi Trophy
1960	GP Nations
1961	Baracchi Trophy

Tour de France

1959	6th
1960	33rd
1962	8th
1964	DNF

BALLON D'ALSACE

The Ballons are the three highest summits at the southern end of the Vosges in eastern France. When the Ballon d'Alsace, the Tour's first mountain, was introduced in 1905, organiser HENRI DESGRANGE predicted that nobody would be able to ride it. In fact RENÉ POTTIER did it twice, even overtaking Desgrange's car. His MEMORIAL stands at the summit.

The Ballon is 1,247m high. It has been a stage FINISH in 1967 (LUCIEN AIMAR), 1969 (EDDY MERCKX), 1972 (BERNARD THÉVENET) and 1979 (PIERRE-RAYMOND VILLEMIANE).

(*See* MOUNTAINS for how Desgrange was reluctant to include the Pyrenees and how crossing the TOURMALET on foot nearly killed his assistant.)

FRANCO BALMAMION
b. Nole Canavese, Italy, Jan 11 1940

Franco Balmamion was a classy Italian rider who rarely made it successfully across the Alps. He won consecutive Giros in 1962 and 1963 – although without winning a stage – and a good career promised in the Tour de France. But the talent didn't transfer well: he rode five times and finished three. He did finish third to

ROGER PINGEON and JULIO JIMENEZ in 1967, but never again got into the top ten.

Winner

1962	Giro d'Italia, Milan-Turin, Tour Apennines
1963	Giro d'Italia, Championship Zurich
1967	Tour Tuscany, National championship

Tour de France

1963	DNF
1967	3rd
1969	39th
1970	12th
1971	DNF

JULES BANINO

b. Nice, France, Nov 16 1872, d. Nice, France, Jun 12 1947

The Frenchman Jules Banino, a policeman from the Mediterranean coast, was the Tour's oldest ever rider. (*See* AGES for the youngest and oldest winners.) He rode the Tour in 1921 and then again in 1924, when he was 51. He finished on neither occasion.

Banino was an adventurer of a kind impossible to find these days. He didn't finish in 1924 because he had been disqualified for finishing outside the time limit, the result of being blinded by dust from unmade roads. But he still had to get home to Nice, so he set off just ahead of the race because it happened to be going that way. In those days the Tour started at night and the leaders, already cracking along at a good pace, were alarmed to hear that a rider was ahead of them in the darkness. The pace picked up and the riders grew ever more angry.

The race had two categories, the aces and the rest, and the aces didn't expect also-rans to show them up. So they picked up the pace to 35km/h on the rutted roads and took the descents at 50km/h. Finally they spotted a lone figure in the headlights of the cars leading the way.

'Who are you?' they demanded.

'I'm Jules Banino, an amateur. I'm just riding home at my own pace.'

The reference to 'my own pace' and its unintended insult to men who'd just spent an hour chasing him wasn't taken lightly. OTTAVIO BOTTECCHIA, normally a placid man, began thumping him. Then Jean Alavoine joined in, giving him a great kick that knocked Banino into a ditch. To make things worse, the incident happened to be seen by Alavoine's supporters. They assumed something dastardly had happened and, ignoring Banino's protests, began hitting him with sticks. The off-duty policeman was in such a state that it took several hours before he was ready to complete his ride home.

The writer Roger Dries claimed that Banino would do almost anything for a challenge. In his *Le Tour de France de Chez Nous* he wrote, 'You saw him in all the sports events ever organised. There was a swimming meeting? He'd be the first to turn up, perched on his bike, and he'd dive into the sea and take part. A pole-climbing contest? Banino would be there. He once even took on the same wager as the Count of Monte Cristo [hero of the book by Alexandre Dumas], tying himself in a sack and being thrown into the Mediterranean, at Tabau-Capeu. He almost drowned. He had to be pulled out in a hurry and was hardly breathing when they got to him.'

Tour de France

1921	DNF
1924	DNF

GINO BARTALI

b. Ponte a Ema, Italy, Jul 18 1914, d. Ponte a Ema, Italy, May 5 2000

Two great stars emerged in ITALY on each side of the second world WAR. They were so different in character that they divided the country in the 1950s in the way that RAYMOND POULIDOR and JACQUES ANQUETIL split FRANCE in the 1960s. And they became such rivals that they viewed each other with suspicion even when they were in the same NATIONAL TEAM. (*See* ALFREDO BINDA for why they were like 'a cat and a dog in the same sack.')

The first was Gino Bartali, whose star years began before the war, and the other was FAUSTO COPPI, who came to his peak when peace returned. Their careers are forever interlinked.

Gino Bartali looked like a boxer but soared like the angels that he worshipped. He won the Tour in 1938 and 1948, with ten years and a war between the two victories. He won the Giro three times, Milan-San Remo four times, and the Tour of Lombardy three times. And all this he would tell you at length because he was also a boaster.

Bartali was born in July 1914. His family was considered typically Tuscan, which means hard-headed, hardworking, deeply traditional, and religious. Their third son inherited all these traits. He began work in a bicycle repair shop and started racing when he was 13. His early canniness with MONEY led him to sell races he would have won in exchange for first prize. He may not have won them, but he did pocket both first and second prizes, which was useful because his father Torello was a poorly paid labourer.

In 1935, when he was 20, Bartali won the MOUNTAINS competition in the Giro for the first time. By his 22nd birthday he had won both the Giro and the Tour of Lombardy. His reputation in Italy was already secure, but outside the country he was untested.

His first Tour, in 1937, looked like confirming foreign suspicions that he was just another Italian – successful at home but weak where it mattered. By the third stage he was more than eight minutes down, creeping to 10:06 after the BALLON D'ALSACE. And then on the GALIBIER, a road of potholes and loose stones, he reached the col 1:14 ahead but, more important, with greater leads over the top riders overall. He finished in Grenoble secure in the yellow JERSEY, 9:18 up on Edward Vissers of BELGIUM, 9:55 on ERICH BAUTZ of GERMANY, 16:35 on SYLVÈRE MAES, another Belgian, and 23:35 on the Frenchman ROGER LAPÉBIE.

Bartali, confirming his nickname of 'the Pious', had his jersey blessed by a priest next morning. It did little good. His team-mate Jules Rossi skidded in front of Bartali on a wooden bridge over the river Colau just as he was chasing a break. Bartali was thrown over the parapet. Another team-mate, Francesco Camusso, plunged into the water to save him.

Bartali struggled out, his arm and knee bleeding, and his breathing painful because of a blow to the chest. Remarkably, he struggled on to the FINISH at Briançon with the help of a lot of pushes. The sight of him in a yellow jersey covered in mud and blood caused a sensation. He had lost 'only' 10 minutes, though, and kept his first place. Still more astonishingly, although the injuries grew more painful and he lost the race lead, he got through the rest of the Alps and retired only when the race got to MARSEILLE.

Next summer Bartali mastered the entire Tour, beating FÉLICIEN VERVAECKE, the Belgian runner-up, by 18:27, and the third man, Victor Cossan of FRANCE, by 29:26. After watching the Italians waving their green-white-and-red flags and chanting Bartali's name, the author Georges Briquet wrote, 'These people had found a superman. Outside Bartali's hotel at Aix-les-Bains an Italian general was holding back the crowd by shouting, "Don't touch him – he's a god!"' Italy began a public subscription for Bartali's benefit and Italian dictator Benito Mussolini himself contributed.

Bartali survived the war, unlike Mussolini (who was hanged upside down in the Piazza Loreto in Milan, where the first Giro started). He came back to racing aged 34, lacking race practice and worried enough to make a point of memorising the numbers of two dozen riders he didn't recognise. A lot of old faces had vanished in the conflict and youngsters had come along to replace them.

Many other riders had the same worries as Bartali, and the 1948 Tour started with all the dignity of an upturned beehive. Attack after attack went away, but a downpour sent riders grasping for waterproofs. The jackets hid riders' numbers, and Bartali looked around for just one man he could recognise.

He fastened on the first to pass and only eventually realised it was the Belgian ace BRIEK SCHOTTE. In the words of JEAN-PAUL

OLLIVIER, Bartali clung to him with the desperation of a man in a shipwreck. The two hurtled into the TRACK at Trouville and Bartali secured the yellow jersey. At Lourdes, at the foot of the Pyrenees 'Gino the Pious' sent a telegram to Pope Pius XII asking for benediction. Then he entered the shrine of Bernardette Soubirous, the Saint of Lourdes, and prayed not that he should win – 'Only I can do that,' he conceded – but that he shouldn't fall.

As it happened it was Italy itself that nearly fell, and a peculiar Tour became even stranger. In mid-July a young law student had shot the Communist leader Palmiro Togliatti as he was leaving the Chamber of Deputies in Rome, and the country was threatened with acute civil disturbance. The politician lay in a coma with wounds to his neck and back, and angry communists occupied factories and seized broadcasting centres in the capital.

On the Tour's rest day at Cannes, Bartali went to the beach with his team-mates, a bottle of vermouth and several packets of cigarettes. They decided to leave the race if Togliatti died, and assumed that the next day's stage, from Cannes to Briançon, would be their last. That night the prime minister, Alcide De Gasperi, called Bartali, begging him to win the Tour in order to distract the country from civil chaos. Bartali obliged by winning three stages in a row and the Tour itself by nearly 14 minutes. Togliatti woke from his coma, enquired after the Tour, and urged the country to calm down. Politicians who had come close to fighting each other in the Chamber of Deputies all applauded Bartali's victory, and the crisis was averted. (And *see* PIERRE BEUFFEUIL for another presidential intervention.)

In 1950 Bartali's Tour career took another odd turn. The race had reached the Pyrenees, and Bartali had been dropped on the AUBISQUE by JEAN ROBIC. But the Italian made up ground over the TOURMALET and then rode with Robic over the Aspin, which starts at a right-hand corner at the foot of the Tourmalet.

What happened next is unclear, but it appears Bartali and Robic brushed shoulders or wheels and fell. There was a commotion, and Bartali claimed that SPECTATORS were so angry

that Robic, a Frenchman, had fallen, that they punched him, and one of them even threatened him with a knife. On the other hand LOUISON BOBET, who was passing as it happened, said, 'I'm pretty sure that in the time it took me to pass him, Bartali wasn't struck, and I think he mistook as blows what was just as attempt to get him back in the saddle.' A hunt for the knifeman brought only recollections of some man who happened to be slicing a sausage and still had the knife in his hand as he went to help.

Bartali won the stage despite the fall and FIORENZO MAGNI, the leader of Italy's second team, took the yellow jersey. All seemed to have ended well for Italy. An hour later, though, Bartali said he was going home and taking the Italian team with him. JACQUES GODDET and FÉLIX LÉVITAN, the organisers, couldn't dissuade him when they visited him at the Hôtel de France in Lourdes, even though they assured him it was an isolated case because FRANCE loved him. But Bartali answered, cigarette between his lips, 'I have no intention of risking my life to a madman even if he is the only one of the species.'

Such was Bartali's influence that Magni, who was leading the race for the theoretically rival Italian *Cadetti*, shrugged and said, 'I'll do what Gino does,' and packed his own bags as well. (And *see* SPONSORS for why Magni was laughed at for signing up with a face-cream company – but started a trend in the process.)

Of all his wins, Bartali rated most highly the Tour of Switzerland in 1946, when he saw off challenges from the home favourites, FERDY KÜBLER and HUGO KOBLET, and also from Fausto Coppi.

Bartali never enjoyed a comfortable relationship with Coppi until both men had left top competition. Their paths crossed first on January 7 1940 when Eberrardo Pavesi, the MANAGER of the Legano team, told Bartali he had signed Coppi to support him in the Giro. Bartali is said to have frowned because Coppi looked so weak. But the new boy quickly moved from supporter to rival, winning the Giro when he chased and passed a break on the Abetone climb, and eventually won by four minutes.

Bartali was not amused, and had organised the whole Legano team in chase. Their rivalry lasted 20 years. Both climbed off rather than help the other win in the 1949 world championship at Valkenburg, HOLLAND.

Such was Bartali's frustration that he even searched Coppi's luggage for the drugs he suspected him of using. 'I hurried to the waste basket and to the bedroom table,' he said in his memoirs. 'I swiped all the flasks, bottles, phials, tunes, cartons, boxes, suppositories. I gathered them all up.' He demanded that a DOMESTIQUE, Primo Volpi, should sample them. Volpi began riding 'like a star', Bartali said. This convinced him that he should look even more closely at Coppi's 'scientific preparation', the favoured term of the day.

'I became so expert in the use of this pharmacy,' he said, 'that I knew in advance how Fausto would go in the stage. I could work out from the products how and when he was going to attack me.' Bartali protested his own innocence, telling RENÉ DE LATOUR that 'only once in my life was I crazy enough to accept something a trainer handed me in a race; [It] put me in a ditch, with my heart pounding like a steam engine, my head dizzy.' But the truth is that in retirement both he and Coppi sang songs on television telling of how they had doped themselves.

Bartali raced as a professional from 1935 to 1954, finishing his last Tour in 11th place a year earlier, aged 39. Unwise investments lost him a lot of money but he also gave much of it away. He supported humanitarian causes and during the war helped rescue Jews hidden in a convent by smuggling documents on his bicycle. (*See* JEAN ROBIC for similar activities.)

Bartali was never a warm man. His favourite assessment of life was, 'Everything's wrong; we must start all over again.' The best that PIERRE CHANY could say in his favour was that while he frequently boasted of what had happened on remote mountains with few witnesses, he never told the same story differently. In retirement he hosted a satirical television programme and appeared in films.

Bartali liked recognition, always stopping to sign autographs, even when driving a car in the Giro. He never lost his intense religious belief, and ate with a statuette of the Madonna on his table. But the years robbed him of his money, his slimness, his voice and his mind. 'In later life don't become like Gino Bartali,' MIGUEL INDURAIN was warned by his MANAGER, José-Miguel Echavarri.

Bartali died of a heart attack at his home near Florence in 2000, when he was 85; he had been given the last rites 10 days earlier. The prime minister, Giuliano Amato, sent condolences. The president of the European Commission, Romano Prodi, called him 'a symbol of the most noble sportsmanship'. The Italian Olympic Committee announced two days of mourning, marked by a minute's silence before sports events.

Faustino Coppi, Fausto's son, said, 'With Bartali's death, a piece of my father's memory dies too.'

Winner

1935	Tour Basque Country, National championship
1936	Giro d'Italia, Tour Lombardy
1937	Giro d'Italia, National championship, Tour Piedmont
1938	Tour de France, Tre Valle Varesine
1939	Milan-San Remo, Tour Lombardy, Tour Piedmont, Tour Tuscany
1940	Milan-San Remo, Tour Lombardy, National championship, Tour Tuscany
1945	Tour Lazio
1946	Giro d'Italia, Tour Switzerland, Championship Zurich
1947	Tour Switzerland, Milan-San Remo
1948	Tour de France, Championship Zurich, Tour Tuscany
1949	Tour Romandie
1950	Milan-San Remo, Tour Tuscany
1951	Tour Piedmont
1952	Tour Reggio Calabria, National championship, Tour Emilia
1953	Tour Emilia, Tour Tuscany

1937	DNF	Stage win Aix-les-Bains—Grenoble, and Yellow Jersey
1938	1st	Stage wins Montpellier—Marseille, Digne—Briançon, and Yellow Jersey and Mountains leader
1948	1st	Stage wins Paris—Trouville, Biarritz—Lourdes, Lourdes—Toulouse, Cannes—Briançon, Briançon—Aix-les-Bains, Aix-les-Bains—Lausanne, Metz—Liège, and Yellow Jersey and Mountains leader
1949	2nd	Stage win Cannes—Briançon, and Yellow Jersey
1950	DNF	Stage win Pau—St-Gaudens
1951	4th	
1952	4th	
1953	11th	

HONORÉ BARTHÉLEMY

b. Paris, France, Sep 25 1890, d. Paris, France, May 12 1964

Frenchman Honoré Barthélemy had one of the worst CRASHES in cycling history. On the stage to Aix-en-Provence in 1920 he fell heavily and climbed back on his bike, groggy and bleeding. He was so battered that he had to turn his handlebars up the other way because he couldn't bend his back. Within a few minutes he realised something even worse had happened: what he thought was blurred vision was blindness in one eye. A flint had gone into it.

The astonishing thing is that he finished not only the stage but the Tour, coming eighth despite semi-blindness and constant pain. As if that wasn't enough, he also had a broken shoulder and a dislocated wrist. Crowds carried him in triumph when he got to the PARC DES PRINCES.

Losing an eye didn't stop Barthélemy from racing. He replaced it with a glass eye that he would take out whenever the roads were dusty – which was generally. The socket would then become infected so he would fill it with cotton wool. 'It makes no difference to the view but it's softer and I always like a bit of pampering,' he said with irony.

The writer ALBERT LONDRES came across him by the roadside in the 1924 Tour, on the stage from Brest to Les Sables d'Olonne, a distance of 412km. 'Another rider has stopped by the side of the road,' he wrote later. 'He's not repairing his machine but his face. He's got one real eye and one glass one. He takes the eye out to wipe it. "I've only had it four months; I'm not used to it."

'He tapped the socket. "It's got pus in it."

'You in pain?'

'"No, but my brain's leaking."'

(*See* Albert Londres for the confessions of HENRI PÉLISSIER about DOPING in that year's Tour.)

The false eye wasn't a great success and often fell out. Later in that year's race Barthélemy was reduced to getting down on his knees at the FINISH line to see where it had rolled. 'I spend all the prizes I win on buying new eyes for the ones that I lose in races,' he grumbled.

Barthélemy rode the Tour eight times between 1919 and 1927 but finished only the first three, coming third in 1921.

Winner

| 1921 | Paris-St-Étienne |

Tour de France

1919	5th	Stage wins Bayonne—Luchon, Marseille—Nice, Nice—Grenoble, Grenoble—Geneva
1920	8th	
1921	3rd	Stage win Geneva—Strasbourg
1922	DNF	
1923	DNF	
1924	DNF	
1925	DNF	
1927	DNF	

MICHELE BARTOLI
b. Pisa, Italy, May 27 1970

Michele Bartoli is a talented rider with more successes in northern Europe, particularly BELGIUM, than is often the case for an Italian. But hopes that he would repeat the formula in the Tour de France, if only to win a stage, have come to nothing. He has ridden the race four times, never improving on the 19th place he took in his debut in 1996, and he has never taken a stage. It is not too late, but time is running out.

Bartoli is the son of an AMATEUR rider, Graziano Bartoli, whose career ended after a CRASH. He named his first son after MICHELE DANCELLI, his hero and the winner of Milan-San Remo in 1970, and was rewarded when his son began showing interest in cycling when he was only eight.

Michele Bartoli turned pro in 1992 and a year later won his first race, the Sicilian Week, including two stages. He formed part of the Italian invasion of Belgium that began in the 1990s and overturned years of indifference to races in the cold north – a change driven by the presence of the Tour of Flanders in the World Cup competition. He won the Flèche Brabançonne in the snow in 1994, and the Three Days of De Panne in 1995. His Tour of Flanders win in 1996 was his first World Cup victory and his fondest memory.

And then it all looked like going wrong when he crashed in the Tour of GERMANY in 1999, broke his kneecap and ripped a knee tendon. It took a complicated operation and 18 months of convalescence to put it right. 'I swung from dreaming of becoming a cyclist again to periods of deep doubt,' he said during the 2000 Tour, where he said his fitness didn't match his morale and eventually quit the race.

This produced mixed feelings in ITALY: the fans didn't want to lose one of their biggest classics hopes, but some have criticised him as a selfish, brazen, self-regarding, Ferrari-driving Flash Harry. Nonetheless, there is always more to anyone's personality than is revealed by his public image and Bartoli says, 'I love being cuddled by my grandmothers. They go on doing it as they did when I was a boy. The trouble is distance; since December 1997 [my wife] Alessandra and I have lived in Monaco.'

His BROTHER Mauro was also a professional briefly before working in the family woodworking business.

Winner

1993	Sicilian Week
1994	Flèche Brabançonne
1995	Three-days De Panne
1996	Tour Flanders, GP Fourmies, Tour Reggio Calabria, Tour Veneto, Tour Emilia
1997	World Cup, Liège-Bastogne-Liège, GP Frankfurt
1998	World Cup, Liège-Bastogne-Liège, GP Gippingen, GP Suisse, Tour Reggio Calabria, Three-days Panne De Panne, Tour Romagna
1999	Flèche Wallonne, Flèche Brabançonne, Tirreno-Adriatico
2000	GP Plouay
2001	Het Volk
2002	Tour Mediterranean, Amstel Gold

Tour de France

1996	19th
1997	DNF
2000	DNF
2001	33rd

MARINO BASSO
b. Rettorgole, Italy, Jun 1 1945

ITALY's Marino Basso rode the Tour four times between 1967 and 1972, finishing three times. He won six stages but never finished better overall than 63rd (1970, an improvement of one place over 1967). As a SPRINTER he wouldn't realistically have expected to do better, because fast finishers always find their bulk a problem in the MOUNTAINS.

For half a decade Basso was one of the fastest, but also one of the least predictable, sprinters in the bunch, winning 13 stages in 13 Giros, and six stages in a single Tour of SPAIN

(1975). He took the world championship at Gap, France, in 1972, having built up just about enough lead over FRANCO BITOSSI to be able to throw both arms into the air. Sometimes he'd win by pinning his rivals to the edge of the road, at other times by leading out with 300 metres to go and daring anyone to come by. However he did it, he rarely lost a sprint from 1968 to 1972, making him the MARIO CIPOLLINI of his day.

Like Cipollini, Basso liked the good life. He took to it in a big way with girls and sports cars after his world championship and while he could still win. He retired to become a team MANAGER.

Winner

1969	Trofeo Matteotti, Tour Piedmont, Tre Valle Varesine
1972	World championship, Tour Sardinia
1973	GP Gippingen
1977	Coppa Placci

Tour de France

1967	64th	Stage wins Caen—Amiens, Pau—Bordeaux
1969	DNF	Stage win Roubaix—Woluwe-St-Pieter
1970	63rd	Stage wins Angers—Rennes, Divonne—Thonon, Ruffec—Tours
1972	82nd	

CHRISTOPHE BASSONS
b. Mazamet, France, Jun 10 1974

Speaking out about DOPING during the 1999 Tour cost Christophe Bassons his place in the race, his share of his team's prizes, and ultimately his career.

Bassons was lucky to turn professional in 1996 with no more to his career than the French AMATEUR national TIME TRIAL championship in 1995. He joined the Festina team but wasn't considered good enough to ride the Tour. That meant he was still at home in 1998 when Festina's SOIGNEUR, WILLY VOET, was caught on the Belgian border with a carload of drugs destined for Bassons' team-mates. (*See* FESTINA SCANDAL.)

Riders were arrested and questioned. In September 1998 *Le Parisien* printed some of the Festina riders' statements, including comments by Armin Meier and CHRISTOPHE MOREAU that Bassons was the only member of the team not using drugs. Newspapers immediately contacted him. He gave as many as eight interviews a day and began writing a column for *Le Parisien*. Most of his comments were innocuous and often dispelled rumours about doping. Riders didn't like him talking about the subject publicly but he was ignored, if not forgiven, so long as he said nothing damaging.

The 1998 Tour had almost failed to get to Paris at all as some riders were thrown out and others just walked out. The Tour authorities billed its successor in 1999 as a race of 'renewal', and riders were said to have learned their lesson. A similar claim had been made in 1968 after the death of TOM SIMPSON. (*See* STRIKES for riders' attitude to attempts to crack down on drug-taking.)

Bassons dismissed this so-called renewal as an 'illusion' when the peloton kept moving at 50km/h. 'I am not the only clean rider,' he said, 'but there aren't many who can say, "I don't take drugs".' Some riders 'used to ride like they were continually going downhill'.

Some riders ignored Bassons, others shunned him, many insulted him. Some told him he would never again win a race, which indeed he didn't. In the end LANCE ARMSTRONG rode up alongside and told him that he shouldn't be in the Tour given his attitude. Bassons reported the encounter in his column: 'He told me it was a mistake to speak out the way I do and asked me why I was doing it. I told him that I'm thinking about the next generation of riders. Then he [Armstrong] said, "Why don't you leave, then?"' Armstrong confirmed the conversation. Bassons was repeatedly in tears because of the stress.

At 5.30am on July 16 he packed his bags after a night worrying about now open threats from other riders and informed his MANAGER, MARC MADIOT, that he had abandoned. It was the

11th stage and he disappeared in a journalist's car – an action which led organiser JEAN-MARIE LEBLANC to wonder if he had been 'manipulated by the press'. That had an irony considering that Leblanc had himself been a journalist seeking riders' confidences for L'ÉQUIPE, the newspaper owned by the same ASO group that owns the Tour and, ironically, *Le Parisien.*

In February 2000 Xavier Jan, a representative of riders in Bassons' by then former team, La Française des Jeux (the state lottery), said he wouldn't get a share of its prizes from the 1999 Tour. Traditionally riders pool their winnings and an overall winner gives his prizes to every-one else (a tradition formalised in France by LOUISON BOBET and the MANAGER of the French team, MARCEL BIDOT; *see* DOMES-TIQUES for more.) Jan said, 'Bassons rode only for himself . . . So, in keeping with the team's rules, we have decided not to pay him for the work he didn't do.' Jan denied it had anything to do with his doping comments.

Bassons raced again in 2000 for Jean Dela-tour, remarking, 'I still don't know what many riders think of me and some still won't talk to me.' He was with Jean Delatour when his book, *Positif,* appeared with more details of doping practices, thus ending his career.

Bassons had an unusually high education for a bike rider, with a degree in civil engineering. He was considered an intellectual in a sport where reading books makes a rider a bit of a boffin. After retiring as a pro, he began working with the sport and youth ministry in BOR-DEAUX and studied to become a sports instruc-tor. He also took part in a series of question-and-answer sessions with, among others, Voet, the now repentant soigneur, whose cache of drugs had triggered off the scandal in the first place.

(*See* PAUL KIMMAGE for another rider whose career ended after talking about drugs.)

Tour de France

1999   DNF

STEVE BAUER
b. Sainte-Catherine, Canada, Jun 12 1959

Steve Bauer is Canada's greatest success. After coming second to Alexi Grewal of AMERICA in the 1984 Olympic road race, he gained a place in BERNARD HINAULT's La Vie Claire team in 1985. After joining the 7-Eleven team in 1990, Bauer came within millimetres of beating EDDY PLANCKAERT of BELGIUM in the Paris-Roubaix race, saying it was 'OK to finish second at Roubaix'. He then got into a crucial break in the Tour and spent 10 days in yellow. He was the second Canadian to lead the race after ALEX STIEDA had first done so in 1986.

'People said I was lucky but I made that luck,' he said. 'I knew the JERSEY would be selected by a break that day, so I was at the front from the START of the stage looking for one to go. When it happened, we got the gap up to about a minute and a half. At 60km to go I thought, "OK, they'll reel us in now." But then all of a sudden, boom! The gap grew: four, six, seven minutes. That was the amazing surprise.'

He finished 27th in Paris although this was not his best performance. Two years earlier he had come in just one place off the final podium. No Canadian has ever finished in the first three.

Bauer's career was tinged with unhappiness, however. In 1988 there were 12km to go in the world championship in BELGIUM. The Canadian and three French riders, including LAURENT FIGNON, were chasing Maurizio Fondriest of ITALY and the local man, Claude Criquélion. Bauer got across to the break just before the FINISH, where he and the Belgian contested the sprint. Bauer's elbow caught the Belgian and Criqélion crashed into the barriers. Within five minutes Bauer was disqualified and threatened with legal action by Criquélion, who saw a fortune vanishing in lost contracts. It took three and a half years for Bauer to be cleared legally.

Bauer rode the Tour 11 times, every year from 1985 to 1995. Then his marriage broke down and he left Europe, joining the Saturn team in AMERICA at the end of 1996. He retired a year later.

RAPHAËL GÉMINIANI said of him, 'Steve Bauer never pretended to be one of the best riders in Europe but the fact that he could rub shoulders with them [an unintended pun given the Criquiélion incident] demands congratulations. If cycling has become more of a worldwide sport then it's because of riders like Bauer and PHIL ANDERSON.'

Winner

1988 GP Americas, Tour Oise, Trofeo
      Pantalica
1989 Championship Zurich

Tour de France

1985	10th	
1986	23rd	
1987	74th	
1988	4th	Stage win Pontchâteau—Machecoul, and Yellow Jersey
1989	15th	
1990	27th	Yellow Jersey
1991	97th	
1992	DNF	
1993	101st	
1994	DNF	
1995	101st	

ERICH BAUTZ
b. Dortmund, Germany, May 26 1913, d. Dortmund, Germany, Sep 17 1986

Erich Bautz won the German national championship in 1937 (a year when it consisted of a points competition over several races), and then caught the train to Paris. Three days later he started the Tour de France. Germans shouted for him on the BALLON D'ALSACE, close to the border, and he was inspired to win alone by four minutes at Belfort. Time BONUSES doubled the advantage of a lone winner so that this comparative outsider in an unfancied NATIONAL TEAM took the yellow JERSEY. He led the favourite, GINO BARTALI, by no less than 12 minutes. Sacks of letters began arriving and over the next three stages he rode brilliantly in his red socks, persuading many in Germany that he could win.

Their hopes died, sadly, when Bartali attacked on the stage to Grenoble and Bautz suffered first a run of punctures on the GALIBIER and then with toothache. In the end he came ninth and JACQUES GODDET wrote, 'Without his bad luck in the Alps, the German champion would have finished with the best. He proved that he was as good on the flat as in the MOUNTAINS and that he deserved his place among the best.'

Bautz returned to racing after the WAR, winning the German championship for a third time in 1950.

Winner

1937 National championship
1941 National championship
1947 Tour Germany
1950 National championship

Tour de France

1936	DNF	
1937	9th	Stage wins Metz—Belfort, Bordeaux—Royan, and Yellow Jersey

BENONI BEHEYT
b. Zwijnaarde, Belgium, Sep 27 1940

BELGIUM's Benoni Beheyt rode three Tours (1963, 1964 and 1965) and won a stage in 1964. But he is best known as the man who tugged RIK VAN LOOY's jersey to become WORLD CHAMPION in 1963. Or did he?

The championship on August 11 1963 was in Ronse, Belgium, and looked like being a benefit for the home crowd. Beheyt was in the leading group with van Looy, the team leader and favourite. Van Looy had offered each of the Belgian team the equivalent of £300 to help him win a third rainbow JERSEY. Belgian teams are notorious for internal splits, though, because of the intensity of competition between riders and SPONSORS in such a small country (in fact, just half a small country, because cycling is concentrated in the Dutch-speaking north). Gilbert Desmet saw his own chance on the run-in to the FINISH and attacked. He was caught, but positions in the breakaway group changed in the chase and Beheyt found himself alongside van Looy.

It has never been clear what happened next, but photos show Beheyt's hand on the pockets of van Looy's jersey. Beheyt insisted he was fending him off, whereas van Looy's supporters claimed that he was tugging their man back. TOM SIMPSON, who had himself been tugged by van Looy in the sprint, recalled, 'Van Looy was shouting desperately for someone to give him a wheel to pace him to the front. He asked Benoni Beheyt but was told he had cramp. Beheyt was foxing and, taking the inside, had gone to the front under his own power. As I was told, van Looy saw him and switched across the road trying to ward him off. Just about side by side, Beheyt got hold of van Looy's jersey and I reckon he must have said to himself, "Should I push him? Should I hell!" And so he pulled him as his captain was trying to push him away, and he took the title by inches.'

Van Looy was diplomatic about the incident, but Beheyt's career was effectively over. He rode the Tour twice after his world championship but only because the race was once again open to sponsored trade teams rather than NATIONAL TEAMS. He and van Looy were in different teams – Beheyt with WIEL'S-Groene Leeuw, and van Looy with the stronger Solo-Superia – and van Looy was in no position to keep him out. In the 1964 Tour Beheyt even won the stage from Orléans to Versailles and the Tour of Belgium in same year. But he was never again allowed to win where van Looy had any say. He stopped racing in 1968 with 19 victories as a professional to his credit and aged just 27.

Beheyt still appears at races, notably as one of the reporters working on the race radio at Liège-Bastogne-Liège.

Winner

1963   World championship, Ghent-
          Wevelgem, GP Fourmies
1964   Tour Belgium

Tour de France

1963   49th
1964   49th   Stage win Orléans—Versailles
1965   47th

BELGIUM

Belgians have won the Tour de France 18 times, more than any other nationality except the French (36). The total is still more impressive because these successes are concentrated in the northern, Dutch-speaking region of Flanders, an area of only five million people compared to the 60 million of FRANCE. Not until 1933 did Belgium pick a rider, Georges Lemaire, who had French rather than Dutch as his first language. (*See* JAN AERTS for more on Lemaire.) Even EDDY MERCKX, who comes from the officially bilingual but in practice largely French-speaking capital of Brussels, was as much at home in Dutch as French.

Belgian riders rode the Tour from its origin, with Marcel Kerff, Jules Sales and Julien Lootens (riding under the name Samson) taking part in 1903. Lootens finished sixth and Kerff seventh. Sales did not finish.

The first Belgian to be consistently prominent outside his own country was Cyriel van Houwaert (sometimes written Hauwert), who travelled to Paris in 1907 to persuade the bike-maker LA FRANÇAISE to SPONSOR him in Paris-Roubaix. The French company didn't consider him worth the cost of PACEMAKERS needed in those days, and sent him off with just a couple of free tyres. They soon saw their error. Van Houwaert – French riders pronounced it *Ven'-ouvert*, or 'empty stomach' – left La Française's riders behind and the team's directors began negotiating with him in mid-race. He got the pacemakers he needed. He came second because of a CRASH but his reputation was made.

Van Houwaert won Paris-Roubaix in 1908, the year in which he also won Milan-San Remo. Paris-Roubaix's historian, Pascal Sergent, wrote, 'A fanfare announced the arrival of the first man but nobody was sure who it would be. It turned out to be a black mass, a sort of apparition, and the Belgians in the crowd began rejoicing when they realised it was van Houwaert. In fact he collided with a grounds-man as he came into the stadium and crashed. He got back on instantly and finished the required six laps [of the track].'

Belgians quickly established themselves in international races and became celebrated for their toughness, especially on bad roads and in poor weather. The first Belgian Tour winner was ODILE DEFRAYE in 1912. Ten thousand people lined the streets of Roeselare when he got home. He inspired others and in 1913 no less than 22 of the 51 riders with professional contracts were Belgian.

Defraye was followed by PHILIPPE THYS, who won in 1913, 1914 and 1920, FIRMIN LAMBOT (1919, 1922) and LÉON SCIEUR (1921). Between them they won seven Tours in succession. That did little for the sales of L'AUTO, the organising newspaper. The more the Belgians won, the less the French bought the paper. Despite their success, Belgians often believed that HENRI DESGRANGE, editor, organiser and chief official, penalised their riders unjustly to limit their chances.

All nations have their time, though, and Bel-gium's ran out after Lambot in 1922. There were just intermittent successes after that, and then nothing until the end of the 1960s. Bel-gium fell into a long period of introspection. Many blamed the rise of CRITERIUMS and the fat fees demanded by AGENTS such as Jean van Buggenhout for producing riders of tremen-dous speed who could win well-paid single-day races, but lacked the endurance or desire to ride races with real MOUNTAINS.

Then came Eddy Merckx. He was feast and famine – feast for him, year after year, but famine for everyone else. Appropriately enough for a nation divided by language, Merckx's surname with its improbable collec-tion of consonants was Flemish, but by calling himself Eddy rather than Ward (the Flemish abbreviation of Edward) he also bonded with the French-speaking south. Merckx turned professional in 1965, winning nine races in his first year and 20 in his second, including Milan-San Remo. He went on to win the Tour five

times (1969, 1970, 1971, 1972, 1974), the Points competition in 1969, 1971 and 1972, and the Mountains title in 1969 and 1970.

And yet his achievement was curiously counter-productive. Other riders began to compete not to win but for second place. His superiority was so great that in the 1971 Super Prestige Pernod, the forerunner of the World Cup, he won twice the number of points of the second, third, fourth and fifth riders combined. And the best Belgium could count on inter-nally was a one-sided popularity contest between Merckx and FREDDY MAERTENS. It meant Belgian cycling once more had a vacuum when he retired in 1979, and one that, bar Lucien van Impe's sole success in 1976, has still to be filled.

ROMAIN BELLENGER
b. Paris, France, Jan 18 1894, d. Cahors, France, Nov 25 1981

Romain Bellenger, a hefty man of 1.78m (which was big for the 1920s), was a giant of the years after the first world war. He turned pro for the ALCYON team in 1919 and raced for them until 1925, finishing third in the Tour of 1923. That success could have come earlier: he was the best French rider in the 1921 Tour until he stopped to drink at a mountain spring. The water was too cold and he collapsed with cramp and then diarrhoea, and finally gave up on the Col de Portet d'Aspet.

Bellenger made a habit of winning the stage from Le Havre to Cherbourg, along the north-west coast. He took it four years in five, in 1921, 1922, 1924 and 1925.

Tour de France

1920	DNF	
1921	DNF	Stage win Le Havre—Cherbourg
1922	DNF	Stage win Le Havre—Cherbourg
1923	3rd	Stage win Strasbourg—Metz, and Yellow Jersey
1924	8th	Stage wins Le Havre—Cherbourg, Metz—Dunkirk
1925	11th	Stage win Le Havre—Cherbourg
1929	DNF	

JOSEBA BELOKI
b. Lazkao, Spain, Aug 12 1973

The gnome-like Spaniard Joseba Beloki (just 1.74m and 56kg), known as 'Joe Bloke' to his less respectful British fans, was born into a cycling family. His father was a reasonable AMATEUR and his uncle, Ramon Murillo, had been a professional in the 1970s. Beloki spent every Sunday afternoon at finish lines with them. 'A bike in the Beloki family is like a *toro* with the *ganaderos* who breed the great bulls,' he said once.

Beloki turned professional in 1998 and within three years had twice come third in the Tour. Until 2000, he had never completed a three-week Tour, starting the Tour of SPAIN in 1999 but pulling out early. Moreover, he had never ridden a TIME TRIAL longer than 25km. He started the 2000 Tour de France in realistic mood, telling his parents (with whom he still lives in the Basque city of Vitoria), 'If you want to watch me race, come to the Pyrenees because I don't expect to get to Paris.'

He started the race as a DOMESTIQUE, but crept into sixth place after the HAUTACAM stage because of his climbing ability. Then he trailed round behind LANCE ARMSTRONG and JAN ULLRICH, profiting from their personal battle. He stuck close to them on MONT VENTOUX, moved into third place overall and held it to the end. Even in the time trial, a relative weakness for him as for all climbers, he finished fifth, holding off CHRISTOPHE MOREAU, his Festina team-mate and closest challenger, by 30 seconds.

He repeated the performance in 2001, once more finishing behind Armstrong and Ullrich. His team was delighted, with the possible exception of Marcel Wust, his room-mate during the Tour. Beloki relaxes to tapes of Basque folk music, and confessed, 'Marcel hated it. He is fluent in seven languages but he couldn't understand any of it.'

In 2002 Beloki came second by sticking with almost the same tactics – rarely attacking, generally following.

The writer Andrew Hood has provided another angle on Beloki's personality. His unassuming manner reminded him, Hood said, of 'a boy scout with all the honour badges for perfect attendance'.

Winner

2000	Tour Asturias
2001	Tour Catalonia
2002	Montjuich

Tour de France

2000	3rd
2001	3rd
2002	2nd

JEAN-FRANÇOIS BERNARD
b. Luzy, France, May 2 1962

The Frenchman Jean-François Bernard (who is always known as Jeff), rode the Tour eight times but never improved on his third place in 1987. It is for that race that he will always be remembered, and particularly for the TIME TRIAL from Carpentras to the top of MONT VENTOUX. Bernard swapped his bike at the foot of the climb and beat the eventual winner in Paris, STEPHEN ROCHE, by more than two minutes. He rode the barren section between the Chalet Reynard and the summit in the unusually high GEAR of 51x19 to take the yellow JERSEY.

He said, 'I knew the night before that I was going to do a ride. I'd trained on the Ventoux and I knew I had good legs. I knew I was doing well the moment I heard the crowd shouting for me.' He was convinced he had won the Tour. But the next day he wasn't so sure.

'The others ganged up against me,' he said. 'The moment I punctured they attacked, especially the Système U team under [MANAGER] CYRILLE GUIMARD, with LAURENT FIGNON, CHARLY MOTTET and the MADIOT BROTHERS. I punctured on a narrow road, which explains the delay before I got going again.' The team's car apparently had trouble passing other riders and cars to reach him. 'And then nobody would work with me.' He blamed the rivalry on the unpopularity of his manager, Paul Koechli, and on widespread support for the popular Roche.

Things got worse when he was held up again at the FEEDING AREA and then broke his gears. By the day's end at Villard-de-Lans he'd slid to third place behind Roche and the new leader, PEDRO DELGADO. But Bernard won the time trial at Dijon and scraped onto the podium in Paris. 'I am the only rider to have dominated the two time trial stages of a Tour without being the final winner,' he said. 'Everybody else who has won the time trials has also won the Tour.'

Outside the Tour his regret is never having won the Grand Prix des Nations, where he finished second in 1987 and third in 1986. 'It is always at the end of the season and I was worn out,' he said. 'I never trained specifically for it but I always came up against riders who had, like Charly Mottet or SEAN KELLY.' Bernard stopped racing in 1996 and now runs a clothing company.

Winner

1986   Tour Mediterranean
1987   GP Rennes, Tour Emilia
1992   Paris-Nice, Critérium International

Tour de France

1986	12th	Stage win Nîmes—Gap
1987	3rd	Stage wins Carpentras—Mont Ventoux, Dijon—Dijon, and Yellow Jersey
1988	DNF	
1990	DNF	
1991	14th	
1992	39th	
1993	49th	
1994	17th	
1995	34th	

EVGUENI BERZIN
b. Viborg, USSR, Jun 3 1970

Evgueni Berzin was Russia's big hope when in 1994 he won Liège-Bastogne-Liège at the age of 23. Two months later he beat MIGUEL INDURAIN to win the Giro d'Italia, wearing the leader's JERSEY for 19 days. The following year he came second. It seemed all the more remarkable because Berzin looked even younger than he was.

Berzin's fans in ITALY, where he lived, called him Eugenio rather than Evgueni and begged him to take Italian nationality. They and he expected great things in the Tour but they never happened. He rode four times from 1995 to 1998 and finished only twice. He did come 20th during his second attempt, and wore the yellow jersey. But for a man who had dominated the Giro at just 23, it wasn't enough. *Vélo* in FRANCE labelled him *Le roi de la désillusion* – the king of disillusion.

In 2000 Berzin was thrown out of the Giro for exceeding the permitted haematocrit (red blood cell) level, a quasi-DOPING offence. Critics say early success spoiled him. Friends said he wasn't willing enough to go training. 'Could do better' seems the verdict on a man who dominated Indurain at the Giro but did little at the Tour – or ultimately anywhere else.

Winner

1994   Giro d'Italia, Liège-Bastogne-Liège, Tour Appenines
1995   Bicyclette Basque

Tour de France

1995	DNF	
1996	20th	Stage win Bourg-St-Maurice—Val d'Isère, and Yellow Jersey
1997	DNF	
1998	25th	

PAOLO BETTINI
b. Cecina, Italy, Apr 1 1974

Little Paolo Bettini began racing when he was seven, riding for his village team in ITALY, La California in Tuscany. Talent showed from the start with a succession of wins as he moved up through the categories, and in 1997 he abandoned work as a mechanic to turn professional.

Bettini's debut Tour was in 2000, when he won the transitional stage (a day in between one strategically important area and another, usually the MOUNTAINS) from Agen to the foot of the Pyrenees at Dax. The climbs won him the Mountains jersey that day, but he lacked the climbing ability to win the competition overall.

Bettini, who is known mostly for his sprinting ability, has said of himself, 'I'd still like to ride for the general classification in a big tour, but for the moment, even when I'm on form, there are still 20 men ahead of me. I did finish seventh in the Giro in 1998, but most people forget that I was [lucky enough] to be allowed to gain 16 minutes on a breakaway on one stage.'

Winner

2000	Liège-Bastogne-Liège
2001	Championship Zurich, Coppa Placci,
2002	Liège-Bastogne-Liège, World Cup

Tour de France

2000	DNF	Stage win Agen—Dax, and Mountains leader
2001	70th	

PIERRE BEUFFEUIL
b. L'Eguillé, France, Oct 30 1934

The almost unknown Pierre Beuffeuil would have been completely unknown had he not missed an important bit of news during the Tour in 1960.

On Saturday July 16 the president, Charles de Gaulle, let the organisers know that he would be at the foot of his garden in Colombey-les-Deux-Églises as the race passed. Tour organiser JACQUES GODDET drove alongside the national champion HENRY ANGLADE, who happened to be alone and on his way back up to the peloton after having a pee, and said, '*Mon cher* Henry, do you think the riders would find it inconvenient to stop and say *bonjour?*' Anglade was astonished. Stop the race to shake hands? Such a thing had never happened before. But the other teams agreed, and brakes squealed as the race entered the village. There,

as promised, was de Gaulle, an admiral, and a minder, Roger Tessier.

'We have stopped to salute you, Monsieur le Président,' Goddet said. At which de Gaulle looked down his long nose and, pretending he'd never imagine such a thing would happen for one so modest, said, 'Oh, but it wasn't necessary.' He spotted Anglade's French championship JERSEY and told him he knew all about him, then he saw the *maillot jaune* of GASTONE NENCINI, whom he told he knew about from the television. And then he walked round shaking hands. But not with a handful of Belgian riders who, unaware of the presence of a foreign president, and not understanding why everyone had stopped, thought a STRIKE had started and were having a pee at the back of the crowd.

Nor did the president shake hands with Beuffeuil, who was another rider who knew nothing of the stop, because at the crucial time he had been still chasing back to the race after puncturing. Beuffeuil couldn't believe his luck when he found the whole race halted by the roadside. He put his head down and hammered on to the FINISH at Troyes. He won the stage, one of only two in his career, and has dined out on the story ever since.

(*See* TOMMASO DE PRA for another rider who won because nobody else was racing.)

Tour de France

1956	31st	
1960	31st	Stage win Besançon—Troyes
1961	28th	
1962	50th	
1963	47th	
1966	71st	Stage win Montluçon—Orléans

BIANCHI

The Italian BIKE company Bianchi and its blue-green bikes (the colour is officially called *celeste*) have had a long association with racing in general and the Tour in particular, thanks to its SPONSORSHIP of riders and teams.

The firm was founded in Milan in 1885 by 21-year-old Eduardo Bianchi, the owner of a small bike shop. Sales picked up quickly and Bianchi moved to a larger workshop, pioneering the use of pneumatic tyres in Italy. In 1895 he had enough of a reputation to be asked to provide an open-framed machine for Italy's Queen Margherita, and to teach her to ride.

Bianchi began sponsorship with Giovanni Tommaselli who won the Grand Prix de Paris on one of Bianchi's bikes in 1889. But it was the firm's links with FAUSTO COPPI that confirmed its place in cycling history. Coppi won the Giro d'Italia and the Tour de France on a Bianchi in 1949, followed by the world championship at Lugano in 1953. Other WORLD CHAMPIONS who rode Bianchis include FELICE GIMONDI in 1973, MORENO ARGENTIN in 1986 and GIANNI BUGNO in 1992 and 1993.

Bianchi shared sponsorship with the *extra-sportif* companies Carpano and Faema as times changed and bike factories could no longer afford the cost of teams alone. (*See* SPONSORS for more on *extra-sportifs*.) Bianchi was missing from the peloton from 1967 to 1972, and then left road-racing again in 1990 to concentrate on mountain-bike racing.

The firm returned to the road in 1998 when they backed MARCO PANTANI's Mercatone Uno team. But the liaison proved embarrassing because Pantani became embroiled in DOPING inquiries. In 2002 company official Christophe Soubra said, 'These last years [have] been something else. I think that everyone has understood that we need to start again with another team.' Bianchi supplied bikes to the German Coast team in 2003.

MARCEL BIDOT
b. St-Lyé, France, Dec 31 1902, d. St-Lyé, France, Jan 26 1995

Marcel Bidot rode the Tour every year from 1926 to 1930, when he came fifth, and then again in 1932. He was a good team man and a popular choice for France but not a dependable winner. He won two stages and in 1929 wore the yellow JERSEY but that was almost as far as he went as a rider. He won no big races other than Paris-Rouen, hardly a classic, in 1920.

What makes Bidot remarkable is that he was MANAGER of FRANCE's Tour team in the 1950s and 1960s, probably the richest period in its history.

Bidot came into cycling in 1920, when he worked in Troyes as a clerk for the French bank Crédit Lyonnais (SPONSOR of the yellow jersey in 2003). His father, a café owner, had also raced, and was then running the local club. When Marcel turned professional in 1923 he earned ten times the 200 francs a month he had received at the bank.

Bidot rode his first Tour in 1926. At 5,745km this Tour was the longest in history, with some days of more than 400km. The longest stage was 435km over broken roads from Metz to Dunkirk. Stages began at midnight and finished the following night with gaps sometimes measured in hours rather than seconds. It became known as the 'Tour of Suffering', a title far from discouraged by HENRI DESGRANGE's officials. They watched Bidot closely when he broke a pedal and began pedalling with just his left foot. They watched him, too, when he bound the broken pedal to the crank with a leather strap because, under the RULES, riders were responsible for their own repairs. Finally they let him take a bike from a SPECTATOR, but only on condition that he use his own wheels. Bidot pressed on, riding on a bike the wrong size, and finished the day exhausted.

Then his freewheel broke in the Pyrenees, which meant he had to ride up the Col d'Aspin in the GEAR that he planned to ride down it. Riders in the Tour weren't allowed derailleurs. He pressed on to cover not only that climb but four other cols including the TOURMALET. That day only half the field managed to struggle through awful weather to Luchon, and at midnight Desgrange had to send out search parties to find riders sheltering in inns and houses. Bidot, of whom Desgrange once said, 'He doesn't know how to suffer; he will never finish the race,' finished an hour and a half behind the stage winner, LUCIEN BUYSSE.

Two days later, after a rest, the race set off towards the Alps. Desgrange now accused Bidot of controlling the race with his team (team tactics were still banned). Finally he pronounced,

'Bidot can ride any race he likes [this time next year] except the Tour de France.' In fact Bidot did ride the Tour, although he didn't finish.

As if all this weren't enough, a judge again stepped in as Bidot struggled to remove a punctured tyre on the IZOARD. Bidot recounted, 'There I was in the Casse Déserte [a wilderness of strangely shaped rocks]. My fingers were solid with cold and I couldn't unstick the tyre from the rim. I tried to do it with my teeth. Impossible. Several minutes went by and then along came Meunier, the driver of the Alcyon car, and he threw me a penknife. The commissaire made sure I couldn't get to it. "I forbid you to pick it up," he said. I had to get the tyre off with a wing nut [the wheel bolt].' Despite all that he finished third at Briançon.

Desgrange almost warmed to him then: 'Bidot has a sluggish mentality,' he said, 'he has no drive, he's lazy and doesn't have much of a head. I believe he could have won that stage. But he's strong, fit, he climbs and descends well, and he doesn't stop at water fountains. A man who can ride his first Tour like that suggests he has courage.'

Bidot became France's team manager in 1952 in succession to his brother Jean, who had moved to the gear company Simplex (*see* GEARS for Simplex's contribution to bike technology). The rules insisted that French managers should have no connection with the bike trade, partly to avoid favouritism and partly because, without that rule, it is unlikely that partisan team sponsors would have agreed on the appointment of such a manager.

Bidot, who until that time had worked in the champagne business, led the team in 12 Tours. He won six – with LOUISON BOBET (1953, 1954, 1955), with JACQUES ANQUETIL (1957, 1961), and with ROGER PINGEON (1967) – and in his estimation could have won three more: with ANDRÉ DARRIGADE but for the unexpected win of ROGER WALKOWIAK in 1956; with ROGER RIVIÈRE had he not crashed into a ravine in 1960; and with RAYMOND POULIDOR had he not crashed on the road to Albi in 1968.

Bidot became famous for writing team selections on the back of a cigarette packet. 'Journalists never stopped remembering those Gitane packets,' he said. 'It brought me a cheque for 100,000 francs from the *Régie des Tabacs* (the state tobacco monopoly) because they reckoned I'd earned it in the publicity I'd given them.' French teams were never easy to pick because riders were often rivals with conflicting ambitions. To bind his team together Bidot even had to resort to a written contract to establish who was assigned to what role. (*See* DOMESTIQUES for details.)

His career as manager ended with the switch from national to sponsored teams in 1969 (*see* NATIONAL TEAMS), a decision he still regrets. 'It was a really sorry move because it was only about money,' he said. 'Cycling lost most of its romance and those who wanted trade teams then are the very ones who now want to bring back national teams.'

He lived until 1986 in the house he bought in St-Lyé, his home town, with the 51,900 francs he won in the 1930 Tour.

(*See* PIERRE DUMAS for Bidot's comments on the extent of DOPING.)

Winner

1920	Paris-Rouen
1924	Paris-Bourges
1929	National championship

Tour de France

1926	10th	
1927	DNF	
1928	8th	Stage win Brest—Vannes
1929	16th	Stage win Marseille—Cannes, and Yellow Jersey
1930	5th	
1932	30th	

BIKES

The first bikes in the Tour were single-speed roadsters weighing up to 20kg, two and a half times as much as a modern machine. The hubs were typically 1.20m apart compared to less than 1m today, so riders would roll rather than bounce over bad roads. Surfaces stayed poor for decades; MARCEL BIDOT remembered of the 1926 Tour, 'In the rain, the MOUNTAIN roads became bogs. A lot of riders had conventional wired-on tyres but no brakes. There was no tarred surface, only stones and pebbles.'

Early bikes had no toe-straps on the pedals, and sometimes primitive brakes that pressed not on the rim but on the tread of the tyre, which were wide and measured in inches, typically 28 x 1⅜in. Pierre Desvages of FRANCE used a BSA freewheel in 1903, but he was alone, and for years riders used fixed wheels. Freewheels didn't become popular until ÉMILE GEORGET raced down mountains on one in the 1907 Tour, and won six stages.

JOANNY PANEL in 1912 was the first rider known to have used a derailleur, but he didn't make a mark, and riders remained suspicious of the mechanism's supposed unreliability. Derailleur gears were considered fit only for everyday riders, not athletes. In fact Tour organiser HENRI DESGRANGE banned riders from using them even after they had become widespread. He saw them as a way of diluting the battle of men against adversity which he thought so important, so Tour riders had to use their fingers to move the chain between the two sprockets on each side of the wheel, or turn the rear wheel round to pick the right gear. (*See* GEARS for more.)

Desgrange's successor JACQUES GODDET allowed gears in 1937, but even then stipulated that riders must use Super-Champion derailleurs. RENÉ VIETTO, who later made the first seven-speed gear by welding extra sprockets to a five-speed, refused to do this and switched his Champion for a Simplex. A row broke out between Goddet, who had a contract with the makers of Super-Champion, and Vietto, who was similarly contracted to his friend Lucien Juy of Simplex (*see* GEARS for

Juy's contribution to bike technology). POLICE intervened when officials started a tug-of-war by trying to snatch the bike back from Vietto, who compromised by starting with no gear at all.

Vietto also pioneered double chainrings after the WAR and was first to carry his bottle on the down tube instead of the handlebars. Other riders insisted he would wobble as he reached for it. But they saw the light soon afterwards, although riders carried their second bottle in a handlebar cage until the end of the 1960s.

When it came to tyres, many riders used conventional wired-on models when the Tour began, but stuck-on tubulars were also popular. These were thick and heavy with double-thickness cotton bodies. High pressures were unwise on the rough roads. There was always a temptation to fit lighter tyres that would turn faster. In 1921 a spate of punctures led Desgrange to write, 'Riders' tyres are having a bad press at the moment. You'd be right to think that there is nothing wrong in their quality, only the understandable desire of riders to use lighter and lighter ones. On the TRACK they're little thicker than cigarette paper but on bad roads like those round Tréport and Le Havre the result of the race can be decided by a flint.' (*See* HONORÉ BARTHÉLEMY for how a rider's life was indeed changed by a flint.) In 1923 he even considered a minimum weight, or in effect thickness, of tyres.

MARCEL BIDOT said that riders in his time carried three spare tyres looped round their shoulders, but even that was often not enough. Riders continued to carry spares that way until the fashion died in the 1950s. Thereafter they carried them under the saddle, and eventually not at all thanks to the advent of easily accessible service cars.

Better design, pressure and lightness mean that wired-on or clincher tyres, once the preserve of leisure riders, were used by 60 per cent of the field in 2000. The rest stayed loyal to stick-on tubulars.

Desgrange also stood out against metal rims. He said these were liable to shed their tyres when they heated up on descents and the rubber cement that held the tyres in place began to melt. Rims were made of light wood until 1935, when aluminium versions appeared.

The takeover by aluminium and other light materials is now complete. In 1973 LUIS OCAÑA was the first to use titanium – for a headset and bottom bracket – after discussions with an engineer at Sud-Aviation, the aircraft maker in Toulouse. In 2000, 60 per cent of frames were aluminium, 25 per cent of carbon and 15 per cent alu-carbon, marking the disappearance of steel frames. ITALY and France each made 35 per cent of frames in the Tour, the USA a further 20 per cent. Five per cent had aluminium front forks; the rest were carbon. Traditional steering columns have all but gone. Only 10 per cent of riders preferred them to the newer Aheadset and similar patterns.

Vietto's welded-together gears have also progressed. Despite his innovation, freewheels developed only slowly from four speeds (1940s) to five (1950s) to six (1960s) and so on, averaging one tooth a decade until the nine or ten now standard. Riders still prefer two chainrings over three, saying the extra width of a triple places their feet too far apart. That means 18 or 20 gears are now standard, 18 for bikes equipped by Shimano of Japan and 20 for Italian manufacturer Campagnolo. (*See* JULIEN MOINEAU for how he pulled off a stunt with a giant chainring and a table of beer.)

More and smaller sprockets meant a change in derailleur design. Gear mechanisms hang further forward to engage more teeth on the smallest sprockets. Until design changes during the 1970s, the strain was too great and teeth sometimes broke. EDDY MERCKX pioneered an 11-tooth sprocket on the Valenciennes-Forest stage of the Tour in 1970. The innovation continued as Philippe Louviot fitted an electronic derailleur made by Mavic in 1992, but it hasn't caught on. Shimano is currently experimenting with gears operated by compressed air.

Frames changed little until 1979. They became smaller and then larger with fashion, but modern low-profile machines did not appear until BERNARD HINAULT tried one in 1979. About 20 per cent of bikes in 2000 had sloping top tubes. The shape of frames is now limited by UCI (Union Cycliste Internationale) rules.

Narrow handlebar extensions known as tri-bars are standard in TIME TRIALS. They were pioneered in 1989, when GREG LEMOND used them twice to get into a lower position to reduce wind resistance. The American 7-Eleven team used them as well, but LeMond made them famous when he beat LAURENT FIGNON in the final time trial to win the Tour. Officials didn't have time to consider whether a second set of handlebars breached the rule demanding only three points of contact (saddle, pedals and bars). Tri-bars, so called because they were popular in triathlons, became so widely used that the question became redundant. But worries about crashes in the peloton meant that from 1998 their use was restricted to time trials. 'A bicycle must be fitted with a handlebar that can be steered with complete safety under all circumstances,' said Alain Rumpf, road co-ordinator of the UCI, the sport's governing body.

(*See* OTTAVIO BOTTECCHIA for why LeMond's bike had a curious link to a Tour winner's unexplained death. *See* CHRIS BOARDMAN for more on tri-bars and other developments.)

Disc wheels and clipless pedals – known in France as 'automatic' pedals – appeared in 1985. In 1986 THIERRY MARIE fitted a back support and vortex cone to his saddle and won the prologue. Officials didn't notice this until afterwards, resulting in confusion as they allowed the result to stand but banned the support.

The supply of bike components is dominated by Shimano, which supplies 50 per cent of bikes, and Campagnolo, which has 40 per cent of the pro market.

ALFREDO BINDA
b. Cittiglio, Italy, Aug 11 1902, d. Cittiglio, Italy, Jul 19 1986

The move to clipless pedals (*see* BIKES) has removed the link between this Italian champion and the modern world. Alfredo Binda's record may have slipped the mind, but his name has survived for decades on a brand of high-quality toe-straps.

Binda was the first professional WORLD CHAMPION on the road, a title he won three times. He was also national champion four times, won five Giros and 41 stages, and four Tours of Lombardy, and he also broke the world 10km, 20km and 50km records. Binda would have won a sixth Giro in 1930 had the organiser not paid him the equivalent of first prize to stay away for fear the race would become too predictable. In the same year, by contrast, HENRI DESGRANGE broke a personal principle and paid him to start the Tour de France.

Binda was born in the Italian village of Cittiglio but was brought up in Nice, France. He worked as a bricklayer in his teens and rode the TRACK at Pont Magnam in his spare time. He was good at it although it soon became clear he was also a talented CLIMBER on the road. (*See* RENÉ VIETTO for how he passed on that talent.) This combination of ability in the MOUNTAINS and speed on the flat was unbeatable.

On June 27 1927 he became the first world professional road champion, on the Nurburgring circuit in GERMANY. Fifty-five started that race and only 18 finished after more than six and a half hours. Binda beat COSTANTE GIRARDENGO by 7:15. Desgrange watched with fascination as he went on to pile victory upon victory, but couldn't persuade the Italian to ride the Tour. This hurt Desgrange, especially because Binda lived in France.

But Binda was more interested in the Giro, and he was particularly interested in the world championship, which he wanted to win again. In 1929 the Belgian Georges Ronsse had won it for the second successive year, with Binda in third place, and the Italian wanted revenge.

'I didn't want to use up my energy in the Tour,' he said. 'In the end I was forced into it. Emilio Colombo [head of *La Gazzetta dello Sport*, the newspaper behind the Giro] came to see me as an emissary of Henri Desgrange. Desgrange wanted me in the Tour to give it extra prestige in its new formula [of NATIONAL TEAMS]. I wasn't very keen and he offered me a contract equivalent to what I'd get for riding a track meeting. My rate for each stage was what I'd have been paid in a vélodrome. He knew I wouldn't get as far as Paris.'

It seems certain Desgrange swore him to secrecy about the contract. Nine years earlier he had written, 'I hope the day will never come when organisers of races on the road will pay riders in the way that track directors do.' Binda stayed silent for half a century, until in 1980 he admitted it to journalists at his Milan apartment on the eve of the Giro.

In fact Binda rode an impressively erratic Tour in 1930, losing an hour on the stage from Bordeaux to Hendaye, then winning the next two stages to Pau and Luchon in the Pyrenees, then pulling out and going on to win the world title again. He won his third world championship in 1932 and his last Giro in 1933, including six of its stages, but his career dwindled quickly as he grew older. He stopped racing in 1937 and became MANAGER of the Italian national team. That gave him the thankless job of uniting the great rivals FAUSTO COPPI and GINO BARTALI.

'It was like being asked to put a cat and a dog in the same sack,' he said. 'It was no good pretending they were friends. Their rivalry wasn't an attitude they adopted out of vanity. It was real and never-ending.' He said the solution was to prevent their disputing with each other. 'That would have been pointless. Instead I had to show them I was boss and win them over to my ways. I had to turn two men accustomed to giving orders into obedient boys.'

In 1949 he summoned them both into a room at the Hotel Andreola at Chiavari, with just officials from the Italian federation as witnesses. 'I asked them to listen to me and not to ask questions until I'd finished,' he said. 'Then I talked . . . one hour, two hours, three. . . . Finally I could say, "Gentlemen, I've finished. Now I hope that you understand how and why an Italian team can't be and mustn't be beaten in the Tour de France." I'd been talking for five and a quarter hours. Then Coppi and Bartali got up and shook my hand.

'Later I got, without having asked for it, a signed promise by Coppi and Bartali that they would obey me blindly, whatever happened, follow my orders, never dispute them either in public or in private.'

Binda allocated each of them five DOMES-TIQUES, which French journalists interpreted as a split. He realised the rumour could only help Italy and didn't deny it as Coppi went on to win, with Bartali second. In fact the two stars used different GEARS and needed riders ready with appropriately equipped bikes in case of problems.

Binda is remembered now in a museum in Cittiglio. (And *see* MEMORIALS for other riders' monuments.)

Winner

1922	Nice-Puget-Nice
1923	Marseille-Nice, Circuit Var, Nice-Annot-Nice, Mont Chauve, Nice-Puget-Nice
1925	Giro d'Italia, Tour Lombardy
1926	Tour Tuscany, Tour Piedmont, Tour Lombardy, National championship
1927	World championship, Giro d'Italia, Tour Tuscany, Tour Lombardy, National championship, Tour Piedmont
1928	Giro d'Italia, Tour Veneto, National championship
1929	Giro d'Italia, Milan-San Remo, National championship
1930	World championship
1931	Milan-San Remo, Tour Lombardy
1932	World championship
1933	Giro d'Italia

Tour de France

1930	DNF	Stage wins Hendaye—Pau, Pau—Luchon

FRANCO BITOSSI

b. Camaioni, Italy, Sep 19 1940

Franco Bitossi developed the reputation of a man it was unwise to overlook in the closing phase of a race. Ignore him for a moment and he would launch an attack of such ferocity that many likened it to having a knife plunged in their back. His frenetic sprinting gave him the NICKNAME of '*cuore mato*' (mad heart).

Bitossi was discovered by FIORENZO MAGNI in 1961. His home, as with many Italians, was more the Giro than the Tour. In the Giro he won 21 stages in 16 rides, as well as the MOUNTAINS prize three times, and the Points competition twice. His tally in the Tour was disappointing by contrast, with just four stages – two each in 1966 and 1968 – and the Points competition in 1968.

It wasn't that he lacked talent. To finish eighth in the Tour as a SPRINTER (1968) is no small achievement. To win the Mountains competition in one major Tour and the Points competition in another is extraordinary. In 1972 he would have been WORLD CHAMPION if he hadn't let the race slip through his fingers to MARINO BASSO. And at 36 he won the national championship for the third time (1970, 1971, 1976). He just never clicked in the Tour.

Bitossi retired on medical advice with heart problems which would briefly immobilise him in the middle of races. It gave his nickname a poignant double meaning.

Winner

1965	Tour Switzerland, Championship Zurich, Tour Lazio
1967	Tour Lombardy, Tirreno-Adriatico
1968	Championship Zurich, Milan-Turin, Tour Tuscany
1970	National championship Tour Emilia, Tour Catalonia, Tour Lombardy
1971	National championship, Tour Romagna
1972	Tour Reggio Calabria
1973	Tour Emilia, Tour Veneto
1974	Trofeo Matteotti, Tour Romagna
1976	Tour Friuli, National championship

Tour de France

1966	17th	Stage wins Dieppe—Caen, Briançon—Turin
1968	8th	Stage wins Lorient—Nantes, Albi—Aurillac, and Points winner

BLACKBOARD MAN

Being blackboard man is the best job on the Tour apart from being a rider. Known as the *ardoisier* (slate man) in FRANCE, he rides on the back of a motorbike between the bunch and the break to pass on rider numbers and split times. He can also shout information such as which teams are chasing. Nobody sees more of the racing.

The current blackboard man is Joseph Lappartient, who rides pillion behind Christian Bourguignon. Their information comes from RADIO TOUR and their own stopwatch. Lappartient writes down the lead riders' numbers, then the time difference, followed by a horizontal line and the numbers of the chasers or, if the bunch is together, a large circle. If nothing is happening, he writes 'RAS' – *rien à signaler* (nothing to report).

The job was crucial before SATELLITE POSITIONING, because it was the only way the riders knew exactly what was going on. And it also stopped the coming and going of MANAGERS as they drove to the front to see the situation for themselves. Now team officials can watch television as they drive – RALEIGH's Peter Post was first to fit a TV in a team car – and satellites and transponders pinpoint race positions to a few seconds. That news can be passed to riders through their radio EARPIECES. Not all riders have earpieces, though, and many like the reassurance of the blackboard and the questions they can ask Lappartient.

The blackboard man's first job as the bunch rolls away is to chalk up a rider's name and the words '*bon anniversaire*' (happy birthday). It may not be cutting edge but you'd never get service like that from a computer.

In 2002 the job went to 37-year-old Michel Bationo from Ouagadougou, capital of Burkina Faso (*see* FAUSTO COPPI for Burkina Faso's links with his death). Bationo had done the job on the country's national tour for nine years, which was taken over in 2001 by the SOCIÉTÉ DU TOUR DE FRANCE. French officials overheard him say during a radio interview that he'd always dreamed of being *ardoisier* on the world's largest race, and so they gave him the chance.

(*See* HENRY ANGLADE for how the blackboard man helped a downhill race with GASTONE NENCINI.)

JEROEN BLIJLEVENS
b. Rijen, Holland, Dec 29 1971

Dutch names are never easy; Jeroen Blijlevens is pronounced Yuh-ROON BLAY-lay-f'ns. The surname means 'happy life', which makes it odd that he's best known for a fight. This happened on the last day of the Tour in 2000. Blijlevens had just ridden right round FRANCE only to be thrown out of the race and given a one-month suspension – a week longer than the race he had just ridden – within minutes of getting off his bike.

As the 2000 race ended, and cameramen hurried after the winner LANCE ARMSTRONG, a more spectacular show began closer to the line. Blijlevens, who had grown increasingly irritated all through the Tour with the riding of the American BOBBY JULICH, now approached Julich and began hurling abuse. The American just smiled back. This apparent sarcasm made Blijlevens boil over and he pushed him backwards. Now Julich was equally annoyed and retaliated by throwing his helmet at him. A fight started and Julich's eyebrow and chin were cut. Film and TV crews turned from Armstrong and hurried over.

Even Julich's MANAGER, Roger Legeay, got

abuse as the Dutchman shouted his frustration with the American. Blijlevens was led away, informed that it had all been his fault, and thrown out. He was then fined and suspended for a month from the start of the following season. He dismissed the incident later, saying, 'These things happen. It had more to do with the moment. You have to be intense to compete and sometimes that causes a problem. It's part of sport.'

Julich told journalists, 'He can't sprint any more so he picks on me. He was mad at me from two laps before the FINISH when I brought Magnus Backstedt to the front. If the cameras hadn't been there, I'd have hit him back.'

(And *see* MAGNUS BACKSTEDT for his role in LAURENT JALABERT's loss of the yellow jersey.)

Winner

1997   Veenendaal-Veenendaal
1999   GP Denain, GP Escaut

Tour de France

1995   DNF   Stage win Fécamp—Dunkirk
1996   128th Stage win Lac de Madine—Besançon
1997   126th Stage win Le Blanc—Marennes
1998   DNF   Stage win Plouay—Cholet
2000   DNF
2001   DNF

CHRIS BOARDMAN
b. Hoylake, England, Aug 26 1968

Chris Boardman rode the Tour's fastest PROLOGUE at his first attempt at the Tour in 1994. His 55.152 km/h in Lille beat MIGUEL INDURAIN by 15 seconds. The yellow JERSEY he won was BRITAIN's first since TOM SIMPSON 32 years earlier. By the time his career ended in 2000 he had won an Olympic gold medal and two versions of the hour record.

Boardman first showed talent when he won a British 10-mile TIME TRIAL championship for boys in 1984. Racing alone against the clock is

the dominant part of the sport in Britain, and Boardman progressed through the senior distances to become one of the best in the country. But his only significant win in road racing as an AMATEUR was the Tour of Lancashire in northern England in 1993.

He came to international notice when he won the Olympic 4,000m pursuit in Barcelona in 1992. The success attracted extra attention because he rode a carbon-fibre bike with one front fork and two sets of handlebars, one set extending forward in a tri-bar position and the others fitted sideways to the top of the front fork. (*See* BIKES for the history of other developments.) The monocoque frame was made by the Lotus sports car company in Norfolk and designed by a local bike guru, Mike Burrows.

Boardman's gold medal was Britain's first in Olympic cycling since Harry Ryan and Thomas Lance won the tandem sprint in 1920. Boardman even had small Olympic rings tattooed behind his right shoulder. 'I wanted to immortalise my title,' he said, 'and I chose a discreet souvenir.'

He turned professional in FRANCE in August 1993 but his lack of road-racing experience showed. The 'new boy almost sank without trace,' said *Cycling Weekly*. 'Somehow he survived the initial nerve-racking months and by the season's end had scored stage wins in the Dauphiné Libéré (both *en ligne* and against the watch), and the Tour of Switzerland.' (*En ligne* means massed-start, a conventional race.)

Boardman was never wholly happy in France. His wife and four children stayed at home near Liverpool and he flew back to see them as often as he could. He said, 'To succeed, you've got to make the sacrifices, live abroad and do the performances. I was the exception; I did it the other way round, did the performances and got my place in the [professional] team. Living at home was a bit of a compromise but if I'd gone the normal route and lived in France, I wouldn't have made the grade. I wasn't hard enough.'

Handicapped in most races by relatively poor climbing, he was nevertheless a potential winner in any time trial. He won the Tour prologue in 1994, 1997 and 1998, and also the Grand Prix des Nations (1996), the GP Eddy Merckx (1993 and 1996) and the world time trial championship in 1994. To this he added the world hour record in Bordeaux in 1993 (52.270km) and again in 1996, when he rode 56.375km in Manchester. In October 2000, just before he retired, he rode the hour again on the same sort of bike that EDDY MERCKX had used in 1972 (since which time BIKES had changed as much as vaulting poles, and with the same effect on records). A new standard had been established for riders on more traditional machines. Boardman beat Merckx's 49.431km by 10 metres.

He suffered two major setbacks at the Tour. In 1995 on a rainswept prologue course at St Brieuc, he crashed and was hit by his own support car and broke his ankle. Three years later, after winning the Dublin prologue, he touched the wheel of a team-mate on the second stage to Cork and crashed in the yellow jersey, knocking himself unconcious and out of the race.

He retired in 2000 after being diagnosed with an illness, similar to osteoporosis, which couldn't be treated as he would have wished without breaching DOPING rules.

Winner

1993   Chrono Herbiers, GP Merckx, World
       hour record
1994   World time trial championship
1996   GP Nations, Critérium International,
       GP Merckx, Chrono Herbiers,
       World hour record
2000   World hour record

Tour de France

1994   DNF   Stage win Lille—Lille, and
             Yellow Jersey
1995   DNF
1996   39th
1997   DNF   Stage win Rouen—Rouen, and
             Yellow Jersey and Points leader
1998   DNF   Stage win Dublin—Dublin, and
             Yellow Jersey and Points leader
1999   119th

LOUISON BOBET
b. Saint-Méen-le-Grand, France, Mar 12 1925,
d. Biarritz, France, Mar 13 1983

PHILIPPE THYS of BELGIUM was the first rider to win three Tours (1913, 1914 and 1920), but it was FRANCE's Louis 'Louison' Bobet who was first to win three in a row (1953, 1954, 1955).

Bobet rode his first Tour in 1947 when he was 22. He didn't finish, but he justified the confidence shown in him by finishing fourth the following year and even winning two stages and wearing the yellow JERSEY. He improved on that with third place in 1950. But it was in 1953 that he spread his wings, almost literally. He rode away from the field across the Vars and IZOARD in an era when the summits were still little better than loose rock, and he won by more than five minutes at Briançon.

He rode into Paris a French winner on the Tour's 50th anniversary, and there to meet him were MAURICE GARIN, GUSTAVE GARRIGOU, LUCIEN BUYSSE, Philippe Thys, ROMAIN and SYLVÈRE MAES, ANDRÉ LEDUCQ, ANTONIN MAGNE, GEORGES SPEICHER, ROGER LAPÉBIE and FERDY KÜBLER.

Bobet's performances were superb but, according to the writer RENÉ DE LATOUR, 'he didn't look good on a bike' and had 'the legs of a footballer'. Bobet was never popular with other riders, who laughed at his early habit of bursting into tears when things went wrong and called him 'Cry-baby'. They also disliked what they saw as his arrogance and his lofty social aspirations. RAPHAËL GÉMINIANI, one of few riders strong enough to confront him, teased him for his love of evening dress and polite company. He remembered how Bobet had blushed when a society lady asked about a well-publicised operation for a saddle boil. Bobet had looked uncomfortable as he searched for the right words.

'Ours is a difficult *métier*,' Géminiani remembered him explaining with embarrassment. 'You understand, *madame*, that we ride many kilometres a year. It gives us certain difficulties.'

'Difficulties?' the woman asked in puzzlement, as other riders listened with amusement.

'With our . . . with our . . .' Bobet blushed.
'With our, er, pockets.'

'With your pockets, Monsieur Bobet?' At which Géminiani interrupted with an exasperated 'Oh for heaven's sake, "Zonzon", tell her you've got bloody balls.'

Zonzon was a diminutive of Louison, and a NICKNAME he detested. Nor was his cause helped by the fact that while Louison is a diminutive of Louis in Brittany, elsewhere in France it's a woman's name. Bobet, to his detractors, was the 'Boy Named Sue'.

The British rider BRIAN ROBINSON said of him, 'He was not easy to approach. He was a private man, really, and a little moody. He would soon sulk if things weren't going right for him.' But Bobet was idolised in BRITAIN, and in 1954 he distributed prizes at the British Best All-Rounder time trialling competition night at the Royal Albert Hall in London, giving one of his yellow jerseys to winner Vic Gibbons.

He followed his second Tour victory in 1954 by winning at Solingen, GERMANY, to become the first French WORLD CHAMPION since Magne in 1936. The following year brought him that record third win. His career effectively ended when he and his brother Jean crashed their car outside Paris in autumn 1960, and he never fully recovered.

Bobet enjoyed a prosperous retirement. After opening shops around Paris selling men's shirts, he sold them in 1962 to invest the equivalent of £250,000 in his Institute for Thalassotherapy, a sea-cure centre at Quiberon, on the Brittany coast. He also started his own small airline, although it was mainly to fly himself and his staff around. It was a brief career, though, because he died young after a long illness, the day after his 58th birthday.

In 1991 the Tour passed through the village of St-Méen-le-Grand in Brittany where Bobet had been born above a baker's shop in the rue de Montfort. The postmaster, Raymond Quérat, was convinced the local hero had been forgotten. He appealed to readers of *Ouest-France*, 'Please write if you, too, think that Bobet was a truly great son of France.'

Hundreds of letters, films and photographs arrived from all over the country, and an exhibition opened in the village in March 1993.

(*See* ROGER LÉVÈQUE for why Bobet was yellow jersey in 1951 even though he shouldn't have been. And *see* DOMESTIQUES for how Bobet bound his team together by volunteering to give away his prizes.)

Winner

1949	Critérium As, Tour Ouest
1950	Critérium As, National championship
1951	Milan-San Remo, Critérium International, Tour Lombardy, National championship
1952	Paris-Nice, Critérium International, GP Nations
1953	Tour de France, Critérium As
1954	Tour de France, World championship, Critérium As
1955	Tour de France, Tour Luxembourg, Tour Flanders, Dauphiné Libéré
1956	Paris-Roubaix
1959	Bordeaux-Paris

Tour de France

1947	DNF	
1948	4th	Stage wins Bordeaux—Biarritz, San Remo—Cannes, and Yellow Jersey
1949	DNF	
1950	3rd	Stage win Gap—Briançon, and Mountains winner
1951	20th	Stage win Montpellier—Avignon
1953	1st	Stage wins Gap—Briançon, Lyon—St-Étienne, and Yellow Jersey
1954	1st	Stage wins Brasschaat—Lille, Grenoble—Briançon, Epinal—Nancy, and Yellow Jersey
1955	1st	Stage wins Roubaix—Namur, Marseille—Avignon, and Yellow Jersey
1958	7th	
1959	DNF	

GUIDO BONTEMPI
b. Gussago, Italy, 12 Jan 1960

Many Italian riders who succeed in ITALY do not do well abroad. They have tended to avoid riding in the cold of northern Europe until the World Cup forced them there. Guido Bontempi was an exception, a man who could ride 11 Tours between 1982 and 1995 and finish all but two (1982 and 1989), and who in 1992 became one of fewer than two dozen riders to have finished the Tour, Giro and the Tour of Spain in the same year, (respectively 75th, 40th and 62nd).

That was also the year he broke away in the last 10km of the Tour stage to Wasquehal, on the Franco-Belgian border, to win alone. It was his sixth and final stage win in the Tour. Bontempi's record in the north also includes Ghent-Wevelgem in 1984 and 1986, and both Paris-Brussels and the GP Harelbeke in 1988. He works now as a MANAGER.

Winner

1982	Tour Friuli
1983	Tour Piedmont
1984	Ghent-Wevelgem
1986	Paris-Brussels, Coppa Placci, Tour Reggio Calabria, Tre Valle Varesine, Ghent-Wevelgem
1987	Tour Puglia, Tour Friuli
1988	GP Harelbeke, Tour Friuli
1990	Tour Puglia
1991	Tre Valle Varesine

Tour de France

1982	DNF	
1985	112th	
1986	92nd	Stage wins Villes-sur-Mer—Cherbourg, Clermont-Ferrand—Nevers, Cosne—Paris
1987	119th	
1988	106th	Stage win Pornichet—La Baule, and Yellow Jersey
1989	DNF	
1990	122nd	Stage win Castillon-La-Bataille—Limoges
1991	96th	

Tour de France (continued)

1992	75th	Stage win Nogent-sur-Oise—Wasquehal
1994	90th	
1995	89th	

BONUSES

Tour organiser HENRI DESGRANGE decided in 1923 that riders needed more incentive than just their prizes. He decided to give each day's winner a small time credit, known as a bonus (*bonification* or simply *bonif* in French).

He was frustrated with the way his race was going, for he was convinced that riders were forming combines instead of riding as individuals, as the RULES insisted. And he was frustrated because he was certain that SPONSORS were encouraging riders to collaborate in order to make sure their own favourites won. (*See* NATIONAL TEAMS for the consequence of Desgrange's frustration.)

Desgrange wanted man-to-man combat right to the line, and so in 1923 he offered a two-minute bonus to the first rider to finish each day. The first to win a bonus was Robert Jacquinot of FRANCE after a stage from Paris to Le Havre.

The bonus rose to three minutes the following year, and in 1932 Desgrange went still further, offering four-, three- and one-minute bonuses to the first three, and a further three minutes to anyone who could win by three minutes. (*See* OTTAVIO BOTTECCHIA for the influence that had on Tour history.) That innovation proved too much, and in 1933 bonuses were back to just two minutes for the stage winner, falling again to 1:30 for the stage winner and 45 seconds for the runner-up in 1934.

In 1937 bonuses doubled the time gap of a lone winner, so that ERICH BAUTZ of GERMANY looked for a while like getting the better of the race favourites. MOUNTAIN bonuses were introduced in 1939. That year, too, the last rider overall was thrown out of the race from the second day onwards. The same thing happened from the third to the 18th stages in 1948.

The bonus in 2002 was 20 seconds for the stage winner, 12 seconds for second place, and eight for third. There were no finish bonuses on the last stage or in the TIME TRIALS. Intermediate sprints have bonuses of six, four and two seconds.

(*See* JACQUES ANQUETIL for how he gave away bonuses to thwart RAYMOND POULIDOR.)

BORDEAUX

The Tour has been to Paris every year since 1903 (*see* PARC DES PRINCES and CHAMPS ELYSÉES) but nowhere outside the capital beats Bordeaux, the major city of south-west FRANCE, for Tour visits. The race had been there 78 times by the end of 2003 compared to 58 for Pau.

Bordeaux is located little more than 100km north of the Pyrenees, making it a prelude to or a conclusion of the MOUNTAINS. The Bordeaux stage FINISH used to be on the city's TRACK until the bankings were removed in 1979 to make more room for football. It is now in the city centre.

The first winner at Bordeaux was Charles Laeser of Switzerland on the first Tour in 1903.

In 1966 Bordeaux was the scene of impromptu drug raids to which riders responded, the next morning, by climbing off their bikes five kilometres outside the city at La House. (*See* STRIKES.)

SANTIAGO BOTERO

b. Medellín, Colombia, Oct 27 1972

Blue-eyed Santiago Botero's career has been as up-and-down as his COLOMBIA countryside. In the 2000 Tour he lost 11:58 to LANCE ARMSTRONG on the climb to HAUTACAM where the American laid the base of his Tour win, only to win the long stage through the Alps to Briançon five days later and take the MOUNTAINS prize.

Then the opposite happened in the Tour of SPAIN in 2001, where he won the first long TIME TRIAL but ruined his chance of overall victory by suffering in the mountains.

In 2002 the mountains winner of 2000 once more went to bits in the hills, this time on MONT VENTOUX, only to ride away alone over the Allos, Vars and IZOARD to finish the race only one place short of the podium.

He says he enjoys spirited attacking and is prepared to take the consequences. 'I am not a tactician and I don't like those who ride a tactical race,' he said in 2002.

Winner:

2002 World time-trial championship, Classique Alpes

Tour de France:

2000	7th	Stage win, Draguignan-Briançon and mountains winner
2001	8th	
2002	4th	Stage wins, Lanester-Lorient, Vaison la Romaine-Les Deux Alpes

OTTAVIO BOTTECCHIA

b. San Martino di Colle Umberto, Italy, Aug 1 1894, d. Gemona, Italy, Jun 15 1927

ITALY's Ottavio Bottecchia hardly had a good start in life, what with his wing-nut ears, long, thin legs, 'skin like an old saddle, wrinkles that looked like scars,' as one contemporary wrote, and 'the awkwardness of a peasant'. Nor did he have a good ending, for he was found dead by the roadside in circumstances which have still never been explained.

Bottecchia grew up in a poor family, working with horses as a carter. To bring more money into the house he raced at weekends. In the first world war bicycles were seen as useful substitutes for horses, and Bottecchia served as a cycling soldier in the dark green uniform and broad-brimmed plumed hat of the *Bersaglieri* (light infantry). A lieutenant in a machine-gun company on the Italian-Austrian border saw him ride across a col with a gun on his back, and was impressed. He persuaded Bottecchia that he could have a career as a cyclist when the conflict was over. Bottecchia was taken prisoner before the war ended, but it was a cyclist that he became when he was released.

In 1923 he came fifth in the Giro d'Italia and was recruited for Automoto, the French BIKE-maker team, on the recommendation of the journalist Fabio Orlandini. Automoto wanted to expand into Italy and was prepared to recruit a man whose only French was the one curious phrase, 'No bananas, lots of coffee, thank you.' The bosses weren't disappointed: Bottecchia came second in the 1923 Tour to the French favourite HENRI PÉLISSIER, who predicted 'Bottecchia will succeed me.' And he did. Having become the first Italian to wear the yellow jersey the previous year, in 1924 Bottecchia became the first man to lead the race from beginning to end, and the first Italian to win the Tour.

He won 'on one leg', as he put it, helped by HENRI DESGRANGE's generous time BONUSES. Every day's winner got three minutes snipped from his time; Bottecchia won four stages, including the first and the last, and therefore got 12 minutes. Not that that was all that won him the race; the runner-up, NICOLAS FRANTZ of LUXEMBOURG, would have finished more than 20 minutes down even without the bonuses.

Bottecchia should have been a hero, but he was a humourless man who kept himself away from other people. He was also a socialist at a time when Italy swung to fascism, and rarely missed a chance to urge Italians not to be dominated by the right. This gave him the reputation of a moraliser, especially among people who weren't then feeling dominated or threatened. The general view was that he would be better to stick to cycling, which he knew, rather than preaching, which he didn't.

Aware of the adverse feelings he aroused, Bottecchia switched his yellow jersey for a less visible violet one when the 1924 Tour passed through Italy on the ninth stage from Toulon to Nice. (*See* PAUL DUBOC for another rider who hid for fear of being lynched.) It must have hurt him to take off the yellow jersey for the day, for he was so proud of it that he wore it on the train all the way home from Paris rather than pack it away.

Bottecchia won again in 1925, although this time with reduced bonuses and without leading from start to end. In 1926 Benito Mussolini transformed Italy into a single-state dictatorship and Bottecchia protested still more. On June 3 1927 he was found unconscious in a field outside Peonis, his skull cracked, his collarbone and other bones broken.

Bottecchia's body lay some distance from his bike, which was undamaged, and was found on a straight, safe road on which there were no skid marks from either a bike or a car. Many theories have been suggested to explain why he had come off his bike in good weather and on a road he knew well, why he and his bike were lying so far apart, and why his usual training partner hadn't been with him.

There were rumours, and even claims by the priest who gave him the last rites, that fascists had killed him. Ten years later in America, an Italian dying of stab wounds after a brawl on a New York waterfront said that he had been employed as a hit-man to do the job. In true Hollywood style he named a godfather, Berto Olinas, but no such man was ever found. There was just no evidence of a fascist plot and – while this is hardly conclusive – Mussolini was among the first to contribute to a fund to his memory.

The most popular tale is that a farmer threw a rock to scare him away from his grapes. The farmer had apparently admitted his guilt as he lay dying. The rock had hit him by mistake, he said, causing Bottecchia's death. But again this story reeks of invention. Grapes aren't ripe in June, so Bottecchia would hardly be stealing them for his thirst. The farmer said he was too far from Bottecchia to recognise him, the most famous cyclist in Italy, and yet if that was true he would have needed the strength of an Olympic shot-putter to throw a rock that far. But if he had been close enough to have spoken to him normally, why throw a rock? And wouldn't Bottecchia have found an unattended field if he wanted to steal grapes?

The death remains a mystery. The name lives on, though: Greg LeMond beat LAURENT FIGNON on a Bottecchia bike to win the Tour in 1989. (*See* GREG LEMOND for why that bike threw judges in a spin and revolutionised TIME TRIALS.)

Winner

1924   Tour de France
1925   Tour de France

Tour de France

1923   2nd   Stage win Le Havre—Cherbourg
1924   1st   Stage wins Paris—Le Havre,
              Bayonne—Luchon, Luchon—
              Perpignan, Dunkirk—Paris, and
              Yellow Jersey
1925   1st   Stage wins Paris—Le Havre, Les
              Sables—Bordeaux, Bordeaux—
              Bayonne, Dunkirk—Paris, and
              Yellow Jersey
1926   DNF

ALBERT BOURLON
b. Sansergues, France, Nov 23 1916

The 1947 Tour is usually remembered as the one which JEAN ROBIC won on the last day, reputedly causing the previous leader, PIERRE BRAMBILLA, to bury his bike in the garden in disgust. But there is another story.

The 1947 race was the first after the WAR, and it was particularly hard both because of the route and because many riders lacked fitness. Many of the established stars had died or stopped racing, and there were many unknown faces at the start. Nothing was predictable. (*See* GINO BARTALI for the effect that a race with strangers created.)

The stage from Carcassonne to Luchon was 253km long and had barely moved 300m when a lean-legged rider, sitting low on his bike, raced off by himself. Eyebrows rose, people wondered who the man might be and also about the foolishness of what he'd done, but that was all.

The man was Albert Bourlon, riding for the REGIONAL TEAM of Centre-Sud-Ouest, a hotchpotch of riders not good enough for the FRANCE team, and he had no idea how long he would be away. Riders attack early usually because their talent isn't enough to do it when it matters and because the bunch rarely chases. That pleases the SPONSOR because it gives an often poorly paid rider a long time in the public eye and maximum return for little outlay.

As Bourlon guessed, the bunch didn't chase. The best he had managed by then was 35th in his first Tour, and that had been nine years earlier in 1938. For many of the intervening years he had been a prisoner-of-war of the Germans. He had never won a stage, never won a big race, and never looked likely to.

Undeterred by any of this, Bourlon pressed on, crouched low over his top tube, eating regularly, keeping his pace even. He went over the Col d'Ares, over the Col de Port and then the Portet d'Aspet, and showed no weakness. On the contrary, he gained half an hour. His strength couldn't last, but nobody would have expected that, after eight hours and 10 minutes and 253km (less those first 300m). He was all in when he crossed the line after the Tour's longest lone break. Although he lost 14 minutes when the chase finally started, he still averaged 31km/h. Sixteen minutes passed before the Belgian NORBERT CALLENS reached the finish, and another six minutes before everyone else arrived. (*See* Callens entry for the man who 'lost' his yellow JERSEY.)

Sadly, Bourlon never recovered from that huge effort. He lost 45 minutes over the MOUNTAINS of the Pyrenees that followed and finished 21st in Paris. He never rode the Tour again.

Tour de France

1938   35th
1947   21st   Stage win Carcassonne—
              Luchon

JONATHAN BOYER
b. Moab, USA, Oct 8 1955

Jonathan 'Jacques' Boyer represented a second coming for the USA, a nation which had had more cycling talent than any country in the

19th century, but had lost interest in the sport between the wars. (*See* AMERICA for history and the unknown Joseph Magnani.)

The revival came with Boyer, who joined the ACBB club in western Paris after the 1973 junior world championship. From there he turned professional in 1977 for Lejeune-BP, a team that combined a small Parisian BIKE-maker and a giant oil company. Boyer was said to have been paid the equivalent of about £420 a month.

He was to have ridden the Tour straight away, but a crash and a stomach virus put him out of it. Recovery took a year, and involved a trip home to Carmel, in California, and conversion to vegetarianism. He returned to France in 1980 to finish fifth in appalling weather in the WORLD CHAMPIONSHIP at Sallanches. EDDY MERCKX said of him, 'I think he has a very great talent and that America will be the land of the future of cycling.'

The world championship course was said to have been designed for BERNARD HINAULT, who turned the race into a process of attrition. Hinault did indeed win it and his MANAGER, CYRILLE GUIMARD, offered Boyer a place in their team in 1981 and picked him to ride for the Frenchman when the Tour started in Nice on June 25. Boyer took to describing himself as 'the American champion' because of his ride at Sallanches, and the organiser, FÉLIX LÉVITAN, encouraged him to wear a stars-and-stripes jersey to which he wasn't entitled. Lévitan was already nurturing ideas of attracting American sponsors. (*See* Lévitan entry for how America spelled the end of his career.)

Boyer was 25, the first American to ride the Tour. His vegetarianism, deep religious belief and other aspects of his personality led Guimard to call him a '*marginal*', a French word which carries hints of crankiness, hippiedom and lack of conventionality. To satisfy his meat-less diet, for instance, Boyer arrived for the START in Nice with 50kg of dried fruits, nuts and Californian dates. He would be in constant touch with doctors in Illinois, he said, to check his health.

Boyer came ninth on the longest day – 259km from Le Mans to Aulnay-sous-Bois – and finished 32nd in Paris. Thanks to him, American cycling had come a lot further than the 3,753km he had pedalled from Nice.

Boyer rode as a professional until 1987, including Paris-Roubaix six times, the Tour of Switzerland six times, the Giro three times and the Tour de France five times. He came 10th in the 1982 world championship in BRITAIN after breaking clear in the last mile but being chased down by his fellow American, GREG LEMOND. The pair had never been friends but then became committed rivals.

The assessment of Ed Pavelka, editor of *VeloNews* and later of *Bicycling*, is that 'Boyer was too far ahead of the curve – a lone US eagle in the Tour. Those of us in cycling were in awe, but that's about as far as it went for his celebrity. I remember *Sports Illustrated* doing a feature story about him. This seemed huge at the time because finally someone noticed. Boyer broke major ground for US cycling, but I'm willing to bet that the average European would recognise his name before the average American.'

The British writer Geoffrey Nicholson called Boyer 'slightly dandified', and said his earnest-ness was a constant talking point. According to the reporter Dennis Donovan, journalists took pity on his loneliness in a French-speaking team and offered him girlie mags. 'Thank you but no,' Boyer replied. 'I have my Bible and that is all I require.'

His religious earnestness made his downfall still more abrupt. In July 2002 he faced 10 charges of molesting an underage girl who was part of his church community in California. Questioned by journalists, he made the some-what understated comment that 'It's a very unfortunate situation.'

The girl, who was 11 at the time of the first incidents, said Boyer insisted on speaking French as he molested her. He was jailed for a year.

(*See* PDM AFFAIR for Boyer's role in the mysterious mass withdrawal.)

Tour de France

1981	32nd
1982	23rd
1983	12th
1984	31st
1987	98th

FERDI BRACKE

b. Hamme-Durme, Belgium, May 25 1939

The Tour's records should show Ferdinand Bracke among its winners. And he would have been but for a collapse of nerves.

Bracke was a tall (1.84m), lean Belgian with extraordinary talent against the clock. He was born in Dutch-speaking Flanders, at Hamme-Durme, but as a child moved to the French-speaking south near Charleroi. That meant he was unusual for Belgian riders at the time in speaking French and Dutch equally well (*see* EDDY MERCKX) even though his mother spoke no French at all when the family moved.

Bracke started racing in 1957 and in 1962 won the Grand Prix des Nations, at that time virtually the world TIME TRIAL championship, when he was just an INDEPENDENT (semi-professional). He was barely known outside Belgium.

He turned fully professional with the PEUGEOT team, and rode his first Tour in 1963, finishing 21st. This showed he was competent if not talented in the MOUNTAINS, a rarity for a time-triallist. Between 1963 and 1977 he rode the Tour nine times, finishing six times and coming third in 1968. It was that third place that could have been victory. (*See* JAN JANSSEN for why the 1968 Tour was almost halted due to rioting.)

Two Belgians and a Dutchman were within three minutes of each other in the first three places at the start of the final time trial on the last day. HERMAN VAN SPRINGEL was the leader, the Dutchman JAN JANSSEN was second, and Bracke third. Of the three, Bracke was not only potentially the fastest but had a proven track record – literally. In 1964 he had been the world pursuit champion, a title he won again in 1969.

Many in Belgium were convinced they would have the top two places on the podium, with either the pug-faced and mournful-looking van Springel or the quiet, gentle and grey-haired Bracke topping it. They were to be disappointed. Van Springel led by a fraction at 40km but for the remaining 14km Janssen gained steadily on him to win the Tour without ever having previously worn the yellow JERSEY.

And Bracke? Stage fright overcame him. He didn't even come third of the three. ROGER PINGEON beat him by six seconds. Bracke finished 1:23 behind Janssen, although he was still fast enough to keep his third place overall.

Marcel de Leener wrote in *Cycling* that 'Bracke cannot suffer and he lacks the essential ability to read a race. If he had the brain of RIK VAN STEENBERGEN and the guts of RIK VAN LOOY, he would be a superchampion.'

It was this that led doubters to doubt his hour record in 1967, including a number of JACQUES ANQUETIL supporters. Anquetil had broken the hour record in September 1967 but had been denied ratification when he refused to take a dope test in the middle of the track. A champion, he insisted, should not be forced to go into a tent and urinate in front of a crowd. A sample he gave on returning to Rouen was refused. The row was still going on – whether Anquetil was within the UCI's rules or not – when Bracke beat the record anyway.

Bracke's 48.093km on October 30 was the first ride at more than 30mph. It took place on the Olympic track in Rome, which Bracke preferred to the more popular Vigorelli in Milan because the drier atmosphere was less likely to provoke his mild asthma. And he passed the dope test. The claim that the track had been mismeasured arose through a combination of Bracke's tendency to flop when it mattered, his contrast with Anquetil in personality and record, and his choice of Rome. The claim was not true, but it speaks volumes of how Bracke was perceived that it could even have been considered.

Anquetil was less than complimentary. 'People have written that I have cast doubt on Bracke's record,' he said, 'but that is simply false and absurd. I suppose, as a joke, I may have asked "But how did he do it?" but nothing more than that . . .' Anquetil was aggrieved for the rest of his life that the French sports minister had sent a telegram of congratulations to Bracke, a Belgian, but had never done so to Anquetil the Frenchman.

Bracke should have won more. His one success on the road was the Tour of SPAIN in 1971, when he beat LUIS OCAÑA on home ground. He spent all his career with Peugeot and retired after 17 years to manage, briefly, the Old Lord's Whisky team and the country's women's team in world championships. His grey hair and height gave him the NICKNAME 'Grey Eminence'.

Winner

1962   GP Nations
1966   Baracchi Trophy
1967   World hour record, Baracchi Trophy
1964   GP Lugano
1970   GP Wallonia
1971   Tour Spain

Tour de France

1963	21st	
1964	DNF	
1965	DNF	
1966	32nd	Stage win Chamonix—St-Étienne
1968	3rd	
1969	57th	
1971	58th	
1976	77th	Stage win Fleurance—Auch
1977	DNF	

PIERRE BRAMBILLA

b. Villarbeney, Switzerland, May 12 1919,
d. Grenoble, France, Feb 13 1984

Pierre Brambilla, a rider of complicated national background, was the man who lost the 1947 Tour on the last day. Legend – unconfirmed – maintains that he went home and in despair buried his bike in his garden.

A Swiss-born Frenchman of Italian descent, Brambilla rode the Tour in a team labelled as ITALY but made up largely of Italians and near-Italians living in France. The WAR hadn't long finished, and this was as close as the Tour authorities felt they could come to fashioning a team of Italians. It was 1960 before the first German team appeared after the war, although individuals had ridden before then in mixed teams. (*See* GERMANY.)

Brambilla took the yellow JERSEY at St-Brieuc. It was unlikely he would lose it before Paris, and there was a tradition that the race leader should not be attacked on the last day. But this was a tradition not respected by the Frenchman JEAN ROBIC, who had made himself even more unpopular than usual by boasting that he felt 'irresistible'.

The last stage was from Caen to Paris. The riders were leaving Rouen by the Côte de Bonsecours to the east when Robic attacked, in the words of PIERRE CHANY, 'with ferocious energy'. Brambilla tried to match him but couldn't manage it, and slipped back to the main field. There he pleaded for help but was refused. The repercussions from the war were obvious, and feelings still ran high against Italians; unpopular though Robic was, at least he was French and not Italian.

Those in the break were equally unhappy about working with Robic but he did deals to keep it going. Turning to EDOUARD FACHLEITNER, also in the FRANCE team, he was reputed to have said, 'You can't win the Tour because I won't let you get away. So let's ride together and I'll give you 100,000 francs.' Fachleitner agreed, the break stayed away, Briek Schotte took the stage, and Robic won the Tour. Brambilla didn't even come second. That honour went to

Fachleitner, at 3:58, and Brambilla was pushed back in a single day by 10:07.

It's worth pointing out that the journalist PIERRE CHANY, who was there at the time, attributes the bribe story to RENÉ VIETTO, 'who would say anything to discredit Robic; having followed the stage, I can say that Robic deserved his win.'

Brambilla buried his bike, it's said, because he never wanted to ride the Tour again. But in fact he rode four more times, every year from 1948 to 1951, and took part in tourist competitions after that. One of JOCK WADLEY's regrets was that he had ridden with Brambilla in one such event and had never thought to confirm the burial story.

Winner

1946 Tour Ouest

Tour de France

1947	3rd	Yellow Jersey and Mountains winner
1948	DNF	
1949	26th	
1950	11th	
1951	36th	

ERIK BREUKINK

b. Rheden, Holland, Apr 1 1964

HOLLAND's Erik Breukink came to cycling late. Until he was 16 he had preferred football, which he played with a team called the Dierense Boys. His father, Willem, was a director of the Gazelle BIKE factory and took him to races when there were no matches on, but the bug bit only when he was 16 in 1980.

Breukink quickly made a mark as an AMATEUR and rode the team TIME TRIAL at the 1984 Olympics in Los Angeles, although the Dutch weren't placed (the medallists were ITALY, Switzerland and the USA).

His pro career got off to a bright start. He won the MOUNTAINS competition in the Tour

of Switzerland in 1986, then came third (1987) and then second (1988) in the Giro. His battle in 1988 with ANDY HAMPSTEN (the eventual winner) was the feature of the race. In the following year's Tour he won the PROLOGUE in LUXEMBOURG to get his only yellow JERSEY.

Holland was ready to fete him as a potential winner, but it never happened. It sometimes seemed that he only had to start the Tour de France to submit himself to suffering and lost time. In 1990 he changed bikes three times on the TOURMALET in an effort to settle in, but never succeeded. In 1991 he walked out of the Tour in the mysterious mass retirement known as the PDM AFFAIR. In 1993 he started with injuries after being struck by a car, and his left knee hurt so much that he abandoned in the MOUNTAINS.

It all became more than he could bear, and he retired after the 1997 race to work in PR for the Rabobank team and as a television commentator. He said of his new career, 'It is good to stay with the Tour, although my wife wasn't so impressed because she'd hoped we'd have a holiday.'

Winner

1988 Tour Basque Country, Critérium International
1989 Montjuich
1990 Tour Ireland
1991 GP Merckx, Tour DuPont
1992 Tour Piedmont
1993 Tour Holland, Tour Asturias, Critérium International, National championship

Tour de France

1987	21st	Stage win Bayonne—Pau
1988	12th	
1989	DNF	Stage win Luxembourg—Luxembourg, and Yellow Jersey
1990	3rd	Stage wins Fontaine—Villard-de-Lans, Lac de Vassivière—Lac de Vassivière
1991	DNF	
1992	7th	
1993	DNF	

1994	29th
1995	20th
1996	34th
1997	52nd

BRIGADE ORANGE

The construction and logistics crew who work around the Tour wear bright orange overalls. Hence their affectionate title, the *Brigade Orange*. They build the START, the FINISH, and the compound known as the VILLAGE where riders, journalists and SPONSORS gather each morning before the off. They measure the temperature of the road and water it if it looks like melting, and even repair broken stretches of tarmac – a tradition that goes back to when the Tour paid to repair the road over the AUBISQUE in 1910 (*see* MOUNTAINS) – and build ramps over the worst *ralentisseurs* (speed humps) in the road.

The brigade works in two teams, one working on that day's stage and the other on the following day's. They rarely see each other. The first takes down the work that the second puts up – and at breathtaking speed. The start village is already being demolished as the last people leave; brigade members wait along the finishing straight to whip away the barriers the moment the last riders and cars are in.

(And *see* LAURENT JALABERT for the link between barriers, a policeman's camera, a CRASH and a boy who later broke a world record.)

BRITAIN

Britain has played a surprisingly large part in Tour history for a nation where road racing is not only a minor sport, but was actually banned for decades.

A Briton – James Moore of Bury St Edmunds – won the world's first recognised BIKE race, in Paris on May 31 1868, and then the first long place-to-place road race, Paris-Rouen, on November 13 1868. But those events were in FRANCE, where Moore had emigrated with his parents in 1853. In Britain things were different; in 1878 there was even a legal attempt to drive cyclists off the road. That failed, but discontent against cyclists in general and races in particular continued to increase. Its peak came on July 21 1894, on the main road from London to Edinburgh, about 60 miles north of London. Three racers panicked a woman who was leading a horse and carriage; the riders swerved off the road, their bikes were ruined, and the woman complained to the police.

The British governing body, the National Cyclists' Union, demanded that road races should be discontinued for fear that all cyclists would suffer. Many clubs moved their events to the TRACK. In 1897 the NCU banned road racing and, while a rebel organisation arose to run TIME TRIALS, the choice of the name 'time trial' shows how much organisers tried to disguise the idea of a race. Competitors rode alone at dawn against the clock, and courses and dates were referred to in code and were given no pre-publicity. Riders dressed from neck to ankle in black to be 'inconspicuous', and carried bells to show how responsible they were.

The sport developed abroad, but British riders heard little about it. Time trials became the substance of the sport, acquiring respectability and a huge following. Then, with the second world WAR, the change came. Suddenly the roads were empty and there was little traffic to upset, equine or motorised. This seemed, to a Wolverhampton enthusiast called Percy Stallard, an opportunity that could hardly be missed.

Stallard wrote to the NCU in December 1941: 'I can never understand why massed-start road racing is not indulged in on the public roads of this country. I have raced in France (three times), GERMANY, BELGIUM, Denmark and should have competed in ITALY in 1939. . . . In Belgium I was honoured to compete in a road race that was witnessed by an estimated crowd of 250,000. It is amazing that this is the only country in Europe where this form of sport is not permitted. . . . There would be no better time than now to introduce this form of racing to the roads.'

The NCU said no, but Stallard ran a race anyway. It went from Llangollen to Wolverhampton on June 7 1942, and Stallard was banned for life. Fifty competitors, too, were suspended, but this proved to be the NCU's greatest mistake. With nowhere to go, their opponents started their own organisation, the British League of Racing Cyclists. Thousands of cyclists unhappy with the NCU switched their allegiance.

The BLRC started a road-racing programme, organised Tours of Britain, recognised INDEPENDENTS (semi-professionals), and allowed them to race against AMATEURS (which the other two organisations did not). However, it did not invent massed-start racing – the NCU had always allowed that, provided races were held on airfields and other private roads. The NCU even picked teams for the world championships and in 1937 sent a team to the Tour de France (of which more later).

What the BLRC showed was that the police, far from acting against racing on public roads, were prepared to support it. That support cooled after a time, but by then the principle was established. The BLRC and the NCU fought a bitter battle which brought both so near to bankruptcy that they merged on February 1 1959 to form the British Cycling Federation, now called simply British Cycling.

Before that, though, in 1937, the NCU had sent Britain's first team to the Tour de France. The first Britons to ride were CHARLES HOLLAND of Birmingham and Bill Burl of London. They were joined by a French Canadian, Pierre Gachon, in a team representing the British Empire. None finished.

It took another decade and a half before a Londoner called Derek Buttle started Britain's first full professional team in 1952 (See HERCULES.). The Hercules team began racing in 1953, and in 1955 provided much of the first fully British team in the Tour. Out of it came BRIAN ROBINSON, the most successful British rider of the period, but in 1956 the team folded because of accounting difficulties. (See HERCULES, too, for the ill-fated ANC-Halfords venture in 1987.)

Not discouraged, in the 1960s another generation of Britons tried again. This time British cyclists rode for French and Belgian teams, although there were British NATIONAL TEAMS in the Tour in 1960 and 1961. In 1962 TOM SIMPSON became Britain's first yellow jersey, although he was not riding for Britain but for the Leroux-GITANE team. In 1965 he became Britain's first professional road WORLD CHAMPION of the century. Britain fielded more national teams in the 1967 and 1968 Tours, although Simpson died in 1967 after collapsing on MONT VENTOUX.

The country was still hindered, though, by the absence of a British-sponsored team along the lines of Hercules. Such sponsorship as existed was going into cut-price teams of independents (semi-professionals), a category abolished by the sport's governing body, the Union Cycliste Internationale, in 1966. Some riders and a few sponsors formed professional teams, but riders such as Colin Lewis and ARTHUR METCALFE still had other jobs, and rode the 1967 and 1968 Tour de France in their holidays.

Denied British sponsorship, ambitious riders went to work in foreign teams. ROBERT MILLAR came fourth in the 1984 Tour and became the only British rider to win the Mountains jersey. SEAN YATES wore the yellow jersey in 1994 and CHRIS BOARDMAN wore it in 1994, 1997 and 1998.

In 1987 there was one other attempt to field a British team, the ANC-Halfords team, but this dissolved into chaos, as described in journalist Jeff Connor's book, *Wide-eyed and Legless*.

The Tour has been to Britain twice. In 1974 it went to an unopened bypass near Plymouth to promote a shipping line from Roscoff in Brittanny. The TRANSFER was not a success. Riders disliked the long journey; Customs were suspicious of so many BIKES; organiser JACQUES GODDET forgot his passport; little of the publicity CARAVAN made the crossing; there were fewer SPECTATORS than forecast; the stage was was ridden by a very sullen group of riders; and the sprint at the end was won by the little-known HENK POPPE. Next day the *Daily*

Mirror's headline was, '*Tour de France:* can 40 million Frenchmen be wrong?'

The second visit was in 1994 to mark the 50th anniversary of D-day (*Jour J* in France), and it was a success. After a stage from Cherbourg to Rennes passed the Normandy landing beaches, Francisco Cabello won the stage from Dover to Brighton and Nicola Minali the next day's race to Portsmouth. Crowds lined the route to see Boardman, who had won the PRO-LOGUE at Lille, and eventual winner MIGUEL INDURAIN, who amused home fans by tactfully remembering to say that the climbs he most feared were the TOURMALET, the GALIBIER and, referring to a locally feared hill outside Brighton, the 'côte de Ditchling Beacon'.

(*See* PHIL ANDERSON and GEORGES PASSERIEU for riders born in Britain but successful for other nations; *see* DAVID MILLAR for a rider born outside Britain but of British nationality.)

BROADCASTING

The Tour's organising paper, *L'AUTO*, at first wanted only its own journalists to follow the race. Then in 1922 it realised it was missing publicity and allowed in 10 other press cars. Radio joined in 1929 when Jean Antoine and Alex Virot *of L'Intransigeant* broadcast for Radio Cité. They were only a partial success because they had just set up their gear and were starting to broadcast at the START at Le Vesinet when the riders set off, leaving them with little to say. Coverage quickly improved and on July 12 1932 the pair recorded the sound of the Tour crossing the AUBISQUE and broadcast it using phone lines.

Television came to the Tour in 1949 when valve cameras at the PARC DES PRINCES watched RIK VAN STEENBERGEN win the stage from Nancy, with FAUSTO COPPI in his yellow JERSEY. There were only a few thousand television sets in France, mostly in Paris, so few people watched.

Subsequently, reporters followed the race on a BMW motorbike and in a Jeep, and filmed stages on two 16mm cameras as technology improved. The film was put on a train or plane to Paris and broadcast at noon next day.

Alex Virot, the pioneer of Tour broadcasting, died at the microphone of Radio LUXEM-BOURG in 1957. He and his driver, René Wagner, crashed into a dried-up riverbed on the stage from Barcelona to Ax-les-Thermes.

The first celebrity commentator was Robert Chapatte, who first followed the Tour for television in 1957. Chapatte was there for the first live coverage, on the Aubisque on July 8 1958. The next live coverage was on the PUY-DE-DOME near Clermont Ferrand in 1959, the first year that stage finishes outside Paris were shown on the same day, although still on film. They were broadcast at 8.30pm thanks to a staff of 50 doing the filming, editing and transmission. Modern TV coverage really began on June 16 1960 when motorcycle cameraman François Magnen followed riders down the IZOARD at 80km/h.

Pictures are now provided by the state channel France 3. Its Paris headquarters is within walking distance of where the Michaux family first put pedals on a bicycle, and also of the home of James Moore, winner of the world's first recognised bike race in 1868. (*See* BRITAIN.) France 3's expert on the race is the 1975 and 1977 winner BERNARD THÉVENET. He worked until 2001 with Patrick Chêne, the youthful-looking head of sport who first broadcast news of the DOPING scandal involving PEDRO DELGADO in 1988. (*See* Delgado's entry for details.) Chêne was followed in 2001 by Christian Prudhomme. He and other broadcasters work from studios beyond the FINISH. France 3 takes the cabin closest to the line and broadcasts the last three hours of the flatter stages and the mountain stages in their entirety. The motorbike reporters are Jean-René Godart and the much-loved JEAN-PAUL OLLIVIER. The old valve cameras that caught van Steenbergen on camera have been replaced by digital versions weighing less than 2kg.

French TV has 300 staff on the race, four helicopters, two aircraft, two motorbikes, four race cars, 35 other vehicles and 20 full-size cameras. Its pictures go to 160 countries with a claimed audience of 100 million. That gives it the world's third largest viewing figures after the summer Olympics and the soccer World Cup. Among the most prolific re-broadcasters of France 3's pictures is the satellite service Eurosport, for whom the colour commentator is LAURENT FIGNON.

The main radio stations are the news channel France Info, with Georges Goujon and the veteran Jean-Paul Brouchon, and the middle-of-the-road channel France Inter with Jean-François Rhein and Fabrice Abgrall. Radio coverage is also provided on Europe 1 and RTL. These and France Inter can also be heard outside France on long wave; France Info can be picked up on the audio channel of satellite television.

The travelling entertainment shows that Europe 1 put on in stage towns each evening of the Tour inspired the former controller of BBC Radio 1, Johnny Beerling, to start the Radio 1 Roadshow in 1973.

British television coverage of the Tour began in 1963 on the ITV programme Wide World of Sport. The commentator was the *Daily Telegraph* reporter David Saunders. The programme's founder, John Bromley, died in 2002. Until then there had been only intermittent radio reports by journalists such as JOCK WADLEY.

The Tour internet site, www.letour.fr, gives minute-by-minute updates.

(*See* ERIK BREUKINK, FINISH, RADIO TOUR and RONAN PENSEC for more on broadcasting.)

MAURICE BROCCO

b. Fismes, France, Jan 28 1883, d. Erigné, France, Jun 26 1965

The Frenchman Maurice Brocco never finished the Tour and won only one stage. But he did give us the word DOMESTIQUE for a rider employed to sacrifice his own chances to help his team leader win.

The background is that the first tour organiser HENRI DESGRANGE allowed sponsored teams to take part but insisted that their riders

should compete as individuals. Tactics weren't allowed, and even cooperation on the road, such as sharing the pace, was frowned on. The word that Desgrange detested was 'combines'.

In 1911 Brocco – known as Coco – lost any chance of winning the Tour when he suffered badly in the last 20km of the stage to Chamonix. Consequently, he began selling his services to whoever offered most. He approached FRANÇOIS FABER, who had been suffering equally badly as the race neared Perpignan. Faber was in danger of being eliminated for slipping outside the time limits and so, a deal done, Brocco waited for him and paced him to the FINISH.

Desgrange wanted to disqualify Brocco straight away but hesitated because he feared the rider would appeal to the national governing body, the UVF. Desgrange had no proof, and wasn't sure he would win the case, even though the UVF was so in awe of him that it rarely denied him what he wanted. He did, though, castigate Brocco in the Tour paper *L'AUTO*, writing, 'He is unworthy. He is no more than a *domestique* [servant].'

Brocco was hurt but not repentant. At the start of the stage from Luchon to Bayonne he smirked at Desgrange, an austere figure whom few dared to approach, and said, 'Today, monsieur, we are going to settle accounts.' The phrase had two possible meanings: either he planned to make amends to Desgrange or he planned to cash in once again.

Not surprisingly, Desgrange followed him. He watched him ride the TOURMALET with the yellow JERSEY, GUSTAVE GARRIGOU. 'So, am I forbidden to ride with him?' Brocco taunted.

On the next climb, the AUBISQUE, Brocco dropped Garrigou, passed PAUL DUBOC (who had been poisoned; *see* his entry) and took the lead with ÉMILE GEORGET. Once more he challenged Desgrange, 'So, do I have the right to stay with him?' Desgrange, a proud man, again felt ridiculed but couldn't prove anything. And then Brocco pulled off the move he thought would secure the issue but which proved his undoing. He dropped Georget, the so-called king of the CLIMBERS, and won alone from Garrigou by 34 minutes.

Brocco smirked when he saw Desgrange. Moments later he was less happy. The director told him to pack his bags and catch the train for Paris. Desgrange informed his readers that anyone who could ride with such flair clearly hadn't been trying earlier in the race, had clearly been selling his services rather than win the race. 'He deserves his punishment,' he wrote. 'Immediate disqualification.'

Winner

1910 Paris-Brussels

Tour de France

1908 DNF
1910 DNF
1911 DNF Stage win Luchon—Bayonne
1912 DNF
1913 DNF
1914 DNF

BROOM WAGON – *See* voiture balai

BROTHERS

Talent sometimes runs in families, sometimes between father and son (EDDY MERCKX and his son Axel are examples), but more usually between brothers. The earliest may have been the Garin brothers: MAURICE GARIN, who rode in 1903 (1st and three stages) and in 1904, when he was disqualified; his brother César also rode in 1904 and was also disqualified. (*See* THE 1904 AFFAIR.)

The greatest number of brothers riding at the same time from the same family is three, Henri, Francis and Charles Pélissier. HENRI PÉLISSIER rode in 1912 (DNF), 1913 (DNF but won one stage), 1914 (2nd and three stages), 1919 (DNF but won one stage), 1920 (DNF but won two stages), 1923 (1st and three stages), and 1924 and 1925 when he also didn't finish. FRANCIS PÉLISSIER rode in 1919 (DNF but won one stage), 1920 (DNF), 1923 (23rd), 1924 and 1925 (both DNF), and 1927 (DNF but won one stage). CHARLES PÉLISSIER rode in 1929 (28th

and won one stage), 1930 (9th and eight stages), 1931 (14th and five stages), 1933 and 1934 (both DNF), and 1935 (13th and two stages).

ANTONIN MAGNE and his brother Pierre: Antonin rode the Tour in 1927 (6th and one stage), 1928 (6th and two stages), 1929 (7th), 1930 (3rd and one stage), 1931 (1st and one stage), 1933 (8th), 1934 (1st and two stages), 1935 (DNF), 1936 (2nd and one stage) and 1938 (8th and two stages). Pierre was less talented but still rode the Tour in 1927 (15th), 1928 (10th), 1929 (9th) and 1930 (6th) and won the stage from ÉVIAN to Pontarlier in 1928.

ROGER LAPÉBIE and his younger brother Guy: Roger rode in 1932 (23rd and one stage), 1933 (29th), 1934 (3rd and five stages), 1935 (DNF), 1937 (1st and three stages). Guy rode the Tour in 1948 (3rd and one stage), 1949 (DNF) and 1952 (DNF).

LOUISON BOBET and his younger brother Jean: Louison rode in 1947 (DNF), 1948 (4th and two stages), 1949 (DNF), 1950 (3rd and one stage), 1951 (20th and one stage), 1953 (1st and two stages), 1954 (1st and three stages), 1955 (1st and two stages), 1958 (7th) and 1959 (DNF). Jean rode in 1955 (14th) and 1957 (15th).

ROGER DE VLAEMINCK and his brother Erik both rode the Tour. Roger was the more talented on the road, particularly in single-day races, while Erik won seven world cyclo-cross championships. Nevertheless, while Roger the roadman started the Tour in 1969, 1970 and 1971, and finished none of them (although he did win a stage in 1970), Erik the off-road specialist finished 51st in 1968 and won a stage, didn't finish in 1969, and came 62nd in 1971.

Also from BELGIUM were the Planckaert brothers. JO PLANCKAERT rode in 1997 but didn't finish. EDDY PLANCKAERT rode in 1981

(DNF but won one stage), 1982 and 1984 (both DNF), 1986 (DNF but won one stage), 1988 (115th) and 1989 and 1990 (both DNF). Their father Willy was also a Tour rider, riding in 1966 (40th and two stages) and 1967 and 1968, finishing neither year.

In FRANCE, there were PASCAL SIMON and his brothers Régis, Jérôme and François. Pascal rode in 1980 (28th), 1982 (20th and one stage), 1983 (DNF but yellow jersey), 1984 (7th), 1985 (20th), 1986 (13th), 1987 (53rd), 1988 (17th), 1989 (13th), 1990 (35th) and 1991 (57th). Régis Simon rode in 1984 (111th), 1985 (100th and one stage), 1986 (93rd) and 1988 (123rd). Jérôme Simon rode in 1984 (36th), 1985 (24th), 1987 (42nd), 1988 (19th and one stage), 1989 (18th), 1990 (22nd), 1991 (23rd) and 1992 (27th). François Simon rode in 1993 (57th), 1994 (43rd), 1995 (59th), 1996 (86th), 1997 (32nd), 1998 (57th), 1999 (30th) 2000 (58th), 2001 (6th and yellow jersey), 2002 (DNF).

Also in France, MARC MADIOT and his brother Yvon: Marc rode in 1982 (30th), 1983 (8th), 1984 (35th and one stage), 1985 (26th), 1987 (47th), 1988 (66th), 1989 (34th), 1991 (115th) and 1992 (70th). Yvon Madiot rode in 1984 (46th), 1985 (72nd), 1986 (10th), 1987 (73rd), 1988 (DNF), 1989 (47th), 1990 and 1991 (DNF), 1992 (67th).

STEPHEN ROCHE of IRELAND and his brother Laurence: Stephen rode in 1983 (13th), 1984 (25th), 1985 (3rd and one stage), 1986 (48th), 1987 (1st and one stage), 1989 (DNF), 1990 (44th), 1991 (DNF), 1992 (9th and one stage) and 1993 (13th). Laurence rode in 1991 and came 153rd.

From SPAIN there were MIGUEL INDURAIN and his brother Prudencio. Miguel rode in 1985 and 1986, when he didn't finish, 1987 (97th), 1988 (47th), 1989 (17th and one stage), 1990 (10th and a stage), 1991 (1st and two stages), 1992 (1st and three stages), 1993 (1st and two stages), 1994 (1st and one stage), 1995 (1st and two stages) and 1996 (11th). Prudencio rode in 1993 (126th), 1996 (58th), 1998 (DNF) and 1999 (76th).

LAURENT JALABERT and his brother Nicolas: Laurent rode in 1991 (71st), 1992 (34th, Points winner and one stage), 1993 (DNF), 1994 (DNF), 1995, (4th, Points winner and one stage), 1996 (DNF), 1997 (43rd), 1998 (DNF), 2000 (54th), 2001 (19th, Mountains winner and two stages) and 2002 (42nd, Mountains winner). Nicolas rode in 1997 (135th), 1998 (49th), 2000 (DNF) and 2001 (115th). Laurent made it a condition of team contracts that there was a place, too, for his younger brother.

JOS BRUYERE
b. Maastricht, Holland, Oct 5 1948

There are only so many ambitions in life. For BELGIUM's Jos Bruyere – born in HOLLAND but of Belgian nationality – it seemed good enough to win the first AMATEUR Flèche Ardennaise in 1969, splitting the field. But what happened next was unbelievable. A man called Jean Crahay approached him and asked, 'My friend EDDY MERCKX wonders if you'd be interested in riding for him.' For Bruyere it was like being offered keys to the Mint.

He and Merckx became allies, Bruyere being what writers at the time liked to call a 'faithful lieutenant'. He dedicated himself to a man he considered a god. When Merckx won Milan-San Remo (as he did seven times, four with Bruyere in support) Bruyere too lifted his arms. He worked so hard for Merckx that even the great man himself had to ask him to slow down. Bruyere towed the bunch along in Paris-Nice in 1970, and rode so hard that nobody could or would come by. Finally Merckx urged him, 'Take it steady, you'll get your chance to win.'

'I'm not riding to win,' Bruyere said. 'I'm doing it to stop anyone attacking you.' Merckx responded by taking Bruyere with him from SPONSOR to sponsor as he changed teams. So Bruyere was never out of work. And he could also win on his own account. He won Liège-Bastogne-Liège in 1976 and 1978 and the semi-classic Het Volk in 1974, 1975 and 1980. He wore the yellow JERSEY in 1974 and 1978 Tours, holding the second one until the Alps and missing the podium in Paris by one place.

It may be pushing it to say the heart went out of him when Merckx retired in 1979, but he had only one more major win and never rode the Tour again.

Winner

1974	Het Volk
1975	Tour Mediterranean, Het Volk
1976	Liège-Bastogne-Liège
1978	Liège-Bastogne-Liège
1980	Het Volk

Tour de France

1970	50th	
1971	60th	
1972	26th	Stage win Auxerre—Versailles
1974	21st	Yellow Jersey
1977	DNF	
1978	4th	Yellow Jersey

JOHAN BRUYNEEL
b. Izegem, Belgium, Aug 23 1964

Johan Bruyneel was a moderate professional for 12 years – although coming third in the 1995 Tour of SPAIN while helping LAURENT JAL-ABERT to win is hardly 'moderate' – and then went on to become a still more successful team MANAGER. Bruyneel rode six Tours and finished four. In 1993 he finished seventh and won what was until 1999 the fastest ever road stage in Tour history, but he is better remembered for being the only man to cling to MIGUEL INDURAIN in BELGIUM in the 1995 Tour.

Indurain attacked in the last part of the stage from Charleroi to Liège. Bruyneel, an unfancied rider but one performing in front of his home (Belgian) crowd, saw his chance and went with the break. Indurain attacked again on the Côte des Forges (*see* STAN OCKERS) and this time only Bruyneel could stay with him. Indurain began riding so hard that Bruyneel said 'it was like riding behind a motorbike'. Indurain had a reason. Astonishingly, the race leader, BJARNE RIIS, had missed the break. Going like a motorbike was the way he was going to win the Tour. The Spaniard built the two of them a 50-second lead, but not surprisingly started tiring in the outskirts of Liège, and ultimately Bruyneel came by to win easily and take the yellow JERSEY. Indurain may have been disappointed that he didn't have the stage, but the Tour was still young, and there were still the TIME TRIALS to come. And there he would be unbeatable. Indurain, as Bruyneel had discovered, was devastatingly fast when he needed to be. Indurain won the Tour and Riis, the one-time leader, came third.

Bruyneel retired after the 1998 Tour and became manager of the new US Postal team. There he led LANCE ARMSTRONG to Tour victory.

Winner

1990	Tour Avenir
1991	GP Frankfurt
1992	GP Nations, Coppa Placci

Tour de France

1990	17th	
1991	35th	
1993	7th	Stage win Evreux—Amiens
1995	31st	Stage win Charleroi—Liège, and Yellow Jersey
1996	DNF	
1998	DNF	

GIANNI BUGNO
b. Brügg, Switzerland, Feb 14 1964

Though not a pure SPRINTER, Gianni Bugno had the speed to beat some of the best finishers around when he needed to. Thus he denied a WORLD CHAMPION's JERSEY to STEVEN ROOKS and MIGUEL INDURAIN in 1991, and to LAURENT JALABERT in 1992.

Bugno – Italian despite being born in Switzerland – turned professional in 1986 and rode the Tour eight times, finishing all but once (1994). His best year was 1991, when he came second. There was much speculation that he could win in 1992 by combining his brute power with his ability in the MOUNTAINS. But his undoing proved to be the TIME TRIALS. Indurain beat him by four minutes and that was that. Bugno had no hope of pulling the deficit back in the mountains, and ended both physically and mentally beaten in third place behind Indurain and Claudio Chiappucci.

FRANCESCO MOSER said of him, 'He had the motor to be a great rider but not the character to be great. He lacked personality, he wasn't hard enough, too easily happy with what he'd achieved.'

Bugno's career ended not as a Tour winner but as a DOMESTIQUE for the Mapei team. He retired at the end of the 1999 season to work for a salvage company in Turin. In 2001 he returned to the Tour, piloting his helicopter to ALPE D'HUEZ, where he had won in 1990 and 1991. Among his passengers, despite his remarks, was Moser.

Winner

1986	Tour Appenines, Tour Friuli, Tour Piedmont
1987	Tour Appenines
1988	Tour Calabria, Tour Appenines
1989	Tre Valle Varesine
1990	Giro d'Italia, Milan-San Remo, World Cup, Wincanton Classic, Tour Trentino
1991	World championship, Bicyclette Basque, San Sebastian Classic, National championship
1992	World championship, Milan-Turin, Tour Lazio, Tour Emilia
1993	GP Gippingen
1994	Tour Flanders
1995	Trofeo Matteotti, Tour Mediterranean, National championship

Tour de France

1988	62nd	Stage win Ruelle—Limoges
1989	11th	
1990	7th	Stage wins St-Gervais—Alpe d'Huez, Pau—Bordeaux
1991	2nd	Stage win Gap—Alpe d'Huez
1992	3rd	
1993	20th	
1994	DNF	
1995	53rd	

MAX BULLA
b. Vienna, Austria, Sep 26 1905, d. Jan 1990

Max Bulla was the first Austrian to wear the yellow JERSEY, a remarkable feat because he was a TOURISTE-ROUTIER. It was in 1931, when it was still possible to ride the Tour as a private entrant. The teams paid for and organised their riders' accommodation and other needs, but tourists organised their own affairs as they went. (*See* JULES DELOFFRE.)

The rules were particularly complicated because the tourists set off 10 minutes after the aces. Far from discouraging them, the time gap often inspired the tourists, and on the second stage four of them not only caught the aces but passed them. Bulla won the stage from Caen to Dinan and took the yellow jersey. He kept it into the Pyrenees but lost his lead when ANTONIN MAGNE opened the gap that eventually won him the Tour. Bulla finished 15th.

Bulla's record includes the first Tour of Switzerland, in 1933, along with three of its stages. He also came fifth in the Tour of SPAIN in 1935.

Winner

1931	Championship Zurich
1933	Tour Switzerland

Tour de France

1931	15th	Stage wins Caen—Dinan, Montpellier—Marseille, Grenoble—Aix-les-Bains, and Yellow Jersey
1932	19th	
1933	DNF	
1936	DNF	

LUCIEN BUYSSE
b. Wontergem, Belgium, Sep 11 1892, d. Deinze, Belgium, Jan 3 1980

The Buysse family was a Belgian cycling dynasty. MARCEL BUYSSE came third in the Tour in 1913, his son Albert was a star on the six-day circuit with nine wins in the 1930s, and

Achiel won the Tour of Flanders in 1940, 1941 and 1943. And then there was the family's Tour winner.

Lucien Buysse, Marcel's brother, looked as though he'd never do it. He rode his first Tour in 1914 but didn't finish. The WAR then intervened and cost him five further years. He failed to finish again in 1919 but improved gradually until he came second in 1925. By then he was 32 and the chance of going one place better the next year seemed slight. It seemed even more remote when his daughter, one of four children, died during the race. Buysse carried on only because his family begged him to.

Far from losing heart, he led a stage over four Pyrenean MOUNTAINS by 25 minutes. The weather was the worst the Tour had known. Only 16 riders arrived within the time limit and many ended up taking shelter in bars and houses. Others finished by car. In Paris, Buysse, the winner by 88 minutes on NICOLAS FRANTZ, prayed aloud to his daughter, saying, 'I thought of you during all the hardest hours of the race.'

His record also included third in Bordeaux-Paris in 1926, second in Liège-Bastogne-Liège in 1920, and third in the same year's Paris-Roubaix.

Winner

1926 Tour de France

Tour de France

1914	DNF	
1919	DNF	
1923	8th	Stage win Perpignan—Toulon
1924	3rd	
1925	2nd	Stage wins Nîmes—Toulon, Toulon—Nice
1926	1st	Stage wins Bayonne—Luchon, Luchon—Perpignan, and Yellow Jersey
1929	DNF	
1930	DNF	

MARCEL BUYSSE
b. Wontergem, Belgium, Nov 11 1889, d. Oct 3 1939

Marcel Buysse was the oldest of the Buysse dynasty. (*See* LUCIEN BUYSSE.) He rode the Tour four times, coming 3rd in 1913 with six stage wins, and won the Tour of Flanders in 1914.

How far this relentless hard man of Belgian cycling would have gone will never be known; his career ended just after the first world WAR, which he survived only to die at the start of the next.

Winner

1914 Tour Flanders

Tour de France

1912	4th	
1913	3rd	Stage wins Brest—La Rochelle, Luchon—Perpignan, Grenoble—Geneva, Geneva—Belfort, Longwy—Dunkirk, Dunkirk—Paris
1914	DNF	
1919	DNF	

CAFÉ RAIDS

Among the Tour's SPONSORS there is always a drinks supplier, including firms such as the ÉVIAN mineral water company and Coca-Cola. These days bottles are carried to the riders in trays on motorbikes, and this is done for several reasons. First, DOPING RULES forbid riders from the old practice of taking drinks from SPECTATORS, or at least force them to face the consequences of what they drink; claims that riders were doped by onlookers handing up bottles were common in the early days of drug tests. (*See* PIERRE DUMAS.)

Second, riders now drink as much as they can whereas until the 1970s the custom was to drink little. 'Driest is fastest,' as JACQUES ANQUETIL put it. And third, organisers grew embarrassed at so-called 'café raids'.

It was commonplace for riders to help themselves to what they wanted as they rode, and shopkeepers seemed happy enough with the arrangement. In 1924 ALBERT LONDRES wrote: 'Number 247 is walking; he's out of tyres. "I've had five punctures," he says. "Five. I've got no tyres left." So the owner of the bike shop at 90 rue de St-Vulfran gives him a tyre, and 247 rides off without paying. It's the usual practice.'

For years DOMESTIQUES were told to raid café shelves and refrigerators to bring drinks to their leaders. TOM SIMPSON used to send riders for Cokes, which sometimes annoyed helpers so much that, according to VIN DENSON, they once tipped some out and peed into the bottle to top it up. 'He didn't seem to notice but he was as angry as hell when we told him,' Denson says.

Café raids rarely annoyed the owners, who just sent a bill to the organisers. But they were embarrassing for a prestige event, and the practice died out when riders were first allowed to take drinks from their team cars, and then to do so from special drinks motorbikes.

NORBERT CALLENS
b. Wakken, Belgium, Jun 22 1924

The yellow JERSEY who never got to wear it, Norbert Callens was one of the lesser riders in Belgium's team in 1949. He was there to ride for RIK VAN STEENBERGEN, BRIEK SCHOTTE, MARCEL KINT and STAN OCKERS, but the early days of every Tour are unpredictable, and often offer a moment for minnows to show themselves. Callens wasn't exactly an unknown – he had won the Tour of Belgium in 1945 and been the next rider home after ALBERT BOURLON's record break in 1947 – but winning a stage of the Tour would surpass all that.

And so in 1949 he slipped into a break with César Marcelak of the Ouest-Nord REGIONAL TEAM and another Belgian, Florent Mathieu. He outsprinted them in Boulogne after 211km to lead van Steenbergen by 3:03 and RAPHAËL GÉMINIANI by 4:36. It may have caused an upset in the team – he had taken the yellow jersey from his team-mate Roger Lambrecht and therefore put both him and the team at risk – but for Callens it was the greatest day of his career.

Sadly, next morning his SOIGNEUR let the team's truck leave with the jersey inside. The Belgian journalist Albert van Laethem lent him a yellow sweater but Callens regretted the event for the rest of his life. He lost the lead next day to Jacques Marinelli of the Ile-de-France team and never rode the Tour again.

Winner

1945   Tour Belgium
1949   Tour Flemish Ardennes

Tour de France

1947   DNF
1948   DNF
1949   DNF   Stage win Brussels—Boulogne,
             and Yellow Jersey

ROBERT CAPA

The most evocative pictures of the Tour are in black and white, and they consist not so much of the racing as of riders washing in buckets in barns, or fat policemen directing the race with provincial pomposity, or the bunch clambering up a grass bank to avoid some unseen obstacle. Many of these were taken by Robert Capa – real name Andrei Friedmann – who followed the race in 1939 for *Match*, later *Paris-Match*, on a motorbike driven by a friend called Taczi. He used the 35mm Leica that he preferred as a war photographer, and which traditional photographers considered too small. (They preferred the 2¼-square format of 120 film.)

Capa was born in Budapest, Hungary, in October 1913, and left home at 18 to work as a darkroom apprentice in Berlin. He fled Germany with the rise of the Nazis and settled in Paris with his Polish fiancée Gerda Taro. His new name was their private joke: 'Robert Capa' was supposed to be a talented but unknown photographer who happened to be visiting France. This Capa was very rich, and wouldn't let Gerda sell his pictures to newspapers for less than 150 francs, or three times the going rate.

The trick worked, but the secret didn't last long. Lucien Vogel, the editor of *Vue*, worked out that Gerda's humble 'darkroom assistant' and the 'rich American' were the same person. Far from being upset, Vogel sent Capa to the Spanish civil war, where his picture of a soldier dying with his rifle raised in the air made him the most famous photographer of his generation.

Capa emigrated to America after covering the 1939 Tour de France, and worked for *Life*, where he founded the Magnum picture agency with Henri Cartier-Bresson. He died on May 25 1954 after stepping on a mine while covering the war in French Indochina, now Vietnam.

CARAVAN

HENRI DESGRANGE conceived the Tour as a race of individuals. The riders might be in teams sponsored by BIKE factories, but they were to race as individuals. There were to be no TACTICS, and he insisted that riders from the same sponsor must not help each other win. However, despite Desgrange repeatedly warning the sponsoring factories about this, they took no notice. Things came to a head in 1929 when riders in the ALCYON team were clearly working for their best rider, MAURICE DEWAELE, even though he was ill and oughtn't have won. 'My race has been won by a corpse,' Desgrange complained, angry at how Dewaele's team-mates had brought him back from the dead.

Desgrange's solution was to banish trade teams, and he decreed that, from 1930, everyone would ride in NATIONAL TEAMS. That satisfied his ideals, and the idea was well received by SPECTATORS, who could now identify themselves with riders representing their country. But it brought a real financial headache for the Tour. Until then, sponsors had paid their riders' costs. Obviously, they wouldn't foot the bill if they couldn't field their own teams, and so Desgrange had to pay for riders' hotels, food and equipment. His solution was to charge stage towns for the publicity that the race would bring them, and to open the Tour to advertising.

The commercial possibilities of the crowds that lined the road of the Tour had already struck some companies. Paul Thévenin of the Menier chocolates firm had tried to follow the race to give away samples, only to find spectators had gone home when he passed by. Desgrange's plan was to let his proposed advertising cavalcade, which immediately became known as 'the caravan', go in front instead. Thévenin was delighted, handing out tons of samples and 500,000 policeman's hats marked with Menier's name. The company also brewed hot chocolate in the MOUNTAINS and handed it to fans, riders and officials.

Along with Menier in that first caravan were many other companies promoting products, such as La Vache Qui Rit, Graf, Biscottes Delft, Esders and Noveltex.

Before long the procession of advertisers took longer to pass than the race itself. The order was decided by the contract each firm had drawn up with the SOCIÉTÉ DU TOUR DE FRANCE. And since it was an exercise in selling that had to get its message over in just a few seconds, the advertisers weren't always restrained. On July 10 1935 the journalist Pierre Bost grumbled in the journal *Marianne* ('Marianne' is the national symbol of FRANCE), 'That Monsieur Henri Desgrange earns a lot of money in this month of July is incontestable. That he gets it, for the most part, on contracts for the advertising which mushrooms around the whole spectacle, is obviously not very glorious. The caravan of 60 vividly painted trucks extolling the virtues of an aperitif, or of underwear, or of rubbish bins, presents a shameful sight. It shouts, it plays bad music, it's ugly, it's sad, it's horrible – it's the vulgarity of money.

'That Monsieur Desgrange accepts parasites on the course is fair enough; but at least he could impose a minimum level of decency. The day that Monsieur Desgrange, who is very intelligent, understands that, he will sort the matter out with two strokes of his pen; and I never give up hope of one day seeing among the staff of the Tour de France a commissaire of good taste.'

Bost's wish hasn't been totally realised. The advertising caravan sets off two hours ahead of the race and extends for 25km. More than 200 cars and trucks throw out cheap souvenirs – in 1994 the GAN insurance company got through 170,000 hats, 80,000 badges, 60,000 plastic bags and 535,000 eight-page newspapers. They weighed 32 tonnes.

Staff are told to hand over goods or at least throw them only at spectators' feet, but that's not always achieved in the rush to get samples to the maximum number of people in the minimum time. No vehicle is allowed to stop. In 2000 a boy named only as 'Philippe' was hit by a car and killed beside his parents on the Avignon-Draguignan stage. As a result, the size of the caravan was cut and police imposed radar speed checks. But even so a boy of seven, Melvin Pompele, died near Retjons in 2002 after running in front of the caravan to join his grandparents. Speed was not an issue, police said, and urged parents to keep their children under control.

Many of the caravan staff are students recruited through agencies. Advertisers pay the equivalent of about £12,500, plus the expense of staff and advertising for three vehicles to precede the race. Each vehicle that goes past is the subject of enthusiastic comment from the voice of the Tour (announcer and commentator), DANIEL MANGEAS.

Jean-Pierre Lachaud, who has been in charge of the caravan since 1989, after first joining it for a summer job in 1983, says the hardest days are in the smaller mountains, where narrow roads make it difficult to keep moving. His worst experiences include a racing car that couldn't run slowly enough, and a team bus that jammed on the Col de Joux-Plane. Spectators pushed it out of the way just seven minutes before the race arrived.

The caravan reaches the FINISH an hour before the riders.

FABIO CASARTELLI

b. Como, Italy, Jul 16 1970, d. Tarbes, France, Jul 18 1995

Fabio Casartelli, ITALY's Olympic champion in Barcelona in 1992, was the third rider to die in the Tour. On July 18 1995 he was among several riders who fell on a bend going down the Col de Portet d'Aspet. The others rode on, but Casartelli hit a stone block shielding the drop. His heart stopped three times before he reached hospital in Tarbes, and he died as a result of brain damage. The rest of the riders gave Casartelli's family the equivalent of £60,000 from the next day's prizes, and the Tour donated the same amount.

The Casartelli MEMORIAL near the site is a winged wheel in white marble on a grey marble base, on which is set a sundial. Casartelli's team MANAGER, Jim Ochowicz, says it symbolises 'his life, his Olympic victory and his death'. The Tour organisers paid their respects to him there in 1999, on the rest day.

The bike Casartelli was riding is in the Madonna del Ghisallo chapel near his home town of Como, Italy. In 2001 ERIK DEKKER gave his World Cup winner's JERSEY to the Fabio Casartelli Foundation; he had finished second to Casartelli in the 1992 Olympic road race.

The other riders who died while racing in the Tour were FRANCESCO CEPEDA and TOM SIMPSON.

(*See* ADOLPHE HELIÈRE for a rider who died on a rest day.)

Tour de France

1994	DNF
1995	DNF

FRANCESCO CEPEDA

b. Sopuerta, Spain, Mar 8 1906, d. Grenoble, France, Jul 17 1935

The first rider to die during the Tour was the Frenchman ADOLPHE HELIÈRE, who went swimming on the rest day in Nice in 1910 and drowned after being stung by a jellyfish. But the first to die while racing was SPAIN's Francesco Cepeda. His front tyre rolled off the rim on July 14 1935 and he fell over a cliff on the way down the GALIBIER. Cepeda was pulled out half-conscious, with blood streaming down his face, and quickly slipped into a coma. He died three days later in hospital in Grenoble.

Jules Merviel of FRANCE also came close to dying during the same race. He rode into a lorry while leading the stage from Cannes to Marseille, and was severely injured. The other riders to die were TOM SIMPSON on MONT VENTOUX in 1967, and FABIO CASARTELLI on the Portet d'Aspet in 1995.

Tour de France

1930	27th
1931	DNF
1933	DNF
1935	DNF

PINO CERAMI

b. Misterbianco, Italy, Mar 28 1922

Giuseppe 'Pino' Cerami was born Sicilian but his parents emigrated to Belgium in 1927, and their son became a Belgian citizen. He started racing in 1937, turned professional in 1947, and raced until 1963, a remarkable 26 years of which 15 were as a pro.

Cerami rode for RIK VAN STEENBERGEN for much of his career, happier as a DOMESTIQUE than having to find the confidence to win for himself. His success in the Tour of Belgium in 1957 was an aberration, and while the race counted for a lot at home it mattered little abroad. Then over Easter 1960 van Steenbergen didn't turn up for Paris-Roubaix because he had done too little training, and initially Cerami felt lost. But '*Qui ne tente rien n'a rien*' (nothing ventured, nothing gained) as they say in Roubaix, so off he went. He ventured, he gained, he won alone.

'That day after Paris-Roubaix was one of the hardest of my life,' he said. 'I was a team man. Nobody wanted to talk to me. Suddenly I had every journalist in the world on my doorstep. I wasn't used to it.' At 38 he had finally got his confidence. After that he couldn't be stopped, winning the Flèche Wallonne that same year and Paris-Brussels the next year, and making himself so popular that a race was named after him. The GP Pino Cerami is now one of BELGIUM's most popular events.

Cerami retired in 1963 after 58 wins. His farewell gesture was to win a Tour stage from Bordeaux to Pau, where he sneaked off alone with a kilometre to go and beat the great SPRINTER, ANDRÉ DARRIGADE.

Winner

1957	Tour Belgium
1960	Paris-Roubaix, Flèche Wallonne
1961	Paris-Brussels, Flèche Brabançonne, Antwerp-Ougrée
1962	Antwerp-Ougrée

Tour de France

1949	DNF	
1957	35th	
1958	DNF	
1962	81st	
1963	DNF	Stage win Bordeaux—Pau

CHAMPS ELYSÉES

These days it seems natural that FRANCE's greatest sports event should finish on Paris's grandest avenue, but it hasn't always been the case. In fact it was used as the START long before it hosted the finale.

The first time the Tour came to the Champs Elysées was 3am on July 13 1908, when riders signed on under gaslight in the Place de la Concorde. Large crowds turned out and 'an army of cyclists', as the papers put it, joined the 111 competitors riding in procession along the Champs Elysées to the true start at the Pont de la Jatte. But only 110 riders set off together from there. The 111th, Ernest Goujon, started 25 minutes later with a note from the boss of the Café de la Grande-Jatte, the start venue, explaining he'd been delayed on the way but hadn't quit the race. Goujon got to Roubaix,

272km away, 7hr 53min after GEORGES PASSERIEU. But he was far from being last man, who was Pierre Desvages, another Frenchman, at 8hr 51min. (*See* BIKES for Desvages' role in technical history.)

The Tour had always finished in Paris, although never in the centre of it until the Champs Elysées was first used in 1975. The 1903 and 1904 races finished outside the Restaurant du Père Auto in the western suburb of VILLE D'AVRAY. The finishers then rode in procession to the PARC DES PRINCES TRACK at the southern end of the Bois de Boulogne. In 1905 the last kilometre to the track was a TIME TRIAL, and from 1906 the race went straight to the Parc and finished there.

The Parc hosted the finish until 1967, when ROGER PINGEON won. After that it was demolished, and the finish moved to the PISTE MUNCIPALE at Vincennes. The *"cipale"*, on the edge of the Bois de Vincennes in the south-east, lay inside the Périphérique ring road, and therefore the Tour finished for the first time in Paris rather than its suburbs (the distinction between inner and outer Paris is marked). But the Vincennes track could never be more than a stopgap because the stadium and track were deteriorating and there was limited space for SPECTATORS.

At the start of the 1970s the Tour authorities began suggesting that the race should finish on the Champs Elysées, the greatest of the avenues designed by the 19th century architect Georges Haussmann for his city of light. The Champs Elysées linked the Arc de Triomphe, where the pioneering Paris-to-Rouen race had started in 1868 (*see* BRITAIN), with the Place de la Concorde, where the Tour started in 1908.

The city didn't say yes immediately. Negotiations continued, and in 1974 the mayor – and later president – Jacques Chirac agreed. So in 1975 half a million spectators watched WALTER GODEFROOT outsprint Rik van Linden on the Champs Elysées. Until then the avenue, 1,910m long and 70m wide, had been closed only for the military procession on Bastille Day.

The closing stage into Paris is now little more than a procession, far different from the time when JEAN ROBIC took PIERRE BRAMBILLA's yellow JERSEY on the last day in 1947. Now the day traditionally starts with champagne for the leader, and riders laugh, joke and play about for photographers. A few trivial attacks may be tried for a last stab at publicity, but the rest of the riders will be saving energy and nerves for the final laps through Paris. The pace rises terrifyingly as the world's longest bike race comes to an end.

To win on the Champs Elysées is a question more of prestige than any influence on the result, although the sprinters' competition for the green jersey, by contrast, can last right to the line. ERIK ZABEL couldn't be sure until the final metres in 2001 that he had beaten STUART O'GRADY. 'That was the most emotional of my six green jerseys,' he said. In 2002 he lost it equally narrowly to another Australian, ROBBIE MCEWEN.

The most exciting finish between contenders for overall victory was when the first two, BERNARD HINAULT and JOOP ZOETEMELK, broke away in the last kilometres in 1979. (See GREG LEMOND for how he won the closest Tour in history on the Champs Elysées in 1989.)

PIERRE CHANY

A book of interviews with the French journalist Pierre Chany has the words 'L'homme aux 50 Tours de France' (the man with 50 Tours de France) on the cover. It was a proud boast but unfortunately proved to be inaccurate, a forecast forced by publishing schedules, because Chany died of pleurisy on June 18 1996 just weeks before his 50th Tour. He left behind at his home in Créteil a library of the books he'd written and tens of thousands of newspaper and magazine articles printed in 15 languages.

Chany was born in Langéac in the Haute Loire area on December 22 1922, and moved to Paris when his parents took over a café in the rue Guillaume Bertrand in the 11th arrondissement (district) near the Père Lachaise cemetery (where his friend and fellow cycling writer Antoine Blondin is buried).

Chany raced as an AMATEUR, but his career was interrupted by the war. Because he had

been trained as a locksmith, he was forced by French police to open the lock on a house that hid Jews, who were all shot. Repelled by the complicity of fellow Frenchmen, he joined the Forces Françaises de l'Intérieure, the Resistance movement known as les fifis (the girlies) because of its initials. On his 21st birthday he was betrayed and arrested.

The GMR, the French riot police, smashed his fingers and then handed him over to the Germans, who threw him into jail. But Chany escaped while being transferred to an army barracks in Clermont-Ferrand, and joined a Resistance group based in Algeria. When peace came he became a reporter at La Marseillaise, Le Sport and Ce Soir, and then joined the Tour paper L'ÉQUIPE at the start of the 1950s, becoming head of cycling. The editor and Tour organiser JACQUES GODDET called him 'a sacred animal of the profession'.

In the 1950s and 1960s riders, especially French riders at their peak, were willing to share their inside stories. Chany's insider knowledge, and his unparalleled closeness to JACQUES ANQUETIL, gave him an impressive understanding of what was happening in cycling. His contempt for races he didn't think were up to standard was legendary.

Chany enjoyed a joke. In 1964 he dressed up the singer Dalida as a man and smuggled her into his Tour car to thwart Goddet's rules banning women. The story ran over two pages in Miroir Sprint. Goddet could see a good news story, Chany said, and never mentioned it. He took the same view when Chany dressed up as a rider and joined in the night-time section of the marathon Bordeaux-Paris as Goddet dozed. Chany's anecdote doesn't say which year this happened.

Chany, for a long time a heavy drinker, wasn't always the healthiest of men. He died of pleurisy when he was 73, after falling ill during the PROLOGUE of the Dauphiné Libéré. L'Équipe wrote on June 19 1996, 'Our paper has lost one of those who have made themselves masters of history and sports journalism.'

The first reporter to follow 50 Tours was in fact JACQUES AUGENDRE.

CHEATS

It's not surprising that an event as long and unsupervised as the Tour should be prone to cheating. In the early days competitors rode alone or in small groups, separated by intervals of hours. Checking them was impossible, especially when stages went on through the night. It seems improbable that there wasn't something underhand going on even in the first Tour in 1903, but without judges it's hard to know. What makes this likely is that there was so much cheating in 1904.

Cheating in 1904 was undertaken both by riders and SPECTATORS. Riders took lifts by car, or clung on to them, or rode in their slipstreams. Another ruse was to tie a length of wire to a door handle and grasp the other end between the teeth with the help of a cork. A rider could thus be towed along while appearing to grimace with effort. But with the cheating came a Draconian enforcement of the rules and many of the leading riders were disqualified and others penalised (*see* 1904 AFFAIR). Such was the chaos HENRI DESGRANGE announced the end of his race, which had been ruined 'by the blind emotions' it had aroused.

Those passions were also evident among spectators in 1904. They not only helped their favourites but also felled trees across the road to delay others. One night a group of fans started beating up riders, and the next night waited for the police and officials who had stopped them. The roving reporter and organiser GÉO LEFÈVRE was forced to fire his gun on the Col de la RÉPUBLIQUE near St-Étienne to disperse a gang waiting for him and his race.

In Lyon a car full of rival fans tried for six kilometres to force MAURICE GARIN (the 1903 winner) and Lucien Pothier into a ditch. HENRI CORNET claimed he had been fed poisoned chicken and collapsed and fell asleep over his handlebars. Jean-Baptiste Dortignacq had itching powder put into his JERSEY. LOUIS TROUSSELIER was accused of smashing ink stands so other riders couldn't sign the control documents that proved they had gone the right way.

Riders and spectators scattered nails on the road. In 1905 about 125kg of nails were found on stage one between Paris and Nancy. Only Dortingnacq managed to avoid a puncture, and only 24 of the 60 starters reached the FINISH. It took a STRIKE by the riders to persuade Desgrange not to cancel the race.

In fact nail-scattering was so bad in 1905 that an inventor called Cavalade produced a puncture-proof tyre which he demonstrated in the Café Sion during the rest day at Toulouse. A reporter wrote, 'Dortignacq got on the inventor's bicycle, rode quickly, then slowly, jumped on the pedals, balanced on the nails and jumped the bike on to them. There was no puncture, the nails falling from the tyres at the first turn. . . . All the Tour riders tried it. . . . The bike was convincing and the riders warmly thanked M. Cavalade, who put the invention at their disposal, without obligation, for the stages still to come.'

In its early years some people didn't want the noise and confusion that the Tour might bring to their town, and tried to sabotage it. They scattered nails, turned signposts around, and jeered as riders passed. Desgrange compromised by moving the FINISH out of town centres when he could.

There have also been more immediate forms of sabotage. PAUL DUBOC was poisoned in 1911 by food or drink supplied by a rival MANAGER – Duboc was in second place and had won two stages. GUSTAVE GARRIGOU, who stood to gain most and thus unfairly got the blame, had to be disguised to escape a lynch mob waiting for him in Duboc's hometown of Rouen. Duboc still finished second overall.

Garrigou himself recalled of 1910, 'We were riding from Nîmes to Perpignan for the eighth stage. I took care the previous night, as always, to take my ALCYON cycle up into my room at Nîmes. It might have seemed a needless precaution because our team had so far dominated the Tour. The only scuffling for places was between ourselves. Anyway, I forgot to lock my door, a mistake which cost me dear.

'We were going through Lunel at about 3am when my front wheel gave up, ball bearings spilling everywhere. Someone had done a good job of unfixing the hub, and I hadn't noticed a thing. So I had to find a mechanic – at 3am – and then search for bearings of the right size to replace those I had lost. I lost an hour and a half because of that. And I had been within seconds of [my big rival] FABER.'

There were no marshals in the early Tours, and riders were given route sheets and told to sign control sheets to prove they'd gone the right way. There was an incentive to take short cuts. At a shepherd's suggestion, ÉMILE MASSON SR and PHILIPPE THYS once took a goat track on the Peyresourde, but lost more time than they gained. Others went further. In 1906 Maurice Carrère, Henri Gauban [see HENRI PÉPIN] and Gaston Tuvache were disqualified when they caught a train to Dijon, only to stumble into Tour officials studying a map at the station exit.

In 1928 Francis Bouillet and Arsène Alancourt hitched a lift after being dropped by the bunch. Their truck skidded and fell into a gully, but they climbed out and caught a passing taxi. When they got to the finish they demanded that their manager should pay the fare. Amazingly, they weren't disqualified – the RULES said riders could drop out and be drafted back in. Bouillet started again three days later.

HENRI ALAVOINE exploited Desgrange's prickly nature by engaging him in lengthy debates in which both grew ever angrier. Desgrange was once so busy arguing that he didn't notice Alavoine clinging to his car and getting a free ride up a climb.

In 1937 ROGER LAPÉBIE was warming up at Luchon when he noticed someone had sawn through his handlebars. Suspicion fell on the national team of BELGIUM, whose riders had accused Desgrange of wanting Lapébie to win. In 1938 GEORGES SPEICHER, the 1933 winner and WORLD CHAMPION, was disqualified for hanging on to a car.

DOPING became prevalent after the WAR. Until then riders had used strychnine or ether, but the mass production of amphetamine during the war changed that. 'We have seen riders reduced to madness under the effect of the heat or stimulants,' wrote Antoine Blondin. 'Some coming back down the hairpins they thought they were climbing, others brandishing their pumps and accusing us of murder.' (And see MONT VENTOUX.)

In 1955 JEAN MALLÉJAC of FRANCE was taken to hospital after collapsing on Mont Ventoux with his legs still turning phantom pedals. According to the local paper, 'He struggled, gesticulated, shouted for his bike, wanted to escape so much that he had to be strapped down.' (See Malléjac entry.) TOM SIMPSON died on the same mountain in 1967 after taking drugs.

Dutch riders discovered at the end of the 1990s that if they hooked their feeding bags over the wing mirror of a car they could get an easy ride up a MOUNTAIN without it being obvious. The trick had to stop when officials began using helicopters to watch the race.

In 1998 the Tour came close to not reaching Paris at all, when some riders were arrested and others walked out. A Belgian SOIGNEUR, WILLY VOET, had been found with a carload of drugs destined for the Festina team. This led to police raids on teams, arrests, charges and suspensions of leading riders such as RICHARD VIRENQUE. (See FESTINA AFFAIR.)

In 2002 JACKY DURAND, one of his team officials and a team car were thrown out after Durand took a tow in the mountains.

(See too LA FRANÇAISE, JULIEN MOINEAU, LUCIEN PETIT—BRETON.)

CLAUDIO CHIAPPUCCI
b. Uboldo, Italy, Feb 28 1963

Claudio Chiappucci was born to be a racing cyclist. As a boy his father Arduino told him how he had fought alongside FAUSTO COPPI in the WAR, and had shared his belongings when they were taken prisoner by the British. Arduino Chiappucci encouraged his son to race, and lived just long enough to see him become a professional. He died from cancer the day after his son's first professional race, in Laigueglia in 1985.

Chiappucci rode through the 1989 Tour unnoticed in 81st place, which made his impact all the greater in 1990. He was so little known outside ITALY that the Tour paper *L'ÉQUIPE* provided a guide to pronouncing his name, as well as the information that his widowed mother had a dress shop, that he'd been a good cyclo-cross rider . . . but little else. That made the surprise even greater when he started a break within 10km of the start of the first stage. He, STEVE BAUER, RONAN PENSEC and Frans Maassen beat the bunch by 10 minutes. (*See* Steve Bauer entry for his comments.) Bauer took the yellow JERSEY with Maassen second and Chiappucci at nine seconds.

Chiappucci took the jersey after the 12th stage, the 33km TIME TRIAL from Fontaine to Villard-de-Lans, and would have held it to Paris but for losing time in the Pyrenees. GREG LEMOND took over the lead in the final TIME TRIAL, but he was rattled enough by this stylish newcomer to refer to him as 'Cappuccino or whatever his name is', for which he later apologised. Chiappucci finished second overall at 2:16.

Chiappucci's most dramatic Tour ride wasn't that opening stage, however. It was on Saturday July 18 1992, on the stage from St-Gervais, at the foot of Mont Blanc, to SES-TRIERE just across the Italian border. Among the MOUNTAINS en route was the ISÉRAN, the Tour's classic col, 2,770m high.

Chiappucci needed an epic ride to win the Tour because MIGUEL INDURAIN had come to the race so fit from the Giro that he had averaged 49km/h in the first major TIME TRIAL in LUXEMBOURG, beating Chiappucci by five and a half minutes. Consequently, Chiappucci needed to produce something special as the bunch prepared for the 254km to Sestriere.

Chiappucci arrived at the start with a monitor meter strapped to his chest. These days heart monitors are standard, but then they were almost unknown. Chiappucci was obviously planning something serious. And so it turned out. He attacked with 233km to go and as the attack developed Indurain was reduced to chasing personally to defend his lead, with his team-mates incapable of maintaining the the pursuit.

Had Indurain not been such a superb athlete, Chiappucci would have won the Tour.

He rode like a hero as five cols followed each other, his heart monitor consistently logging 175 beats a minute. For many, just to finish within the time limit was the most they could hope. Eighteen didn't succeed. Yet at the end Chiappucci only beat Indurain by only 1:45, not enough to win the Tour. His domination in the mountains, though, was total, and he amassed 410 points against the 245 of the Mountains runner-up, RICHARD VIRENQUE.

Chiappucci never did win one of the major tours, although he came second in the Tour de FRANCE in 1990 and 1992, and third in 1991. In 1991 and 1992 he came second in the Giro, and was third in 1993.

Those close to him remember a man of bragging self-confidence. 'He got a kick out of putting other riders down,' said STEPHEN ROCHE. Others recall his scoffing at rivals such as GIANNI BUGNO – 'Did you see him trying to stay with me, with his mouth open gasping for air?' But the way he rode brought a breath of fresh air to the sport, and was a reminder of the era of long lone attacks.

With his NICKNAME of *El Diablo* (the devil) Chiappucci was an impressive figure, but the end of his career was marred by positive blood-DOPING tests in the Tour of Romagna in 1997 and in the same year's WORLD CHAMPIONSHIP. And this raised speculation that his ride to Sestriere may have been the start of the so-called EPO era of doping which culminated in the FESTINA SCANDAL of 1998. Nevertheless, Chiappucci had earned his position as a man of sheer panache and entertainment. (*See* DEVIL.)

Winner

1989	Coppa Placci, Tour Piedmont
1991	Milan-San Remo, Tour Basque Country
1992	Tour Appenines, Tour Trentino
1993	San Sebastian Classic, Japan Cup
1994	Tour Catalonia, Tre Valle Varesine, Japan Cup
1995	Montjuich, Japan Cup, Tour Piedmont

1989	81st	
1990	2nd	Yellow Jersey
1991	3rd	Stage win Jaca—Val Louron, and Mountains winner
1992	2nd	Stage win St-Gervais—Sestriere, and Mountains winner
1993	6th	Stage win Tarbes—Pau
1994	DNF	
1995	11th	
1996	37th	

EUGÈNE CHRISTOPHE

b. Malakoff, France, Jan 22 1885, d. Paris, France, Feb 1 1970

Eugène Christophe, who came from an area on the edge of Paris called Malakoff, was a stocky man with a mournful expression that belied a happy personality. For many years he sported a big moustache like an ancient Gaul's, and was known as *Le Vieux Gaulois*. Less formally, SPECTATORS shouted for 'Cri-Cri', and fellow riders called him 'Hippo' because he performed well in the mud and rain.

Christophe never won the Tour but in 1919 he was the first to wear the *maillot jaune*. (*See* JERSEYS; and *see* PHILIPPE THYS for another claim to this title.) He wasn't impressed by the honour, saying that for the rest of the race spectators shouted that he looked like a canary. The journal *La Vie au Grand Air* put him on its cover, the first time the yellow jersey was pictured in colour. He also claimed a place in Tour legend when he had to walk down the TOURMALET with his broken bike before repairing it in a smithy.

This happened in 1913 when he was 28 years old and the race favourite. That Tour was a scrap between the big teams, PEUGEOT and ALCYON, and the biggest battleground was the sixth stage from Bayonne to Luchon. It included the AUBISQUE, Gourette, Soulor, Tourmalet, Aspin and Peyresourde.

Christophe and Thys went clear on the Tourmalet and were halfway down the descent when, as Christophe recalled, 'All of a sudden, about 10 kilometres from Sainte-Marie-de-Campan down in the valley, I feel that something is wrong with my handlebars. I pull on my brake and stop. I see my fork is broken. I can tell you now that my fork was broken, but I would not have told you at that time because it was bad publicity for my firm. So there I was, left alone on the road. When I say road, I should say the path. I thought that maybe one of these steep pack trails would lead me straight to Ste-Marie-de-Campan. But I was crying so badly I couldn't see anything. With my bike on my shoulder, I walked for all of those 10 kilometres.

'On arriving at the village I met a young girl who led me to the blacksmith on the other side of the village. Monsieur Lecomte was the name of the blacksmith. He was a nice man and wanted to help me, but he wasn't allowed to. The regulations were strict. I had to do all the repair myself. I never spent a more wretched time in my life than those cruel hours in M. Lecomte's forge.'

At one point Christophe allowed a seven-year-old called Corni to pump the bellows for him, while his own hands were occupied with the broken bike and a hammer. As a result, the chief official, a man called Mouchet, fined him a further 10 minutes, later reduced to three. Christophe made it to Luchon at 8.44pm, 29th and still faster on the day than 15 others.

Lecomte's forge is no longer there, but a small house stands on the site with a plaque from the French cycling federation on its wall. Appropriately for a man so dogged by bad luck, it spells his name wrongly as 'Cristophe'. The forks have also disappeared; Peugeot took them and Christophe never saw them again.

History repeated itself in 1919 on the 468km stage from Metz to Dunkirk. Again Christophe's forks broke but this time there was a bicycle factory a kilometre away, although he still had to mend his bike alone. He was delayed almost two hours and dropped from first to third. The Tour paper L'AUTO's readers sent him the money he'd lost in prizes: contributions ranged from three francs to 500, given by Henri de Rothschild. It took 20 lists in the paper to name all of the donors. In all they donated 13,310 francs, more than he would have won by finishing first.

Then came a third incident. In 1922 he hit a block of stone coming down the GALIBIER and once again broke his forks. A priest offered Christophe a bike which he declined because it had bad brakes. The Lord might look after a *curé* on a badly maintained bike, he said, but his own record wasn't so dependable. 'That accident didn't upset me as much as the others,' he recalled. 'By then I was a bit of an expert.'

Christophe's hardships were severe, but his victory in the 1910 Milan-San Remo takes some beating. The weather, good all week, had turned to snow. It was too deep to ride the Turchino pass, then just a track, so Christophe began to walk. Suffering from exposure, he dragged himself under a rock, unable to go further, and froze so much that all he could move was his head.

A chance passer-by found him and got him to a café where the barman stripped him, wrapped him in a blanket, sat him by a fire, and refused to let him leave. Then Cyril van Hauwaert and Ernest Paul, the next two riders, came in. Neither of them was wholly conscious: Paul hadn't even noticed he had lost a shoe, and and van Hauwaert put his hands into the fire to restore sensation. Before the innkeeper would let him go Christophe had to lie about having arranged a meeting with a man who would drive him to San Remo. He won the race, but spent weeks in hospital. It was another year before his health recovered.

In retirement Christophe used to visit the offices of L'ÉQUIPE, L'Auto's successor, on a heavy Camille Foucaux bike with flat handlebars fitted with muffs and a Torpedo coaster hub-brake. A restaurant nearby called itself Le Vieux Gaulois in his honour. His name was also preserved for decades in a brand of toe-clips.

Winner

1910	Milan-San Remo
1920	Bordeaux-Paris, Paris-Tours
1921	Bordeaux-Paris

Tour de France

1906	9th	
1909	9th	
1911	DNF	
1912	2nd	Stage wins Longwy—Belfort, Belfort—Chamonix, Chamonix—Grenoble
1913	7th	
1914	11th	
1919	3rd	Yellow Jersey
1920	DNF	
1921	DNF	
1922	8th	Yellow Jersey
1925	18th	

MARIO CIPOLLINI
b. Lucca, Italy, Mar 22 1967

Italy's Mario Cipollini is the most extrovert sprinter and entertainer of the current era, a man whose mere presence in the front line meant he would win – and at least once with enough panache to wave triumphantly to SPECTATORS while in full flight.

But the Italian's place in Tour history is hard to assess because for all his delight in racing on the flat, Cipollini has never bothered with the Tour beyond the start of the MOUNTAINS, riding seven times between 1992 and 1999 but never finishing. Tour RULES insist every rider must intend to ride the distance, and eventually organiser JEAN-MARIE LEBLANC pointedly sidelined the Italian in both the 2001 and 2002 Tours by not selecting his team. After the second exclusion he said, 'Cipollini merited a place in the Tour and he would probably have won two or three stages. But he would have pulled out at the foot of the Pyrenees and his team doesn't strike me as strong enough to finish the Tour.'

Cipollini didn't admit to any cynicism in abandoning the race, but insisted he had been 'treated no better than meat on a butcher's slab'. And because of the climate of suspicion that followed the FESTINA AFFAIR of 1998, and the rejection of riders and teams associated with drug-taking, he objected to the possible implications of Leblanc's decision. 'I have never once been implicated in a doping affair,' he said, 'and I'd have thought I merited better.'

Cipollini at his peak is unbeatable, revelling in sprint wins slavishly established by a team which clears a path for him through the fastest finishes. From 1993 to 1999 he won at least one stage in the first week of every Tour he started. The exception was 1994 when he was recovering from a CRASH. In 1993 and 1997 he wore the yellow JERSEY, and by the turn of the century he had 12 stage wins in six Tours.

Such was his dominance of the sprints in 1999 that he won four stages in a row, one at RECORD speed, but then had a disastrous 2000. While he was freewheeling in Tuscany and trying to secure the zip of his jersey he crashed and hit his face on the road, after which he needed 30 stitches and missed the Tour. His SPONSOR told him to ride the Tour of SPAIN to earn his money only for him to be thrown out and suspended for three months for punching Francisco Cerezo. Cipollini claimed Cerezo had insulted him the previous day and a fight began when the two arrived to sign on. Cerezo was cut beneath the left eye and needed three stitches in his forehead.

'What happened in Spain was the worst moment in my career and finished off a terrible year,' Cipollini said. He won only six races all year – almost a zero for a man who by that time had won 146. Next year the Tour told him to stay at home, a decision that angered many but made the race more open.

The author Matt Rendell said of the Italian, 'Over 25 years, Mario has taken a physique blessed with innate physical gifts and moulded it into a ruthless sprinting machine. Part of this relentlessly single-minded project has been to refuse even to begin the mountain stages of major tours in order to protect his muscle shape. Any improvement in his climbing would jeopardise his pure speed. That means near invincibility in his ideal race profile – the long, flat sprint finish where victory depends on positional sense, a high-speed lead-out, and blinding maximum speed – but vulnerability where matters are complicated by no more than a few curves, a slight gradient, and a cross-wind. And as a stage racer, Super Mario doesn't even register on the screen.'

He may never have finished the Tour, let alone won, but Cipollini brought more colour to the Tour than many who did both. No stunt was too much. He would pose nude and with topless models. In 1997 he wore shorts of a different colour each day, matching the green JERSEY, the yellow and the American flag of his BIKE-maker. He was fined every day. In 1998 officials stopped him riding in IRELAND in a green jersey labelled 'Peace'. Mobile phones were banned during races, it's said, because he was spotted phoning friends from the middle of the bunch. (And see EARPIECES.)

In 1999 he dressed in a toga alongside a stripper billed as Cleopatra for a Tour stage start. More fines followed when he and his team turned up next morning dressed in silver jerseys marked *Veni, vidi, vici* (I came, I saw, I conquered) in honour of his four stage wins. He also rode with a picture of Pamela Anderson on his handlebars.

After 40 stage wins and two points titles at the Giro, in 2002 he crowned his career by winning the world championship at Zolder, Belgium – in a sprint, of course.

Winner

1991 GP Escaut, Tour Syracuse
1992 Ghent-Wevelgem
1993 Escant, GP Hovelbeke Ghent-Wevelgem
1995 Trofeo Luis Puig
1996 National championship
1999 Trofeo Luis Puig
2002 Milan-San Remo, Ghent-Wevelgem, World championship

Tour de France

1992	DNF
1993	DNF Stage win Luçon—Les Sables, and Yellow Jersey
1995	DNF Stage wins Perros Guirec—Vitré, Alençon—Le Havre
1996	DNF Stage win 's Hertogenbosch—Wasquehal
1997	DNF Stage wins Rouen—Forges-les-Eaux, St Valery-en-Caux—Vire, and Yellow Jersey and Points leader
1998	DNF Stage wins Chôlet—Châteauroux, La Châtre—Brive
1999	DNF Stage wins Laval—Blois, Bonneval—Amiens, Amiens—Maubeuge, Avesnes-sur-Helpe—Thionville

CIRCUIT DE FRANCE – *See* WAR

THIERRY CLAVEYROLAT
b. La Tronche, France, Mar 31 1959, d. Vizille, France, Sep 7 1999

Thierry 'Clavette' Claveyrolat – the NICKNAME means cotter pin and referred to his size – was a stage and MOUNTAINS winner in a career that ran from 1983 to 1994. Like many CLIMBERS, he was let down by poor TIME TRIALS, which he hated. His peak was the 1990 Tour, when he won the St-Gervais stage beneath Mont Blanc and finished the race in the mountains JERSEY. The next year he won in nearby Morzine.

Claveyrolat retired in 1995 and opened a bar called L'Étape (the stage) in the Place du Château at Vizille, near his home in Notre-Dame-de-Mesage, south of Grenoble. The sign was in red and white polkadot (the Mountains leader colours) and the walls lined with pictures and jerseys from his 12 years as a professional.

The business was a success but Claveyrolat did not live to enjoy the benefits. He became depressed after causing a traffic accident which

left a family of four badly injured, and he shot himself at home in September 1999. (*See* RENÉ POTTIER for another rider who killed himself; and *see* HENRI PÉLISSIER for a Tour winner who was murdered.)

Winner

1989	GP Marseillaise, Tour Limousin
1990	Bicyclette Basque, Boucles Parisiennes
1993	GP Plouay, Trophée Grimpeurs, Tour Haut-Var

Tour de France

1985	29th	
1986	17th	
1987	DNF	
1988	23rd	
1989	DNF	
1990	21st	Stage win Geneva—St-Gervais, and Mountains Jersey
1991	27th	Stage win Bourg d'Oisans—Morzine
1992	33rd	
1993	28th	

CLIMBERS

Some of the cruellest jokes are the most true. The joke about climbers is that the heavens compensated for their closeness to angels by making them devilishly ugly. Few have stopped female hearts. For every boyish LUCIEN VAN IMPE there has been a JULIO JIMENEZ or ROBERT MILLAR, a man whose lean looks and pointed nose led him to being called 'the Maggot' and described as 'like a Dickensian chimney-sweep'.

Climbers are admired because they do their work alone. SPRINTERS on the other hand aren't seen until the FINISH, when their team-mates wind up the speed in the last mile so the sprinter can glory in the last 200 metres. There is a perception, therefore, that sprinters profit from the work of others.

Climbing hills on a bicycle is something that everybody knows is hard. Mountains on the Tour can be 20km long, and one day can include seven of them. To see a man ride away from the field in such circumstances is something everyone can understand and admire. Climbers exploit a simple truth: that every extra degree of incline adds disproportionate agony. Acceleration is hard or even impossible for most riders, and yet that is just how many climbers succeed. They may ride most of the time no faster than other riders, but for moments they can accelerate enough to open gaps on those who try to stay with them.

That ability depends on the balance between weight and power. Most classic climbers have been small men, like MARCO PANTANI. Their strength and in particular their weight are small compared to those of a sprinter and even of a time triallist. But visible lack of strength doesn't matter so much when there's not much load to be shifted. That relative weakness means climbers also pedal faster, sometimes at 95 revs a minute.

Other tiny men to have succeeded as climbers include VICENTE TRUEBA (first to win the Mountains competition in 1933), RENÉ VIETTO, CHARLY GAUL and FEDERICO BAHA-

MONTES. Of them, Gaul was unusual in riding at his own pace until the opposition crumbled.

Climbers can be taller and heavier in physique provided they are also proportionately stronger. A big lever exerts more power than a small one, so tall riders have succeeded in the mountains. Men like STEVEN ROOKS, GERT-JAN THEUNISSE and RICHARD VIRENQUE lack the acceleration of pure climbers, but they have the power to ride fast all the way to a summit, keeping the pace high enough to discourage true climbers, or giving way to the little men on the longest ascents but powering past them on shorter ones. Virenque lacks the punch of a true climber but has won five Mountains competitions by always being there or thereabouts on qualifying climbs, however small.

There remain a few riders simply dogged enough not to be dropped, like JACQUES ANQUETIL, 'who can drop nobody but whom nobody can drop,' as his reputation had it. Others are simply so strong that they overcome their weight. EDDY MERCKX and JAN ULLRICH are examples.

KINGS OF THE MOUNTAINS

1933	Vicente Trueba	1961	Imerio Massignan	1982	Bernard Vallet
1934	René Vietto	1962	Federico Bahamontes	1983	Lucien van Impe
1935	Felicien Vervaecke	1963	Federico Bahamontes	1984	Robert Millar
1936	Julian Berrendero	1964	Federico Bahamontes	1985	Luis Herrera
1937	Felicien Vervaecke	1965	Julio Jimenez	1986	Bernard Hinault
1938	Gino Bartali	1966	Julio Jimenez	1987	Luis Herrera
1939	Sylvère Maes	1967	Julio Jimenez	1988	Steven Rooks
1947	Pierre Brambilla	1968	Aurelio Gonzalez	1989	Gert-Jan Theunisse
1948	Gino Bartali	1969	Eddy Merckx	1990	Thierry Claveyrolat
1949	Fausto Coppi	1970	Eddy Merckx	1991	Claudio Chiappucci
1950	Louison Bobet	1971	Lucien van Impe	1992	Claudio Chiappucci
1951	Raphaël Géminiani	1972	Lucien van Impe	1993	Tony Rominger
1952	Fausto Coppi	1973	Pedro Torres	1994	Richard Virenque
1953	Jesus Loroño	1974	Domingo Perurena	1995	Richard Virenque
1954	Federico Bahamontes	1975	Lucien van Impe	1996	Richard Virenque
1955	Charly Gaul	1976	Giancarlo Bellini	1997	Richard Virenque
1956	Charly Gaul	1977	Lucien van Impe	1998	Christophe Rinero
1957	Gastone Nencini	1978	Mariano Martinez	1999	Richard Virenque
1958	Federico Bahamontes	1979	Giovanni Battaglin	2000	Santiago Botero
1959	Federico Bahamontes	1980	Raymond Martin	2001	Laurent Jalabert
1960	Imerio Massignan	1981	Lucien van Impe	2002	Laurent Jalabert

What all climbers need is good resistance to oxygen deprivation. Mountains have to be ridden on the edge of anaerobia, the point at which the lungs can take in no more air. As the riders climb the air gets thinner and therefore the oxygen less. Mountains have to be ridden on a fine line where the effort of climbing comes close to using all the available oxygen. The effect becomes noticeable at 1,500m and is marked at the top of mountains like the TOUR-MALET and MONT VENTOUX which rise to around 2,000m.

LAURENT JALABERT said he felt bad above 1,500m, and his climbers' prizes in 2001 and 2002 came not because he battled with the best but because he broke away alone at a significant time.

Few climbers are good descenders. 'You always have to give them plenty of space,' said STEPHEN ROCHE. The theory is that climbers don't have the weight to lean into corners at speed or to stay in a straight line over bumps. BENOIT FAURE lost the Tour in 1930 because he lost more time going down the AUBISQUE, Soulor, and the Tourmalet than he had gained in riding up them.

Federico Bahamontes sometimes took downhill corners with one foot out of the pedal, like a speedway rider. He stopped at the top of the GALIBIER in his debut Tour in 1954 and ate an ice cream as he waited for the rest to catch him because he was nervous about riding down the hill alone. (*See* Bahamontes entry for why.)

The days of climbers like Gaul, who won a stage by 12 minutes in 1958, are over. Riders had only ten gears in the 1960s, the top one high enough for sprinting, the lowest for climbing, with little chance of finding exactly the right ratio between them. The Campagnolo chainset that most riders used could not take rings small enough to match the low gears riders can use today. Stages were longer and roads rougher than today, which meant riders were more tired when they got to the biggest climbs; and they had to dodge loose rocks and even unsurfaced stretches, and therefore use heavier wheels and tyres than modern riders would tolerate. Today roads are smooth and riders have 20 gears with the option of 30, which means a smaller step between each and more chance of finding the right ratio. 'Riders of the 1960s were indisputably better than those of today,' said PIERRE CHANY, who saw 49 Tours.

Spectators have now been largely dissuaded from pushing the no-hopers at the back during climbs, although CHEATING still happens. The Frenchman JACKY DURAND, famous for long lone attacks on the flat but a poor climber, was thrown out of the 2002 Tour for hanging onto a car. (*See* Durand entry for details). Those who know they can't compete settle for riding in the GRUPPETTO, the group of unhappy souls who tag along at the back, aiming only to finish inside the day's time limit.

CLUB DU TOUR

The Tour de France is nothing if not commercial. There were once so many SPONSORS for various JERSEYS, competitions, and other awards that the communist newspaper *L'Humanité* sneered that lust for sponsorship would one day mean a prize for the prettiest smile. By the late 1970s, the quantity of commercial interests and advertising had become so great that people began to wonder if the race would be better run by the government than drowned in advertising.

Far from cutting back, however, organiser FÉLIX LÉVITAN told the race PRESENTATION in 1981 that the number of small-time sponsors could even increase. He opened the books (*see* Lévitan entry) to show that his race cost 'not a centime' in taxes and, by implication, how much the taxpayer would have to pay if the sponsors were abandoned and the race handed to the government.

Lévitan was on the losing side, though. In 1987 a row over sponsorship for the Tour of America cost him his job, and JEAN-MARIE LEBLANC began undoing the mess when he took over as organiser in late 1988. Leblanc cut the trophies from 12 to six, and the JERSEYS to four. He also reduced the main sponsors to a so-called 'Club du Tour', limiting their number to give them greater exclusivity and better advertising. In 2002 these sponsors consisted of the following names:

1. The bank Crédit Lyonnais, which began sponsoring the yellow jersey in 1987. After the FESTINA SCANDAL, Crédit Lyonnais said it was reconsidering its support in view of DOPING problems, but it has now signed until 2008. It sponsors other events belonging to the SOCIÉTÉ DU TOUR DE FRANCE such as Paris-Roubaix, Paris-Nice, the TOUR DE L'AVENIR, the Grand Prix des Nations and the Critérium International.
2. The supermarket chain Champion, which has been in the Tour since 1993 as sponsor of the competition for best CLIMBER.
3. The betting company PMU (Pari Mutuel Urbain), the equivalent of the British Tote. PMU joined in 1990 to sponsor the SPRINT- ERS competition (green jersey). The large green cardboard hands which it distributes have proved the advertising success of the race, but in 2002 for a few days they weren't handed out at the finish because ROBBIE MCEWEN had complained he'd sprinted into one at 40mph after a SPECTATOR had waved it in his face.
4. The drinks firm Nestlé Aquarel, which joined the Tour in 2001 to sponsor the competition for the best YOUNG RIDER. Aquarel's contract runs until the end of 2003. A brand of mineral water aimed at the middle market, the company sprays water mist over hot spectators as they wait for the race.

Beneath the main sponsors come partners and suppliers, which include the TV satellite provider Astra, the watch firm Festina, the drinks companies Coca-Cola and Café Grand'Mère, the insurer AGF, and the tyre company Michelin. AGF insures the Tour, Nike provides the main jerseys, Festina times the race, France Télécom establishes communications, Coca-Cola sponsors the stage winner, Sodexho provides buffets, Coeur de Lion sponsors the COMBATIVITY AWARD, Mavic looks after riders with mechanical problems, Miche-

lin supplies maps, Kawasaki the photographers' motorbikes, and Norbert Dentressangle carts everything about in articulated lorries.

COLOMBIA

Colombia was the only country to take up FELIX LÉVITAN's offer in 1983 of a place in the Tour to teams from outside Europe. (See AMA- TEURS for full story.) Colombia is a mountainous country. It has a single coastline divided by the umbilical cord of Panama. Travel from one city to another almost certainly requires crossing part of one of three branches of the northern Andes, and as a cyclist being able to climb is the only way to get on.

Cycling took off in Colombia in the 1950s. The Vuelta a Colombia was the only event to tie the country together after it collapsed into lawlessness after the killing of the Liberal leader in 1948. Colombian fans realised how good their local heroes were when FAUSTO COPPI and HUGO KOBLET visited in 1958 and were thoroughly beaten.

However, it wasn't until 1980 that the country sent a team to Europe. They were not a team of professionals but sponsored amateurs for the TOUR DE L'AVENIR (the amateur and semi- pro race that shadowed the main Tour). In 1975 Brazil's coffee crop had been wrecked, and Colombia began selling all the coffee it could produce, and at record prices. That gave the money for diversification of the economy and the chance to sell other products abroad. Among these was Postobón, a soft drink made by a firm which backed Colombian Tour de l'Avenir riders. In 1980 Alfonso Flórez of the Postobón team took the lead on stage six, gave the mighty Russian team a pasting in the mountains, and won in Paris.

The Colombian team sent to the professional Tour was backed by a battery maker, Varta, but the riders still had the same amateur status as those at the Tour de l'Avenir. Even so, 35 Colombian journalists turned up. 'The racket they made was deafening,' says Eurosport reporter David Duffield. 'In those days broadcasting cubicles were flimsy wood and canvas and all you could hear was these frantic Spanish voices. And they all chain-smoked and the area was deep in cigarette ends.'

Flórez may have won the Tour de l'Avenir, but the professional race was different. It was too fast and the cobbles were more than he could manage. He retired after Pau, on the first stage in the Pyrenees, the place he was expected to succeed. Only five Colombians finished, but Patrocinio Jimenez wore the polka-dot (Mountains leader) jersey for five days, and Edgar 'Condorito' Corredor beat LAURENT FIGNON on every mountain stage, the only rider to do so.

The best rider during Colombia's initially brief but intensive impact on the Tour was LUIS HERRERA, given the NICKNAME of the 'Gardener of Fusagasuga' because he once worked in the fields as a flower-picker. Known as Lucho, he rode the Tour seven times (*see* entry for details), came seventh in 1985 and won two stages and the polka-dot jersey; he came fifth and won the mountains competition in 1987, and in 1988 he was sixth.

The Colombian talent pool dwindled as soccer took over from cycling as the national craze. Café de Colombia, which backed the later professional ventures, pulled out when the international coffee agreement collapsed in 1989. Nevertheless, Colombians haven't disappeared. Herman Buenahora rode six times and came 10th in the 1995 Tour. Alvaro Mejia also rode six times and finished fourth in 1993. Fabio Parra finished eight Tours, coming third in 1988 with a stage win. The startlingly blue-eyed SANTIAGO BOTERO came seventh in 2000, eighth in 2001 and fourth (with two stage wins) in 2002. His record was marred by a six-month suspension in 1999 for DOPING.

COMBATIVITY AWARD

The word 'combativity' sits less easily in English than the *combativité* of French. 'Aggression' has other connotations – although fights between riders are not unknown: CHRISTOPHE MOREAU, for instance, was penalised two minutes and fined 400 Swiss francs for taking a swing at Carlos Sastre on the Col de la Core in 2002 having accused the Spaniard of trying to elbow him off LANCE ARMSTRONG's wheel. (And *see* LUCIAN AIMAR, JEROEN BLIJLEVENS and MARIO CIPOLLINI for other fights.)

In fact, the award goes to the most competitive rider, the one who has done most to liven up the day's stage. It began in 1908 when Théo Vienne, editor of *Sports Populaires*, suggested a '*prix de courage*'. He was joined in his idea by *L'Éducation Physique*, which announced that 'the rider having finished the course, even if unplaced, and who is particularly distinguished for the energy he has used, will receive 100 francs and the Vermeil medal of *L'Éducation Physique*.'

The modern award began when the Tour offered the equivalent of £100 a day in 1952. It is judged by JEAN-MARIE LEBLANC, BERNARD HINAULT and a handful of reporters such as Philippe Bouvet of the Tour paper *L'ÉQUIPE*, Gérard Holtz of French television, and the veteran radio man, Jean-Paul Brouchon, of France-Info. The most competitive rider has been marked since 1998 by a red rather than black number on his back. The winner in 2002 was LAURENT JALABERT.

(*See* ARTHUR METCALFE.)

FAUSTO COPPI

b. Castellania, Italy, Sep 15 1919, d. Tortona, Italy, Jan 2 1960

The Italian *campionissimo* Fausto Coppi defined an era. You were pre-Coppi, post-Coppi or you rode with him, in fear of a man who from 1946 to 1954, according to PIERRE CHANY, was never caught once he had broken clear of the field. In 1949 he was first to win the Tour and Giro in the same year, a feat repeated in 1952.

EDDY MERCKX says, 'It is flattering to be called the best in the world, but what would Coppi have achieved if he had not lost six years to the WAR?'

Coppi was born in 1919 in Castellania, in a road now called the Via Fausto Coppi, and ran errands for a butcher 20km away in Tortona. His first race prize was a bunch of sausages. He turned INDEPENDENT (semi-professional) in 1939 and won six races. In 1940 he turned professional and won the Italian pursuit championship and the Giro. He was national road champion in 1942, and broke the world hour record later that year, when he again won the national pursuit championship.

Coppi was kept out of the early part of the war by officers who were keen to keep him on his bike. But in 1943 a new commander arrived, and soldier number 7375 of the 38th Infantry was sent to Tunisia in March. His was a short war. He was taken prisoner by the British between Mateur and Medjez-el-Bab on April 13. There he shared plates and cutlery with the father of CLAUDIO CHIAPPUCCI.

The British moved him to Italy in February 1945 to work at an RAF base at Caserta. Until the war ended he was employed as a batman to an officer who knew nothing about bike racing and had never heard of Coppi. When it was over Coppi rode part the way home on his bike, and hitched a lift the rest of the way in a lorry full of other prisoners and internees. On Sunday July 8 1945 he won the Circuit of the Aces in Milan at 42km/h after four years with no racing. The next year he won Milan-San Remo.

He rode humpbacked and narrow-shouldered. And yet, said ANDRÉ LEDUCQ, 'he seems to caress rather than grip the handlebars. His long legs extend to the pedals with the joints of a gazelle. At the end of each pedal stroke his ankles flex gracefully, a movement which would be wonderful to analyse in slow motion on a cinema screen – all the moving parts turn in oil. His long face appears like the blade of a knife as he climbs without apparent effort, like a great artist painting a water colour.'

Coppi's rival was GINO BARTALI, whose Legnano team Coppi joined as a DOMESTIQUE in 1940. Bartali was dubious when he heard the news from the MANAGER Eberrardo Pavesi as he sat in his house on January 7. Coppi was too fragile for stage races, he thought. The truth

soon dawned. Coppi stayed with Bartali after a CRASH on the first day of that year's Giro, and then survived by his side as a series of attacks sent the rest of the team spinning off the back.

Any remaining worries about fragility vanished when Coppi set off after a breakaway group, passed it on the Abetone pass, and won by four minutes. Bartali was so unamused by this upstart employed as his helper that he organised the Legnano team in chase. But Coppi still won overall. Their rivalry lasted close on 20 years.

ITALY split between Bartali the religious 'peasant' and Coppi the slicker. The writer Curzio Malaparte said, 'Bartali belongs to those who believe in tradition ... he is a metaphysical man protected by the saints. Coppi has nobody in heaven to take care of him. His manager, his masseur, have no wings. He is alone, alone on a bicycle. . . . Bartali prays while he is pedalling; the rational Cartesian and sceptical Coppi is filled with doubts, believes only in his body, his motor.' (See ALFREDO BINDA for how the two rivals were finally united.)

In the 1948 Tour, Bartali won two days running at Lourdes and Toulouse, then every stage in the Alps, and claimed the overall title in Paris. Next year Coppi caught Bartali on the IZOARD and Bartali realised his career was over. Bartali shouted, 'It's my birthday. Let's finish together. Tomorrow you'll win the Tour.' Coppi agreed: Bartali won in Briançon but Coppi took the Tour – by 28: 27. Organiser JACQUES GODDET had to double the money for second place to keep other riders interested.

Coppi was plagued not only by crashes and mechanical mishaps but also by misjudgment. At the centre of it was Giulia Occhini. The broadcaster JEAN-PAUL OLLIVIER describes her as 'strikingly beautiful with thick chestnut hair divided into enormous plaits'. Giulia and her husband, an army captain and doctor called Enrico Locatelli, had married two weeks after meeting. They had a child, Loretta, in 1946 and settled on the Adriatic coast. Locatelli worked all day, spoke little when he returned home, and had no interests other than cycling. His hero was Coppi.

Giulia knew nothing of cycling but agreed to join her husband at the Tre Valle Voresini race on August 8 1948, where Locatelli would see both Coppi and Bartali close up. By chance a traffic jam halted them behind Coppi's car. It was the first time Giulia had seen him, and she was entranced. That evening she pursued him to his hotel, persuaded a helper to bring him to the lobby, and badgered him for a photograph. He signed it 'With friendship to . . .', then asked her name and added it.

Giulia pursued him like a groupie. He began spending more time with her than with his wife, Bruna. Rumours spread in strait-laced Catholic Italy, but nobody knew who the woman was. Finally Luigi Boccaccini of *La Stampa* saw her at St-Moritz in 1954, waiting for Coppi to finish a race. She was wearing a white raincoat. Coppi went over to hug her, the paper's camera snapped, and next day she was pictured as *La Dama in bianco di Fausto Coppi* – Coppi's woman in white. The scandal had broken, and it had brought with it the intense shame of adultery.

Giulia moved in with her lover. But the scandal was so great that the landlord of their new flat in Tortona made them leave the same night. They moved into a hotel at Casteletto d'Orba but reporters found them and once more they had to move out. They bought the Villa Carla, near Novi Ligure, but police raided them at midnight to see if they were sharing a bed. Pope Pius XII asked Coppi to return to his wife, and refused to bless the Giro while he remained in it. Bartolo Paschetta, president of the Italian National Sports Centre, wrote on July 8 1954, 'Dear Fausto, yesterday evening St Peter [the Pope] made it known to me that the news [of the adultery] had caused him great pain.'

Coppi asked for a divorce but was refused. Divorce was still against the law in parts of Italy. The request inflamed the country even more, and the house was broken into and Coppi's best clothes stolen. The strain told. In 1959 he was first to be dropped in the Tour of SPAIN, every day. Promoters cut their races to 45km to be sure he would finish. PIERRE CHANY called him

'a magnificent and grotesque washout, a weary and disillusioned man, ironical towards himself; nothing except the warmth of simple friendship can penetrate his melancholia.'

Interviewed on television after he retired, Coppi was asked of that period, 'Did you take drugs?', to which he replied 'Only when necessary.'

'And how often was it necessary?'

Coppi hesitated and smiled. Then he said 'Practically all the time.'

On December 10 1959 he left for a racing and safari trip to Upper Volta, the country north of Ghana now called Burkina Faso. The trip had been arranged by RAPHAËL GÉMINIANI, who was accompanied by JACQUES ANQUETIL, HENRY ANGLADE, ROGER RIVIÈRE, ROGER HASSENFORDER and a journalist from *L'ÉQUIPE*, Maurice Maurel.

In Upper Volta an estimated 20,000 watched Anquetil win a 70km exhibition race in a sprint, after which the group relaxed at a dance and met the president, Maurice Yameogo, who was 'democratically seated on a garden chair' as the report put it. Maurel remembers Coppi looking tired and ill, and then not enjoying the travelling and hunting that followed. Maurel and Coppi left Upper Volta after a final meal on December 17 and flew back to Paris with Géminiani as the rest of the party stayed for a final day.

From Paris Coppi flew to Turin, telling Giulia the trip was 'interesting' but that the hunting and the country itself was a disaster and he'd have to be paid a lot to go back. He looked yellow and wrinkled, she said, although next day he seemed better and they went shooting together; the next day they went to a local football derby.

On December 26 Coppi felt he had flu. The diagnosis was confirmed by a family doctor, Professor Giovanni Astaldi, on December 29. It developed into an intense fever, with Coppi sweating, vomiting and intensely thirsty. On January 1 1960 he was taken to a clinic at Tortona. News reached doctors that Géminiani had developed the same symptoms in France.

Géminiani's illness was diagnosed as malaria, much less easily treated then than now. Tortona, on the other hand, insisted Coppi had bronchopneumonia. A priest asked if he wanted to make a final confession but Coppi's tongue was too furrowed to reply. He died at 8.45am on Saturday January 2 1960. In the general distress, Giulia's printed announcement of his death got the date wrong. The year had just changed but the announcement said 'January 2 1959'.

Questions about Coppi's medical treatment were asked in the Italian parliament. His obituary ran endlessly in *La Gazzetta dello Sport* and for two pages in *L'Équipe*, where Goddet wrote, 'We would like to have cried out to him: "Stop!" And as nobody dared to, destiny took care of it.'

The tributes to Coppi were many and various; some of them extraordinary. A recovered paraplegic walked to the funeral, attributing his miraculous cure to the day Coppi gave him 10,000 lire. The cycling aristocracy including Anquetil, Bartali, LOUISON BOBET, and ROGER RIVIÈRE were among thousands of mourners. There were 300 metres of wreaths. Coppi was buried in earth from the Izoard. A director of *La Gazzetta dello Sport* wrote, 'I pray that the good God will one day soon send us another Coppi.'

Winner

1940 Giro d'Italia
1941 Tour Emilia, Tour Veneto, Tour Tuscany, Tre Valle Varesine
1942 World hour record, National Championship
1946 GP Nations, Milan-San Remo, Tour Lombardy, Tour Romagna
1947 Giro d'Italia, GP Nations, Tour Lombardy, Tour Romagna, Tour Emilia, Tour Veneto, National Championship
1948 Milan-San Remo, Tour Lombardy, Tour Emilia, Tre Valle Varesine
1949 Tour de France, Giro d'Italia, Milan-San Remo, Tour Lombardy, Tour Romagna, Tour Veneto
1950 Flèche Wallonne, Tour Reggio Calabria, Paris-Roubaix
1951 GP Lugano
1952 Tour de France, Giro d'Italia, GP Lugano, Tour Mediterranean

Winner (continued)

1953 World championship, Giro d'Italia, Baracchi Trophy
1954 Tour Lombardy, Baracchi Trophy
1955 Tour Appenines, Tre Valle Varesine, Baracchi Trophy
1956 GP Lugano
1957 Baracchi Trophy

Tour de France

1949 1st Stage wins Les Sables—La Rochelle, Briançon—Aoste, Colmar—Nancy, and Yellow Jersey and Mountains winner
1951 10th Stage win Gap—Briançon
1952 1st Stage wins Metz—Nancy, Lausanne—Alpe d'Huez, Bourg d'Oisans—Sestriere, Bagnères-de Bigorre—Pau, Limoges—Puy-de-Dôme, and Yellow Jersey and Mountains winner

HENRI CORNET

b. Desvres, France, Aug 4 1884,
d. Prunay-le-Gillion, France, Mar 18 1941

Henri Cornet of FRANCE was the youngest winner of the Tour, a month short of his 20th birthday in 1904. (*See* AGES.) In fact Cornet came fifth, but the first four riders, including winner MAURICE GARIN, were disqualified for cheating. (*See* 1904 AFFAIR.)

He never won the Tour again and only once – in 1908 – finished in the top 10, when he came eighth. For that reason Cornet is often portrayed as an unworthy winner who succeeded only because others failed. In fact the situation is more complicated.

The complications start with the fact that Cornet wasn't his real name. He was born Henri Jaudry in the town of Desvres, near Calais. Second, Cornet himself could have been disqualified in 1904 but was instead just warned about his conduct. Third, in addition to allegedly cheating, Cornet also claimed to have been cheated against.

Cornet was a cheerful individual with wide-spaced blue eyes, a nose described as trumpet-like, and a generous mouth that readily spread into a smile. His sense of fun gave him the NICKNAME of '*le Rigolo*' (the joker). It's not clear whether anyone called him that before the Tour in 1904 or if it was invented by HENRI DESGRANGE to popularise a competitor unknown to most readers of *L'AUTO*, the Tour paper.

As an AMATEUR Cornet won Paris-Honfleur in 1903, which encouraged him to enter the 1904 Tour. He was one of 105 entrants, of whom 88 made the start at MONTGERON on July 2. Alongside names like Garin and HIPPOLYTE AUCOUTURIER he was unknown. His SPONSOR, Cycles JC of Paris, was also tiny compared to PEUGEOT and LA FRANÇAISE, the big names of the day.

The 1904 race was a catalogue of cheating. Cornet was one of many accused of taking a lift in a car – there were many similar claims, including one that some riders caught a train. Cornet was cleared of the charge but was still warned to behave himself. At one stage he appeared to faint, collapsing over his handlebars. Years later he said that he had been given poisoned chicken. (*See* PAUL DUBOC for another rider poisoned during the Tour.)

There was so much cheating – probably more than the officials or the inquiry by the French cycling association ever discovered – that the results are worthless. Cornet finished second to Aucouturier on the third stage, from Marseille to Toulouse, beating a small group by eight minutes, and beating the last man, Julien Gabory, by six hours. Aucouturier was among those thrown out, though, so Cornet was given the victory and Aucouturier's prize of 400 francs.

Stage four was also affected by disqualification and Cornet ended up third rather than sixth. On stage five he moved from fourth to second. Stage six took the riders back to Paris and Cornet came seventh at 11:50. In the revised result, though, he was third. Put together, Cornet moved from fifth to first overall and became the second and still the youngest winner of the Tour.

He rode another seven times but never with the same success because, says the cycling historian Jacques Seray, the standard of racing went up. But, he adds, he 'was not the weakling that he was made out to be after he finished several hours behind Garin in 1904. Just remember that he won Paris-Roubaix in 1906.' He also came third in Paris-Roubaix in 1905, third in Bordeaux-Paris in 1905, second in 1906 and fifth in 1907.

Cornet was never the healthiest rider, though, and had repeated heart problems. These brought his career to an end just before the first world war. He ran a bike shop and died in 1941 after a hospital operation that followed a heart attack.

Winner

1904	Tour de France
1906	Paris-Roubaix
1910	Paris-Alençon

Tour de France

1904	1st Stage win Marseille—Toulouse
1905	DNF
1907	DNF
1908	8th
1909	DNF
1910	16th
1911	12th
1912	28th

CRASHES

Cycling is a fast sport that demands balance. Things rarely go wrong, but if they do the consequences can be serious, decisive – or grimly amusing. Stéphane Bergès, for instance, skidded in a storm in the French championship in 2000 and crashed on his right shoulder. The road had been made slippery by SPECTATORS who'd painted their heroes' names on it. And on whose name had he skidded? His own.

FRANCESCO CEPEDA of SPAIN was the first rider to die on a bike in the Tour when he fell down a ravine near Bourg-d'Oisans in 1935 and broke his skull. He died in Grenoble three days later. The second was BRITAIN's TOM SIMPSON, who collapsed and died on MONT VENTOUX on July 13 1967. Drugs were subsequently found in his bloodstream. The third casualty was FABIO CASARTELLI of ITALY, who crashed going down the Col de Portet d'Aspet on July 18 1995.

Riders have also been seriously injured without being killed. Jules Merviel of FRANCE came close to dying in 1935 when he rode into a timber lorry while leading alone from Cannes to Marseille. He died five years later in a traffic accident while he was cycling in Toulon. Another Frenchman, ROGER RIVIÈRE, broke his back when he crashed off the road while going down the Col de Perjuret in 1960. He had taken so many painkillers that he was too numb to pull the brakes.

In 1920 HONORÉ BARTHÉLEMY was blinded in one eye in a fall but finished the Tour with several broken bones (*see* his entry for details) and continued his racing career with a glass eye.

LUIS OCAÑA of Spain crashed on the Col de Mente in 1971 when EDDY MERCKX missed a bend in rain and fell. Ocaña tried to avoid him and hit a low wall. He got up with only mild injuries only to be knocked back down when JOOP ZOETEMELK ran into him in blinding rain. He was then hit in the small of the back as he lay on the road when both JOAQUIM AGOSTINHO and Vicente Lopez-Carril also came to grief.

Ocaña did race again after leaving hospital, and returned to win the Tour in 1973. But he was never the same man and committed suicide in 1994. (*see* Ocaña entry for details.)

Other crashes looked dramatic but caused little harm. WIM VAN EST was wearing HOLLAND's first yellow JERSEY when he skidded and fell on the AUBISQUE in 1951. He tumbled down the mountainside and ended up on the one small ledge that could have saved him from certain death. He had to be pulled out with a car towrope to which had been tied all the team's spare tyres. They stretched so much that the Dutch had to leave the race.

GINO BARTALI of Italy also pressed on after a fall into a river in 1937. He was in the yellow jersey and chasing a break when his team-mate Jules Rossi skidded in front of him on a wooden bridge over the river Colau. Bartali flew over the parapet, and colleagues and spectators feared he had broken his back or drowned. Another team-mate, Francesco Camusso, plunged into the water to save him. Bartali clambered out, his arm and knee bleeding and his chest painful from a blow. Colleagues pushed him to the FINISH at Briançon, where the sight of the race leader covered in mud and blood caused a sensation. Nevertheless he got through the rest of the Alps and retired only when the race got to Marseille.

There was a mass pile-up in 1999 when the race crossed the Passage du Gois causeway to the Ile de Noirmoutier. For a part of each day the causeway is covered by high tides, but the race was scheduled to miss them. Only too late was it realised that the receding sea would leave slime. Brakes went on, wheels locked, BIKES skidded, and riders fell amid the mayhem. Accounts say 10 riders fell, but photographs suggest at least 12, of whom seven plunged off the edge of the causeway onto the wet sand. Holidaying people on the beach pushed them back up to the road, where they lay moaning as others attacked. AMERICA's Jonathan Vaughters and the Dutchman Marc Wauters were too badly hurt to continue. Another Dutchman, Michael Boogerd, cut his chin, lip, knee, and arms but struggled on. (*See* EARPIECES for how the race developed after the crash.)

The FINISH is always a danger. ANDRÉ DARRIGADE, the French SPRINTER and winner of 22 stages, survived when a 70-year-old official stepped on to the PARC DES PRINCES in 1958. Their heads cracked at 60km/h. Darrigade cracked his skull but the official was thrown into the air and died.

BERNARD HINAULT lost control and crashed in a finish sprint at St-Étienne in 1985. He fell on his head and broke his nose. He carried on and won his fifth Tour.

DJAMOLIDINE ABDOUJAPAROV broke a collarbone on the CHAMPS ELYSÉES while sprinting head-down in 1991. He hit a roadside barrier and flew over the handlebars. There were just 60 metres of the 3,914km race to go.

LAURENT JALABERT was severely injured on July 3 1994, when a policeman stepped into the road to take a photograph at Armentières. Wilfried Nelissen crashed into the man and brought down Jalabert, who landed on his face and needed extensive hospital treatment. Nelissen broke a collarbone. The twist to this story concerns a boy who ran from the crowd and picked up the battery from the policeman's broken camera (which he still has). The boy's name was Arnaud Tournant, then no more than any other young enthusiast. In 2001 Tournant won three world championships and became first man to ride a kilometre in less than a minute.

On Bastille Day 1999 a spectator nearly ruined the chances of ITALY's Beppe Guerini on the ALPE D'HUEZ. A teenage photographer named only as Richard stepped out to take a photo and misjudged the distance through his lens. Riders rely on spectators stepping back at the last moment but Richard didn't. Guerini tumbled off but climbed back on and won the stage.

Hundreds of journalists tried to find Richard but he'd vanished. Later that evening, though, he turned up at Guerini's hotel to apologise. Neither spoke the other's language but their smiles showed the incident was forgiven.

In 2001 a mentally disturbed driver crashed into the barriers at 60km/h at Colmar and injured four spectators.

Onlookers have been killed or injured by the CARAVAN (*see* entry for details) and a motorbike radio crew crashed into a river gully and died in 1957 (*see* BROADCASTING for details). In 1975 the BIANCHI team car swerved on the Col d'Allos to get round parked press cars, crashed through the safety barriers, and fell an estimated 150m. The occupants of the car survived, although the MANAGER, Giancarlo Ferretti, was streaming with blood and his MECHANIC was left unconscious.

Victims of crashes are looked after during the race by the Tour's medical team, led by Dr Gérard Porte, who has been with the Tour since 1972, and has been its chief doctor since 1982.

He succeeded PIERRE DUMAS, who said his problem in dealing with serious casualties was finding out for the hospital doctors what drugs the riders had taken. (*See* DOPING.)

CRITERIUMS

Criteriums are minor races on short circuits, usually in provincial towns and villages. In BELGIUM they are called *kermiskoersen*, or village-fair races, which accounts for their alternative name of 'kermesses'.

Stars rode criteriums only occasionally before the WAR, leaving them to *régionaux* – local riders. Roads were bad, few riders had good cars, and the top men travelled only when they had to, collecting their MONEY from road races, salaries and occasional TRACK appearances. The situation changed in Belgium, a compact country easy for travel, when Jean van Buggenhout, a former track rider, set up as an agent, and then began to coordinate and organise races, and negotiate contracts. (*See* AGENTS for more.)

Bringing big names to small circuits allowed organisers to sell sponsorship and charge admission. That meant more money, better riders and larger crowds. The highest money went to the Tour winner, and the tradition grew that he would give his prizes from the Tour to the rest of his team. (*See* DOMESTIQUES for more.) This was because he could earn more from appearances than he had earned in the Tour. JACQUES ANQUETIL asked the equivalent of £250, 50 or 60 days a year in the 1960s and still more after he had won five Tours.

Fees ranged down in value from the JERSEY winners at the top down to the bottom of the field, where even just finishing the Tour would

add a little to a contract. The LANTERNE ROUGE (last man) was always a sympathy-puller, particularly if he had suffered unusually or had an odd story. ABDEL KADER-ZAAF, who fell asleep under a tree on July 28 1950 and set off in the wrong direction (*see* his entry) found he could ask the equivalent *of* £180, or 10 times his previous fee despite not finishing the race.

SEAN KELLY says, 'It was the done thing. You had the whole of August free and everybody rode them. Now you have the World Cup and there are events in August like the San Sebastian Classic and they're far more important.'

These developments and the rise in PRIZES and riders' salaries (*see* MONEY) after the GREG LEMOND era meant riders no longer had to race as often to make a living. That left them fresher and faster for the races that really mattered. Consequently, it cost more to persuade them to ride criteriums. Reliable figures are hard to come by, but Jan Ullrich was asking Dutch organisers the equivalent of £15,000 a ride when he wore the yellow jersey in 1997, or more than three times as much as the Dutch winner JOOP ZOETEMELK in 1980. But deals were possible. The 1997 criterium at Boxmeer, says Dutch journalist Peter van Leeuwen, paid the equivalent of around £22,000 to attract Ullrich, Points winner ERIK ZABEL, and two teammates from their Telekom team.

Jean-Michel Bordenave, organiser of the criterium at Monein, FRANCE, says, 'The first thing I have to do before anything else can happen is find financial partners so I can put together 60,000 euros (£40,000). That takes about six months. The best circuit is in a town centre. You have to make sure the spectators get the best possible view, give them the best spectacle. Our circuit is 1.2km long, quite hilly and fairly difficult. We get an action-packed race that lasts two hours and in general the public go home delighted.'

Criteriums are furiously fast, but the result is less important than the show. Van Leeuwen says, 'The audience knows that they're a combination of cycling and amusement, and they drink beer and rush to the fences when the riders are passing. They all know that the winner isn't going to come from a little team like Vlaanderen 2002 or Collstrop "because we don't know them".'

Despite this, part-time bookmakers sit in Belgian bars and take bets from spectators on the day's result.

Traditionally the local star and the day's big attraction get a chance to show themselves off the front, but sometimes this can go wrong. ERWAN MENTHÉOUR recalled LAURENT JALABERT going off the front. After a while he was not only showing himself but gaining a dangerous lead. In the end a rider was deputed to allow himself to be lapped so he could speak to Jalabert as he caught him.

'The boys want to know what you're playing at,' he said. 'You were supposed to show yourself and then ease up.'

'What do you mean "and then ease up"?' Jalabert asked. 'I've been waiting for you for the last ten laps.'

Breaking the unwritten rules is not appreciated. When a young BERNARD HINAULT started beating the big names for *primes* (intermediary prizes) in the Circuit de Châteaulin in Brittany in 1975, no less a figure than EDDY MERCKX warned him to share them if he expected to win any more.

The classic criterium in Holland for many years was the Acht van Chaam. *Acht* means 'eight' in Dutch and describes the course. The organiser, Ad Coenraads, told van Leeuwen, 'Of course the riders made some deals in the past. But sometimes it went wrong, too. In 1981 Roy Schuiten won when the local hero, Johan van der Velde, was supposed to win. After his victory it was "over and out" for Schuiten in the peloton.'

Criteriums are still standard for Dutch amateurs, but events and crowds for professionals are dwindling here as elsewhere. Chaam attracted 80,000 people in 1980 but fewer than 25,000 20 years later, by which time it had been forced to change to a conventional road race. There were 65 events in Holland in 1980, but only two dozen at the end of the millennium.

Criteriums do best in countries on a winning wave. The more domestic riders succeed, the more enthusiastically they are welcomed home as conquering heroes. Criteriums are also more popular in northern Europe than in the south. Five wins by MIGUEL INDURAIN from Spain and four by an American, LANCE ARMSTRONG, have therefore done little to improve matters on the criterium circuit. Neither viewed criteriums with much enthusiasm.

The main French post-Tour events in 2002 were at Lisieux (July 30), Camors (July 31), Lamballe (August 1), Dijon (August 2), Monein (August 3), St-Martin-de-Landelles (August 4), Castillon-la-Bataille (August 6), Marcoles (August 7), Chaumeil (August 8), Dun-le-Palestel (August 10), Vayrac (August 11), Montmarrault (August 12), Lusignan-Petit (August 14), Vergt (August 15), Riom (August 17), Quillan (August 18) and Châteauroux (August 23). Events tend to keep their order year after year except when the occasional event disappears or a new one appears.

(*See* HENRY ANGLADE for how he was denied the Tour de France to protect other riders' criterium fees.)

CROIX DE FER

With a gradient of 4.7 per cent, the Croix de Fer (Iron Cross) is not the toughest MOUNTAIN in the northern Alps, but it is 31.5km long and 2,068m high. The Tour rode it for the first time in 1947, when the Italian Fermo Camellini was first across on his way to winning two stages and finishing seventh in his first Tour.

The Croix de Fer is one of the most scenic climbs on the Tour, lying between the Arc and Romanche valleys. SPECTATORS stand ten deep because of high banks on each side of the single-track road.

ÉMILE DAEMS
b. Genval, Belgium, Apr 4 1938

SPRINTERS are not expected to win in the MOUNTAINS. Their natural ground is the flat, simply because their bulk should reduce them to the GRUPPETTO when the big climbs start, leaving them to struggle home as best they can each day. But sometimes a clever head can count more than a climber's legs, as BELGIUM's Émile Daems proved in 1962.

The stage from Antibes to Briançon that year was the first to go over the Restefond, at 2,802m the highest col the race has ever tackled. The closing section of the road wasn't even surfaced. After that it was to go over the Vars and IZOARD. The bunch was apprehensive but also overawed by JACQUES ANQUETIL – the Frenchman had won the previous year and in 1957. He was the favourite again in 1962. Anquetil was not an outstanding CLIMBER, but he was a man who rarely lost more than he could make up afterwards.

Spotting the race's caution, and thinking he had nothing to lose in a stage where he would otherwise finish way down, Daems went off alone. He was caught but not overtaken by CHARLY GAUL (the very man whom organiser JACQUES GODDET had relied on for great things when he had included the Restefond in his Tour route), and by the two race favourites, Anquetil and RAYMOND POULIDOR. Goddet, standing on the seat of his car and peering out like a tank commander through the sun roof, prepared to watch the two favourites and the legendary climber fight out his epic stage. He was less than delighted when a thick-thighed sprinter – and a Belgian at that – won instead. For him, the stage's 241km and a massive nine hours and 20 minutes of racing had been wasted. To Daems, of course, it was not only his third stage win of that year's Tour but the greatest win of his life.

Life returned to normal soon afterwards, of course. Poulidor won next day over the Luitel, Porte, Cucheron and Granier despite a painful hand, beating HENRY ANGLADE and FEDERICO BAHAMONTES by 2:30, and Anquetil by more than three minutes. It took him to third place but still 1:08 from Anquetil's second place and 5:43 on the yellow JERSEY, JO PLANCKAERT. He needed to do still better; next day was the TIME TRIAL and Anquetil would be unbeatable. And he was. He beat ERCOLE BALDINI by 2:59 in 68km and Poulidor by 5:01 and won the Tour de France.

As for Daems, he knew he'd never win. But he did finish second to RUDI ALTIG in the points competition and got to Paris in 13th place, 27:17 down.

Winner

1960 Tour Lombardy, Circuit Ouest, Tour Appenines
1961 Tour Sardinia
1962 Milan-San Remo
1963 Paris-Roubaix

Tour de France

1961	DNF	Stage win Roubaix—Charleroi
1962	13th	Stage win Pont l'Evêque— St-Malo, Montpellier— Aix-en-Provence, Antibes— Briançon
1963	67th	
1964	DNF	

JEAN-PIERRE DANGUILLAUME
b. Joué-les-Tours, France, May 25 1946

There's a lot to be said for having the right genes. FRANCE's Jean-Pierre Danguillaume couldn't have had a better set of them. Four generations of his family have been successful riders as AMATEURS or INDEPENDENTS.

Jean-Pierre is the nephew of Camille Danguillaume, who had the novelty of being filmed during his win in the 1944 Grand Prix of Europe by a cameraman in a bike-drawn taxi. There was no wartime petrol for a car. Camille, who was born on June 4 1919, won more than 100 races, including Liège-Bastogne-Liège in 1949. He died in a CRASH with a motorcyclist during the French national championship on the Montlhèry car circuit in June 1950.

Jean-Pierre's own career began when he won Paris-Vailly at the age of 18, and then the Peace Race, the Communist world's top amateur race in 1969. He won seven stages of the Tour de France and came third to HENNIE KUIPER and ROGER DE VLAEMINCK in the world championship at Yvoir, BELGIUM, in 1975. He had 325 wins before retiring to become MANAGER of Mercier-BP.

He now follows the Tour de France as a PR man for Coca-Cola.

Winner

1971	GP Plouay
1973	Critérium International
1974	Midi Libre, Trophée Grimpeurs
1975	Paris-Bourges

Tour de France

1970	64th	Stage win Tours—Versailles
1971	18th	Stage win Bordeaux—Poitiers
1972	21st	
1973	22nd	Stage win Belfort—Divonne
1974	13th	Stage wins St-Lary-Soulan— Tourmalet, Bagnères-de- Bigorre—Pau
1975	DNF	
1976	22nd	
1977	35th	Stage wins Rouen—Roubaix, Altkirch—Besançon
1978	DNF	

JEAN DARGASSIES
b. Grisolles, France, Jul 15 1872, d. Grisolles, France, Aug 7 1965

In popular imagination the village blacksmith is seen as a giant of a man who spits on his hands before performing feats of enormous strength. Jean Dargassies, a great, bearded man who had been a blacksmith at the village of Grisolles in south-west France, matched this picture exactly.

Never yet having found a muscular task that defeated him, he was undaunted by the first Tour de France in 1903. In fact he turned up in Paris not even sure about what he had entered. Dargassies had only recently bought a BIKE, and the shop owner, having told him he looked a strong lad, suggested he should ride this Tour de France he'd seen advertised. The Tour was to pass through their village, and it'd be good to get everybody to turn out to see him.

'Well, if you think so, I will,' Dargassies said, and he caught the train to Paris. There he presented himself to the young entries clerk, GÉO LEFÈVRE, whom Dargassies had never heard of before, and certainly didn't know as the person who had had the idea of a Tour de France in the first place.

'Tell me, have you ever raced?' Lefèvre asked.

'No,' Dargassies said, 'but I've ridden from Grisolles to Montauban and back and I didn't even have to try. I'm a blacksmith, so I'm not worried by tiredness.'

He wasn't, either. He finished 11th, halfway down the field and 13 hours behind winner MAURICE GARIN, but seems not to have won a franc. Undeterred, he rode again in 1904 and finished fourth, this time winning 1,000 francs. In fact he had finished tenth at 13 hours, but there was so much cheating in the 1904 Tour and so many disqualifications that he was moved up six places. (See HENRI CORNET, and 1904 AFFAIR.)

Dargassies rode again in 1905 when he didn't finish, and then again in 1907 when he was employed as a pioneer DOMESTIQUE, often described as a valet, by the 'Baron' HENRI PÉPIN. (See entry for details.) He and Henri Gauban paced the 'Baron' round the Tour, joined him at the best hotels, and ate in the most expensive restaurants, not caring that they finished the Roubaix—Metz stage 12 hours and 20 minutes behind ÉMILE GEORGET. After this the organisers introduced time limits. Their little group increased to four later in the race when they found another rider, Jean-Marie Teychenne, collapsed in a ditch. They pulled him out, cleaned him up, and enrolled him into their party.

Dargassies didn't finish that year because Pépin decided part-way through the fifth stage, from Lyon to Grenoble, that he had had enough, and instructed his PACEMAKERS to take him to the nearest railway station. There he is said to have paid them, as promised, more than what they would have collected had they won the Tour and caught the train home to near BORDEAUX. Pépin died of 'athleticism' in 1914.

Dargassies returned to Grisolles and died in 1965.

(And see MONEY.)

Tour de France

1903	11th
1904	4th
1905	DNF
1907	DNF

ANDRÉ DARRIGADE
b. Narosse, France, Apr 24 1929

Dédé Darrigade – Dédé is French for Andy – was the Tour's star SPRINTER in the 1950s, making the first stage a speciality in the days when this was a conventional race and not a PROLOGUE TIME TRIAL. The winner of the first stage has to win only that day to get the yellow JERSEY. In any other stage he has to make up all the time lost to all of those riders ahead of him.

Darrigade's talent gave him the Tour's first yellow jersey five times, a record still unequalled. In all he won 16 yellow jerseys and 22 stages – only EDDY MERCKX (34), BERNARD HINAULT (28) and ANDRÉ LEDUCQ (25) have won more. His technique was not the late rush of a classic sprinter but a build-up from far out, daring others to stay on his wheel. That panache won him more affection than many sprinters get.

Darrigade was involved in a fatal CRASH at the PARC DES PRINCES in 1958 when a security man stepped on to the track to take a photograph. (See CRASHES for a similar incident involving LAURENT JALABERT.) The two of them hit heads and the security man died next day. Darrigade survived, although with a cracked skull, and came third in the same year's world championship. He won that championship the next year, 1959, and also came third in 1957. He was French national champion in 1955.

Darrigade came from the Landes region of south-west France (the word means 'bogs' but it's more a huge region of conifer woods bordering the Atlantic). He still lives there, running a newspaper shop on the coast at Biarritz. His office on the first floor has a small display of newspaper articles about his career, including the front page of *Miroir Sprint* (*see* PUBLICA-TIONS) with the simple number 22. It was published when he won his record number of stages, appropriately further along the same coast on the track at BORDEAUX, in 1964. The picture shows him just to the left of the centre of the finish straight, his thinning blond hair swept back, and his mouth open in its characteristic surprised expression beneath his generous nose. Behind him are WARD SELS, BENONI BEHEYT and JAN JANSSEN.

'Those wins never became dull or routine,' he says. 'Each one was an immense pleasure. What's more, I had the chance to race alongside great champions such as LOUISON BOBET and JACQUES ANQUETIL.' For much of his Tour career he rode not so much with stars as for them, a super-DOMESTIQUE who could be guaranteed to pull out sprint wins.

'I was always considered a team-man,' he said. 'I never had pretensions to be anything else. In the days when the Tour had NATIONAL TEAMS, MARCEL BIDOT [the legendary MAN-AGER who made his selections on the back of a cigarette packet] always saw me as just that.' (*See* Bidot entry.).

Darrigade was particularly close to Anquetil, balancing his impulsive character against what he calls the 'bizarrely calm' nature of the great Norman. 'Quite often I had to say to him, "If you don't get going, you'll lose the Tour",' he says. Anquetil often turned to him for advice.

Raphaël Géminiani said, 'Darrigade was the greatest French sprinter of all time and he'll stay that way for a long time. The mould has been broken. But he wasn't just a sprinter. He was an *animateur* [activator] who could start decisive breaks; he destroyed the image of sprinters who just sit on wheels.'

Winner

1954 Tour Picardy
1955 National championship
1956 Tour Lombardy, Baracchi Trophy
1959 World championship, Critérium International
1960 Manx Premier

1953	37th	Stage win Luchon—Albi
1954	49th	
1955	49th	Stage win Colmar—Zürich
1956	16th	Stage win Reims—Liège, and Yellow Jersey
1957	27th	Stage wins Nantes—Granville, Libourne—Tours, Tours—Paris, and Yellow Jersey
1958	21st	Stage wins Brussels—Ghent, Quimper—St-Nazaire, Luchon—Toulouse, Béziers—Nîmes, Aix-les-Bains—Besançon, and Yellow Jersey
1959	16th	Stage wins Mulhouse—Metz, Bagnères-de-Bigorre—St-Gaudens, and Yellow Jersey and Points winner
1960	16th	Stage win Caen—St Malo
1961	32nd	Stage wins Rouen—Versailles, Pontoise—Roubaix, Aix-en-Provence—Montpellier, Périgueux—Tours, and Yellow Jersey and Points winner
1962	21st	Stage win Spa—Herentals, and Yellow Jersey
1963	DNF	Stage win Luchon—Toulouse
1964	67th	Stage wins Lisieux—Amiens, Bayonne—Bordeaux
1965	93rd	
1966	62nd	

DATES

Looking for a reason to celebrate? Here are the anniversaries of Tour history.

1868 James Moore wins the first recognised bike race meeting
1869 First place-to-place race, Paris-Rouen, also won by Moore
1902 Nov 20 GÉO LEFÈVRE has idea of running the Tour
1903 July 1 First Tour starts
1905 First col, the BALLON D'ALSACE
1908 COMBATIVITY AWARD
1910 Pyrenees introduced, including the TOURMALET and AUBISQUE VOITURE BALAI introduced

1910	ADOLPHE HELIÈRE first to die during race
1911	Alps introduced, including the GALIBIER
1913	Tour changes from points to times
1914	First Australian riders DON KIRKHAM and Ivor Munro
1919	July 19 Yellow JERSEY introduced
	First FEEDING AREA
1921	First press cars for regional and foreign journalists
1922	Cols de Vars and IZOARD
1924	ITALY wins first Tour with OTTAVIO BOTTECCHIA
	ALBERT LONDRES writes Les forçats de la route (Convicts of the Road)
1926	First START outside Paris, at Évian
	First Japanese rider KISSO KAWAMURO
1927	Record 24 stages, the flat ones as team TIME TRIALS
1928	Riders split into regional teams and individuals
1930	NATIONAL TEAMS replace SPONSORS
	First direct radio BROADCASTING
1931	First Austrian Yellow Jersey MAX BULLA
1932	First German Yellow Jersey KURT STOPL
1933	MOUNTAINS competition starts; first winner VICENTE TRUEBA
1934	First individual TIME TRIAL
1936	Third-stages introduced, three mini-stages in one day
	First Swiss Yellow Jersey PAUL EGLI
1937	Derailleur GEARS allowed
1939	First mountain time trial
	REGIONAL TEAMS
1947	First winner on last day JEAN ROBIC
1948	Daily prize for Yellow Jersey
1949	First Tour-Giro double FAUSTO COPPI
1951	MONT VENTOUX
	First Dutch Yellow Jersey WIM VAN EST
1952	Mountain finishes, ALPE D'HUEZ, SESTRIERE, PUY-DE-DOME
1953	Points jersey introduced
1954	First foreign start Amsterdam
1955	Photo-finish introduced
	First Spanish Yellow Jersey MIGUEL POBLET
1960	First train TRANSFER, Bordeaux—Mont-de-Marsan

1962	Highest col, Restefond (2,802m)
	Return to trade-sponsored teams
	First extra-sportif sponsors
	First British Yellow Jersey TOM SIMPSON
1963	First Irish Yellow Jersey SHAY ELLIOTT
1964	JACQUES ANQUETIL first to win five Tours
1966	DOPING checks
1967	First PROLOGUE
	Return to national teams
	Last finish on PARC DES PRINCES
1968	Doping checks at finishes
	First finish at Piste Municipale, Valenciennes
1969	Return to sponsored teams
1971	First plane transfers, Le Touquet—Paris and Marseille—Albi
1973	First titanium equipment, LUIS OCAÑA
1974	First sea transfer, to Plymouth
1975	First finish on CHAMPS-ELYSÉES
	First red polka-dot Mountains Jersey
	First YOUNG RIDER Jersey
1978	Yellow Jersey disqualified, MICHEL POLLENTIER
1980	Tour run by SOCIÉTÉ DU TOUR DE FRANCE
1981	First Australian Yellow Jersey PHIL ANDERSON
1983	First 'open' race, with COLOMBIA
1984	First Red Jersey for intermediate spirit points
1986	First North American Yellow Jersey, Canada's ALEX STIEDA
	First American winner GREG LEMOND
	RECORD number of starters: 210
1987	Furthest start from France: Berlin
	First East European Yellow Jersey LECH PIASECKI
1988	First Tour VILLAGE
1989	Smallest winning margin: 8 seconds by Greg LeMond
1990	Tour returns to three jerseys, yellow, green and polka-dot
1994	First tunnel transfer, to Folkestone
1998	First visit to IRELAND
	GPS satellite-positioning introduced
	Red number for COMBATIVITY AWARD

FRED DE BRUYNE

b. Berlaere, Belgium, Oct 21 1930, d. Seillans,
France, Feb 4 1994

'A champion who didn't leave his address,' as
one writer said of BELGIUM's Fred De Bruyne.
Meaning that he could have achieved more but
wasn't recognised for what he did.

De Bruyne started racing in 1947 after abandoning his studies and going off to see what he
could do in the sport. He was just 1.70m and
weighed 68kg, but for Belgium he was a giant in
waiting. The country hadn't won a Tour since
SYLVÈRE MAES in 1939. By the 1950s it was getting desperate and De Bruyne carried its hopes.
To that extent he disappointed. He rode six
times but never finished better than 17th
(1955), although he did win six stages.

In single-day races, though, he was in his ele-
ment. In a glorious period from 1956 to 1959
he won Liège-Bastogne-Liège three times,
Paris-Nice twice, and Milan-San Remo, the
Tour of Flanders, Paris-Roubaix and Paris-
Tours once each. In 1957 and 1958 he won the
Challenge Desgrange-Colombo, a forerunner
of the World Cup.

De Bruyne's career ended after a series of
bike CRASHES and, in 1960, a serious car crash
in Paris. From 1961 to 1977 he worked for
Belgian radio and television, where he was
much loved but sometimes believed to be the
worse for drink. Belgian TV became famous for
showing close-ups of riders' feet. 'Look at his
feet, look at his feet!' De Bruyne would say,
insisting he could tell a rider's condition by
the way he pedalled. Directors and cameramen
were obliged to follow his commentary, which
was fine for viewers of Belgium's Dutch-
language television but a puzzle for viewers
watching Eurovision in other countries and
hearing a different commentator.

De Bruyne stopped broadcasting in 1978 to
become MANAGER of the FLANDRIA team,
moving from there to Daf in 1979 and to
Aernoudt in 1983. In 1984 he joined Peter Post
as PR manager with Panasonic. He was never as
good a commentator as he was a cyclist, and
never as good a manager as he had been a commentator. He left Belgium to live in the south of

France in Seillans, the same village as his friend
RAPHAËL GÉMINIANI. There he wrote biogra-
phies of RIK VAN LOOY, RIK VAN STEENBERGEN,
Peter Post and PATRICK SERCU, and an autobiography, *Memoires*.

Géminiani says, 'Fred De Bruyne was a
master of the classics: intelligent, crafty, devi-
ous but very strong and an excellent tactician.
He knew how to impose his authority. He
wasn't a sprinter like van Looy or van Steenbergen but he had a good fast finish which meant
he got in the results of the biggest classics. Elegant, extremely gentle, he came out of the
world of cycling with ease. These days that
doesn't mean much, but then attitudes were
different: once a Fleming, always a Fleming. We
spent 10 happy years together.'

Winner

1956	Milan-San Remo, Liège-Bastogne-Liège, Paris-Nice
1957	Paris-Roubaix, Tour Flanders, Paris-Tours
1958	Liège-Bastogne-Liège, Paris-Nice
1959	Liège-Bastogne-Liège

Tour de France

1953	52nd	
1954	36th	Stage wins Vannes—Angers, Luchon—Toulouse, Nancy—Troyes
1955	17th	
1956	20th	Stage wins Liège—Lille, St-Malo—Lorient, Bordeaux—Bayonne
1957	DNF	
1959	31st	

ODILE DEFRAYE

b. Rumbeke, Belgium, Jul 14 1888, d. Bierges,
Belgium, Aug 21 1965

Odile Defraye (sometimes written Defraeye,
the style before spelling reform) was the first
Tour winner from BELGIUM. He crushed the
opposition in 1912 and won three stages, but
his victory was tainted when an entire French

team stormed out of the race insisting he had cheated.

Odile Defraye turned professional in 1909 after winning most of his AMATEUR races. Compulsory army service ruined his chances in that year's Tour. Returning to civilian life in 1912, he joined the French ALCYON team. However, the owners wanted an all-French team for their national Tour and planned to leave him at home. They relented when salesmen in Belgium insisted they needed him to sell the firm's bikes, and he was enrolled on condition that he ride for GUSTAVE GARRIGOU, the winner the previous year. Defraye repaid them by outsprinting his leader on the second stage, from Dunkirk to Longwy.

Things changed for good when saboteurs scattered nails in the MOUNTAINS between Grenoble and Nice and ruined Garrigou's chances. Whether this was vandalism or was aimed against particular riders has never been established. Defraye felt obliged to wait as Garrigou changed his tyre. That took longer in those days than now, and it became obvious in the long chase back to the race that the Belgian was stronger than his captain. Finally Garrigou told him to go on alone and Defraye finished the day, tied for first place, whereas Garrigou lost 40 minutes.

Defraye went on to win three stages, and finished in Paris as Belgium's first winner. But victory was blemished by claims of collusion. The allegation was that Belgians riding for rival teams had contrived to help Defraye and to hinder the Frenchman OCTAVE LAPIZE, who was lying second. Lapize said in particular that FIRMIN LAMBOT, who rode for Le Globe, had helped Defraye on the Col des Aravis. He and his LA FRANÇAISE team walked out on the ninth stage.

That caused uproar in Belgium, which probably saw little wrong in Belgians securing the win of one of their own. Ten thousand lined the streets of Roeselare when Defraye got home.

He was never the success they hoped for, though, winning one Tour but never finishing another. What's more, his win wasn't as convincing as it looked. The race was decided not on time but points, so the order of finish each

> **Trivia note:** Defraye won Milan-San Remo in 1913 and, like LOUIS TROUSSELIER after the 1905 Tour, gambled away all his winnings the same night. He is remembered at the national bike museum in Polenplein, Roeselare, where a hall is named after him.

day was more important than the winning margin. Defraye's rival was the Frenchman EUGÈNE CHRISTOPHE, but since Defraye could outsprint him, he had only to finish just ahead to pick up more points, while Christophe, on the other hand, was forced to go off on long lone attacks. Yet however far he finished ahead of Defraye, he still picked up only the same points. Had the race been decided on time, the result would have been closer and the race more exciting. Realising this, organiser HENRI DESGRANGE changed back to a timed race the following year.

Winner

1911 National championship
1912 Tour de France, Tour Belgium
1913 Milan-San Remo

Tour de France

1909 DNF
1912 1st Stage wins Dunkirk—Longway, Nice—Marseille, Perpignan—Luchon
1913 DNF
1914 DNF
1919 DNF
1920 DNF
1924 DNF

ERIK DEKKER
b. Hoogeveen, Holland, Aug 21 1970

Erik Dekker, a lean, crop-haired, toothy Dutchman, has had an erratic career mixing happiness and misery. Turning professional in September 1992, after he had finished second to FABIO CASARTELLI in the Olympic road race, he had half a dozen good results immediately afterwards, but then featured almost nowhere. He won the Tour of Sweden in 1994 and 1995 but that was hardly enough to set the clogs dancing.

At the Tour, and now riding for Rabobank, Dekker was riding the stage to Fribourg when his MANAGER, Adri van Houwelingen, decided to make something of the fact that Dekker was leaner and faster than he had been before.

'Stop fetching bottles for the others and have a go at winning,' he told him. Next day, at Colmar, Dekker came fifth to NEIL STEPHENS. His confidence was restored but two still fairly lean years followed, his health suffering from a series of crashes. Then he was suspended from racing at Verona in 1999 after being informed the night before the world road championship that his red blood cell count was too high.

A year later, in 2000, Dekker won a hat trick of stages: at Villeneuve-sur-Lot, Revel and Lausanne. All were in lone breaks. By Revel he had ridden 625km alone ahead of the race. At Vitré he could have won again, had the bunch not swept him up with 400 metres left of a 151km ride with JENS VOIGT.

At Villeneuve Dekker wept with joy. 'I'm an emotional guy,' he said later. 'It was my first big win in a stage race. But the tears were to do with the way it happened. In the last few kilometres I knew I was pretty safe, and when you're riding alone and you're safe, you have time to get emotional.'

Van Houwelingen said in 2001 after Dekker had won another stage at the Tour, 'It's always very difficult to analyse him. He won those three stages and yet each one was in a different way. He's not a SPRINTER, nor a pure *rouleur* [a word difficult to translate but which implies someone who can ride fast for long periods], nor a CLIMBER, and yet he belongs among the very best riders in the world.'

Dekker, his wife Petra and their two sons, live not in HOLLAND but a kilometre across the border at Meerle in BELGIUM, where tax is less onerous.

(*See* GRUPPETTO.)

Winner

1994	Tour Sweden
1995	Tour Sweden
1997	Tour Holland
1999	GP Merckx
2000	San Sebastian Classic, Tour Holland
2001	World Cup, Amstel Gold, GP Merckx, Ruta del Sol
2002	Tirreno-Adriatico

Tour de France

1994	101st	
1995	70th	
1996	74th	
1997	81st	
1998	DNF	
1999	107th	
2000	51st	Stage wins Limoges—Villeneuve-sur-Lot, Bagnères-sur-Bigorre—Revel, Évian—Lausanne, Combativity Winner
2001	91st	Stage win Colmar—Pontarlier
2002	136th	

RENÉ DE LATOUR

The journalist René de Latour brought continental professional racing to a generation in BRITAIN thanks to 120 articles he wrote for the monthly magazine *Sporting Cyclist* during the 1960s. (*See* PUBLICATIONS for other cycling magazines.)

De Latour was born in New York on September 30 1906, the child of a French father and Belgian mother. His family moved to France and in 1917 de Latour appointed himself interpreter to American soldiers, taking them to the Folies Bergères when he was only 11. Interpreting for the Canadian Willie Spencer at the Vélodrome d'Hiver got him into professional racing, and he joined *Paris-Soir* as a cycling journalist in 1932, where one of his jobs was to help set up the Grand Prix des Nations. He was later race director of the TOUR DE L'AVENIR.

JOCK WADLEY, *Sporting Cyclist*'s editor, described him as 'an undemonstrative man who may appear sullen ... His humour is dry and, to an Englishman, rather stern.' Asked what had happened to British riders in the TOUR DE L'AVENIR, de Latour answered 'I don't know; I wasn't that far back.'

He retired to Quiberon in Brittany, and died in 1986 after a stroke, aged 79.

PEDRO DELGADO

b. Segovia, Spain, Apr 15 1960

SPAIN'S greatest rider was MIGUEL INDURAIN, the first man to take five Tours in a row. Just before him, though, there was another fine Spanish rider, Pedro Delgado.

Delgado was born a sickly child and 'not much to look at physically' according to his parents, Victorina and Julio. He spent three months in bed with hepatitis before his 12th birthday.

'I got my first bicycle when I helped my brother Julio, much more determined than me, on his paper round for the local paper, *El Adelantado de Segovia*,' he recalled. 'But I wanted a racing BIKE, and after saving I was able to buy my first racing bike which cost me 5,000 pesetas. It was made of iron but it was marvellous.'

He was introduced to racing by a school friend, Frutos Arena, whom he joined on training rides. In autumn 1974 Delgado rode his first race, wearing running shorts, a T-shirt and trainers. It was the provincial championship of Segovia, but to this day he doesn't know where he came in the confusion of categories and age groups.

He won a stage of the TOUR DE L'AVENIR in 1979 and had three offers to turn pro. But he was 19, and because of his studies and compulsory military service he delayed the decision until the summer of 1982. His Tour de France career started in 1983 and he made steady progress, coming 15th that year and sixth in 1985.

By 1987 he was a real force, and his race-long duel with STEPHEN ROCHE in that Tour was an epic. Delgado became race leader after ALPE D'HUEZ but he needed more than just 21 seconds on Roche to keep his JERSEY until Paris. The TIME TRIAL was still to come at Dijon, where Roche was likely to be the stronger. Delgado, therefore, attacked on the climb to La Plagne and gained a lead of two minutes. He seemed to have won the Tour.

But two things combined to deny the dream. First, he started weakening three kilometres from the FINISH. And second, Roche rode so hard to catch him that the Irishman drove himself to the point of collapse on the line and needed oxygen. Delgado hoped Roche would take time to recover, but he got over the effort quickly, took the lead back in the time trial, and relegated Delgado to second in Paris.

Delgado eventually won in the 1988 Tour, taking the lead from STEVE BAUER by 25 seconds when the race again reached Alpe d'Huez. Next day he won a hilly TIME TRIAL from Grenoble to Villard-de-Lans, and nobody was left to threaten him. He held the lead to the end to finish 7:13 up on STEVEN ROOKS of HOLLAND.

But victory was tainted. Rumours were already spreading when the race reached BORDEAUX on July 19 that Delgado had become embroiled in a DOPING scandal. The news that he had tested positive for probenicid was confirmed on French television on July 20.

The sensation was spectacular. Ten years earlier, another rider – MICHEL POLLENTIER – had taken the yellow jersey on the same mountain – Alpe d'Huez – and had lost it the same day, also for doping. Pollentier tried to disguise what he had taken by using someone else's urine for the control. By taking probenicid Delgado was alleged to have done the same thing chemically, because the substance interferes with what the kidneys secrete. In particular, it can hide the remains of anabolic steroids.

Gérard Porte, the Tour's doctor, was furious that the news had broken before the re-run of the test, to which Delgado was entitled. But then it emerged that the leak had come from a source close to the Tour's own management. Why, nobody knows, but the speculation was that whoever leaked the news wanted it out of the way so the race could continue in peace.

Another twist followed when lawyers found that although probenicid had been banned by the International Olympic Committee, that decision was not to be ratified by cycling's regulatory body, the UCI, until after the Tour. Delgado, in fact, had no case to answer.

Feelings were mixed but heated. Fellow riders either felt sympathy for a colleague who had been branded a drug-taker but had taken nothing illegal, or viewed him as a fraud. The view in Spain, however, was more unanimous, so much so that the Spanish sports minister, Javier Gomez-Navarro, flew to Paris so that he and technical experts from the Spanish sports authorities could press for Delgado's acquittal. In Madrid, meanwhile, angry fans threatened the French embassy.

On July 21, the second test confirmed the first. The UCI called its race officials to a conference, where it announced after a long meeting that Delgado could continue, since cycling hadn't yet banned probenicid. The one Spanish official on the UCI, Javier Iturbe, had not been included at the meeting, but the result was announced by the UCI president, Luis Puig, another Spaniard. Sceptics were not impressed.

Frustration grew on the same day when the Dutchman GERT-JAN THEUNISSE was penalised 10 minutes for taking steroids, the very drugs that probenicid was said to mask. Next day riders went on STRIKE at Clermont-Ferrand, ostensibly against ill-defined tests, but also because many riders considered the penalties hadn't gone far enough. Eric Boyer, who was fifth overall, said Delgado 'took a big risk, he cheated and he lost; he was runner-up last year and perhaps he didn't want to be second again.'

Delgado still insists he did nothing wrong, and that has remained the view in Spain. The argument was that he had been tested at least 10 times before Alpe d'Huez; only one sample

had shown traces of any substance, and even that had not been anything illegal. The incident set off years of bad feeling between FRANCE and SPAIN, and the remnants of that hostility did nothing to make the FESTINA AFFAIR easier in 1998. (See Festina entry.)

Delgado came to the Tour in 1989 anxious to restore his name, but things went wrong from the START. There was nobody the crowds wanted to see more at the PROLOGUE in LUXEMBOURG than the controversial Spaniard they had learned to call by his NICKNAME, Perico. But Delgado didn't turn up at his allocated time. The timekeeper called for him and officials looked for him but he was still absent when his start time came.

The rules state that the clock starts running at the moment a rider is due to start a time trial, and carries on running until he turns up. When Delgado did show up, the clock was already at 2min 40sec.

'Even today I can't explain what happened,' he says. 'I wanted to shine from the first pedal. I went to warm up, which I never usually did. I wanted to get away from the press who hassled me all the time and I also wanted to keep my concentration. I meant to arrive just before the start. It was this and nothing else that made me late; none of the press meditations about my late start [that he had been basking in adulation and signing autographs or was merely attracting attention to himself] were true. I called myself stupid.

'The worst repercussion wasn't so much the time lost so stupidly but that I couldn't forgive myself and lost a night's sleep over my own anger.'

There were two stages next day, 135km in the morning and a team TIME TRIAL in the afternoon. Delgado was tired and his team stressed. Delgado's Reynolds team lost five more minutes.

He struggled back to finish third, just 3:34 down on race winner GREG LEMOND, and came fourth in 1990, but his career was beginning to fizzle out and he was soon eclipsed by Indurain.

Delgado was a curious, penny-pinching man who logged every kilometre he drove and every peseta he spent so he could claim them back in expenses. He works now as a newspaper columnist and as a TV commentator during the Tour.

RAYMOND DELISLE

b. Ancteville, France, Mar 11 1943

Raymond Delisle rode 12 Tours and finished 11 in a row. Not one passed without his 'animating' them, as his fellow Frenchmen say. So much so that in his early days ROGER PINGEON begged him to calm down for his own sake.

On Bastille Day 1969 Delisle won the Castelnaudary-Luchon stage in the blue, white and red of national champion. But greater success, and especially the yellow JERSEY, looked like eluding him. And then came 1976. The race reached the Pyrenees, where the MOUNTAINS opened with a stage from Port-Barcarès to the ski station at Pyrenees 2000 (so called because of its altitude). Delisle knew the area and attacked on the Col de Jau. Nobody took any notice; LUCIEN VAN IMPE didn't see him as a threat in the CLIMBERS' competition, and

RAYMOND POULIDOR's team thought it better to stick with their leader. Delisle, after all, was a man who had never finished in the first 10.

They underestimated him. Delisle beat the favourites by seven minutes and took the *maillot jaune*. He kept it next day because the stars were more concerned with saving their energy before another bout in the mountains. Then the real race started over the Menté, Portillon, Peyresourde and Pla d'Adet, and Delisle's days of glory were over. Even so, he finished fourth in Paris.

He rode one more Tour, finishing ninth in 1977, then retired and took on a seventeenth-century hotel in Normandy which he still runs.

JULES DELOFFRE

b. Cateau, France, Apr 22 1885, d. Caudry, France, Oct 13 1963

Jules Deloffre was a TOURISTE-ROUTIER with unusual talent. Touriste-routiers were casual entrants who were allowed to ride provided they made all their own arrangements. They had to raise the cost of their accommodation themselves, so if there were no prizes there could also be no bed. Deloffre, from the Pas-de-Calais region, would arrive at the FINISH, blackened by sun after 10 hours in the saddle, take a drink from a barrel, borrow a chair from a café, and use it to perform acrobatic tricks in the street. He then went round the crowd with his cap out for centimes. He still managed to finish four Tours in the top 20. He also finished sixth in Bordeaux-Paris in 1924.

Every July since 1985 a CRITERIUM has been held in Deloffre's memory at Cateau, his birthplace.

Tour de France

1908	DNF
1909	16th
1910	15th
1911	15th
1912	21st
1913	12th
1914	36th
1920	DNF
1921	26th
1923	DNF
1925	DNF
1926	DNF
1927	DNF
1928	DNF

VIN DENSON
b. Rensby, England, Nov 24 1935

One of cycling's most charming men and a born story-teller, Vin Denson was one of a collection of British riders who went to FRANCE in the 1960s to try for a career as a professional. His background was that he had finished four times in the top 12 of the British Best All-Rounder time-trialling competition (comprising the best average speeds over 50 and 100 miles and 12 hours), and had come seventh in the AMATEUR Tour of BRITAIN in 1959, and fifth in 1960.

Denson turned INDEPENDENT (semi-professional) in 1961 and fully professional in 1963. The following year he became a DOMES-TIQUE for RIK VAN LOOY, of whom he says, 'He was always pleading he was short of money and would only pay out half what he had promised.' Of the four years he spent with JACQUES ANQUETIL, though, he says, 'Brilliant, the best of my career.'

Denson's successes include the 1965 Tour of LUXEMBOURG and a stage of the Giro d'Italia in 1966. Italian SPECTATORS at the Giro would appear to be pushing foreign riders on hills, but would in fact be pulling their brake cables. 'You'd not only be delayed, you'd be fined for being pushed as well,' he said. 'And when we were chasing Gianni Motta through Naples they were chucking rubbish at us from balconies – tomatoes, spaghetti, old newspapers, anything.'

Denson lost his will to race professionally in 1967 when his friend TOM SIMPSON died on MONT VENTOUX. (*See* BARRY HOBAN for why Denson didn't win the memorial stage.) He wanted the British team to abandon and go to the funeral, but was persuaded to continue. 'I kept crying and thinking I could see Tom in the peloton,' he said.

He tried another year on the Continent, raced briefly in Britain and won the Vaux GP, the biggest domestic race, and then retired to run a timber preservation business near Harlow, Essex.

Denson still rides a bike. One of his early supporters, the cycle dealer Ron Kitching, said, 'He's a character, always laughing, one of the smiling giants of the world. They don't overpower you with their size, they overpower you with their friendship.'

Winner

1965	Tour Luxembourg
1968	Vaux GP

Tour de France

1961	DNF
1964	72nd
1965	87th
1966	DNF
1967	DNF
1968	62nd

TOMMASO DE PRA
b. Mortara, Italy, Dec 16 1938

ITALY's Tommaso De Pra was an unknown who, like PIERRE BEUFFEUIL in 1960, enjoyed a single moment of fame. Where Beuffeuil had won a stage because he didn't know he was supposed to stop and say hello to Charles de Gaulle (*see* entry for details), De Pra took the yellow JERSEY in 1966 because the rest of the race decided to hold a go-slow at the moment he attacked between Bayonne and Pau. This was a follow-up to a STRIKE they had held the previous day after DOPING controls were applied in BORDEAUX. (*See* DOPING and STRIKES.)

The bunch allowed De Pra to gain 10 minutes, delighted that their action had been given greater impact by forcing the Tour's organisers to honour an unknown. He eventually finished just ahead of Willy In't Ven of BELGIUM, and two minutes ahead of JAN JANSSEN and the bunch.

It was a safe gesture: De Pra's win had come on a stage that included the AUBISQUE, but next day De Pra finished 45th and 6:56 down, never troubling the finish line judges again. And who finished three places back from him in the same group? Pierre Beuffeuil.

De Pra rode the Tour again in 1971 but, as had been the case in 1966, didn't finish then either.

Tour de France
1966	DNF	Stage win Bayonne—Pau, and Yellow Jersey
1971	DNF	

JO DE ROO
b. Schore, Holland, Jul 5 1937

Johannes De Roo was the youngest of three sons of a Calvinist farm worker in Zeeland, the most south-westerly province of HOLLAND. His father refused to let his brother Jaap become anything so frivolous as a cyclist, but relented in Jo's case.

De Roo was handicapped as a Tourman by being big in size and a poor CLIMBER. But he started five Tours, finished three and won three stages. His talent was in single-day races, winning the Tour of Lombardy, Paris-Tours and Bordeaux-Paris in 1962, Lombardy again in 1963, and the Tour of Flanders 1965. In 1962 he won the Super Prestige Pernod, forerunner of the World Cup.

That record could have been better had he not arrived as a professional in 1959, an era when Holland had no professional teams. The then leading Dutch MANAGER, Kees Pellenaars, had been unable to find a SPONSOR and had temporarily left the sport. De Roo rode instead as a DOMESTIQUE for JACQUES ANQUETIL, a rare Dutchman in a French team. JAN JANSSEN, who rode for the French Pelforth brewery, was another. But while Janssen felt at home in France, and spoke fluent French which he had learned before going there, De Roo was always happier among fellow Dutchmen. In 1965, when Pellenaars (*see* DOPING and WIM VAN EST) started the Televizier team, De Roo joined it.

But by then most of De Roo's best results were behind him. Janssen invited him to ride the Tour with him in the Dutch NATIONAL TEAM in 1968, but De Roo declined, and retired to open a household goods shop in Zeeland. He sold it when he divorced and he lives now in his father's house with his second wife. He still rides a bike.

Winner
1960	Tour Sardinia
1961	Manx Premier
1962	Bordeaux-Paris, Tour Lombardy, Paris-Tours

1963 Paris-Tours, Tour Lombardy
1964 National championship
1965 Tour Flanders, National championship
1966 Het Volk

Tour de France

1960	DNF	
1964	43rd	Stage win Montpellier—Perpignan
1965	55th	Stage win La Rochelle—Bordeaux
1966	DNF	Stage win Montpellier—Aubenas
1967	76th	

HENRI DESGRANGE

For many years the yellow JERSEY carried the initials '*H D*', in honour of the Tour's first boss, Henri Desgrange, known to almost everyone as *Ash-Day* (the French pronunciation of his initials).

Born in Paris on January 31 1865, Desgrange began work as a clerk in a legal office after leaving school. There, according to legend, he upset a woman client by cycling to work with bare calves, presumably in the baggy plus-fours of the time, with no socks between knee and ankle. Early stubbornness showed when his bosses are said to have demanded he choose between his work and the way he dressed on his way there. Desgrange walked out.

Not working gave him more time to train, and he rode regularly at the TRACKS that surrounded central Paris in those days. One of them, the Buffalo – so called because of Wild West shows that had been held on the site – had been opened in April 1893 with money provided by Clovis Clerc, the director of the Folies Bergères. Clovis knew a lot about putting on a good show, but little about cycling, so he had turned to Desgrange for advice on the track's design after reading newspaper articles he had written. A month later, on May 11 1893,

Desgrange used the track to establish the world's first ratified hour record.

There had been other such contests, but until then none under agreed conditions; Desgrange rode 35.325km to improve on the 35.100km of an Italian called Braida, and established the world's first recognised mark. The record stood until October 10 1894, when Jules Dubois, another Frenchman, extended it to 38.220km on the same track.

Desgrange also set records over distances of 50km and 100km, over 100 miles and six hours. His reputation was such that in 1894 he could write a training book, *La Tête et Les Jambes* (Head and Legs), and see it sell well. It is written as an exchange of letters between a young rider (presumably Desgrange as a novice) and his coach (the older and wiser Desgrange). He was also able to find backers to open the PARC DES PRINCES track outside western Paris in 1897.

Desgrange changed jobs frequently, working for *La Bicyclette* and also in public relations for the car and tyre-maker Adolphe Clément. Ten years older than Desgrange, Clément had raised enough money making car and bike tyres to start building cars of his own. From 1899 he used engines made by Albert de Dion and his partner Georges Bouton.

Clément and de Dion (often described as a count, although the title had disappeared after the French Revolution) were among the largest advertisers in a newspaper called *Vélo*, which mixed sport with general news and comment. They were both strongly right-wing, and fell out with the paper's editor, Pierre Giffard, over the guilt or innocence of Alfred Dreyfus.

The Dreyfus Affair split France at the end of the nineteenth century. The man at the centre of it, a Jewish army captain, was accused and then convicted in 1894 of passing secrets to the Germans. The issue, which had strong overtones of anti-Semitism, divided right from left, conservative from liberal, country from city, religious believers from non-believers. The army had assumed that Dreyfus, once accused, would shoot himself. Instead the issue went to a series of trials with trumped-up evidence. Dreyfus was imprisoned on Devil's Island, and France remained split.

Infuriated by Giffard's insistence that Dreyfus was innocent, Clément, de Dion and other advertisers pulled their advertising from *Vélo* and opened up a rival paper. Clément was sure that few people knew more about writing and sport – or cycling, at any rate – than the man who had been handling his public relations. In a rush job, and apparently lacking other candidates, they appointed Desgrange to run their new paper, *L'AUTO*, which appeared on October 16 1900.

Desgrange may have been good on a bike, but he was less talented off it. So short was he of ideas that all he could do was copy his rival's paper, starting with the title, which he called *L'Auto-Vélo* until Giffard brought a court case complaining of unfair trading. From then on, the best Desgrange could think of doing was what others had already done, only bigger, such as running a second Bordeaux-Paris as well as other races.

L'Auto's circulation stayed low for two years, which was bad enough. But worse, *Vélo* was still a success, whereas the plan had been to drive Giffard out of business. *L'Auto*'s investors finally demanded new ideas, or new men at the top. Characteristically, Desgrange had no ideas of his own when he called a crisis meeting in the boardroom on the first floor of the newspaper's office in the rue du Faubourg Montmartre. The only hope was an idea hesitantly offered by a young rugby and cycling writer called GÉO LEFÈVRE, whom Desgrange had poached from Giffard.

Lefèvre suggested a race so long that nobody else could match it. Desgrange, to clarify what his employee meant, asked if he meant a 'Tour de France'. The title had been used before to publicise record attempts, but this was the first time it had been employed in its modern sense.

Even then Desgrange wasn't convinced. Looking at his watch, he ended the meeting with the observation that it was lunch time, and took Lefèvre up the street to the Taverne Zimmer, where the idea wasn't discussed further until coffee. Desgrange said he would mention the subject to the company accountant, Victor Goddet, who, he was sure, would dismiss it, thus saving Desgrange the need to make a decision. Instead, Goddet was enthusiastic. Legend says he was so grateful for any idea that might save the paper that he pointed at the safe and said, 'It's all in there; have what you need.'

Even then indecision reigned. It took a while for the idea to appeal to riders, who asked to have the daily distance cut, the prices increased, and a small daily fee paid before they would enter. And Desgrange was so uncertain that the race would work that he stayed away from the START at MONTGERON, the suburb where the first race began on July 1 1903. He did the same when the race went into the MOUNTAINS for the first time in 1910, and in 1904 he very nearly threw in the whole project after mass cheating and disqualification. (*See* 1904 AFFAIR.).

However, the moment the race began to look like a success, and certainly when the circulation of *L'Auto* began to soar, Desgrange was only too keen to associate himself with the race and never disclaimed the nickname of 'Father of the Tour'. Lefèvre, its true originator, had long since been sent off to write about other sports.

To be fair, Desgrange ran the new race with an enthusiasm and a dictatorial control without which it might never have grown into what it has now become. In retrospect some of his ideas seem bizarre. But it's important to remember that he was a person of his time, with strong views on man's strength and independence, and that he had nothing to serve him as a model. Factors such as the enormous distances of the stages in the pioneering days, or Desgrange's refusal to allow modern accoutrements like derailleur GEARS, or his insistence that riders should mend their own BIKES however badly damaged (*see* EUGÈNE CHRISTOPHE for an example) were, like his refusal to allow team TACTICS or collusion, just Desgrange's way of keeping his race a pure competition between men and not between machines and their makers. And he always struggled to find new ways of running the race, whether on points (*see* tactics entry) rather than time, or as a TIME TRIAL (*see* HUBERT OPPERMAN) rather than first-over-the-line.

Sometimes riders rebelled. HENRI PÉLISSIER led a walkout over a petty rule that competitors should not remove clothing as the day heated up. (*See* Pélissier entry.) MARCEL BIDOT said Desgrange was 'a driven man and a boss who tolerated no disagreement'. PIERRE CHANY wrote, 'He knew the imperfections of his work, which was still in progress, but it was as if he didn't see them. He rejected advice, certain of his authority and decisions, powerful in a world where his word had the force of law. He followed a narrow path between the interests of cycling in general and his own, a way of thinking that justified his reputation as a despot.'

Desgrange became the Tour's organiser, chief official, writer and almost everything else. His style was histrionic, as when he wrote of Paris-Brest-Paris: 'There are four of them. Their legs, like giant levers, will power onwards for sixty hours; their muscles will grind up the kilometres; their broad chests will heave with the effort of the struggle; their hands will clench on to their handlebars; with their eyes they will observe each other ferociously; their backs will bend forward in unison for barbaric breakaways; their stomachs will fight against hunger, their brains against sleep. And at night a peasant waiting for them by a deserted road will see four demons passing by, and the noise of their desperate panting will freeze his heart and fill it with terror.'

The 'emperor' was 71 when he fell ill in 1936, and had a kidney operation just before the Tour started. He ignored doctors' orders and followed his race, padding his car to minimise the pain, but it got too much at Charleville, two days after the START. Desgrange was replaced by JACQUES GODDET, son of the man who had reputedly pointed at the safe in his office at *L'Auto* and told Desgrange to take what he needed. Desgrange himself departed for his villa at Beauvallon on the Riviera, and died there on August 16 1940.

Earlier that summer France had capitulated to the German invasion and the government had moved to Vichy. *L'Auto* continued to publish, and as a result was closed down after the Liberation. As for Dreyfus, whose arrest had set the whole thing off, he was cleared of the trumped-up charges in 1906, but it was not until 1998 that President Jacques Chirac apologised to his descendants.

The initials *H D* returned to the yellow jersey in 2003 to mark the Tour's 100th birthday.

(*See* BONUSES, CARAVAN, DOPING, GALIBIER, ALBERT LONDRES, NATIONAL TEAMS, SPONSORS.)

DEVIL

Television gives occasional glimpses – and riders get irritatingly frequent ones – of a SPECTATOR dressed in a red devil's outfit, jumping up and down or running about with a trident which he shakes wildly.

Didi Senff is the name of this character, a 48-year-old German who was once a novelty but has since become an annoyance whom riders throw things at if they get the chance. Since 1993 Senff has run along shouting at riders and followers. He was first seen in Andorra, chasing CLAUDIO CHIAPPUCCI whose NICKNAME of *el Diablo* was then widespread. Undiscouraged by the reception he gets from riders, Senff paints warning red tridents a few hundred metres from where he stands so they have time to throw bottles and other rubbish at him.

Everything on the Tour has SPONSORS, and Senff too is backed – by a company making clutch fluid. Journalist William Fotheringham said, 'There was a brief surreal touch when an Italian turned up in an angel outfit and the two

stood on opposite sides of the road. But that was nothing compared to the man we saw dressed as Jesus who waved at us from a cross in the Périgord.'

In 1997 a streaker ran along the CHAMPS ELYSÉES. The French are not familiar with the streaking phenomenon, have no word for it, and had to have the novelty explained by news readers. The streaker was a certain Xavier Clément, a 30-year-old actor, who was fined the equivalent of £210 for 'sexual exhibition'. Friends who had dared him to do it bought him lunch in compensation.

(*See* SPECTATORS.)

ERIK DE VLAEMINCK

b. Eeklo, Belgium, Mar 23 1945

Erik is the brother of ROGER DE VLAEMINCK, and he is a man whose fiery talent burnt away into the cinders of drugs and personality disorders.

The two (*see* BROTHERS for other siblings) were as different in talent as they were in looks. Roger was called 'the Gipsy', partly for the way he roamed Europe to find teams, but also for his lean face and dark complexion. Erik (the often-seen 'Eric' is the French spelling of his name) was fairer and squatter, with a round, sometimes vacant-looking face lacking strong features. His talents were in cyclo-cross rather than the road – although he did win a Tour stage and finished twice (in 1968 and 1971), whereas Roger never finished the race.

Both brothers rode cyclo-cross, and in 1968 Erik was the world professional champion and Roger was the amateur champion. But Erik went further and became the greatest in history, winning the title of WORLD CHAMPION every year from 1966 until 1973, with the exception of 1967 when his bike broke. Erik De Vlaeminck floated where others bumped, and rode where others had to run. At Crystal Palace, London, in 1973, the organisers of the world championship had put a long downward rake of stone steps to force riders to get off and run in, and they were astonished to see De Vlaeminck accelerate and skim over them.

That talent extended to the road as well, and in 1969 he won the Tour of Belgium and came third in the same year's Ghent-Wevelgem, one place behind his brother. But success came at a price. Erik De Vlaeminck had repeated DOPING problems, and in 1973 went into psychiatric hospital for detoxification. Four years later he was arrested and investigated for presenting forged prescriptions after trying to crash through a police barrier. Wild stories are known all over Belgium about what he is supposed to have done while drugged up, but De Vlaeminck won't confirm or deny them.

'I never talk about that period of my past,' he says forcefully. What happened drove a rift between him and his brother that has never closed.

BELGIUM gave De Vlaeminck a licence for just one day at a time in 1978, when he said he wanted to stop driving a dumper-truck for the parks department in Eeklo and come back to racing. But things have changed now. Rehabilitated, he works as national cyclo-cross coach. At the 2002 world championship he gained his 29th medal as a manager.

De Vlaeminck's 26-year-old son Geert was also a talented cyclo-cross rider, but died of a heart attack during a race at Heist op den Berg in 1993.

(*See* ROGER DE VLAEMINCK for spelling variations of his surname.)

Winner

1966	World cyclo-cross championship
1968	World cyclo-cross championship
1969	Tour Belgium, World cyclo-cross championship
1970	Paris-Luxembourg, World cyclo-cross championship
1971	World cyclo-cross championship
1972	World cyclo-cross championship
1973	World cyclo-cross championship

Tour de France

1968	51st	Stage win Arlon—Forest
1969	DNF	
1971	62nd	

ROGER DE VLAEMINCK

b. Eeklo, Belgium, Aug 24 1947

Roger De Vlaeminck was a man of enormous talent whom circumstances prevented from achieving a better record in the Tour. He rode three times, winning a stage, but he never finished. By contrast, his older brother ERIK DE VLAEMINCK – by far the less talented roadman – rode three Tours, finished two and also won a stage.

Roger De Vlaeminck was a powerful rider with a strong sprint, and was good enough in a TIME TRIAL to win smaller stage races. But he was a poor CLIMBER, which limited his range. He also spent much of his time with Italian teams who saw the Tour as less important than the less mountainous Giro, and it was in the Giro that he won the Points JERSEY in 1972, 1974 and 1975. De Vlaeminck's other problem was his dislike for France, which was reputed to go so far as refusing even to speak French, the *lingua franca* of bike-racing and Belgium's other national language together with Dutch.

The exception to his Francophobia was the Paris-Roubaix race, which he rode 14 times, won four times, and finished on the podium on a further five occasions. Only once did he give up, after a puncture in 1980 – the first he'd had in a race notorious for wrecking bikes. His worst place was seventh. De Vlaeminck's winning margin of 5: 21 in 1972 is a record, and *L'ÉQUIPE* gave him the headline 'Monsieur Paris-Roubaix' after he won for the fourth time in 1977. Ironically, his one Tour stage win came at Valenciennes, a key point in Paris-Roubaix.

He was also a good cyclo-cross rider (*see* ERIK DE VLAEMINCK for details and for his relationship with his brother) as well as a six-day rider, and he won 16 classics. Only the world road championship eluded him, although he finished second to HENNIE KUIPER in 1975.

Roger was both loved and disliked by Belgians – loved for the aggressive way he rode and for his successes, but disliked by rival supporters for lack of tact when speaking of other riders. He was close to EDDY MERCKX but a permanent rival of FREDDY MAERTENS. In 1977, when Belgians took the first four places in the

Tour of Flanders – the most important race of the year for a Belgian – De Vlaeminck was jeered at when he won. He had ridden on Maertens' wheel for 60km only to win the sprint to the finish by six lengths, thus defying the convention that a rider who does all the work in a break is allowed to win at the end.

Maertens crossed the line in tears, and De Vlaeminck had to be shielded from his angry supporters. 'I told Freddy I couldn't work with him but I didn't promise to let him win the sprint,' he said, attempting to justify his action.

De Vlaeminck began to race in 1964, turned professional in 1969, and retired in 1984. He lives on a farm with his girlfriend and their son, Eddy, and is often seen at races.

> *Trivia note:* The brothers' surname is sometimes written Devlaeminck, as one word. Asked which version he preferred, Roger said he didn't much care.

Winner

1969	Het Volk, National championship
1970	GP Escaut, GP Gippingen, Kuurne-Brussels-Kuurne, Liège-Bastogne-Liège
1971	Flèche Wallonne, Four-days Dunkirk, GP Harelbeke, Kuurne-Brussels-Kuurne
1972	Paris-Roubaix, Milan-Turin, Tirreno-Adriatico, Coppa Placci
1973	Milan-San Remo, Tour Tuscany, Tirreno-Adriatico, Trofeo Matteotti
1974	Tour Lombardy, Paris-Roubaix, Milan-Turin, Coppa Placci, Tirreno-Adriatico, Tour Veneto
1975	Tour Switzerland, Championship Zurich, Tour Lazio, Trophée Pantalica, Critérium As, Paris-Roubaix, Tirreno-Adriatico, World Cyclo-Cross championship
1976	Tour Emilia, Tour Lazio, Tour Lombardy, Tirreno-Adriatico
1977	Tour Flanders, Tour Piedmont, Paris-Roubaix, Tirreno-Adriatico
1978	Tour Friuli, Milan-San Remo

MAURICE DEWAELE

b. Lovendegem, Belgium, Dec 27 1896,
d. Maldegem, Belgium, Feb 14 1952

Not many Tour de France winners have been called a 'corpse' by the organiser. But that was the fate of Maurice Dewaele of BELGIUM in 1929.

In this Belgian's case, HENRI DESGRANGE was greatly upset because, like FIRMIN LAMBOT in 1919, Dewaele had won largely through another rider's misfortune. For Lambot it was EUGÈNE CHRISTOPHE's broken bike, which Christophe had to mend himself. (And *see* JOOP ZOETEMELK for another win at someone else's expense.) For Dewaele victory came because the race leader, the regional rider VICTOR FONTAN, had broken his chain, punctured, and then fallen into a ravine in the Pyrenees. (*See* FRANCESCO CEPEDA, WIM VAN EST and ROGER RIVIÈRE for other riders who fell off MOUNTAINS.)

Dewaele (pronounced *de-WAH-luh*) took the *maillot jaune* only to suffer with it in turn. His agony on the GALIBIER was so great that he was still unconscious when the next day's stage was to start. Desgrange agreed to a request from his SOIGNEUR to delay the race by an hour, and Dewaele revived – and was illegally nursed and protected to the Paris finish by colleagues in the ALCYON team. (*See* Alcyon entry for background.) Desgrange couldn't understand why rivals hadn't attacked him and how Dewaele had finished only four minutes down despite the climbs. Positive that illegal TACTICS

and other types of collusion had been used to 'ruin' the Tour, he moaned, 'My race has been won by a corpse.'

The following year Desgrange turned his back on SPONSORS and ran the race instead for NATIONAL TEAMS.

(And *see* MEMORIALS.)

DISTANCES

The length of the Tour de France has varied wildly over the years. It grew as HENRI DESGRANGE realised that riders could cope with a race longer than any previously organised, and as he grew convinced that his perfect event was one so tough that only one rider would finish.

There were no restrictions on the overall length, the number of stages or the length of stages until after TOM SIMPSON died in 1967, after which the UCI (Union Cycliste Internationale) progressively introduced rules about maximum lengths, rest days and the number of long races in the calendar.

The list of race distances should be read with the understanding that early races were estimated rather than measured. Accuracy increased over the years as cars and their odometers became more dependable. They became still more accurate with the introduction of SATELLITE POSITIONING.

Distances (continued)

The shortest and longest distances exclude short TIME TRIALS and PROLOGUES. In some cases the shortest distances were of split stages and riders were required to ride once or twice more the same day.

(See RECORDS for the longest, shortest, fastest and slowest Tours.)

DISTANCES

Date	Distance (kms)	Stages	Shortest stage	Longest stage
1903	2,428	6	268	467
1904	2,428	6	268	467
1905	2,994	11	171	342
1906	4,545/4,637*	13	259	421
1907	4,488	14	254	415
1908	4,488	14	254	415
1909	4,497/4,507*	14	254	424
1910	4,734	15	216	424
1911	5,343	15	289	470
1912	5,289	15	289	470
1913	5,287	15	321	470
1914	5,380	15	323	470
1919	5,560	15	315	482
1920	5,503	15	300	482
1921	5,485	15	272	482
1922	5,375	15	260	482
1923	5,386	15	260	482
1924	5,425/5,488*	15	275	482
1925	5,440	18	189	433
1926	5,745	17	189	433
1927	5,340/5,398*	24	103	360
1928	5,476	22	120	387
1929	5,257/5,286*	22	133	366
1930	4,822	21	132	333
1931	5,091	24	102	338
1932	4,479/4,520*	21	99	382
1933	4,395/4,409*	23	91	293
1934	4,470	23	81	293
1935	4,338	21	81	325
1936	4,418/4,442*	21	67	325
1937	4,415	20	37	263
1938	4,687/4,694*	21	48	311
1939	4,224	18	70	311
1947	4,642/4,655*	21	165	314
1948	4,922	21	166	286

Date	Distance (kms)	Stages	Shortest stage	Longest stage
1949	4,808/4,819*	21	134	340
1950	4,773	22	96	314
1951	4,690	24	142	322
1952	4,898	23	149	354
1953	4,476	22	103	345
1954	4,656	23	131	343
1955	4,495	22	102	275
1956	4,498	22	125	331
1957	4,669/4,686*	22	134	317
1958	4,319	24	129	320
1959	4,358	22	119	331
1960	4,173	22	108	248
1961	4,397	21	136	309
1962	4,274	22	147	271
1963	4,138/4,210*	21	118	285
1964	4,504	22	118	311
1965	4,177/4,188*	22	147	299
1966	4,322/4,329*	22	111	265
1967	4,758/4,779*	22	104	359
1968	4,492	22	112	243
1969	4,117	22	111	329
1970	4,254	23	95	270
1971	3,608	20	19	257
1972	3,846	20	28	257
1973	4,090	20	76	248
1974	4,098	22	112	249
1975	4,000	22	94	260
1976	4,017	22	71	258
1977	4,096	22	70	258
1978	3,908	22	96	244
1979	3,765	24	120	248
1980	3,842/3,895*	22	92	276
1981	3,753	24	97	259
1982	3,507	21	122	246
1983	3,809	22	145	299
1984	4,021	23	83	338
1985	4,109	22	52	256
1986	4,094	23	85	258
1987	4,231	25	79	260
1988	3,286	22	38	232
1989	3,285	21	92	259
1990	3,504	21	119	301
1991	3,914	22	115	286
1992	3,983	21	141	268
1993	3,714	20	158	285
1994	3,978	21	149	271

Date	Distance (kms)	Stages	Shortest stage	Longest stage
1995	3,635	20	155	261
1996	3,765	22	46**	262
1997	3,950	22	148	262
1998	3,875	21	148	252
1999	3,870	20	144	237
2000	3,662	21	138	255
2001	3,458	20	142	233
2002	3,282	20	142	226

* Historians disagree; where they also disagree over the shortest and longest stages, the figure given is an average.

** Stage shortened by bad weather; shortest unaffected stage: 64km.

DOMESTIQUES

Cyclists realised from the start that it was easier to ride behind someone else than it was to lead. Most of a rider's energy on the flat is spent breaking into the mass of air in front of him. That resistance increases disproportionately with speed, and riders soon learned that taking turns in leading and then sitting behind other riders led to faster races.

The next step, apparent from the first years of the Tour, was to rely not only on like-minded rivals but to employ friendly riders of your own. They are known these days as '*domestiques*', the French word for servants, and many riders have been content to go through their careers in service to others in this way. If they couldn't be sure of winning, they would rather get a reliable wage and a share of the star man's prizes. Domestiques give up their BIKES, chase rivals, and let the stars ride in their slipstreams. The idea that a team works for its leader may be unique to cycling.

The word itself was an insult coined for MAURICE BROCCO in 1911. (*See* entry for details.) Brocco had found himself unable to win the Tour that year, and had offered his help to whoever would pay. HENRI DESGRANGE wanted to throw him out, but couldn't gather enough proof against him. Brocco tried to get back into the organiser's good books by domi-

nating the race thereafter, but the tactic backfired. Desgrange decided that if the man could ride that well, he must surely have sold himself for hire on days of poorer performance. Brocco, he said scathingly, was just a *domestique*, and deserved his disqualification.

Desgrange stood out for a long time against the TACTICS that made domestiques important. It was the way the ALCYON team rode for MAURICE DEWAELE in 1929, securing victory for him even though he was sick, which made Desgrange despair of trade teams and decide instead to organise his race by means of NATIONAL TEAMS.

The gap in Desgrange's logic was that in trying to get rid of one form of team racing, he had merely formalised another. From 1930 the role of the domestique, which in reality had already existed for three decades, was formalised in the Tour as it had long been in other races. But there was a further twist. In sponsored teams, riders were either stars or the helpers of stars, and each knew his job. Most countries had enough sponsored teams to accommodate the nation's best riders, and enough lesser riders to service them.

National teams in the Tour were different, though. Each country, even those like FRANCE, ITALY and BELGIUM which, at least in some years, had more than one team, naturally wanted all their stars to ride together. But patriotism alone wasn't always a strong enough force to bring together in collaboration men who rode all year as rivals, sometimes disliked each other, and always had a commercial interest in being the best.

In Italy, it took ALFREDO BINDA hours of negotiation to get FAUSTO COPPI and GINO BARTALI to cooperate. (*See* Binda entry for details.) In France, JACQUES ANQUETIL would never ride in the same team as RAYMOND POULIDOR. In fact, France was so aware of commercial pressures on its team that only MANAGERS who had no connection with any SPONSOR or team could be selected for the job.

The French manager was MARCEL BIDOT (*see* entry for history and how he chose his teams on a cigarette packet). It was he who formalised the tradition whereby Tour winners should not keep their prizes but give them to their team (see CRITERIUMS for why). Bidot asked each of his riders for a forecast before the 1953 race.

'Can you win?' he asked.

'I don't think so, but I can get in the top five,' they said, and so on.

LOUISON BOBET answered 'Yes, I can win if the rest will block for me. And if I win, I'll give all my prizes to my team-mates.' The rest of the team looked surprised and then dubious, but it was a good offer in a commercial world and nobody had a better one. They consented.

The team's formal agreement eventually read as follows:

Members of the French team give Marcel Bidot the right to collect the prizes and *primes* [intermediary prizes] they win in the Tour. He will share and distribute the sums won *pro rata* with the stages ridden. He will have the right to include a rider who has given total satisfaction before leaving the race for reasons beyond his control. Any rider who does not ride for the team despite several warnings risks having his share of the prizes reduced or total exclusion from the combine. Should a member of the team win, he will give all his prizes to the team except for 200,000 [old] francs which he can keep for his expenses.'

This formalised an arrangement used in ITALY by FAUSTO COPPI in 1949 and by HUGO KOBLET in 1951 and was known as riding 'Italian style'.

STEPHEN ROCHE says he never kept a penny of what he won as team leader, not just in the Tour but in *all* races. 'I was paying a lot of tax. If I won £10,000, I'd have to give half of it to the tax man, so I'd only have £5,000 left. Compared to the wages, the prizes are just an extra, especially after tax, so it meant less to me than other guys. So I used to give 10 per cent to the team staff and the rest to the team for getting me there. That wasn't so common when I started but now it's getting so that it's expected.'

Old-style domestiques, men who slogged endlessly without hope of winning, have all but disappeared. The American writer Jack Olsen wrote of this kind of domestique that he 'may have lost his toenails from the constant forward pressure in his cycling shoes, his backside may be pocked by suppurating ulcers and his mind so addled by amphetamine that he is not sure of his name, but he is a hero, a major athletic figure, a finisher in the Tour de France.'

The British journalist Geoffrey Nicholson wrote, 'To a degree it was an apprenticeship, but many domestiques burnt out whatever talents they had brought into the sport before they had a chance to display them. In compensation, they ate well, dressed well and stayed in better hotels than they would even have entered if they had stayed at home. Above all they enjoyed the reflected glory of famous events and the envy of their peers. But the financial rewards were poor – since there were always more applicants than jobs – and at the end of the season it was back to the farm to wait and see if their contract would be renewed.'

Reasons for the virtual disappearance of old-style domestiques are complex, but they include higher social expectations, education and work conditions. Semi-educated men no longer regard breaking their backs on a bike as the only alternative to back-breaking work on the land. Greater health and fitness mean that more riders are potential winners than before. And that has combined with the World Cup ranking system to make riders as aware of their own chances as of their star's.

The worldwide classification of professionals by result was started in 1984 by the magazine *Vélo* and then adopted by Hein Verbruggen of the UCI (Union Cycliste Internationale) as the basis of the World Cup. The existence of an accurate way of ranking riders has led to a defined bargaining measure, a huge rise in salaries, and a different atmosphere.

MANAGER MARC MADIOT said in 1990, 'Solidarity? Don't make me laugh. I don't believe it. Or rather, I don't believe it exists any more. It's all gone with the way cycling has changed. It was there when I started racing, in 1982. I remember in my first Tour how Maurice Le Guilloux, who had tendinitis, finished the race without once turning the pedals. I can still see him, bouncing from rider to rider as they pushed him in the peloton for two days to Paris. Today, just eight years later, it goes without saying that even his team-mates would have dropped him.'

Riders now reckon that each point they collect in the World Cup is worth as much as £470. Times are hard, or at any rate uncertain, for the handful of riders still prepared to sacrifice their own careers for those of others, though such riders are nevertheless admired. Jacques Michaud of the Swiss team, Phonak, said in 2002 that a few old-style domestiques still exist. 'They're recognised by their managers and their leaders; they're capable of riding at 60km/h when it's needed. Super-domestiques like that are rare on the market but I would rather have someone with no World Cup points and who'll work hard for his team than someone with 200 who'll ride only for himself.'

Even so, there are signs that the old star system is returning. The US Postal team that helped LANCE ARMSTRONG to four successive wins between 1999 and 2002 was in the mould of those of the 1950s and 1960s where riders laid down their life for a friend, or at any rate a boss. Armstrong had the luxury (and the money to buy it) of riding for hours behind a line of team-mates each day as they brought back breakaways. Then, still fresh when his army was wasted, he could ride away alone to victory.

In 1952 the Italian domestique Andrea Carrea became *maillot jaune* by mistake, and was terrified to have won it. FAUSTO COPPI had told him to join in a break of three on the stage from Mulhouse to Lausanne, to keep an eye on it and do nothing to make it go faster. He didn't need to: it won by five minutes even without help from the tall, permanently morose Carrea. This gave the unknown Italian the yellow JERSEY, which he took from another Italian, FIORENZO MAGNI. Carrea had to be pushed up the steps to the podium, terrified of how both Magni and Coppi would react.

PIERRE CHANY wrote, 'At last the peloton put in an appearance, among the riders being Coppi and Magni. When the latter spotted Carrea decked in yellow he scowled and the new leader's teeth began to chatter. Then Coppi slowly finished his ride. He pointed at Carrea and burst into deep laughter. Only then did the poor fellow start waving his bouquet and smiling at the photographers.

'Next morning Carrea was up early and began his day, as usual, by cleaning Coppi's shoes. Later in the afternoon the *campionissimo* [Coppi] overwhelmed the opposition on the ALPE D'HUEZ and put everything back into proper order.'

DOPING

Cycling is built on excess and suffering. No other sport running solely on muscle power lasts as long. Fatigue will make a runner fall over or a high jumper lose his technique, but a bike keeps its rider upright and pedalling. Only rowers, supported by their boats, know anything like it.

The original point of a BIKE race was that it should extend beyond the travel distances of ordinary people, from one city to another so far away that it was known only by name. But originator GÉO LEFÈVRE's conception of the Tour de France was slightly different – a race so much longer than anything else that nobody could top it. His boss HENRI DESGRANGE saw the point clearly. He said a perfect Tour would be so hard that only one rider could finish.

It was hardly surprising that drugs became a feature from the start, given the gruelling conditions, the extravagant prizes (riders could win many times a workman's annual salary) and the riders' scant education. As long ago as 1896, the British manager and coach Choppy Warburton was so strongly implicated in a supposed doping sensation at Catford TRACK in South London that he was banned for life.

Confused and erratic riding by Jimmy Michael, Britain's first world champion, was attributed to the contents of a bottle Warburton had been seen to give him. Warburton had also treated another Welshman, Arthur Linton, in Bordeaux-Paris in May 1896. Linton died two months later and his obituary in *Cyclers'*

News, by 'one who knew him', says, 'I saw him at Tours, half-way through the race, at midnight, where he came in with glassy eyes and tottering limbs, and in a high state of nervous excitement.... At Orléans at five o'clock in the morning, Choppy and I looked after a wreck – a corpse as Choppy called him, yet he had sufficient energy, heart, pluck, call it what you will, to enable him to gain 18 minutes on the last 45 miles of hilly road.'

Only Warburton knows what he gave him, but heroin is the most popular claim. Heroin, cocaine and strychnine were the commonest early drugs but these weren't strictly performance enhancing. Not until anabolic steroids appeared in the 1970s did drugs actually make riders go faster; painkillers that worked on the muscles and, later, amphetamines that worked on the brain, only enabled a rider to ignore the agony of effort. That may have let riders push themselves harder, but there was no physiological change of the sort that steroids and the later more sophisticated drugs were to produce.

Amphetamine was first made in 1887, and its derivative, Benzedrine, appeared in 1934. That was perfectly timed for the second world war, when British troops alone got through 72 million tablets. Production by both sides in the war was so huge that, even though its side-effects (principally impairment of judgement) were so obvious by 1943 that the RAF abandoned it, untold millions of tablets remained available for the commercial market.

Many of these found their way into cycling, being bought and sold between riders, or supplied by medical quacks known as SOIGNEURS. It would be unfair to condemn this practice too much because in 1957 the American Medical Council was reported as saying, 'Clinical experience of more than twenty years had conclusively demonstrated that amphetamine sulphate is one of the safest drugs available to medical practice.'

The problem is that the feeling of well-being produces first mental dependence, and then physical tolerance of increasing doses. The Dutch MANAGER Kees Pellenaars told of a rider at a training camp, 'The boy ... raced as though he was powered by rockets. I asked him if he wasn't perhaps using something and he jumped straight up, climbed on a chair and from deep inside a closet pulled out a plastic bag of pills. There were 5,000 of them, excluding hormone preparations and sleeping pills. I took the 5,000 bombs away, to his own relief. Later he seemed to have taken too many at once and he slept for a couple of days on end. We couldn't wake him up. We took him to hospital and they pumped out his stomach. They tied him to his bed to prevent anything going wrong again. But somehow he had some stimulant and fancied taking a walk. A nurse came across him in the corridor, walking along with the bed strapped to his back.'

The Belgian journalist Willem van Wijnendaele, founder of the Tour of Flanders, wrote of Leandro Faggin in the 1956 world track championships, 'He was in a shocking state half an hour before his ride against the general favourite. . . . His feverish eyes were deep into his face and he kept licking his dry lips as though he had a thirst but nothing to help it. They were signs [of amphetamine doping] that no doctor could mistake, and we all knew he had taken something. I pointed him out to several colleagues and in no time there was a crowd of soigneurs, journalists and managers, all having a look. Someone shouted, "Nobody smoke in case there's an explosion . . .".' Faggin died aged just 37.

FAUSTO COPPI said on television that he had taken drugs only 'when necessary'. Asked how often that was, he replied: 'Almost always.'

Changing attitudes, and above all the work of PIERRE DUMAS, made dope tests inevitable. Tests in BELGIUM during 1965 showed 37 per cent of professionals were using drugs. Yet the first tests in the Tour, in 1966, led riders to STRIKE against what they saw as interference in their personal freedom. Events were against them, however. JEAN MALLÉJAC had collapsed on MONT VENTOUX in 1955 and been taken to hospital with his mouth foaming, his body twitching and his legs still turning phantom pedals. Then came TOM SIMPSON's death on the same mountain in 1967. Colin Lewis, who shared his hotel room, recalled how his leader had paid a pusher more for one consignment of amphetamine than Lewis was paid all year to ride his bike.

Even so JACQUES ANQUETIL argued that Simpson had died not because of the amphetamine and alcohol he had taken, but because the culture of drug-testing meant he couldn't use 'safer' drugs of his own choice. It was an odd argument and not widely accepted, but it speaks much about the attitude of the time that it could have been made at all.

It became easy to detect amphetamine, although it was still used, and a race now began for drugs that couldn't be detected. Variations on anabolic steroids became popular, and cyclists began to change in appearance from emaciated men with thin skin and sunken cheeks (amphetamine is an appetite suppressant) to muscular men with crash wounds that took a strangely long time to heal (a symptom of steroid use).

It took considerable time to perfect a test for steroids. But in 1978 three riders were caught at the world championship and, after a chase through the medical textbooks to find odder and odder drugs of the same family, the emphasis moved in the late 1980s to drugs which worked on the blood.

The basic equation is that the more oxygen that blood can carry, the more power goes to muscles. The most popular drug that assisted this process was EPO, which at first proved impossible to detect. Under EPO's influence the Tour changed from a race where riders struggled in the MOUNTAINS, their mouths gasping for air, to an event where they appeared to cruise without effort. The best that doctors could do was to set a limit to red corpuscles in the blood (the haematocrit level) and to suspend riders who exceeded it.

In 1998 customs officials stopped the soigneur WILLY VOET with a carload of EPO and other drugs destined for the Festina team (*see* FESTINA AFFAIR), and police raids, arrests and walkouts almost brought the Tour to an end. Next year CHRISTOPHE BASSONS (*see* his entry for details) was hounded out of the Tour for speaking out about EPO use. But the EPO era started to close in 1999 when doctors at Châtenay-Malabry, France, perfected a test for discovering it.

Many riders, grand and unknown, have tried to cheat the tests. MICHEL POLLENTIER was found with a contraption of rubber tubes attached to a bottle of someone else's urine after he had won the yellow JERSEY on ALPE D'HUEZ in 1978. Willy Voet, in his book *Massacre à la Chaine* (*Breaking the Chain* in the legally censored English-language version) tells of a classic winner (named in the French version) who was found positive because the mechanic who had supplied the urine (concealed up the rider's backside in a condom with a tube attached for urinary realism) had himself whiled away the tedium of the race by dipping into the team's drug stocks.

In 2000 the SOCIÉTÉ DU TOUR DE FRANCE was criticised during the Festina trials for doing too little. So in 2001 it paid for anti-doping campaigns, lectured riders and officials before the START in Dunkirk, and made competitors sign an anti-drug agreement.

What concerns campaigners today is the uncertainty about the side-effects of the new 'body-altering' drugs. Drug-taking in the amphetamine era was self-limiting, because a rider who took too much wouldn't sleep and would have to abandon the race. Amphetamine was taken for a specific performance, and for most the consequences were short-term. But it is too soon to assess the long-term medical consequences of the drugs of the modern era. Early takers of anabolic steroids are only now in middle age and there is no certainty what will happen to users of EPO and the catalogue of other dubious substances that riders pump into themselves in the pursuit of cycling glory.

(*See* BIANCHI, PDM AFFAIR, PAUL DUBOC, PIERRE DUMAS, FESTINA AFFAIR, ALBERT LONDRES, JEAN MALLÉJAC, GERT-JAN THEUNISSE, WIEL'S AFFAIR.)

> ***Trivia note:*** a drug-taker is a *chaudière* (a boiler) and has *allumé les phares* (turned on his headlights).

JEAN DOTTO

b. St-Nazaire, France, Mar 27 1928, d. Ollioules, France, Feb 20 2000

Jean-Baptiste Dotto, born in FRANCE of Italian nationality but naturalised in 1937, was a classy CLIMBER and in 1955 became the first French-man to win the Tour of SPAIN. Dotto rode 13 Tours and finished fourth in 1954 behind LOUISON BOBET. His wife, who chronicled his career, calculated that he had led over 68 cols, which made him arguably the best French climber of all time. Despite that he never wore the MOUNTAINS JERSEY. He retired to run a bar in Cabasse, from where he looked out onto the square named after him. He died in February 2000 after a long illness. (*See* MEMORIALS for other riders' tributes.)

Winner

1952	Dauphiné Libéré
1955	Tour Spain
1960	Dauphiné Libéré

Tour de France

1951	23rd	
1952	8th	
1953	DNF	
1954	4th	Stage win Briançon—Aix-les-Bains
1955	DNF	
1956	19th	
1957	10th	
1958	DNF	
1959	15th	
1960	35th	
1961	8th	
1962	58th	
1963	28th	

PAUL DUBOC

b. Rouen, France, Apr 2 1884, d. Paris, France, Aug 1 1941

Sometimes riders blossom late. The French-man Paul Duboc was just such a case. In 1911 he was 27, a former carpenter, and not regarded

as a threat even though he'd come 11th in the 1908 Tour and fourth in that of 1909.

But in the 1911 Tour he rode into his own near the Mediterranean, and won the stage into Perpignan. Next day came the first stage in the Pyrenees, and he broke clear on the Portet d'Aspet and won in Luchon. That took him to within seven points of the leader, GUSTAVE GARRIGOU. The race was then decided on points rather than time, and Duboc could easily make up seven points on the next day's epic stage that crossed the Peyresourde, Aspin, TOURMALET and AUBISQUE on the way to Bayonne.

Duboc attacked immediately the stage started at 3:30am. He had 10 minutes over the Tourmalet, dropped to the FEEDING AREA at Barèges, and rode on to Argelès and the Aubisque. And there, climbing the open-sided road, he wobbled and fell in front of a car which only just missed him. Duboc lay on the road, and began writhing with vomiting and diar-rhoea. Riders kept passing all the time as he lay there for an hour and a quarter, but couldn't intervene because giving or receiving help would bring disqualification.

In the end his MANAGER, Paul Ruinart, despaired and gave him an emetic to clear his stomach completely. Duboc, still groggy, wobbled off to the stage finish, zigzagging from the verge to the open drop. Extraordinarily, he still finished the stage 21st, 3hr 47min behind MAURICE BROCCO and Garrigou. (*See* MAURICE BROCCO for his role in coining the word *domestique*.)

Rumours spread instantly, with many blam-ing Garrigou, since he seemed the only obvious beneficiary. Duboc had clearly been poisoned, and Garrigou, therefore, must have done it. Angry crowds shouted and threatened Gar-rigou as the race passed. The Tour provided the leader with a bodyguard, but matters got worse as the race approached Duboc's home town of Rouen. Notices had been posted in his name there, proclaiming, 'Citizens of Rouen, I would be leading the race if I hadn't been poisoned. You know what you have to do when the race crosses the city.' They were signed in Duboc's name.

In fact Garrigou was innocent, and he and Duboc – who had recovered quickly – were eating at neighbouring tables in La Rochelle when news of the threats reached them. Duboc offered to go ahead and calm the city. But HENRI DESGRANGE hit on another idea and disguised Garrigou with a moustache, new vest and different goggles. Then he asked the bunch to stay together until after Rouen, with Garrigou in its centre. The mob looked for Garrigou but failed to spot him. Fights started when people realised they had been fooled. But it was too late. Garrigou won the Tour and Duboc came second, 18 points down.

So who did it? There had been a control point in Argelès, and Duboc remembered taking a bottle from SPECTATORS chanting his name as he signed the book. It could have been anyone who'd given it to him. But someone must have arranged it; someone must have poisoned the drink. In time suspicion fell on FRANCOIS LAFOURCADE, a man with a reputation for 'wonder' drinks. Lafourcade is said to have confessed some years later and was banned for life, but the details were never published. (*See* MOUNTAINS for Lafourcade's more honourable part in Tour history.)

Duboc carried on riding the Tour until 1927, when he was 43, but never won it. He then stopped racing, went back to work as a carpenter and died from a work injury in 1941.

Winner

1909 Tour Belgium

Tour de France

1908	11th	
1909	4th	Stage win Brest—Caen
1911	2nd	Stage wins Marseille—Perpignan, Perpignan—Luchon, Bayonne—La Rochelle, Cherbourg—Le Havre
1912	DNF	
1913	DNF	
1914	31st	
1919	8th	
1923	18th	
1926	27th	
1927	DNF	

LAURENT DUFAUX
b. Montreux, Switzerland, May 20 1969

Dufaux has been a professional for 12 years, winning the Dauphiné Libéré twice and stages in the Tours of France and SPAIN. His career ended under a cloud, when he was suspended for seven months after the FESTINA AFFAIR. He returned to finish fourth in both the Tour de France and Tour of Spain in 1999, but in a season without wins. He said he would retire at the end of 2001, when he was 32, because of a prostate problem, but he reappeared to ride the Tour again in 2002, and didn't finish.

Winner

1991	Coppa Placci, Route Sud, National championship
1993	Dauphiné Libéré
1994	Dauphiné Libéré
1995	Route Sud, Tour Burgos
1998	Midi Libre, Tour Romandie
2000	Championship Zurich

Tour de France

1992	DNF	
1994	35th	
1995	19th	
1996	4th	Stage win Argelès-Gazost—Pamplona
1997	9th	
1998	DNF	
1999	4th	
2000	DNF	
2002	DNF	

Trivia note: the 1908 rider Marcel Berthet, who didn't finish the race, was also poisoned. In his case it was by his servant, who had dosed him with arsenic for seven years. He survived. Nobody knows what happened to the servant.

PIERRE DUMAS

More than anyone else in cycling, Pierre Dumas exposed the extent of drug-taking in the sport and fought against it, often with bitter opposition from riders themselves.

Dumas became head of the Tour medical service in 1952 when he was offered the job at short notice. Until then he had been more of a judo fan, a black belt, and he knew little of cycling. But in July 1952 he cancelled his climbing holiday in the Alps and went straight to the race.

Dumas was medical chief of the Tour until 1969, and head of DOPING controls until 1977. It was an era, he said, which began with 'magic, medicine and sorcery', and ended with steroids.

'When I came to the Tour in 1952,' he said, 'there were SOIGNEURS, fakirs, who came from the six-days. Their value was in the contents of their case, which was their commercial worth. Riders took anything they were given, even bee stings and toad extract. In 1953 and 1954 it was all magic, medicine and sorcery. After that they started reading drug catalogues.' Then came amphetamines and cocktails of drugs. 'This was the second period, semi-scientific. They'd take cocktails, painkillers and then a stimulant, then something to overcome the effects and help them sleep,' he said.

The extent of the problem was explained by the French MANAGER, MARCEL BIDOT: 'Three-quarters of the riders [in the 1950s] were doped. I am well placed to know since I visit their rooms each evening during the Tour. I always left frightened after these visits.'

Some of it was pure quackery. Dumas spoke of 'medicine from the heart of Africa ... healers laying on hands or giving out irradiating balms, feet plunged into unbelievable mixtures which could lead to eczema, so-called magnetised diets, and everything else you could imagine.' Riders injected themselves with drugs in front of him because they saw nothing wrong with the practice itself, or the dirty needles they used, or any of the drugs they employed.

In 1959 Dumas intercepted a package – addressed to a soigneur – that contained enough strychnine 'to kill a whole regiment'.

On another occasion he found 50 capsules of amphetamine on its way to a soigneur who had looked after JACQUES ANQUETIL. The soigneur told him the drugs were for his own use.

'I offered to inject him myself,' Dumas explained in an interview with the Tour paper L'ÉQUIPE, 'but he refused. I said, "You're a little shit, you are; it's fine for the other guys but not for you."'

In 1960 Dumas found the Italian rider GASTONE NENCINI receiving a primitive blood transfusion in his hotel room, following a technique practised by Scandinavian long-distance runners. This involved giving blood, storing it, and then transfusing it back into themselves in order to restore their lost red corpuscles. The result was supercharged blood of the sort that EPO (see DOPING) would later mimic chemically.

Dumas was not happy that such practices were being carried out by unqualified team-helpers. Convinced that the practice went beyond just one rider, he met the team's doctors after the FINISH at Briançon and tried to intervene. This was reputed to be the world's first meeting between a drugs campaigner and sports doctors or faux-doctors.

In 1964 Dumas led the International Sports Medicine Federation's demands to the sport's governing body, the UCI (Union Cycliste Internationale), that it should test riders in the 100km team TIME TRIAL at the Olympic Games in Tokyo. It was in the 100km race at the Games in Rome in 1960 that a Danish rider, Knut Enemark Jensen, had collapsed and died. Jensen had taken amphetamine and a drug called Ronicol, which dilated blood vessels. The combination was fatal in the Italian heat.

The tests in Tokyo weren't important for the results – in fact only inoffensive drugs were found – because there were as yet no drugs limitations at the Olympics. But it was the first time tests had been conducted at such a large event, thanks largely to Dumas. The tests were carried out under the supervision of four officials from the UCI and the French sports minister, Maurice Herzog.

Dumas and Herzog were already working on FRANCE's first anti-doping law. It was published in November 1964, and known as *la loi Herzog*. Charles de Gaulle passed it in July 1965 with only one change, from the English-sounding *le doping* to *le dopage*. It demanded that a competitor in any sport 'submit to any inspection, even without notice, in particular to any clinical or biological examination of their person.'

The law, hurriedly passed and not based on experience, was full of loopholes. Its definitions were weak and there were too many chances for riders to claim that they had been drugged by someone else – a bottle handed up by SPECTATORS was always a popular excuse – and were therefore victims rather than culprits.

The clumsiness of the Tour's first drug controls at BORDEAUX in 1966 added fuel to riders' claims that their privacy and right of choice were being transgressed, and it led to a STRIKE. In addition to the traditional strikers' chants and protests there was a personal as well as professional dimension to the campaign against Dumas. The extent of the protest, and the risk it posed to the good order of the race, laid the Tour authorities open to charges that they were lukewarm about Dumas's tests.

Things changed when TOM SIMPSON died on MONT VENTOUX on July 13 1967. Dumas, alerted by a policeman who told him there had been a *pépin* (a bit of a fuss), found Simpson apparently dead on the roadside. He gave him oxygen and artificial respiration but Simpson – whom Dumas said was 'well known' as a drug-taker – didn't respond.

From then on Dumas had the law and public sentiment on his side, although for many years he had still not won round many of the riders (*see* RUDI ALTIG for an example). The medical service expanded, and Dumas was joined in

1972 by Gérard Porte, who became the service's head in 1982 and remains so today. Dumas retired in 1997 and died an invalid in eastern Paris, aged 78, in February 2000.

JACKY DURAND
b. Laval, France, Feb 10 1967

There are two ways to make a name and please SPONSORS. You win, or you fail with flair. The chunky Frenchman Jacky 'Dudu' Durand lacks the ability to do the first dependably – although he won the Tour of Flanders in 1992 – but his talent at the second is incomparable. So much so that the magazine *Vélo* runs a monthly 'Jacky-metre', set out like a car odometer. By the end of 2001 it showed he had ridden 32,177km, raced 16,524km, and been in breaks for 2,270km.

No stage is too inconsequential, except in the MOUNTAINS, for Durand to spend hours in the lead by himself or with a few others. He is often swept up in the last half an hour, or is too tired to win even if the break does stay away. But the time he spends under the TV camera justifies his wages.

'I've spent my whole career knowing I'll never win the Tour,' he said in 2000, 'so I rely on my media value. If I do something, it gets in the papers. Sometimes, 100km of riding alone in the Tour de France has more significance than a win in another race.'

That 'except in the mountains' is significant. Durand is too tall – 1.86m – to be a good CLIMBER, but he has developed his own techniques. There were complaints in 2001 that he had, to put it tactfully, made the most of cars and motorbikes alongside him on the cols. In 2002 race officials caught him red-handed on the 12th stage, hanging on to a team car on the stage to Plateau de Beille. (*See* CHEATS for other wheezes.)

It hadn't done him a lot of good – he finished 162nd of 167 left in the race – but it kept him within the time limit. Officials threw him out along with the car's driver, Martial Gayant (*see* LAURENT JALABERT), and fined Durand the equivalent of £90.

But there have been stage wins as well. Two came in trademark breakaways, the third when he set the fastest time among the early starters in the St-Brieuc prologue in 1995 and then saw the rain wash out the favourites' hopes.

Winner

1991 GP Isbergues
1992 Tour Flanders
1993 National championship
1994 National championship
1998 Paris-Tours

Tour de France

1992 119th
1993 121st
1994 DNF Stage win Bergerac—Cahors
1995 DNF Stage win St-Brieuc—St-Brieuc, and Yellow Jersey
1996 115th
1998 65th Stage win Brive—Montauban
1999 141st
2000 74th
2001 127th Mountains leader
2002 DNF

DYNAPOST

You can write to riders during the Tour by addressing your envelope with the name, the stage town and then 'Dynapost, France'. Allow time for it to reach France and then another couple of days. A mobile sorting office at each stage FINISH will deliver your mail. Metal racks for each team are emptied a couple of hours after each day's racing. The most popular rider ever is RICHARD VIRENQUE, who got 1,800 letters a year at his peak but only 589 in 2000. Dynapost is part of *La Poste*, the French post office.

In 1906 the Tour offered to post the result of each stage to anyone who sent 50 centimes in stamps or a prepaid envelope.

MARTIN EARLEY

b. Dublin, Ireland, Jun 15 1962

Martin Earley was Ireland's Third Man, the one always forgotten in pub quizzes after SEAN KELLY and STEPHEN ROCHE. (In fact he was the Fourth Man, since SHAY ELLIOTT preceded all of them, but he was of a different era.)

Earley showed promise with 12 AMATEUR wins in FRANCE, and rode the first of seven Tours in 1985. He was a DOMESTIQUE rather than a leader, but he did win a stage in 1989 when he was riding for Kelly in the PDM team. Earley broke clear of three riders 750m from the end of the stage from La Bastide d'Armagnac to Pau. (See MEMORIALS and HENRY ANGLADE for the significance of this village in cycling history.)

In 1991 Earley was one of the first of the team to pull out of the race in a mysterious mass withdrawal that became known as the PDM AFFAIR (see entry for more). The circumstances were never satisfyingly explained.

Earley rode in the 1992 Tour, finished 80th, and retired to open a practice as a sports therapist in Stoke-on-Trent, England.

Tour de France

1985	60th
1986	46th
1987	65th
1988	DNF

Tour de France (continued)

1989	44th	Stage win La Bastide d'Armagnac—Pau
1990	DNF	
1991	DNF	
1992	80th	

EARPIECES

The use of earpieces – *oreillettes* in French – is controversial. Riders – some, not all, because a few don't like the concept – tape the earpiece in place and carry a radio weighing 200–350gm in their jersey pocket. To it is linked a microphone, which is either clipped on the outside of the jersey or more usually on the braces of a rider's shorts. Riders can then talk to and receive instructions from their MANAGERS as they ride. Effective transmission is up to seven kilometres, although this may go down to three kilometres in bad weather and sometimes less in the MOUNTAINS.

The radios aren't perfect. They work fine when a rider is stationary but less predictably when he is on the move.

The idea of wiring up riders first occurred to the American coach Ed Burke. His pursuit team for the world TRACK championships in 1988 turned up with small radios in their helmets so they could hear his instructions from the grandstand. Like tri-bars (see BIKES), earpieces came into use before the sport's governing body, the UCI, could make a decision about them, and it was some time before it decided to ban them on the track.

The use of two-way radios was popularised on the road by the Motorola team in 1992 (Motorola makes mobile phones). The manager, Jim Ochowicz, fitted out PHIL ANDERSON with a receiver the size of a cigarette packet, which was carried in his jersey pocket with a wire to an earpiece. Under his saddle was a transmitter with a range of a little more than a kilometre.

Paul Sherwen, the team spokesman, said, 'It's all standard Motorola equipment. The listener is based on one of our pagers. We've given up on helmet radios because this is easy to set up and it means the rider doesn't have to wear a helmet.'

Others in the Tour experimented with conventional mobile phones. These were larger then and much heavier, so the idea didn't catch on. But mobile phones were still banned, it's said, after race officials caught MARIO CIPOLLINI phoning friends in the middle of a race.

Motorola's advantage in having earpieces showed when Anderson punctured on one stage and his call to Ochowicz came 30 seconds before the news came on RADIO TOUR. It was then only a matter of time and technological progress before everyone went the same way. Other companies began experimenting with race radios – the Swiss audio equipment company Phonak even sponsors a Tour team – and they are now so general that, though the UCI doesn't like the idea and has banned them for under-19s because of a fear they would diminish the value of tactical experience, there seems little chance of turning back the clock.

Some would like to do just that, saying they take spontaneity and the advantage of riders' experience out of racing, creating riders who are the puppets of the managers watching the race on TV as they follow in their cars. These critics point out how they helped destroy Alex Zülle's hope of winning the Tour in 1999 after a CRASH on a slippery road between the island of Noirmoutier and the mainland, when a dozen riders fell. Teammates of ABRAHAM OLANO and LANCE ARMSTRONG were told to attack, and they were able to react unnaturally quickly because of earpieces, say critics, with the result that Zülle lost six minutes.

BERNARD HINAULT says that with earpieces 'riders become no more than simply pedalling machines'. Earpieces 'lessen the importance of a rider's tactical sense'.

Supporters of earpieces deny they have a bad influence and say that talking to riders this way prevents the need to drive beside them in the race. Vincent Lavenu, manager of the AG2R team, said in 2002, 'I consider it a real plus when it comes to TACTICS. Riders have access to much more information with earpieces. And they can react much faster to changes in the race. Before that, the manager had to drive up alongside the race, approach a rider, discuss what to do, and in that time the break could get several minutes.'

Michel Gros, boss of the French Jean Delatour team, said older riders take longer to get used to earpieces. Some, like ANDREI TCHMIL, always refused, but younger ones accept them as normal.

There are no agreed frequencies, and teams trade wavelengths at the start of each season. They also use scanners to eavesdrop on rivals.

(*See* BLACKBOARD MAN.)

PAUL EGLI
b. Durnten, Switzerland, Aug 18 1911, d. Durnten, Switzerland, Jan 23 1997

Egli was first Swiss to wear the yellow JERSEY, which he collected when he won the opening stage in 1936 from Paris to Lille in a storm. He also came second in the WORLD CHAMPIONSHIP in 1938, and third in 1937, but he never again did well in the Tour.

Winner

1934 Championship Zurich
1935 Championship Zurich, National championship
1936 National championship
1942 Champion Zurich

Tour de France

1936	DNF	Stage win Paris—Lille, and Yellow Jersey
1937	29th	
1938	31st	

VJATCHESLAV EKIMOV
b. Vyborg, USSR, Feb 4 1966

In January 2001 Russia named Vjatcheslav Ekimov its rider of the 20th century. It was an honour nobody disputed except perhaps on chronological grounds, since he had been born in the USSR, which had come into being only in 1917. And the Russian Federation which awarded him the title was founded only in 1991, a year after Ekimov turned professional.

Although 12 Tour rides from 1990 never saw him finish better than 18th (1995), he did win the stage from Aix-les-Bains to Mâcon in 1991. He also won stages of the Tour of Spain and the Tour of Switzerland in 1999 and came second in the 1998 Tour of Holland.

He won the 1990 world pursuit championship and the individual TIME TRIAL on the last day of the Sidney Olympics in September 2000.

Winner

1992	Championship Zurich
1994	Veenendaal-Veenendaal
1996	Three Days De Panne
1997	National championship
1988	Tour Regio
2000	Olympic time-trial, Three Days De Panne, GP Merckx

Tour de France

1990	55th	
1991	42nd	Stage win Aix-les-Bains—Mâcon
1992	65th	
1993	35th	
1994	36th	
1995	18th	
1996	21st	
1997	44th	

Tour de France (continued)

1998	38th
2000	55th
2001	82nd
2002	58th

ALBERTO ELLI
b. Guissano, Italy, Mar 9 1964

Determination pays. Alberto Elli rode his first Tour in 1990, and rode it every year for a decade without even a stage win. Then in the first race of the new millennium he took the yellow JERSEY. It was quite something for someone who had won only 25 races (other than CRITERIUMS) since turning professional in 1987, although he did come second in the Italian national championships of 1998 and 1999, and in Milan-San Remo in 1997.

Elli rode his first 10 seasons in Italian teams before moving to FRANCE and the Casino team in 1997. He then moved to GERMANY and Deutsche Telekom.

Winner

1993	Trofeo Matteotti
1996	Tour Luxembourg
1997	Midi Libre
1998	Tour Murcia
2000	GP Wallonia, Tour Luxembourg

Tour de France

1990	72nd	
1991	91st	
1992	28th	
1993	17th	
1994	7th	
1995	33rd	
1996	15th	
1997	30th	
1998	29th	
1999	17th	
2000	84th	Yellow Jersey

SHAY ELLIOTT
b. Dublin, Ireland, Jun 4 1934, d. Dublin, Ireland, May 4 1971

In 1998, when the Tour rode through Kilmaconogue in Co Wicklow, Ireland, the organiser JEAN-MARIE LEBLANC walked into the village churchyard to lay a wreath on the grave of Shay Elliott, IRELAND's Tour de France pioneer.

Elliott went to race in FRANCE when abroad truly was a different place; cars were loaded aboard ferries by crane, and borders required passports and customs formalities. He became the first Irishman to wear the yellow JERSEY, and in 1962 would have been WORLD CHAMPION at Salo in ITALY had he not given the victory to his brother-in-law JEAN STABLINSKI of France. Even PIERRE CHANY, who was hardly likely to side against a Frenchman, said Elliott was 'in superb condition'.

Elliott's career started as oddly as it ended. In 1954 he walked onto the stage of the Gresham Hotel in Dublin, a round-faced 19-year-old, to receive congratulations for being best CLIMBER in the recently completed Tour of Ireland. It was an odd moment, because there was no prize to give him. And it was an odd success for a rider who hardly had a climber's whippet-like shape. Instead, he was promised a month at the Simplex training camp in Monte Carlo.

Simplex was then one of the biggest makers of GEARS, and it had engaged the old 1930s pro CHARLES PÉLISSIER, brother of the more turbulent HENRI PÉLISSIER, to pass on his wisdom to AMATEURS from all over Europe. The 1947 Tour winner JEAN ROBIC and the then un-known CHARLY GAUL visited the camp from time to time.

Elliott set off from Victoria station in London on January 1 1955 and registered his bike through to Monte Carlo, where it would arrive two days after him, having transferred trains in Paris. After spending his time at the camp, he threw in his job as a panel-beater near his home at Crumeley, Dublin, moved briefly to Nice, and then went to the ACBB club in the Paris suburb of Boulogne-Billancourt where accommodation was arranged for him by the journalist Jean Leulliot, organiser of Paris-

Nice. (*See* STEPHEN ROCHE for another Irishman whose path to the top was through the ACBB.) Elliott won numerous races, including the prestigious Paris-Evreux, and that December ended his AMATEUR career at the Vélodrome d'Hiver in Paris with the world 10km record.

He won his first pro race, the GP Isbergues, in 1956. In 1958 he won the points competition in Paris-Nice and then in 1959 won the Belgian semi-classic Het Volk by riding the last 30km with just FRED DE BRUYNE. In 1962 he showed his class by leading the Tour of SPAIN for nine days and finishing third.

Elliott was sturdy in the style of old-time *flahutes*, the name given to 1930s Belgian riders who never weakened whatever the conditions. He had the strength to influence any race and enough of a sprint to win it. That he did less than he might have done had to do with Elliott's own financial circumstances.

Elliott found his talent could more dependably be turned to profit by selling it to others. (*See* MAURICE BROCCO.) In the autumn of 1962 he broke away in the world championship with his brother-in-law, JEAN STABLINSKI, and declined to chase when the Frenchman attacked. 'I couldn't chase my friend,' he said as he collected his silver medal. But there may have been more to it than friendship. Apart from anything else, both rode for the same SPONSOR, the Helyett cycle company.

The favour was repaid during the Tour de France in 1963. Stablinski slowed a break for Elliott to get back after he had punctured. Six kilometres from the FINISH at Roubaix, he let Elliott attack and win not only the stage but Ireland's first yellow jersey. In three days he had lost it, but he'd never had any illusions.

He could have won the 445km London-Holyhead in 1965, but instead blocked Albert Hitchen in the sprint to let TOM SIMPSON win. Pictures show him braking to hold back Hitchen and let Simpson by. Elliott never let talent take him as high it could, because there was more money in renting it to others. Ironically, in the end money worries were his undoing.

When Elliott's marriage to Stablinski's sister

Marguerite started to falter, he moved from Paris to Loctudy in Brittany, where his money disappeared in a failed hotel venture, and little more came in as his talent dwindled. He accepted a cheque from the *Sunday People* to spill the beans on DOPING and bribery.

'I knew times were hard for him,' said JOCK WADLEY, who had known him since sharing his room at the Simplex camp, 'but nobody knew just how hard until he had to do that.' The article, bland though it was, made things worse because the peloton ostracised him and made it clear he would never again win a race on the Continent. Those who snubbed him included many he had helped.

He returned to Dublin in 1967 when he was 33, and set up a metalworking business with his father. Two years later his wife Marguerite returned to France, and Elliott tried a racing comeback in BRITAIN. In April 1971 his father died, and Elliott was found dead soon afterwards in his garage with a shotgun beside him.

Winner

1956	GP Isbergues
1958	GP Sigrand
1959	Het Volk, Manx Trophy, GP Denain
1965	Tour Oise

Tour De France

1956	DNF	
1958	48th	
1959	DNF	
1961	47th	
1963	61st	Stage win Jambes—Roubaix, and Yellow Jersey
1964	DNF	

JOSÉ-MARIA ERRANDONEA
b. Irun, Spain, Dec 12 1940

Sometimes history is made in a moment, while the fame of it lasts little longer. The Tour's first PROLOGUE, at Angers in 1967, was won by SPAIN's now forgotten José-Maria Errandonea. It seemed for a long time that RAYMOND POULIDOR had won it and would take his first yellow JERSEY. Then Errandonea beat him by six seconds.

It was the only mark he made on the Tour. He was afflicted by a boil and pulled out minutes after the start of the third stage and never rode the race again.

Tour de France

1966	56th	
1967	DNF	Stage win Angers—Angers, and Yellow Jersey

FERNANDO ESCARTIN
b. Biescas, Spain, Jan 24 1968

Find a MOUNTAIN on a hot day, and Fernando Escartin was your man. Escartin came third in the 1999 Tour after winning the Piau-Engaly stage in the Pyrenees. He was 31, and was probably convinced such a thing would never happen.

Escartin spent years riding for TONY ROMINGER, and then led the Spanish KELME team. Like LUCIEN VAN IMPE, he showed no ambition to win the Tour itself and seemed happy to follow the best through the mountains. Then things changed, and by his 11th season he had become an attacker who could leave rivals suffering.

However, as so often for a climber, his ambitions were limited by poor TIME TRIALS.

Winner

1995	Tour Aragon, Tour Mining Valleys
1997	Tour Catalonia

Tour de France

1992	45th	
1993	30th	
1994	12th	
1995	7th	
1996	8th	
1997	5th	
1998	DNF	
1999	3rd	Stage win Saint-Gaudens—Piau-Engaly
2000	8th	

JACQUES ESCLASSAN
b. Castres, France, Sep 3 1948

Jacques Esclassan of FRANCE rode for the PEU-GEOT team throughout his professional career, from 1972 to 1979, and won 26 races. They included a stage of the Tour of SPAIN (1973) and stages of the Tour de France every year from 1975 to 1978. He was a talented team man who won the Tour's Points competition in 1977.

Winner

1974 Étoile Bessèges
1975 Critérium International
1977 Route Sud

Tour de France

1973	68th	
1974	75th	
1975	DNF	Stage win Versailles—Le Mans
1976	80th	Stage win Beaulieu—Divonne
1977	28th	Stage win Morcenx—Bordeaux, and Points winner
1978	61st	Stage wins Brussels—St-Amand-les-Eaux, Valence d'Agen—Toulouse
1979	DNF	

ÉTAPE DU TOUR

The *Étape du Tour* (Tour stage) is the chance for wannabes and Sunday racers to tackle a stage of the Tour. The magazine *Vélo* organises a mass ride – a race for those in front, survival for the other 6,500 – over the route of one of each year's stages, usually two or three days before the race tackles the stage. Riders start in bunches of 500 with a time limit – generally about 12 hours – according to the length and severity of the ride. The 'winner' of the first *Étape* was Christophe Rinero, who won the MOUNTAINS competition in the Tour in 1998.

The route is named a few weeks after the Tour PRESENTATION in Paris, and entries open at the start of the year. Accommodation in the START town fills within weeks. Details are available on www.letapedutour.com

DAVID ETXEBARRIA
b. Abadiano, Spain, Jul 23 1973

A minuscule CLIMBER, 1.63m tall with a fearsome finishing sprint, David Etxebarria won the Bicyclette Basque in June 1999 and at that year's Tour won two stages: a hilly day into St-Flour and then another into Pau. But it was a single flare of talent. In 1997 he didn't finish and he came no better than 34th in 2001 and 60th in 2002 when leading the Basque Euskaltel team. He is ambitious, and has been described by his colleagues as a perfectionist, but Etxebarria is really in his element in races of up to a week. The three weeks of the Tour are too long and and the mountains too tough for him to shine.

Winner

1996 Tour Avenir
1999 Bicyclette Basque

Tour de France

1997	DNF	
1999	12th	Stage wins St-Galmier—St-Flour, Lannemazan—Pau
2000	DNF	
2001	34th	
2002	60th	

ÉVIAN

The French city of Évian on the banks of Lake Geneva was the first city outside Paris to run the START of the Tour, which had always started in Paris before. (*See* CHAMPS ELYSÉES, MONTGERON and PARC DES PRINCES for more.) This is how it happened.

In 1926 HENRI DESGRANGE was walking through the corridor of his race headquarters when he crossed with Luzien Cazalis, his assistant.

'We've got to reduce the time between the Alps and getting to Paris,' Desgrange said. 'Riders in bunched promenades do nothing for excitement or morale and bore the public.'

'Shame you can't move the MOUNTAINS, then,' Cazalis joked.

Even Desgrange couldn't move mountains, but he could move the start – to Évian. Riders went from Paris by train and officials by car. The Tour then circuited FRANCE anticlockwise before returning to Évian and riding via Dijon to Paris. It added up to 5,745km in 17 stages, the longest Tour there'd been, and included a 433km day from Metz to Dunkirk. The winner was LUCIEN BUYSSE who, in the words of JACQUES AUGENDRE, 'imposed his superiority in the infernal stage of four Pyrenean cols from Bayonne to Luchon under glacial rain.'

Évian, a spa town, supplied the Tour's water and drinking bottles during the 1960s. (*See* CAFÉ RAIDS, FEEDING AREAS.)

FRANÇOIS FABER

b. Aulnay-sur-Iton, Luxembourg, Jan 26 1887,
d. Garency, France, May 9 1915

François Faber rode through knee-deep puddles, won in the mountains in a gale that twice blew him off his bike, and ran to the FINISH with a bike that had a broken chain. That was in 1909. His MANAGER, Alphonse Baugé, called him 'the god who came down to ride a bicycle.' He was the 'Giant of Colombes', a man so popular in the Tour's pioneering years that he received 300 letters after each race and, after his heroism of 1909, poems and marriage proposals as well. (*See* PHILIPPE THYS for Baugé's role in the mystery of the *maillot jaune*.)

Colombes is a suburb of north-western Paris, on the banks of the Seine, and Faber was the 'Giant of Colombes' because he lived there. But in fact he was from LUXEMBOURG, having been born in that country in 1887. He was 'the Giant' because he was 1.86m and 91kg, enormous for the era.

He rode his first Tour in 1906 when he was 19, and in 1908 became the first foreigner in the top three. In 1909, aged 22, he became the first foreign winner. No victory could have been tougher. It rained day after day. Snow, rain, wind, mud and frost created knee-deep ruts that sent 50 riders home in a week. Freezing rain fell for all 398km of the second stage from Roubaix to Metz, but Faber rode the last 200km alone. He rode 110km of the next day by himself as well, over the iciness of the BALLON D'ALSACE, and finished 33 minutes ahead of the next man.

The next day 3,000 SPECTATORS turned out at 2am to watch him start. He rode the Col de Porte in 70 minutes in a gale which twice blew him off, and despite being knocked down by a horse which kicked his bike 15 metres away. He rode on despite potholes, puddles which covered his calves, and broken chains. Twenty thousand fans waited for him at Lyon, reaching for him, trying to touch him.

He took all five stages between Roubaix and Nice, all alone, and also won into BORDEAUX. At the PARC DES PRINCES his chain broke again and he ran more than a kilometre to the FINISH. Spectators rose to their feet to cheer him (*see* HONORÉ BARTHÉLEMY for another man mobbed at the Parc). He would have won the following year as well had a run of punctures on the last day not stopped him beating OCTAVE LAPIZE. He came second instead.

Faber died in the French Foreign Legion in May 1915, aged 28. Appropriately for a hero of enormous strength and resistance to suffering, he had gone to the help of a colleague injured during an offensive at Garency. He was carrying him back from no man's land when he was shot in the back and killed.

Faber was the first of only three riders from Luxembourg to win the Tour. The others were NICOLAS FRANTZ in 1927 and 1928, and CHARLY GAUL in 1958.

(*See* MAURICE BROCCO for Faber's role in the coining of the word DOMESTIQUE.)

Winner

1908 Tour Lombardy
1909 Tour de France, Paris-Tours, Paris-Brussels
1910 Paris-Tours
1911 Bordeaux-Paris
1913 Paris-Roubaix

Tour de France

1906 DNF
1907 7th
1908 2nd Stage wins Metz—Belfort, Belfort—Lyon, Nîmes—Toulouse, Nantes—Brest
1909 1st Stage wins Roubaix—Metz, Metz—Belfort, Belfort—Lyon, Lyon—Grenoble, Grenoble—Nice, Bayonne—Bordeaux
1910 2nd Stage wins Roubaix—Metz, Belfort—Lyon, Nice—Nîmes
1911 DNF Stage wins Longwy—Belfort, Grenoble—Nice
1912 14th
1913 5th Stage wins Nice—Grenoble, Belfort—Longwy
1914 9th Stage wins Belfort—Longwy, Longwy—Dunkirk

EDOUARD FACHLEITNER
b. Santa Domenica, Italy, Feb 24 1921

Edouard Fachleitner was born in ITALY and had a German surname, but rode for FRANCE because his family had taken naturalisation. He was instrumental in the success of JEAN ROBIC on the last day of the 1947 Tour.

Robic had broken the tradition that the race leader, in this case PIERRE BRAMBILLA, should not be attacked on the final day. Robic accelerated on a hill outside Rouen, Fachleitner cooperated because Robic was reputed to have paid him 100,000 francs, and they caught a small breakaway group, dropping Brambilla. (*See* Brambilla entry for full story.)

Fachleitner rode the Tour twice more but didn't finish on either occasion. He is less remembered for his second place in 1947 than for the way he phoned home every evening to talk to his dog.

Winner

1948 Dauphiné Libéré
1950 Tour Romandie

Tour de France

1947 2nd Stage win Nice—Marseille
1948 DNF
1949 DNF
1952 DNF

FALSE NAMES

Riding under a false name was common when cycling started. Many saw bike races the way amateur runners see marathons now, as fun events. And while they didn't wear fancy dress – although J. T. Johnson came seventh in the Paris-Rouen race in 1869 wearing jockey's silks and carrying a whip 'to fend off dogs' – they did adopt false names. Also in the field were a Miss America (who was English), a Peter The First, and riders known just as A.C.D. and G. de M. The trend lasted into the new century, with Julien Lootens competing in the first Tour in 1903 as Samson (*see* BELGIUM.)

LUCIEN PETIT-BRETON, winner of the 1907 and 1908 Tours, was really Lucien Mazan. He called himself Petit-Breton to keep his father from knowing he was riding BIKE races. HENRI CORNET, winner in 1904, was really Henri Jaudry, although the reason for the change has been lost. JEAN STABLINSKI, WORLD CHAMPION in 1962, had his name changed during the Peace Race by French reporters who couldn't manage the Polish original of Edward Stablewski. Why he became Jean rather than Edouard is anybody's guess.

The Tour's most persistent failure, GEORGES GOFFIN of Liège, also rode as Georges Nemo. (*See* Georges Goffin entry for details.) Again, the reason is lost.

BENOÎT FAURE

b. St-Marcellin, France, Jan 11 1900, d.
Montbrison, France, Jun 16 1980

Tiny in size, Benoît Faure was the greatest TOURISTE-ROUTIER of them all, a brilliant CLIMBER who lived halfway up a hill at Lucenol in FRANCE. Touriste-routiers were riders who had been allowed to take part as individuals provided they found their own hotels and made their own arrangements.

Some were remarkably good (*see* touriste-routier entry for examples), and Faure was among the best. In 1930 he broke away between Pau and Luchon in the Pyrenees, rode over the AUBISQUE, then the Soulor, and had five minutes on the TOURMALET. On the way down he was caught by ALFREDO BINDA, Pierre Magne and ANDRÉ LEDUCQ because, like many climbers, he was too light to be a good descender, and he bounced too much on the ruts and loose rocks. Binda won, Leducq became *maillot jaune* and Faure came fifth.

Big teams offered Faure a place several times, but he turned them down. Tour organiser HENRI DESGRANGE even paid his fare to Paris so he could lecture him on joining the powerful ALCYON team and warn him, as Faure recalled, about 'the things that were likely to happen to me if I didn't'. But he stuck with his own SPONSOR, Le Cheminot (The Railwayman), for half what Alcyon were offering.

'I'd been a touriste-routier, a loner, too long,' he said. 'I wasn't a good team man and I liked the freedom of riders who were without any obligation.'

Just once, in 1931, was he tempted into the French team, where his job was to ride for ANTONIN MAGNE against ITALY. 'Instead, I went after a 2,000-franc *prime* [intermediary prize) and started a rare old battle in which the Italians happily joined. They took the first three places. Magne was mad with me, the whole team too, but maddest of all was Henri Desgrange. He'd written a book called *La Tête et les Jambes* (Head and Legs). A rider needed both head and legs, he said. But Benoît just stumbled along on his legs.'

Benoît Faure's legs took him to third place in

Bordeaux-Paris in 1936 and 1937, and fourth in the 1933 Tour of Switzerland.

Tour de France

1926	23rd	
1929	15th	Stage win Cannes—Nice
1930	8th	
1931	13th	
1932	12th	
1933	DNF	
1935	12th	

FEEDING AREAS

Riders use 5,000 calories on ordinary days and up to 8,000 in the MOUNTAINS. That's 3,000–5,000 more than in normal life, and so they eat and drink as they ride. Their jerseys have pockets in the back and, in earlier times, had one across the chest to hold food. The first Tours went on so long that riders stopped at bars. ÉMILE MASSON recalls not only eating at a restaurant with PHILIPPE THYS, but waiting for riders who came in after them. (*See* Masson entry for details). Later there were CAFÉ RAIDS as DOMESTIQUES fetched drinks for their leaders.

At first riders ate whatever they fancied, usually something sweet and substantial, like honey, meat sandwiches, and even cold porridge. Later they preferred fruit, sandwiches and sugar lumps. More recently they have gone for commercial energy bars and sports drinks.

Modern riders can eat or drink where they like but, for safety's sake, food can only be handed up from the roadside in set areas 500–1,000 metres in length, called *zones de ravitaillement*, or *ravitos* for short. These were introduced in 1919, and until the 1950s they consisted of rows of tables on which food was heaped for riders to stop and collect. Gradually this changed, and the custom grew for MANAGERS to stand with cloth bags called *musettes* over their extended arms. Today's riders loop their arms through the straps as they pass, swing the bag round their necks, and transfer the contents to their pockets. They then throw away the bags, which are collected by SPECTATORS. Drinking bottles – the Tour gets through 35,000 a year – are also eagerly sought after as souvenirs.

There are penalties for taking roadside food outside *ravitos*. In 1970, before he became Tour organiser, JEAN-MARIE LEBLANC was fined for joining LUIS OCAÑA and JAN JANSSEN for a picnic under a tree. This had been set up as a publicity stunt for their Bic team, and the publicity it brought handsomely justified a fine amounting to the equivalent of £4.

Managers are allowed to hand out food and drink from cars, but not in the first 50km or the last 20km of a stage. Officials watch out for riders who hang onto their bottles too long in the MOUNTAINS; managers and riders know to the second how long both can hold the bottle as it's pushed through the car window, thus giving the rider an illicit tow.

Tradition says riders do not attack in the feeding area – 'burning the control' as it's called – but it has happened. In 1969 the LANTERNE ROUGE (last rider), PIERRE MATIGNON, used the *ravito* to beat Eddy Merckx in a lone break to the PUY-DE-DOME. *(See* Matignon entry for details; and *see* JULIEN MOINEAU for how a table of beer bottles won him a surprise stage.)

FESTINA AFFAIR

Festina is a Spanish watch-making firm based in Andorra which ran a Tour team in FRANCE. Its star riders were RICHARD VIRENQUE and the 1997 WORLD CHAMPION, Laurent Brochard. These were among the riders who flew to Dublin for the START in 1998, while officials and helpers took the ferry to England and then across the Irish Sea to meet them.

Among them was a balding 53-year-old Belgian SOIGNEUR called WILLY VOET (pronounced 'foot'). Like everyone else driving a car in the Tour, he had been to the Tour's headquarters at Issy-les-Moulineaux to collect the vehicle, a white Fiat, allocated to Festina. After checking the advertising attached to the car, he had then left.

Subsequent inquiries show that he took a roundabout route, going through Switzerland and Germany and then into Belgium. Voet had in fact long lived in France, but the team's doctor, Erik Rijckaert (pronounced 'raycart'), was resident in Ghent. At 8am on Tuesday July 7 1998 Voet set off for an appointment at Rijckaert's house, where he was to collect ten boxes of medical drips. Belgian wholesalers sold their drips in plastic containers rather than the inconvenient glass used in France. Plastic is easier to throw away.

Behind the seat of his car, Voet already had 234 doses of the blood-enhancing drug EPO, 80 bottles of growth hormone, 160 capsules of testosterone, and 60 blood-thinning tablets. These he had collected from a supplier in a car park near Bordeaux airport a month earlier.

At 6am on Wednesday July 8 Voet had just enough time to dose himself up with a '*pot belge*', a phenomenally potent cocktail of cocaine, heroin, amphetamine and steroids, before continuing his journey. The *pot belge* was already well known in Belgian cycling, but Voet said later that he only realised what the contents were when a TV journalist told him two months afterwards.

Both Rijckaert and Voet knew the stash of drugs meant huge trouble if detected, and Rijckaert's last words were to warn Voet to be careful. And he was careful, turning off the E17 motorway near Roubaix and approaching the French border on a back road.

Normally there would be no customs inspectors at a place like Neuville-en-Ferrain, for continental borders have been open since the Schengen agreement of June 1985. Why the border was patrolled at that moment, and whether the inspectors knew Voet was about to cross somewhere – and if so who tipped them off – are lasting mysteries. Voet says he took that crossing by chance, and was confident his car wouldn't be examined. Customs were usually interested only in lorries. He was more concerned that they would spot he was as high as a kite after his *pot belge*.

Apparently they didn't. Instead, they took the unusual step of searching Voet's car – and again the question is why, unless they already knew team cars could carry drugs – and found the Festina team's drugs cache.

Voet was taken to Lille police station. Then detectives found more drugs at the Festina warehouse in Lyon, and Voet confessed, suspecting he was to become scapegoat for an organised DOPING operation of which he was only a part. The MANAGER, Bruno Roussel, admitted the team had a doping fund, claiming later that he had lost control of the team to the doctor, Rijckaert. He regretted this development, but pointed out that at least Rijckaert ensured systematic drug-taking would be medically supervised.

Voet confirmed this, saying afterwards, 'Erik [Rijckaert] was one of the precursors of organised doping regimes within teams. For him there was no alternative: success meant using doping products. But he tried to channel it, to organise it so that riders didn't risk their health. He introduced them to doping to some extent, but with clarity of thought that cost him dearly.' Rijckaert, too, ended up in jail.

More raids followed, sweeping through Festina riders' rooms. Virenque, Alex Zülle and Laurent Brochard were all implicated, but allowed to continue on the Tour. The manager Roussel was declared *persona non grata*. At the same time it emerged that a Dutch team, TVM, was also under investigation after its car had been halted earlier in the year.

The Tour threw out all the Festina riders just before 11pm on Friday July 17. Virenque met Tour organiser JEAN-MARIE LEBLANC, pleading his innocence and begging to be allowed to continue. Leblanc refused, but the Festina riders insisted they would ride the following day's TIME TRIAL regardless – although in the end they didn't.

No fewer than 23 people had been arrested by the rest day. Riders were questioned in hotels, held in police stations, and stripped and tested for drugs. Riders from the TVM team were also arrested. LAURENT JALABERT, a member of the Spanish ONCE team, protested at the way newspapers were reporting events, and clashed with his future team manager BJARNE RIIS. A Spanish official was questioned and the Spanish teams left the race, Jalabert

with them. Others followed. There were STRIKES on July 24 and 29 as riders grew both angrier and more confused. The Mountains leader, Rodolfo Massi, was arrested, and medicaments and money were found in his room. He was released on bail on condition he had no further links with professional cycling. Leblanc was in tears. Things grew more bitter and for a while it looked as though the Tour itself would be abandoned. Only negotiations set up by Riis between riders and organisers stopped this happening.

France had had doping laws since July 1965 (*see* PIERRE DUMAS) but enforcement had been left largely to the sport. (*See* STRIKES and DOPING for police raids at Bordeaux.) Now the government had started a clean-up through its communist sports minister, Marie-George Buffet. Under police interrogation Zülle, Armin Meier and LAURENT DUFAUX crumbled and began to name names. (*See* CHRISTOPHE BASSONS for the unusual result of his being named as a non-taker of drugs.)

Riders were fined and suspended. Those who admitted doping got six months' suspension. Those who denied it but were found guilty, like Virenque, got nine. Roussel was arrested and questioned, admitted his guilt and then left the sport to become an estate agent. Voet was given a suspended sentence and declared *persona non grata*. Rijckaert spent three months in prison and died shortly afterwards.

The SOCIÉTÉ DU TOUR DE FRANCE demanded compensation, but the court sent it packing, saying it had done too little to prevent the problem. In 2001 Leblanc organised a lecture at the START of the race in Dunkirk under the slogan, 'Doping – we're all losers', and demanded riders sign a pledge. (*See* also CHEATING.) The most important development, though, has been that a test had now been found for EPO (pronounced *aypo* in France). The usually fast massed stages of the first week now saw riders split by up to 20 minutes, and they were once more seen gasping for air in the MOUNTAINS. (*See* CLIMBERS.)

(*See* JEAN MALLÉJAC, FRÉDÉRIC MONCASSIN, TOM SIMPSON.)

May 1998	French sports minister Marie-George Buffet updates the doping law, but parliament delays it six months for consideration.
June 1998	French cycling decides to test French riders outside races.
July 8 1998	Voet arrested.
July 17 1998	Festina team disqualified after Roussel and five riders confess.
July 28 1998	Director and doctor of TVM team questioned.
July 29 1998	Riders strike. Doctor of the ONCE team questioned. Tests confirm drugs in TVM team's car.
Oct 30 1998	French sponsors sign a good-conduct agreement.
Nov 30 1998	Lab tests confirm eight Festina riders took EPO and other drugs. Virenque denies it.
Dec 4 1998	TVM team doctor freed, and inquiry dropped against the director.
Dec 6 1998	Virenque says he'll stop racing.
Dec 14 1998	Brochard, Christophe Moreau and Didier Rous suspended until May. Pascal Hervé agrees not to race in the same period.
Jan 26 1999	French tests show more than half of riders have medical anomalies.
Mar 26 1999	Virenque questioned.
May 8 1999	Drugs trade dismantled in France and a 'doctor' and lawyer jailed.
May 18 1999	Voet publishes his confession, *Breaking The Chain*.
June 16 1999	The Tour asks Virenque to stay away.
July 3 1999	Tour starts with Virenque included at UCI's insistence.
Dec 29 2000	Virenque suspended for nine months from February 2001 and fined.

LAURENT FIGNON
b. Paris, France, Aug 12 1960

A grumpy, sometimes sharp-tongued rider who (until he grew a beard) looked rather like women's tennis legend Martina Navratilova, Laurent Fignon also stood apart because of his spectacles, his ponytail, and his scholarly aspect. The other riders called him '*le Professeur*', partly in mockery but also because he'd been to medical college.

Fignon won the Tour for FRANCE in 1983 and 1984, but he never won the hearts of Frenchmen. Even JACQUES ANQUETIL, who could be cold but did sometimes speak about his feelings, had more fans. Fignon was inclined to win and then say he'd done nothing special, that he'd simply felt good, that he was paid to win races, and so on ... Not the stuff of romance.

His first Tour win, in 1983, was a good one, but it was marred because the man he had to beat, PASCAL SIMON, gave up the yellow JERSEY only because he had been riding for six days with a broken shoulder and had surrendered to the pain on the ALPE D'HUEZ stage. His other rival, JOOP ZOETEMELK, had been caught in a DOPING test. From there it was a clear run for Fignon, but not a road paved with glory.

In 1984, therefore, Fignon rode the Tour with a point to prove, racing through the Pyrenees and dominating on the flat. Any chance that BERNARD HINAULT would challenge him disappeared in the two TIME TRIALS, when he was denied his usual advantage. Hinault did try to break him on ALPE D'HUEZ, but Fignon rode in his wake and cracked him 10km before the end. By Paris his lead was 10:32.

Some years after his retirement Fignon became organiser of the Paris-Nice race, the winner of which has in many years also gone on to win that summer's Tour. However, in 2002 Fignon was forced by financial difficulties to hand control of the race to the SOCIÉTÉ DU TOUR DE FRANCE.

(*See* GREG LEMOND for details on how Fignon lost the Tour on the very last day.)

Winner

1982 Critérium International
1983 Tour de France
1984 Tour de France, National championship
1986 Flèche Wallonne
1988 Milan-San Remo, Tour EEC
1989 Giro d'Italia, GP Nations, Critérium As, Milan-San Remo, Tour Holland, Baracchi Trophy
1990 Critérium International

Tour de France

1983	1st	Stage win Dijon—Dijon, and Yellow Jersey
1984	1st	Stage wins Alençon—Le Mans, Les Échelles—La Ruchère, Bourg d'Oisans—La Plagne, Morzine—Crans-Montana, Villié-Morgon—Villefranche, and Yellow Jersey
1986	DNF	
1987	7th	Stage win Bourg d'Oisans—La Plagne
1988	DNF	
1989	2nd	Stage win Bourg d'Oisans—Villard de Lans, and Yellow Jersey
1990	DNF	
1991	6th	
1992	23rd	Stage win Strasbourg—Mulhouse
1993	DNF	

FILMS

Pour Un Maillot Jaune is a delightful 30-minute film of the 1965 Tour by the French director Claude Lelouch. Black-and-white and colour film of the race and events around it are linked by a sound track of rather poorly edited music and sometimes exaggerated sound effects. But in general the result is charming. The mountain sequences are dramatic and hotel-room scenes of SOIGNEUR Luis Guerlache's massages entertaining. Watch for briefings by RAPHAËL GÉMINIANI and his dismay at being caught dozing in his car, and of a rider lowering his handlebars as he rides. You can see FEDERICO BAHAMONTES as he abandons the race, and FELICE GIMONDI winning despite coming to a halt in the mountains.

Claude Lelouch was a distinguished film director who won two Oscars for *Un Homme et Une Femme*. His documentary films include *Loin de Vietnam* (Far from Vietnam), made in 1967 as a protest against the Vietnam war.

Vive le Tour by another talented director, Louis Malle (1932–1995), was made in 1962 and lasts only 18 minutes. Unlike *Pour Un Maillot Jaune* it is narrated (in a French accent in the English version). The film is good on the suffering of the riders, and takes a look at DOPING. 'All the riders that day told us they had eaten bad fish,' says the narrator as yet another rider drops into a ditch during the WIEL'S AFFAIR.

Dustin Hoffman followed several stages of the 1984 Tour to make a film provisionally titled *The Yellow Jersey*, but it was never completed. Other films include *Pour le Maillot Jaune* in 1939 (not to be confused with Lelouch's 1965 *Pour Un Maillot Jaune*), starring Albert Préjean and Meg Lemonnier, sister-in-law of Tour organiser JACQUES GODDET; and *Autour du Tour*, a documentary by Jacques Ertaud in 1975.

(*See* ROBERT CAPA for the story behind striking black-and-white photos of the Tour.)

FINISH

Stages usually end at around 5 pm, but the Tour paper *L'ÉQUIPE* publishes a timetable each day for three likely speeds. Stages often used to finish on TRACKS, but most are now in town centres. A few are in the MOUNTAINS.

The finish is known in French as *l'arrivée*. The last structures are erected about three hours before the finish is due, and red-overalled men from ESP Publicité paint advertisements on the road. The crowd starts to gather four hours before the riders arrive, and there's no chance of getting near the line with an hour to go.

SPECTATORS are entertained by a variety of turns: by men on flexible BIKES, by Tour commentator DANIEL MANGEAS' interviews with former stars, by rushing for hats and key rings from race SPONSORS, and sometimes by a stage show. Souvenir shops are open for business. Large TV screens up the road from the finish show the race so those who can't see the line get a better view.

The inflatable arch for the red triangle (the *flamme rouge*), marking the last kilometre, goes up at the same time as the arch across the finish and the grey shell-like winners' podium, which inflates from a truck. It's there that the JERSEYS are presented and guests are introduced to riders by BERNARD HINAULT.

The CARAVAN arrives two hours before the finish, and the first team trucks and buses come in with an hour to go, followed by journalists and others. Beyond the finish are the BROADCASTING positions, with French TV closest to the line at ground level, and radio on the upper level. Opposite is the grandstand for guests. The white DOPING van is alongside the podium, its side windows shielded by grey plastic. Riders have to report within 35 minutes after their appearance on the podium. Beyond that is the stage for TV shows and then a catchment area for the caravan.

Behind the whole lot is the *zone technique*, 3,000sq metres of broadcasting equipment and astonishing lengths of cables. The engineers rarely show any interest in the race beyond watching portable televisions to see how close it is so that they know when they will have to stop eating their salads and start work. *Vélo* names the hotels at which riders are staying, although not which teams are staying where. Riders arrive at their hotels by bike or team bus and go indoors quickly, with only a handful of autograph hunters satisfied. The chance that a rider will emerge again is slim.

The Tour used to finish in Paris on the PARC DES PRINCES until 1967, when it moved to the PISTE MUNICIPALE in the Bois de Vincennes in western Paris. It stayed there until 1975 when it moved to the CHAMPS ELYSÉES. (*See* separate entries for more; and *see* CRASHES for finishes that ended in disaster.)

FLANDRIA

Flandria, a Belgian BIKE company, sponsored teams from 1960 to 1979. It ran BELGIUM's strongest team as the 1960s moved into the 1970s. In 1969 the Flandria team included ERIK and ROGER DE VLAEMINCK, WALTER GODEFROOT, Éric Leman, and the WORLD CHAMPION Jean-Pierre Monseré. Monseré died on March 15 1971 in a CRASH in his second year as a professional when a car drove onto the circuit.

Never high-paying, Flandria sought everchanging secondary SPONSORS to keep going. It once even signed a backer halfway through the Tour. Subsidiary backers included Velda (a meat company), Lano (carpets) and Mars (confectionery).

In 1975 BRIEK SCHOTTE was replaced as MANAGER by the colourful Lomme ('Some people feel I exaggerate!') Driessens. Scarcely any world champions have failed to benefit from his advice, it would seem. Driessens built up the so-called Three Musketeers of FREDDY MAERTENS, Marc Demeyer and MICHEL POLLENTIER. All ran into DOPING scandals. Driessens demanded exhausting work schedules – more than 200 races for Maertens in 1977 – and successes became fewer and fewer. He was replaced in 1978 by FRED DE BRUYNE but the decline continued.

The Flandria firm's finances were as shaky as its team's. It was weakened by a row between Flandria's founders, the brothers Aimé and Remi Claeys, who eventually divided their factory in Zedelgem in December 1956 and ran separate businesses. The Flandria Ranch nightclub, backed by Maertens among others, was never a success and burned down in 1978. Flandria itself went bankrupt in 1981.

VICTOR FONTAN

b. Nay, France, Jun 18 1892, d. Saint-Vincent, France, Jan 2 1982

Victor Fontan was shot twice in the leg in the first world war, and could hardly have expected to ride the Tour. But he did, even getting to be picked for the Tour when he was 36 (*see* AGES, and *see* FRANÇOIS FABER and OCTAVE LAPIZE for stars who died in the war). Until then he had rarely competed outside south-west France.

In 1928 Fontan rode the Tour in the colours of a local SPONSOR, Elvish-Wolber, a team so weak that he spent most of his time nursing his colleagues through the race, and losing time himself. The 1928 Tour was run as a team TIME TRIAL until it got to the MOUNTAINS and strong riders with weak team-mates were therefore at a disadvantage.

Fontan's chance came when the rules let him ride for himself, and he won the stage from Les Sables d'Olonne to Bordeaux (285km). He was so far down – 1h 45 – that the leaders didn't worry when he set off to win the stage from Hendaye to Luchon, 387km across the Pyrenees. He pulled off a startling lone ride, cheered by crowds who came to see their local man, and took seven minutes on NICOLAS FRANTZ of ALCYON and LUXEMBOURG. Fontan finished seventh in Paris, 5:07:47 behind Frantz.

The arithmetic, though, showed the positions would have been reversed had it been Fontan who'd ridden for the strong Alcyon team and Frantz for the little Elvish-Wolber. The five hours by which Fontan lost the Tour were the five hours that he was delayed by his team.

Inspired, he rode again in 1929 and achieved what 12 months earlier had been unthinkable: he not only took the yellow JERSEY but did it at BORDEAUX, near his home in the Pyrenees. Or rather, he took *a* yellow jersey. Uniquely there were three because Fontan, ANDRÉ LEDUCQ and Frantz were all on equal time after the stage from Les Sables, the stage that Fontan had won the previous summer.

He and the others lost their *maillots jaunes* to GASTON REBRY on next day's stage to Bayonne, still lying equal but now in second place. A day

later Fontan got back into yellow, this time alone after a stage from Bayonne to Luchon.

The following day's race over 363km from Luchon to Perpignan started in early morning darkness. After only seven kilometres Fontan slipped into a gutter. The fall didn't hurt but it broke the bike's forks. Fontan set off by moonlight to find a replacement, walking from house to house, getting people out of bed. Villagers, astonished to see the leader of the Tour de France on their doorstep, eventually found him one. He pedalled into the night and regained some time with his broken machine on his shoulder. The rules said he had to finish on, or at any rate with, the bike on which he had started. Disillusioned, he abandoned.

Louis Delblat of *L'Écho des Sports* protested, 'How can a man lose the Tour de France because of an accident to his bike?' and he campaigned for MECHANICS to follow the race with spares.

Tour de France

1924	DNF	
1928	7th	Stage wins Les Sables—Bordeaux, Hendaye—Luchon
1929	DNF	Yellow Jersey
1930	DNF	

FOREIGN VISITS

The first Tour to leave FRANCE was in 1906. It went to Alsace, which France had lost to GERMANY in a war 30 years earlier. It also crossed into ITALY and SPAIN. The next year it entered SWITZERLAND. It visits BELGIUM almost every year, and has twice been to BRITAIN as well as starting in IRELAND. Suggestions made in the 1980s of starting in AMERICA were dismissed when too few Concordes were available to transfer riders and race staff.

The most complicated foreign START was Berlin in 1987, when the city was marking its 750th anniversary. Germany was then still divided into East and West, and Berlin was surrounded by East Germany. Plans to enter East Germany were abandoned when the difficulties became too much, and the race had to travel through it in quarantine. West Berlin wasn't a lot easier. The police objected to how many officers were needed – more than at any time in West Germany's brief history, it was said – and residents were upset at traffic congestion caused by closed roads. Some campaigned to cancel the race.

The 2004 Tour will start in Liège, Belgium, after speculation that the choice would be Strasbourg. (*See* TRANSFERS.)

FOREIGN STARTS

1954	Amsterdam
1958	Brussels
1965	Cologne
1973	The Hague
1975	Charleroi
1978	Leiden
1980	Frankfurt
1982	Basle
1987	Berlin
1989	Luxembourg
1992	San Sebastian
1996	's-Hertogenbosch
1998	Dublin
2002	Luxembourg
2004	Liège
2006	possibly Tenerife

JEAN FORESTIER
b. Lyon, France, Oct 7 1930

Jean Forestier may not have been among the greats but it wasn't for lack of heart. In 1955 in Paris-Roubaix he jumped clear in rain on the rise to Mons-en-Pévèle with 30km to go. The stars hesitated, not sure how to take this unrated Frenchman, then set off in chase. Among them were FAUSTO COPPI, HUGO KOBLET and LOUISON BOBET. But they left it too late, and Forestier had enough time at the end to stand in the TRACK centre and watch Bobet and Coppi sprint for second.

He won the Tour de France Points competition in 1957, and in 1958 the Super Prestige Pernod, forerunner of the World Cup.

Winner

1954	Tour Romandie
1955	Paris-Roubaix
1956	Tour of Flanders
1957	Critérium National, Tour Romandie
1960	Circuit Flemish Regions
1962	Tour Var

Tour de France

1953	39th	
1954	27th	Stage win Le Puy—Lyon
1955	32nd	Stage win Bordeaux—Poitiers
1956	12th	Stage win Aix-en-Provence—Gap
1957	4th	Yellow Jersey and Points winner
1958	DNF	
1959	34th	
1960	DNF	
1961	35th	Stage win Chalon-sur-Saône—St-Étienne
1962	36th	

FRANCE

France is the birthplace of organised BIKE racing. There must have been informal races for as long as people had ridden bikes, but the first recognised formal events were held in the Parc de St Cloud in western Paris on Friday May 31 1868. Crowds turned out in top hats and posh frocks to watch riders race the 1,200 metres from the park's fountains to the gates and back again.

The winner was the youngest competitor, a 19-year-old called James Moore whose blacksmith father and illiterate mother (she signed her son's birth certificate with an X) had emigrated to Paris from Bury St Edmunds, Britain, when he was four. Their son gained from becoming a friend of the Michaux family, who had a coach repair business nearby, for it was Michaux who provided the bikes on which he won at St-Cloud, and then again in Paris-Rouen on November 7 1869, then the world's longest place-to-place race.

Paris-Rouen was run by the journal *Le Vélocipède*, ostensibly to promote cycling but without doubt also to increase its sales. France's early dominance of cycle racing was due to a large extent to the way papers promoted longer and longer races to increase their sales. The Tour de France started in 1903 for no other reason than to help the paper *L'AUTO* out of a sales slump. (*See* HENRI DESGRANCE and GÉO LEFÈVRE for details.)

The Tour quickly became the dominant force in cycling, and bike-makers such as ALCYON and PEUGEOT immediately saw how a victory by a rider on one of their machines would multiply sales. (*See* also SPONSORS and GITANE.) That led to bigger and stronger teams and therefore more rivalry and more professionals.

French riders dominated the first half of the 20th century and into the 1960s, and often found themselves with more good riders than would fit easily into one team. In conventional sponsored teams that was no problem, and led to the excitement of clashes between fellow Frenchmen such as JACQUES ANQUETIL and RAYMOND POULIDOR in the 1960s. However, from 1930 until 1960 the Tour organisers had insisted on NATIONAL TEAMS. (*See* National Teams entry for the difficulties created.)

France won in those years despite rather than because of that system. It's a tribute to the persuasive powers of the manager, MARCEL BIDOT, that he bound together rivals and sometimes personal enemies such as LOUISON BOBET, Jacques Anquetil and RAPHAËL GÉMINIANI. (*See* Bidot entry; and *see* DOMESTIQUES for how Bidot did it.) Many Frenchmen look back on national teams with affection.

France was the first country to have a full professional team sponsored by a company outside the bike trade. As the cost of running teams became too much for bike-making factories already affected by declining sales, sponsors withdrew and their riders were left without employers. Raphaël Géminiani went outside the bike industry to seek sponsorship from the St-Raphaël aperitif company that shared his name (*See* SPONSORS), and the future looked safer. Jacques Anquetil had some

of his best years in the red, white and pale blue of St-Raphaël.

As elsewhere, though, France quickly banned sports sponsorship by alcohol and tobacco companies, and sponsors became harder to find. DOPING scandals in the 1960s and 1970s did little to help the cause. The prestige of the Tour de France – the *raison d'être* of French racing – was tarnished, and so was the status of the once god-like riders who won it. The growth of television advertising after deregulation in 1974 (before which French television was in government control) and the advent of commercial local radio in 1984 also reduced the attraction of team sponsorship.

It is a strange fact about French politics that it was the Socialist party, normally associated with state control, which lessened state controls on broadcasting and created independent radio stations. But, while it was doing that, it was also running the Renault car factory, the Gitane bike factory and the Elf oil company. So when in different combinations these companies ran teams from 1978 to 1985, the riders they put into the intensely capitalist Tour (including BERNARD HINAULT) were effectively riding as state employees.

The same also applied to Poulidor when he rode for GAN, the state-owned Groupe

Assurance Nationale insurance giant. (*See* FÉLIX LÉVITAN for why it was proposed that even the Tour itself should be nationalised.)

France since Hinault has been in a prolonged lull. LAURENT FIGNON, who lacked Hinault's fire, won nevertheless in 1983 and 1984, but in 1989 was denied a win by eight seconds by GREG LEMOND. Since then France has persistently regretted its absence from the top of the podium. It's not that riders don't finish well – there have been many in the first three or wearing one of the main JERSEYS – but they don't get right to the top step.

LAURENT JALABERT delighted France by winning the MOUNTAINS competition in 2001 and 2002. But Jalabert was not at the start of his career but at the very end. Halfway through the 2002 race he said it would be his last, and that he would retire at the end of the season. RICHARD VIRENQUE, the only other Frenchman of global status, has won the mountains title five times. But this was achieved, say critics, not by dominating in the way of classic CLIMBERS of the past or even like LANCE ARMSTRONG today, but mainly by gathering points steadily and in a calculating way. And Virenque's career (if not his popularity) was tarnished anyway by the FESTINA AFFAIR of 1998.

Successors may take a while to emerge, but there are promising young riders. In 2002 Tour organiser JEAN-MARIE LEBLANC let some of them ride the Tour while excluding veterans like MARCO PANTANI, stained by a dope inquiry, and MARIO CIPOLLINI, who has persistently pulled out at the mountains when his chances as a SPRINTER have been over. (*See* entries for details). The decision to showcase smaller teams, particularly at the expense of Pantani and Cipollini, was criticised. But many in France will see it as the only way to return to the glories of Bobet, Anquetil and Hinault.

NICOLAS FRANTZ

b. Mamer, Luxembourg, Nov 4 1899, d. Luxembourg, Jan 1 1985

Nicolas Frantz was LUXEMBOURG's second Tour winner after François Faber, thanks to a controversial decision by HENRI DESGRANGE. In the 1927 Tour Desgrange made the 16 flat stages of the race a virtual team TIME TRIAL, setting teams off at intervals to be sure they raced as hard as they could. The formula meant good riders with weak teams stood less chance than moderate teams of all-round ability. As a result, Frantz was gifted with an easy win. (*See* VICTOR FONTAN for the greatest victim of this arrangement.)

Desgrange repeated the idea in 1928 and Frantz won again, although not so easily because his frame broke on a level crossing near Longuyon, with 100km to go before the stage FINISH at Charleroi. His ALCYON team went into panic mode, the firm's representative insisting Frantz should be taken to the nearest Alcyon shop and given a replacement. But the MANAGER, Ludovic Feuillet, pointed out that this would take an hour, and a row started when the rep began worrying about the bad publicity a broken frame would cause his company.

The argument was still going on when someone spotted a woman watching with her bike by her side. It was good enough, despite its wide saddle, mudguards and bell, and Frantz jumped on. In earlier years he would have been penalised up to an hour, but the rule about starting and finishing the race on the same bike had recently been dropped. So Frantz got to Charleville 28 minutes down, although he still managed to ride the last 100km at 27km/h. He was only the second rider to wear the yellow JERSEY from START to FINISH.

Frantz was a perfectly groomed man with thick hair brushed back from his forehead without a parting. He was almost obsessively careful and methodical. In the 1927 Tour he packed 24 jerseys, 24 pairs of shorts, 24 pairs of socks and 24 sets of underwear, one for each day of the race. ANDRÉ LEDUCQ, who shared a hotel room with Frantz, said that when he got back after a brief ride on a rest day he 'found Nicolas meditating in front of a panoply of things lined up on the table: jumpers, leggings, woollen gloves and . . . an electric lamp! I asked him what it was for and he said in his terse way, "It's dark up there . . . and cold, very cold"'.

Frantz raced only for the Tour, rarely finding classics important. After the WAR he became a national selector. (And *see* HUBERT OPPER-MAN.)

Winner

1922 National championship
1923 National championship
1924 National championship
1925 National championship
1926 National championship, Tour Basque Country
1927 Tour de France, Paris-Brussels, National championship
1928 Tour de France, National championship
1929 Paris-Tours, National championship
1930 National championship
1931 National championship
1932 National championship
1933 National championship
1934 National championship

Tour de France

1924	2nd	Stage wins Briançon—Gex, Gex—Strasbourg
1925	4th	Stage wins Brest—Vannes, Vannes—Les Sables, Luchon—Perpignan, Évian—Mulhouse
1926	2nd	Stage wins Brest—Les Sables, Bordeaux—Bayonne, Perpignan—Toulon, Toulon—Nice
1927	1st	Stage wins Bayonne—Luchon, Toulon—Nice, Strasbourg—Metz, and Yellow Jersey
1928	1st	Stage wins Paris—Caen, Vannes—Les Sables, Marseille—Nice, Strasbourg—Metz, Dieppe—Paris, and Yellow Jersey
1929	5th	Stage wins Les Sables—Bordeaux, Dieppe—Paris, and Yellow Jersey
1932	45th	

GALIBIER

Just as the TOURMALET is the most celebrated MOUNTAIN in the Pyrenees, so the Galibier, 2,645m high, is the epic climb of the Alps. It came to the Tour on July 10 1911 on the stage from Chamonix to Grenoble, when it was topped for the first time by ÉMILE GEORGET. He, PAUL DUBOC and GUSTAVE GARRIGOU were the only riders not to walk.

The north side is the more difficult, and starts in Valloire at 1,430m after the short descent of the Télégraphe. The road starts to climb seriously after Plan Lachat (1,960m) with sections of 13 per cent. It takes eight kilometres to climb 700 metres in height. The last section eases in time to give a spectacular view of glaciers in the south.

The climb from the south begins at the Col du Lautaret at 2,058m. It averages 7.8 per cent but the kilometre after the old tunnel is 12 per cent.

The Galibier inspired HENRI DESGRANGE to write an 'Act of Adoration': 'Oh Sappey, Oh Laffrey, Oh Col Bayard, Oh Tourmalet! I will not shirk from my duty in proclaiming that beside the Galibier you are nothing but pale babies; in front of this giant we can do nothing but take off our hats and bow.'

Of the first crossing, he wrote, 'Today, my brothers, we gather here in common celebration of the divine bicycle. Not only do we owe it our most pious gratitude for the precious and ineffable love that it has given us, but also for the host of memories sown over our whole sports life and which today has been made concrete. In my own case I love it for its having given me a soul capable of appreciating it; I love it for having taken my heart within its spokes, for having encircled a part of my life in its harmonious frame, and for having constantly illuminated me with the victorious sparkle of its nickel plates. In the history of humanity, does it not constitute the first successful effort of intelligent life to triumph over the laws of weights?'

The Desgrange MEMORIAL on the mountain won the Grand Prix de Rome for Bertola, its creator. It was inaugurated when the Tour passed on July 19 1949.

The old route is no more than a stone track that splits off from the main road, indicated for years by a temporary sign. The track turned off soon after the Galibier bridge and went through a stone-faced tunnel. The new road, the D902, is where the race has gone since the road opened in 1938. The original pass was 2,556m, but with the closing of the tunnel and the road going closer to the peak, it is now 2,645m.

MAURICE GARIN

b. Arvier, Italy, Mar 3 1871, d. Lens, France, Feb 18 1957

Maurice Garin won the first Tour de France in 1903, and also the second – until he and three others were disqualified. He was born on the

French-Italian border at Arvier where, legend says, his father exchanged him for a wheel of cheese (although legend does not add to whom or for what). Nor do we know just why his parents moved not simply from ITALY but right across FRANCE to the Belgian border.

At some stage the Garins took French nationality and their son – just 1.65m tall and 61kg – ran a BIKE shop in Roubaix from 1895 to 1901, and also worked for a while as a chimney sweep. He was often pictured with a floppy moustache and a cigarette.

Garin rode his first race in 1892 and showed immediate talent. In 1894 he won a 24-hour race in Liège, and two years later a similar race, the Bol d'Or, in the Parc de Vincennes in Paris. His success made him an immediate favourite when the first Tour started at MONTGERON in 1903. He won the first stage, Paris to Lyon, and led throughout to win in Paris three weeks and 2,400km later. His adopted town of Lens organised a parade to welcome him home.

However, Garin is known less for having won that first Tour by 2hr 49min, two and a half days ahead of the *LANTERNE ROUGE* (last rider), than for having been disqualified, with three other leaders, from the second. They were accused of hanging onto cars, taking short cuts, and even taking a train (*see* 1904 AFFAIR). On November 30 1904 the Union Vélocipédique de France announced there had been a *violation des réglements*. It disciplined 29 riders. Several – Garin and his brother César, LUCIEN POTHIER and HIPPOLYTE AUCOUTURIER – were disqualified. Garin was banned for two years, Pothier for life. The winner was now HENRI CORNET, 20 years old.

But why was the decision delayed four months? The UVF's official, Léon Breton, needed time to investigate, before he dared revive the emotions that had made July 2–24 1904 so eventful. Of this Tour JACQUES AUGEN-DRE's *Panorame d'un Siècle* (Panorama of a Century) cites 'protests and barricades on the course. Aggression against riders and officials on the Col de la République and at Nîmes. Multiple irregularities . . .' The journalist Michel

Nicolini says, 'If they'd taken the decision [to disqualify Garin] at the FINISH there'd have been a riot, and officials would have been lynched.'

Garin said, 'The cycling federation had numerous protests after the race finished. It was said that little Lucien Pothier had been seen hanging on a car during the first stage, Paris-Lyon, that I should have won. It's possible, but I wasn't involved. Despite that I was declassified because he and I belonged to the same team. It still makes me angry.'

Garin refused to race again immediately after his suspension ended, turning out only in 1911 for Paris-Brest-Paris, where he came 10th. In the meantime he ran the garage and filling station which he had bought in the rue de Lille with his prizes from the second Tour before disqualification. He called it *Au champion des routiers du monde* and he ran it until he died on February 19 1957, a month short of his 86th birthday. *L'ÉQUIPE* wrote, 'Garin rode a bike as heavy as lead, which demanded enormous strength, power and will. He rode more on pure strength than suppleness. His almost inexhaustible energy let him win the toughest races.'

Garin lies now in section F3 of the Cimetière Est, off the rue Constant Darras between Lens and Sallaumines. The assistant gravedigger there, Maurice Vernaldé, remembers running errands to see him at his garage. He says, 'He was an old man, a bit stooped, but he still had that enormous moustache. He never lost interest in cycling and he loved talking about it. But I was just a boy then, and old men, they like to tell the same tale over and over again, don't they? I didn't have the patience.'

Vernaldé's memories confirm that whatever Garin said publicly about alleged cheating, he was more open in private and with the safety of years. 'He admitted it,' Vernaldé says. 'He was amused about it, certainly not embarrassed, not after all those years. There wasn't the same significance to the Tour then, of course, and he used to laugh and say, "Well, I was young . . ." Maybe at the time he said he didn't [cheat], but when he got older and it no longer mattered so much . . .'

Even though Garin lived in Lens for 55 years, the town has provided no MEMORIAL. Even the place where he had been buried was forgotten. It took the gravedigger, Jean-Marie Jasniewicz, 15 years to realise Garin was one of his charges, and then only because Italian television had arrived to make a documentary.

Vernaldé believes Garin deserves a memorial for winning the first Tour. 'Had he been a politician or a footballer, he would have one,' he says. 'But the truth is that he won't get one, not because he won the first Tour but because of the way he won the second.' (*See* CHEATS, LA FRANÇAISE.)

Winner

1897 Paris-Roubaix
1898 Paris-Roubaix
1902 Bordeaux-Paris
1903 Tour de France

Tour de France

1903   1st Stage wins Paris—Lyon, Bordeaux—Nantes, Nantes—Paris
1904 DNF

GUSTAVE GARRIGOU

b. Vabre-Tizac, France, Sep 24 1884, d. Esbly, France, Jan 28 1963

A dapper dresser and as skinny as a broom, Cyprien Gustave Garrigou rode eight Tours from 1907 to 1914, finished them all, won in 1911, came second three times, twice third and also fourth and fifth. He rode 117 stages, won eight, finished in the first five in 65, and in the first ten in 96.

Garrigou showed talent right from the start, winning Paris-Amiens as an AMATEUR, and as a result turning professional in 1907. Some riders have difficulty when they step up a class. Not Garrigou. In that year he won the French national championship, the Tour of Lombardy, the Paris-Brussels race, and came second in the Tour.

His win in the 1911 Tour was deserved – not least because HENRI DESGRANGE gave riders 5,400km to ride in 15 stages. But he was helped by a succession of retirements and by the poisoning of his closest rival.

In the 1911 Tour Garrigou took the lead from the first stage. One by one the favourites dropped out of the running or just dropped out – LUCIEN PETIT-BRETON in a CRASH, OCTAVE LAPIZE exhausted on the BALLON D'ALSACE, FRANÇOIS FABER exhausted in the Alps (*see* MAURICE BROCCO for his involvement). ÉMILE GEORGET was clear on the Ballon d'Alsace only to be knocked down by a car on the descent.

The most dramatic episode, though, involved PAUL DUBOC. He was Garrigou's only challenger when he suddenly collapsed on a track on the AUBISQUE and was violently ill. Inquiries showed he had been poisoned. (*See* Duboc entry for details.) Garrigou was innocent, but angry mobs of Duboc supporters couldn't see who else could have done it, and they jeered and threatened the race leader so violently that he had to be disguised for his safety. (*See* Duboc entry.) Duboc recovered to come second, but Garrigou's winning position was nevertheless strengthened by Duboc's mishap.

Garrigou's career came to an end with the first world war. He began a second career as a businessman at Esbly, near Paris where, in 1937, the Tour paper L'AUTO found him and asked him about his memories. Garrigou spoke of 'summits that only the eagles could get to. The highest summits in Europe. That was the bad side, the bad roads. Not even a road, just donkey tracks ... and I'm being polite. It wasn't anything superhuman because we weren't supermen, and I'm the proof, a man like anybody else, with four GALIBIERS in my pocket, then the TOURMALET, where I won five sovereigns because I rode all the way up without walking. It was our job. The prizes, the *primes* [intermediary prizes], the contracts. I was a professional. It was just life.'

Garrigou died on January 28 1963, when he was 78, after a career that also included victory in Milan-San Remo in 1911, second place in

Milan-San Remo and third in Bordeaux-Paris in 1907, second in the Tour of BELGIUM in 1908, second in Bordeaux-Paris in 1911, and third in 1912.

(And *see* ALCYON, CHEATS, ODILE DEFRAYE, GEARS.)

Winner

1907 Paris-Brussels, National championship, Tour Lombardy
1908 National championship
1911 Tour de France, Milan-San Remo

Tour de France

1907	2nd	Stage wins Bayonne—Bordeaux, Nantes—Brest
1908	4th	
1909	2nd	Stage win Nantes—Brest
1910	3rd	Stage win Nantes—Brest
1911	1st	Stage wins Paris—Dunkirk, Brest—Cherbourg
1912	3rd	
1913	2nd	Stage win Perpignan—Aix-en-Provence
1914	5th	Stage win Grenoble—Geneva

CHARLY GAUL
b. Pfaffenthal, Luxembourg, Dec 8 1932

In 1989, when Charly Gaul received the Tour de France medal from JEAN-MARIE LEBLANC, it celebrated not just the career of a legendary CLIMBER but also a comeback from the near-dead.

Gaul, one of three winners from LUXEMBOURG (the others were FRANÇOIS FABER and NICOLAS FRANTZ) was cycling's most gifted climber of the 1950s. Pierre About of *L'ÉQUIPE* called him the 'Angel of the Mountains'. He was so adored that at his peak he received 60 letters from women a day, some so outrageous that his team-mate Marcel Ernzer swore after reading them that he'd never marry.

Charly Gaul (pronounced *Gowl*) was ambitious enough as an AMATEUR to join the Simplex training camp run by CHARLES PÉLISSIER.

(*See* SHAY ELLIOTT for details.) He went on to win the Flèche du Sud twice and also the Tour of the Twelve Cantons. Turning professional in 1953 he came a surprise third in the Tour of Luxembourg. That was the year he rode his first Tour de France, but he finished neither that race nor the 1954 edition.

Things changed in the 1955 Tour when he came third and won two mountain stages and the mountains title. In 1956 he fell to 13th place but won another two stages, and also the climbers' competition. That was the year he won the Giro d'Italia with three stages, including one across the Dolomites in such awful weather that 57 abandoned. (*See* HENRY ANGLADE for how he and GASTONE NENCINI held a private downhill race at the Giro.) Gaul soared on in the snow on the Monte Bondone until he'd made up the 15 minutes that the stars had had on him, and then went on to gain enough to win the Giro as well. It started the reputation of Gaul as the man who triumphed in bad weather but, equally true, suffered in the heat. He won the Giro again in 1959, the first non-Italian to win the race twice.

However, Gaul was an erratic rider, alternately brilliant and mediocre. And he was a comparatively poor one-day rider, although he did take the bronze medal in the 1954 WORLD CHAMPIONSHIP, and won the Luxembourg national championship six times.

In the 1958 Tour Gaul won all the TIME TRIALS, including the first one, in which he beat JACQUES ANQUETIL by seven seconds before the 1957 winner pulled out due to illness. He won the climb of MONT VENTOUX by 31 seconds and the last mountain stage of the race by more than eight minutes.

Gaul may have been arrogant, but his competence was so great that he could tell LOUISON BOBET exactly where he would attack in the 1958 Tour, and dare him to follow. Gaul was bitter at how Bobet and Nencini had attacked during the 1956 Giro as he stood by the roadside for a pee. It not only cost Gaul the lead and an 80km chase, but it also forced him to pioneer the technique of urination from the saddle. Papers took to calling him *Monsieur Pipi*, which hurt even more.

At Briançon he sought out his tormentor and worked at his self-doubt. (*See* Bobet entry for examples). 'You're ready, Monsieur Bobet?' he said, ironically formal. 'I'll attack on the Luitel climb. I'll even tell you which hairpin. You want to win the Tour? Easy. I've told you what you need to know.' The stage set off for Aix-les-Bains, 219km away. With his usual blank expression and staring blue eyes, Gaul rode with his saddle low, his bars high. He rode patiently. The Luitel would come soon enough.

Then he moved as he had forecast, pedalling fast. Race leader RAPHAËL GÉMINIANI begged Bobet to help chase, but the taunting had demoralised him. Gaul had 5:30 at the top of the Col de Porte, 7:50 on the Cucheron, 12:20 at the FINISH beside Le Bourget lake. He had moved from nowhere to third. Bobet finished more than 19 minutes behind and Géminiani arrived in tears, branding Bobet a Judas. By the end of the week Gaul had won the Tour by more than three minutes.

But Gaul was torn by inner demons. He spoke little and had few friends, and he foamed at the mouth as he rode. By 1962 he was a shadow of himself, and he rode his last race on the track at Nierdekom in 1965. He opened a bar near the railway station in Luxembourg then abandoned it six months later to live as a recluse in the Ardennes.

The 'Angel of the Mountains' developed a belly, double chin and grey beard. He parted from his second wife. He refused to answer the phone. He became a recluse in the forest and lived without piped water or electricity. Journalists who came for stories were sent packing. Gaul rarely spoke or smiled; his only company was his dog Pocki. A magazine pictured him fishing, and challenged readers to recognise him.

And then something happened. In 1983, 25 years after his Tour de France victory, life began again for Charly Gaul. He married for a third time, and began speaking publicly. But he was still confused and forgetful. Years, riders and races were muddled. The minister of sport offered him a job as an archivist, hardly an obvious choice of job for a man who had lost his memory, but perhaps a good way for him to reclaim it. He organised races to raise funds for cancer research. He is beginning to remember how great he was. He says he couldn't accept life after a career in the saddle.

All is not yet right, as his guest appearance during the 2000 Tour showed. But at least the angel was back on earth, if no longer flying.

Winner

1954 Circuit 6 Provinces
1955 Tour Sud-Est
1956 Giro d'Italia, Tour Luxembourg, National championship
1957 National championship
1958 Tour de France
1959 Giro d'Italia, Tour Luxembourg, National championship
1960 National championship
1961 Tour Luxembourg, National championship
1962 National championship

Tour de France

1953	DNF	
1954	DNF	
1955	3rd	Stage win Thonon—Briançon, Toulouse—St Gaudens, and Mountains winner
1956	13th	Stage wins Les Essarts—Les Essarts, Turin—Grenoble and Mountains winner
1957	DNF	
1958	1st	Stage wins Châteaulin—Châteaulin, Bédoin—Mont Ventoux, Briançon—Aix-les-Bains, Besançon—Dijon and Yellow Jersey
1959	12th	Stage win St-Étienne—Grenoble
1961	3rd	Stage win St-Étienne—Grenoble
1962	9th	
1963	DNF	

BERNARD GAUTHIER
b. Beaumont-Monteux, France, Sep 22 1924

Few riders have had their photos taken quite so often as Bernard Gauthier – or few riders, at any rate, whose successes did not merit such exposure. With a Tour career that ran from just after the WAR to the start of the 1960s, Gauthier was a cameraman's dream, perfect for pictures because of his endless and ever-changing grimaces.

He began racing in occupied FRANCE in 1941 and won the Drôme regional championship. More local successes followed, but he had to wait until 1947 and the recovery of cycling after the war before he could turn professional. He then immediately won three races, came sixth in the Grand Prix des Nations, and 22nd in the Tour.

Gauthier won a stage in the following year's Tour, and in 1950 wore the yellow JERSEY. He won it by a second after getting into an unremarkable break of seven that won the Liège-Lille stage by three and a half minutes on the main field. Gauthier kept the jersey for seven days until the race reached the Pyrenees, when it was taken by FIORENZO MAGNI after a stage won by GINO BARTALI. (*See* their entries for how an alleged knifeman led both to abandon the Tour.)

Gauthier's strength lay in the very races that weakened everyone else, not least Bordeaux-Paris. He rode and won that race four times, exhausted after more than 500km and often battered by accidents. In the 1954 race 'Nanar' lost control behind his derny, the pacing motorbike used for the daylight section, and crashed to the ground, banging his head. There he lay in a dazed state before climbing back on his bike, still groggy, to get to Paris.

Gauthier's career included second places in the Tour of Flanders (1951), Paris-Brussels (1951) – when his lone break ended just three kilometres from the line – and Milan-San Remo (1955).

It was Gauthier who got RAYMOND POULIDOR started as a professional. Gauthier saw Poulidor in a CRITERIUM and recommended him to his MANAGER, the old Tour star ANTONIN MAGNE. Poulidor stayed all his career with Magne's Mercier team and so did Gauthier, riding as the younger man's DOMESTIQUE until he retired in 1962 to live in Grenoble at the foot of the Alps.

Winner

1951	Bordeaux-Paris
1952	Tour Sud-Est, GP Alger
1953	GP Pneumatique
1954	Bordeaux-Paris
1956	Bordeaux-Paris, Critérium As, National championship
1957	Bordeaux-Paris
1958	Tour Sud-Est

Tour de France

1947	22nd	
1948	24th	Stage win Liège—Roubaix
1949	DNF	
1950	17th	Yellow Jersey
1951	26th	
1952	63rd	
1953	75th	
1955	46th	
1959	DNF	
1960	79th	

GEARS

The earliest bikes had neither gears nor chain – Leonardo Da Vinci is credited with the idea of a chain and cog in the 15th century but it made no progress – and pedals were fixed by crank to the hub of the front wheel. Riders sat above the wheel and the effective gear was limited by the length of their legs. Bikes of that sort, with a small trailing wheel at the rear, were known in Britain as penny-farthings after two common coins of widely different sizes. Purists refer to an 'Ordinary bicycle', the name it acquired in the 1880s when inventors produced bikes driven via a chain to the back wheel.

At first there was only a single gear. The one rear sprocket could be changed but not during a ride. Nor could riders freewheel – and even when they could, many preferred to stick to fixed wheels, on which the pedals turned all the time the bike was in motion. They believed – as some TIME TRIAL riders in BRITAIN continued to believe into the 1950s – that they got a smoother, faster and mechanically more reliable ride.

Tour de France riders were originally free to use freewheels, but in the first Tour of 1903 only one rider, Pierre Desvages, is ever named as doing so. Desvages used a freewheel made by BSA and came 20th, but the other riders were more conservative, and also suspicious. They preferred to fix sprockets to both sides of their back wheels, one larger than the other, and pick the right moment to jump off, undo the nuts, turn the wheel and lace the chain on to another sprocket (bigger for hills, smaller for the flat and going downhill).

ROGER LAPÉBIE said, 'We had big fork ends at the back of the bike to make adjustments possible. In the MOUNTAINS we used a 44-tooth ring at the front with a 22 and 24 on one side and 18 and 20 on the other. On the flat we had a 50-tooth ring at the front with 16, 17, 19 and 20 sprockets at the back. Flexibility and speed were important. You had to change gear at the right moment. On the flat you would put it in the right gear, or you would go as far as you could up the hill and then change.

'You could lose a race if you didn't change gear at the right moment. If a good rider stopped to change gear, everybody might attack together and he would never see them again. There was a lot of psychology involved.' Riders who knew the course were prone to bluff by spinning the wheel twice, which meant they ended up on the same gear while rivals were tricked into changing into a higher gear before a hill.

FIRMIN LAMBOT rode up to PHILIPPE THYS, the race leader in 1920, and said, 'The course is flat from here on: why are you staying in your little gear?' Thys trusted him, got off to turn the wheel . . . and Lambot sprinted away. When Thys got back, he was angry he'd been cheated, and made a point of outsprinting Lambot when the stage ended in Strasbourg.

Not having to stop and move the chain or turn the wheel was obviously going to be an advantage. But riders had grown conservative. JOANNY PANEL invented a gear called the Chemineau, complete with indexed handlebar lever, and used it in the 1912 race; but rivals were unimpressed, considering it unreliable when Panel failed to finish. HENRI DESGRANGE

disliked gears because they got in the way of his ideal of a pure battle between men in which machines were incidental. He banned gears in the Tour before they had a chance to catch on.

But things were different among leisure riders, who became increasingly swayed by the views of the French writer Paul de Vivie (1853–1930). De Vivie ran a bike shop in St-Étienne and in 1887 founded the magazine *Le Cycliste*. There, under the name Vélocio, he wrote articles insisting that gears were the future. Even into old age he set out every day to to make his point by riding the Col de la République outside the town (he preferred the traditional name of Col de Grand Bois). His MEMORIAL is in a lay-by at the summit.

De Vivie's campaigning had some success with leisure riders, and by 1912 they were using gears that could handle up to five sprockets. But racers remained adamant: gears, says historian Ralph Hurne, 'were for tearaways, tourists, softies and vicars – and definitely not for racing.'

In the end, of course, modern life overwhelmed old attitudes. In 1928 the French engineer Lucien Juy made the Simplex double-pivot derailleur. This, unlike earlier inventions, hung with its own chain tensioner beneath the freewheel, just like a modern gear. Earlier gears, and even the popular Osgear on sale for a few years after the war, had a wheeled and sprung arm behind the bottom bracket to press down on the chain and take up the slack.

Juy was the inventor of the modern derailleur if anybody was, but it was a gadget that evolved rather than simply appeared. Tullio Campagnolo, on the other hand, definitely invented the quick-release hub, although this got off to a muddled start.

Legend says that in 1927 Campagnolo punctured on the Croce d'Aune pass while racing in the GP della Vittoria. It was mid-November and his hands were so cold in the snow on the Dolomites that he couldn't undo the wing-nuts to remove his wheel and change the tyre. He is said to have muttered, '*Bisogno cambiá qualcosa de drio!*' (Something must change at the back).

Because of his difficulty in undoing the wing-nuts with his cold hands, Campagnolo invented a quick-release hub, worked by cam and lever rather than nuts. He patented it in February 1930, but its reception was unenthusiastic: riders stubborn about gears were dubious about anything as apparently flimsy as a lever, and many were still using wing-nuts even at the start of the 1950s.

Campagnolo then turned to rivalling Juy's Simplex derailleur. His mind was still on his quick-release hub, though, and his Cambio Corsa gear in 1940 reflected this. It had two levers and rods on the right seat stay, one to move prongs that pushed the chain sideways, the other to work the wheel release to move the wheel to take up the surplus slack chain.

To change gear, the rider loosened the wheel with one lever, then used the other to move the chain. The wheel lock was then re-tightened, the whole operation being done while still riding. GINO BARTALI was happy with it, but FAUSTO COPPI persisted only because of sponsorship commitments.

Awkward though both the Simplex and Campagnolo were, they were better than unbolting a wheel and turning it. Thus they became standard in races, but still not in the Tour. The only people who could use them were *TOURISTE-ROUTIERS* because they rode, in effect, for the fun of it. (*See* entry for details.) Desgrange saw them as more *touriste* than *routier*. But when *touriste-routiers* began riding past the established stars on the MOUNTAINS, the Tour started to look ridiculous. However, Desgrange still stood firm.

The change came after he fell ill during the 1936 Tour, handed control to JACQUES GODDET, and never returned. Goddet may have wanted gears in the Tour – allowing them was one of his first decisions in 1937 – but he penalised Félicien Vervaecke 10 minutes for anticipating the decision in 1936. The severity of the penalty was a recognition of just how much difference gears could make.

Double chainrings – introduced in 1947 – doubled the number of available gears and allowed each ratio to be closer to the next. The opportunity for riders always to have the right gear for the conditions pushed up speeds and improved the shelter that riders got from each other. TACTICS changed, and races became a succession of attacks taking riders off the front rather than attrition which shed them from the back.

New designs followed from both Simplex and Campagnolo until, by the early 1960s, the standard rear gear was a collapsible parallelogram on which spring-loaded jockey wheels both guided the chain to the right sprocket and took up the slack. Simplex slowly lost its place in the market, along with other makers such as Mavic and Sun-Tour, and Campagnolo was in turn challenged by the Japanese company Shimano. The two now have the market effectively to themselves. (*See* BIKES for market distribution.)

FRANCE, once the world's leading equipment-maker, couldn't cope with the challenge from Campagnolo. Shimano's arrival hit it even harder. Gerald O'Donovan, the businessman behind the dominant RALEIGH team in the 1970s (equipped by Campagnolo) said, 'The problem was getting the French to agree on a common set of parts. They just could not get their game together. I still believe today that the French component industry shot itself in the foot by failing to cooperate with one another. They would have been in a much stronger position to resist oriental competition. But there, I am forgetting that M. Chauvin was French.'

Gears have seen more development than any other part of the bike. From having to unbolt the back wheel and turn it round in the 1930s, riders now have potentially 30 gears operated in defined clicks by a small lever set behind the brake lever. The smallest sprocket has fallen from 14 in the 1960s to 11. (*See* BIKES for this and other changes.) The closeness of gear ratios and the simplicity of gear-changing have pushed speeds markedly higher; riders can now always find precisely the right pedalling speed for any condition. Not only can they change gear without reaching for the lever, they can even change while they're out of the saddle.

A flick of the finger has replaced returning to the saddle and reaching down to a lever on the frame or the end of the handlebars.

The only common link with the past is the wire that links levers and gears. But even that may change. In the 1992 Tour Philippe Louviot experimented with Mavic electronic gears. And Shimano has tested gears powered by compressed air.

(*See* JEAN-FRANÇOIS BERNARD, RENÉ VIETTO.)

AB GELDERMANS
b. Beverwijk, Holland, Mar 17 1935

HOLLAND's best Tour rider of the early 1960s, Albertus Geldermans was a rider of catlike smoothness and grace who spent most of his career as DOMESTIQUE for JACQUES ANQUETIL. In 1959 he finished a surprising sixth in the WORLD CHAMPIONSHIP at Zandvoort, and rode his first Tour the next year. There he came 12th, which made him head of Holland's NATIONAL TEAM the next year. But he punctured in the TIME TRIAL, then crashed going down the Col de Schlucht when Horst Oldenburg of GERMANY fell in front of him. Geldermans broke his collarbone.

In 1962, when he next rode, the Tour was for trade teams, and Geldermans was a *knecht* (domestique) for Anquetil. A break of 15 went off on the sixth day, on the stage from Dinard to Brest, and Anquetil ordered Geldermans to get up to it and keep an eye on what happened. The group stayed away, and Geldermans finished fifth to become yellow JERSEY. He kept the lead for two days.

Winner

1960 Liège-Bastogne-Liège, Tour Germany
1961 Four-days Dunkirk
1962 National championship

Tour de France

1960	12th	
1961	DNF	
1962	5th	Yellow Jersey
1963	24th	
1964	38th	
1965	DNF	
1966	69th	

RAPHAËL GÉMINIANI
b. Clermont-Ferrand, France, Jun 10 1925

A great character, storyteller and mischief-maker, Raphaël Géminiani is one of the most colourful riders in cycling history and a man whose vision changed the sport permanently.

Géminiani came from the Michelin tyre town of Clermont-Ferrand. His father had emigrated from Italy and ran a BIKE shop in the city, and Raphaël worked with him after he left school at 12, trueing wheels and welding frames. It was inevitable that he would start racing, and he showed early promise when he won the Premier Pas Dunlop for under-16s. The Premier Pas ('first step' in French) was a race to pick out promising young riders, and Géminiani won by breaking away on the last hill in front of a home crowd in Clermont-Ferrand. In sixth place was another rider who would go far, young LOUISON BOBET.

Géminiani and his elder brother Angelo began racing against professionals after the WAR, and in 1946 Raphaël won a contract from the Métropole team. Its MANAGER, ROMAIN BELLENGER, had seen him in the Circuit des Six Provinces. That led in 1947 to a place in a French Sud-Ouest-Centre REGIONAL TEAM in the Tour, although he didn't finish because of severe sunburn.

Géminiani was a strong and above all tactically astute rider, but he came into cycling at a time when FRANCE was at its strongest. Thus he was overshadowed by others, notably LOUISON BOBET and JACQUES ANQUETIL, whom he later managed. There were too few places in some of the NATIONAL TEAMS of those days, and Géminiani's strong views didn't always make him the friends necessary to secure his selection.

Although he rode his first Tour in 1947, it wasn't until he was 33 in 1958 that he got his first yellow JERSEY. This arose from his anger at being sidelined from the main France team when Anquetil thought Géminiani and Bobet together would be too much to handle. He was put instead into another regional team, Centre-Midi, and he didn't take the slur lightly. 'Every time I wore the tricolour [national] jersey I did it honour,' he wrote in his autobiography. 'And I did it a lot: three times in the Giro, twice in the Vuelta. And I was dismissed without a care.'

Géminiani set out to make life miserable for the official French team. When a Belgian supporter gave him a donkey as a gift, he promptly named it Marcel and offered it to MARCEL BIDOT, the MANAGER who had bowed to Anquetil's wishes and kept Géminiani out. (*See* Bidot entry for how he picked his teams on the back of cigarette packets.) With his flair for publicity, Géminiani made sure there were photographers around when he gave Bidot the donkey.

Géminiani's anger lasted throughout the race. He would get into important breaks, sabotage initiatives by Bobet by chasing or not chasing as the case demanded, and use his tactical brain – one of the greatest the sport has known – to undermine whatever the main team tried.

After days of disruption, the time came for a positive move. He chose the 13th stage from Dax to Pau, encouraged by the knowledge that even Bobet had said he'd be a danger in the MOUNTAINS. The action started when FEDERICO BAHAMONTES attacked, forcing the other great climber, CHARLY GAUL, to retaliate. Géminiani set off with him, knowing Gaul would outpace the bunch on the climbs. He also knew he would be dropped by him, but by then Gaul would have taken him far enough ahead for him to win the yellow JERSEY.

Pulling it on as he stood on the podium, Géminiani commented on how the situation had changed, how he was now the leader and not the disrupter. 'Now the others will have to come looking for me rather than the other way round,' he said.

Géminiani's triumph had an affect he couldn't have forecast. His NICKNAME was *le grand fusil* (loosely 'Top Gun'), but after so many years on the fringes he was more of a loose cannon, and thrived when he had a free hand. But 'from that moment,' his manager Adolphe Deledda recalled, 'he became more cautious. He was no longer the spontaneous, happy Géminiani that we'd known. He had to suppress his personality to win the Tour. Until then, he'd ridden on TACTICS and the need to impress his rivals. We drank champagne that night. We knew it was going to be difficult.'

Géminiani lost his jersey after four days, then regained it by beating new leader Vito Farer, in a TIME TRIAL up MONT VENTOUX. Gaul won there and then produced the ride of his life on the Briançon—Aix-les-Bains stage, so cocky that he told Bobet, whom he disliked, on precisely which climb he would attack. Gaul rode alone over the mountains in one of the most crushing rides the post-war Tour has seen. (*See* Gaul's entry for details.)

France crumbled, or perhaps they were taking revenge on their outcast. Géminiani begged Bobet to help limit the damage, shouting in the rainstorm that Gaul would cost both of them the Tour if he was allowed to stay away. But Bobet was physically weak and spiritually demoralised, and refused to help. Anquetil pulled out with a lung infection. So Géminiani chased on alone, flaying himself. But nobody could have stopped the little LUXEMBOURG climber and Géminiani lost his jersey and with it the Tour. He finished the stage in tears of anger and disillusion, calling Bobet a Judas.

Géminiani's influence went further than his race record. He was one of the era's most popular riders with fans and yet, apart from the Midi-Libre in 1951, the only important race he won was the French national championship in 1953. He retired in 1960 after catching malaria on a racing and hunting trip to Upper Volta (now Burkina Faso) with Fausto Coppi at the end of the previous year. (*See* FAUSTO COPPI for details.) Coppi died but Géminiani survived.

Géminiani made his mark on the history of the Tour when he arranged to bring in team sponsors from outside the cycle industry. He had for some time sponsored himself through his Géminiani bike company. (In fact the bikes were made by Cizeron of St-Étienne or by Mercier, but they bore his name, a common procedure also followed by Louison Bobet.) There was too little money to engage a good team, and so Géminiani went to the aperitif company, St-Raphaël, that shared his name, and arranged a sponsorship deal. (*See* SPONSORS for details.) Jacques Anquetil won the 1962, 1963 and 1964 Tours in St-Raphaël's colours of red, white and pale blue.

Géminiani also managed EDDY MERCKX's Fiat team in 1977 and STEPHEN ROCHE in La Redoute in 1984.

Géminiani lives in Seillans in southern France (*see* also FRED DE BRUYNE), and according to friends still watches races, bangs café bars in frustration at the monotony of modern cycling, and swears each race will be the last he'll watch. And then a week later he'll turn up again. His nickname of *le grand fusil* was coined by Louison Bobet in 1955, and he said it was in recognition of the way he rode. But it could also have hinted at Géminiani's generous nose.

(*See* DOMESTIQUES, FILMS, FERDY KÜBLER.)

Winner

1950 Trophée Grimpeurs
1951 Midi Libre, Trophée Grimpeurs
1953 National championship

Tour de France

1947	DNF	
1948	15th	
1949	25th	Stage win Lausanne—Colmar
1950	4th	Stage wins Nice—Gap, Briançon—St-Étienne
1951	2nd	Stage win Limoges—Clermont-Ferrand, and Mountains winner
1952	11th	Stage wins Nancy—Mulhouse, Toulouse—Bagnères-de-Bigorre
1953	9th	
1954	DNF	
1955	6th	Stage win Briançon—Monaco

Tour de France (continued)

1956	49th	
1958	3rd	Yellow Jersey
1959	28th	

JEAN-PIERRE GENET

b. Brest, France, Oct 24 1940

Jean-Pierre Genet was the man who upset the king of Belgians. King Baudouin (r.1951–93) was too good-mannered to say so, but the reason he had turned out in Marche-en-Famenne in 1971 was to to see a compatriot, either EDDY MERCKX or HERMAN VAN SPRINGEL, win a Tour stage in BELGIUM.

Instead, the little-known Frenchman Genet stood on the podium and said, 'When I set off, it wasn't with the idea of winning.' He and José Gomez-Lucas had broken clear and ridden 46km across Belgium as an increasingly frantic chase set up behind them. Merckx and his Molteni team wanted the royal honour, and teams with the best SPRINTERS wanted the victory. But they got the timing wrong. Genet crossed the line five seconds before them and a second ahead of Gomez-Lucas. It was all that remained of what had been a two-minute advantage.

Genet rode 13 Tours, won three stages and wore the yellow JERSEY in 1968.

Tour de France

1964	78th	
1965	75th	
1966	DNF	
1967	88th	
1968	41st	Stage win Aurillac—St-Étienne, and Yellow Jersey
1969	68th	
1970	82nd	
1971	26th	Stage win Nancy—Marche-en-Famenne
1972	DNF	
1973	46th	
1974	67th	Stage win Lodève—Colomiers
1975	DNF	
1976	43rd	

ÉMILE GEORGET

b. Bossay, France, Sep 21 1881, d. Chatellerault, France, Apr 16 1960

Émile Georget was first to climb the GALIBIER, on July 10 1911. Just as OCTAVE LAPIZE had accused officials of being 'murderers' on the first AUBISQUE climb in 1910, so Georget approached them on the Galibier in 1911, filthy and dripping, and sneered, 'That'll keep you quiet for a bit.'

Émile Georget was morally the winner of the 1907 Tour, although he actually finished in third place. The race was an example of the bitter competition between the ALCYON and PEUGEOT teams. (See EUGÈNE CHRISTOPHE for another example.) The previous year's winner, RENÉ POTTIER, had committed suicide, leaving LOUIS TROUSSELIER of Alcyon and Georget of Peugeot as the remaining favourites.

Georget won five of the first eight stages. But then he crashed at the checkpoint at Auch on the hot stage from Toulouse to Bayonne. His team-mate, Gonzague Privat, gave him his BIKE and Georget rode on. But the RULES said a rider must finish on the machine on which he'd started, and since bikes were impounded by POLICE after each stage there was no hope of getting away with it.

Alcyon protested, demanding that Georget be thrown out of the race. But the organisers weren't going to disqualify a French favourite like Georget, and compromised by relegating him to last place on the stage. That kept him in the race but with no chance of winning. Alcyon weren't happy with that and went on STRIKE. That lost the race a lot of its competition and cleared the way for LUCIEN PETIT-BRETON, another Peugeot rider. He became a new man once in the lead and rode to Paris without finishing outside the top three.

This was the first Tour to visit Germany, crossing the politically difficult Alsace-Lorraine region to reach Metz. (See GERMANY for what happened and for the unflattering light in which it put FRANCE.) It was also the race in which the 'Baron' Pépin de Gontaud rode with two 'valets' (see HENRI PÉPIN for more) and to

which ALFRED LE BARS cycled the 270km to the START.

Winner

1910	Bordeaux-Paris, National championship
1911	Paris-Brest-Paris
1912	Bordeaux-Paris

Tour de France

1903	DNF	
1905	4th	
1906	5th	Stage win Paris—Lille
1907	3rd	Stage wins Roubaix—Metz, Metz—Belfort, Lyon—Grenoble, Nice—Nîmes, Nîmes—Toulouse, Brest—Caen
1908	DNF	
1910	DNF	Stage win Metz—Belfort
1911	3rd	Stage win Chamonix—Grenoble
1912	DNF	
1913	DNF	
1914	6th	

GERMANY

The Tour first went to Germany in 1906, when HENRI DESGRANGE sent Alphonse Steinès (see MOUNTAINS) to Metz to meet the governor. He was to ask permission to cross the area of France lost to Germany after defeat in the battle of Sedan, which ended the Franco-Prussian war in 1870. Both the governor and Berlin agreed. Desgrange then drew up a course of 4,637 km, or 1,600km longer than the previous year.

The assistant organiser, Victor Breyer, reported that the French from the annexed areas cheered French riders and even French cars. German police, he said, not only behaved impeccably but declined to halt speeding drivers and riders. 'You'd never get that from a French policeman,' he wrote.

It wasn't the only unfavourable comparison the French would draw with their own country. Formalities on passing back out of Germany were *minutieuses* (meticulous), according to one report. 'Woken from a deep sleep, obliged to get up in three minutes, the German customs men appeared before us correctly dressed in new uniforms. At the French border, by contrast, it was simply distressing. Smelly, covered in mud, their clothes patched and discoloured, backs bent, squashed *képis* on dirty bodies, the two officials charged with nosing around on behalf of the tax authorities and who represented France revolted us.' The delays were long enough to force the judges to organise a second START. *L'AUTO* cheekily but 'very seriously' offered a public appeal to dress its frontier officials properly.

The first German to ride the Tour was Ludwig Bartelmann in 1903. The first complete team was in 1930, the first year of NATIONAL TEAMS. Consisting of Félix Manthey, Rudolph Wolke, Herbert Nebe, Adolf Schön, Oskar Thierbach, Alfred Siegel, Hermann Buse and Oscar Tietz, only Buse, a Berliner, was known outside Germany. He had won that year's Liège-Bastogne-Liège. Nevertheless they finished third best team and Schön came 10th.

The first German in the yellow JERSEY was KURT STÖPEL in 1932.

After the second war no Germans were invited to the Tour until 1955. Then two individuals, Heinz Müller and Gunther Pankoke, rode with Luxembourger CHARLY GAUL in an international team. Müller had been WORLD CHAMPION in 1952 but abandoned the Tour after four days; Pankoke got to Paris in 37th place.

The first German team after the war was fielded in 1960, although more individuals had ridden in mixed teams, including Lothar Friedrich, who came 12th in the 1958 Tour. Germany suffered through rarely having its own trade teams. Riders had to look elsewhere for SPONSORS but there were RULES limiting the number of foreigners in each team. The best could do it, though, and RUDI ALTIG won the yellow jersey in 1962 and 1964 for St-Raphaël of FRANCE, and in 1966 for the Italian sponsor Molteni.

DIDI THURAU blossomed in the last quarter of the 21st century, but riches came only at the millennium's end, with ERIK ZABEL dominating the sprinters (*see* entry for details) and JAN ULLRICH winning the Tour in 1997 and the Olympic road race in 2000.

The Tour has started in Germany three times: in Cologne in 1965, in Frankfurt in 1980 and in Berlin in 1987, the city's 750th anniversary. Plans to enter East Germany in 1987 were abandoned; the organisers decided West Berlin was already difficult enough. (*See* FOREIGN VISITS; and *see* also HENNIE KUIPER, REGIONAL TEAMS.)

FELICE GIMONDI

b. Sedrina, Italy, Sep 29 1942

Snaggle-toothed Felice Gimondi was one of the Tour's most popular winners. He was just 22 when he won in 1965 after being put into the race at the last moment, and his youth and shy smile won him many fans. Gimondi's win is colourfully portrayed in the FILM *Pour un Maillot Jaune*, including the moment when he briefly ground to an exhausted halt among SPECTATORS in the MOUNTAINS.

Gimondi benefited from JACQUES ANQUETIL's decision not to try for a sixth win. The Frenchman was tired of claims that his habit of winning Tours in the TIME TRIALS had made the race dull. 'My contracts won't get better if I win again,' he said, 'but they'll go down if I fail; I'll stay at home.'

The decision put the focus on RAYMOND POULIDOR and, so far as ITALY was concerned, on the more favoured Gianni Motta and VITTORIO ADORNI. It didn't seem to matter, then, when the novice Gimondi joined two unfancied Belgians, Vic van Schil and Bernard van der Kerkhove, when they broke away on the stage to Roubaix. Gimondi came second behind van der Kerkhove, then next day won Roubaix-Rouen and gained both the yellow jersey and more than three minutes on Poulidor.

Van der Kerkhove took back his lead when Gimondi missed a break of nine on stage seven but the Italian was back in control after the first MOUNTAIN stage, from Dax to Bagnères-Bigorre. Poulidor all but broke Gimondi on

MONT VENTOUX but it wasn't enough and Gimondi not only survived but won the final TIME TRIAL into Paris.

Gimondi never made a career of the Tour because he and his SPONSORS were happier in the Giro. Nevertheless he followed his win in 1965 with two MOUNTAIN stages in 1967 and second place to EDDY MERCKX in 1972. His last Tour was 1975, when he came sixth.

Gimondi was a stylish and much-loved rider who won all three major stage races – the Tour in 1965, the Giro in 1967, 1969 and 1976, and the Tour of SPAIN in 1968 – but had enough class to win classics as well, including the Tour of Lombardy (1966, 1973), Milan-San Remo (1974), Paris-Roubaix (1966) and the world championship of 1973.

Gimondi now works as a team manager and lives in an expensively furnished 18-room mansion near Bergamo, which has prompted his NICKNAME of 'the Aristocrat.' When MARCO PANTANI won the Tour in 1998, and became the first Italian to win since Gimondi 33 years earlier, the two men embraced on the finishing line.

Winner

1964 Tour Avenir
1965 Tour de France
1966 Paris-Brussels, Paris-Roubaix, Tour Lombardy, Coppa Placci
1967 Giro d'Italia, GP Lugano, GP Forli, GP Nations, Tour Lazio
1968 Tour Spain, Critérium As, GP Forli, GP Nations, National championship
1969 Giro d'Italia, Tour Romandie, Tour Appenines, GP Forli
1970 Trofeo Matteotti
1971 GP Wallonia, Tour Piedmont, GP Forli
1972 Tour Catalonia, Tour Appenines, GP Lugano, National championship
1973 World championship, Tour Puglia, Tour Piedmont, GP Forli, Tour Lombardy
1974 Milan-San Remo
1976 Giro d'Italia, Paris-Brussels

Tour de France

1965	1st	Stage wins Roubaix—Rouen, Aix-les-Bains—Mont Revard, Versailles—Paris, and Yellow Jersey
1967	7th	Stage wins Divonne—Briançon, Limoges—Puy-de-Dôme
1969	4th	Stage win Digne—Aubagne
1972	2nd	
1975	6th	Stage win Auch—Pau

COSTANTE GIRARDENGO

b. Novi Ligure, Italy, Mar 18 1893, d. Novi Ligure, Italy, Feb 9 1978

ITALY dominated cycling at the end of the twentieth century, as it had in the FAUSTO COPPI era of the 1950s. But the first great Italian was Costante Girardengo, who won Milan-San Remo six times (1918, 1921, 1923, 1925, 1926, 1928), and the national championship in every peacetime year from 1913 to 1925. Coppi was often called the *campionissimo*, but the first to be given the title of champion of champions was Girardengo.

Italy on the eve of the first world war was desperate to do something in the Tour de France. Its best riders had all preferred the Giro d'Italia, and the best it had done in the Tour was sixth place in 1907 (Eberado Pavesi), and two stage wins in 1912 (Vicenzo Borgarello). Girardengo had won the national championship for the first time in 1913, and enthusiastic fans were sure that he was the man to change their fortunes in FRANCE. He wasn't then the great rider that he was to become and Automoto, his SPONSOR, wouldn't accept him as leader in 1914 above LUCIEN PETIT-BRETON and LOUIS TROUSSELIER, two former winners. Girardengo settled for being a DOMESTIQUE on the condition that he could make his own race if he had the chance.

That opportunity came quickly when he sprinted to fourth in the first stage, from Paris to Le Havre. The man who beat him then, PHILIPPE THYS, went on to win the Tour. For Italy's great hope, though, that was as good as it got. He lost 72 minutes next day after several

CRASHES, crashed badly again on stage six, and abandoned well behind the race and without team-mates. The race was a disaster for Automoto: Petit-Breton pulled out after nine stages and Trousselier came 38th.

Girardengo returned to Italy and never rode the Tour again. It was a loss. Many believed the mature Girardengo could have won easily. Instead, the first Italian winner was OTTAVIO BOTTECCHIA in 1924.

(*See* HENRI PÉLISSIER.)

Winner

1913	National championship
1914	National championship, Milan-Turin
1915	Milan-Turin
1918	Milan-San Remo, Tour Emilia
1919	Tour Lombardy, National championship, Giro d'Italia, Milan-Turin, Tour Piedmont, Tour Emilia
1920	National championship Milan-Turin, Tour Piedmont
1921	Milan-San Remo, Tour Lombardy, National championship, Tour Emilia
1922	Tour Lombardy, National championship, Tour Emilia
1923	Giro d'Italia, Milan-San Remo, National championship, Tour Tuscany, Milan-Turin, Tour Veneto
1924	National championship, Tour Tuscany, Tour Piedmont, Tour Veneto
1925	Milan-San Remo, National championship, Tour Veneto
1926	Milan-San Remo, Tour Veneto
1928	Milan-San Remo

Tour de France

1914	DNF

GITANE

Gitane is a French BIKE firm which is now close to celebrating half a century since it came into the Tour de France. That was in 1957, and in 2002 Gitane was still in the peloton with the Big Mat team. Among its winners it has had JACQUES ANQUETIL, BERNARD HINAULT and LAURENT FIGNON.

Gitane began in 1926 when a blacksmith mechanic called Brunelière opened a workshop in stables at Machecoul, south-west of Nantes. He began making two or three bikes a day, first under his initials, GMB, then as Marbru. The name changed to Gitane in 1930 supposedly, legend says, to celebrate the way Brunelière travelled round France to sell his bikes; but *gitane* means not gypsy but gypsy-*woman.*

Anquetil won the Tour on a Gitane in 1957. Encouraged, the firm started the Gitane team in 1959 with RAPHAËL GÉMINIANI, who finished third to CHARLY GAUL in 1958 (*see* Géminiani's entry for his role in extending cycling sponsorship still further.) Anquetil won again in 1961 and 1963, and the following year production rose to 500 bikes a day. Brunelière retired in 1970 but growth continued, and in 1972 the firm exported 185,000 bikes in addition to those sold in France.

In 1976, Gitane's motorbike business brought it into the state-owned Renault group, so when Hinault won the Tour for Renault and Gitane (1978, 1979 1981 and 1982) he did so as a state employee. Gitane came out of government ownership in 1985. Its bikes are now made at Cycleurope de Romilly, where PEUGEOT and France's RALEIGH bikes are also made.

JACQUES GODDET

Jean-François ('Jacques') Goddet was the Tour's second organiser. He ran the race from 1936 to 1987 and, with FÉLIX LÉVITAN, brought the Tour into its modern era. The sight of Goddet in tropical khaki and a pith helmet, peering through the roof of his red car like a tank captain, is the classic image of the Tour in the 1960s and 1970s.

Jacques Goddet was the son of Victor Goddet, the accountant at L'AUTO who gave HENRI DESGRANGE the money to start the Tour in 1903. Jacques Goddet and his father – who died in 1926 – spent many days at the Vélodrome de Paris-Est. In 1924 he went to work for his father's paper, in the rue du

Faubourg-Montmartre in Paris. But family links brought no passport to the Tour; he wasn't allowed to follow it for four years, and then for only two days. But in 1928 he sat spellbound in his car for 710km through the Pyrenees. He saw VICTOR FONTAN win at Luchon after more than 16 hours in the saddle, on cols that he remembered 'were no more than mediocre earth paths, muddy, stony'.

Goddet returned next year and followed every Tour until 1989, except in 1932 when he went to the Olympics, and in 1981 when he was ill. In 1936 Goddet took over from Desgrange as organiser. His immediate change was to allow GEARS from 1937, although Félicien Vervaecke was heavily penalised for anticipating the decision in 1936. (*See* GEARS for more.)

The WAR interrupted Goddet's changes, coming weeks after SYLVÈRE MAES won the 1939 Tour. GERMANY invaded France in 1940, the nations came to an armistice on June 22, and the government moved to Vichy.

France has only recently come to terms with its shameful moments in the war, and one of the worst of these was in 1942, when 9,000 French policemen rounded up 13,000 Jews and imprisoned them in the Vélodrome d'Hiver TRACK near the Eiffel Tower. There they suffered appallingly in the heat, dirt and bad conditions before being shipped to a holding station at Drancy and from there to Auschwitz. Only 400 returned.

Goddet owned the *Vel d'Hiv'* track where they had been held, and had rented it before the war for fascist meetings. In 1942 he handed over the keys when the police demanded them. It's dangerous to judge one era against the attitudes of another, and it may well be that Goddet had no choice and that, so far as the fascist meetings were concerned, he was happy to hire the hall to anyone. PIERRE CHANY, who knew Goddet well, claimed he had no choice, and that he had also printed Resistance newsletters and had stood out against Desgrange's decision to publish a weekly called *Savoir Vite*, which carried German propaganda. (*See* Chany entry for other wartime experiences, and for practical jokes played on Goddet.)

L'Auto was closed down on August 17 1944 after France was liberated, its doors literally nailed shut for continuing to publish during the Occupation. Goddet at once established a successor, *L'ÉQUIPE*, on the opposite side of the road, in a building owned by the now sequestered *L'Auto* company. The new paper appeared for the first time on February 28 1946 (*see L'Équipe* for more.)

Goddet's style echoed that of Desgrange, and the heroic approach he cultivated. Thus he wrote not of finish lines but *les arrivées magistrales* (masterly finishes), or of LOUISON BOBET 'accepting gallantly the delay attributed to him by the celestial handicapper'. Jean Cocteau said, 'The last of the troubadours, [Goddet] sings the Tour like an adventure novel.' The British journalist Geoffrey Nicholson wrote, 'Brisk but courteous, he took an avuncular interest in the welfare of his riders and knew each by name. He often came into the press room to type out his daily column, which was full of battlefield oratory. But unlike most correspondents, who dressed as though they had just crawled out of a foxhole, Goddet was immaculate.'

Goddet saw the race develop from the era of attrition and backbreaking toil that it had been under Desgrange into the speed-based competition we recognise now. His 'avuncular' manner, as Nicholson put it, could be deceptive; under the gentle exterior was a clear, determined vision of what his race should be and the place that riders had in it. When riders walked across the FINISH line at Valence d'Agen in 1978 because they thought there were too many split stages and too many early starts, he dismissed their protest. 'It's necessary to keep the inhuman side to the Tour,' he said. 'Excess is necessary.' (*See* STRIKES for more.)

Goddet was fond of BRITAIN and even attended a school near Oxford – at least until he broke his arm at rugby and went home. He could speak good English although he rarely did. He took an amused interest in the few English-speaking journalists (so few that most were somehow assumed to be 'from *The Times*') who followed the Tour – but employed a press officer, Louis Lapeyre, whose way of dealing with them was to refuse to speak to any of them, let alone in English. The Tour in Goddet's day may have started to look further afield (*see* COLOMBIA) but it was distinctly French.

In 1983 the decision to bring in AMATEURS (*see* entry for details) produced a public split from Félix Lévitan, his co-organiser. The two were said to work well together professionally – Goddet on the sporting side of the race, Lévitan on the commercial – but to dislike each other personally. In the end, time caught both men out as their insistence on dozens of sponsors made the race tawdry, and critics even suggested that it should be taken into government control. (*See* Félix Lévitan and JEAN-MARIE LEBLANC entries.)

In 1987 a row blew up over alleged cross-financing of a race in America, and on March 17 1988 Lévitan turned up for work to find his office locked and a bailiff ready to go through his drawers and files. Lévitan left that day, protesting his innocence, and indeed nothing has ever been proved. Goddet died on December 15 2000, a year after being elevated to *grand officier* of the Légion d'Honneur, the equivalent of a knighthood. He was 95 and still had his own office at *L'Équipe*.

On his death President Jacques Chirac called Goddet 'one of the inventors of French sport'. The prime minister, Lionel Jospin, said, 'France and journalism have just lost an exceptional man. He made the Tour de France, through his 50 years at its helm, the most popular French sports event and the one most known across the world.'

Goddet is commemorated by a MEMORIAL at the Col de TOURMALET.

(*See* ROGER LÉVÈQUE, PUBLICATIONS.)

WALTER GODEFROOT
b. Ghent, Belgium, Jul 2 1943

The Tour had wheeled along the CHAMPS ELYSÉES before 1975, but it had never finished there. (*See* entry for history.) Then the era of TRACK finishes, first at the PARC DES PRINCES,

then the PISTE MUNICIPALE, came to an end. From 1975 the world's greatest bike race would finish on the world's most glorious avenue.

The French naturally wanted a Frenchman to win on that great first occasion. But it turned out to be a battle between two Belgians – Rik van Linden, the Points leader, who sprinted too soon, and the cooler Walter Godefroot, who got his timing right. This continued Godefroot's tradition of winning at least one stage in each of the seven Tours he had ridden. The Champs Elysées in 1975 was his 10th and last stage, completing 150 victories that included Paris-Roubaix by three minutes in 1969, and the 1968 Tour of Flanders. His sprint declined as he got older but his hardness didn't. He became a DOMESTIQUE for FREDDY MAERTENS but he could still win the Tour of Flanders in 1978, ten years after his first win.

Two decades later he was back on the Champs Elysées, not as a winner but a MANAGER of winners BJARNE RIIS (1996) and JAN ULLRICH (1997).

Godefroot looked like a boxer when he raced, complete with broken nose, and yet he spoke with a gentle voice. Now he looks fleshier and balder, and has the appearance of an absent-minded accountant projected suddenly into daylight. But he has lost none of his hardness, as he showed in his handling of the 2002 crisis surrounding Ullrich. (*See* JAN ULLRICH for details.)

Winner

1965	National championship
1966	A travers Belgique
1967	Liège-Bastogne-Liège
1968	A travers Belgique, Ghent-Wevelgem, Tour Flanders
1969	Paris-Roubaix, Critérium As, GP Gippingen, GP Escaut, Bordeaux-Paris
1970	Championship Zurich, Tour Reggio Calabria
1972	National championship
1974	GP Frankfurt, Championship Zurich, Four-days Dunkirk
1976	Bordeaux-Paris
1978	Tour Flanders

Tour de France

1967	60th	Stage win Angers—St-Malo
1968	20th	Stage wins Forest—Roubaix, Royan—Bordeaux
1970	29th	Stage wins Rennes—Lisieux, Lisieux—Rouen, and Points winner
1971	DNF	Stage win Clermont-Ferrand—St-Étienne
1972	44th	Stage win Royan—Bordeaux
1973	65th	Stage win Nancy—Mulhouse, Fleurance—Bordeaux
1975	51st	Stage win Paris—Paris

GEORGES GOFFIN
b. Liège, Belgium, Apr 1 1883, d. unknown

The record of BELGIUM's Georges Goffin, who came from Liège and also rode as Georges Nemo, was one of persistent failure. Goffin started three Tours and abandoned them all on the first day. It is a record unlikely to be beaten. Almost nothing is known about him, including why he rode under different names. (*See* FALSE NAMES for other examples.)

Tour de France

1909	DNF
1911	DNF
1922	DNF

JEAN GRACZYK
b. Neuvy-sur-Barangeon, France, May 26 1933

Jean Graczyk was a classic *rouleur-sprinter* (roadman/sprinter), a man like ANDRÉ DARRI-GADE who could push up the speed and still win a sprint. And like Darrigade he was a blond-haired shock trooper for JACQUES ANQUETIL, a man less concerned with winning the Tour for himself than with livening it up for others.

Graczyk, known by his NICKNAME of 'Popof', was the son of Polish immigrants, as was JEAN STABLINSKI. He could be quiet off his

BIKE, but he was the opposite on it. He was a poor CLIMBER, but his popularity meant he could rely on pushes from SPECTATORS.

Winner

1957	Tour Sud-Est
1959	Paris-Nice
1960	Critérium International

Tour de France

1957	DNF	
1958	14th	Points winner
1959	35th	Stage win Rouen—Rennes
1960	13th	Stage wins Dieppe—Caen, Luchon—Toulouse, Briançon—Aix-les-Bains, Troyes—Paris, and Points winner
1962	38th	
1963	72nd	
1964	76th	

ROBERT GRASSIN
b. Le Mans, France, Sep 17 1898, d. Gien, France, Jun 26 1980

Robert 'Toto' Grassin was the man who rode 300km of one stage of the Tour with two BIKES – one which he pedalled and another on his shoulder. (*See* VICTOR FONTAN and LÉON SCIEUR for other examples.)

HENRI DESGRANGE insisted that riders should complete the race on – or at least with – their own bikes. Grassin was riding the 1922 Tour when his forks broke between Le Havre and Cherbourg. A break like that would suggest he must have completed much of the stage. But in fact Grassin had ridden only the first 65km of a day that was 364km long.

He tried to repair the bike *(see* also EUGÈNE CHRISTOPHE) for a reputed three and a half hours before abandoning the attempt and borrowing a spare to complete the stage. He then set off with the bike on his shoulder to complete the last 300km and satisfy the judges. He reached the FINISH 2:44:32 behind the winner, ROMAIN BELLENGER. (*See* RAPHAËL GÉMINIANI for Bellenger's role in his career.)

That was a long gap, or a rather short one, depending on your view of how fast a man could race with a bike on his back. There may be some doubt about Grassin's claim that it took three and a half hours to repair the bike, but it's still remarkable. Bellenger himself took 15:7:53 for the stage, and riders were still coming in three hours behind Grassin.

Grassin walked out of the race in displeasure, and abandoned the road to become a pace-follower, riding behind giant motorbikes. He became world motor-pace champion at Amsterdam in 1925 and came third at Brussels in 1930. He was a favourite with the spectators at the Vélodrome d'Hiver in Paris. (*See* JACQUES GODDET for the Vélodrome's dark history.)

Tour de France

1922   DNF

GRAND PRIX DU TOUR DE FRANCE – *See* WAR

GRUPPETTO

Few riders can make the pace in the MOUNTAINS. The rest hope only to get through the day fast enough not to be eliminated on time – all riders have to finish within a set percentage of the winner's time. '*Gruppetto*' is the Italian word for the no-hopers who combine to ride fast enough to make sure they do stay in the race, slow enough to race again another day. The French call it '*l'autobus*'.

The Danish rider Brian Holm said, 'You get to the mountains and everyone gets in the gruppetto. Everyone knows who they're riding with. Eventually you panic because of the time limit and the group can explode. You help each other out, but you don't make friends there. You give each other things like food and water, but only because you expect to get something back. A guy may be suffering but you might need him later if you want someone to help you ride on a flat piece between the mountains.'

Sometimes the race can run so far behind time that a break puts everyone at risk. In 2001

the bunch – including favourites LANCE ARMSTRONG and JAN ULLRICH – arrived 35:54 behind ERIK DEKKER in a soaking stage to Pontarlier. The whole lot could have been thrown out, leaving barely a dozen in the race, but for a rule that eliminations don't apply if more than 20 per cent of the starters finish outside the limit. Asked what it meant to win by such a margin, Dekker said, 'It means being out in the rain for half an hour less than the others.'

But even this wasn't a record. In 1926 the weather was so awful on the TOURMALET that LUCIEN BUYSSE was shaking with cold as he crossed it with 35 minutes' lead. The rest were worse. Only 16 got to the FINISH within the limit – known in French as the *délai* – and many hadn't arrived by nightfall. HENRI DESGRANGE was reduced to phoning people in Luchon to ask if they had a car and, if they had, would they drive around in the mountains looking for his riders. Many did, and they found them shivering and dangerously tired in chalets and shelters. They weren't all down in Luchon until just before midnight. Desgrange gave the race a day off, but still 24 riders didn't make it to the START.

(*See* LUCIEN VAN IMPE.)

LEARCO GUERRA
b. San Nicolo Po, Italy, Oct 14 1902, d. Milan, Italy, Feb 7 1963

Learco ('the Locomotive') Guerra not only won the 1934 Giro d'Italia, but also took stages two to six, then stages nine to 12. He finally took stage 14 to complete 10 winning days out of a possible 17. In 1932 he won stages one, four, six, eight, nine and 13 and finished fourth. In 1935 he took five more stages and again came fourth. He was Italian national champion every year from 1930 to 1934.

Guerra rode the first of two Tours in 1930 in a rare excursion out of ITALY. It was the first year of NATIONAL TEAMS and Italy needed him. He came second, wore the yellow JERSEY and won three stages. He could have won overall, too, and for 60km he thought he had. No one could have been more disappointed.

ANDRÉ LEDUCQ was the *maillot jaune* by the time the Tour reached the Alps in 1930. He crossed the GALIBIER six seconds ahead of Guerra and 15 seconds behind team-mate Pierre Magne. Leducq left his hands off the brakes and rode down the other side at 80km/h. It was a risk he had cause to regret – he crashed and Guerra, alerted, plunged on faster and safer.

Behind him, Leducq slowly recovered consciousness. His team-mate Pierre Magne pulled him back on his BIKE and they pressed on to the Télégraphe. There a pedal fell off Leducq's bike. MARCEL BIDOT, France's most successful MANAGER (*see* Bidot entry for details), borrowed one from a SPECTATOR and Leducq set off again. Guerra now had up to 15 minutes, the leader on the road, the virtual winner of the Tour de France.

Sadly for him Bidot's French team of ANTONIN MAGNE, Pierre Magne and CHARLES PÉLISSIER (*see* HENRI PÉLISSIER and SHAY ELLIOTT for more on Pélissier) chased furiously for 60km and caught Guerra just before the FINISH at ÉVIAN. Guerra had lost the Tour and Leducq went on to win it by 14:19 – about the same gap as Guerra had had on the road from the Galibier.

He came second again in 1933, this time to GEORGES SPEICHER, winning stages at Charleville, Aix-les-Bains, Grenoble, Pau and Paris. His career ended with the WAR.

(*See* ALFREDO BINDA for why he was talked into the 1930 Tour and then abandoned it.)

Winner

1930 National championship
1931 World championship, Tour Reggio Calabria, National championship
1932 Tour Tuscany, National championship
1933 Milan-San Remo, National championship
1934 Giro d'Italia, Tour Piedmont, Tour Lombardy, National championship
1935 Tour Romandie

Tour de France

1930 2nd Stage wins Caen—Dinan, Marseille—Cannes, Nice—Grenoble, and Yellow Jersey
1933 2nd Stage wins Lille—Charleville, Évian—Aix-les-Bains, Aix-les-Bains—Grenoble, Tarbes—Pau, Caen—Paris

CYRILLE GUIMARD
b. Bouguenais, France, Jan 20 1947

Cyrille Guimard was a good rider – nearly 100 wins in eight seasons – and an even better MANAGER, who made Tour winners of LUCIEN VAN IMPE, LAURENT FIGNON and BERNARD HINAULT.

Guimard wore the yellow JERSEY in the 1972 Tour despite being a SPRINTER. He set out to keep it through the MOUNTAINS but it cost him dear. In 1969 he had injured his knee in an accident with a car when he was training, and had spent a week in a coma. The operation couldn't bring the knee back to its original condition, and in 1972 it grew so bad in the mountains that he couldn't walk and had to be carried to his bike every day.

The pain grew worse as he battled with EDDY MERCKX, now in the lead, over MONT VENTOUX. MECHANICS modified his bike in an attempt to make it easier to ride and he somehow still managed to came second to LUCIEN VAN IMPE on the ORCIÈRES-MERLETTE stage, and came close enough to threaten Merckx again.

Guimard spent the rest day in bed, and the pain in his knee eased. Going through the Alps, Merckx won two stages, Guimard the next one. That left a 28km stage over Mont Revard, as tough as it was short. Merckx however decided to bring Guimard, literally, to his knees and piled on the pressure. Guimard didn't crack. Instead he nipped by as the Belgian raised his hands in victory, and beat him by 10cm.

Guimard now couldn't pedal at all and even the other, previously good, leg started to hurt. He abandoned the Tour two days before the finish while second overall and leading the points competition.

Guimard was among the first modern team MANAGERS who concerned themselves with training and diet as well as TACTICS and management. He worked in the Renault-GITANE team with Dr Armand Megret, who became French federation doctor and founder of year-long DOPING tests for French riders. (*See* PIERRE DUMAS and STRIKES for more on dope controls; *see* too BERNARD HINAULT.) He also worked on aerodynamics with the aero-technology institute at St-Cyr-l'École near Paris. (*See* LUCIEN VAN IMPE for the story of how Guimard helped the Belgian win the 1976 Tour de France and *see* JEAN-FRANÇOIS BERNARD.)

Winner

1972	Midi Libre, Paris-Bourges, Tour Oise
1975	GP Plouay

Tour de France

1970	62nd	Stage win Limoges—La Rochelle
1971	7th	
1972	DNF	Stage wins Angers—St-Brieuc, Merlin-Plage—Royan, Valloire—Aix-les-Bains, Aix-les-Bains—Mont Revard, and Points leader
1973	DNF	Stage win Roubaix—Reims
1974	DNF	Stage win Châlons-sur-Marne—Chaumont

ALFRED HAEMERLINCK

b. Assenede, Belgium, Sep 27 1905, d. Ghent,
Belgium, Jul 10 1993

Fred Haemerlinck, from Antwerp, was one of
BELGIUM's iron-hard all-rounders between the
wars. He rode only one Tour, in 1931, but won
two stages and wore the yellow JERSEY. His
talent ranged from riding the TRACK – from
1931 to 1938 Antwerp had one of Europe's best
– to coming fourth in the WORLD CHAMPI-
ONSHIP in 1933, and third in the Tour of Flanders in 1929 and 1932.

Tour de France

1931	DNF	Stage wins Paris—Caen, Les Sables—Bordeaux, and Yellow Jersey

ANDY HAMPSTEN

b. Great Plains, USA, Apr 7 1962

Andy Hampsten is an example of how bike-
racing in AMERICA has different roots from its
European version. In Europe cycling was, like
boxing, a way for men of humble origins to
leave their village and rise above a life in the
fields or down the mine. Elsewhere, where
cycling is a minor sport (as in the USA), racing
means going against the trend, justifying what
you do, constantly explaining. That takes intelligence and determination.

Hampsten was the son of English professors
at a university in Grand Forks, North Dakota.
He got his first BIKE at 12 and – most unlike a
European rider – went to the library to find
articles about cycling in foreign newspapers.

He rode his first race when he was 15, not in
the US but in Cambridge, when he was on holiday in BRITAIN. Successes began to accumulate
when he returned to America, and he became a
member of the national team in 1979. His
strength was such that he was picked for the
TIME TRIAL team at two world junior championships even though he was more of a
CLIMBER. His team came third in 1979 and
second in 1980.

A conversation in spring 1985 with DAVIS
PHINNEY and Ron Keifel, another professional
(*see* AMERICA for more background), persuaded Hampsten to join the new 7-Eleven
professional team as a climber for the Giro
d'Italia. There he won the Gran Paradiso stage
after MANAGER Mike Neel told him exactly
how to ride. Italian papers, which hadn't taken
the new American team seriously, called him
'the champion punk-rock climber' because of a
blond streak in his brown hair.

He joined BERNARD HINAULT's La Vie Claire
team next year, won the Tour of Switzerland,
and finished the Tour de France fourth and best
YOUNG RIDER in 1986. Then a year later he
moved back to 7-Eleven and stayed with the
team as it became Motorola. (*See* EARPIECES for
the team's influence on race technology.)

His greatest win was the 1988 Giro, which he took 'on a day to make strong men cry', according to the Australian rider Alan Peiper, by riding alone over the Passo de Gavia in a snowstorm. He took the leader's JERSEY and kept it until the FINISH in Milan.

Hopes that Hampsten would repeat that success in the Tour were undermined by his poor ability as a time triallist. He changed his training to build more muscle on his skinny frame, but the increase in bulk and cruising power spoiled his climbing, so he accepted that he'd never win the Tour. Instead he pulled off a gem of a win on the ALPE D'HUEZ stage in 1992, winning by 1:17.

Hampsten stopped racing in 1996 and lives now with his wife Linda and their daughter Emma on a wine and olive farm in the Maremma hills in Tuscany.

Winner

1986 Tour Switzerland
1987 Tour Switzerland
1988 Giro d'Italia
1992 Tour Romandie
1993 Tour Galicia

Tour de France

1986	4th	
1987	16th	
1988	15th	
1989	22nd	
1990	11th	
1991	8th	
1992	4th	Stage win Sestriere—Alpe d'Huez
1993	8th	

ROGER HASSENFORDER
b. Sansheim, France, Jul 23 1930

Roger Hassenforder was a man who won hearts and friends more through his pranks and sense of humour than his results. He rode six Tours and finished only one, although he won seven Tour stages.

'Hassen', from the Colmar region of eastern France, came to cycling when he was 19, having previously been a footballer. He was so far behind in his first race that the judges went home. In his second, friends found him exhausted in a ditch. The race was 200km long, and he had taken only two oranges to eat.

In 1950 in the army, though, he began training on the TRACK in Reims and showed talent, even beating FAUSTO COPPI. He moved to the road and came to notice when he took the yellow JERSEY in the first week of the 1953 Tour. He won it from FRITZ SCHAER after getting into a break from Dieppe to Caen that was won by JEAN MALLÉJAC (see Malléjac entry for drama at the foot of MONT VENTOUX), pushing Schaer to second by 48 seconds. Hassenforder wore it for four days until the Pyrenees, when Schaer took it back again. In the 1956 Tour he won three stages.

Hassenforder provided good entertainment in a serious sport. He was a natural joker, known as 'the Clown', 'the Bandit', or simply 'Hassen', but as a cyclist he was handicapped by being a poor CLIMBER. Maybe his sense of fun arose because he was laughing in relief, happy simply to be alive, for as a boy he had had a very close call. He had buried wartime shells and other ammunition in a field with cans of petrol, called it the 'Hassenforder atom bomb', and lit a trail of gunpowder towards it. He was running for a trench when the 'bomb' blew up, and he had to be taken to specialists in Switzerland for treatment to burns on his legs and back.

Hassenforder's trick in races was to snatch hats from SPECTATORS. All went well until one day he picked a woman whose hat was tied under her chin. He also set pigeons loose at a UCI (Union Cycliste Internationale) banquet in Paris. The birds panicked and knocked clouds of dust from the chandeliers. In 1956 he took a lap of honour at the PARC DES

PRINCES sitting on the handlebars and facing backwards.

He now runs a restaurant and hotel called Chez Roger Hassenforder in a timbered 17th-century building in Kaysersberg, Colmar. The sign outside shows a rider in a yellow jersey riding a penny-farthing. His home is full of skins and stuffed animals from his career as a big-game hunter. 'Such things were permitted then,' he says.

Winner

1953	Tour Sud-Est
1954	Critérium International
1956	Critérium International
1958	Critérium International

Tour de France

1953	DNF	Yellow Jersey
1954	DNF	
1955	DNF	Stage win Metz—Colmar
1956	50th	Stage wins Rouen—Caen, La Rochelle—Bordeaux, Toulouse—Montpellier
1957	DNF	Stage wins Metz—Colmar, Alès—Perpignan
1959	DNF	Stage win Nantes—La Rochelle

HAUTACAM

It was on the 1,560m climb of Hautacam near Lourdes that LANCE ARMSTRONG set up his victory in appalling weather in 2000. Many consider this to be one of the great stages of Tour history. It was the first mountain stage of the Tour, and an initial break had crumbled and left only the unknown JAVIER OTXOA in the lead. Armstrong went off alone into the wind and rain and left his challengers rooted, pushing JAN ULLRICH into second place overall by four minutes.

Otxoa still won the stage but, like the epic stage in 1964 on the PUY DE DÔME between JACQUES ANQUETIL and RAYMOND POULIDOR, the winner didn't matter. Armstrong finished

at 42 seconds but took the race lead, never to lose it.

ROBERT MILLAR said, 'First set of mountains and it's game over for everyone but Lance Armstrong. From that epic cold, wet day through the Pyrenees all the other challengers have been racing or rather surviving for the podium places.'

BJARNE RIIS rode the field off his wheel there in 1996 and beat RICHARD VIRENQUE by 49sec.

ADOLPHE HÉLIÈRE
b. Rennes, France, Feb 2 1888, d. Nice, France, Jul 14 1910

The virtually unknown Frenchman Adolphe Hélière has the misfortune not only to have been the Tour's first fatality, but also not even to have been riding his BIKE when it happened. He went swimming in the sea on a rest day in Nice in 1910, was stung by a jellyfish . . . and drowned. Riders who died during the Tour were FRANCESCO CEPEDA, TOM SIMPSON and FABIO CASARTELLI. (*See* their entries for details.)

Tour de France

1910	DNF

ROBERTO HERAS
b. Béjar, Spain, Feb 21 1974

Roberto Heras, a quiet Spanish CLIMBER whose character changes to excitement on his BIKE, turned professional in August 1995 on the advice of SPAIN's former champion, Laudelino Cubino, who introduced him to Alvaro Pino, MANAGER of the KELME team. He rode his first pro race near his home at Béjar in the west of the country, but won nothing in his first two years. Then he rode the 1997 Tour of Spain and won a stage and came fifth overall. In 2000 he won the race and came fifth in his first Tour. In 2001 and 2002 Heras provided the main support to LANCE ARMSTRONG in the mountains, going so fast on the climb to La Mongie in 2002 that the American asked him to slow down.

HERCULES

Before the war, Britain was inexperienced at massed-start road-racing because the British governing body, the National Cyclists' Union, had banned it for decades for fear the police would drive all cyclists off the road. (*See* BRITAIN.) Therefore, the Birmingham BIKE-maker Hercules' venture into sponsorship had been of long-distance TIME TRIAL specialists who attacked mainly city-to-city records.

British cyclists had first ridden the Tour in 1937, with CHARLES HOLLAND and the Londoner Bill Burl. None of that so-called British Empire team finished. However, during the war Continental-style road-racing came to Britain, causing a violent dispute over amateurism between the sport's governing bodies, as there were now not only INDEPENDENTS (semi-professional riders) in the British cycling world, but also a small group of full professionals riding TRACK races at Herne Hill in south London.

One of these professionals, Derek Buttle, approached Hercules in 1952 with the idea of running a team for the Tour de France. He and the company's representative, Mac McLachlan, agreed the deal at the Cora Hotel, near Euston station.

'He asked what we wanted and we settled on £500 a year plus bonuses,' Buttle says. The first team was Buttle, Dave Bedwell, Dennis Talbot and Clive Parker. They raced in Britain in 1953 and then, as the team expanded to six, spent a season riding Continental races before tackling the Tour in 1955 with a full squad of 12 to choose from.

The manager, a former Manchester track rider called Syd Cozens, took them to a training camp near Marseille where Bedwell finished second to JACQUES ANQUETIL at Fréjus, and outsprinted ANDRÉ DARRIGADE in the Tour of Picardy. It was a promising start, but to the established stars these races were for training and less important than to the new arrivals. The Tour would be different.

The selection for the Tour was: Dave Bedwell, Tony Hoar, Stan Jones, Fred Krebs, Bob Maitland, Ken Mitchell, Bernard Pusey, BRIAN ROBINSON, Ian Steel and Bev Wood. Pusey abandoned on stage two, and Wood on stage three, as did Bedwell, who dropped further and further back after puncturing. Jones went out on stage seven, Steel on stage eight, Maitland on stage nine, and Krebs and Mitchell in the MOUNTAINS on stage 11, Mitchell with saddle boils. Just two got to Paris, Robinson 29th at 1:57:10 and Hoar as LANTERNE ROUGE (last rider) at 6:06:01. Their mud-speckled bikes were displayed at the national cycle show at Earl's Court in London.

Within weeks the team was fired. Just what happened has never been clear. Some blamed the decline of the cycle trade, and saw the whole Tour venture as an expensive swan song. Others said the team was too strong at home but not strong enough to keep abroad. And there were claims that Hercules were faced with enormous costs but not enough receipts to make the books right.

The collapse was a disaster for most of the team. There was no way back for pros to the AMATEURS in those days. Nor could they revert to riding as independents, because independents rode against amateurs and amateurs weren't allowed to compete with former professionals. A few went abroad, but only Robinson made a success of it, in 1958 becoming the first Briton to win a stage (*see* his entry for details). The others were stranded and, like Buttle, stopped racing.

'It had been a good time,' Buttle says, 'but there was no way I could race in England and no way I could afford to go round Europe without a sponsor.'

There has never been a purely British team in the Tour since, with the exception of the

NATIONAL TEAMS in 1967 and 1968. In 1987 the ANC-Halfords team included two Frenchmen and a Czech. The venture was bigger than an inexperienced manager, minor riders, and a small sponsor like ANC-Halfords could handle. The team fell apart in rows over money, management and tactics. Only Malcolm Elliott (94th), Guy Gallopin (133rd), Kvetoslav Palov (103rd), and Adrian Timmis (70th) finished the 1987 Tour for ANC-Halfords, and Timmis complained he had ridden the Tour de France for three weeks without being paid.

LUIS HERRERA

b. Fusagasuga, Colombia, May 4 1961

The Colombian Luis Herrera was born in a farmhouse surrounded by palm trees and banana plants, on a hill outside Fusagasuga, 50km from Bogota. He worked in the fields, picking flowers, which gave him his NICKNAME of *el jardinerito* (the little gardener). As a child he is said to have had a pet rat which he led on a string, and which grew to a metre in length.

The Tour's financial chief, FÉLIX LÉVITAN, had heard how in Colombia BIKE racing was second only to soccer in popularity, and was richly financed (*see* COLOMBIA for details), so he invited the country to ride the 1983 Tour. (*See* AMATEURS for story.)

Herrera, a sad-looking and sometimes impenetrable man, rode his first Tour in 1984. He waited as BERNARD HINAULT and LAURENT FIGNON fought a personal duel on the ALPE D'HUEZ, and then rode away while they were preoccupied with each other. 'His climb of the Alpe was a thing of beauty,' says the writer Chris Sidwells. 'His wiry legs simply stroked the pedals round with a rhythm all of his own.' Herrera became the first South American to win a stage. (*See* also RAUL ALCALA.) Next year he won the MOUNTAINS JERSEY and two stages, after reaching a tacit agreement with BERNARD HINAULT. (*See* Hinault entry for details.) A million people are said to have turned out to welcome 'Lucho' home.

Herrera won the mountains competition again in 1987 and also the Tour of SPAIN. But he stopped racing in 1992. Life for Colombian riders had rarely been happy, due to uncertainty over SPONSORS (*see* COLOMBIA) and disagreement with the management style of LUIS OCAÑA, the former Tour winner. Ocaña, they said, wanted to turn them immediately into experienced European professionals rather than let them progress.

Colombian riders were also uncomfortable with the style of European racing. Few Colombian events were longer than 160km, but the climbs could be as long as 50km. Tour mountains, by contrast, are around 20km. And Colombian descents were straight and not full of hairpins like the Alps.

Herrera could do little but climb. On the right day, that was more than enough. But it would never win him the Tour. He tried to improve his time trialling and his speed on the flat but, like RENÉ VIETTO and ANDY HAMPSTEN, the better he got at one the worse he got at the other. He also couldn't sprint.

In a reference to the steroids and the EPO era (*see* DOPING) he said, 'When I started seeing riders with fat arses climbing like aeroplanes, I understood. I preferred to stop.'

He returned to Colombia to live with his wife, Judith, a former model, and went into business as a cattle breeder with his brother, Rafael. When he stopped racing his fortune was put at $5 million, and the cattle business increased it. His wealth and celebrity made him a target for kidnappers. In 2000 he was taken by the Revolutionary Army Force of Colombia, marched seven hours through the jungle to a hideaway and then released 20 hours later unhurt. He has never said how much was paid to free him. Rumour has it that he still pays protection money.

Raphaël Géminiani said, 'Lucho Herrera was one of the greatest climbers of his generation, a pure, light, true flyer. But that was in Colombia. We never saw the best of him in Europe. A Tour of Spain, two Dauphiné Libérés, that's nothing for a man with such talents as a climber. He preferred to be the best in Colombia. He didn't want to adapt to European cycling because ambition wasn't his cup of tea. It was a shame for him but above all for Colombians, who are real cycling fans.'

A little bit of Colombia remains where Herrera made his name in the Tour. When a volcanic eruption killed 25,000 people in a single night in the Colombian town of Armero in November 1985, France provided humanitarian relief. In recognition, Herrera brought with him two lumps of the brown lava when he came to the 1986 Tour. They were put under the bridge by the last but one bend to the Alpe d'Huez, near the chapel, together with a commemorative plaque.

Winner

1985	Tour Colombia
1986	Tour Colombia, RCN Classic
1987	Tour Spain
1988	Dauphiné Libéré, Tour Colombia
1991	Dauphiné Libéré
1992	Tour Aragon

Tour de France

1984	27th	Stage win Grenoble—Alpe d'Huez
1985	7th	Stage wins Pontarlier—Avoriaz, Autrans—St-Étienne, and Mountains winner
1986	22nd	
1987	5th	Mountains winner
1988	6th	
1989	19th	
1991	31st	

STÉPHANE HEULOT
b. Rennes, France, Mar 20 1971

There's nothing like starting the Tour as French champion, at least as far as the French are concerned. That's what Stéphane Heulot of Rennes did in 1996, and he came with a record of doing his national tricolour proud wherever he raced.

In 1996 he switched from the Banesto team, where he'd been an also-ran to MIGUEL INDURAIN, to join the French GAN team, backed by a insurance company, which gave him more freedom. On the fourth stage, from Soissons to Lac de Madine, Heulot got into a break that went clear after Fère-en-Tardennois. The bunch didn't take it seriously. The race had ridden less than an hour and there were 194km to go.

The lead built to 17:40 and still nothing happened behind. With 100km to go, it seemed unlikely they'd be caught. And they weren't. The lead was eventually cut to 4:33 but '*Le jour de gloire est arrivé!*' as the Marseillaise has it. The stage went to the youngest rider, 23-year-old Cyril Saugrain from the cut-price Aubervilliers team, and Heulot pulled on the *maillot jaune* over his French champion's jersey.

But the fairy tale didn't have a happy ending. The day had been hard and the weather next day was bad. Rain fell and Heulot developed tendinitis. The Alps were on the horizon with the Cormet de Roseland as the first major test. In unrelenting rain Heulot, whose knee was swollen and painful, called for the Tour doctor, Gérard Porte, and winced as he explained that he could barely push the pedals. Halfway up the climb he rolled to a halt on the left of the road, a rock face by his shoulder, and walked to his team car in tears.

Winner

1996	GP Cholet, Trophée Grimpeurs
1999	Tour Limousin

Tour de France

1996	DNF	Yellow Jersey
1997	20th	
1998	13th	
1999	14th	
2000	DNF	
2001	40th	

BERNARD HINAULT
b. Yffiniac, France, Nov 14 1954

Bernard Hinault was born on his grandparents' farm in the hamlet of La Clôture near Yffiniac in Brittany, the heartland of French cycling. His parents Joseph – a railway worker – and Lucie imagined he'd work in a bank, but his talent as an athlete began to show on his daily bike rides to the École du Sacré-Coeur in St-Brieuc when he was 13. Friends couldn't stay with him when they got to the Côte d'Yffiniac.

Hinault's first interest, though, was cross-country running – at 14 he finished 10th in the French championship in Compiègne, north of Paris. He spent three years as a runner and then, on May 2 1971 when he was 16, he borrowed his brother Gilbert's BIKE for his first race, in the hamlet of Planguenoual. He dominated the race and disposed of the few who could stay with him by starting the sprint 700m from the line. He won 12 of the 20 races he rode that year, and was French junior champion the next season.

In 1975 he turned professional for GITANE, beginning an extraordinary career which not only made him the third rider (after JACQUES ANQUETIL and EDDY MERCKX) to win the Tour five times, but also one of the few riders to govern the sport both from the saddle and the boardroom table.

In 1977 he won Ghent-Wevelgem and Liège-Bastogne-Liège, a victory he repeated by ten minutes in 1980, when cold and wind forced other riders out a dozen at a time. The cold affected Hinault's arms so badly that it took three weeks to get proper movement in his right index and middle fingers.

Hinault rode his first Tour in 1978 and won. He repeated it the following year, 1979, when the suspense continued right up to the closing hour. The finale along the CHAMPS ELYSÉES is important for everyone, especially the French, who naturally want their man to win in their capital, but it's rare for the race leader to do more than ride round in the bunch. But in 1979, Hinault and his runner-up, JOOP ZOETEMELK, broke away in the last kilometres and fought all the way to the FINISH. Hinault's second Tour win wasn't in doubt, but he wasn't going to let a Dutchman win a stage in Paris, and he didn't. Anyway, Zoetemelk's contentment at coming second was short-lived; a few days later he was found positive in a DOPING test and denied his place on the stage.

Zoetemelk was destined to ride in the shadow of greater and certainly more adventurous riders. (*See* entry for details.) In 1980 he beat Hinault to win the Tour at last, but such was Hinault's status that the race became known as 'the War of Hinault's Knee' rather than the 'Tour that Zoetemelk Won'.

The problem in Hinault's right knee, which newspapers discussed with a gravity normally reserved for dying kings, showed for the first time when he couldn't take his turns on the front of the line in the team TIME TRIAL between Compiègne and Beauvais. Doctors diagnosed it as tendinitis, a problem which had afflicted 50 other riders and which was never explained. Hinault rode on through continuing bad weather to the foot of the Pyrenees. He spent long stretches of the stage from Agen to Pau alongside his team car talking to his MANAGER, CYRILLE GUIMARD, whose own chance of a win in the Tour had been wrecked by knee problems. (*See* entry for details).

At 10.30 that evening Guimard called the organisers, JACQUES GODDET and FÉLIX LÉVITAN, from their meal. Hinault was close to tears as Guimard explained that his rider – who had been treated for more than a week by the Tour's doctor, the appropriately named Philippe Miserey – could no longer continue.

Then Hinault vanished. Newspapers sent reporters all over France to find him, particularly to Brittany. In the end he turned up near Lourdes at the home of his team-mate Huber Arbes, who had left the race after a CRASH. It was a pleasing coincidence that Lourdes, a stronghold of the Catholic faith, should shelter two sick men in what the writer Geoffrey Nicholson once described as a 'sport of unspoken Catholicism'.

Zoetemelk meanwhile was dismissed as having won the Tour only because Hinault couldn't. (*See* Zoetemelk entry for more.)

Hinault's most dramatic Tour was his fifth, in 1985. It was an extraordinary year for a man of 31, in which he won both the Tour and the Giro, dominating in the MOUNTAINS, in time trials, and wherever else he pleased. He won the Tour PROLOGUE at Plumelec, then beat

STEPHEN ROCHE by 2:20, CHARLY MOTTET by 2:26 and GREG LEMOND by 2:34 in the 75km time trial to Strasbourg. He rode what was then an innovation – a low-profile bike with a solid, spokeless back wheel – and he wore a streamlined helmet, another innovation.

The race continued to the Pyrenees with Hinault mastering LeMond – a team-mate but a challenger nevertheless – and LUIS HERRERA, the climbing revelation from COLOMBIA. With Herrera and the other Colombians he reached an unspoken agreement that he would do nothing to obstruct their dominance in the mountains if they would leave him unchallenged for the yellow JERSEY.

That left LeMond. The American had been brought into the La Vie Claire team to develop his ability or (reports vary) to stop him getting in the way of Hinault's fifth Tour win. The two agreed to work for whoever was better placed, which Hinault settled by winning the prologue and the time trial. That's how it would have stayed had Hinault not crashed at 300m from the FINISH at St-Étienne, breaking his nose. This affected his breathing, and he struggled to hold Roche, now his biggest threat for the overall race, on the stage to LUZ-ARDIDEN. The Irishman pulled away with LeMond, faithful to the agreement, riding on his wheel without helping.

LeMond realised he was stronger than Roche and their companion, Eduardo Chozas of SPAIN, but his manager ordered him to do nothing, promising LeMond that Hinault was only 40 seconds behind. Those 40 seconds were actually 1:15, and LeMond lost that plus whatever time he might have gained by attacking. Some say this cost him the Tour. LeMond said he felt cheated and 'burned' because Hinault had been his hero. (See LeMond entry for more, especially the epic 1986 Tour.)

Hinault rode his last race, a cyclo-cross, on November 14 1986. His farewell party – which featured a hook on which to hang his BIKE – attracted ROGER LAPÉBIE, JACQUES ANQUETIL and FÉLIX LÉVITAN. He says he has never ridden a bike since and works now as a cattle breeder, as does Herrera. (See Herrera entry for how this led to his kidnapping.) But Hinault's influence

on cycling and the Tour has grown rather than faded. He is now an 'adviser' for the SOCIÉTÉ DU TOUR DE FRANCE, a title which disguises his actual influence. Hinault has an important role in deciding the race's route and the strategic advances or obstacles it includes. He has a higher rank than any other former rider, close not only to JEAN-MARIE LEBLANC and his deputy Daniel Baal but also to Hein Verbruggen, the head of the UCI (Union Cycliste Internationale), the sport's governing body, as well as to the managers and top riders who influence the sport.

He is an outspoken campaigner against doping, and in 2002 called for a lifetime ban on those caught. 'Some of them get a year's suspension,' he says, 'and then start all over again. They just don't understand.'

His infamously short temper – he was a regular contender for the journalists' *Prix Citron* (lemon) for the sourest rider – seems to have abated, at least enough for him now to look after each day's guests as they meet the race leaders on the podium.

(*See* EARPIECES, STRIKES.)

Winner

1976	Paris-Camembert, Tour Limousin
1977	Dauphiné Libéré, Ghent-Wevelgem, GP Nations, Liège-Bastogne-Liège, Tour Limousin
1978	Tour de France, Tour Spain, Critérium International, National championship, GP Nations
1979	Tour de France, Flèche Wallonne, GP Nations, Dauphiné Libéré, Tour Lombardy
1980	World championship, Giro d'Italia, Tour Romandie, Liège-Bastogne-Liège

Winner (continued)

1981	Tour de France, Amstel Gold, Paris-Roubaix, Critérium International, Dauphiné Libéré
1982	Tour de France, Giro d'Italia, Critérium As, Tour Luxembourg, GP Nations
1983	Tour Spain, Flèche Wallonne
1984	Four-days Dunkirk, Tour Lombardy, GP Nations, Baracchi Trophy
1985	Tour de France, Giro d'Italia
1986	Tour Valencia

Tour de France

1978	1st	Stage wins St-Emilion—Sainte-Foix-la-Grande, St-Dier—St-Étienne, Metz—Nancy, and Yellow Jersey
1979	1st	Stage wins Luchon—Superbagnères, Luchon—Pau, Brussels—Brussels, Évian—Avoriaz, Dijon—Dijon, Auxerre—Nogent-sur-Marne, Le Perreux—Paris, and Yellow Jersey and Points winner
1980	DNF	Stage wins Frankfurt—Frankfurt, Liège—Spa-Francorchamps, Liège—Lille, and Yellow Jersey
1981	1st	Stage wins Nice—Nice, Nay—Pau, Hasselt—Mulhouse, Alpe d'Huez—Le Pleynet, St-Priest—St-Priest, and Yellow Jersey
1982	1st	Basle—Basle, Martigues—Martigues, St-Priest—St-Priest, Fontenay-sous-Bois—Paris, and Yellow Jersey
1984	2nd	Stage win Montreuil—Noisy-le-Sec, and Yellow Jersey
1985	1st	Stage wins Plumelec—Plumelec, Saarbrücken—Strasbourg, and Yellow Jersey
1986	2nd	Stage wins Nantes—Nantes, Briançon—Alpe d'Huez, St-Étienne—St-Étienne, and Yellow Jersey and Mountains winner

GEORGE HINCAPIE
b. New York, USA, Jun 29 1973

George Hincapie – 1.90m tall and 79kg – is a powerful DOMESTIQUE for his fellow American LANCE ARMSTRONG, a role that has overshadowed his own talent.

Hincapie came to Europe after a junior career that ran up 10 national titles. He is a nearly-man with repeated places in the first six but only rarely a win. In 2002 alone he came second in the Haribo Classic, third in the Three Days of De Panne, fourth in the Tour of Flanders, third in Ghent-Wevelgem, and sixth in Paris-Roubaix.

His one big win came from outsprinting Leon van Bon to win Ghent-Wevelgem in 2001. He just missed winning the last stage on the CHAMPS ELYSÉES in the 1997 Tour, when he was caught with less than 200m to go. Nor was that his only disappointment: he won the American championship that same year but had the JERSEY pulled from his back within minutes when officials insisted he had ridden behind a team car. He won again next year, this time without dispute.

Winner

1998	National championship
1999	GP Atlanta
2001	Ghent-Wevelgem

Tour de France

1996	DNF
1997	104th
1998	53rd
1999	78th
2000	65th
2001	71st
2002	59th

BARRY HOBAN
b. Wakefield, England, Feb 5 1940

Barry Hoban remains BRITAIN's most prolific stage winner. In March 1962 he packed in a job as a colliery apprentice, went to Arras in northern France, and stayed abroad for 18 years.

He began as an INDEPENDENT (semi-professional) in the Bertin-Porter 39 team for the equivalent of £30 a month, arranged through the Yorkshire cycle dealer Ron Kitching. André Bertin, a cycle dealer, gambler and whisky importer, was Kitching's business contact. Hoban didn't finish his first three races but then things clicked and he won 16 races in his first season and had 50 placings in the first five.

He rode the TOUR DE L'AVENIR in 1963 and won the bunch sprint at BORDEAUX, the TRACK where he would twice win in the professional Tour. He finished the race 16th.

Hoban's decision to turn professional for RAYMOND POULIDOR's Mercier-BP team in 1964 angered Bertin, who had ideas of building his own pro team around Hoban. 'He's an idiot,' he said. 'He'll end up as nothing but a DOMESTIQUE to Poulidor.' Which turned out true. Even so, in that first year he won two stages of the Tour of SPAIN, a stage of the Midi-Libre, and rode his first Tour, finishing 65th.

His first Tour stage win was on July 14 1967, the day after TOM SIMPSON, the leader of the British NATIONAL TEAM, died on MONT VENTOUX. How it happened is disputed. VIN DENSON says he had himself been offered the stage, as Simpson's closest friend, through riders' spokesman JEAN STABLINSKI, but that Hoban rode off the front instead. Hoban says he remembers nothing but finding himself at the front. 'I don't count that stage win after Tom's death. It was symbolic – a gesture to Tom. It just happened. Stablinski, WALTER GODEFROOT and a dozen of the older guys in the peloton got together and said that they would ride *piano, piano* [slowly] in Tom's memory. The British guys were told to ride at the front. The next thing I knew was that there was a gap behind me.'

His first proper win – odd for a SPRINTER – came at Sallanches in 1968, where there were five MOUNTAINS in the 200km from Grenoble as well as a hilltop finish. Hoban rode away on the drop to Albertville, had eight minutes on the Aravis where he won a prime (intermediary prize) in honour of HENRI DESGRANGE, and won alone by six seconds. Next year he won on successive days at BORDEAUX and Brive.

In 18 years Hoban rode 12 Tours and finished 11. His last stage win – the eighth – was at Bordeaux in 1975. His last Tour was in 1978, and his last Continental win was at Germigny-l'Eveque in 1980.

There were no homecoming parties for Hoban, and no offers to work in cycling as a MANAGER or coach. He said, 'My one regret is that I am not known for what I did over there. No one knows who the hell Barry Hoban was. It would be nice to be known for what I did for the sport and not be pushed into oblivion as if it didn't count. Over here, it's, "So you rode the Tour a few years ago: so what?"'

He rode briefly in BRITAIN before joining the cycle trade. He lives now in central Wales with his wife Helen, who had been married to Simpson.

Winner

1966	GP Frankfurt
1970	Vaux GP, Manx Premier
1971	GP Fourmies
1974	Ghent-Wevelgem, Paris-Bourges

Tour de France

1964	65th	
1967	62nd	Stage win Carpentras—Sète
1968	33rd	Stage win Grenoble—Sallanches
1969	67th	Stage wins Mourenx—Bordeaux, Libourne—Brive
1970	DNF	
1971	41st	
1972	70th	
1973	43rd	Stage wins Montpellier—Argelès, Bourges—Versailles
1974	37th	Stage win Avignon—Montpellier
1975	68th	Stage win Angoulême—Bordeaux
1977	41st	
1978	65th	

HOLLAND

The Netherlands is too crowded for many big races and the main racing programme is based around CRITERIUMS. These are as popular as in BELGIUM, but run on circuits of two or three kilometres rather than the 10km or more found in Belgium. That makes it surprising that the country has produced so many good Tour riders. On the other hand, the smallness of the country, and therefore the lack of potential SPONSORS, meant that until RALEIGH came along in 1976 there were few teams of international strength. And Raleigh, of course, was from BRITAIN. (*See* Raleigh entry for why it had a Dutch team.)

Holland's big chance came with the change to NATIONAL TEAMS in 1930, but even then it did not come immediately. No Dutch team was invited until 1936, when Albert van Schendel (15th), Antoon van Schendel (32nd), Theo Middelkamp (23rd and a stage win) and Albert Gijzen (DNF) rode, just four against the 10 apiece fielded by larger nations such as FRANCE, BELGIUM and GERMANY.

The country's first yellow JERSEY was WIM VAN EST in 1951. He lost it in a CRASH when he fell down the mountainside on the AUBISQUE and had to be pulled out with a rope fashioned from the team's spare tyres. (*See* Aubisque entry for details.) Holland won the team competition in 1953, a golden year in which Dutchmen won five stages and WOUT WAGTMANS came fifth.

The first Dutch Tour winner was JAN JANSSEN in 1968. By then the Tour had returned to trade teams and, with Holland again unable to find rich sponsors, he rode for the Pelforth brewery in France. Janssen took the race on the last day by 38 seconds, having never worn the leader's jersey until Paris.

The golden period for the Netherlands was 1976–1983, thanks to the RALEIGH team under Peter Post as manager. It amassed two world road championships (GERRIE KNETEMANN 1978, JAN RAAS 1979), the 1980 Tour de France (JOOP ZOETEMELK), the Amstel Gold Race in 1978, 1979 and 1980, the Tour of Flanders in 1979 and Ghent-Wevelgem in 1980. It also

collected 15 world championships, five World Cups, 77 Tour stages, the Giro d'Italia, 37 classics and 55 national championships.

Dutch riders have often been good CLIMBERS, despite their extremely flat home countryside, and so many have won on ALPE D'HUEZ that thousands of Dutchmen habitually camp out there to support them (*see* Alpe d'Huez entry).

(*See* also FOREIGN VISITS, PROLOGUE, START.).

CHARLES HOLLAND
b. Birmingham, England, 1908, d. Dec 1989

Charles Holland of Birmingham and Bill Burl of London were the first British riders to start the Tour, in 1937. They rode with the French-Canadian Pierre Gachon as a British Empire team. Gachon quit on the first day and Burl was thrown out the next for being so far behind. Holland rode on until the MOUNTAINS and retired only because of a broken pump.

Holland had little experience of road racing, at least in the conventional sense. British cycling authorities had banned road racing for fear that it would lead the police to drive all cyclists off the road. (*See* BRITAIN for why.) Most racing in Britain was done alone and against the clock at dawn. The only chance to ride in a massed bunch was an occasional race on an airfield or on the Isle of Man.

A separate nation, the Isle of Man was prepared to extend its TT motorcycle week to bring in cyclists. The first race was in 1936, one lap of the 61km mountain circuit (the current race is three laps), and Holland won. That success, and his experience of road racing at the 1932 Olympics in Los Angeles (where he finished 16th), plus coming fourth in the 1934 world championship race in Leipzig, convinced Holland there was more to cycling than time trialling. And so he turned professional for RALEIGH in May 1937 to ride the six-day TRACK race at Wembley. Sadly, neither limited road racing nor riding alone against the clock was adequate preparation for repeated fast laps of a steep track. He crashed on the second day and broke a collarbone.

As a professional, though, he was available for the Tour, where the organisers were looking for more teams. Since British cycling was amateur, and based on time trial or track racing, Holland's selection was automatic. Nothing seems to be known about his team-mates Burl and Gachon.

The French took a liking to the English rider, nicknaming him Sir Holland, and let him stay at their hotels. More usefully, they took pity on his innocence, gave him advice, and helped him from their spares van. Holland rode for 15 days and 3,200km until he was stopped by lack of a pump, when he punctured 30m behind the leaders on the Col de Port in the Pyrenees. Heat had warped the pump washer and he couldn't get his replacement tyre beyond half-pressure.

He punctured twice more on the descent and ran out of tyres. The French mechanics were elsewhere, looking after their own riders, and Holland was stranded. A tourist lent him a tyre but it wouldn't stay on the rim. Then the pump snapped in the middle. He struggled on but officials had left the next FEEDING AREA, and he pulled off his number despite encouragement from Belgian journalists.

'I asked a press car for a lift to Luchon,' he said. 'They would not give me a lift but drove alongside trying to persuade me to carry on, and even grabbed me by the jersey and pulled me along. I think they would have done anything to have kept me in the Tour but I did not wish to finish this great race unless it was by my own efforts.'

He came back to England, and started preparing for the professional world championship, but he broke his collarbone again and didn't race properly until 1938. Then he settled down to trying to beat long-distance records (*see* HERCULES for more history), breaking Land's End-London, Liverpool-Edinburgh and Edinburgh-York.

His career ended with the war, when he joined the Royal Corps of Signals. By 1945 he was too old to pick up where he'd left off, and he ran two shops in Perry Bar, Birmingham, and another on the other side of the city in Sheldon. In 1974 and 1975 he won the year-long veterans' time trialling championship.

Holland died aged 81 in December 1989.

Tour de France

1937   DNF

GUY IGNOLIN
b. Rochecorbon, France, Nov 14 1936

FRANCE's Guy Ignolin won an epic stage into Turin during his first Tour in 1961. The day started in Grenoble, and Ignolin attacked soon after the start, taking with him another French-man, Emmanuel Busto. The pair were away for 247km of the stage's 250km, and Ignolin won even though Busto was fresher, having kept behind the leader and done none of the work. Their lead on the next rider, Carlo Brugnami of ITALY, was 11:10.

Ignolin rode mainly for JACQUES ANQUETIL, who won that year's Tour by leading from the first day, but Ignolin had the talent to win two more stages of the Tour in 1963, and even beat his master in the Circuit d'Aulne in 1965. He retired at the end of 1968 after nine years as a professional, and ran a newspaper and cigarette shop.

Winner

1962 GP Fourmies
1965 Circuit Aulne, GP Télégramme, Tour Morbihan

Tour de France

1961 59th Stage win Grenoble—Turin
1962 78th
1963 37th Stage wins Bagnères-de-Bigorre—Luchon, Aurillac—St-Étienne
1967 DNF

RAYMOND IMPANIS
b. Berg-Kampenhout, Belgium, Oct 19 1925

Round-faced Raymond Impanis, whose looks betrayed his Italian roots beneath the Belgian nationality (*see* PINO CERAMI and MAURICE GARIN for other riders of Italian origin), oozed class but rarely bothered to put it to effect. He preferred to be at home in slippers than out training. He was 'the despair of Belgium', according to RAPHAËL GÉMINIANI. Too much of a homebody to love the life of an interna-tional racing cyclist, he nonetheless did manage to win three stages of the Tour (1947 and 1948) and, in 1954, the greatest Belgian prize, the Tour of Flanders.

His successes ranged from the Vannes-St-Brieuc TIME TRIAL in 1947 (*see* RENÉ VIETTO) to victory in Paris-Nice in 1960, when he was 35. His name lives on in cycling in the form of the Raymond Impanis bike route through country lanes in Belgium's Kampenhout region. (*See* MEMORIALS for tributes to other riders.)

Winner

1949 A Travers Belgique
1951 A Travers Belgique
1952 Ghent-Wevelgem
1953 Ghent-Wevelgem
1954 Paris-Roubaix, Tour Flanders
1957 Flèche Wallonne
1960 Paris-Nice

1947	6th	Stage win Vannes—St Brieuc
1948	10th	Stage wins Toulouse—
		Montpellier, Montpellier—
		Marseille
1949	DNF	
1950	8th	
1953	23rd	
1955	13th	
1956	33rd	
1963	66th	

INDEPENDENTS

Cycling started, unlike most sports, as a way to make money. In 1869 James Moore (*see* BRITAIN) won 1,000 francs (almost impossible to translate into modern currency but an astonishing prize) when he won Paris-Rouen. First prize in the 1903 Tour was 3,000 francs, more than a thousand times the daily rate for a workman.

There were two consequences. First, the sport relied on full-time riders who had time to travel to races, ride, and travel home. And second, because some riders had time and others didn't, a gulf opened between professionals and those who remained AMATEURS. (*See* amateurs entry for how a definition of amateurism troubled nations for years.)

The cycling authorities' solution was to bridge the gap with an 'Independent' category. Independents could accept sponsorship, wear advertising, and receive a wage. They could ride against amateurs or professionals but, since amateurs and professionals couldn't compete with each other in the same events, independents couldn't ride against both at the same time.

There was even an independents' Tour de France in 1911, covering 3,000km in 14 stages, a forerunner of the TOUR DE L'AVENIR. Some reports say there were 200 riders and others put the total at an extraordinary 650. The first two places went to René Guenot (who rode the professional Tour in 1913 but didn't finish) and a now unknown rider called Valotton. Third place went to the 1923 Tour winner, HENRI PÉLISSIER. (*See* Pélissier entry for how he was killed; and *see* ALBERT LONDRES for how Pélissier spilled the beans on DOPING.)

Independents were expected to decide after two years whether to turn professional or revert to amateurism. A number made the full step, but most didn't, since many riders saw being an independent as a pinnacle in itself. In Britain there were not many true professionals (*see* HERCULES), and riders who could no longer be sure of international selection as an amateur turned independent. Then they couldn't turn pro without going abroad like BARRY HOBAN did, and couldn't ride again as amateurs because of the country's rules.

In BELGIUM, where professional racing flourished, independents still outnumbered both pros and amateurs. There was little point in staying amateur if sponsors were prepared to offer at least a bike and a jersey that a rider would otherwise have to buy for himself. The sport's governing body, the Union Cycliste Internationale (UCI), finally despaired of the situation and did away with the category in 1966.

MIGUEL INDURAIN
b. Villava, Spain, Jul 16 1964

A tall, quiet, and not particularly fascinating character, SPAIN'S Miguel Indurain was an extraordinary athlete, and the first man to win five successive Tours (1991, 1992, 1993, 1994, 1995). With a heart rate of 29 at rest, and lungs that could suck in eight litres of air, he was a rider who merely had to turn on the power in order to dominate. It was a shame that he didn't have the ability to excite of EDDY MERCKX, or the grittiness and temper of BERNARD HIN-AULT. 'He doesn't ride to impress the crowds but to prove to himself he remains the strongest,' wrote JACQUES AUGENDRE.

Miguel Indurain Larraya started cycling in his village of Villava in the Spanish province of Navarra, in the foothills of the Pyrenees. He rode his first race at 11, winning a sandwich and a drink. He went on to join the local club, and took out his first racing licence in 1978.

There may be journalists who now claim they saw all along that he was to be one of the sport's greats. But there weren't many at the time. Indurain's first three Tours ended with two abandons and then 97th place in 1987. The change came in 1990 when he came 10th and won in the MOUNTAINS at LUZ-ARDIDEN.

In 1991 the race looked certain to go to GREG LEMOND, who had won three Tours and looked like taking a fourth. But Indurain won the 73km TIME TRIAL on the eighth stage and, though this didn't immediately threaten the American, it moved Indurain to fourth overall, 2:17 behind LeMond. Then came the 13th stage. Indurain and CLAUDIO CHIAPPUCCI broke away for 60km after the TOURMALET; Chiappucci won that contest, but Indurain took the yellow JERSEY. By the last time trial, Indurain was well in control and victory that day only cemented that fact. Though nobody realised it, he had won the first of five successive Tours.

In LUXEMBOURG next year he won the first long TIME TRIAL by three minutes as he completed a clean sweep of the time trials. For three years thereafter there was no doubt, after the first long time trial, about who would win the Tour. 'It seemed every Tour de France time trial in the early 1990s,' wrote Cycling, 'was marked by one image: a fixed grin mounted on rock-solid shoulders bursting out of a skin suit – yellow or blue and white Banesto – above deeply tanned legs which could have been sculpted from mahogany or teak, whirling a massive gear, eating up the road.'

Indurain was expected to go for six wins, but his career fizzled out in the 1996 Tour when he was dropped by leaders in the Alps and Pyrenees and finished 11th. He won that year's Olympic time trial, but by then relations with his team were souring. First Indurain protested that he had been 'press-ganged' into riding the 1996 Tour of Spain. Then Spanish newspapers said he was asking for a wage of the equivalent of £6,000,000, while his SPONSOR, the Banesto bank, was offering little more than half that.

Things grew so bitter that in 2000 Indurain announced his relations with his old bosses, José-Miguel Echavarri and Unzue Eusebio, were now 'non-existent'. 'We say hello, that's all,' he said. 'It's such a shame to lose such friendships all because of one season.'

In January 1997 Indurain called a press conference in Pamplona and said, 'Today I wish to announce my retirement from professional cycling.' His statement ended, 'I think I have spent enough time in the sport; my family are waiting.' (See LAURENT JALABERT for a similar sentiment.) The era was over.

EDDY MERCKX said, 'In stage racing, Indurain will leave a gap which is hard to fill. With or without the record-breaking sixth Tour his greatness remains the same. He was a great time triallist rather than a born winner.' BERNARD HINAULT added, 'He always drew the line when he was racing; for him it was to win the Tour, and he raced only to gain that objective.'

Neither comment is unrestrained praise, and both could be taken as criticism, implying that Indurain – like JACQUES ANQUETIL – had just one unusual ability that compensated for much else, and that in concentrating entirely on the Tour, where he could exploit that talent, he was less than a coureur complet.

However, those five successive wins make Indurain the greatest rider in Tour history, even though he never achieved the popularity of riders who did only half as well. It wasn't that he had enemies; he simply lacked fans. He didn't openly speak French, which made him a mystery to the French, and he only occasionally rode important races other than the Tour, which made him a puzzle to everyone else. 'The best documented fact about Miguel Indurain is that journalists have struggled to find out interesting facts about [him],' wrote William Fotheringham.

His trainer, Sabino Padilla, recommended that after retirement he should carry on riding a bike for his health. Indurain had kept all the bikes on which he won the Tour, as well as the one on which he broke the hour record, but now he wanted another. Spanish papers had a lot of fun when they reported how Indurain, buying a bike with his own money for the first time in at least 17 years, had gone to a shop in Pamplona to find one. The shop assistant, startled to recognise his customer, began explaining choices of sprockets, wheels, chainsets and so on. He soon realised, it was said, that Indurain had little idea what he was talking about and left him to look around.

After a while he chose a Cannondale mountain bike and, spotting the price tag, gasped, 'What? This bike costs half a million pesetas [£2,500]?', and walked out saying he would think about it and maybe come back next week. In the end he did come back, and bought a Cannondale R4000, the top of the range.

Indurain lives in Pamplona with his wife Marisa and their children Miguel and Jon. He concedes he's not as fit as he was. 'I still ride in shorts and jersey as if I was racing,' he said in 1998. 'But these days I've got chicken-skin [surface fat] on my legs. A group of Sunday tourists caught me and dropped me.'

He is also a member of the Spanish Olympic committee and runs a charity, named after him, which gives money to promising Spanish AMATEURS. At the end of 1999 he was named Spain's athlete of the century with 60 per cent of the votes.

His strength is best summed up by a description from the 1995 Tour, when JOHAN BRUYNEEL said that riding behind him to Liège was like taking pace from a motorbike (*see* Bruyneel entry for details).

(And *see* MONEY.)

Winner

1986 Tour Avenir, Tour Murcia
1987 Tour Mining Valleys
1988 Tour Catalonia
1989 Paris-Nice, Critérium International
1990 Paris-Nice, San Sebastian Classic
1991 Tour de France, Tour Catalonia
1992 Tour de France, Giro d'Italia, Tour Catalonia, National championship
1993 Tour de France, Giro d'Italia
1994 Tour de France, Tour Oise, World hour record

Winner (continued)

1995 Tour de France, Midi Libre, Tour Galicia, Dauphiné Libéré, World time trial championship
1996 Dauphiné Libéré, Bicyclette Basque, Olympic time trial championship, Tour Asturias

Tour de France

1985	DNF	
1986	DNF	
1987	97th	
1988	47th	
1989	17th	Stage win Pau—Cauterets
1990	10th	Stage win Blagnac—Luz-Ardiden
1991	1st	Stage wins Argentan—Alençon, Lugny—Mâcon, and Yellow Jersey
1992	1st	Stage wins San Sebastian—San Sebastian, Luxembourg—Luxembourg, Tours—Blois, and Yellow Jersey
1993	1st	Stage wins Puy-de-Fou—Puy-de-Fou, Lac de Madine—Lac de Madine, and Yellow Jersey
1994	1st	Stage win Périgueux—Bergerac, and Yellow Jersey
1995	1st	Stage wins Huy—Seraing, Lac de Vassivière—Lac de Vassivière, and Yellow Jersey
1996	11th	

IRELAND

Ireland's role in modern cycling starts with the basics – the tyres. For it was John Boyd Dunlop (1840–1921), who patented the blow-up bicycle tyre in 1888, and Dunlop was an animal doctor in Belfast. He sold his rights to the entrepreneur and TRACK racer W. H. Du Cros, with whom he'd been exploiting his new tyres, and settled in Dublin.

Ireland's first star was Harry Reynolds from Balbriggan, a round-faced man with a centre parting. In 1895 he won the Surrey 100-Guinea Cup at Kennington Oval in London, and then the world amateur sprint championship in Copenhagen in 1896. This was followed by a long period of silence on the international scene, not helped by a split between the Irish Cycling Association (formed 1892), which had international recognition but was weak outside cities, and the Gaelic Athletic Association (1884), which appealed to nationalist feelings and was strong in the countryside. The birth of the Irish Free State in 1922 brought into existence the National Athletic and Cycling Association to run the whole sport, but clubs in Northern Ireland joined the National Cyclists' Union in BRITAIN instead.

The NACA refused to keep itself to the south, and was banned as a result by the sport's governing body, the Union Cycliste Internationale. Irish riders could no longer compete at the Olympics or anywhere else abroad. Still more bodies were created, and even in Ireland many struggled to understand who ran what in a small sport in a small country. (*See* BRITAIN for a similar dispute.)

In 1978 the three surviving organisations agreed to run the sport between them, which worked until 1988 when the UCI insisted on only one association per country. Only after a court hearing did the Federation of Irish Cyclists, later renamed the Irish Cycling Federation and then Cycling Ireland, emerge from half a century of fighting.

Much of what was accomplished by Irish riders came about despite the conflict, and sometimes despite the rules. SHAY ELLIOTT went to FRANCE to race, and in 1963 became the first Irishman to wear the Tour's yellow JERSEY. SEAN KELLY won the year-long Super Prestige Pernod (forerunner of the World Cup) in 1984, 1985 and 1986, and the World Cup in 1989. Kelly also won the Tour points competition in 1982, 1983, 1985 and 1989, and the yellow jersey for a day in 1983. In addition, he won Paris-Nice every year from 1982 to 1988. STEPHEN ROCHE won the Tour, Giro and world championship in 1987. Cycling Ireland's offices in Dublin are called Kelly Roche House.

Ireland has fallen quiet since the remarkable period from Elliott to Roche, although the Sligo teenager Mark Scanlon won the junior world championship in HOLLAND in 1998 and was signed by the French AG2R team for 2003.

(And *see* MARTIN EARLEY, FESTINA AFFAIR, FOREIGN VISITS, PAUL KIMMAGE, WILLY VOET.)

ISÉRAN

The Iséran is the Tour's classic col, 2,770m high. The cycle-tourist and author Tim Hughes has written, 'Purists argue that this is the highest genuine col in Europe, maintaining that roads that go higher are either dead ends to the tops of mountains . . . or artificially contrived to go higher than they need.'

The Iséran haul runs from Bourg-St-Maurice or can be reached by a zigzag from the south side. On that side it starts in Lanslebourg, rising short and steep to the Col de Madeleine (not the famous one) at 1,650m. The rise then continues gently through a valley to Bonneval-sur-Arc at 1,835m. Then the climb really starts as it loops into a valley. After that comes another steep section through snow. The average gradient is 4.2 per cent. The descent on the other side has long straights, tight hairpins and a dozen tunnels over a distance of 40km. The tunnels are unlit.

The first rider to top the Iséran in the Tour was FÉLICIEN VERVAECKE of BELGIUM in 1938. The Tour's first MOUNTAIN TIME TRIAL was over the Iséran from Bonneval to Bourg-St-Maurice in 1939, and it was won by SYLVÈRE MAES. Weather makes the pass difficult for the Tour because it is often blocked by snow until the start of July. The mountain was abandoned in the 1996 Tour because of snow, and the stage to SESTRIERE, won by BJARNE RIIS, started at Monètier-les-Bains instead.

ITALY

Italian cycling has developed alongside but separate from the sport in the rest of Europe. The main reasons for this include: the mountains on the northern border, which provided an obstacle to travel for many decades; the fact that most of Europe's big competitions have been in northern France or Belgium, adding to travel difficulties, and the fact that Italy has no neighbours except those who live on the other side of large mountains.

Given all that, it is surprising that cycling should have developed at all. Almost all that can be said of Italy could also be said of the peninsula that holds Norway and Sweden, which at least have ferry links to the south, but cycling never reached the level of passion in Scandinavia which it occupies in Italy.

The 'alongside but separate' formula is typified by the national tour, the Giro d'Italia. This started in 1909 for exactly the same reason as the Tour de France, namely commercial rivalry between newspapers. In FRANCE it was the new paper *L'AUTO* against *Vélo*, in Italy it was the new *La Gazzetta dello Sport* challenging *Corriere dello Sport*.

Having a major national tour of their own, combined with native insularity, made Italian riders reluctant to travel. They had SPONSORS who had no commercial interests outside Italy, and were often unknown outside their country.

The first Italian to ride the Tour was Giovanni Gerbi, who had the misfortune to be clubbed to the ground on the Col de la RÉPUBLIQUE in 1904 when SPECTATORS tried to help their favourites and hold back rivals. (*See* 1904 AFFAIR for more.) Gerbi didn't finish then or in 1906, but he did come 20th in 1908. It was Gerbi, incidentally, who won the first Tour of Lombardy in 1905, then a race over muddy rutted tracks but now a classic.

The first Italian team in the Tour was sponsored by Legnano in 1910. Legnano (*see* GINO BARTALI for more) was the Italian BIKE-maker which won the Giro team prize repeatedly: 1922–1923, 1925–27, 1929, 1931–33, 1936 and 1957. But in the 1910 Tour the Italian connection was slight: Pierino Albini (11th), Ernest Azzini (13th) and Louis Azzini (17th), all from Milan, were outnumbered by six Frenchmen.

The first Italian stage winner was Vicenzo Borgarello, who won stages at Perpignan and Le Havre in 1912. He finished 13th overall.

Italy's first hope for a win was Costante Girardengo in 1914. He wasn't then the great rider he was to become (he won Milan-San Remo in 1918, 1921, 1923, 1925, 1926 and 1928, and was national champion in every peacetime year 1913–25). His SPONSOR, Automoto, told him to ride for the former winners LUCIEN PETIT-BRETON and LOUIS TROUSSELIER, but to take any chance that turned up.

Ambition made sure Girardengo saw that chance on the first stage, from Paris to Le Havre, and he came fourth to the man who went on to win, PHILIPPE THYS. Next day he crashed several times on rough roads and lost 72 minutes. Then he crashed again on stage six and abandoned, well behind the race and without team-mates.

Girardengo's failure was eventually made good in 1924 by OTTAVIO BOTTECCHIA, the first Italian winner, and the first rider to lead from start to finish. He won 'on one leg', as he put it, because of the three-minutes time benefits for each of his four stage wins. (*See* BONUSES for why; and *see* Bottecchia entry for his refusal to wear his yellow JERSEY through Italy, and his mysterious death.)

Italy's greatest days ran from 1938, when Gino Bartali won his first Tour, to 1952 when FAUSTO COPPI won his second and last. Both men's careers were badly affected by the WAR – Bartali's wins came in 1938, the last year of peace, and then again in 1948 – and many have said that Coppi, whose career didn't start properly until he was 26, could have been better than even EDDY MERCKX.

Bartali and Coppi were rivals in cycling, and opposites both on and off the bike. Bartali was an all-rounder with talent as a CLIMBER, so that each time he won the Tour he also won the MOUNTAINS competition. He was deeply religious and not easy to like. (*See* Bartali entry for details.) Coppi was a superb rider alone but weak in a sprint, a likeable atheist whose life was ruined by an adulterous affair that scandalised conservative Italy. (*See* Coppi entry for details.) Each was obsessively jealous of the other, and ALFREDO BINDA says his greatest achievement as a MANAGER was to get both to cooperate in the same team. (*See* Binda entry for more.)

There have been superb Italian riders since Coppi. FELICE GIMONDI was just 22 when he won in 1965. But for every level-headed individual who made a mark, there has always been a character like MARCO PANTANI whose life was a shipwreck.

Pantani became the first Italian winner since Gimondi when he won in 1998, a win even more extraordinary because his leg had been broken in a crash in 1995 when he hit a car on a descent in Milan-Turin. He was a brilliant climber, but his life after the Tour success was a succession of DOPING inquiries and suspensions. (*See* entry for details.) The whole of Italian cycling then became embroiled. The police raid on the 1998 Tour (*see* FESTINA AFFAIR) was dramatic, but small compared to the raid on the 2001 Giro. There were tales of a rider leaping through a window to avoid detention, of drugs being thrown into the sea and hidden under bushes, of police carrying away drugs literally by the bucketful. As many as 40 faced trials. More raids followed that year and the next.

IZOARD

At 2,361m the Izoard is the highest pass regularly crossed by the Tour, and a place of race legend.

The first rider to cross it in the Tour was PHILIPPE THYS in 1922. In 1923 HENRI PÉLISSIER won his first Tour at 34 by breaking away on it. In 1926 MARCEL BIDOT fought to prise off a punctured tyre with frozen fingers and a wing-nut after officials refused to let him use anything else. (*See* Bidot entry for more.) In 1949, FAUSTO COPPI caught GINO BARTALI there, and Bartali realised his career was over. He shouted, 'It's my birthday. Let's finish together. Tomorrow you'll win the Tour.' Coppi agreed; Bartali won in Briançon but Coppi took the Tour – by 28:27. Coppi was buried in earth brought from the Izoard.

In 1953 LOUISON BOBET rode away across the Izoard to win by more than five minutes at Briançon. Television's first motorbike pictures were broadcast there in 1960. (*See* BROADCASTING.)

The MOUNTAIN is on the D902 from Queyras to Briançon, a climb of 20km from Briançon, and 31km from Guillestre. Its most striking feature is the landscape of spikes and hollows called the Casse-Deserte, just before the top on the southern side. There are MEMORIALS in the rock there to Bobet and Coppi, their backs to each other, with the inscription by the writer Antoine Blondin, '*Rien n'y pousse sauf des coureurs qu'on pousse et produisent des amendes*' (Nothing pushes [moves] there except the riders, who are punished for being pushed). The memorials were restored in 2000 by the town of Briançon and re-commemorated in a ceremony presided over by Tour organiser JEAN-MARIE LEBLANC.

The top gives a spectacular view of all the Alps with Mont Blanc at their centre. MONT VENTOUX is just visible to the south.

LAURENT JALABERT
b. Mazamet, France, Nov 30 1968

FRANCE's best all-round talent at the end of the twentieth century rode the last day of the 2002 Tour on a bike dotted with red spots. The maker's name had been replaced by the words '*Merci, Jaja*'. The bike celebrated how the country's most popular rider since RAYMOND POULIDOR had yet again won the MOUNTAINS jersey in what he'd just announced would be his retirement year.

Jalabert was born in Mazamet, east of Toulouse, where the Quai Cazeneuve has been named the Place Laurent Jalabert. He trained as an electrical mechanic before being conscripted into the army, where he became its cycling champion thanks to generous time for training. 'I have never done anything but ride a BIKE,' he said.

Jalabert turned professional in 1989 for Toshiba. Team-mates remember him as a timid man anxious to impress. Teased for drinking wine where the others abstained, his colleague Martial Gayant laughed, 'You, you drink alcohol, you're as healthy as a horse . . . you'll make a good rider.' Later, pouring wine for him, he said, 'Here, have a glass of Jaja.' Jalabert's NICK-NAME had been created.

Philippe Le Fut, his first friend among the pros, said, 'His first race was the Tour of Valencia. We were warming up before the prologue when he tapped me on the shoulder and said, 'Look, that's SEAN KELLY.' He was just like a kid.' Jalabert's first win was the Tour of Armorica that season.

He moved to the ONCE team of SPAIN in 1992, and in 1994 bagged seven stages and the points competition of the Tour of Spain. Hopes that he could do the same in the Tour vanished on July 3 when a policeman stepped into the road at Armentières to take a photo. (*See* below.) Wilfried Nelissen smashed into the policeman, breaking his collarbone and bringing down Jalabert, who landed on his face. He was taken to hospital for jaw and facial surgery.

> **Trivia note:** the policeman's camera broke open when it hit the road at Armentières. A boy picked up a battery and kept it. His name was Arnaud Tournant. In 2001 he won three world championships and became the first man to ride a kilometre in less than a minute.

He returned better than ever in 1995 to win Milan-San Remo, Paris-Nice, the Critérium International, the Flèche Wallonne, and the Tour of Catalonia; the points competition and a stage of the Tour de France; and five stages and overall victory in the Tour of Spain. In 1997 he became world TIME TRIAL champion. That was when the Place Laurent Jalabert in Mazamet was named, and in October 1997 he unveiled a plaque that hailed him as 'Number one in the world since 1995', and 'World time trial champion 1997.'

He conceded in 2000 that he would never win the Tour, because he felt sick – *'mauvaises sensations'* – above 1,500m. On that year's stage to HAUTACAM he was nine minutes down and struggling for breath where LANCE ARMSTRONG won his yellow JERSEY and the Tour. 'The humility of the man to come in with the also-rans was impressive beyond words,' said one reporter.

The stage result marked another twist to a bizarre race. Jalabert had been in yellow through Brittany, and but for a *coup de pissette* – a Pisspot Rebellion – might still have been leading as far as the Pyrenees and Hautacam. He had nothing to fear from an easy stage to Tours, but after 10km of the stage he stopped for a pee. It is not polite to attack a yellow JERSEY in such circumstances, but unwittingly MAGNUS BACKSTEDT did so. Backstedt was 30 places down, far enough to discourage a chase. But then JACKY DURAND went as well, and he was in the top half dozen. Durand's attack gave everyone permission to do the same.

Jalabert's team chased hard before giving up, deciding that losing the *maillot jaune* was bad enough, but it would be worse to exhaust themselves two days before the Pyrénées. Jalabert slid from first to 10th. 'I was disappointed. I was *very* disappointed,' he said. 'It would be bad enough to lose it in a legitimate attack, but to lose it like that . . .'

In 2001 he fell out with ONCE's charismatic MANAGER Manolo Saiz over the team's restructuring, and joined a new Danish team run by BJARNE RIIS, Denmark's first Tour winner in 1996. The two had clashed during the FESTINA AFFAIR *(see* entry) but Jalabert said the issue had been forgotten.

'I would have ridden for a French team,' he said, 'but they had all allocated their budget at the time I knew I was leaving ONCE.' It is a disappointment for France that he never rode for a French SPONSOR.

Riis told him to train less, and to drop the daily five-hour sessions at 27km/h that he had been doing under Saiz. And Jalabert made another important decision on Tour tactics. Knowing his breathing was not up to man-to-man racing at altitude, he tried riding away alone. After a lone win through the undulating first world war battlefields to Verdun, he won again, finishing alone after being in a break through the mountains to Colmar on Bastille Day. Six stages later he freewheeled away from the field going down the Portet d'Aspet – few riders could match him downhill – and stayed away until he was caught by LANCE ARMSTRONG six kilometres from the Pla d'Adet.

The result was that a self-confessedly average climber ended up winning the 2001 mountains JERSEY. In 2002 he won it again with the same tactic. In that Tour, though, he told journalists gathered in the TRACK on the rest day at BORDEAUX on July 16 that this would be his final season. 'I miss my family too much to keep leaving them,' he said. *(See* MIGUEL INDURAIN for a similar comment.) He'd decided at the start of the year, he said, but he hadn't wanted people to think he was giving up because of a fall from grace.

The rest of the race was lined with banners reading, 'We'll miss you, Jaja.' Some had pictures of a panda; *L'ÉQUIPE*'s cartoonist, Chenez, had once drawn him as a panda because of his swarthy looks and thick eyebrows, and the image had stuck, promoted by cartoons drawn during French TV's live coverage. *(See* BROADCASTING for history of Tour television.)

Retirement doesn't trouble him. 'I've never done anything but ride a bike. I'll be happy to do nothing at all,' he said. A private man who rarely shows his thoughts, he has no ambition to become a manager or have any other official job. With Sylvie, his wife who years ago had presented him with a bouquet when he won his first race, he plans to live in retirement with their four children in a suburb of Geneva close to the French border. The couple's only flamboyances are a Wurlitzer jukebox in their sparsely decorated home and a Ferrari. Their telephone number is ex-directory.

(*See* CRITERIUMS, MONEY.)

Winner

1989 Tour Armorica
1990 Paris-Bourges
1993 Tour Rioja
1995 Tour Spain, Milan-San Remo, Paris-Nice, Flèche Wallonne, Tour Catalonia, Critérium International
1996 Midi Libre, Paris-Nice, Tour Valencia, Route Sud, Classique des Alpes
1997 Flèche Wallonne, Paris-Nice, Tour Lombardy, World time trial championship, Milan-Turin
1998 National championship, Classique des Alpes, Tour Asturias
1999 Semana Catalana, Tour Basque Country, Tour Romandie
2000 Tour Mediterranean, Semana Catalana
2001 San Sebastian Classic
2002 San Sebastian Classic, Tour Haut-Var

Tour de France

1991 71st
1992 34th Stage win Roubaix—Brussels, and Points winner
1993 DNF
1994 DNF
1995 4th Stage win St-Étienne—Mende, and Yellow Jersey and Points winner
1996 DNF
1997 43rd
1998 DNF
2000 54th Yellow Jersey

Tour de France (continued)

2001 19th Stage wins Huy—Verdun, Strasbourg—Colmar, and Mountains winner
2002 42nd Mountains winner

JAN JANSSEN
b. Nootdorp, Holland, May 19 1940

Once every 21 years since the WAR, the Tour has been won on the last day. In 1947 the winner was JEAN ROBIC, in 1968 Jan Janssen, and in 1989 GREG LEMOND.

The 1968 Tour was also unusual in another way – Paris had been torn by '*les évènements*', the civil disorder of those times. The riots and strikes started as a student dispute, and expanded across France in a wave of undefined discontent climaxing in a national strike by nine million people. Enough people died as cobbles were hurled and shots fired to justify a memorial in the Père Lachaise cemetery in eastern Paris. The Tour looked like being a victim, perhaps even being cancelled. (*See* FESTINA AFFAIR for another Tour on the verge of cancellation.) But the rioting paused wherever the Tour went by.

The last day started at Melun, on the edge of the Fontainebleau forest near Paris, with the Dutchman Jan Janssen 16 seconds behind HERMAN VAN SPRINGEL of BELGIUM. These two and a group of other riders including the Belgian hour record holder FERDI BRACKE were within three minutes of each other. There was just a 54km TIME TRIAL to the PISTE MUNICIPALE to sort out the winner.

Bracke was the favourite, but he was notorious for stage fright, and dropped out of the running early. Van Springel led by a fraction of a second at 40km but from there on Janssen gained rapidly and at the end he had 38 seconds on van Springel and won the Tour. He, his wife Cora and their daughter Karin burst into tears. That yellow JERSEY was the only one he'd worn and the margin he'd taken it by was the smallest ever, until the eight seconds that separated LeMond and LAURENT FIGNON in 1989 – a battle which Janssen was there to see.

Janssen was WORLD CHAMPION in 1964, when he beat VITTORIO ADORNI and RAYMOND POULIDOR at Sallanches, and then he almost won again in 1967 when he was beaten by EDDY MERCKX. In his book *Eddy Merckx, Coureur Cycliste*, Merckx named Janssen as one of the few he considered a 'true athlete'. His sprint made him a favourite in any race he rode, but he was handicapped by being only a moderate CLIMBER.

The end came for Janssen in the Tour of LUXEMBOURG in 1972, when he heard the race radio announce the winner, and also the news that Janssen was 15 minutes behind. 'I can't tell you what a blow that was,' he said. 'Jan Janssen at 15 minutes, winner of the Tour de France, former WORLD CHAMPION, winner of Paris-Roubaix, winner of Paris-Nice, all the big races. There and then I decided to do a couple more races and *hup*, I was done.'

A quiet and likeable man, Janssen opened a BIKE factory in Putte, on the Dutch-Belgian border, after he retired, and in 1990 sold it to Union. He was often called 'the Professor' – like Laurent Fignon after him – for his intelligence, his glasses, and because he made a point of learning French before riding his first Tour. He spent his best years in the yellow, white and blue of the French Pelforth brewery.

(And *see* SPRINTERS.)

Winner

1962	Championship Zurich
1964	World championship, Paris-Nice
1965	Tour Holland
1966	Bordeaux-Paris, Flèche Brabançonne
1967	Tour Spain, Paris-Roubaix, Paris-Luxembourg
1968	Tour de France
1969	GP Isbergues

Tour de France

1963	DNF	Stage win Angers—Limoges
1964	24th	Stage wins Champagnole—Thonon, Monaco—Hyères, and Points winner

Tour de France (continued)

1965	9th	Stage win Barcelona—Perpignan, and Points winner
1966	2nd	Yellow Jersey
1967	5th	Marseille—Carpentras, and Points winner
1968	1st	Stage wins Seo-de-Urgel—Canet-Plage, Melun—Paris, and Yellow Jersey
1969	10th	
1970	26th	

ZENON JASKULA
b. Gorzow, Poland, Jun 4 1962

Cycling in eastern Europe developed separately from the west. The east sent teams to events such as the Tour of BRITAIN (the Milk Race) and to world championships, and it had an international tour in the Peace Race, run between Warsaw, Berlin and Prague. But mainly it concentrated on Olympic TRACK events, and its riders won every world sprint and pursuit title from 1977 to the fall of the communist bloc in 1990.

Attempts in 1983 to persuade east European AMATEURS to ride the Tour de France ended in failure. (*See* Amateurs entry for background.)

As the Cold War came to an end, east European amateurs began riding experimentally in western professional races, and then joined as full professionals. Poland's Zenon Jaskula like many others from the Eastern Bloc, became a pro in Italy with the Diana team and then rode for the Italian GB-MG team, run by the Belgian MANAGER Patrick Lefevere. It was Lefevere who gave Jaskula his second ride in the Tour in 1993.

Jaskula never excited, but he did move into third place overall in the Pyrenees. He then won the 16th stage, from Andorra to St-Lary-Soulan, after leading over the Pla d'Adet and beating TONY ROMINGER and the overall leader, MIGUEL INDURAIN. He reached Paris in third place, the first east European to finish on the podium.

He also won the Tour of Portugal in 1997 but did little else and retired in 1998.

JERSEYS

Riders in the first Tours rode in whatever clothing they liked. Few riders at that time could either afford clothing used just for sport or indeed see the need for it. Advertisements at the start of the 20th century show riders in tight knee-length shorts not unlike modern shorts, and short-sleeved vests with low, square-cut collars and a row of buttons.

Those advertisements were mainly for TRACK meetings, where riders dressed like runners. Pictures of road riders leaving MONT-GERON for the START of the 1903 Tour show jumpers, flat caps and plus fours – trousers cropped under the knee and held by elastic or tucked into socks. Others show them in jackets and shorts and long socks. In other words, they wore whatever they chose.

By 1906 riders such as RENÉ POTTIER are shown in tights and jerseys with what look like primitive team colours. But still there was little consistency and no advertising. The interest of SPONSORS in riders had been recognised from the start, but only from 1913 were riders listed by their teams rather than as individuals who happened to be sponsored. They then began to compete formally in team colours. It's hard to say when makers' names began appearing on jerseys, but PHILIPPE THYS is shown with advertising in 1913. Within 10 years almost all riders wore some sort of lettering across their chests.

Sponsored teams were standard until 1930, when Tour organiser HENRI DESGRANGE,

unable to prevent sponsors from employing team TACTICS and thus spoiling his idea of a race between individuals, created NATIONAL TEAMS. From 1930 until 1961 riders rode in the colours of their country or REGIONAL TEAMS concocted to make up numbers.

Trade, or sponsored, teams returned in 1962 and have remained ever since, apart from 1967 and 1968 when national teams were briefly reintroduced. The reason, it was said, was because organisers JACQUES GODDET and FÉLIX LÉVITAN believed sponsors were the culprits behind a STRIKE that followed a DOPING check in 1966. (*See* entries and PIERRE DUMAS for more.)

There are exceptions to the wearing of team colours: individual jerseys are worn to identify the WORLD CHAMPION (white jersey with rainbow bands), the various national champions (colours based on their national flags), and the race category leaders. The rider with least accumulated time wears yellow; the rider with best accumulated placings each day (points leader) wears green, often called the SPRINTERS' jersey; and the best CLIMBER wears a white jersey with red blobs, or polka-dot. The best YOUNG RIDER wears white.

The first leader, MAURICE GARIN in 1903, did not wear a yellow jersey but a green armband. Officially, the first yellow jersey was EUGÈNE CHRISTOPHE of FRANCE on July 18 1919, when journalists and officials asked for a way to pick out the leader among the 11 left in the race. There was no presentation of the jersey when this was decided, after the 10th stage, from Nice to Grenoble. Christophe just pulled on his *maillot jaune* in a hotel, but he never liked it and was jeered at and called a canary for the rest of the race.

Christophe is the 'official' first, but PHILIPPE THYS of BELGIUM, who won the Tour in 1913, 1914 and 1920, said that he too had been given one in 1913. Tour authorities take his claim seriously, but say that nobody is alive to confirm it.

Legend says the jersey is yellow to match the colour of paper that *L'AUTO* used to distinguish it from the green of its rival, *Vélo*. Another account says it was the only colour available during post-war shortages. Jerseys had been ordered from Paris by Tour officials, and the only colour in large enough quantities at late notice was the unpopular yellow.

The yellow jersey was made of wool and changed little until the 1960s, apart from the disappearance of floppy collars, neck buttons, and front pockets. Acrylic jerseys in the 1980s made riders sweat and were abandoned in favour of Rovyl, a material used for underwear. Lycra then took over, and the only change since then has been that the podium jersey opens at the back like a straitjacket so that tired riders don't have to tug it over their heads.

Embroidery was so expensive that until 1969 team sponsors printed their names on patches of material the size of half a handkerchief, and fixed them to the jersey with pins (and from 1970 by stitching). From 1978 the names were printed by 'flocking', blowing cotton fluff at stencilled glue in a way that had become common for team jerseys. Silk-screen printing in the 1980s meant sponsors' names could be printed easily, with a stock of names held for each team at the finish.

The *maillot jaune* used to carry Henri Desgrange's initials on the left breast. In 1969 these were transferred to the sleeve to make room for the jersey's first sponsor, Virlux. The emblem of the clothing company Coq Sportif appeared at the same time at the foot of the zip. In 1972 the Desgrange initials returned to the front of the jersey but on the right, with a new sponsor, the ice-cream maker Miko, which had replaced Virlux in 1971, on the left. Coq Sportif appeared on the sleeves. In 1974 the initials went back on the left breast and '*Miko*' moved to the right. In 1984 *HD* was replaced by '*Le Tour*'. The initials will reappear in 2003 to mark the Tour's centenary.

The first rider to wear yellow from START to FINISH was OTTAVIO BOTTECCHIA in 1924, followed by NICOLAS FRANTZ in 1928. In 1929 there were three yellow jerseys on the same day when NICOLAS FRANTZ, ANDRÉ LEDUCQ and VICTOR FONTAN tied – Desgrange hadn't considered the need for tie-breaks. In 1971 EDDY

MERCKX refused to wear yellow for a day because he had only won it after LUIS OCAÑA crashed. Nor did FERDY KÜBLER wear it after FIORENZO MAGNI had pulled out because spectators had threatened his compatriot GINO BARTALI. (*See* Magni entry.)

In order to protect the fabled *maillot jaune* riders are not allowed to wear team colours featuring too much yellow. Among teams that have had to change colour are Dr Mann of BELGIUM in the 1960s and ONCE of SPAIN in recent seasons.

The climbers' competition, where the leader each day now wears a polka-dot jersey, began in 1933 (although prizes were offered in 1930 by the Menier chocolates company, pioneer of the CARAVAN), but there were no prizes attached to the wearing of it until the following year. The first company to pay a daily prize to the race leader was the wool firm Sofil in 1948, which offered the equivalent of £90. And the first post-war sponsor for the polka-dot was Vitteloise, followed by Cuir [leather] de France. The current sponsor is the Champion supermarket chain. The distinctive polka-dot jersey – *maillot à pois* in French – was ridiculed when it appeared in 1975 but now, of course, is much loved. The design, chosen by Tour organiser FÉLIX LÉVITAN, is based on jerseys he saw at the Vélodrome d'Hiver in Paris in the 1930s.

The points competition, where the leader each day wears a green jersey, began in 1953 to mark the 50th race, when it was called the Grand Prix du Cinquentenaire. It was won by

FRITZ SCHAER of Switzerland. Green jersey points go to the riders finishing highest each day, and the competition therefore favours sprinters, who have a greater number of suitable finishes. They can also pick up extra points in intermediate sprints called *primes*. The first jersey carried the name of its sponsor, La Belle Jardinière. The current backer is Pari Mutuel Urbain or PMU, the betting company.

The leading teams have been named from the start, with La Française-Dunlop winning in 1903. The most successful trade team is the French BIKE company ALCYON, which won in 1909–1912 and 1927–29. Top NATIONAL TEAMS are FRANCE and BELGIUM, with 10 wins each. Yellow hats to identify the best team have been tried, appearing and disappearing over the years, but have rarely appealed to spectators. Other innovations since abandoned include a team points award, and a red or white jersey combining all the other jerseys for the best rider in all the jersey competitions combined.

The COMBATIVITY AWARD leader wears a number printed in red and white, and gets the equivalent of £9,000.

JULIO JIMENEZ

b. Avila, Spain, Oct 28 1934

The journalist Geoffrey Nicholson summed it up when he wrote that 'Julito' Jimenez was 'a small birdlike figure ... [who was] also balding, grey-faced and never looked particularly well, but on the first steep slope he would prance away as though he had springs in his calves.'

Jimenez was to CLIMBERS what MICHEL POLLENTIER was to *rouleurs* (riders fastest on the flat), pug-ugly but fascinating and effective. He won the MOUNTAINS category three years in a row but never the Tour, mainly because like his fellow Spaniard FEDERICO BAHAMONTES he would lose on the way down all he had gained on the way up.

Jimenez was not only a bad descender but also dreadful in TIME TRIALS, which meant he had just a week in each Tour to make his name or finish in obscurity. He rarely disappointed,

however, winning five mountain stages in the mid-1960s.

Jimenez opened a business in his home town of Avila when he left cycling, but sold it shortly afterwards to put his feet up. He sometimes makes animated appearances on retro features on French television, and speaks lively Franco-Spanish with a fluency he never showed on his bike. The irony is that while he is more articulate than Bahamontes, he never had the same recognition or popularity in SPAIN. This may be because Bahamontes was the more complex personality (*see* entry for details), and rode the high mountains with an air of almost puzzled distraction, whereas Jimenez sweated and slogged his way up. He and Bahamontes drive the length of Spain for appearances, sometimes together, but it's Baha the crowds look for first.

(And *see* PUY-DE-DÔME.)

Winner

1964	National championship
1967	Trophée Grimpeurs

Tour de France

1964	7th	Stage win Perpignan—Andorra, Brive—Puy-de-Dôme
1965	23rd	Stage wins Dax—Bagnères-de-Bigorre, Briançon—Aix-les-Bains, and Mountains winner
1966	13th	Stage win Bourg d'Oisans—Briançon, and Mountains winner
1967	2nd	Mountains winner
1968	30th	

ARNE JONSSON

b. Copenhagen, Denmark, Nov 28 1931

Arne K. Jonsson would have passed unnoticed into history had he not given up the 1960 Tour before it started – because he had no shoes.

Jonsson and Bent Ole Retvig rode the 1959 Tour as Danes in the International team along with BRIAN ROBINSON and SHAY ELLIOTT. They joked that the free meals and hotels they got in the Tour made it cheaper than most races they went to. Retvig lasted until stage seven, Jonsson for two more.

They were picked for the International team again in 1960, although by then Robinson had left to lead a British team that included a young TOM SIMPSON. Conscious again of not spending more money than they needed to, Jonsson, Retvig and another Dane, Leif Hammel, entered a series of races, each taking them one step nearer to the Tour START in Paris. They arrived at midnight before the race. But by next morning thieves had emptied their car.

The riders borrowed all they needed, but Jonsson couldn't find shoes that fitted him. Inconsolable, he abandoned the Tour without turning a pedal. Retvig borrowed shoes, but his feet were bloody and aching by the first day. When he retired, he inadvertently took the British novice Tony Hewson out of the race as well. Hewson had ridden with Retvig in the previous summer's International team and stopped to help as Retvig tended his bleeding feet. They lost so much time before Retvig finally decided he wasn't going on that Hewson was obliged to climb into the *VOITURE BALAI* in depression. The remaining Dane, Hammel, lasted five days.

Jonsson and Retvig now live on the French Riviera, where they own building complexes.

Tour de France

1959	DNF
1960	DNF

BOBBY JULICH
b. Corpus Christi, USA, Nov 18 1971

A good time trialist and decent climber, Bobby Julich was the surprise of 1998. He didn't win a stage, but came second, third and fourth in TIME TRIALS. If he had taken 16 seconds less in each he would have taken second place above JAN ULLRICH. The next year he didn't finish, which was typical of his roller-coaster career. Success 'became like an albatross,' he said. 'It

happened like a bolt out of the blue and I couldn't take it in. There was so much expectation.'

Julich's career started at 14 with the Red Zinger Mini-classic in AMERICA in 1985, where he won his age category. In 1987 he won the American junior championship, and at 19 came fifth in the DuPont tour against GREG LEMOND and ERIK BREUKINK. He turned professional two years later and was about to leave for Europe when his SPONSOR, Rossin, collapsed. Not until 1995 did he get to Europe, riding with LANCE ARMSTRONG in the Motorola team for two seasons before joining the French Cofidis team.

In 1996, when he was 24, Julich spent 12 days leading the MOUNTAINS competition in the Tour of SPAIN. That was an 'up' part of the roller coaster. Then a 'down' came with suspected heart problems. 'Up' returned when he won third place in the 1998 Tour. Then in 1999, when he was expected to challenge for first place, an 80km/h downhill CRASH in a Tour time trial took him to hospital in Metz with a broken elbow and ribs. In 2000 he struggled through the mountains in the GRUPPETTO and finished in 48th place – after a fight on the CHAMPS-ELYSÉES with JEROEN BLIJLEVENS (*see* Blijlevens' entry for more). He came 18th in 2001 and 37th in 2002.

Tour de France

1997	17th
1998	3rd
1999	DNF
2000	48th
2001	18th
2002	37th

HANS JUNKERMANN
b. Sankt-Tonis, Germany, May 6 1934

In 1960 Hans Junkermann led the first NATIONAL TEAM from GERMANY with eight riders against the 14 of SPAIN, BELGIUM, FRANCE and ITALY. Only the main nations were allowed full squads.

Junkermann rose from 33rd to fourth, thanks to a break with ROGER RIVIÈRE and GASTONE NENCINI that gained 14 minutes at Lorient. He could have built on that, but cautiousness stopped him attacking when he could, and he came fourth in Paris. He finished one place further back the following year.

In 1962 he left the Tour in the midst of the WIEL'S AFFAIR, a disappointing episode in a career that promised much but delivered less.

Winner	
1957	Championship Zurich
1959	Tour Switzerland, National championship
1960	National championship
1961	National championship
1962	Tour Switzerland
1963	GP Frankfurt

Tour de France	
1960	4th
1961	5th
1962	DNF
1963	9th
1964	9th
1965	25th
1967	11th
1972	DNF

GERBEN KARSTENS
b. Leiden, Holland, Jan 14 1942

Gerben Karstens, a lively and witty man, was the son of a lawyer in the Dutch university city of Leiden. His parents had given him a good education in the hope he would follow his father into law. Instead he opted to become an agricultural engineer. That led to a row and Karstens, needing money more quickly than a farming career would provide, became a professional cyclist instead.

His sense of humour made Karstens a favourite with journalists and other riders, and his legs – among the fastest on the road – made him a man who could win both a TIME TRIAL (he was Olympic 100km team champion in 1964) and a sprint. And in 1965 he showed he was pretty nippy as a *rouleur* (fast-moving on the flat) as well, winning Paris-Tours at 45km/h, a record for a race run without GEARS (a novelty of that year that wasn't repeated).

Karstens won six stages of the Tour, starting in 1965 with a 20km lone break for the penultimate stage to Versailles. In 1966 he won a bunch sprint in Bayonne, and in 1976 he led over the Col d'Aspin, the sign of a real all-rounder. His humour showed in 1977 when he lay on the road after a CRASH; photographers and TV cameras took pictures of him, apparently close to dying. He waited until they'd finished, had a good laugh, got up, and went on his way. The Tour organisers JACQUES GODDET and

FÉLIX LÉVITAN weren't amused, and gave him a ticking off.

Karstens had 91 wins as a professional, including 14 stages of the Tour of SPAIN. His downfall was DOPING. In 1974 he was penalised 10 minutes in the Tour for taking the test after the time limit on stage four. He was denied the 1969 Tour of Lombardy and 1974 Paris-Tours after failing tests.

(*See* BERNARD THÉVENET for how Karstens' absence gave him his break in the Tour.)

Winner

1965 Paris-Tours
1966 Critérium As, National championship
1968 GP Fourmies
1973 Critérium As
1974 Tour Haut-Var

Tour de France

Year	Place	Notes
1965	59th	Stage win Auxerre—Versailles
1966	46th	Stage wins Tournai—Dunkirk, Bordeaux—Bayonne
1967	30th	
1969	65th	
1971	63rd	Stage win Basle—Fribourg
1972	60th	
1974	61st	Yellow Jersey
1975	50th	
1976	84th	Stage wins Lacanau—Bordeaux, Paris—Paris
1977	52nd	
1978	DNF	

KISSO KAWAMURO

Daisuke Imanaka, who rode in 1996 but didn't finish, has often been billed as the first Japanese in the Tour. But the honour goes to Kisso Kawamuro, a TOURISTE-ROUTIER in 1926 and 1927. The oversight is possibly forgiveable: Kawamuro abandoned both races on the first day and was never heard of again.

Tour de France

1926 DNF
1927 DNF

SEAN KELLY
b. Waterford, Ireland, May 24 1956

The strangely unemotional Sean Kelly became not only IRELAND's most successful rider, but also for four seasons the best rider in the world. He won Paris-Nice seven times, so often that undenied rumours said he was paid to stay away in year eight for fear of killing any remaining interest. His toughness and above all his sprint made him a king of the classics. He was slower than MARIO CIPOLLINI, but didn't need a team of lead-out men (*see* SPRINTERS) to guide him through the rough house of the last 400 metres. The one talent he lacked was as a CLIMBER which, along with a dislike of hot weather, denied him the Tour title.

John James Kelly was born in Waterford, near his family's 20-hectare farm in Carrick-on-Suir. He rode his first race when he was 14, on August 4 1970, on the edge of the town. His brother Joe had joined a new cycling league and John, known as Sean to avoid confusion with his father (also called John), followed him.

Tony Ryan, who helped organise the race, said, 'I didn't know who this lad was. When asked for his name he looked at Joe and said, "I'm his brother." When asked did he do much cycling he replied, "A little." He didn't look much so we let him off three minutes ahead of the scratch group [in a handicap race, the slowest riders start first]. They never got near him.'

Ryan drove him through the snow to Cork on St Patrick's Day 1972 for the Irish junior championship. Kelly won, and won again in 1973, followed by wins in the SHAY ELLIOTT memorial race in 1974, a stage of the Tour of BRITAIN in 1975, and the AMATEUR Tour of Lombardy in 1976.

Kelly moved to FRANCE to join the ACBB club in Paris (*see* STEPHEN ROCHE, who made the same move) and then in 1977 to Vilvoorde in BELGIUM to turn professional as a DOMESTIQUE in the FLANDRIA team of MICHEL POLLENTIER. (*See* Pollentier entry for his dramatic disqualification from the Tour.) Kelly's early role was as lead-out man for FREDDY MAERTENS. But once he'd learned TACTICS and self-sufficiency from the avuncular Jean de Gribaldy, Flandria's self-styled 'count' and deputy MANAGER took him off to other teams to which Kelly seemed to owe no allegiance other than the right to win in their name.

He won Paris-Nice for the first of seven times in 1982, winning four stages, and that summer won the SPRINTERS' competition of the Tour and third place at the world championship. His success rolled on, and he won the season-long Super Prestige Pernod, forerunner of the World Cup, in 1984, 1985 and 1986. He also won the first World Cup in 1989.

He won the Tour's green JERSEY (as points winner) four times, in 1982, 1983, 1985 and 1989, which was then a record, and wore the yellow jersey for a day in 1983. His single-day wins range from the cobbles of Paris-Roubaix to the lone ride against the clock in the Grand Prix des Nations in 1986. He won the 1988 Tour of SPAIN.

His last big win was Milan-San Remo in 1992, after which he had quieter years until he retired in 1994 when he was 38, after a career of 193 wins in 18 years. When he rode his last race in December 1994, BERNARD HINAULT, LAURENT FIGNON, ROGER DE VLAEMINCK, EDDY MERCKX and STEPHEN ROCHE joined a crowd of more than 1,200 at Carrick-on-Suir. A square named after him in the town is, in the Irish way, actually triangular.

Kelly still sounds like what he began as, a farmer's boy who had planned to be a bricklayer and had somehow ended up doing well on a bike. His biographer, David Walsh, says, 'His inability to communicate with strangers was a problem which surfaced with increasing regularity as Kelly achieved success on a bike. After winning a stage of the Tour of Britain Milk Race as a 19-year-old he was interviewed on Irish radio. It was said afterwards that Kelly was the 'only man who ever nodded in answer to a question on the radio.'

One of the few times his emotions showed was in his rivalry with another hard-guy sprinter, Eric Vanderaerden, a rivalry so intense that in 1986 there was a fight during the sprint in the sixth Tour stage at Reims, and both were placed last in the bunch.

Off the bike he had an unaffected manner remarkable for its honesty and lack of self-aggrandisement. Years spent in Belgium and France had taught him to end sentences with an interrogative *hein?* And, like a Frenchman, he also 'made' everything: 'I made an interview' etc. The bizarre accent he had acquired led British journalists at the 1981 world championship in Czechoslovakia to hold a sweepstake on what they thought he'd said in an interview. Since the piece was destined for Irish radio, they assumed that the engineer in Dublin would provide the answer. Instead he said, 'Sure I don't know what the boy is saying, but put me down for a pound anyway.'

Kelly lives now where he grew up, at Carrick-on-Suir, and works during the summer as a commentator for Eurosport.

Walsh says, 'Calculating the extent of Kelly's earnings is difficult and a task which gets no assistance from the rider himself. Kelly's joke is that journalists think of the biggest telephone number they know and work from there; that they are totally unrealistic. From the very beginning Kelly appreciated the importance of making his life on the bike pay. "Professional sportsmen might say different things but they compete, in the first place, for the money. If they claim otherwise, they lie."'

(And *see* AGENTS, GREG LEMOND, PDM AFFAIR.)

Winner

1977	GP Lugano, Circuit l'Indre
1980	Three-days De Panne
1982	Paris-Nice, Tour Haut-Var
1983	Tour Lombardy, Paris-Nice, Tour Switzerland, Critérium International, GP Isbergues
1984	Liège-Bastogne-Liège, Paris-Roubaix, Paris-Tours, Paris-Nice, Critérium International, Paris-Bourges, GP Plouay, Critérium As, Tour Basque Country, Tour Catalonia
1985	Tour Lombardy, Critérium As, Paris-Nice, Nissan Classic
1986	Critérium As, Paris-Nice, GP Nations, Milan-San Remo, Paris-Roubaix, Tour Catalonia, Nissan Classic, Tour Basque Country
1987	Paris-Nice, Critérium International, Nissan Classic, Tour Basque Country
1988	Tour Spain, Ghent-Wevelgem, Paris-Nice, Catalan Week
1989	Liège-Bastogne-Liège, World Cup
1990	Tour Switzerland
1991	Tour Lombardy, Nissan Classic
1992	Milan-San Remo, Trofeo Luis Puig

Tour de France

1978	34th	Stage win Mazé-Montgeoffroy—Poitiers
1979	38th	
1980	29th	Stage wins Voreppe—St-Étienne, Auxerre—Fontenay-sous-Bois
1981	48th	Stage win Besançon—Thonon
1982	15th	Stage win Fleurance—Pau, and Points winner
1983	7th	Yellow Jersey and Points winner
1984	5th	
1985	4th	Points winner
1987	DNF	
1988	46th	
1989	9th	Points winner
1990	30th	
1991	DNF	
1992	43rd	

KELME

Kelme, a Spanish sports shoe company based in Elche, near Alicante on the Costa Blanca, is the longest-serving SPONSOR in the sport, from 1979 to the present. Diego and José Pepe Quiles began Kelme in 1977. Two years later the Tour of SPAIN offered them the MOUNTAINS competition and a minute a day of TV advertising, and the brothers agreed. That led to an approach by Rafael Carrasco for them to take on the little Transmallorca team of which he was MANAGER. This became the Kelme team in 1979. Its first leader was the CLIMBER Francisco Paco Galdos, who had come fourth to BERNARD THÉVENET in the 1977 Tour, his highest placing.

A Kelme team first rode the Tour in 1980, when Vicente Belda in 20th place was best finisher. The company used its team to expand into the USSR and into COLOMBIA, taking on riders from both countries. Co-sponsors with Kelme have included the Iberia airline, the Colombian airline Avianca, and the Costa Blanca tourist board.

KERMESSES – See CRITERIUMS

PAUL KIMMAGE
b. Dublin, Ireland, May 7 1962

Paul Kimmage's father Christy was an Irish international, and the genes showed when Kimmage came sixth in the 1985 AMATEUR world championship. He rode as a professional in IRELAND's golden period of SEAN KELLY, STEPHEN ROCHE and MARTIN EARLEY.

Kimmage started the Tour in 1986, 1987 and 1989, but finished on only the first occasion. He retired on July 13 1989 when the Tour reached Toulouse, and went back to Ireland to work as a cycling and rugby writer for the *Irish Independent* in Dublin. His book *Rough Ride* in 1990 described his failure and the role of DOPING in cycling. 'I was never a cheat, I WAS A VICTIM,' he insisted, complete with the capitals, after describing how he had finally agreed to take drugs to race.

He wrote, 'The Tour de France was no ordinary race. A syringe did not always mean doping. In a perfect world it would be possible to ride the Tour without taking a single medication. But this was not a perfect world. We were not doping, we were taking care of ourselves. The substances taken were not on the proscribed list, so how could we be doping?

'The line between taking care of yourself and doping becomes very thin. Most cross it without ever realising they have. They just follow the advice of a team-mate or SOIGNEUR.'

Kimmage described how he finally relented, describing his first race as a drugged rider as one of the easiest he had ridden – 'My mind had been stimulated. Stimulated by amphetamines. I believe I am invincible, therefore I am.'

Former cycling colleagues, particularly Roche, shunned him. He didn't figure in the Tour's celebrations when the race started from Dublin in 1998. (*See* FESTINA AFFAIR for links between Dublin, DOPING and WILLY VOET.) Roche, who had denied widespread doping, said, 'He [Kimmage] has to wake up some time and realise what he's doing to the sport in general. Yes, it's OK to wake everybody up to the danger of drugs, I do agree, but at the same time there's a limit as to what you can say. He said it once, OK, but he keeps saying it again.'

Kimmage says his hero is CHRISTOPHE BASSONS, who wrote about drugs in 1999 and wrecked his career. (*See* Bassons entry for details.)

Tour de France

1986	131st
1987	DNF
1989	DNF

MARCEL KINT
b. Zwevegem, Belgium, Sep 20 1914, d. Kortrijk, Belgium, Mar 23 2002

BELGIUM's Marcel Kint, known as the 'Black Eagle' because of his beaked nose and the colour of his jersey, rode as a professional from 1935 until 1951. He rode the Tour five times, winning six stages, and took Paris-Roubaix in 1943 and the Flèche Wallonne in 1943, 1944 and 1945.

Kint was cycling's longest-serving WORLD CHAMPION, winning the title at Valkenburg in 1938 ahead of the Swiss riders Paul Egli and Leo Amberg. Unable to defend it until 1946 because of the WAR, he came close to winning it again only to be caught in the final kilometres by Hans Knecht of Switzerland, in front of his home crowd in Zurich. Kint had nothing left, and Knecht dropped him to win by 10 seconds.

What made defeat more bitter was the fact that Knecht had been helped to the front by Kint's own team-mate, RIK VAN STEENBERGEN, who also wanted to win. World championships are supposed to be for individuals rather than nations, but only in principle, never in fact. There was uproar.

The rift with van Steenbergen didn't last, though, and the two became regular partners in six-day TRACK races. (*See* RUDI ALTIG for why riders took part.) Then a severe crash in the 1947 Paris six-day cracked his skull and kept him out of racing for two years, after which he returned to win Ghent-Wevelgem in 1949.

Kint, who died aged 87 at his home in Kortrijk in 2002, was a leader of the school of hard Belgian roadmen for whom guts and courage were more important and often more successful than beauty and speed. It is said, for instance, that Kint trained on salted fish to get him used to the heat-induced thirst of southern France during the Tour.

Winner

1938	Paris-Brussels, World championship
1939	Antwerp-Ghent-Antwerp, National championship
1940	Tour Belgium
1943	Tour Belgium, Flèche Wallonne, Paris-Roubaix
1944	Flèche Wallonne
1945	Flèche Wallonne, Tour Flemish Ardennes
1949	Ghent-Wevelgem

Tour de France

1936	9th	Stage win La Rochelle—La Roche-sur-Yon
1937	DNF	Yellow Jersey
1938	9th	Stage wins Briançon—Aix-les-Bains, Aix-les-Bains—Besançon, Strasbourg—Metz
1939	34th	Stage wins Bordeaux—Salies de Béarn, Troyes—Paris
1949	DNF	

DON KIRKHAM
b. Lyndhurst, Australia, 1880, d. 1929

Don Kirkham was one of Australia's first riders in the Tour, competing in 1914 with Ivor Munro and sponsored by Phebus-Dunlop along with GEORGES PASSERIEU. They came respectively 17th at 11:53:39, and 24th at 12:38:57.

In 1929 Kirkham was cycling home to his farm after winning a 100-mile race when he was knocked off by a drunken motorist. Delays in finding a doctor meant his injuries led to pneumonia and tuberculosis, from which he died.

Tour de France

1914	17th

JAAN KIRSIPUU
b. Tartu, USSR, Jul 17 1969

Russian by birth, Estonian after independence, and living in St-Alban-Leysse in the Savoie department of France, Jaan Kirsipuu has remained faithful to the same management team throughout his pro career, although the name sponsor has changed several times: he rode for Chazal from 1992 to 1995, for Petit Casino and Casino from 1996 to 1999, and then for the AG2R life assurance company from 2000.

He is hefty as cyclists go, 73kg and 1.79m. That bulk took him to four sprint wins in the 2001 Four-days of Dunkirk, beating his previous best of three in the previous year's Tour of

Poland, and taking his Dunkirk tally to 12. In 1999 he led the Tour for six days from St-Nazaire to Metz, losing his JERSEY 'because I ran out of gas and I had bad morale,' he said. 'I tried to cope with all the journalists and by the end of the week I was exhausted with all the inquiries. I don't look for publicity; what's important is to win races.'

Kirsipuu's stage to Rouen in 2002 was his 100th as a professional.

His MANAGER, Vincent Lavenu, says, 'I don't know what his limits are except in the high MOUNTAINS. He has exceptional acceleration. He can hold 1,550 watts over five seconds, it's unbelievable. He can ride 53x11 or 54x11 in a sprint.'

Despite all that pure speed and power, Kirsipuu has yet to finish a Tour, and is always dropped in the mountains. His brother Tomas was also a professional, riding for KELME in 1989.

Winner

1993 GP Isbergues
1997 GP Cholet, Tour Vendée
1998 GP Cholet, Route Adélie, National Championship, GP Denain, Circuit Sarthe
1999 GP Cholet, Tour Vendée, Tour Oise, National championship
2000 Classic Haribo, Tour Vendée
2001 GP Denain, Route Adélie, National championship
2002 Kuurne-Brussels-Kuurne, Classic Haribo

Tour de France

1993 DNF
1994 DNF
1995 DNF
1997 DNF
1998 DNF
1999 DNF Stage win Montaigu—Challans, and Yellow Jersey and Points leader
2000 DNF
2001 DNF Stage win Commercy—Strasbourg, and Points leader
2002 DNF Stage win Soissons—Rouen

KISSING GIRLS

Twice as many kissing girls get on the rostrum as riders, because there are two for every SPONSOR. Their origins are obscure but FRANCE has always been keen on kissing as a greeting and so they have probably been there from the start.

The first kissing girls were wives or daughters of local bigwigs. Not all were attractive and, to judge by the revulsion on the faces of some women called on to kiss a snot- and mud-caked winner, they may have thought the same of the riders. On a good day, old-style kissing girls – or women – went to work with gusto. A picture of OCTAVE LAPIZE in 1910 shows him overwhelmed by a buxom madame in a feather boa.

The history isn't clear, but it seems the Tour may later have insisted that kissing girls had to be beauty queens. Now the girls work for individual sponsors and travel with the race in company uniforms.

GERRIE KNETEMANN
b. Amsterdam, Holland, Mar 6 1951

Gerrie Knetemann (pronounced *Herry Kuh-nay-tuh-munn*) rode as a professional for 17 years, starting 13 Tours and reaching Paris in all but two. His 10 stage wins are equalled in HOLLAND only by RALEIGH team-mates JAN RAAS and JOOP ZOETEMELK.

Knetemann's glory year was 1978 when he took the yellow JERSEY on the sixth stage, lost it two days later to JOS BRUYÈRE in the TIME TRIAL, won the 18th stage into Lausanne, and crowned his Tour by winning on the CHAMPS ELYSÉES. By the end of the year he was WORLD CHAMPION.

After more yellow jerseys Knetemann's career went into decline following a fall in the A Travers la Belgique race, a Belgian semi-classic, on March 24 1983. He took months to recover. He did ride the Tour again after that, but won nothing. After 127 wins as a pro, he became national coach.

Knetemann's wit, inventive expressions and odd use of words made him popular in Holland

and he had regular BROADCASTING spots long before his career finished.

Winner

1974	Amstel Gold
1976	Ruta del Sol, Tour Holland
1977	GP Frankfurt, Four-days Dunkirk
1978	Tour Mediterranean, World championship
1980	Tour Mediterranean, Tour Belgium, Tour Holland
1981	Tour Holland
1982	Three-days De Panne
1983	Tour Mediterranean
1985	Amstel Gold
1986	Tour Holland
1987	Tour Sweden

Tour de France

1974	38th	
1975	63rd	Stage win Tarbes—Albi
1976	DNF	
1977	31st	Stage wins Saint-Trivier—Dijon, Montereau—Versailles
1978	43rd	Stage wins Morzine—Lausanne, St-Germain-en-Laye—Paris, and Yellow Jersey
1979	30th	Stage wins Fleurance— Fleurance, Dijon—Auxerre, and Yellow Jersey
1980	38th	Stage win Agen—Pau
1981	55th	Yellow Jersey
1982	47th	Stage wins Beauraing— Moeskroen, Valence d'Agen— Valence d'Agen
1984	103rd	
1986	84th	
1987	89th	
1988	DNF	

HUGO KOBLET

b. Zurich, Switzerland, Mar 21 1925, d. Uster, Switzerland, Nov 6 1964

Switzerland's Hugo Koblet was the epitome of sleekness: silky under effort, his saddle low, but a picture of elegance with his straight back and long arms. Dark goggles below his left elbow gave the image of a ski playboy. A French journalist wrote, 'He had not an enemy at all; his ready and kindly smile came from deep down inside, and one knew from the start that this was a genuine, gentle man with a natural warmth of character.'

His trademarks were comb, sponge and cologne, held in a narrow extra back pocket on his jersey. If he could win alone, he would take his hands from the bars and run the comb through his thinning hair, then freshen his face with the cologne before crossing the line. He was the exact opposite of his fellow Swiss, FERDY KÜBLER.

Koblet won the Giro and the Tour of Switzerland in 1950, the Tour and the Grand Prix des Nations in 1951, three medals in the world professional pursuit, and two second places in the Giro. Pope Pius XII fêted him and GINO BARTALI at the Vatican in June 1950.

In 1951 *'le bel Hugo'* produced one of the Tour's legendary rides on the Brive—Agen stage. He rode clear on a hill and kept going for 135km. At first the rest took no notice. But insouciance grew to concern and then anger. FAUSTO COPPI, Bartali, LOUISON BOBET, RAPHAËL GÉMINIANI, STAN OCKERS and JEAN ROBIC set into a team pursuit to bring him back. But they never caught sight of him. Koblet entered the long finish and lifted his hands, still pedalling smoothly. He reached for his comb, eau-de-cologne and sponge. He rode into the last kilometre a groomed gentleman, and won by 2:35.

After puncturing three days later on the TOURMALET, he waited for help before dropping Bartali, Bobet, Ockers and Géminiani as he chased to the summit. He took the yellow

> **Trivia note:** Koblet was having a hard time from FRANCOIS MAHÉ in the 1951 Tour of Switzerland. So Koblet demoralised him in the mountains by riding hands off beside him to comb his hair. Mahé gave up and dropped back.

JERSEY with victory in Luchon and kept it to Paris. Géminiani was second, 22 minutes behind. The singer Jacques Grello, who was following the Tour for *Parisien Libéré*, nicknamed him the 'Pedaller of Charm'.

Koblet liked to look around during races, taking in the chateaux or the countryside. He was a fan of AMERICA, where he toured and raced several times. But his power diminished suddenly after 1951. His style was still faultless but the power had gone. Jean Bobet wrote, 'We saw him in 1953 getting an odd sickness above 2,000m, then above 1,500m, then above 1,000m. We saw him unable to get over even the tiniest hill and we were witnesses to his disappearance. His face grew older and his personality sombre.' That year the bunch waited for him in the Giro to make sure he got back on after a CRASH.

By 1953 he was a shadow of the man who'd won at Agen two years before. In 1954 he was dropped and two days later, on the 13th stage from Luchon to Toulouse, he climbed off. It wasn't the end: there was enough of a recovery to win a stage in the Tour of SPAIN, but only after RIK VAN STEENBERGEN and MIGUEL POBLET eased back to give him a farewell win.

Koblet stopped racing in 1958, and lived with the carefree elegance he had shown on the bike. He spent much of what he earned on a convivial lifestyle, going on a tour of the Americas in the hope of regaining his health. He opened a garage near the Hallenstadion TRACK in Zurich but lost his money. Then he worked as a journalist for Swiss radio.

But the debts grew, and his wife left him. On November 2 1964 the white Alfa-Romeo he was driving left a bend at 120km/h just outside Zurich and hit a pear tree. The speed was shown by the jammed speedometer. The head of the medical team said after an operation that lasted four hours, 'He has only a two per cent chance of survival.' That evening he added, 'Only a miracle can save him.' Koblet died three nights later, at 1.45am. His death was considered a suicide by many although experts dismissed the idea at an inquiry. He was 39.

(*See* ROGER LÉVÈQUE.)

Winner

1950	Giro d'Italia, Tour Switzerland, GP Zurich
1951	Tour de France, GP Nations, Critérium As, GP Zurich
1952	Championship Zurich
1953	Tour Romandie, Tour Switzerland
1954	Championship Zurich, GP Martini, GP Zurich
1955	Tour Switzerland, National championship

Tour de France

1951	1st	Stage wins La Guerche—Angers, Brive—Agen, Tarbes—Luchon, Carcassonne—Montpellier, Aix-les-Bains—Geneva, and Yellow Jersey
1953	DNF	
1954	DNF	

FERDY KÜBLER
b. Marthalen, Switzerland, Jul 24 1919

For every kilometre that his fellow Swiss HUGO KOBLET rode as a picture of elegance, Ferdy Kübler rode like a wild man, bobbing, weaving and foaming. No man struggled so hard for wins, nor grimaced as much as Kübler, except BERNARD GAUTHIER perhaps (*see* Gauthier entry for more.)

Kübler enjoyed taunting riders and MANAGERS, dropping back to team cars to warn in broken French, 'Ferdy attack soon, you ready?' And then, a few minutes later, 'Ferdy big horse. Ferdy attack now. Your boys ready?' When he once more dropped back to tell RAPHAËL GÉMINIANI, 'Ferdy attack now, FRANCE ready?', the Frenchman said in deliberate, equally bad French, 'Ferdy shut up now or Ferdy get head knocked in.'

Kübler began racing when he was 19 but during the WAR he could race only in neutral Switzerland. He won the Tour of Switzerland in 1942 but raced abroad only from 1947. He immediately went to the Tour de France and won two stages, but surprised everyone by giving up before the end.

Ferdy Kübler *(continued)*

In 1949 he took on FAUSTO COPPI and GINO BARTALI in the Alps, and gained 10 minutes. But three punctures stopped him, forcing him to wait for a MECHANIC once he'd used all his spares. But at that moment the Swiss car was stranded with a breakdown of its own, and next morning Kübler called it a day.

In 1950 he satisfied his fans by winning the 78km TIME TRIAL from Dinard to St-Brieuc, but greater excitement was to come. The race was nearing the summit of the Aspin when JEAN ROBIC and GINO BARTALI brushed against each other and fell off. SPECTATORS angry at Robic's downfall surged round Bartali, and one seemingly threatened to stab him, although it's more likely he was waving a sandwich knife. Bartali took exception and ITALY went home even though FIORENZO MAGNI was leading. Magni was riding for the B team, the *Cadetti*, and cynics said Bartali couldn't stand being upstaged.

That meant Kübler took over the yellow JERSEY (although he refused to wear it next morning as a mark of respect to Bartali and Magni) and with it the Tour. (*See* EDDY MERCKX and JOOP ZOETEMELK for other riders who refused to wear yellow.) His Tour was far from an empty victory, however, for he won two more stages and worked up nine and a half minutes on the second man, STAN OCKERS.

The first year Kübler crossed MONT VENTOUX, in 1955, Géminiani warned him it wasn't 'a mountain like any other' and he should take it easy. Kübler replied, 'Ferdy also racer not like others; Ferdy grand champion win at Avignon.' He attacked 10km from the top, followed by LOUISON BOBET and Géminiani. But then he became delirious, foaming at the mouth and weaving about. His MANAGER, Alex Burtin, jumped out of his white Jeep and ran beside him, urging him to take it easier.

But Kübler only swore at him in German and pushed on. He crashed several times on the descent, then stopped at a bar on the outskirts of Avignon. Once outside he got back on his bike and was about to set off in the wrong direction when a drinker turned him round.

> *Trivia note:* Kübler refers to his giant Mercedes as his 'Trabby', the popular name for the notorious, fume-belching East German Trabant.

'Stand clear,' Kübler shouted. 'Ferdy's going to explode!'

That evening he announced he was giving up racing and went to his room, covered with plasters from his falls. He slept badly and announced, 'He is too old, Ferdy, he is too sick; Ferdy killed himself on the Ventoux.' He left the Tour and never rode it again.

Kübler later bought a flower shop in Zürich. He also managed the Italian Gazzola team, led by CHARLY GAUL. In 1983 the Swiss voted Kübler their greatest sportsman of the previous half-century. Now retired, he still works in public relations for the Tour of Switzerland. His first name is often written *Ferdi*, but that's the way French-speakers spell it. Kübler writes it Ferdy.

Kübler drank little during a race, sharing JACQUES ANQUETIL's theory that 'driest is fastest' (*see* CAFÉ RAIDS). His beaky nose gave him the nickname 'the Eagle of Adilswil', the village where he grew up, and the similarly beak-nosed TOM SIMPSON called him Uncle Ferdy.

Winner

1942	Tour Switzerland
1943	Championship Zurich
1948	Tour Romandie, Tour Switzerland, GP Zurich, National championship
1949	GP Zurich, National championship
1950	Tour de France, GP Lugano, National championship
1951	World championship, Liège-Bastogne-Liège, Flèche Wallonne, Tour Switzerland, Tour Romandie, National championship
1952	Liège-Bastogne-Liège, Flèche Wallonne
1953	Bordeaux-Paris
1954	National championship
1956	Milan-Turin

Tour de France

1947	DNF	Stage wins Paris—Lille, Strasbourg—Besançon, and Yellow Jersey
1949	DNF	Stage win Rouen—St-Malo
1950	1st	Stage wins Dinard—St-Brieuc, Menton—Nice, St-Étienne—Lyon, and Yellow Jersey
1954	2nd	Stage wins Caen—St-Brieuc, Toulouse—Millau, and Points winner
1955	DNF	

HENNIE KUIPER

b. Denekamp, Holland, Feb 3 1949

Hennie Kuiper and ERCOLE BALDINI are alone in winning not only Olympic gold medals but also the world professional road championship. It was by winning the 1972 Olympic road race in Munich that the Dutchman Kuiper, who spoke with a stammer and wore his hair in a fringe, gained a contract with the German Rokado team. He was a poor SPRINTER and had to get his wins through lone breaks, for which he built quite a name. In 1975 he won the world championship in BELGIUM.

Kuiper started 12 Tours, winning none but twice coming second, beaten by BERNARD THÉVENET in 1977 and JOOP ZOETEMELK in 1980. He was never lucky, crashing in 1976 and 1978, and failing to finish in 1983 and 1985. Even so he won three stages, including ALPE D'HUEZ in 1977 and 1978. He spent his best years with the RALEIGH team, but was overshadowed by JAN RAAS and other more spectacular riders.

Kuiper disliked Peter Post, the team's dominating MANAGER. 'My character and Peter Post's are totally different,' he once said. 'I was still a youngster. And when you're young and you have some sort of problem, you need to discuss it. But that was almost impossible. Post is as hard as stone. I can be hard as well but the difference was much too big.'

He left Raleigh and rode under FRED DE BRUYNE for the Dutch car-maker DAF. 'I then went to PEUGEOT specifically to win the Tour.

Maurice de Muer was the team leader and everything was aimed at the Tour. The team rode in my service in the Tour, or that was the way it was supposed to be. But for the French the Tour is the biggest of all and they do not work happily for someone else. I had a two-year contract but ... I was fourth in 1979 and in 1980 I was second, but for a team like Peugeot that wasn't enough.'

Kuiper retired after 74 wins to live in Putte, near the Belgian border, a few streets from JAN JANSSEN. He managed the Deutsche Bundespost team in 1991 before it evolved into Deutsche Telekom with JAN ULLRICH and ERIK ZABEL.

Winner

1975	World championship, National championship
1976	Tour Switzerland
1981	Tour Flanders, Tour Lombardy
1982	GP Wallonie
1983	Paris-Roubaix
1985	Milan-San Remo

Tour de France

1975	11th	
1976	DNF	Stage win Le Touquet—Bornem
1977	2nd	Stage win Chamonix—Alpe d'Huez
1978	DNF	Stage win St-Étienne—Alpe d'Huez
1979	4th	
1980	2nd	
1981	30th	
1982	9th	
1983	DNF	
1984	56th	
1985	DNF	
1988	95th	

KARL-HEINZ KUNDE

b. Cologne, Germany, Aug 6 1938

One of the tiniest cyclists to ride the Tour, Karl-Heinz Kunde was 1.59m and weighed 49kg. Not surprisingly, he became known as 'the Flea', like BENOIT FAURE.

Kunde took the yellow JERSEY in 1966, just days after his compatriot RUDI ALTIG had held it for 11 days. But unfortunately for Kunde, his PEUGEOT team couldn't help him. It was a team of stars like FERDI BRACKE, ROGER PINGEON and TOM SIMPSON, but such was Kunde's ability as a CLIMBER that the best they could hope was that they'd be able to hang on. And nobody saw him as a possible WINNER.

Kunde kept the jersey for five days but, tired out by having to defend his own chances, he was wiped out when JULIO JIMENEZ of SPAIN attacked on the stage from Bourg d'Oisans to Briançon. Kunde struggled to hang on but his time was over.

'Karl the Tiny has been beaten by a giant,' said JACQUES GODDET of the battle with Jimenez, who was himself only a little taller. Kunde finished the Tour ninth.

Tour de France

1964	16th	
1965	11th	
1966	9th	Yellow Jersey
1967	DNF	
1968	DNF	
1972	20th	

FRANÇOIS LAFOURCADE

b. Lahontan, France, Nov 8 1881,
d. Western Front, Aug 10 1917

François Lafourcade was the first rider over the Col d'AUBISQUE when the Tour crossed it for the first time in 1910. Organiser HENRI DES-GRANGE had been too scared of his reputation and the possibility of disaster, and stayed away when the race went into the MOUNTAINS for the first time, sending his deputy, Victor Breyer, instead. Breyer and the rest waited so long for the race to appear that they feared the riders had gone home, been ambushed or – as the riders had themselves feared – been eaten by bears. Eventually Lafourcade passed without speaking to them, but the next man, OCTAVE LAPIZE, accused them of being 'assassins', and said he was giving up as soon as he'd got down to the valley.

Lafourcade could then have won the Tour but, unfortunately for him, Lapize decided to carry on after all and passed him. Instead Lafourcade finished the Tour 14th.

Lafourcade was implicated in the poisoning of PAUL DUBOC (*see* entry for details).

Tour de France

1907	13th
1908	DNF
1909	DNF
1910	14th
1911	DNF
1912	28th

LA FRANÇAISE

La Française was the BIKE company to which MAURICE GARIN, his brother César and LUCIEN POTHIER were attached in the first Tour in 1903. It had links with the Clément family which had helped found *L'AUTO*. Critics said the paper was so keen that one of Clément's men should win in the 1904 Tour, especially Garin, that officials handed him food and denied it to the others. (*See* 1904 AFFAIR). Just why they gave him food is now lost to history, but certainly he was unfairly helped, perhaps because GÉO LEFÈVRE, the travelling reporter and chief official, was in awe of him.

A row broke out when one paper wrote, 'It was the *La Française* company that provided the money for the race, and therefore its riders had to finish for it to get its money's worth.' This stung organiser HENRI DESGRANGE, who was already convinced the race had been killed off by the 'blind emotions' that had led mobs to attack some riders and to help others to cheat. He was forced to write a long denial, stating, '*L'Auto* is a public company and any shareholder can check its expenses. It is therefore simple, and it will be simple, in a month, to see who has paid and who will be paid the prizes and the costs of the race.'

In 1912 the whole team pulled out when OCTAVE LAPIZE broke off halfway through a chase, turned in the road, and stopped. He began to complain of illegal combines, telling reporters, 'How can I fight in conditions like these? Everybody is working for ALCYON. The Belgians are all helping DEFRAYE whether they belong to his team or not. I've had enough of it and I'm pulling out.'

(And *see* CHEATS, MONEY.)

ROBERTO LAISEKA

b. Guernica, Spain, Jun 17 1969

Roberto Laiseka was riding for a team promoting the Spanish Basque region, and had no great achievements behind him, when he won the stage from Tarbes to LUZ-ARDIDEN in 2001. He was by then 32 and well into his career, but he took more than a minute on LANCE ARMSTRONG and JAN ULLRICH as they wrestled with each other for 144km before finishing hand-in-hand in third and fourth.

Tour de France

2001	28th	Stage win Tarbes—Luz-Ardiden
2002	46th	

FIRMIN LAMBOT

b. Florennes, Belgium, Mar 14 1886, d. Borgerhout, Belgium, Jan 19 1964

Firmin Lambot of BELGIUM had a wide, thin mouth and a permanently sad expression suggesting, rightly, that he permanently feared the worst. For example, he always rode with 500 francs in his pocket, so that he could buy a new bike if he had to.

For a man who worried so much about his own misfortunes, Lambot profited handsomely from the misfortunes of others. When EUGÈNE CHRISTOPHE's forks broke during the Metz-Dunkirk stage in 1919, the delay of two hours lost Christophe the race and allowed Lambot to win.

The 1922 Tour was even more eventful. Lambot benefited first from Christophe suffering another set of broken forks that cost him 47 minutes in the Pyrenees, and then from a bad day in the MOUNTAINS for Jean Alavoine, who lost the yellow JERSEY to Hector Heusghem. That should have been the end of it, but then Heusghem wrecked his BIKE in a pothole and collected a one-hour penalty for switching to a team-mate's machine instead of setting about a repair as the rules insisted. Heusghem would have won the Tour but for that penalty, and the honour went instead to Lambot, 37 years old and the first rider to win without taking a stage.

(And *see* LÉON SCIEUR, PHILIPPE THYS.)

Winner

1919	Tour de France
1922	Tour de France

Tour de France

1911	11th	
1912	18th	
1913	4th	Stage win Aix-en-Provence—Nice
1914	8th	Stage win Bayonne—Luchon
1919	1st	Stage win Metz—Dunkirk, and Yellow Jersey
1920	3rd	Stage wins Les Sables—Bayonne, Bayonne—Luchon
1921	9th	Stage win Toulon—Nice
1922	1st	Yellow Jersey
1923	DNF	
1924	DNF	

LANTERNE ROUGE

The *Lanterne Rouge* (red lamp) is the term used to describe the last rider in the overall standings each day. Arsène Millocheau was the first to be so called in 1903, after losing 15 hours between Lyon and Marseille and 10 hours on the final stage. He reached Paris 64 hours and 47 minutes behind winner MAURICE GARIN.

At first there was no sympathy for the *Lanterne Rouge*. In 1939 and 1948 the last rider overall was thrown out of the race, from the second stage onwards in 1939, and from the third stage in 1948. But then attitudes changed, and the idea of a poor rider who had struggled round FRANCE as a DOMESTIQUE, sometimes in the face of injury and illness, was enough to bring him CRITERIUM contracts. Riders sometimes even held their own slow-bicycle races at the back to see who could come last.

That sort of race was going on in 1969 between PIERRE MATIGNON and another Frenchman, André Wilhem. Matignon was 86th with two days to go, a position helped by being docked 15 seconds for DOPING on stage 14, and finishing stage 19 last – 8:48 behind BARRY HOBAN.

Even Wilhem couldn't go that slowly, so on stage 20 to the PUY-DE-DOME he changed tactics and attacked. So too did Matignon, so successfully that he won by 1:25 on EDDY MERCKX. Merckx, offended at being shown up on a prestige stage by a rider whose name he didn't even know, set off on the sort of chase that only hurt pride can produce. The Puy gave Matignon his greatest day of an admittedly easily overlooked career, and so everybody was happy, because Wilhem rode into Paris as the last man, just as he wanted, and Merckx won the Tour.

Lanternes Rouges often played to their role, as when Roger Chaussabel posed with a Chinese lantern in 1956. He said ironically, 'I can't ride fast, I can't climb, I can't sprint ... I'm a complete roadman. A Tourman, therefore.' Londoner John Clarey (63rd at 2:43:28 in 1968) delighted photographers by having his moustache sprayed each morning 'with rose fertiliser for added strength'.

Tony Hoar was a popular *Lanterne Rouge* behind LOUISON BOBET in 1955. (*See* HERCULES for origins of the British team; *see* ARNE JONSSON for how being kind-hearted took him out of the Tour.) Hoar would tackle the stars each day only to find his build undid him after 120km. He was so far back in Monaco

that he kept in the race only by claiming he'd been delayed by crowds who'd given up waiting for him.

Guy Million played on his name in 1957 when he finished bottom of the prize list and 4:41:11 behind JACQUES ANQUETIL. Gerhard Schönbacher of Austria was *Lanterne Rouge* in both 1979 and 1980.

GUY LAPÉBIE

b. Saint-Geours-de-Marenne, France, Nov 28 1916

Guy Lapébie turned pro after winning the Olympic team pursuit in Berlin in 1936 and coming second to another Frenchman, Guy Charpentier, in the road race. Hopes that he and his brother Roger would form a good road team and an even better six-day team on the TRACK foundered when a knee injury ended ROGER LAPÉBIE's career just as Guy's was starting (*see* Roger Lapébie entry). Guy paired on the track instead with Arthur Seres and Émile Carrara.

Guy Lapébie still makes guest appearances at stage finishes at BORDEAUX, near his home.

Tour de France

1948	3rd	Stage win Dinard—Nantes
1949	DNF	Stage win La Rochelle—
		Bordeaux
1952	DNF	

ROGER LAPÉBIE

b. Bayonne, France, Jan 16 1911, d. Pessac, France, Oct 12 1996

Roger Lapébie was a difficult man, constantly arguing with organisers and other riders. In 1937 he was the first rider to win the Tour on GEARS, which the previous organiser HENRI DESGRANGE hadn't allowed, but his victory was tainted by accusations of cheating and a STRIKE by angry riders from BELGIUM.

Lapébie won his first race at 15, on the TRACK. His family, including BROTHER ROGER LAPÉBIE, then moved north up the coast from Bayonne to BORDEAUX. There, under the guidance of the local club, he switched to road racing, and delighted fans with his attacking style. He won his first road race in 1929. Several quiet years followed before he won the French national championship and six other important races in 1933.

Lapébie rode his first Tour in 1932, taking a stage and finishing 23rd. A row with Henri Desgrange meant he was not one of the leaders in the French team for 1933, but he still finished 29th even as a DOMESTIQUE. Almost in revenge he had a superb year in 1934, winning five stages and finishing third.

Lapébie and Desgrange then had yet another row – there were so many that it hardly matters what they were about – and Desgrange contrived to keep him out of next year's FRANCE team, forcing him to ride as an individual – not quite a TOURISTE ROUTIER but nevertheless not in a team. He walked out on the 12th stage, which led to a fresh row. This was still going on in 1936, so this time Lapébie refused to ride at all.

Not until 1937 did rider and organiser come to terms. That year Lapébie had a superb Tour, winning three stages and overall victory. But not, of course, without incident.

The race started in bad humour. The background was that French riders had won every Tour from 1930 to 1934, after which two Belgians had won in a row, ROMAIN MAES in 1935 and the unrelated SYLVÈRE MAES in 1936. The French were as reluctant to see a third foreign win as the Belgians were keen to secure one. There was skulduggery when Lapébie, warming up at Luchon, found his handlebars had been sawn through (*see* CHEATS).

'It was done by someone close to the Belgians,' he said. 'They were staying in the same hotel. I put new bars on but they had no bottle cage. I was penalised every time someone handed a bottle up. I lost five minutes on the TOURMALET and panicked. I wanted to stop.' Instead he found a mountain spring and came round enough to press on.

He was repeatedly warned for being pushed by SPECTATORS. 'I said, "I can't stop the crowds

pushing me. I'm asking them not to." In fact I was quietly asking them to push me harder,' he said later. But matters went still further. Belgian riders had already claimed that Lapébie had held onto a car in the Alps, and things came to a head on a stage through the Pyrenees that included the Peyresourde, Aspin, Tourmalet and AUBISQUE.

Lapébie was seven and a half minutes down but, astonishingly, made up the gap. Then, equally astonishingly, he lost it again. On the Aubisque it became clear what was going on: where there were cars to be grabbed, Lapébie was grabbing them. He went from one to another on the Aubisque, then rode behind the cars of French journalists. The Belgians were furious – but not as furious as they became when Desgrange penalised him only a minute and a half.

Things took a bizarre turn when the French threatened to STRIKE if the penalty was increased, and counter-claimed that Sylvère Maes had been helped by another Belgian, Gustave Deloor, who was not part of the Belgian national team. And indeed he had been helped. Maes was in yellow when he had punctured on the stage to Bordeaux. Lapébie attacked immediately and got a lead of 2:33. Maes replaced the tyre and set off with Deloor in pursuit.

What made the row still more convoluted was that the Belgians, who could hardly deny they had cheated, then turned on a railway signalman. This man, they insisted, had spotted Maes and Deloor when they were only 75m from getting back to Lapébie, and had lowered a level crossing gate in front of them. Maes and Deloor pushed their BIKES under the barrier, ran across the tracks and remounted. That upset French spectators, and Maes was pushed and jostled when he got to Bordeaux.

Judges shrugged and said railways operated to their own schedules so there was nothing to be done. Then they penalised Maes a further 30 seconds, which reduced his lead to just 25 seconds and caused such anger that the Belgian MANAGER, Karel van Wijnendaele, took the team home. Crowds turned out in Brussels to welcome them. Van Wijnendaele, the founder of the Tour of Flanders, went back to work as editor of *Sportwereld* and received 20,000 letters from angry fans. The Belgian cycling association paid the team the prizes they had missed.

Lapébie won the Tour by more than seven minutes, but the row went on. Desgrange turned against him because he had been pushed, and he wasn't asked back in 1938. He followed instead as a reporter. In 1939 his career ended when he broke a kneecap in the Bordeaux-Paris race. He stayed in the sport as a driver for French television, and died aged 85 in October 1996.

Winner

1933	Paris-St-Étienne, GP Echo d'Alger, Paris-Angers, National championship
1934	Critérium International, Paris-Vichy, Paris-St-Étienne
1935	Paris-St-Étienne
1937	Tour de France, Paris-Nice, Critérium International
1938	Paris-Sedan

Tour de France

1932	23rd	Stage win Gap—Grenoble
1933	29th	
1934	3rd	Stage wins Charleville—Metz, Metz—Belfort, Cannes—Marseille, Montpellier—Perpignan, Perpignan—Ax-les-Thermes
1935	DNF	
1937	1st	Stage wins Briançon—Digne, Saintes—La Rochelle, La Rochelle—La Roche-sur-Yon, and Yellow Jersey

OCTAVE LAPIZE

b. Paris, France, Oct 24 1887, d. Verdun, France, Jul 14 1917

Louis Octave Lapize, known as *Frisé* or Curly, was that rare performer, a rider who could climb and sprint, and who could also outwit opponents. Lapize could perform as well on the TRACK, riding six-days and setting motor-paced records, as onroad and cross-country – in 1907 he was both the French road and cyclo-cross champion.

His MANAGER, Paul Ruinart, said, 'Lapize will be the best rider of his generation. He can and must win everything because he has all the gifts of a perfect cyclist.'

He turned professional in 1909 and won the first of three Paris-Roubaix races. The only criticism of him was that he did no more work than was necessary, which some interpreted as wheel-sucking. These critics were glad to see, therefore, that the champion couldn't cope when it counted, pulling out disillusioned after three days of his first Tour in 1909.

Next year, the first time the Pyrenees were included (*see* MOUNTAINS for the background story), Lapize was a different man and turned the race into a personal battle with the giant Luxembourger, FRANÇOIS FABER.

The epic stage was from Luchon to Bayonne, and Lapize went off in attack straight away. He rode over the TOURMALET, Aspin and Peyresourde – then just tracks of mud, grass and stone – and reached the last climb of the day, the AUBISQUE. Then for the first time he faltered and was overtaken by a regional rider, FRANÇOIS LAFOURCADE. Lapize, suffering badly now, reached the top 15 minutes behind him. Seeing officials waiting for him, he hissed just one word: 'Assassins.' A moment later he told Victor Breyer, deputising for Tour organiser HENRI DESGRANGE (who had claimed sickness rather than witness what he feared would be the debacle of sending riders through the mountains), that he was going to quit the race at the foot of the hill and go home.

The anger must have cleared his mind, though, because Lapize then dropped at reckless speed down the winding, unfenced, and above all unsurfaced descent of the Aubisque. (*See* WIM VAN EST for how he fell over the edge.) He caught and then dropped Lafourcade and finished ahead of him and his other key rivals by 10 minutes. The rest of the race followed in during the next seven and a half hours. Lapize finally took the yellow jersey from Faber on the stage to Brest, and a win in Caen on the next stage sealed his victory.

Lapize never again finished the Tour because, he said, riders ganged up on him. 'When I stop for a piss, they all take to their heels,' he complained. 'When someone else stops, they take no notice.' In 1913, a year notorious for combines, Lapize got so sick of it that he sat outside a bar near Brest and said he'd had enough. However, he cashed in on his name with a make of BIKE.

Lapize volunteered the moment war began in 1914, and joined the fledgling French air force. Shot down as a fighter pilot above Pont-à-Mousson, near Verdun, he died aged just 29. His MEMORIAL is at the summit of the Tourmalet.

(*See* LA FRANÇAISE.)

Winner

1909 Paris-Roubaix
1910 Tour de France, Paris-Roubaix
1911 Paris-Brussels, Paris-Roubaix, Paris-Tours, National championship
1912 Paris-Brussels, National championship
1913 Paris-Brussels, National championship

Tour de France

1909 DNF
1910 1st Stage wins Lyon—Grenoble, Perpignan—Luchon, Luchon—Bayonne, Brest—Caen, and Yellow Jersey
1911 DNF
1912 DNF Stage win Grenoble—Nice
1913 DNF
1914 DNF Stage win Perpignan—Marseille

L'AUTO

L'Auto was the paper that started and organised the Tour de France in 1903. It owed its origins to the Dreyfus Affair, when in 1894 Captain Alfred Dreyfus, a Jewish army officer from the Swiss border and the highest-ranking non-Catholic in the army, was accused of selling secrets to the Germans. Evidence was fabricated and Dreyfus was shipped off to Devil's Island.

The case split France. A rally was held on Auteuil racecourse near Paris on June 3 1899, where the president, Émile Loubet, who had acquitted Dreyfus to stop the country tearing itself apart, was attacked by anti-Dreyfus demonstrators who shouted, 'Resign! Resign!' and climbed on his platform to clout him with a stick.

Among those arrested by the police was Albert de Dion, a car-engine maker and founder of the Automobile Club de France. They took him to Santé prison where he was visited by a newspaper editor called Pierre Giffard, who ran a sports-and-politics paper called *Le Vélo* and wanted de Dion's story. Giffard already knew de Dion as a major advertiser in his paper.

Giffard was a passionate Dreyfus supporter and the two argued bitterly, Giffard saying he would no longer tolerate de Dion's advertising in his paper or, according to another account, de Dion saying he wanted nothing more to do with it. Either way, Giffard and de Dion became enemies.

De Dion decided to force Giffard out of business by setting up a rival paper. To achieve this he turned to the tyre-makers Adolphe Clément, Edouard Michelin and others to put up money for the new venture. Clément said his PR man, HENRI DESGRANGE, who had written a cycling book and in 1893 had set the first ratified world hour record, would make a good editor.

> **History note:** the Dreyfus affair was indirectly responsible not only for the Tour de France but also for a substantial change in French life. Such was the reaction to a man so many believed innocent that the right-wing government was swept from power in 1899, the status of the army fell, and new laws limiting the influence of the church led to the separation of church and state in 1905. France itself pleaded guilty in 1998. More than a century after it happened, President Jacques Chirac apologised to Dreyfus' descendants for the way the country had persecuted him.

The first issue of *L'Auto-Vélo* appeared on October 16 1900, and was printed on yellow paper because Giffard's *Le Vélo* used green. But circulation stuck at 20,000, the owners lost money, and doubts began to arise about Desgrange. On November 20 1902 there was a crisis meeting in the boardroom at *L'Auto*'s office in 10 rue du Faubourg Montmartre, Paris. 'What we need is something to nail his [Giffard's] beak shut,' Desgrange said. After a while one of Desgrange's employees, GÉO LEFÈVRE, said, 'Let's organise a race that lasts several days, longer than anything else. Like the six-days on the track but on the road.' Desgrange replied, 'If I understand you right, *petit Géo*, you're proposing a Tour de France?'

The race in 1903 brought immediate success for *L'Auto*, which printed a special edition within seven minutes of the FINISH and sold it instantly. *L'Auto* printed 14,178,474 papers in 1903; by 1913 it was 43,641,875. In 1921 it added pictures of the race and during 1922 circulation rose to more than 600,000 a day. On November 20 1904 *Le Vélo* went out of business. Giffard's beak had been nailed shut.

In 1914 Desgrange ordered the youth of France to war against 'those dirty bastards' the Germans. In the second world war, however, the paper wasn't so sure. *L'Auto* changed to *L'Auto-Soldat*, publishing war news. Circulation fell. It was shut on August 17 1944 at the time of the Liberation for cooperating with the Germans.

The company owned a building on the other side of the road and it now rented this to a new paper, *L'ÉQUIPE*, edited by JACQUES GODDET, who had been a leading journalist with *L'Auto*. (*See* Goddet entry for details.) Thus *L'Équipe* took over from *L'Auto*.

APO LAZARIDES

b. Marles-sur-Mines, France, Oct 16 1925, d. Nice, France, Oct 30 1998

Jean-Apôtre Lazarides was the son of a Greek couple who emigrated from Athens, living first in the Calais area before recrossing France to live on the Côte d'Azur. Just 1.63m tall, he was a talented CLIMBER and won a stage in the Circuit des Six-Provinces (which became the Dauphiné-Libéré) and Marseille-Monaco in his first year as a professional in 1946.

He and his brother Lucien rode for RENÉ VIETTO, the 1934 MOUNTAINS winner, and Apo was wholly in his thrall. In 1947 Vietto had an aching foot and told a doctor to cut off a toe on the rest day. 'I'll be lighter in the MOUNTAINS,' he said. He then turned to Lazarides and ordered him to lose a toe as well.

'But why?' he protested. 'I don't need to.'

'Because I say so,' said Vietto, and Lazarides went ahead. For the rest of his life he walked with a wobble. Vietto's toe, by the way, is in a bar in Marseille, preserved in formaldehyde.

The following year, the now nine-toed Lazarides suffered like everyone else in weather so bad that only 44 of the 120 starters finished. PIERRE CHANY said he came across him 'standing frozen on the quagmire descent of the GALIBIER, a candle of ice hanging from his chin.' Just up the road, Chany said, two Italians were sharing a single pair of leg-warmers.

Vietto became a team MANAGER after he retired, running the Helyett team during the 1950s. Lazarides joined it, hope overruling experience. But poor Apo – 'the Greek kid' – got nothing but criticism. Whatever went wrong, it was because Lazarides hadn't tried hard enough. After the Giro in 1951, Vietto said, 'I have never attended such a long funeral; it was 5,000km long and my team followed the whole way. They call themselves racers but they were more like mourners.' But Vietto relented enough to take some of the team to the opera at La Scala, where a lone singer silenced the

audience with her performance. Suddenly
Vietto hissed, 'Apo?'
 'Sssh!' said the audience.
 'Apo, you see the woman on the stage?'
Lazarides said he did.
 'Well she's doing what she's paid for, you
bastard.'
 Lazarides' record includes coming second in
the 1948 world championship, one second
behind BRIEK SCHOTTE of BELGIUM. He
stopped racing in 1956 and died in Nice in 1998
after a long illness, aged 73.

Winner

1949 Trophée Grimpeurs

Year	Result
1947	10th
1948	21st
1949	9th
1950	28th
1951	DNF
1954	13th
1955	39th

LEADER

The leader of the Tour is the rider who has
taken least accumulated time to reach the stage
finish each day. He wears a yellow JERSEY. The
record is held by EDDY MERCKX with 96 days in
the lead.

LEADERS OF THE TOUR

96 days	Eddy Merckx
78 days	Bernard Hinault
60 days	Miguel Indurain
51 days	Jacques Anquetil
46 days	Lance Armstrong
39 days	Antonin Magne
37 days	Nicolas Frantz
35 days	André Leducq
34 days	Louison Bobet
33 days	Ottavio Bottecchia
26 days	Romain Maes, Sylvère Maes, René Vietto
22 days	Laurent Fignon, Joop Zoetemelk, Greg LeMond
20 days	Gino Bartali
19 days	Fausto Coppi, Didi Thurau, André Darrigade
18 days	Rudi Altig, Maurice Dewaele
17 days	Roger Pingeon, Jan Ullrich, Luis Ocaña
16 days	Bernard Thévenet
15 days	Pedro Delgado
14 days	Steve Bauer, Gastone Nencini, Léon Scieur, Bjarne Riis, Philippe Thys
13 days	Maurice Archambaud, Georges Speicher, Eugène Christophe
12 days	Kim Andersen, Vincent Barteau, Lucien van Impe, Ferdy Kübler, Wout Wagtmans, Antonin Rolland
11 days	Jos Bruyère, Gilbert Desmet, Hugo Koblet, Georges Vandenberghe
10 days	Felice Gimondi, Pascal Lino
9 days	Phil Anderson, Georges Groussard, Freddy Maertens, Fiorenzi Magni
8 days	Camille Buysse, Gerrie Knetemann, Claudio Chiappucci, Rudy Pevenage, Roger Walkowiak, Henri Pélissier
7 days	Jan Adriaenssens, Federico Bahamontes, Bernard Gauthier, Learco Guerra, Cyrille Guimard, Jean Majerus, Jos Planckaert, Pascal Simon, Herman van Springel, Erich Maechler, Gustaf van Slembrouck, Jean Rossius, Igor Gonzalez de Galdeano

6 days   Lucien Aimar, Robert Cazala, Vito Favero, Roger Lévèque, Francesco Moser,
         Fritz Schaer, Félicien Vervaecke, Chris Boardman, Mario Cipollini, Marco Pantani,
         Stuart O'Grady, Jaan Kirsipuu
5 days   Charly Mottet, Jean Alavoine, Adelin Benoit, Firmin Lambot, Jean Malléjac,
         Jorgen Pedersen, Francis Pélissier, Bernard van de Kerckhove, Eric Vanderaerden,
         Cédric Vasseur, Erich Bautz, Karl-Heinz Kunde
4 days   Gilbert Bauvin, José Catieau, Alberto Elli, Shay Elliott, Wim van Est,
         Raphaël Géminiani, Roger Hassenforder, Jos Hoevenaars, Robert Jacquinot,
         Laurent Jalabert, Roger Lapébie, Nello Lauredi, Hector Martin, Eddy Pauwels,
         Gerrit Voorting, Italo Zilioli, Alexa De Silva, Thierry Marie, Rolf Sorensen, Alex Zülle,
         Johan Museeuw, Rafael Di Paco, Louis Mottiat
3 days   Jean Diederich, Jean Goldschmit, Charly Grosskost, Roger Lambrecht, Georges
         Lemaire, Émile Masson, Charles Pélissier, René Privat, Jan Raas, Willy Schroeder,
         Julien Stevens, Michel Vermeulin, Teun van Vliet, Stéphane Heulot, Wilfried Nelissen,
         Stephen Roche, Jelle Nijdam, David Millar, François Simon
2 days   Henry Anglade, Theo Beckman, Romain Bellenger, Pierre Brambilla, Johan Buysse,
         Roger Delisle, Aimé Dossche, Victor Fontan, Jean Fontenay, Jean Forestier, Charly Gaul,
         Ab Geldermans, Jacques Hanegraaf, Jan Janssen, Gerben Karstens, Ludo Peeters,
         Jean Robic, Aldo Ronconi, Ward Sels, Johan van der Velde, Rik van Steenbergen,
         Klaus-Peter Thaler, Rolf Wolfshohl, Ronan Pensec, Flavio Vanzella, Ivan Gotti,
         Jacky Durand, Laurent Desbiens, Christophe Moreau, Jean-François Bernard,
         Martial Gayant, Erik Zabel, Rubens Bertogliati
1 day   Jean Aerts, Nicolas Barone, Jean-René Bernaudeau, Yves Bertin, Marcel Bidot,
         Max Bulla, Norbert Callens, Andrea Carrea, Tomasso De Pra, Marcel Dussault,
         Paul Egli, Jean Engels, José-Maria Errandonea, Amédée Fournier, Dominique Gaigne,
         Jean-Louis Gauthier, Jean-Pierre Genet, Félix Goethals, Jean Groussard,
         Yves Hamerlinck, Hector Heusghem, Sean Kelly, Marcel Kint, Jean-Claude Lebaube,
         Léon Le Calvez, Paul Le Drogo, Desiré Letort, Rik van Looy, François Mahé,
         Arsène Mersch, Willi Oberbeck, Miguel Poblet, Giancarlo Polidori, Gaston Rebry,
         Raymond Riotte, Giovanni Rossi, Gregorio San Miguel, Jos Schepers, Patrick Sercu,
         Tom Simpson, Jos Spruyt, Alex Stieda, Kurt Stöpel, Willy Teirlinck, Adri van der Poel,
         Wim van Est, Rini Wagtmans, Henk Lubberding, Erik Breukink, Luc Leblanc,
         Richard Virenque, Sean Yates, Johan Bruyneel, Evgueni Berzin, Frédéric Moncassin,
         Bo Hamburger, Marc Wauters, Jens Voigt

Eleven riders have abandoned while leading: in 1927 FRANCIS PÉLISSIER (*see* HENRI PÉLISSIER) was forced out by illness; in 1929 VICTOR FONTAN abandoned after hunting from door to door for a spare bike; in 1937 SYLVÈRE MAES and in 1950 FIORENZO MAGNI left after trouble with French SPECTATORS; in 1951 WIM VAN EST fell off the AUBISQUE; in 1965 Bernard van de Kerckhove pulled out through sickness; in 1971 LUIS OCAÑA crashed on the Col de Mente; in 1978 MICHEL POLLENTIER was thrown out after cheating a DOPING check on ALPE D'HUEZ; and in 1983 PASCAL SIMON broke a shoulder but struggled on for six days; .

A knee injury ended BERNARD HINAULT's chances in 1980. ROLF SORENSEN broke a collarbone after hitting a traffic island on the run in to Valenciennes in 1991; in 1996 STÉPHANE HEULOT quit with tendinitis in his knee; and in 1998 CHRIS BOARDMAN hit a wall two days after winning the PROLOGUE.

ALFRED LE BARS

b. Morlaix, France, Mar 14 1888, d. St Pol-de-Leon, France, Jan 13 1984

Few riders enter history for what they did on the way to the Tour rather than what they did on the Tour. The Frenchman Alfred Le Bars would have stayed unknown had it not emerged that he had cycled to the START of the 1907 Tour all the way from Morlaix, 500km to the west.

'There was no way of getting to the start in Paris other than by BIKE,' he said. 'So I rode it in eighteen and a half hours. And I wasn't even in cycling clothes. When I got there, I went to see Alphonse Baugé, the MANAGER of the Labor bike factory. He made it really hard for me to have a bike. I'd paid my five francs entry fee and L'AUTO [the organising paper] gave me the five francs a day it was paying riders who weren't linked with professional concerns. And so I managed to ride.'

Le Bars crashed on an unsurfaced road four kilometres from the start and had to borrow a bike from a SPECTATOR, but he still finished 26th overall of the 33 finishers after 28 days.

Tour de France

1907	26th
1909	19th

JEAN-MARIE LEBLANC

b. Nueil-sur-Argent, France, Jul 28 1944

Jean-Marie Leblanc is the former professional and cycling journalist who took over as competitions director of the Tour in late 1988. He succeeded Jean-François Naquet-Radiguet, who had held the post for a year after JACQUES GODDET and FÉLIX LÉVITAN before leaving for a job in television.

Leblanc had been a student of law and economics at Lille university. His father, who had raced before the WAR and knew his son's ambitions on a bike, insisted he should get an education. Jean-Marie rode his first unlicensed race in 1961 and won his first real one at Bousies in May 1962. On leaving university he was torn

between becoming a professional cyclist or a journalist. A 'proper' job seemed more reliable and so, having always wanted to write for *La Voix du Nord* in Lille, he asked the sports editor, Émile Parmentier, for a part-time job so he could carry on training.

'I know you,' Parmentier said. 'You're a local rider. You can start next week.' Leblanc was so astonished that he still remembers the phone box he was standing in.

Leblanc's career as a rider was unsensational. Paradoxically, given his current role as upholder of dignity and RULES, he is best remembered for stopping for a picnic during the 1970 Tour. His MANAGER, Maurice de Muer, had arranged this as a publicity stunt for the Bic team. Leblanc was joined under a tree by LUIS OCAÑA and JAN JANSSEN, and each was fined the equivalent of £4 for taking food outside a FEEDING AREA.

That was the third and last of Leblanc's Tours, and he returned to journalism to become chief cycling correspondent of *L'ÉQUIPE*. From there he moved in 1988 to running the Tour, continuing a tradition, broken only by Naquet-Radiguet (a drinks salesman), that the race is organised by a journalist.

Leblanc said, 'My first preoccupation has been to restore the Tour's sporting credibility. We have simplified the Tour, which had become incomprehensible to the public, and cut the trophies from 12 to six, with just four classifications: the yellow JERSEY, the winner of the stage, the polka-dot jersey for the best CLIMBER, and the green jersey for the points competition. Cutting the number of *partenaires* has increased their visibility, which means we can charge them higher prices and so offer bigger prizes. We want to match the sort of prizes offered in the greatest sports events in the world'.

HENRI DESGRANGE had seen his race as bigger than the sport, and had made and broken officials. Goddet and Lévitan had at the very least been protective of 'their' race. But while Leblanc is close to Hein Vebruggen, head of the sport's governing body, the UCI, and holds a role close to it, he follows rather than creates RULES.

A tubby and widely popular man, Leblanc is also a talented musician. In 2000 he strolled out of a press conference at Dax, spotted a band playing nearby, and borrowed a clarinet to join in. 'And the man can blow that horn, too,' said Jeremy Whittle of *Procycling*.

(And *see* RADIO TOUR.)

Tour de France

1968	58th
1970	83rd

LUC LEBLANC
b. Limoges, France, Aug 4 1966

Luc Leblanc rode seven Tours and was WORLD CHAMPION in 1994. In June 1978, when he was 11, a car hit him and his eight-year-old brother Gilles as they were walking through their village of Nieul, near Limoges. Gilles died an hour later, and Luc spent six months in hospital.

His left leg is still 3cm shorter than the other, and also weaker. But he was lucky to live, let alone become a BIKE rider. The experience made him deeply religious. At 17 he wanted to become a priest but his near-neighbour RAYMOND POULIDOR persuaded him to continue racing. He took his advice and turned pro three years later. He became a good CLIMBER and friends nicknamed him 'Lucho' in honour of the Colombian LUIS HERRERA, but other riders called him 'St Luke'. (*See* also NICKNAMES.)

His career was a series of successes marred by disappointment and disillusion. He took the yellow JERSEY in the 1991 Tour only to lose it to a still stronger climber next day in the Pyrenean stage to Val-Louron. 'I clung on to MIGUEL INDURAIN as long as I could but I just couldn't do it any longer,' he said, having crossed the line in tears at the sight of the Spaniard standing on the podium in 'his' *maillot jaune*.

Leblanc's national championship victory at Avize in 1992 was tainted by the bitterness of a team-mate, Gérard Rué, who accused him of treachery after their MANAGER, CYRILLE GUIMARD, insisted Leblanc should win instead of him. He became world champion in 1994 when he attacked in the last kilometre, and caused more bitterness when he left Festina and joined the new Le Groupement team; the new team collapsed early the following season.

In March 1999 he told a press conference that his 12 years as a professional had 'ended prematurely' because his Italian SPONSOR, Polti, had signed RICHARD VIRENQUE (disgraced in the previous year's FESTINA AFFAIR) in his place.

'My contract has been prematurely ended,' he said. 'The way it has happened has left me bitter. Polti claimed I had health problems and said I was no longer fit for cycling. Yet I hadn't even seen a doctor. If I'm so unfit for cycling, how come I finished seventh in the Tour of Romandie and second in the French championship?'

In 2002 the UCI, the sport's governing body, suspended the entire Italian Cycling Federation for not paying Leblanc the equivalent of £210,000 that was owed to him by Polti. The case has yet to be fully resolved.

Winner

1988	GP Plouay
1990	Tour Haut-Var, GP Wallonia
1992	Midi Libre, National championship
1994	World championship
1997	Tour Trentino

Tour de France

1990	73rd	
1991	5th	Yellow Jersey
1992	DNF	
1994	DNF	Stage win Cahors—Lourdes-Hautacam
1996	6th	Stage win Chambéry—Les Arcs
1997	DNF	
1998	DNF	

LÉON LE CALVEZ
b. Moelan-sur-Mer, France, Mar 14 1910, d. Créteil, France, Jul 7 1995

Some people take time to make up their minds, others act impetuously. Such was the Frenchman Léon Le Calvez, who turned pro one

Thursday afternoon in 1931 in order to ride Bordeaux-Paris the following weekend. Bordeaux-Paris was the longest race in the world, 601km that year. Le Calvez came fifth to Romain Gijsels, a position he repeated in 1932 and 1935.

Le Calvez rode his first Tour in 1931 and held the yellow JERSEY. He rode just once more before becoming MANAGER of FRANCE's Ouest (West) team in the era of REGIONAL TEAMS. His record includes the 1932 Critérium International and third place to SYLVÈRE MAES in the 1933 Paris-Roubaix.

Winner

1932	Critérium International

Tour de France

1931	DNF	Yellow Jersey
1933	17th	

FERDINAND LE DROGO
b. Pontivy, France Oct 10 1903,
d. Saint-Gildas-de-Rhuys, France, Apr 30 1976

We all like to show off in front of our friends, and Ferdinand Le Drogo had the chance to do so on the 1927 Tour. Organiser HENRI DESGRANGE had decided to run the flat stages of that Tour as TIME TRIALS. Le Drogo, a talented rider against the clock, may have been alone in feeling pleased. Few other riders enjoyed long efforts against the clock.

Le Drogo looked at the map, and saw the route crossed his home area of Brittany, so he decided to win the yellow JERSEY and wear it as he passed his neighbours. After shadowing FRANCIS PÉLISSIER in the rankings for five days, he outsprinted him and received an ecstatic welcome in Dinan. Next day Pélissier abandoned through sickness (*see* LEADERS for other *maillot jaunes* who quit while leading) and Le Drogo pulled on the leader's jersey.

Next day Le Drogo, having done what he wanted, finished the day 52nd, 1hr 21min down. The following day he got off his bike and went home. He rode the Tour once more, in 1929, and didn't finish then either.

Le Drogo came second to LEARCO GUERRA in the 1931 world championship. A contemporary described him as 'as strong as an ox but as naïve as a child'.

Winner

1927	National championship
1928	National championship
1929	Critérium International

Tour de France

1927	DNF	Stage win Cherbourg—Dinan, Yellow Jersey
1929	DNF	

ANDRÉ LEDUCQ
b. St-Ouen, France, Feb 27 1904, d. Marseille, France, Jun 18 1980

A much-loved rider from Marseille, André Leducq was world AMATEUR champion at 20 and winner of 25 stages in the Tour. His tally stayed a record until EDDY MERCKX beat him on the way to his 34 wins.

In 1929 Leducq was one of three riders to wear the yellow JERSEY on the same day. He tied with VICTOR FONTAN and NICOLAS FRANTZ after the stage from Les Sables d'Olonne to BORDEAUX, but Tour organiser HENRI DESGRANGE hadn't considered the need for tie-breaks. These days the issue would be decided by fractions of seconds gained or lost in the PROLOGUE or, failing that, placings in stages in the previous days. But there was no prologue in 1929 and the rules, not having considered the need to split riders with equal times, made no provision for it. Next day the issue was resolved when all three lost their lead to GASTON REBRY, who came third in a three-man break that had gained 3:21 into Bayonne.

Having created history in one way, he then did it in another by becoming the first winner in the new formula of NATIONAL TEAMS in 1930, riding as the head of an unusually strong French team. He won despite losing 15 minutes on the descent of the GALIBIER because of a knee injury. He got back after a 70km chase thanks to the French team, and won the SPRINT at ÉVIAN. (*See* LEARCO GUERRA for fuller story.)

In the 1932 Tour he took the race lead on day three and kept it to the end, gathering five stages.

Leducq got slower as the years passed, and began riding for GEORGES SPEICHER and ANTONIN MAGNE. He raced until 1938, when he crossed the line at the PARC DES PRINCES arm-in-arm with Magne. War broke out the following year. He was detained by German soldiers, and things were going badly, until a German officer said, 'Hey, I know you . . . Leducq,' and after a pause, '*Gut . . . z'est bon*,' and let him go. Leducq told the story to RAYMOND POULIDOR, adding, 'You see Raymond, sometimes it helps to have won the Tour.' Poulidor came second three times and third five times, but never won and never wore the yellow jersey.

Leducq worked after the war for the Mercier bike factory team, and briefly as a MANAGER. Too much had changed, though, and he found modern riders lacked the fun, spontaneity and courage of his generation.

One writer said of him that 'he was liked by women, whom he honoured as frequently as his TRACK contracts.' He spoke English like Peter Sellers' Inspector Clouseau in the *Pink Panther* films, and claimed that his teacher, an Englishwoman, threw him out because he made the others laugh too much. That didn't stop him speaking English whenever he could. The cycle dealer Ron Kitching (*see* BARRY HOBAN for his influence) met him at the Paris cycle show in 1946 and sang *On Ilkley Moor B'aht 'at* with him in a nightclub at 5am. He said, 'All doors opened to Leducq; we never had to wait for a table in a restaurant.' Kitching persuaded him to present the prizes at a pro-am TIME TRIAL at Harrogate, BRITAIN, in 1975.

Winner

1928	Paris-Roubaix, Critérium International
1930	Tour de France
1931	Paris-Tours
1932	Tour de France
1933	Critérium International
1934	Critérium As

Tour de France

1927	4th	Stage wins Dinan—Brest, Charleville—Dunkirk, Dunkirk—Paris
1928	2nd	Stage wins Caen—Cherbourg, Luchon—Perpignan, Perpignan—Marseille, Pontarlier—Belfort
1929	11th	Stage wins Caen—Cherbourg, Perpignan—Marseille, Belfort—Strasbourg, Strasbourg—Metz, St-Malo—Dieppe, and Yellow Jersey
1930	1st	Stage win Vannes—Les Sables, Grenoble—Évian, and Yellow Jersey
1931	10th	Stage win Belfort—Colmar
1932	1st	Stage win Nantes—Bordeaux, Nice—Gap, Grenoble—Aix-les-Bains, Évian—Belfort, St-Malo—Amiens, Amiens—Paris, and Yellow Jersey
1933	31st	Stage wins Marseille—Montpellier, Montpellier—Perpignan
1935	17th	Stage win Rochefort—La Rochelle
1938	30th	Stage win Lille—Paris, and Yellow Jersey

Trivia note: An image of Leducq sitting disconsolately by the road with his head bowed and one arm raised was reproduced as a sculpture by Amo Breker. He called it *Le Guerrier Blessé* (the injured warrior). A significant difference from the original is that the sculpted figure is nude.

GÉO LEFÈVRE

The idea of having a 'Tour de France' is often attributed to HENRI DESGRANGE. The credit really belongs to a cycling and rugby writer called Géo Lefèvre who was then 26 years old.

Lefèvre was a champion of the Stade Français cycling club in Paris who fancied his talent as a writer and threw in his studies to become one. He applied to the largest sports daily, Le Vélo, and was offered a job by its editor, Pierre Giffard. (See L'AUTO for more about Giffard and his downfall.)

Desgrange became L'Auto's editor because he had worked for one of its financiers, the tyre-maker Adolphe Clément. He needed staff, was impressed by Lefèvre's writing style, and offered him a job with more freedom than he was getting from Giffard.

Lefèvre was a straightforward lad, and he told Giffard that Desgrange had approached him but he hadn't yet accepted. If Lefèvre was hoping for advice, or even a pay rise, he got neither. Giffard flew into a not unusual rage and fired him. So Lefèvre went to L'Auto and took Desgrange's offer before that also disappeared.

Desgrange's decision paid off when a crisis meeting was called because Clément and other investors were getting upset at L'Auto's poor sales. Desgrange asked for ideas and Lefèvre, second to be asked, answered, 'Let's organise a race that lasts several days, longer than anything else. Like the six-days on the track but on the road. The big towns will welcome the riders.' Desgrange paused before saying, 'If I understand you right, petit Géo, you're proposing a Tour of France?' He led him out of the building without reaching a decision and took him to the Taverne Zimmer in the Boulevard Montmartre for lunch. They discussed the idea over coffee. The restaurant, now called TGI Friday's, is still there, and a small display marks the meeting.

Desgrange was still not convinced however – he left the decision to the paper's accountant, Victor Goddet, and wouldn't go to the START of the first Tour in 1903, let alone follow it. Travelling with the first Tour de France became Lefèvre's job. He was supposed to follow by bike and train as organiser, referee, judge, timekeeper and statistician. And in the evening he and a colleague, Olivier Margot, were to write a full-page account of the day.

'No car for me, just my bike', Lefèvre recalled. 'So every stage I rode, I did my best to check the race. I followed the riders as far as the closest station where the timetable would let me catch an express train that would get me to the FINISH before the riders.' On the opening day he took his first train to Moulins to watch the riders pass and then another to Lyon. But MAURICE GARIN went faster still and got there before him. 'They are racing even faster than the train,' Lefèvre wrote.

That didn't mean Garin got to a deserted FINISH. He was met by the florid Georges Abran, whose 'role was to wave an immense yellow flag at the start and at the finish and, hat askew, moustache bristling, his face bright red, to sit behind a Pernod at the race café.' The pair were helped by Fernand Mercier, who travelled ahead of the race to set up the finish with L'Auto's local correspondents.

Riders teased Lefèvre, exploiting his youth and enthusiasm, and sometimes coming up to him in the late evening to tell him he ought to be in bed. And Lefèvre had a naïve side that led to the undoing of Garin and LUCIEN POTHIER, when he was persuaded to give them food illegally in the 1904 race. The incident was a factor in the 1904 AFFAIR that led to both men's disqualification. In that same year he was obliged to fire his gun on the Col de la RÉPUBLIQUE to stop a riot of SPECTATORS.

Lefèvre has also been credited with inventing cyclo-cross, when he organised what he called a cross cyclo-pédestre at VILLE D'AVRAY (the original finish of the Tour) in January 1903. He explained, 'Think about a cyclist in wartime. He can't use the main roads; he has to ride or walk across unmade roads and worm his way through the undergrowth and clamber across ditches. Think of that and you'll get the principle of the cross cyclo-pédestre.'

Desgrange steered Lefèvre towards rugby, boxing and aviation the moment the Tour became a success, taking the glory for himself. Lefèvre described his boss as 'a hard man, in the good sense of the word'. It was a generous comment.

Lefèvre moved to L'Auto's successor, L'ÉQUIPE, after the second world war (see

L'Équipe entry for more), became head of the French sportswriters' association, and was a guest at the 50th anniversary of the Tour in 1953. There he saw, with Garin and HIPPOLYTE AUCOUTURIER also in attendance, LOUISON BOBET take the first of three victories. Lefèvre died in 1961 when he was 84.

RENÉ LE GREVÈS
b. Paris, France, Jul 6 1910, d. Saint–Gervais, France, Feb 25 1946

Le Grevès was a sure bet in the Tour. In a pro career that started in 1933 and ended in 1939 – like so many his career was cut short by the war – he rode six Tours, finished five, and won 16 stages. HENRI DESGRANGE said of his powerful style that he was 'the dispenser of justice in charge of punishing the careless and the idle'.

Le Grevès died from injuries he received in a skiing accident on February 25 1946.

Winner

1935	Paris-Tours, Critérium International
1936	National championship
1937	Critérium International

Tour de France

1933	19th	Stage win Rennes—Caen
1934	25th	Stage wins Lille—Charleville, Belfort—Évian, Digne—Nice, La Rochelle—La Roche-sur-Yon
1935	15th	Stage wins Montpellier—Narbonne, Bordeaux—Rochefort, La Rochelle—La Roche-sur-Yon, Nantes—Vire
1936	20th	Stage wins Belfort—Évian, Cannes—Marseille, Marseille—Nîmes, Montpellier—Narbonne, Pau—Bordeaux, Angers—Vire
1937	DNF	
1939	45th	Stage win Dijon—Troyes

Trivia note: Leon Meredith, BRITAIN'S Olympic team pursuit champion in 1908, also died after a skiing accident, on January 29 1930.

GREG LEMOND
b. Lakewood, USA, Jun 26 1961

The hugely popular Greg LeMond, loved for his instant smile, his open manner, and his comeback from the near-dead, was the first American to win the Tour and the first to win a professional world road championship. (*See* AMERICA for earlier American champions.)

For years his sport had been skiing – he rode a BIKE for fitness, not to race. Then a bike-maker called Roland della Santo managed to interest him in a sport that was almost unknown to Americans. LeMond came to cycling after making a name as a skier, but it soon became clear he had talent. Europe found that out when he went to BELGIUM as a junior and won every race for a week before going home, leaving an open-jawed nation behind him.

In 1979 he became world junior champion and late the following year left for Europe with his wife Kathy, whom he'd married when both were 19. They lived first in France and then, when Kathy despaired of speaking French or understanding French culture, in Kortrijk in Belgium.

In 1982 he came second to Beppe Saronni in the world road championship at Goodwood, BRITAIN, and then in 1983 became America's first world champion. The following year he rode his first Tour, finishing third. In 1985 he was heavily tipped to win, but he was then signed from Renault for BERNARD HINAULT's La Vie Claire team, either as the Frenchman's protégé or, by another interpretation, to stop him getting in the way of Hinault's fifth victory.

The two riders agreed to support whichever was better placed, which Hinault made sure was himself by winning the PROLOGUE. LeMond was restricted to being the sorcerer's apprentice, and that was the way it looked like staying until Hinault crashed just before the end of the stage at St-Étienne and broke his nose. That gave him breathing problems as the race headed for the Pyrenees. He could have told LeMond to take his own chances, but instead he told him to shadow STEPHEN ROCHE, a dangerous rival. Roche went clear on the stage to Luchon and took LeMond with him. LeMond did his job but soon realised he was the stronger. He asked team manager Paul Koechli for permission to attack Roche but was refused, and told that Hinault was 40 seconds behind and closing. In fact Hinault was more than a minute behind and making no progress.

LeMond felt bitter when he learnt the truth and had to be placated by his SPONSOR, a businessman, sometime politician and convicted fraudster called Bernard Tapie, who promised him he'd have his chance next year. In 1986, though, Hinault gave little sign of giving the American a clear run at victory. Instead, he said he would give him a hard ride 'as an education'. The tension between them brought echoes of GINO BARTALI and FAUSTO COPPI in the 1950s, when two potential winners also rode for the same team and neither had reason to trust the other.

Hinault didn't beat LeMond in the 1986 Tour, but he did ride alongside him, neither challenging nor helping, always threatening. The greater the tension the faster they went.

The excitement of 1986 was great from the beginning. LeMond fell five minutes behind Hinault on the first stage in the Pyrenees and the Frenchman looked like getting a record sixth win. What changed the situation was the six-hour stage over the TOURMALET, Aspin, Peyresourde and up to Supebagnères which LeMond won by 1:12 over ROBERT MILLAR. That put him 40 seconds behind Hinault. In the Alps at Serre Chevalier he finished 6:26 behind Eduardo Chozas but far enough ahead of Hinault on the stage that included the Vars and IZOARD to take the yellow jersey. The following day LeMond and Hinault were together all the way up ALPE D'HUEZ and crossed the line hand in hand, Hinault showing the master hadn't, as promised, attacked the apprentice, but equally that he hadn't been belittled.

LeMond's worry was that the gap was just 2:45 in his favour with a 58km TIME TRIAL to come. Hinault was better against the clock and had won more than three dozen time trials. Starting ahead of the American and not know-

ing how he was doing, there was every chance Hinault would go flat out and win by three minutes. Even if he wanted to, would he be able to hold back enough for LeMond to win?

As it happened LeMond skidded onto his side on a bend and Hinault won, as predicted. But LeMond lost only 25 seconds and went on to win the Tour. Relations were never good between them. LeMond said he felt he had been 'burned' by a man who had been his hero.

Concerning LeMond's 1986 win, however, Hinault wrote, 'I'd given my word to Greg LeMond that I'd help him win and that's what I did. A promise is a promise. I tried to wear out rivals to help him but I never attacked him personally . . . It wasn't my fault that he didn't understand this. When I think of some of the things he has said since the race ended, I wonder whether I was right not to attack him . . . I've worked for colleagues all my life without having the problems I had with Greg LeMond.'

Then things took an extraordinary turn. On April 20 1987 LeMond was accidentally shot by his brother-in-law during a hunting trip near Sacramento. He lost huge amounts of blood and still has pellets lodged inside him. He was close to dying. Only a helicopter diverted from a road crash saved him.

LeMond tried to come back to racing too soon, not realising how weak he was, and 1988 was dreadful to the point of embarrassment. The next year began as badly and improved only slowly. By mid-season, though, LeMond managed second place in a time trial in the Giro d'Italia, and the situation started to change.

Even so, he was no longer a likely winner when the 1989 Tour started in LUXEMBOURG, and all the bets were on PEDRO DELGADO, who had won the previous year. (*See* Delgado entry for his doping scandal in 1988.) Delgado blundered even before his race started, though, by arriving late at the PROLOGUE. He struggled back to third place, but by then the race was between LeMond and a new French threat, LAURENT FIGNON.

The two were just 50 seconds apart with only the 24km time trial to ride from Versailles to Paris. LeMond clipped forward extensions to his handlebars to bring his arms closer and into a more streamlined position and wore an aerodynamic helmet. Fignon opted for a standard set-up with no helmet. LeMond turned a 50-second deficit into an eight-second win after 3,285km, the closest race in the Tour's history, although he didn't know until 30 seconds before Fignon finished. LeMond's whoop of joy has become one of the Tour's classic moments.

Next morning he and Kathy were pictured in bed under an American flag, drinking champagne. A few weeks later the fairytale comeback was completed when LeMond won the world championship for a second time in Chambéry.

A third Tour win followed in 1990, when he beat CLAUDIO CHIAPPUCCI by 2:16, but that was his last big success. He stopped racing after failing to finish the Tour in 1994 and took up car racing. He also started his own bike company and managed the short-lived Saturn team. His numerous business projects include a bakery chain. He suffers now from muscular myopathy, a wasting disease which has been attributed to the shooting.

(*See* AGENTS, BIKES, MONEY.)

Winner

1982	Tour Avenir
1983	World championship, Dauphiné Libéré, Critérium As
1986	Tour de France
1989	Tour de France, World championship
1990	Tour de France
1992	Tour DuPont

Tour de France

1984	3rd	
1985	2nd	Stage win Limoges—Lac de Vassivière
1986	1st	Stage win Pau—Superbagnères, and Yellow Jersey
1989	1st	Stage wins Dinard—Rennes, Villard-de-Lans—Aix-les-Bains, Versailles—Paris
1990	1st	Yellow Jersey
1991	7th	Yellow Jersey
1992	DNF	
1994	DNF	

L'ÉQUIPE

L'Équipe in FRANCE and *La Gazzetta dello Sport* in ITALY are Europe's largest sports papers. *L'Équipe* was born from the closure of *L'AUTO*, which had been shut down after France was liberated in the WAR because it had continued publishing under the Germans (*see L'Auto* entry for details). The launch of the new paper wasn't possible until February 28 1946, when paper rationing had eased.

JACQUES GODDET founded *L'Équipe* across the road from *L'Auto*'s empty offices. 'Having had to leave number 10 rue du Faubourg Montmartre,' GÉO LEFÈVRE recalled, 'we had to find somewhere to go. *L'Équipe* could rent, on the facing side of the road at 13 rue du Faubourg Montmartre, a little four-room apartment, and to rent it – such irony – from the *L'Auto* company, which owned it.

'The editorial department was in one room, Jacques Goddet had installed his office and the inevitable conference table in the one with the greatest pretensions of being the "salon", and the administrators and accountants were in a third room. The typists were in the fourth. As for me, revelling in the title director of publicity, I was holed up in a cupboard of a few square metres which had once been the toilet.'

When the dust of war settled, the government relinquished its hold on *L'Auto*'s assets and *L'Équipe* left 13 rue du Faubourg Montmartre and moved back across the road. The paper now occupies a white-faced block that faces the Tour de France offices in the suburb of Issy-les-Moulineaux. It sells 350,000 copies on weekdays and more on Saturdays. The paper also runs its own sports TV station.

ROGER LÉVÈQUE
b. St-Nazaire, France, Dec 5 1920

Few people would imagine a concentration-camp survivor would wear the yellow JERSEY. Nor that he could have his yellow jersey taken away only to have it given back to him next morning. But both things happened to Roger Lévèque in 1951.

That year the Tour started in Metz and passed through Paris before returning to finish there at the end of the month. The first Parisian FINISH was on the Longchamps circuit after a stage from Le Tréport. Lévèque, riding with the Ouest-Sud-Ouest REGIONAL TEAM, broke away for 85km and won the stage and two days later he took the race lead.

He lost his *maillot jaune* three days after that in the 85km TIME TRIAL from La Guerche to Angers, which didn't surprise him because he knew he would be well beaten by either HUGO KOBLET or LOUSION BOBET. And sure enough he lost his jersey – only to be rewarded it next morning.

The timekeeper, a man called Adam, refused to accept that Bobet had not beaten Koblet by a second. A row ensued but Adam refused to yield. That evening Koblet and his MANAGER, Alex Burtin, stopped Tour organiser JACQUES GODDET as he walked to his hotel restaurant. They explained the arithmetic, pointing out that Bobet had been 20 seconds down at 60km and had seemingly finished at unbelievable speed whereas Koblet, a specialist, must have slowed to a crawl.

Goddet sent for Adam. On examination his papers showed an error of a minute: Koblet had won. Bobet had the time deducted and Lévèque kept his yellow jersey. Other than his stage win, Lévèque's biggest success was third place in Bordeaux-Paris in 1947. He never rode the Tour again.

Tour de France

1947	24th	
1948	DNF	
1949	31st	
1951	30th	Stage win Le Tréport—Paris, and Yellow Jersey

FÉLIX LÉVITAN

Born in 1911, Félix Lévitan ran the Tour for 25 years alongside JACQUES GODDET. A weasel-faced man, the son of shopkeepers from south-west Paris, he played football and then raced briefly after working at the Vélodrome d'Hiver and PARC DES PRINCES. A favourite jersey that he saw at the *Vél' d'Hiv'* became the design of the polka-dot JERSEY for best CLIMBER in the Tour.

Lévitan became a sports journalist in 1928 when he was 17, and by 1962 had progressed to director-general, chief editor and head of sport at *Le Parisien Libéré*. In that year the paper's owner, Emilion Amaury, signed a sponsorship contract with the Tour. Lévitan joined Jacques Goddet as his deputy. Amaury then named him co-organiser and he stayed until 1987.

Lévitan had particular interest in the commercial side of the sport, and insisted at the PRESENTATION in 1981 that the growing number of SPONSORS and jerseys, which some saw as a commercial mess, was the only way to stop the race passing into government control (as some had suggested). He opened the books to show the race cost 'not a centime' in taxes, the implication being that a state-owned Tour would cost the taxpayer dear.

The gaudy CARAVAN (*see* entry for criticism) was no more heavily commercial, he claimed, than 'soccer, rugby or motor-racing – especially motor-racing with its illegal advertising of tobacco and alcohol.'

Goddet and Lévitan brought the Tour into its modern era, but they ran out of ideas as they grew older. Relations between them were said to be sour. Lévitan became the favoured son when Amaury finally bought *L'ÉQUIPE* in May 1965. But Lévitan's fortunes crashed when Amaury handed over to his son, Philippe. On March 17 1987 Lévitan found his office locked and a court official waiting with a search warrant. He was forced to watch as the bailiff turned out his drawers and cupboards and went through his files. Then he was shown to the door and told not to return.

The row centred on alleged cross-support of a race in AMERICA. Lévitan insisted he was innocent, and sulked after Amaury had cast doubt on his honesty. Nothing was ever proved, but he stayed away until a surprise visit in 1998, and has been a regular visitor since. 'The organisation and I have come to respect each other,' he said.

(*See* STRIKES for how journalists with 'tired eyes' took offence at Lévitan's criticism.)

ALBERT LONDRES

The journalist Albert Londres, born in Vichy in 1884, made his name as a reporter by exposing conditions in penal colonies in French Guyana. In 1924, the year his story appeared, he also followed the Tour and revealed riders' hardships and talked about DOPING. His best known piece was headlined *Les Forçats de la Route* (Convicts of the Road) for *Le Petit Parisien*, which featured conversations with Tour riders, including HENRI PÉLISSIER and his brother Francis at Coutances:

Everybody was there. We had to use our elbows to get into the bistro. The crowd was silent. They said nothing, just looked spellbound into the distance. Three JERSEYS were sitting at the front of the table in front of three bowls of hot chocolate. It's Henri, Francis, and the third is none other than the second, meaning Maurice Ville, who came second at Le Havre and at Cherbourg.

'Had a bang?'

'No,' says Henri. 'It's just that we're not dogs.'

'What's happened?'

'A question of jerseys. This morning at Cherbourg, the commissaire [André Trialoux] approached me and, without saying anything, he lifted my jersey. He was checking that I didn't have [the wrong number of] jerseys. What would you say if I lifted your jacket to see if you had a white shirt? I don't like his manners. That's all.'

'What would have happened if you'd had two jerseys?'

'I could have had 15, but I don't have the right to leave with two and finish with only one.'

'Why?'

'It's the rule. It's not enough that we should race like brutes, we also have to freeze or stifle. That's all part of the sport as well, it seems. Well, I went to find DESGRANGE.

'I haven't got the right to throw my jersey on the road, then?' [The RULES insisted riders fin-ished with as many jerseys as they started, even though stages began at night and finished in mid-afternoon; Pélissier had taken off a jersey in front of Eberardo Pavesi, MANAGER of the rival Legnano team, who had complained to Desgrange.]

'No, you can't throw away Tour property.'

'It's not Tour property, it's mine.'

'I will not hold discussions in the street.'

'If you won't discuss it in the street, I'm going back to bed.'

'We'll sort it out in Brest.'

'That can all be sorted out in Brest because I'm washing my hands of it.' And I washed my hands of it.

'I rejoined the bunch and I said, "Come on, Francis, we're chucking it in."

'And that sounded fine to me,' said Francis, 'because just this morning I'd had a bad stomach.'

'And you, Ville?'

'Me?' Ville replied, laughing like a big baby. 'They picked me up on the roadside. I had painful knees.'

'You have no idea what the Tour de France is,' says Henri. 'It's a cavalry. We suffer on the road. But do you want to see how we keep going? Wait . . .' He gets a phial from his bag. 'That, that's cocaine for our eyes and chloroform for our gums . . .'

'That,' says Ville, emptying his shoulder-bag, 'that's horse ointment to warm my knees.'

'And pills? You want to see the pills?' They get out three boxes apiece. 'In short,' says Francis, 'we run on dynamite.'

Henri continues: 'Have you seen us in the bath at the finish? Come and see us. Take away the mud and we're as white as shrouds. Diarrhoea empties us. In the evenings, in our rooms, we dance a jig like Saint Vitus instead of sleeping . . .

'Look at our laces. Well, they don't go on for ever. They break, and they're made of tanned leather. Think what happens to our skin ... And the nails of our feet. I've lost six out of ten. They fall off little by little every stage. And the Pyrenees ... It's hard labour. All that we get paid for. Unless it can be done only by mules, we'll do it. We're not slackers. But, in the name of God, don't harass us. We accept the torment but we don't want vexations. My name is Pélissier, not Atlas. If I have a newspaper on my chest when I leave, I have to have it when I finish. If not, a penalty. To drink, I have to do the pumping myself. The day will come when they'll put lead in our pockets, because they'll claim that God has made men too light.'

It's a great read, but FRANCIS PÉLISSIER said, 'Londres was a famous reporter but he didn't know about cycling. We kidded him a bit with our cocaine and our pills. Even so, the Tour de France in 1924 was no picnic.'

Londres died on May 16 1932 when a fire killed everyone aboard the *George Philippar* on the way home from China. He wouldn't say why he had gone there except to suggest that he had an 'explosive' story. His name is preserved in a prize for journalists, established in 1933.

HENK LUBBERDING
b. Voorst, Holland, Aug 4 1953

Henk Lubberding was the classic DOMESTIQUE, primarily in the RALEIGH team. He could close gaps or establish breaks. But there was more to him than big legs and a willing head. He was Dutch national champion twice and won Ghent-Wevelgem in 1980. He rode the Tour 13 times, won three stages, wore the yellow JERSEY, and won the YOUNG RIDERS' class in 1978. He finished three times in the first ten.

He now runs courses for company employees under the title '*Teambuilding met Lubberding*'. He also organises winter training camps in the Canaries and works as a driver on the Tour of HOLLAND. His fondest memory is Ghent-Wevelgem, where he rode 70km alone to victory.

	Winner	
1978	National championship	
1979	National championship	
1980	Ghent-Wevelgem	

Tour de France

1977	26th	
1978	8th	Stage win Biarritz—Pau, Best Young Rider
1979	18th	
1980	10th	Stage win Metz—Liège
1981	54th	
1982	46th	
1983	10th	Stage win Roquefort—Aurillac
1984	40th	
1985	82nd	
1986	DNF	
1987	95th	
1988	DNF	Yellow Jersey
1989	119th	

OLAF LUDWIG
b. Gera Thieschitz, East Germany, Apr 13 1960

Olaf Ludwig was the first Tour rider from East Germany, riding in 1990 just after his country vanished with the fall of the Berlin Wall.

Before that, he twice won the Peace Race, often described as the eastern bloc's AMATEUR equivalent of the Tour, with 33 stage wins. Its position as the world's leading amateur race was challenged by the TOUR DE L'AVENIR, but Ludwig won that as well in 1983. He came second in the Olympic Games in 1980 and took the gold medal in 1988.

In 1990 Ludwig rode the Tour with the Dutch team, Panasonic. He took the green points JERSEY on the third stage and then won in a group of nine at Besançon by coming off the wheel of his team-mate, ERIC VAN LANCKER, to beat JOHAN MUSEEUW.

He confirmed his points title on the final stage at the CHAMPS ELYSÉES, where he came third in the sprint and 141st overall. He won his last race in 1996, a farewell gala in his hometown of Gera, by beating his old Peace Race rival, DJAMOLIDINE ABDOUJAPAROV, and his team-mate ERIK ZABEL. It was the last of 57 professional wins. The course was the one on which he rode his first race 23 years earlier, when he was 13. More than 20,000 turned out to say goodbye.

After he retired Ludwig got a job in PR with ERIK ZABEL's Deutsche Telekom team.

(*See* LECH PIASECKI for the first eastern European on the podium and for why the Communist bloc favoured the TRACK over road.)

Winner

1982	Peace Race
1983	Tour Avenir
1986	Peace Race. National championship
1988	Olympic Road championship
1989	National championship
1990	National championship
1991	GP Harelbeke
1992	World Cup, Amstel Gold, A Travers Belgique, GP Fourmies, Kuurne-Brussels-Kuurne, Four-days Dunkirk
1994	GP Frankfurt
1995	Veenendaal-Veenendaal

Tour de France

1990	141st	Stage win Epinal—Besançon, and Points winner
1991	114th	
1992	96th	Stage win La Défense—Paris
1993	DNF	Stage win Marseille—Montpellier
1994	105th	
1995	DNF	

LUXEMBOURG

For a tiny country, Luxembourg has produced enormous stars – literally in the case of FRANÇOIS FABER (*see* entry for why). Three have won the Tour – Faber in 1909, NICOLAS FRANTZ in 1927–1928, and CHARLY GAUL in 1958. Gaul was also best CLIMBER in 1955 and 1956. Arsène Mersch, Jean Majérus, Jean Goldschmit and Jean Diederich, sometimes called Bim, have also all worn the yellow JERSEY.

Gaul and Willy Kemp rode the Tour 10 times, Faber and Marcel Ernzer nine.

The first Luxembourg team was managed in 1936 by Marcel Frick, a journalist with *L'AUTO*. The riders were Mersch, Mathias Clémens, Pierre Clémens, Majérus and Josy Kraus, three of whom finished in the top 10. Around 50 riders from Luxembourg have taken part in the Tour. The most recent START in Luxembourg was in 2002, when the PROLOGUE was won by LANCE ARMSTRONG from LAURENT JALABERT.

LUZ ARDIDEN

Luz-Ardiden, usually ridden after the TOUR-MALET, appeared on the race route thanks to the Tour's search in the 1980s for new finishes. Ski centres liked the publicity and summer trade and so the Tour turned to Luz-Ardiden in 1985. PEDRO DELGADO won that year, and ROBERTO LAISEKA was the last winner there in 2001.

MADELEINE

The Col de la Madeleine in the Grandes Alpes was first climbed in the 1969 Tour, when the road opened. It is one of the most worrying climbs in the Alps, not for its steepness but its descent. Among those who have fallen there are the Dutchman Johan van der Velde in 1983, who went over the edge but landed on a ledge.

The Madeleine climbs from 510m to 1,984m in 38km, with one 3km dip. It is at a persistent gradient of eight or nine per cent. It has been classed as both a first-category climb and as *hors-catégorie* (*see* MOUNTAINS for explanation).

It starts in La Chambre through gardens and vineyards, passes into open pasture with the occasional rocky stretch, and goes up via ski stations to the four big hairpins of the last 400m. There's a café at the top and a map table to point out the other peaks, including Mont Blanc. The sign says the Madeleine is 2,000m, but maps say 1,984m or 1,993m. The Tour says 1,984m.

MARC MADIOT

b. Renazé, France, Apr 16 1959

The Frenchman Marc Madiot won the AMA-TEUR Paris-Roubaix in 1979 and the pro race in 1985. 'Madiot enters into paradise,' said *L'ÉQUIPE*. He won Paris-Roubaix again in 1991 after attacking in the same place as in 1985, at the Carrefour de l'Arbre, and finished alone.

His best Tour finish was eighth in 1983, when he was one of race winner Laurent Fignon's team-mates. He became MANAGER of the La Française des Jeux team, sponsored by a gambling company, when it was created in 1997.

(*See* CHRISTOPHE BASSONS, JEAN-FRANCOIS BERNARD.)

Winner

1981	Tour Limousin
1984	Trophée Grimpeurs
1985	Paris-Roubaix, GP Wallonia
1987	Tour EEC, National championship
1991	Paris-Roubaix
1992	Trophée Grimpeurs

Tour de France

1982	30th	
1983	8th	
1984	35th	Stage win Bobigny—Louvroil
1985	26th	
1987	47th	
1988	66th	
1989	34th	
1991	115th	
1992	70th	

FREDDY MAERTENS

b. Nieuwpoort, Belgium, Feb 13 1952

Freddy Maertens (pronounced *Mah-t'ns*) was the most enigmatic rider of the 1970s and 1980s. He could win more than 50 races one year, next to none the next, then a world championship and eight Tour stages, and then nothing more. Throughout his career he was troubled by DOPING scandals. He has been accused of everything from alcoholism – he was paid for one deal in champagne – to drug addiction. He has denied it all.

No rider has had a career as erratic. His winning record was as follows:

YEAR	WINS	
1973	14	
1974	33	
1975	33	
1976	54	(including World championship and Tour Points title)
1977	53	
1978	18	(including Tour Points title)
1979	2	
1980	1	
1981	11	(including World championship and Tour Points title)
1982	0	
1983	1	
1984	0	
1985	1	
1986	0	
1987	0	

Maertens was the son of a laundry owner from the Belgian coast. He showed promise as a boy when he kept up with passing professionals on a bike loaded with newspapers. At the age of 12 he rode a TIME TRIAL at Ramskapelle and beat riders several years older than himself. His first win was the Criterium of Westhoek in his home village of Lombardsijde on September 20 1966. He then left school a year early to become a racing cyclist and rode his first pro race, Paris-Tours, on October 1 1972, coming 26th. Four days later he won his first professional race, a CRITERIUM at Zwevezele.

That success started a career which included not only eight stages in a single Tour (1976), matching HENRI PÉLISSIER and EDDY MERCKX, but a decade of triumph and anguish. He was thrown out of the Tour of BELGIUM for drug-taking in 1974, won no fewer than eight stages of the Tour in 1976, then in 1977 was disqualified from the Tour of Flanders and the Flèche Wallonne again for alleged drug abuse. However, 1977 turned out to be a great year for Maertens – he not only won the Tour of Spain (picking up the points competition and 13 of the 19 stages along the way) but also won seven stages of the Giro d'Italia before a broken wrist forced him to retire.

When Maertens was suffering with a mystery ailment in early 1979, his medical adviser, Paul Nijs, suggested he go to AMERICA for medical checks including an assessment of his psychological state. The two flew from Amsterdam on May 25 1979, disembarking when their American Airlines DC-10 landed in New York. The aircraft continued to Chicago where an engine fell off as it took off for Los Angeles and all 271 people on board were killed. Nothing in Maertens' life could be straightforward, it seemed.

Meanwhile, rumours spread that he had been admitted to a mental hospital in the US, to which he responded in his autobiography *Niet van horen zeggen* (Not Just Hearsay), 'If I'd been in need of a mental institution at that time, I'd have skipped the long journey and gone to a Belgian one.'

He won just three races during the next two years and then returned in 1981 to win the green JERSEY in the Tour for the third time. He denied doping, specifically the use of cortisone, and credited his success to hard training and being 'judiciously treated' by a doctor. 'I was like everyone else,' he said. 'But, on the big Tours, I took nothing. Amphetamines stay in your urine for three days. I was regularly tested and never found positive.' A few weeks later he became WORLD CHAMPION at Prague.

His was a career with the highest rewards a SPRINTER can achieve, but was punctuated by dawn raids by drugs police and finally financial ruin. He says he earned the equivalent of £1,600,000 in prizes alone, let alone retainers, sponsorship deals and start MONEY – worth twice as much at the time. But he entrusted money to others and made unwise investments, including the ill-fated FLANDRIA Ranch nightclub run by his SPONSOR. The place never succeeded and burned down in 1978.

Flandria itself went bankrupt in 1981 and Maertens says he lost the equivalent of £102,500 in earnings. Belgian tax officials began chasing him. He says, 'I spent a whole year without a salary when Flandria failed. I rode in the hope of being paid at the end of the month and nothing happened. I was riding for nothing during the day and spending the evenings in never-ending meetings with lawyers. When the tax people made their calculations, based on I don't know what, they took me [in 1984] for everything: the house on the coast, the furniture, car, everything. I thought I would never come out of it.' He and his wife Carine moved in with his parents.

Maertens has worked since for a cycle-clothing company and for radio and television, but he has also had long periods of unemployment. 'He should have stayed in cycling a lot longer,' says RAPHAËL GÉMINIANI, 'but he burned the candle at both ends.'

(*See* WALTER GODEFROOT, SEAN KELLY, MICHEL POLLENTIER, STRIKES.)

Winner

1973   GP Escaut, Four-days Dunkirk
1974   Ruta Sol, Tour Luxembourg
1975   Ghent-Wevelgem, Paris-Brussels, Paris-Tours, Four-days Dunkirk, Ruta Sol, Tour Belgium
1976   World championship, Ghent-Wevelgem, Amstel Gold, GP Nations, Critérium As, Flèche Brabançonne, GP Frankfurt, Championship Zurich, Four-days Dunkirk, Baracchi Trophy, National championship
1977   Tour Spain, Tour Catalonia, Paris-Nice, Het Volk, Catalan Week, Tour Sardinia
1978   GP Harelbeke, Het Volk, Four-days Dunkirk, Tour Haut-Var
1981   World championship

Tour de France

1976	8th	Stage wins St-Jean-de-Monts—St-Jean-de-Monts, St-Jean-de-Monts—Angers, Le Touquet—Le Touquet, Nancy—Mulhouse, Auch—Langon, Langon—Lacanau, Montargis—Versailles, Paris—Paris, and Yellow Jersey and Points winner
1978	13th	Stage wins Caen—Mazé-Montgeoffroy, Poitiers—Bordeaux, and Points winner
1981	66th	Stage wins Nice—Nice, Martigues—Narbonne Plage, Roubaix—Brussels, Beringen—Hasselt, Fontenay-sous-Bois—Paris and Points winner

ROMAIN MAES

b. Zerkergem, Belgium, August 10 1913,
d. Groot-Bijgaarden, Belgium, Feb 22 1983

The little Belgian all-rounder Romain Maes led the Tour from beginning to end in 1935 after winning the first stage alone. Angry rivals trying to chase him were held up by a railway crossing and never made up the minute he gained. He became the third rider in the Tour's history to lead throughout. He also ended the domination of French riders, who had won the previous five races.

Romain Maes (pronounced *Mahce*) rode his first race when he was 17 and turned pro in 1933, winning the Tour de l'Ouest. He rode his first Tour in 1934 and twice came second in stages before crashing on the way to Nice and being taken to hospital.

Winning Paris-Lille in the spring of 1935 was a good omen because the first stage of that summer's Tour went the same way. Maes broke away near Béthune and finished alone after the gate at the Haubourdin crossing closed behind him. His good fortune seemed over next day when punctures and other mishaps delayed him more than nine minutes. BELGIUM had to chase for 70km to keep Maes in yellow.

Maes' win was secured when his only rival, the Frenchman ANTONIN MAGNE, who had won the previous year, was hit by a car on the Télégraphe and crashed. Maes won two more stages, including the last into the PARC DES PRINCES, where he again finished alone and collapsed in tears in his mother's arms.

Maes never again finished the Tour, and never again won an important race. Or that's what the record shows. In fact in 1936 he won Paris-Roubaix but the win was erroneously given to the second man, GEORGES SPEICHER, and the judges refused to relent. In 1938 he would have won Paris-Brussels had he not miscounted the finishing laps on the TRACK and stopped one too soon, losing his 100m lead to MARCEL KINT.

Romain and SYLVÈRE MAES, who won the 1936 Tour but was no relation, cashed in on their names by riding track team races together. Romain stopped racing in 1944 and ran a cafe called Le Maillot Jaune near the North station in Brussels. On the wall was a picture of him in his mother's arms in Paris.

Winner

1933 Tour Ouest
1935 Tour de France, Paris-Lille

Tour de France

1934	DNF	
1935	1st	Stage wins Paris—Lille, Nice—Cannes, Caen—Paris, and Yellow Jersey
1936	DNF	
1939	DNF	Stage win Caen—Vire, and Yellow Jersey

SYLVÈRE MAES

b. Zevekote, Belgium, Aug 27 1909, d. Ostend, Belgium, Dec 5 1966

Only once has the Tour been won in successive years by riders with the same name. In 1935 it was ROMAIN MAES and in 1936 the unrelated Sylvère Maes, from Ostend, BELGIUM. It was his third Tour – he came eighth in 1934 and fourth in 1935 – and, except for his success, his most miserable. It rained from beginning to end.

The race was a bitter battle between Belgium and FRANCE, which had had its five-year run of victories broken the previous year. France's hopes rose when MAURICE ARCHAMBAUD took the yellow JERSEY early on, but Maes took over in the Alps and held off another Frenchman, ANTONIN MAGNE, in the Pyrenees. He won the Tour by 26:55.

If that was a miserable Tour because of the weather, then 1937 was worse because of what Maes claimed was a French plot to stop a third Belgian win. Relations had been sour from the start, both nations claiming the other had cheated. Belgium insisted that penalties against them were petty, and complained at what they considered leniency against the French favourite, ROGER LAPÉBIE. Things came to a head when Maes punctured and another Belgian, Gustave Deloor, stopped to help him. Maes was penalised 15 seconds for taking shelter behind Deloor, and Deloor 60 seconds for helping a rider who was not part of his team. Deloor was riding as an individual.

Lapébie made the most of the pair's halt and attacked. The Belgians were within 75m when a level-crossing barrier came down in front of them, and they believed it had been lowered deliberately. Maes and Deloor pushed their BIKES under the barrier, ran across the tracks and remounted. That upset French SPECTATORS, and Maes was pushed and jostled when he got to BORDEAUX. Outraged, Maes pulled his team out and went home. Crowds turned out in Brussels and 20,000 readers wrote angry letters to *Sportwereld*, whose editor (Karel van Wijnendaele, founder of the Tour of Flanders) had been team MANAGER. The Belgian cycling association paid the team the prizes they had missed.

Maes came back to the 1938 Tour and finished 14th. In 1939 he won again after letting RENÉ VIETTO exhaust himself through the

Pyrenees. Maes took a six-minute lead on the IZOARD where Vietto cracked completely and increased it to 17 minutes, eventually winning by 30:38 ahead of Vietto.

He later became manager of the Belgian NATIONAL TEAM and opened a restaurant at Gistel, near Bruges, called the TOURMALET. His NICKNAME was '*le nabot*' (the dwarf).

Winner

1933 Paris-Roubaix
1936 Tour de France
1939 Tour de France

Tour de France

1934	8th	Stage win Caen—Paris
1935	4th	Stage win Perpignan—Luchon
1936	1st	Stage wins Nîmes—Montpellier, Narbonne—Perpignan, Luchon—Pau, Saintes—La Rochelle, and Yellow Jersey
1937	DNF	Stage win Lons-le-Saunier—Champagnole, and Yellow Jersey
1938	14th	
1939	1st	Stage wins Digne—Briançon, Bonneval—Bourg-St-Maurice

ANTONIN MAGNE
b. Ytrac, France, Feb 15 1904, d. Arcachon, France, Sep 8 1983

The Frenchman Antonin Magne's career includes two Tour wins (1931 and 1934), the WORLD CHAMPIONSHIP at Bremgarten, Switzerland, in 1936, the Grand Prix des Nations (then considered the world TIME TRIAL championship) in 1934, 1935 and 1936, and second place in the world championship of 1933 and of the French national championship in 1932, 1933, 1934 and 1936.

Magne began racing when he was 15, turning professional in 1926 when he was 22. He rode his first Tour the following year, winning one stage and coming sixth overall. In 1931 he won for the first time – with the help of an unknown fan.

Sharing a room with ANDRÉ LEDUCQ during that year's Tour, Magne complained he couldn't sleep, so Leducq suggested he should read his mail. One letter, written on a page from a school exercise book, astonished both men. It said, 'Monsieur Antonin Magne, I warn you that Rebry has written to his mother to say that he and Demuysère will make a big attack on the stage from Charleville to Malo-les-Bains. *Salutations*.' It was unsigned but the postmark was from Rebry's village.

Both men fell asleep, not sure if the letter was a joke but resolved to follow GASTON REBRY and Jef Demuysère everywhere on what was the penultimate stage. Next morning was grey, wet, cold and windy. There were long stretches of cobbles, where Rebry excelled. The attack came after 100km, on a cobbled bend. Leducq towed Magne up to the Belgians, who sprinted and dropped them again. The Frenchmen got back, the Belgians attacked, and so it went on. When Magne refused to work as leader, the Belgians threatened, 'Take your turn or you'll eat grass [be pushed off].' But they said it in Dutch and Magne didn't understand, so they forced him to the unsheltered side of the group where he would have to cope with the wind. Getting the message, he took his turn but crashed. The Belgians exploited his misfortune by attacking, but Magne chased back only to suffer more attacks.

Rebry won the sprint at Malo-les-Bains but Magne came second and won the Tour, beating Demuysère into second place overall by 12:56.

He won again in 1934, an extraordinary Tour because Magne led from the second day and FRANCE won 19 of the 23 stages. His victory is famous in Tour history for the self-sacrifice of his 20-year-old team-mate RENÉ VIETTO. Vietto was then little known and was considered a controversial selection with few wins, but he won fans with his youthful looks and his talent as a CLIMBER. By the MOUNTAINS he was third and a possible winner.

He and Magne were in the leading group coming down the Hospitalet pass in the Pyrenees, heading for Ax-les-Thermes. Magne's wheel broke and Vietto sacrificed his chances by handing him one of his own, waiting five minutes by the roadside until mechanics brought him another. In those days there was no neutral service and Vietto had to wait for a slow-moving lorry-load of spares.

The same thing happened next day on the Portet d'Aspet, except that this time Vietto was ahead. Magne shouted to him and Vietto turned in the road and rode back down, once more giving up a wheel and sitting on a parapet with his eyes full of tears. Pictures of the incident suggest he was alone except for the photographer, but they have been cropped to take out a crowd of onlookers, the lone image being pictorially stronger.

Legend says it was a glorious sacrifice. But in fact Vietto said, 'I didn't give him the wheel; he took it. It was a hold-up and I should have complained.' Whatever the truth, it let Magne win the Tour, a victory he secured by winning the Tour's first TIME TRIAL, 83km from La Rochelle to Nantes. Vietto finished fifth overall.

The win brought Magne greater popularity than any athlete had known in France. So much so that he was invited to ride alone along the CHAMPS ELYSÉES before the Tour in front of a crowd said to be larger than for the Armistice in 1918.

The next year, however, the crowd was to be disappointed. Magne abandoned after being hit by a car on the Télégraphe and going to hospital in a farmer's cart which happened to be nearby (*see* ROMAIN MAES). He rode his last Tour in 1938 and crossed the line at the PARC DES PRINCES arm in arm with André Leducq. Both were 34, born 12 days apart, both had made their Tour debuts in 1927, and both had won twice. The judges dithered and declared the stage a tie.

Magne's career ended with the WAR, when he lost all his yellow jerseys in the commotion of the German invasion. (*See* ANDRÉ LEDUCQ for a happier encounter with the enemy.) He became a MANAGER in 1945, particularly of RAYMOND POULIDOR's Mercier team. He was instantly recognisable in his white cowman's coat and through his habit of addressing riders as '*vous*' rather than the more usual and less formal '*tu*'. He had a reputation of being uninterviewable because, already a man of few

words, 'he withdraws into his shell as soon as he meets a journalist,' according to Jean Bobet.

BERNARD GAUTHIER, who rode for him for a decade and a half, said, '*Tonin* was a man with his heart in the sport, not a businessman. He was a kind man, with good advice and complete correctness, who hated injustice.'

Magne was made a Chevalier de la Légion d'Honneur, the French equivalent of a knight, in 1962. He retired in 1970, replaced as Poulidor's team manager by Luis Caput, and concentrated on his farm at Livry-Gargan north-west of Paris, where there is a rue Antonin Magne.

(*See* LOUISON BOBET, CRASHES, BENOIT FAURE.)

Winner

1931	Tour de France
1934	Tour de France, GP Nations
1935	GP Nations
1936	World championship, GP Nations

Tour de France

1927	6th	Stage win Marseille—Toulon
1928	6th	Stage wins Nice—Grenoble, St Malo—Dieppe
1929	7th	
1930	3rd	Stage win Montpellier—Marseille
1931	1st	Stage win Pau—Luchon, and Yellow Jersey
1933	8th	
1934	1st	Stage wins Luchon—Tarbes, La Roche-sur-Yon—Nantes, and Yellow Jersey
1935	DNF	
1936	2nd	Stage win Vire—Caen
1938	8th	Stage wins Béziers—Montpellier, Lille—Paris

FIORENZO MAGNI
b. Vaiano di Prato, Italy, Dec 7 1920

Fiorenzo Magni, an Italian, is the man credited with bringing SPONSORS into cycling from outside the cycle trade. The post-war prosperity of the BIKE business began to dwindle as car sales took off after the second world war, reducing their capacity to sponsor teams. In 1954 Magni approached the Nivea face-cream company and created what is often said to be the first *extra-sportif*. (*See* RAPHAËL GÉMINIANI and SPONSORS for more) The tribute is not wholly deserved because in 1947 there was already a British team of at least semi-professionals backed by the ITP football pools company, but Magni's work brought the first outside backer into mainstream cycling.

His efforts were ridiculed, riders being concerned with the break from tradition and amused that a man not known for his looks (he was prematurely bald) could interest a maker of beauty products. (*See* RAPHAËL GÉMINIANI for how ideas changed.) Their contempt was helped by their dislike for his right-wing views and the way he reacted angrily to anyone who argued with him.

Magni never rode with subtlety. He won by wearing his rivals out, attacking them until they cracked. It was his only tactic, but he would have gone further had his career not coincided with those of FAUSTO COPPI and GINO BARTALI. His climbing was weaker than either of the other two Italians, although his descending was breathtaking. He won the Giro three times, by 13 seconds in 1948, by 1:46 in 1951, and by 12 seconds in 1955, each time by making up on the drops what he had lost on the rises.

That road-handling skill also helped him on bumpy roads. His height, weight and courage kept him upright where others hesitated. It meant that in 1949 he became only the second non-Belgian to win the Tour of Flanders, after Henri Suter of Switzerland in 1923; and in 1951 he became the first rider to win it three times in succession (1949, 1950, 1951).

The oddest incident in Magni's career came when he was leading the Tour in 1950, riding for the second-string Italian team, the *Cadetti*. The leader of the main team, GINO BARTALI, quit the race after claiming that SPECTATORS had threatened him when he had brushed shoulders with JEAN ROBIC near the top of the Aspin and fallen off. (*See* Bartali's entry for more.) The incident, which seems to have been largely imagined, didn't affect Magni, but he was so in awe of Bartali that he packed his bags and left the race with him. FERDY KÜBLER took over the yellow JERSEY but refused to wear it next morning as a mark of respect to Bartali and Magni.

Magni's most dramatic incident on a bike was when he broke a collarbone in the 1956 Giro. Unable to pull on the bars, but determined to continue because he had won the previous year, he asked his MECHANIC to tie a bandage to the handlebars and tugged it with his teeth so he could use his back muscles. He still finished second, 3:30 behind CHARLY GAUL.

(*See* FRANCO BITOSSI, ITALY.)

Winner

1942   Tour Piedmont
1947   Tre Valle Varesine
1948   Giro d'Italia
1949   Tour Flanders, Tour Tuscany, Baracchi Trophy
1950   Tour Flanders, Baracchi Trophy
1951   Giro d'Italia, Tour Flanders, Milan-Turin, Tour Lazio, Tour Romagna, Baracchi Trophy,
1953   Tour Piedmont, Tour Veneto, National championship
1954   Tour Tuscany, National championship
1955   Giro d'Italia, Tour Romagna
1956   Tour Lazio, Tour Piedmont

Tour de France

1949	6th	Stage win St-Sebastian—Pau, and Yellow Jersey
1950	DNF	Stage win Angers—Niort, and Yellow Jersey
1951	7th	Stage win Avignon—Marseille
1952	6th	Stage wins Namur—Metz, Puy-de-Dôme—Vichy, and Yellow Jersey
1953	15th	Stage wins Bordeaux—Pau, Montluçon—Paris

FRANÇOIS MAHÉ

b. Paris, France, Sep 2 1930

A tough and richly talented man, François Mahé of FRANCE rode 13 successive Tours. His record includes second places in the Tour of Spain, Tour of Flanders, Bordeaux-Paris and Paris-Nice. Recognition escaped him, though, because his career coincided with and was overshadowed by those of LOUISON BOBET and JACQUES ANQUETIL. In an era of NATIONAL TEAMS and REGIONAL TEAMS in the Tour he had to work for others rather than take his own chances. He did, though, wear the yellow JERSEY in his first Tour, in 1953.

(*See* HUGO KOBLET.)

Tour de France

1953	10th	Yellow Jersey
1954	15th	Stage win Besançon—Epinal
1955	10th	
1956	DNF	
1957	11th	
1958	DNF	
1959	5th	
1960	14th	
1961	DNF	
1962	20th	
1963	19th	
1964	DNF	
1965	43rd	

MAIL – see DYNAPOST

JEAN MALLÉJAC

b. Dinon, France, Jul 19 1929, d. Landerneau, France, Sept 24 2000

Jean Malléjac, a square-jawed munitions worker from Brest, had enough explosive power on a bike to win the yellow JERSEY in 1953. He took it on the 13th stage, from Albi to Béziers, and held it for five days before losing to LOUISON BOBET. Bobet won the stage across the Vars and IZOARD by 5:23, pushing Malléjac into second place by 8:35. Eventually Bobet won the Tour by 14:18 but, since everybody else had also lost time, Malléjac (who heard while he was leading the Tour that his daughter had been born on his birthday) clung to his second place.

Malléjac made an impression of a different sort in 1955 when he lost control on MONT VENTOUX. JACQUES AUGENDRE wrote, 'Streaming with sweat, haggard and comatose, he was zigzagging and the road wasn't wide enough for him. He'd passed the stage where every pedal seemed to weigh 100kg. He couldn't feel his legs or arms. Colours and shapes dissolved in front of him. He was already no longer in the real world, still less in the world of cyclists and the Tour de France.'

He collapsed 10km from the top and lay on the ground, one foot in his pedal, his legs still working. Tour doctor PIERRE DUMAS put him in the ambulance, where he had a fit, and took him to hospital in Avignon. The *Télégramme de Brest* reported, 'He struggled, gesticulated, shouted for his bike, wanted to escape, so much that he had to be strapped down.'

Dumas was so angry that evening that he said, 'I'm prepared to call for a charge of attempted murder', a reference to whoever had supplied the drugs that Malléjac later denied taking, or perhaps an attack against the organisers for the excesses of their race. Dumas never said which.

Malléjac rode two more Tours before retiring to run a driving school. He died in September 2000.

Tour de France

1952	33rd	
1953	2nd	Stage win Dieppe—Caen, and Yellow Jersey
1954	5th	
1955	DNF	
1956	34th	
1958	DNF	

MANAGERS

The role and nature of managers have changed with the sport and the style of teams. The BIKE companies and accessory-makers who were the only SPONSORS until after the WAR (*see*

RAPHAËL GÉMINIANI and FIORENZO MAGNI for how the change came) quickly realised the link between success in the Tour and increased sales (*see* GITANE for an example). These firms appointed officials, called managers, to look after their riders. The first manager to dominate was 'Père' Ludo Feuillet, a former medical student who ran ALCYON. While other managers saw themselves as sponsors' representatives, Feuillet ran his team with such discipline that it became known as *la taule*, the prison. (*See* ALCYON for more.)

Feuillet's success – Alcyon was best team from 1909 to 1912 – set a style for the rest, and managers became tacticians, personnel managers and negotiators. TACTICS became more important as speeds rose (*see* tactics entry for why), and managers began nominating team leaders whom the rest of the team had to support, sacrificing their own chances. That brought about the development of the DOMESTIQUE. (*See* MAURICE BROCCO for how the word was coined.) It also meant sponsors and tactics played a stronger part than Tour organiser HENRI DESGRANGE felt was healthy for a contest he believed should be a battle between individuals. In 1930 he abolished sponsored teams and picked NATIONAL TEAMS instead. (*See* MAURICE DEWAELE for what provoked this.)

There were now two sorts of manager – those who ran trade teams all year, and those, like MAURICE BIDOT of FRANCE, whose only role was to blend rival cyclists into a national squad for the three weeks of the Tour. Some were more successful than others. Bidot, for example, never brought JACQUES ANQUETIL and RAYMOND POULIDOR together, although he did prompt LOUISON BOBET to formalise a tradition in which the Tour winner gives his PRIZES to domestiques for their help, pocketing his increased CRITERIUM fees instead.

ALFREDO BINDA of ITALY had the same problem of clashing ambitions with FAUSTO COPPI and GINO BARTALI, but hours of negotiation got them to cooperate. (*See* Binda entry for details.)

The next step in the increasing influence of managers came with the decline of the cycle industry after the second world war. Bike companies could no longer afford so many lavish teams, and riders and managers began looking for support outside the industry. The first so-called *extra-sportif* sponsor was the British football pools company ITP in 1947. Other tentative ventures began in SPAIN and Italy. In 1954 Fiorenzo Magni negotiated a contract with the face-cream company, Nivea. Six years later Géminiani's deal with the St-Raphaël aperitif company established the first fully-fledged professional team with an outside backer.

Managers now became sponsor-chasers in winter and team bosses in summer. Bike companies like PEUGEOT stayed in the sport for decades (*see* Peugeot entry for details), but *extra-sportifs* ran teams only for as long as they made commercial sense. Managers were forced to replace firms that left. The more they touted for their teams, the more the notion rose that they 'owned' them. Géminiani took his star riders from St-Raphaël to Ford-France; in the 1980s, Peter Post in effect sold the RALEIGH team to Panasonic, and so it went on.

Teams now no longer belong to any clear organisation. The bewildering number of trademarks on some team JERSEYS make them look more like cycling billboards. Multiple sponsorship means that in effect teams belong to nobody but the sports-management companies at their heart. The first is said to have been France Compétition, a company set up by CYRILLE GUIMARD for the teams he ran in the 1970s and 1980s.

Riders' allegiances also changed. The confessions of the FESTINA AFFAIR of 1998 showed

that the rise of complicated DOPING procedures, such as the use of blood-enhancement drugs in the 1990s, turned riders' allegiance from team manager to team doctor. In Festina's case, said manager Bruno Roussel, his own instructions steadily became less important to riders than the drugs they could receive from the medical team of Erik Rijckaert and the SOIGNEUR, WILLY VOET. Critics said managers had become little more than team-car drivers.

Today, however, the power of managers has started to return, helped by the controversial introduction of EARPIECES (*see* entry for history and explanation) which lets them dictate the race as it progresses.

(*See* JOHAN BRUYNEEL, FRED DE BRUYNE, HENNIE KUIPER, APO LAZARIDES, GREG LEMOND, MARC MADIOT, RENÉ VIETTO.)

DANIEL MANGEAS

Daniel Mangeas, from St-Martin-de-Landelles in Brittany, is the inexhaustible *speaker* (announcer) of the Tour and other races belonging to the SOCIÉTÉ DU TOUR DE FRANCE. The 2002 Tour was his 29th.

A tall man with straggly grey hair and a bearlike stance, he begins the day at the START, where he announces each rider with such enthusiasm that even the weakest feels a winner; and ends it at the FINISH with two and a half hours of questions for the crowd, interviews for passing champions and live commentary. His command of every rider's record, as well as bizarre incidental information, is immense, and made still more impressive by never knowing who will sign on or cross the line next.

As the newspaper *Libération* remarked in 1999, 'He is pushed by a mysterious force, waving his arms, reminding us that Joe Bloggs won the Tour of West Switzerland in the same year as Charlie Farnsbarnes finished one place ahead of Bill Bloke, who himself finished in such-and-such a position the previous year . . . he shouts the successes of the 177 riders without ever neglecting to say that if So-and-so is so strong, it's because he eats only black radish.'

His is an idealised world, the paper concluded. 'He believes in a dream where no cyclists are crooked, where they're all good guys, where all the team doctors are like country GPs sucking gently on their pipes.'

Mangeas works first from the road itself and then, when the CARAVAN starts coming through, from an installation called La Boule, which would look like a horizontally divided orange if it weren't pale blue.

In 2002 the race passed through his village, and he was able to stop to greet his neighbours. (*See* RUDI ALTIG.)

THIERRY MARIE
b. Benouville, France, Jun 25 1963

Thierry Marie was a PROLOGUE star, winning not just in the Tour (at Boulogne-Billancourt in 1986), but also in the Tour of SPAIN and the Tour de l'Aude. At Boulogne-Billancourt his attempt to fit a vortex cone and back support behind his saddle was ruled to be illegal streamlining, although his win did stand.

That ability in prologues should have made him good for no more than half an hour of intense racing. But in the 1991 Tour he won not only the prologue at Lyon but the sixth stage from Arras to Le Havre after a lone break of 234km, one of the longest in history. His motivation may have been that he was crossing his own area, Normandy, and he rode all but the first 25km of the stage alone.

The win put him back in the yellow JERSEY he had lost the day after Lyon, leading SEAN KELLY by 1:04. He kept it a further day before MIGUEL INDURAIN won the 73km TIME TRIAL from Argentan to Alençon.

(*See* BIKES for other technological improvements.)

Winner

1985	Tour Limousin
1988	Tour Holland, Circuit Sarthe
1989	Baracchi Trophy
1990	Paris-Camembert
1992	Tour Oise
1995	Circuit Sarthe

Thierry Marie (continued)

Tour de France

1985	67th	
1986	108th	Stage win Boulogne-Billancourt—Boulogne-Billancourt, and Yellow Jersey
1987	87th	
1988	98th	Stage win Clermont-Ferrand—Chalon-sur-Saône
1989	72nd	
1990	121st	Stage win Futuroscope—Futuroscope, and Yellow Jersey
1991	111th	Stage wins Lyon—Lyon, Arras—Le Havre, and Yellow Jersey
1992	114th	Stage win Montluçon—Tours
1993	DNF	
1994	53rd	
1995	94th	
1996	DNF	

JACQUES MARINELLI
b. Le Blanc-Mesnil, France, Dec 15 1925

NICKNAMES are thrust upon you. And so it was with Jacques Marinelli. It was in 1949, and he was riding the Tour for a second time, in the Ile-de-France REGIONAL TEAM. The previous year he hadn't finished, but this time he was more determined. He came second on the first stage, into Brussels, and went through the next four days attacking relentlessly. He was the surprise of the race.

The fourth stage went from Boulogne to Rouen, and Marinelli slipped into a break of 16. Lucien Teisseire won, but Marinelli came second and took the yellow JERSEY. Next morning, referring to Marinelli's lowly status and his *maillot jaune*, Tour organiser JACQUES GODDET wrote, 'Our budgerigar has been transformed into a canary.' The nickname stuck. Not 'Canary', which would have been flattering, but 'Budgie'.

Leading the race transformed Marinelli for the rest of the Tour. He switched from random attacker to tactician, exploiting the rivalry between FAUSTO COPPI and GINO BARTALI to make sure neither deprived him of his lead.

Thus he kept his jersey for five more stages, all the way to the foot of the Pyrenees, where he lost it to FIORENZO MAGNI. The canary went back to being a budgie, but he still finished on third perch, behind Coppi and Bartali.

Tour de France

1948	DNF	
1949	3rd	Yellow Jersey
1950	DNF	
1951	DNF	
1952	31st	
1954	DNF	

MARIANO MARTINEZ
b. Burgos, Spain, Sep 20 1948

Mariano Martinez, a Frenchman born in Spain with a Spanish name, was the Tour's best CLIMBER in 1978. He also came third in the world championship in 1974.

His son Miguel has done still better: five times WORLD CHAMPION, four times on a mountain bike and once in cyclo-cross, four times European champion, four times national and once Olympic champion again all in mountain biking. He switched to the road in 2002 and finished 44th in his first Tour.

Tour de France

1971	31st	
1972	6th	
1973	12th	
1974	8th	
1975	14th	
1976	42nd	
1978	10th	Stage win Pau—St-Lary-Soulan, and Mountains winner
1979	16th	
1980	32nd	Stage win Serre-Chevalier—Morzine
1981	15th	

ÉMILE MASSON JR
b. Bierset, Belgium, Sep 1 1915

In 1938 Émile Masson won the stage from Besançon to Belfort – 25 years after his father (*see* below) first rode the Tour. Émile finished with Otto Weckerling of GERMANY, 2:08 ahead of the first chasers. Judges couldn't decide which of them had won and gave the stage to both.

Émile was, like his father, a long-distance star, winning Bordeaux-Paris in 1946 and coming second in 1949.

Winner

1938   Flèche Wallonne
1939   Paris-Roubaix
1946   Bordeaux-Paris, National
      championship
1947   National championship

Tour de France

1938   34th   Stage win Besançon—Belfort

ÉMILE MASSON SR
b. Morialme, Belgium, Oct 16 1888, d. Bierset, Belgium, Oct 25 1973

BELGIUM's Émile Masson Sr finished three and a quarter hours behind winner Jean Alavoine on the Bayonne—Luchon stage in 1922. His son, ÉMILE MASSON JR, has explained exactly why in his book, *My father and I, freemasons of Belgian cycling*.

'That day,' his father told him, 'I was flying. I dropped everyone on the first slopes of the AUBISQUE. I knew it would be cold and so I was wearing a thick flannel vest under my jersey. After a few kilometres I was suffocating. I felt like a fish on hot sand. I longed to stop. Three punctures on the descent gave me PHILIPPE THYS as a companion. He said he was suffering from food poisoning. We decided to eat at one of the restaurants in Bagnères-de-Bigorre. No sooner said than done. As we were leaving the place, Jacquinot and Bellenger [ROMAIN BEL-LENGER] turned up to eat. We waited for them and when they'd finished we set off together towards Ste-Marie-de-Campan, where they decided to abandon.

'Philippe and I resolved to press on. With mixed results. On the way up the Peyresourde,

a shepherd suggested we take a short cut on a goat track that went up the side of the mountain. The only solution was to carry our bikes. The stones were slipping beneath our feet and horseflies were biting our legs. We were getting nowhere. Rather than gaining time, we were losing it.' Despite all that Masson finished 12th in Paris after winning two stages on the road back to the north.

He rode as a pro from 1913 to 1925, wearing the yellow JERSEY in 1920. Masson also won Bordeaux-Paris in 1923 and finished second in 1924 and third in 1922, when he was also third in Paris-Roubaix.

Winner

1919   Tour Belgium
1923   Bordeaux-Paris, Tour Belgium

Tour de France

1913   DNF
1919   DNF
1920   5th   Yellow Jersey
1921   DNF
1922   12th   Stage wins Briançon—Geneva,
             Geneva—Strasbourg
1924   DNF
1925   22nd

PIERRE MATIGNON
b. Nantes, France, Feb 11 1943, d. St Michel-de-Chavaignes, France, Nov 1 1987

Pierre Matignon was the LANTERNE ROUGE (last man) who held off EDDY MERCKX to win alone on the PUY-DE-DOME in 1969.

An unknown, curly-haired Frenchman who was never capable of winning the Tour, Matignon was more interested in finishing last and cashing in on the CRITERIUM contracts which tended to come as a result. So was another Frenchman, André Wilhem, but on one memorable occasion when Matignon's impressive dawdling had beaten Wilhem to the LANTERNE ROUGE he attacked instead. The race to be last suddenly became a race to be first, and Matignon attacked as well, picking the FEEDING AREA on the Chavanon climb for his opening salvo.

He had an advantage of five minutes with 30km to go. Four riders set off in chase, including the Portuguese climber JOAQUIM AGOSTINHO. Even so, 20km from the line, Matignon had seven and a half minutes in hand. It began to look as though he could win.

The coiling dead-end of the Puy-de-Dôme is a private road that only occasionally features in the Tour, although it achieved legendary status with the tussle between JACQUES ANQUETIL and RAYMOND POULIDOR in 1964. Pride now persuaded Merckx that this stage belonged to him and he joined in the pursuit, a giant reduced to chasing a DOMESTIQUE whose name he didn't even know, a man who had never before ridden the Tour. Merckx rode with the anger that only upset dignity can produce.

Only Poulidor and Matignon's team-mate Paul Gutty, a CLIMBER from Lyon, could stay with him. Matignon embarked on the last stretches of the Puy and clung to his 500m lead. He began to zigzag with exhaustion. Then he lifted himself again and knew he had cracked Merckx. He won by 1:25, too exhausted to give a victory salute.

Everybody was happy in the end. Matignon had the greatest day of an easily missed career, Wilhem rode into Paris as the last man that he wanted to be, and Merckx won the Tour.

Tour de France

1969   85th   Stage win Brive—Puy-de-Dôme
1972   75th

ROBBIE McEWEN

b. Brisbane, Australia, Jun 24 1972

Robbie McEwen (pronounced *Macky-wenn* in FRANCE) is a born SPRINTER. His talent is in tight finishes where the handling skills learned as a world BMX champion come to the fore.

He took time to settle as a Tour rider, but bounced in at the end of the 1999 Tour to win on the CHAMPS-ELYSÉES soon after his Rabobank team had said they no longer wanted him. FRANCE was desperate to avoid a repeat of 1926, when no Frenchman won at all. Laurent Desbiens and Anthony Morin broke clear in the city, but the Dutch Rabobank team set off in chase and got their man McEwen near the front. Laurent Brochard managed a short lead, but was caught 600m from the line, and McEwen came from behind ERIK ZABEL and Lars Michaelsen to win.

He won the same stage again in 2002 in another battle with Zabel. McEwen had a one-point advantage in the competition for the green (points) JERSEY, and he also had the confidence of knowing he had won on the Champs-Elysées before. Zabel, on the other hand, had six consecutive green jerseys and a stronger team to fight a way through to the FINISH for him. He also had the memory of snatching the green jersey from another Australian, STUART O'GRADY, on the same stage the year before.

However, coming from behind may have given the German a dose of nerves, because he took the last corner too fast, lost his line and gave McEwen his chance. The Australian won and another, Baden Cooke, came second. Zabel finished seventh – one place behind O'Grady. With only four Australians in the race (the other was Bradley McGee, who also won a stage), it was quite a tally.

McEwen was the first Australian to win the points competition, and the second to stand on the podium. The first was PHIL ANDERSON, the best YOUNG RIDER in 1982. McEwen said, 'I finished in the top three in every stage in the first week and that convinced me I had a great chance of going for the green jersey.'

(*See* DON KIRKHAM and RUSSELL MOCKRIDGE for more on Australian pioneers.)

Winner

1996   Luk Cup
2002   Étoile Bessèges, GP Escaut, Paris-
        Brussels, National championship

1997	117th	
1998	89th	
1999	122nd	Stage win Arpajon—Paris
2000	113th	
2002	130th	Stage wins Metz—Reims, Melun—Paris, and Points winner

MECHANICS

Mechanics – *les mécanos* – were first allowed to follow the Tour in 1909, when HENRI DES-GRANGE provided a single vehicle for them. Since then the numbers have grown to several per team, two in cars with the race and another with a truck of spares. The job, said one, was 'like being in the first world war: hours of doing nothing and then minutes of destruction and frantic activity.'

At night they work in hotel garages, cleaning, stripping and changing equipment. Wet days are worst. Riders in 1937 struggled through hub-deep water between Paris and Lille, and JACQUES GODDET, in his first race as organiser, had to find extra shelter for mechanics to make good the damage.

Mechanics and MANAGERS were once allowed to approach riders during the race. Now they must wait until called on RADIO TOUR. They are not allowed to influence the race by creating a bridge between the peloton and the breakaway, and officials will order them to drop back, usually by radio but often also by whistling and waving.

The rise in the number of riders and the need to use narrower roads led the Tour authorities to introduce neutral service cars and motor-bikes to look after riders separated from their helpers. In 2002 this contract was held by the French accessory-maker, Mavic, using yellow cars and motorbikes.

Mechanics can be as overawed as SPECTA-TORS by the riders they help. A *mécano* helping EDDY MERCKX was so overcome by stage fright that he took two minutes to change a front wheel. A photo of FAUSTO COPPI shows a panicking mechanic forcing a back wheel between the front forks. The caption reads, 'Give me a revolver so I can shoot this fool.'

MEMORIALS

JACQUES ANQUETIL has a tall, black marble memorial in a flower bed by the traffic lights in Quincampoix, north of Rouen, his childhood home. Its curved face shows him, high-cheeked and with characteristically swept back hair, and lists his record. He is buried beside the church there. The sports centre in Quincampoix is also named after him. So are buildings at the Piste Municipale in Paris, where there is a further memorial beside the TRACK.

CHARLES, FRANCIS and HENRI PÉLISSIER are commemorated at the same TRACK's entrance by a bronze bas-relief by the sculptor Collarini. Bought by fans at the PARC DES PRINCES, and unveiled there at the end of the 1962 Bordeaux-Paris on May 27, it was moved to the Piste Municipale when the Parc was demolished.

The Brussels authorities said in March 2002 that they would name a railway station in Anderlecht after EDDY MERCKX. The track at Mourenx, FRANCE, is already named after him for his win there in 1969.

TOM SIMPSON's largest memorial is on MONT VENTOUX, near the top on the Bédoin side. There is also a plaque on a house in the square in Bédoin, put there by journalists, a bust of 'a gentleman' at the entrance to the Kuipke track in Ghent, BELGIUM, and a museum in Harworth, BRITAIN.

RAYMOND POULIDOR has a street named after him in Sauvat-sur-Vige, where he was born and where a cycle-dealer called Marquet gave him his first BIKE. The square in Cabasse is named after JEAN DOTTO.

FAUSTO COPPI has a memorial outside the church of the Madonna del Ghisallo, between Como and Bellagio on a key climb in the Tour of Lombardy. His bike, and also those of riders such as FRANCESCO MOSER, FABIO CASARTELLI and GINO BARTALI are inside. The road in which he lived in Castellania is now the Via

Fausto Coppi. Four copper columns in the graveyard list his successes.

Coppi also has a bust on the IZOARD, alongside LOUISON BOBET. The memorials were renovated in 2000 by the town of Briançon in a ceremony presided over by Tour organiser JEAN-MARIE LEBLANC. Leblanc's predecessor, HENRI DESGRANGE, has a memorial just beyond the tunnel on the Galibier. The Tour lays a wreath there as it passes.

The Tour's first great climber, RENÉ POTTIER, committed suicide in 1907 after twice being first to the summit of the BALLON D'ALSACE. His memorial stands at the summit. WIM VAN EST, who fell over the side of the AUBISQUE in HOLLAND's first yellow JERSEY in 1951, has a memorial at the spot, put there by a Dutch businessman.

Near the foot of the TOURMALET at Ste-Marie-de-Campan is a plaque to EUGÈNE CHRISTOPHE, who broke his forks going down the mountain and had to weld them back together in a forge in the village. The workshop is no longer there, but there is a memorial on the side of the house at the spot. The main square is called the Place Eugène Christophe.

At the top of the Tourmalet is a statue commemorating OCTAVE LAPIZE, who won the Tour's first stage through the Pyrenees, and a memorial to former race director JACQUES GODDET. RENÉ VIETTO is remembered at the top of the Col de Braus outside Nice. LUIS OCAÑA has a memorial on the Col de Mente in the Alps.

The journalist Paul de Vivie is remembered at the top of the Col de la RÉPUBLIQUE outside St-Étienne. De Vivie, writing under the name Vélocio, had kept insisting, when it wasn't fashionable, that there was a lot to be said for multiple gears. In St-Étienne itself there is a street named after ROGER RIVIÈRE.

The Place LAURENT JALABERT is in Mazamet, near Toulouse, where he was born. There is a rue ANTONIN MAGNE in Livry-Gargan, near Paris, to celebrate the world champion, Tour winner and successful French team MANAGER.

LUIS OCAÑA and others are remembered at the Nôtre Dame des Cyclistes outside La Bastide d'Armagnac, east of Mont-de-Marsan. Inside are Tom Simpson's white jersey from Paris-Nice, yellow JERSEYS from Merckx, MIGUEL INDURAIN, Ocaña and GREG LEMOND, and WORLD CHAMPION jerseys from JAN RAAS, ANDRÉ DARRIGADE, BERNARD HINAULT and Bobet, as well as bikes from champions of the past.

The RAYMOND IMPANIS bike route runs through country lanes in the Kampenhout region of BELGIUM. Also in Belgium, in Bloemenstraat, Maldegem, is the MAURICE DEWAELE sports centre. BRIEK SCHOTTE has a statue in Kanegem. The journalist PIERRE CHANY has a cyclo-tourist race named after him, as do STEPHEN ROCHE and numerous other riders.

JOOP ZOETEMELK has a bronze statue at the Ahoy track in Rotterdam. Footpaths in Nijmegen are named after WOUT WAGTMANS, Coppi, Simpson, Gerrit Schulte, BERT OOSTERBOSCH and manager Kees Pellenaars.

(*See* JAVIER OTXOA.)

ERWAN MENTHÉOUR
b. Brest, France, Jun 29 1973

A talented but only averagely successful rider, Erwan Menthéour retired from racing in 1999 to write an exposé of DOPING, *Secret Défonce* (Secret High). His book claimed that systematic drug use was at the heart of some teams, that some CRITERIUMS were drug parties (riding on 'just mineral water' would be sacrilege, a MANAGER told him), and that the extent of recreational drug use in the sport needed to be emphasised.

Menthéour told of a party at which a rider's wife, high on a cocktail of heroin, cocaine, amphetamine and other drugs known as a *pot belge*, 'performed a memorable striptease on a table', and how high-ranking officials joined in at other parties. He told of drugged riders giggling as they waited at their team's PRESENTATION for their manager to list his anti-drug promises.

He told too of a drug-fuelled journey round the CRITERIUMS of FRANCE in which he and a friend experimented with ever-stronger drugs until 'we were so out of it that at the motorway junction we didn't turn off to Nantes but went on towards Paris instead'. Of the blood-boosting drug EPO, he wrote, 'You feel as though your kidneys are two balloons of water flopping around the base of your back. Your joints ache and you have trouble seeing. I had atrocious headaches at the Tour of Switzerland when my haematocrit went up to 60 per cent.'

Dismissed as a *raté* or has-been by EDDY MERCKX, his revelations, naming individuals and dating incidents, nevertheless make disturbing reading. He said riders made threatening phone calls as a result of his book. 'They said they knew the number of my car and where my children went to school and so on,' he said.

EDDY MERCKX
b. Meensel-Kiezegem, Belgium, Jun 17 1945

Eddy Merckx was one of the greats of cycling, claimed by many to be the greatest of them all. He won not only all there was to win – including five Tours – but did it by riding away from everyone else. His glamour was helped by matinée idol looks: brown eyes with Betty Boop eyelashes, luxuriant dark hair and a shy smile. Sadly, his looks haven't lasted; the modern Merckx appears to justify BELGIUM's enthusiasm for beer and chips.

It was obvious that Eddy Merckx was going to be special when he became amateur WORLD CHAMPION in 1964 aged 19, and therefore still a junior until the end of the season. Within ten years he had won the Tour five times, the Giro d'Italia five times and the Tour of SPAIN once, as well as almost every classic.

Until Merckx's sudden appearance on the scene, BELGIUM had waited a long time for Tour success. Decades had passed since SYLVÈRE MAES had won in 1936, with rarely a Belgian on the podium. And then a new phenomenon arrived: Merckx. After turning pro in 1965 he won nine times in his first year and 20 in his second, including Milan-San Remo. In 1967 he rode the Giro, coming ninth

and winning two stages including one in the MOUNTAINS. And then he became professional world champion.

The French writer JEAN-PAUL OLLIVIER said, '*Chez* Merckx, there were no clever TACTICS, no camouflage, tactical feints. From the first kilometres, often, other riders just knew what was about to happen.' He could ride harder and faster than everyone else, from the spring classics through the major Tours and on to the Tour of Lombardy. Despite his grand superiority he never relaxed and showed little grace even to lesser lights (*see* PIERRE MATIGNON for a rare error), following on their tails as they led through their home towns. That's an honour accorded to riders almost automatically but Merckx would ride along as well just to make sure no advantage was taken. His domination led the little-known French rider Christian Raymond to NICKNAME him '*le cannibal*' after a remark by his daughter, and it stuck.

Merckx won five Tours in a row from 1969, although not consecutive Tours because he didn't ride in 1973. In 1969 he was first away in the PROLOGUE because his MANAGER, Lomme Driessens, wanted to show him off. There are disadvantages in going first because there's no one to chase, but the benefits are that there's more time to relax afterwards. He lost six seconds to RUDI ALTIG in a wind that many riders didn't have to face, but had the pleasure of taking the yellow JERSEY next day in his Brussels suburb of Woluwe-St-Pierre.

On day seven Merckx attacked on the BALLON D'ALSACE and retook the lead he had ceded to his team-mate, Julien Stevens. He then attacked 200m from the top of the TOUR-MALET, dropped ROGER PINGEON, RAYMOND POULIDOR and others on the descent to Barèges, and had a minute at the foot of the AUBISQUE. By the top he had a staggering eight minutes with 50km to go and no more climbs. JACQUES GODDET wrote simply, 'Merckxis-simo.'

He won that 1969 Tour by 18 minutes. He had the yellow jersey, the points title, the mountain competition, and best team. BEL-GIUM had been waiting 30 years for this and celebrated with Eddy Merckx tea towels, chewing gum, key-rings and T-shirts.

In 1970 he won the prologue, let his team-mate ITALO ZILIOLI wear yellow to lessen attacks on the way to the mountains, and then took over to the end. In 1971 he rode for the Molteni team rather than Faema or Faemino, won the prologue and again passed the lead to a team-mate, RINI WAGTMANS. (*See* Wagtmans entry for the trick he played in the Tour.) But this year he faced his only serious rival throughout his career.

LUIS OCAÑA (*see* entry for details) had won the Tour of the Basque Country and the Tour of Catalonia and come second to Merckx in the Dauphiné Libéré. There he had matched him on many of the climbs the Tour would take and he set out to beat him for the biggest prize of all.

Merckx, astonishingly, didn't react when Ocaña attacked after 17km on the Tour stage from Grenoble. He, JOAQUIM AGOSTINHO and JOOP ZOETEMELK built a lead of 3:10 before Ocaña rode off alone on the col de Noyer at 74km. Merckx and his team chased without help from anyone else but Ocaña never stopped gaining and took the yellow JERSEY by almost nine minutes.

The Belgian tried to take revenge in the Pyrenees but Ocaña resisted. Merckx brought them both down when he skidded in running water going down the col de Mente. Coming down just behind, Zoetemelk swerved to miss Ocaña's service car but hit Ocaña instead. VICENTE LOPEZ-CARRIL and Agostinho then also ran into him. Ocaña left the race in a heli-copter and Merckx declined to wear the yellow jersey in his absence the next morning.

The rematch didn't happen in 1972 because the Spaniard was in bad form, and Merckx didn't ride in 1973. And then in 1974 he won his

fifth Tour, the year an early stage was held in Plymouth, in BRITAIN. He hadn't won any of the spring classics, for the first time since 1966, and he says that 'the wear and tear was beginning to show.' Even the veteran RAYMOND POULIDOR twice climbed better than him in the Pyrenees. But Merckx won the prologue and, overcoming observations that he was no longer the man he was, he took a further six stages, plus the team TIME TRIAL.

He had won the Tour, the Tour of Switzerland and the Giro d'Italia in barely eight weeks.

There was nowhere then but down. Nobody had won the Tour a sixth time. The decline was symbolised in 1975, however unfairly, by the way a Frenchman punched Merckx in the stomach on the PUY DE DOME. Merckx rode on to the finish, then freewheeled back to identify his attacker. The man insisted it had been an accident as the crowd pushed forward but Merckx demanded and received a nominal French franc in damages.

It was a Tour of misery for Merckx because BERNARD THÉVENET caught and passed him on the climb of Pra-Loup – Thévenet still in his big ring. The Frenchman went on to win the Tour by 2: 47.

'I knew that my best years were behind me,' Merckx said, 'but I'm convinced that but for my bad luck [he also broke a cheek bone in a CRASH], I would have won that year's Tour.'

His greatest years were in teams rooted in ITALY although full of Belgians, from the red and white of the coffee-machine maker, Faema, to whom he had gone after PEUGEOT refused to build its team around him, then Molteni (a sausage company for a man who made mince-meat of the opposition) and Fiat.

He won five of the seven Tours he entered and spent 96 days in yellow, 18 more than BERNARD HINAULT. He won on average a race a week for six years. Frankly, it began getting dull. But that didn't stop the crowds. They wanted to see how he would win rather than whether. To this day his popularity is rivalled only by RAYMOND POULIDOR.

Merckx's superiority was so great that in the 1971 Super Prestige Pernod, forerunner of the World Cup, he won twice the points of the second, third, fourth and fifth riders combined. In 1972 he rode 49.431km at Mexico City (altitude: 2,260m) to break the world hour record. It bettered Ole Ritter's 48.653km on the same track in 1968 and stood until 1984 when it was broken with 50.808km by FRANCESCO MOSER. Moser's ride was on a heavily streamlined bike. The record fell repeatedly as bikes improved. The UCI ruled that things had gone too far and, after CHRIS BOARDMAN rode 56.375km in September 1996, decided to use Merckx's record and traditional bike as a standard and, in effect, cross out all the records that followed him. Boardman in turn beat Merckx's record in 2000, riding 49.441km.

Merckx's career trickled to an end at the workaday Omloop van het Waasland near Antwerp in 1979. His health hadn't been what it was and there was nothing left to prove. He is still involved with the Tour de France, providing race BIKES as a SPONSOR and following his son Axel.

(*See* MEMORIALS, JOOP ZOETEMELK.)

Winner

1966 Milan-San Remo, Montjuich, Baracchi Trophy
1967 World championship, Ghent-Wevelgem, Milan-San Remo, Flèche Wallonne, Critérium As, Baracchi Trophy
1968 Giro d'Italia, Paris-Roubaix, Tour Catalonia, Tour Romandie, GP Lugano, Tre Valle Varesine
1969 Tour de France, Liège-Bastogne-Liège, Milan-San Remo, Tour Flanders, Paris-Nice, Paris-Luxembourg
1970 Tour de France, Giro d'Italia, Ghent-Wevelgem, Paris-Roubaix, Flèche Wallonne, Paris-Nice, Critérium As, Montjuich, Tour Belgium, National championship
1971 Tour de France, World championship, Liège-Bastogne-Liège, Milan-San Remo, Tour Lombardy, Dauphiné Libéré, Midi Libre, Paris-Nice, GP Frankfurt, Het Volk, Montjuich, Tour Belgium, Trophée Grimpeurs

1972 Tour de France, Giro d'Italia, Liège-Bastogne-Liege, Milan-San Remo, Tour Lombardy, Flèche Wallonne, GP Escaut, Flèche Brabançonne, Montjuich, Tour Piedmont, Tour Emilia, Baracchi Trophy, World hour record
1973 Giro d'Italia, Tour Spain, Ghent-Wevelgem, Amstel Gold, GP Nations, Liège-Bastogne-Liège, Paris-Brussels, Paris-Roubaix, GP Fourmies, Het Volk
1974 Tour de France, World championship, Giro d'Italia, Tour Switzerland, Critérium As, Montjuich
1975 Amstel Gold, Liège-Bastogne-Liège, Milan-San Remo, Tour Flanders, Montjuich, Catalan Week
1976 Milan-San Remo, Catalan Week
1977 Tour Mediterranean

Tour de France

1969 1st Stage wins Mulhouse—Ballon d'Alsace, Divonne—Divonne, Briançon—Digne, Revel—Revel, Luchon—Mourenx, Créteil—Paris, and Yellow Jersey and Points winner and Mountains winner
1970 1st Stage wins Limoges—Limoges, Valenciennes—Forest, Belfort—Divonne, Divonne—Divonne, Thonon—Grenoble, Gap—Mont Ventoux, Bordeaux—Bordeaux, Versailles—Paris, and Yellow Jersey and Mountains winner
1971 1st Stage wins Mulhouse—Strasbourg, Albi—Albi, Mont-de-Marsan—Bordeaux, Versailles—Paris, and Yellow Jersey and Points winner

Eddie Merckx *(continued)*

Tour de France (continued)

1972 1st Stage wins Angers—Angers,
           Bordeaux—Bordeaux, Pau—
           Luchon, Orcières-Merlette—
           Briançon, Briançon—Valloire,
           Versailles—Versailles, and Yellow
           Jersey and Points winner
1974 1st Stage wins Brest—Brest, Mons—
           Châlons-sur-Marne, Besançon—
           Gaillard, Gaillard—Aix-les-Bains,
           Colomiers—Seo de Urgel,
           Bordeaux—Bordeaux, Vouvray—
           Orléans, Orléans—Paris, and
           Yellow Jersey
1975 2nd Stage win Merlin-Plage—Merlin-
           Plage, Fleurance—Auch, and
           Yellow Jersey
1977 6th

ARTHUR METCALFE
b. Leeds, England, Sep 27 1938 d. Harrogate, England, Dec 11 2002

Arthur Metcalfe rode the 1967 and 1968 Tours during three weeks' holiday from work. Those were the years of NATIONAL TEAMS and Britain had too few full-time professionals to make up the numbers. Metcalfe was riding as a weekend pro in Britain and working during the week for Carlton Cycles.

He only began cycling when he was 18 and his early seasons were restricted by army service. He built a name as an AMATEUR with long lone attacks in the Milk Race (the Tour of BRITAIN), which he won in 1964. In 1966 he won the national road championship and then the year-long TIME TRIAL championship with three straight rides at 50 miles, 100 miles and 12 hours. The double had never before been done.

He turned professional for Carlton after exhausting all he could do as an amateur. He finished the 1967 Tour 69th after riding for team leader TOM SIMPSON. Metcalfe's lone attack on the Tour stage to Bayonne in 1968 won him the day's COMBATIVITY prize.

He recalled, 'I was away for 30 miles and I never recovered. It was the beginning of the end. Until then in Britain we'd only been riding CRITERIUMS on sea-fronts and I was in a hell of a state. Every morning I woke up feeling awful.' It was too much and he abandoned.

He retired to work in insurance and car sales.

Winner

1968 Manx Trophy

Tour de France

1967 69th
1968 DNF

DAVID MILLAR
b. Malta, Jan 4 1977

David Millar began cycling during school holidays to while away the time when he stayed with his mother in High Wycombe, England; he spent school terms in Hong Kong, where his father was an airline pilot. A run of successes in Britain led him to move to St-Quentin, FRANCE, where his club manager Martial Gayant (see LAURENT JALABERT and JACKY DURAND for other stories) described him as 'the next GREG LEMOND'.

He turned professional in 1997, and won the PROLOGUE of the TOUR DE L'AVENIR in that year. The British background of TIME TRIALS and TRACK pursuit races has produced a lot of specialists at short, fast distances; he followed CHRIS BOARDMAN, Hugh Porter, SEAN YATES, BARRY HOBAN and Norman Sheil as a Tour rider with a background as a time trialist. That talent showed again when he won the prologue of his first Tour, in 2000.

That, he said, exposed him to the strains of stardom for the first time, and he was not far from cracking. 'I came reasonably close to thinking about quitting,' he said, 'but I was realistic about it, pragmatic. I locked myself away from journalists and anyone connected with cycling. I was very unhappy; I was just completely lost and I didn't know what I was doing any more. I was getting sick of the lifestyle. I didn't want to get eight years down the line and be living by myself with no friends outside cycling. You see a few ex-pros who have nothing; loads of money but nothing else. All they do is hang around races.'

He decided to miss the world championship and took two months' holiday in Kuala Lumpur, some of it watching car racing, before visiting his father in Hong Kong and going on to Australia. The break did the trick.

His first road stage win at the Tour came from a break on a quiet day from Lavelanet to Béziers in 2002. It was the first by a Briton since Max Sciandri (who is half-Italian) at St-Étienne in 1995. He was helped in the leading break by his hero, Jalabert, who accepted he was no longer a good enough SPRINTER to win. Millar said, 'He attacked first and then I countered. We agreed to ride like that without really talking about it. It was a weird feeling but I just knew that I was going to win.'

Millar lives in Biarritz and rides for a French team, a fact which leads the French (who often mistakenly call him Millard) to see him as almost one of their own. He speaks fluent French with an accent reporters refer to as *à la Jane Birkin* (a British actress well known in France, who in the 1960s recorded a sexually charged song that was banned by the BBC).

The writer Philippe Le Gars says, 'To explain him, you have to look at his Anglo-Saxon spirit, his relaxed style, his lack of typical cyclist culture or even his detachment from his sport. That kind of personality isn't typical; it's far from all the clichés of the champion cyclist.'

His team MANAGER in 2001, Alain Deloueil, said, 'David is anything but a complicated guy. In spirit he is very "anglais", very cool. That type of mentality is very rare in cycling. In fact he is quite an emotional boy, who can often worry about nothing. He always needs to be reassured, you always need to be behind him to reassure him.'

Winner

1999   Manx International
2001   Tour Denmark, Circuit Sarthe

Tour de France

2000	62nd	Stage win Futuroscope—Futuroscope, and Yellow Jersey and Points leader
2001	DNF	
2002	68th	Stage win Lavelanet—Béziers

ROBERT MILLAR
b. Glasgow, Scotland, Sep 13 1958

Robert Millar is a tiny Scottish CLIMBER who in 1984 became the only Briton to win the MOUNTAINS competition. His fourth place in the 1984 Tour is BRITAIN's best ever result.

The writer Robin Magowan said of him, 'With his distinctive pointy nose he looks more like a Dickensian chimney-sweep.' A French writer said his miniature size reminded him of an *asticot*, or maggot.

He was British AMATEUR champion in 1978 when he was 19, and then moved to the ACBB club in Paris which had produced STEPHEN ROCHE, SHAY ELLIOTT and JONATHAN BOYER. Millar won his first race with the ACBB club in a sprint rather than over hills, and then another 12 to become FRANCE's best AMATEUR. In 1979 he won the British title again and came fourth in the world amateur championship in HOLLAND after wrenching his foot loose in the sprint. That near-miss brought him a contract with PEUGEOT, for which the ACBB is a feeder club, but he had no wins for three years.

Millar never got on with Peugeot's MANAGER, Maurice de Muer, and didn't ride the Tour until Roland Berland took over in 1983. In that year's Tour Millar broke away on the Peyresourde, winning by six seconds and moving up 56 places to 27th. He also came second in the mountains competition. On stage 13 he became the first Briton to wear the polka-dot (mountains) JERSEY. Next year he won outright in the mountains and finished fourth overall, behind LAURENT FIGNON, BERNARD HINAULT and GREG LEMOND.

In 1988 he would have won a stage had he not followed the directions of a policeman directing cars at Guzet Neige and taken a wrong turn with Philippe Bouvatier. They were only 300m from the line when Massimo Ghirotto rode by and won.

Millar – Bob to fellow professionals – is the nearest Britain has had to a winner of one of the three major stage races. He finished second in the Tour of SPAIN in 1985 and 1986, second in the Giro in 1987 and fourth in the Tour in 1984.

He led the 1985 Spanish tour for nine days until PEDRO DELGADO ended his hopes on the last but one stage. He and another Spaniard, José Recio, got seven minutes' lead in 60km and won by 6:50. Just what went wrong has never been established. Millar, never an easy person-ality, says he would have been helped had he had more friends in the sport. Equally, he blamed his MANAGER, Roland Berland, for not giving him better time checks. Berland said he hadn't had them from the race organisation. The race organisation said they had been given every three minutes.

That was followed by claims that home riders had ganged up against foreigners. There were even suggestions that the conservative Spanish didn't want a long-haired vegetarian with an ear ring to win their national tour. Why didn't Millar's team-mates help? Because a rail-way crossing had delayed them for several min-utes, they were reported to have said . . . 'Only the train never came.' There were then claims that the Frenchmen in the Peugeot team didn't want their foreigner to win a big tour. It may be some of all of those or none at all.

Millar rode for 15 years as a professional and for six teams, including the 'chaotic' Fagor, the 'professional' Panasonic, 'where I learned more about how to race in six months than in six years with Peugeot' and the ill-fated Le Groupement, which ran out of money and folded in mid-1995, ending his career.

His last big race was that year's Manx Inter-national, which incorporated the national championship. He won alone on a circuit that included three climbs of Snaefell.

He said: 'I first found I could ride the moun-tains when I won the Route de France as an AMATEUR. It's basically a natural thing, the same as sprinting ability is natural.'

In 1997 he became British national coach. 'People who expect me to grovel to them and don't merit it and aren't influential in what I have to do won't get any more respect than they deserve,' he said.

Millar remains a contradiction. He is fiercely Scottish and complains that Scots are called British when they succeed but Scottish when they fail. And yet he lives in the English Mid-lands and rarely speaks well of Glasgow. He is by turns taciturn and even abusive, he has never been an easy man. Of reporters following the Tour he said, '[Those] guys see the race on TV, then ask you what's happened. You see them sleeping during the day because they've been drunk the night before. If I think they're useless, I tell them so.'

(And *see* SPONSORS.)

Winner

1985   Tour Catalonia
1989   Tour Britain
1990   Dauphiné Libéré
1995   National championship

Tour de France

1983	14th	Stage win Pau—Bagnères-de-Luchon
1984	4th	Stage win Pau—Guzet-Neige, and Mountains winner
1985	11th	
1986	DNF	
1987	19th	
1988	DNF	
1989	10th	Stage win Cauterets—Superbagnères
1990	DNF	
1991	72nd	
1992	18th	
1993	24th	

RUSSELL MOCKRIDGE
b. Melbourne, Australia, Jul 18 1928,
d. Melbourne, Australia, Sep 13 1958

Russell Mockridge made up the numbers in a LUXEMBOURG team in the 1955 Tour. It took him a year to recover, he said. He preferred faster races, such as CRITERIUMS and TRACK races where he could make use of a sprint which had beaten sprint champions Reg Harris and Jan Derksen.

Mockridge was a journalist from Geelong, Australia, who left for Europe to try his hand as a pro after winning two Olympic gold medals in 1952. He studied French until he could understand horse-race commentaries on the radio.

Australia's forgotten pioneer, Mockridge died in a road race in Melbourne a few weeks after his 30th birthday.

(*See* DON KIRKHAM for the first Australian Tourman; and *see* PHIL ANDERSON, STUART O'GRADY and ROBBIE MCEWEN for Australian stage winners.)

Tour de France

1955   64th

JULIEN MOINEAU

b. Clichy, France, Nov 27 1903, d. La Teste, France, May 14 1980

The stage from Pau to BORDEAUX in 1935 was on what the French call a *canicule* (dog-day), a time of oppressive, stifling heat. The riders were trudging along sullenly at just 20km/h when they saw an unbelievable sight: rows of SPECTATORS with tables laden with cool beer. They stopped and downed drinks, some loading their jerseys with more. (*See* CAFÉ RAIDS for similar impromptu stops.)

Only one rider decided to press on. Julien ('the sparrow') Moineau had turned up that morning with a 52-inch chainring, unheard of in that era. Shifting his chain onto this monstrosity he won by 15:33, and toasted the bunch with a beer as it followed him in. As well he might. He had organised the stunt himself. The generous beer people with their roadside table were friends, and he'd asked other friends in the bunch to help delay the race as much as possible. (*See* PIERRE BEUFFEUIL for how another impromptu halt won a stage for an unknown.)

Other than that, Moineau's greatest successes were victory in Paris-Tours in 1932 and second place in Bordeaux-Paris in May 1935, improving from third the previous year and fourth the year before that.

Winner

1932   Paris-Tours

Tour de France

1927	8th	
1928	17th	Stage win Grenoble—Évian
1929	DNF	Stage win Bordeaux—Bayonne
1932	25th	
1935	30th	Stage win Pau—Bordeaux

MARCEL MOLINES

b. Chibli, Algeria, Dec 22 1928, d. Sep 22 1986

Marcel Molines may be the only black rider to have won a stage of the Tour. It was in 1950, and he was riding for French North Africa, when the Tour had NATIONAL and REGIONAL TEAMS. The stage from Perpignan to Nîmes was so hot that riders had little inclination to race and even ran into the sea at St-Maxime. (And *see* JULIEN MOINEAU for another halt in the heat.)

Molines broke away with ABDEL-KADER ZAAF with 200km to go, sometimes getting 20 minutes' lead. Zaaf began weaving (*see* entry for details) and collapsed, but Molines went on to win by four minutes.

(And *see* STRIKES.)

Tour de France

1950   DNF   Stage win Perpignan—Nîmes

MONEY

Most accounts of what bike riders earn are apocryphal, inaccurate or at best unconfirmed. It is not in the interests of riders or their AGENTS to deny reports which overestimate their earnings. Indeed some riders have been said to be paid so much that it is clear that the published budget of their team couldn't afford it. In some cases the salaries quoted are for more than one year or include bonuses which may not be paid; in others, earnings include not only salaries but start money, PRIZES and external contracts for product endorsements.

The one certain fact is that, although MAURICE GARIN may have collected nearly ten years' worth of a labourer's earnings by winning the first Tour, riders for many decades afterwards earned less than in other sports. Nor did their prizes keep pace. It was only when JEAN-MARIE LEBLANC took over as organiser in 1988 that the Tour set itself the target of matching the prizes awarded at the Roland Garros tennis tournament in Paris. Until then, Tour prizes had fluctuated greatly over the years, and for a spell included seaside apartments, cars and even works of art of dubious value. (*See* prizes entry for details.)

Riders' wages, too, were uncertain. Many rode for decades for no more than a BIKE, JERSEY and prizes. They did it because it was their only way into professional teams, their only hope of making a name, and a chance to live a life that would never be available as an AMATEUR. Few riders, even those at the top, left the sport rich.

Two things changed the system, which peaked in the 1950s and 1960s and lasted into the 1970s. The first was the French government's extension of *le smic* (the minimum wage) to cyclists. Until then, professional cycling had been seen as a pastime rather than a job. That development continued when in October 2001 the sport set its own minimum wages, riders and SPONSORS agreeing an annual minimum from 2003 of 15,000 euros (£9,600) for new professionals and 18,000 euros (£11,500) for everyone else. In 2004 the

figures will rise to 20,000 euros (£12,800) and 23,000 euros (£14,700).

The other change was riders' own attitudes to what they earned. It's often attributed to GREG LEMOND, who negotiated a reputed 1,400,000 euros (£900,000) with the French businessman Bernard Tapie to ride the 1985 Tour with BERNARD HINAULT in his La Vie Claire team. Winning the Tour and the world championship led to a three-year contract with the Z chain of clothing shops quoted at $5,500,000 (£3.5m) in 1990. The previous record, unconfirmed, was said to be £400,000 paid to SEAN KELLY by the Dutch recording tape maker PDM in 1989.

The Italian magazine *Bicisport* put LeMond's total earnings in 1991 at around £2,700,000, of which a little less than half came from contracts and most of the rest from advertising endorsements. That placed him 35th in the list of sportsmen's earnings, just behind the tennis player Ivan Lendl but well behind the world leader, the boxer Evander Holyfield, said by the American magazine *Forbes* to earn £38,000,000.

The sport couldn't sustain salaries at that level and the Tour de France's estimates say the peak through the rest of the 1990s was 1,320,000 euros (£844,000) a year for MIGUEL INDURAIN, plus his endorsements and prizes. Indurain was reputed to have been offered more to change teams but he stayed where he was and so, in the absence of a wages war, contracts remained steady for most of his career.

The next change came with the arrival of JAN ULLRICH, said in 2001 by the German newspaper *Bild* to earn £1 million a year, and then by LANCE ARMSTRONG with £5,000,000 a year plus £3,200,000 in endorsements. Those figures, however, have not been confirmed and may be journalists' estimates.

The Tour's calculations say LAURENT JALABERT, best-paid of the French riders and reputedly second only to Armstrong, was paid the equivalent of £832,000 a year at ONCE. Disagreements with ONCE about the team's future came too late in 2000 for most SPONSORS to consider him, and his salary was widely said to have fallen when he joined the Danish team CSC in 2001. But not as much as RICHARD VIRENQUE's. He had asked for the equivalent of £1,300,000 a year in 1999, but the FESTINA AFFAIR of 1998 made him damaged goods, and Domo of BELGIUM was the only team prepared to make an offer in 2000 and 2001. The amount was never confirmed but the fact that nobody else was even bidding probably tells all.

The largest teams don't necessarily pay most. Money can go on a few riders paid well or many riders earning less. The biggest teams have up to 80 riders, mechanics and doctors. Below the stars and the thin layer of challengers, the rest earn much the same, about 33,000 euros (£21,000) a year, plus prizes (which teams normally share) and other contracts.

The published budgets of the 10 top teams in 2002 were:

TEAM BUDGETS 2002

World ranking	Team	Budget
1	Fassa Bortolo	5.34 million euros
2	Deutsche Telekom	4.73 million euros
3	Rabobank	4.12 million euros
4	Mapei	7.63 million euros
5	Lotto	3.66 million euros
6	Banesto	5.34 million euros
7	Cofidis	5.34 million euros
8	ONCE	4.58 million euros
9	US Postal	6.1 million euros
10	Domo	6.9 million euros

In March 2002 the UCI (the world body) and the professional cyclists' union discussed a retirement payment of 20,000 Swiss francs for riders of more than 30 who had raced for at least five years.

Bike riders have proved poor money managers. RENÉ VIETTO, HUGO KOBLET, MARC DEMEYER, MICHEL POLLENTIER and FREDDY MAERTENS all invested unwisely and lost most of their earnings. In 1905 LOUIS TROUSSELIER won the Tour and gambled away his prizes and bonuses in a night. They came to 250,000 francs, in those days the equivalent of several years' work for a labourer. (*See* Trousselier entry for more.)

(*See* ERCOLE BALDINI, GINO BARTALI, FERDY KÜBLER.)

MONTGERON

It was at the Café Réveil Matin (the name means 'alarm clock') in Montgeron – now a suburb of southern Paris but then a village – that the first Tour started in 1903. Cyclists liked the place because it cooked good steak and chips. Tour organiser HENRI DESGRANGE knew the family that owned it. Among races to have started in the village was the Éventail from Paris to Tours on July 15 in 1900, when there were 12 starters. A newspaper in 1901 wrote, 'Life in Montgeron would be agreeable if it wasn't for all the cyclists every Sunday.'

The café is still there, signposted from the Route Nationale 19, standing by a T-junction of the Melun and Corbeil roads. A plaque reads:

'Here, in front of the Réveil Matin, on 1 July 1903, the start of the first Tour de France, organised by Henri Desgrange, took place.'

Further notices announce the Tour's 50th visit and another in 1979.

Raymond Potteau, who ran the café until recently, bought the bar from his inlaws soon after the war. They had run it since the 1920s.

MONT VENTOUX

Potteau's barman, Lucienne Robin, worked there for 60 years. The place has now changed hands. You can look into the cellar where the racers changed but there are no souvenirs. They've been stolen.

The start was a carnival of SPECTATORS, drinks salesmen, travelling musicians, officials and riders. 'The men waved their hats, the ladies their umbrellas,' reported an eye-witness. 'You felt they would have liked to touch the steel muscles of the most courageous champions since Antiquity . . . Only muscles and energy will win glory and fortune. Who will carry off the first prize, entering the pantheon where only supermen may go?'

A stage of the 2003 Tour is due to start at Montgeron to mark the race's 100th anniversary.

(And *see* MONEY.)

Mont Ventoux, an old volcano in Provence, is the race's most feared climb. It is neither the longest nor the steepest ascent, but a combination of the airless forest on its lower stretches, and the bleak, often hot and frequently windy stretches of arid stone at the summit make it a terrible climb.

That legend has grown with the near-fatal collapse of JEAN MALLÉJAC in 1955 and the death there of TOM SIMPSON in 1967. Riders have feared it so much and doped themselves so heavily to confront it that, as Antoine Blondin wrote, 'There are few happy memories of this sorcerer's cauldron. We have seen riders reduced to madness under the effect of the heat or stimulants, some coming back down the hairpins they thought they were climbing, others brandishing their pumps and accusing us of murder . . . falling men, tongues hanging

---

ROUTE OF FIRST TOUR

Stage 1   *Paris—Lyon (467km):*
  Montgeron, by RN7 through Melun, Fontainebleau, Montargis, Briare, Cosnes, La Charité, Pougues-les-Eaux, Nevers, St-Pierre-le-Moutier, Moulins, La Palisse, Roanne, Tarare.

Stage 2   *Lyon—Marseille (374km):*
  St-Genis-Laval, Rive-de-Gier, St-Chamond, St-Étienne, Col de la RÉPUBLIQUE, Bourg-Argental, Annonay, Andance, Rhône valley, Tournon, Valence, Montélimar, Orange, Avignon, Orgon, Senas, Aix-en-Provence, Le Pin, St-Antoine, Marseille.

Stage 3   *Marseille—Toulouse (423km):*
  St-Antoine, Salon, Arles, Nîmes, Lunel, Montpellier, Mèze, Montaignac, Pézenas, Béziers, Coursan, Narbonne, Lezignan, Capendu, Carcassonne, Castelnaudary, Villefranche-de-Lauragais, Toulouse.

Stage 4   *Toulouse—Bordeaux (268km):*
  Grisolles, Montauban, Castelsarrasin, Moissac, Valence d'Agen, Agen, Tonneins, Marmande, La Réole, Langon, Podensac, Laprade, Le Bouscat, BORDEAUX.

Stage 5   *Bordeaux—Nantes (425km):*
  Libourne, Barbezieux, Pons, Cognac, Saintes, Rochefort, La Rochelle, Marans, Luçon, La Roche-sur-Yon, Rocheservière, St-Philibert-de-Bouaine, Geneston, Nantes.

Stage 6   *Nantes—Paris (471km):*
  Ancenis, St-Georges-sur-Loire, Les Rosiers, Saumur, Bourgueuil, Langeais, Tours, Montlouis, Amboise, Blois, Mer, Beaugency, Orléans, Patay, Chartres, Rambouillet, Chevreuse, Versailles, VILLE D'AVRAY.

out, selling their soul for a drop of water, a little shade.'

Its quoted height ranges from 1,909 to 1,912m. Historically, the first to cross it was the Italian poet Petrarch, by moonlight on April 25 1336. Car races have been held there from 1902, and early cars also suffered from the absence of oxygen. The first BIKE race was the Circuit du Ventoux in 1935.

The Tour first rode it on July 22 1951, on the 17th stage from Montpellier to Avignon. All the favourites were in the lead group of 12. HUGO KOBLET attacked on the approach to the Chalet Reynard, where a hairpin leads to the bare stretch to the summit, and only RAPHAËL GÉMINIANI, LOUISON BOBET, GINO BARTALI and Lucien Lazarides could stay with him. Lazarides attacked two kilometres from the top and reached the summit alone, followed by Bartali.

Drama came to the climb in 1955, when it was included on the 11th stage, from Marseille to Avignon. Jean Malléjac (*see* entry for more) collapsed and was taken to hospital struggling and shouting. The Belgian, Richard van Genechten also collapsed but was less badly affected.

That was the year FERDY KÜBLER set such a wild tempo that Géminiani warned him to be careful, advice he rejected. (*See* Kübler entry for details.) He began struggling badly in the last kilometre and repeatedly fell on the descent, reaching Avignon 26 minutes behind Bobet and abandoning the race that night.

In 1967 Tom Simpson also began weaving on Mont Ventoux and fell twice in the last kilometres. The Tour's doctor, PIERRE DUMAS, said he was dead by the time he reached him, but Dumas continued mouth-to-mouth resuscitation until an ambulance took the body to hospital. The discovery of drugs in Simpson's stomach and more in his jersey pockets brought doping into focus.

The Ventoux has not always been the cause of grief, though. CHARLY GAUL used the TIME TRIAL up Mont Ventoux as the basis of his Tour victory in 1958.

Seven years later the first road stage FINISH at the summit was in 1965, on the 14th stage from Montpellier. It looked as though RAYMOND POULIDOR would open enough of a gap on FELICE GIMONDI to take the Italian's yellow JERSEY. Poulidor broke away with JULIO JIMENEZ. The two matched each other until, in the last 100m and after the final bend, Poulidor jumped clear and won by six seconds. But his 34 seconds on Gimondi weren't enough to put him in the lead, and Poulidor never did wear a yellow jersey.

The mountain-top finish in 2000 became a battle between LANCE ARMSTRONG and the tiny Italian CLIMBER MARCO PANTANI. The Italian was the better climber but he couldn't shake off Armstrong, who eased off in the last metres to let Pantani win. Armstrong said he did it as a tribute to a troubled star but the temperamental Italian saw it as an insult, claiming that Armstrong had said Pantani had won only because he had been 'allowed' to. The ensuing war of words became the best side-show of the Tour. (*See* Pantani entry for details.)

The classic climb is from Bédoin (296m), where a MEMORIAL to Simpson hangs on a wall in the square. It starts gently and then rises through the steepest section to the St-Estève hairpin at the Chalet Reynard (1,419m). That divides the trees from the open climb to the observatory built at its peak in 1882. The final section, which gets to a gradient of 10 per cent, is closed for much of the year by snow. The temperature at the top is generally 11°C less than at the bottom. The total distance is 21km, with gradients ranging from eight to 14 per cent.

Tom Simpson's main memorial, paid for by fans in BRITAIN and now in sorry shape, is two kilometres short of the summit on the right. It is easily missed in snow or mist. Simpson called

Mont Ventoux 'a great mountain stuck in the middle of nowhere and bleached white by the sun. It is like another world up there among the bare rocks and the glaring sun. The white rocks reflect the heat and the dust rises clinging to your arms, legs and face.'

The fastest ascent was by Lance Armstrong in 50:00 as he chased RICHARD VIRENQUE in 2002.

Tour de France

1996	75th	
1997	19th	
1998	DNF	
1999	27th	
2000	4th	
2001	DNF	Stage win Dunkirk—Dunkirk, and Yellow Jersey and Points leader
2002	DNF	

CHRISTOPHE MOREAU
b. Vervins, France, Apr 12 1971

The likeable Frenchman Christophe Moreau grew up in Reims and then moved to Berlin, where his father had a job. He came to notice in 1994 when he won a silver medal in the French AMATEUR 100km team time-trial world championship. He turned professional in 1995 and came second to Emmanuel Magnien in the TOUR DE L'AVENIR.

In 1998 Moreau was embroiled in the FESTINA AFFAIR, confessed to dope-taking, and was suspended for six months. He returned on May 1 1999. In 2000, he was fourth in the Tour, close behind team-mate Joseba Beloki, whom he had helped through the Alps. In 2001 he won Dauphiné Libéré and also the yellow JERSEY in the Tour de France by winning the PROLOGUE at Dunkirk.

In 2002 Moreau was penalised two minutes and fined 400 Swiss francs for fighting during the Tour on the Col de la Core with Carlos Sastre, a team-mate of LAURENT JALABERT. Moreau accused Sastre of coming too close as he tried to follow LANCE ARMSTRONG's wheel. The Spaniard was penalised 20 seconds and fined 400 Swiss francs for pulling Moreau's jersey.

Moreau met his girlfriend Émilie during the Tour, where she was looking after jerseys for the SOCIÉTÉ DU TOUR DE FRANCE.

Winner

1998 Critérium International
1999 Tour Poitou-Charentes
2001 Dauphiné Libéré

FRANCESCO MOSER
b. Palu di Giovo, Italy, Jun 19 1951

Francesco Moser, for a decade the dreamboat of female Italian cycling fans, couldn't have come from a better family: his brothers Enzo, Aldo and Diego were also professional cyclists.

Moser was one of 12 children. He lost his father when he was 13 and left school to work in the fields. He took up cycling at 18. Two years after turning professional in 1973 he was national champion, and in 1976 became world professional pursuit champion. A year later, at San Cristobal, Venezuela, he won the road race title. A second title looked likely in 1978 on the Nurburgring, West Germany, until he was beaten by GERRIE KNETEMANN.

Moser's weakness was MOUNTAINS, which is why he rode the Tour only in 1975, winning two stages, wearing the yellow jersey for a week and coming seventh. His strength was in the classics, particularly Paris-Roubaix, which he won in 1978, 1979 and 1980. Altogether he won 158 races, plus CRITERIUMS, but for most he'll be remembered for his hour records set in Mexico City in 1984. He beat EDDY MERCKX's record twice, adding more than a kilometre and passing 50km for the first time. Four days later he extended it to 51.151km.

He and his wife Carla live in a villa of carved beams in Palu di Giovo on the edge of the German-speaking area of Italy, formerly part of Austria. He runs a BIKE factory and has 13 hectares of vineyard overlooking Trento. He also works for the organisers of the Giro, Tour of Lombardy and Milan-San Remo.

1974 Paris-Tours, Tour Reggio Calabria,
      GP Forli, Tour Emilia, Tour Tuscany,
      Tour Piedmont, Baracchi Trophy
1975 Tour Lombardy, Midi Libre, Coppa
      Placci, National championship,
      Baracchi Trophy
1976 Tour Appenines, Tour Tuscany, Tour
      Puglia, Tre Valle Varesine
1977 World championship, Flèche Wallonne,
      Critérium As, Tour Tuscany, Tour Lazio,
      Championship Zurich
1978 Paris-Roubaix, Tour Lombardy, Tour
      Catalonia, Tre Valle Varesine
1979 Paris-Roubaix, Tour Emilia, Tour Friuli,
      Ghent-Wevelgem, National
      championship, Tour Veneto, Baracchi
      Trophy
1980 Paris-Roubaix, Tirreno-Adriatico, Tour
      Trentino
1981 Tirreno-Adriatico, National
      championship
1982 Route Sud, Tour Tuscany
1983 Milan-Turin, Tour Friuli, Tour Trentino
1984 Giro d'Italia, Milan-San Remo, Tour
      Lazio, Baracchi Trophy, World hour
      record
1985 Tour Appenines, Baracchi Trophy

Tour de France

1975 7th Stage wins Charleroi—Charleroi,
           St-Gilles-Croix-de-Vie—
           Angoulême, and Yellow Jersey

CHARLY MOTTET
b. Valence-sur-Drôme, France, Dec 16 1962

Charly Mottet, a little French CLIMBER, comes
from an area where rugby is the single passion.
Any hope the Mottet family had that their son
might play for the national XV, however, vanished when he was 10. It was then that he tired
of being hammered by taller and heavier opponents and chose cycling instead.

His all-round talent showed quickly. He
could climb, he could descend fast and he could
hold his own in TIME TRIALS. He showed early

class when he beat MIGUEL INDURAIN in the
TOUR DE L'AVENIR in 1984. With such complete
talent, he was always likely to succeed in hard
races such as the Dauphiné Libéré. He won this
rehearsal for the Tour's alpine stages, held in his
home area, in 1987, 1989, and then in 1992,
beating the world champion GIANI BUGNO and
GREG LEMOND. But the biggest prizes always
escaped him, particularly in the Tour. He rode
10 times, failed to finish only twice and in 1987
and 1991 finished just one place short of the
final podium.

There is a general acceptance that Mottet
consistently refused to resort to DOPING.

He retired from racing after 1994 to work for
the SOCIÉTÉ DU TOUR DE FRANCE, driving
ahead of the Tour to warn of obstructions. 'As a
rider you know nothing of the race except a
blur of faces and that you are the lead actors in
a film,' he says. 'It's not until you join the race
you realise how much is involved.'

He stayed with the Tour until the arrival of
Daniel Baal, the former head of the French
cycling federation, as JEAN-MARIE LEBLANC'S
deputy in October 2001. There was no formal
version for his departure but personality differ-
ences were claimed. He has also managed the
French national road team.

Mottet is not a man given to instant answers.
The writer Jean-Emmanuel Ducoin said:
'Moderation is his religion, softness his music.
Nothing pushes him. "Wait while I think," he
says to the least question. And when he's confronted by a question more convoluted than
the others, his face goes blank as he strokes his
chin thoughtfully in search of inspiration.
"When I have nothing to say, I say nothing," he
says.'

Winner

1984 Tour Avenir
1985 GP Nations, GP Marseillaise, Tour
      Haut-Var, Tour Piedmont
1986 GP Merckx
1987 GP Nations, Dauphiné Libéré,
      Critérium As, Tour Limousin
1988 GP Nations, Tour Lombardy, Tour
      Lazio

Winner (continued)

1989 Dauphiné Libéré, Four-days Dunkirk,
       Tour Lazio
1990 Tour Romandie, Championship Zurich
1991 Classique Alpes, Four-days Dunkirk
1992 Dauphiné Libéré
1993 Tour Limousin, Tour Mediterranean

Tour de France

Year	Place	
1985	36th	
1986	16th	
1987	4th	Yellow Jersey
1988	DNF	
1989	6th	
1990	49th	Stage win Millau—Revel
1991	4th	Stage wins Quimper—St-Herblain, Pau—Jaca
1992	DNF	
1993	40th	
1994	26th	

MOUNTAINS

For many, the mountains *are* the Tour. The flat stages are fast and furious, and the sprints are dramatic, but it's in the mountains that men prove themselves.

The first Tour climb was the BALLON D'ALSACE in 1905, which RENÉ POTTIER rode up all the way at 20km/h despite organiser HENRI DESGRANGE's assertion that nobody would. Desgrange may have exaggerated for the sake of publicity, but he was known to fear that riders would die in the mountains from over-exertion, exposure, brigands, or bears. The man who wore down his resistance to taking the Tour to the mountains was his colleague Alphonse Steinès. Desgrange sent him to survey the Pyrenees in January 1910 as much to get him out of his hair as to seriously consider the mountains.

Steinès looked at the AUBISQUE and persuaded Desgrange to pay 2,000 francs for repairs to the road. But the TOURMALET at 2,114m was impossible in mid-winter. He returned just before the race and persuaded a driver called Dupont to take him across. At 6pm the car ground to a halt in two metres of snow with four kilometres to go. Steinès, in city clothes, got out and walked. He fell several times, got lost, and stumbled soaked and exhausted through the darkness, until he was found by a police search party. It was a disaster he kept from Desgrange. In fact, he telegraphed from the home of *L'AUTO's* correspondent in Barrèges, 'Crossed Tourmalet. Road in good shape. No difficulty for riders. Steinès.'

Twenty-six big names immediately said they wouldn't ride. LUCIEN PETIT-BRETON protested, 'It's murder . . . those bastards want our skin!' GUSTAVE GARRIGOU said, 'People were telling us about avalanches, road collapses, of the killer mountains and the Thunder of God!' Riders told reporters, 'Desgrange is sending us into a circle of death!'

Desgrange sent them over the Peyresourde, Aspin, Tourmalet and AUBISQUE, all on unmade roads. But to protect his reputation, he himself stayed at home, saying he was unwell. Instead, he sent his deputy Victor Breyer and other officials to the top of the Aubisque. The riders were late and they grew worried. Finally a local rider, FRANÇOIS LAFOURCADE, got to the top. He stared at them exhausted and pressed on without speaking.

Then came OCTAVE LAPIZE. He turned to Breyer and the others and hissed, '*Assassins!*' before going on to win the Tour. Desgrange wasn't too upset. In 1911 he introduced the still higher GALIBIER and increased even his own bloated level of hyperbole: 'Oh Tourmalet [and other mountains]!' he declaimed. 'I don't hesitate to proclaim that compared to the Galibier you are but a pale and vulgar baby. In front of this giant there is nothing more for you to do but take off your hats and bow from down below.'

L'Auto wrote of epic battles through the 'mountains of hell', and good reading the stories were, too. Its reporters weren't there, of course, but then nor were the readers. And there certainly were dangers. There were frequent CRASHES and Desgrange urged riders 'to redouble their prudence, all through the mountains, because horses, mules, donkeys, oxen, sheep, cows, goats, pigs can all be wandering untethered on the road.' Climbs are rated 4, 3, 2, 1 and *hors catégorie*, in ascending order according to steepness and length. The assessment is arbitrary, and a medium climb will get a tougher rating if it comes towards the end of a stage rather than at the start. It's the perceived toughness that counts. Even so there are aberrations. The MADELEINE rarely changes its place in the stage, but has always been '1' and *'hors-catégorie'*. And riders are apparently getting weaker because climbs once rated '2' now sometimes appear as '1'. The Alps are longer but shallower than the Pyrenees, averaging gradients of about eight per cent, because they climb in hairpins. Pyrenean climbs may wind but they go straight up, which means sections with 11 per cent gradients.

The weather at the top of the mountains is often far different from that at the bottom, and descents can be bitter. Traditionally SPECTATORS hand out newspapers for riders to put under jerseys as insulation as they cross the summits, but lightweight waterproofs are taking their place.

Mountain-top FINISHES first appeared in 1952. The highest finish is the Col de Granon at 2,413m on the 1986 Tour. The greatest height achieved on the Tour is 2,802m at the Col de

Trivia note: The Col de Péguère was dropped at the last minute in 1973 when advisers said the descent was dangerous. The climb, between Bourg-Madame and Luchon, was 3,5km at a gradient of up to 20 per cent. Rumour said riders put pressure on the organisers for fear they'd be reduced to walking.

Restefond in 1962. The first rider over was FEDERICO BAHAMONTES.

BONUSES for climbs for the mountains competition began in 1934. The first climbers' competition came with the formal publicity CARAVAN in 1930. Paul Thévenin, as well as handing out samples, hats and hot drinks to publicise his Menier chocolate company, announced, 'I am offering 5,000 francs at the summit of each col, and a special prize of 4,000 francs to the first *TOURISTE-ROUTIER* who tops a summit alone with four minutes' lead.'

The first mountain TIME TRIAL was over the ISÉRAN from Bonneval to Bourg-St-Maurice in 1939. It was won by SYLVÈRE MAES.

(*See* EUGÈNE CHRISTOPHE, ISÉRAN, CLIMBERS, HAUTACAM, IZOARD, LUZ ARDIDEN, MEMORIALS, MONT VENTOUX, PUY-DE-DOME, RÉPUBLIQUE.)

FIRST IN THE MOUNTAINS

Alps Mar – *Alpes Maritimes and Provence*   Black For – *Black Forest*   Gd Alps – *Grandes Alpes*

Name	Climb/finish	Height	Year first used	First rider	Location
Agnes	col	1,595m	1988	Millar	Pyrenees
Aigoual	col	1,560m	1987	Contini	Cevennes
Allos	col	2,250m	1911	Faber	Gd Alps
Alpe d'Huez	finish	1,860m	1952	Coppi	Gd Alps
Amic	col	825m	1952	Géminiani	Vosges
Aravis	col	1,498m	1911	Duboc = Georget	Gd Alps
Arcalis	finish	2,240m	1997	Ullrich	Pyrenees
Les Arcs	finish	1,700m	1996	Leblanc	Gd Alps
Ares	col	797m	1910	Lapize	Pyrenees
Aspin	col	1,489m	1910	Lapize	Pyrenees
Aubisque	col	1,709m	1910	Lafourcade	Pyrenees
Aussières	col	1,057m	1976	Bellini	Pyrenees
Avoriaz	finish	1,800m	1975	Lopez-Carril	Gd Alps
Bagargui	col	1,327m	1986	Pensec	Pyrenees

Name	Climb/finish	Height	Year first used	First rider	Location
Ballon d'Alsace	col	1,178m	1905	Pottier	Vosges
Ballon de Servance	col	1,175m	1988	Millar	Vosges
Barraque de Bral	col	610m	1951	Koblet	Cevennes
Bayard	col	1,246m	1905	Maintron	Gd Alps
Berthiand	col	780m	1991	Chiappucci	Jura
Bettex	finish	1,400m	1990	Claveyrolat	Gd Alps
Bonaiga	col	2,072m	1974	Perurena	Pyrenees
Bonhomme	col	950m	1949	Coppi	Vosges
Bonnette – *see* Restefond					
Bordères	col	1,150m	1987	vanVliet	Pyrenees
Bourboule	finish	1,180m	1992	Roche	Massif
Braus	col	1,002m	1911	Georget	Alps Mar
Burdincurutcheta	col	1,135m	1986	Pensec	Pyrenees
Calvaire	col	1,144m	1976	Conati	Vosges
Canto	col	1,725m	1974	Perurena	Pyrenees
Castillon	col	706m	1911	group	Alps Mar
Causse de Larzac	col	825m	1960	Manzaneque	Cevennes
Cauterets	finish	934m	1953	Lorono	Pyrenees
Cauterets	finish	1,320m	1989	Indurain	Pyrenees
Cayolle	col	2,326m	1950	Robic	Gd Alps
Cerdon	col	595m	1907	Garrigou	Jura
Cevennes	col	1,018m	1960	Adriaenssens	Cevennes
Champ du Feu	col	1,100m	1985	Herrera	Vosges
Champ du Messin	col	1,010m	1961	Lach	Vosges
Champs	col	2,095m	1975	Merckx	Gd Alps
Chamrousse	finish	1,730m	2001	Armstrong	Gd Alps
Charbonnière	col	960m	1955	Vitetta	Vosges
Chat	col	1,504m	1974	Aja	Gd Alps
Chau	col	1,430m	1987	Fignon	Gd Alps
Chaubouret	col	1,230m	1950	Kübler	Massif
Chaumeil	finish	860m	1987	Gayant	Massif
Chioula	col	1,450m	1955	Pezzi	Pyrenees
Collet du Linge	col	983m	1957	Bergaud	Vosges
Colmiane	col	1,500m	1973	Torres	Alps Mar
Colombière	col	1,618m	1960	Manzaneque	Gd Alps
Coq	col	1,430m	1984	Arroyo	Gd Alps
Corbier	col	1,325m	1977	Wellens	Gd Alps
Cordon	finish	975m	1968	Hoban	Gd Alps
Core	col	1,373m	1984	Bernaudeau	Pyrenees
Courchevel	finish	2,004m	1997	Virenque	Gd Alps
Crans-Montana	finish	1,670m	1984	Fignon	Gd Alps
Cret de l'Oeillon	col	1,210m	1956	Bahamontes	Massif
Croix de Fer	col	2,068m	1947	Camellini	Gd Alps
Croix Fry	col	1,477m	1997	Jalabert	Gd Alps
Croix Homme Mort	col	1,163m	1971	Danguillaume	Massif
Croix-Morand	col	1,401m	1951	Ruiz	Massif

Name	Climb/finish	Height	Year first used	First rider	Location
Croix de la Serra	col	1,049m	1996	van Bon	Jura
Cucheron	col	1,139m	1947	Robic	Gd Alps
Deux Alpes	finish	1,644m	1998	Pantani	Gd Alps
Donon	col	727m	1961	Bergaud	Vosges
Envalira	col	2,407m	1964	J. Jimenez	Pyrenees
Éspigoulier	col	728m	1957	Stablinski	Alps Mar
Faron	col	665m	1957	Stablinski	Alps Mar
Faucille	col	1,323m	1911	Brocco	Jura
Fontasse	col	537m	1954	L. Lazarides	Cevennes
Font-Romeu	finish	1,800m	1973	van Impe	Pyrenees
Forclaz	col	1,527m	1948	A. Lazarides	Gd Alps
Forclaz de Montmin	col	1,150m	1959	Graf	Gd Alps
Fourches	col	970m	1971	Danguillaume	Massif
Galibier	col	2,645m	1911	Georget	Gd Alps
Glandon	col	1,924m	1947	Klabinski	Gd Alps
Grand Ballon	col	1,424m	1969	van Impe	Vosges
Grand Bois – *see* République					
Grand Cucheron	col	1,188m	1972	Merckx	Gd Alps
Grand St-Bernard	col	2,470m	1949	Bartali	Gd Alps
Granier	col	1,134m	1947	Brambilla	Gd Alps
Granon	finish	2,413m	1986	Chozas	Gd Alps
Grosse Pierre	col	923m	1913	Petit-Breton	Vosges
Guzet-Neige	finish	1,480m	1984	Millar	Pyrenees
Happach	col	1,040m	1971	Zoetemelk	Black For
Iséran	col	2,770m	1938	Vervaecke	Gd Alps
Isola 2000	finish	2,000m	1993	Rominger	Alps Mar
Izoard	col	2,361m	1922	Thys	Gd Alps
Jau	col	1,513m	1976	Delisle	Pyrenees
Joux-Plane	col	1,713m	1978	Seznec	Gd Alps
Joux-Verte	col	1,760m	1981	Alban	Gd Alps
Kreuzweg	col	708m	1967	Tosello	Vosges
Lachamp	col	1,320m	1996	Gualdi	Massif
Laffrey	col	900m	1905	Aucouturier	Gd Alps
Lans-en-Vercors	finish	1,410m	1985	Parra	Gd Alps
Latrape	col	1,110m	1956	Gaul	Pyrenees
Lautaret	col	2,058m	1911	Georget	Gd Alps
Lourdes-Hautacam	finish	1,560m	1994	Leblanc	Pyrenees
Louvesc	col	1,120m	1977	Agostinho	Massif
Luitel	col	1,720m	1956	Gaul	Gd Alps
Luz-Ardiden	finish	1,720m	1985	Delgado	Pyrenees
Madeleine	col	1,984m	1969	Gandarias	Gd Alps
Marie-Blanque	col	1,035m	1978	Pollentier	Pyrenees
Mende	finish	1,045m	1995	Jalabert	Cevennes
Mente	col	1,350m	1966	Galera	Pyrenees
Menuires	finish	1,809m	1979	van Impe	Gd Alps
Meribel	finish	1,750m	1973	Thévenet	Gd Alps

Name	Climb/finish	Height	Year first used	First rider	Location
Millau	finish	835m	1987	Clère	Cevennes
Minier	col	1,270m	1955	Caput	Cevennes
Mollendruz	col	1,185m	1952	Remy	Jura
Mongie	finish	1,715m	1970	Thévenet	Pyrenees
Mont-Cenis	col	2,083m	1949	Tacca	Gd Alps
Montgenèvre	col	1,850m	1949	Bartali	Gd Alps
Montiaux	col	1,030m	1954	Bahamontes	Cevennes
Montsalvy	col	780m	1959	Bahamontes	Massif
Moreno	col	1,065m	1951	Géminiani	Massif
Morgins	col	1,369m	1977	Wellens	Gd Alps
Mosses	col	1,448m	1949	Bartali	Gd Alps
Navacelles	col	600m	1984	De Wolf	Cevennes
Notschrei	col	1,120m	1971	Zoetemelk	Black For
Noyer	col	1,664m	1970	Delisle	Gd Alps
Orcières-Merlette	finish	1,838m	1971	Ocaña	Gd Alps
Ordino	col	1,910m	1993	Rincon	Pyrenees
Ornon	col	1,367m	1966	Otano	Gd Alps
Orres	finish	1,496m	1973	Ocaña	Gd Alps
Pal	finish	1,870m	1993	Rincon	Pyrenees
Perjuret	col	1,028m	1960	Graczyk	Cevennes
Perty	col	1,303m	1958	Dotto	Gd Alps
Petit-St-Bernard	col	2,188m	1949	Bartali	Gd Alps
Peyresourde	col	1,569m	1910	Lapize	Pyrenees
Piau-Engaly	finish	1,800m	1999	Escartin	Pyrenees
Pla d'Adet	finish	1,680m	1974	Poulidor	Pyrenees
Plagne	finish	1,970m	1984	Fignon	Gd Alps
Plainpalais	col	1,173m	1954	Dotto	Gd Alps
Plateau de Beille	finish	1,747m	1998	Pantani	Pyrenees
Plateau de Bonoscre	finish	1,375m	2001	Cardenas	Pyrenees
Platzerwassel	col	1,193m	1967	Aranzabal	Vosges
Pleynet	finish	1,445m	1981	Hiñault	Gd Alps
Plomb du Cantal	col	1,383m	1975	Merckx	Massif
Port	col	1,249m	1910	Lapize	Pyrenees
Port de Larrau	col	1,573m	1996	Virenque	Pyrenees
Port de Lers	col	1,516m	1995	Pantani	Pyrenees
Porte	col	1,326m	1907	Georget	Gd Alps
Portet d'Aspet	col	1,069m	1910	Lapize	Pyrenees
Portillon	col	1,298m	1957	Keteleer	Pyrenees
Portalet	col	1,794m	1991	P. Declerq	Pyrenees
Pradeaux	col	1,196m	1959	Huot	Massif
Pra-Loup	finish	1,630m	1975	Thévenet	Gd Alps
Prapoutel	finish	1,358m	1980	Loos	Gd Alps
Puy Mary	col	1,582m	1959	Bergaud	Massif
Puy-de-Dôme	finish	1,415m	1952	Coppi	Massif
Puymorens	col	1,915m	1913	M. Buysse	Pyrenees
République	col	1,161m	1903	Aucouturier	Massif

Name	Climb/finish	Height	Year first used	First rider	Location
Restefond	col	2,802m	1962	Bahamontes	Gd Alps
Revard	col	1,537m	1965	Gimondi	Gd Alps
Richemont	col	1,060m	2002	Sorensen	Gd Alps
Roche Vendeix	col	1,139m	1951	Ruiz	Massif
Romeyère	col	1,074m	1954	Bahamontes	Gd Alps
Roselend	col	1,968m	1979	Lubberding	Gd Alps
Rousses	col	1,140m	1957	Friederich	Jura
Rousset	col	1,254m	1984	Bernaudeau	Gd Alps
Ruchère	finish	1,160m	1984	Fignon	Gd Alps
Saint-Anastaise	col	1,160m	1996	Savoldelli	Massif
Saisies	col	1,633m	1979	Lubberding	Gd Alps
Salève	col	1,176–1,307m	1973	Ocaña	Gd Alps
Sauveterre	col	1,020m	1954	Varnajo	Cevennes
Schlucht	col	1,139m	1931	group	Vosges
Sentinelle	col	980m	1950	Géminiani	Gd Alps
Serereyde	col	1,290m	1955	Caput	Cevennes
Sestriere	col	2,033m	1952	Coppi	Gd Alps
Sie	col	1,020m	1954	Bobet	Cevennes
Somport	col	1,632m	1991	Leblanc	Pyrenees
Soudet	col	1,570m	1987	Forest	Pyrenees
Soulor	col	1,474m	1912	Christophe	Pyrenees
St-Gervais-Mt-Blanc	finish	970m	1992	Jaermann	Gd Alps
St-Nizier	col	1,180m	1950	A. Lazarides	Gd Alps
Struthof	col		1988	Vichot	Vosges
Superbagnères	finish	1,804m	1961	Massignan	Pyrenees
Super-Besse	finish	1,350m	1978	Wellens	Massif
Super-Lioran	finish	1,326m	1975	Pollentier	Massif
Tamié	col	907m	1933	Archambaud	Gd Alps
Télégraphe	col	1,670m	1911	Georget	Gd Alps
Tende	col	1,320m	1953	Robic	Gd Alps
Thorens	finish	2,275m	1994	Rodriguez	Gd Alps
Tosas	col	1,865m	1957	Bourles	Pyrenees
Tourmalet	col	2,115m	1910	Lapize	Pyrenees
Tourniol	col	1,145m	1987	van Vliet	Gd Alps
Treize Vents	col	600m	1953	Mirando	Cevennes
Turini	col	1,607m	1948	L. Bobet	Alps Mar
Val Louron	finish	1,420m	1991	Indurain	Pyrenees
Vars	col	2,110m	1922	Thys	Gd Alps
Vasson	col	1,700m	1950	Baeyens	Alps Mar
Ventoux	col	1,909m	1951	L. Lazarides	Alps Mar
Vignes	col	860m	1984	Prieto	Cevennes
Villard-de-Lans	finish	1,150m	1988	Delgado	Gd Alps
Vue des Alpes	col	1,283m	1948	Bartali	Jura

JOHAN MUSEEUW
b. Varsenare, Belgium, Oct 13 1965

Johan Museeuw won the World Cup in 1995 and 1996 and proved his place as a star of the one-day scene. The sports paper *Vélo* described this humble Belgian, who still trains with local amateurs and keeps his name listed in the phone book, as the brightest and most articulate rider its reporters had met. Where other stars go off to Spain or Italy or even Australia to prepare, Museeuw joins his friends from his club in Ostend and trains in the wind and rain at home in BELGIUM.

Museeuw began as a footballer, playing left winger for his youth team, Gistel, and in two years becoming best goal-scorer. His dream was to play for Club Brugge but his father, who runs a PEUGEOT garage in the grey village of Gistel, and paces Johan 180km a time behind a motorbike, had been a professional cyclist and saw his son's talent. Johan turned pro for GREG LEMOND's ADR team in 1988.

Museeuw's talent is more in classics than stage races, and he came close to abandoning cycling when sickness forced him out of the Tour in 1991. In 1996 he announced his retirement after a tough season left him exhausted. A week later, on October 13 1996, his 31st birthday, he became WORLD CHAMPION in Lugano, moving from 'hopeless' to 'world's best' in six and a half hours.

Then he broke a kneecap in the 1999 edition of Paris-Roubaix. What looked like eight weeks out of the sport turned into a season. There was

speculation that his leg might be amputated after it became infected. His comeback was in 2000, when he won Het Volk and then a second Paris-Roubaix, crossing the line alone with his leg (and knee) lifted to celebrate his recovery.

Winner

1991	Championship Zurich
1992	GP Harelbeke, National championship
1993	Paris-Tours, Tour Flanders, A Travers Belgique
1994	Amstel Gold, Kuurne-Brussels-Kuurne
1995	World Cup, Tour Flanders, GP Merckx, Championship Zurich, Four-days Dunkirk
1996	World championship, World Cup, Paris-Roubaix, Flèche Brabançonne, National championship
1997	Kuurne-Brussels-Kuurne, Three-days De Panne, Four-days Dunkirk
1998	Tour Flanders, Flèche Brabançonne, GP Harelbeke
1999	A Travers Belgique
2000	Paris-Roubaix, Flèche Brabançonne, Het Volk
2002	Paris-Roubaix, HEW Cup

Tour de France

1988	DNF	
1989	106th	
1990	81st	Stage wins Nantes—Mont-Saint-Michel, Brétigny-sur-Orge—Paris
1991	DNF	
1992	73rd	
1993	50th	Yellow Jersey
1994	80th	Yellow Jersey
1995	73rd	
1996	95th	
1997	DNF	
2001	DNF	

> **Trivia note:** Museeuw auctioned his Paris-Roubaix JERSEY on the internet to help a six-year-old girl with a rare illness. His jersey from the 1998 Tour of Flanders was also auctioned for charity.

NATIONAL TEAMS

The 99 riders who gathered outside *L'AUTO's* offices on Wednesday July 2 1930 were not wearing the colours of the companies that sponsored them but, for the first time, the colours of national and REGIONAL TEAMS.

Since its origin in 1903, HENRI DESGRANGE had insisted his race should be a contest between individuals. He had to accept that many riders would be sponsored, but he disliked the way SPONSORS had become adept at organising their teams to favour an individual rider within the team. That, Desgrange declared, falsified the result. The climax came in 1929 when MAURICE DEWAELE won with the help of team-mates, despite being sick.

'My race has been won by a corpse,' Desgrange sneered, meaning that a 'dead' man had been 'carried' to the finish by riders who should have been his rivals.

Desgrange took his revenge next year by organising the teams himself, with 40 riders representing their countries in teams of eight, 39 riding for French regional teams, and a further 20 riding as individuals, including the 1926 winner LUCIEN BUYSSE in his last Tour.

There were serious flaws in Desgrange's logic. First, he was merely replacing unofficial team racing by a formalised version of the same thing. To this objection he replied that the public would support national teams more enthusiastically than teams of mixed nationality. That would be particularly true in FRANCE, which hadn't won for six years and where his paper *L'Auto* had its commercial interests.

The second flaw was that, without any commercial incentive, sponsors would no longer pay for their riders' hotels, managers, masseurs and other expenses. Desgrange got over the problem by formalising the publicity CARAVAN, the cavalcade of advertising vehicles. He told companies, 'The Tour de France is a publicity medium without equal anywhere in the world. Ten to 15 million SPECTATORS cheer the riders along the roads. You can reach all these people by placing a publicity vehicle in the Tour.'

An informal caravan had followed the race for some years. Companies now signed up to move to the other end of the race, where they would catch spectators before they went home. But there were too few to pay for teams of the size Desgrange wanted. 'Why [teams of] eight?' Desgrange asked. 'I'm going to whisper something in your ear, confidentially. If you've got several hundred thousand francs that aren't doing anything, we can maybe increase the teams to 12.'

That first race had eight riders for FRANCE, BELGIUM, ITALY, SPAIN and GERMANY, and regional teams for the North, Normandy, Midi, Provence, Côte d'Azur, South-east, Alsace-Lorraine, Champagne and Ile-de-France [Paris].

National teams were a success with fans, who could now instantly recognise their riders. Desgrange considered his race had come of age, and had entered a golden period. But the system was unpopular with everyone else. Sponsors asked why they should pay their riders' wages when, for the biggest three weeks of the season, they didn't have a team. They wondered, too, why their riders should ride for commercial rivals just because they happened to be of the same nationality.

What interest, for instance, did the BIKE-maker Mercier have in helping a rider on a Helyett or a GITANE? And what of lesser riders, whose livelihoods depended not on their national team but on supporting a rider who might be the captain of a rival country's team? Would a Dutchman or a German chase JACQUES ANQUETIL, for example, if his salary depended on keeping the Frenchman happy? It was a problem multiplied by every combination of nationality and sponsorship across the race. And even if members of the same team could overcome their commercial rivalry, their personal ambition and sometimes dislike for each other was harder to overcome.

ITALY, with FAUSTO COPPI and GINO BARTALI, and France, with LOUISON BOBET and a whole team of potential winners, were particularly affected. (*See* ALFREDO BINDA and MARCEL BIDOT for how their MANAGERS coped; *see* too RAPHAËL GÉMINIANI for his disillusion in the 'Judas Tour'.) But in practice the system worked tolerably well. And in any case neither riders nor sponsors could object effectively, because just taking part in the Tour, let alone winning it, had become the objective of the year for most of them.

A problem that Desgrange couldn't solve was that some countries had a surplus of riders while others couldn't produce a whole team. While France, Belgium and Italy had to leave riders at home, others were pushed to get their one or two good riders a place. CHARLY GAUL, for instance, won the Tour in 1958 not for LUXEMBOURG but for HOLLAND-Luxembourg. The previous year he rode in a team named,

with obvious despair, Luxembourg-Mixed. It included two Portuguese, a German, and BRIAN ROBINSON of BRITAIN.

A solution of sorts came in 1937 with the reduction of individual entries and TOURISTE ROUTIERS. That made room for more small teams including Britain, or more formally the British Empire (*see* CHARLES HOLLAND). Individuals and *touristes* disappeared in 1938, and some countries got more than one team. France fielded the *Cadets* and *Bleuets* as well as a national selection in 1938. BELGIUM followed in 1939 with Belgium *B*.

National teams lasted until 1961. By then bike factories were struggling to survive at all, let alone to sponsor teams. They petitioned the organiser, JACQUES GODDET, claiming that if they were denied their advertising opportunity of the year, there would soon be no industry and no riders.

Goddet relented. 'The structure of professional cycling is unhappily in a weak state,' he wrote. 'And while I like national teams for their dignity and their symbolic value, it's obvious that this formula would have to be expanded to have any significance. At the moment only five countries can put up a worthwhile team. Trade teams, it seems to me, are therefore the most natural and balanced.' On June 24 1962 riders reappeared in their commercial colours for the first time since 1930.

The Tour has been for trade teams ever since, with the 'experimental' exceptions of 1967 and

1968, when Goddet's colleague, FÉLIX LÉVITAN, reverted to national teams because he believed the sponsors had been behind a STRIKE in BORDEAUX over DOPING checks in 1966. He wrote in *Miroir des Sports*, 'The battle of trade teams . . . has become so sharp that it's close to producing the same problems, all the defects, all the dishonest compromises, that led Henri Desgrange to take his brave decision [to ban sponsored teams] in 1930 . . . The 1967 Tour will be *moralisé*.' Nevertheless, sponsored teams returned on June 28 1969.

There has been talk of reverting to national teams every four years. This was Goddet's original dream, because he had accepted sponsored teams reluctantly. But it has never happened. The exception was the inclusion of COLOMBIA, which was the result of Lévitan's attempt to open the 1983 race to AMATEURS.

(*See* ALFREDO BINDA, LUIS HERRERA, TOM SIMPSON. *See* also PODIUMS for full list of winners by nationality.)

ALI NEFFATI
b. Tunis, Tunisia, Jan 22 1895, d. Apr 1974

Ali Neffati was an 18-year-old Tunisian who rode the Tour in 1913 after getting his first BIKE a night or two earlier. In those days the Tour was open to anyone, and Neffati rode well, always in a fez. That made him a wow with journalists, who recorded that on one of the hottest days – a 470km stage from Brest to La Rochelle – organiser HENRI DESGRANGE had asked him, 'You're not too hot, *mon petit*?' To which Neffati said, 'No, no *missié* [African dialect for *monsieur*] Desgrange, I'm actually rather too cold.'

That day was Neffati's undoing. He climbed off and neither finished that Tour nor the one the following year. Desgrange gave him a job as a messenger at the Tour paper *L'AUTO*, and he moved to its successor *L'ÉQUIPE* after the war.

Tour de France

| 1913 | DNF |
| 1914 | DNF |

GEORGES NEMO – See GEORGES GOFFIN

GASTONE NENCINI
b. Bilancino, Italy, Mar 1 1930, d. Florence, Italy, Feb 1 1980

Gastone Nencini was a tall, thin, dark-haired Italian who smoked heavily and was an amateur painter. Born in a village near Florence, he first came to international attention in the world championship at Varese in 1951, where his long solo break ended only in the last five kilometres. In 1953 he came second to his fellow Italian Ricardo Filippi, and turned professional.

Nencini rarely rode in single-day classics, and never succeeded in them, but he was always in the picture in stage races. He won the 1957 Giro after he, LOUISON BOBET and RAPHAËL GÉMINIANI attacked when CHARLY GAUL had stopped for a pee. Gaul lost his pink JERSEY as race leader and was so bitterly angry, especially with Bobet (whom he disliked for his arrogance), that he threatened to kill him. Gaul then pioneered peeing on the move, gaining the NICKNAME *Monsieur Pi-pi*. (*See* Gaul entry for more.)

Nencini had had a similar trick played on him in 1955, when FAUSTO COPPI and FIORENZO MAGNI attacked him while he was held up by a puncture. There were only two days to go and Nencini lost the Giro.

He won a stage in his first Tour in 1956, then two stages in 1957 when he won the MOUNTAINS competition.

Overall victory came in the 1960 Tour. The deciding day was the 191km stage from St-Malo to Lorient. ROGER RIVIÈRE of FRANCE attacked with 112km to go (*see* Rivière entry for the dispute with HENRY ANGLADE that led to it) and only Nencini, HANS JUNKERMANN of GERMANY and JEAN ADRIAENSSENS of BELGIUM could go with him. Rivière won and Nencini moved into yellow.

Rivière rode wherever Nencini rode. As a world-class pursuiter, he only had to hold Nencini until the TIME TRIAL in the last three days to be sure of stealing the Italian's *maillot jaune*. Nencini, on the other hand, was a classy CLIMBER and nerveless descender. (*See* HENRY ANGLADE for their downhill race in the Giro.) 'A madman *sans pareil*,' said Géminiani. He swept down the Col de Perjuret. Rivière tried to follow but fell over a parapet and broke his back. Nencini stayed in yellow and won by five minutes from his team-mate Graziano Battistini.

Nencini's record also includes second place in the 1964 Championship of Zurich, second in the 1960 Giro, and fourth in the 1955 world championship. It wasn't an untainted record, however. It was when he saw Nencini receiving a blood transfusion in his hotel room that the Tour doctor, PIERRE DUMAS, began his campaign against DOPING. (*See* Dumas entry for more.) Nencini was copying Scandinavian runners, who apparently used to store their own blood and transfuse it back later to boost their red blood cell count. Jean Bobet remembered Nencini offering pep pills to the bunch to get a chase started in a Giro d'Italia.

Nencini stopped racing in 1965, having never properly recovered from a CRASH in Menton-Rome. He died of cancer in 1980. A memorial race inaugurated that year was won by Beppe Saronni, but the race hasn't been held since 1997.

Winner

1956 Tre Valle Varesine
1957 Giro d'Italia, Tour Reggio Calabria
1960 Tour de France

Tour de France

1956	22nd	Stage win Montluçon—Paris
1957	6th	Stage wins Thonon—Briançon, St-Gaudens—Pau, and Mountains winner
1958	5th	Stage win Carpentras—Gap
1960	1st	Yellow Jersey
1962	DNF	

NICKNAMES

HENRI DESGRANGE realised from the start that nicknames would sell his race. Most riders were known only to fans, whereas the Tour was to be a race of excess which even the non-committed could appreciate. And so riders were named 'the Florist' and even 'the Heel-Pedaller', neither of which, it has to be said, caught on. Nor did 'the Bulldog' for MAURICE GARIN. But it set a trend.

Nicknames are usually coined by friends. In cycling they have often been dreamed up by reporters, and because newspapers are published in different languages, not all names cross frontiers. Some, like 'Big Mig' for MIGUEL INDURAIN, are unknown in the rider's own country, – it was invented by the same British journalists who failed to get LANCE ARMSTRONG called 'Big Tex'.

It is names that match a rider's appearance or character that stick. VICENTE TRUEBA was one of numerous riders called 'the Flea'. FERDY KÜBLER and MARCEL KINT were respectively 'the Eagle of Adilswil' and 'the Black Eagle' because of their noses. BERNARD HINAULT was nicknamed 'the Badger' by team-mates Georges Talbourdet and Maurice Le Guilloux because badgers are said to gnaw their victims' bones to a pulp.

LAURENT JALABERT was often called 'the Panda' because of his dark-ringed eyes, but he didn't like the name. 'My children keep seeing wildlife posters in shop windows and saying it's me,' he said. His more popular nickname of 'Jaja' referred to a glass of wine he drank in his first year as a professional. (*See* Jalabert entry for more.)

Bravery was celebrated. GASTONE NENCINI was 'the Lion of Mugello', and there have been numerous Lions of Flanders, helped by the symbol on the Flandrian flag. MARIO CIPOLLINI became 'the Lion King' for his long hair and flamboyant nature. Less flattering was 'Fat Dog' for PHILIPPE THYS because of his legs and the way he leaned over his bike.

FEDERICO BAHAMONTES was the 'Eagle of Toledo', where he lived. HENRY ANGLADE became 'Napoleon' because he was short and bossy. HUGO KOBLET, by contrast, was 'le bel Hugo' and 'the Pedaller of Charm'. RAPHAËL GÉMINIANI was 'le grand fusil' (Top Gun) thanks to LOUISON BOBET, who was called 'Cry-baby' because of an early tendency when confronted by disappointment.

EDDY MERCKX, Mr Merckx to most, was 'the Cannibal' thanks to his man-eating ambition (see Merckx entry for how it started). FAUSTO COPPI was il campionissimo, although the same title has been given to COSTANTE GIRARDENGO. RIK VAN LOOY was 'the Emperor of Herentals' and, before that 'Rik II', to pick him out from RIK VAN STEENBERGEN, who became 'Rik I'.

MARCO PANTANI became 'il pirata' because of his flamboyant headscarf. CLAUDIO CHIAPPUCCI was 'el diablo'. CHARLY GAUL, 'the Angel of the Mountains', was also known as Monsieur Pi-pi (see GASTONE NENCINI).

(And see HENRI CORNET, GEORGES GOFFIN, LUCIEN PETIT-BRETON for riders who used other names.)

WILLI OBERBECK
b. Hagen, Germany, Feb 21 1910

Few riders have been treated as badly by their team-mates as blond-haired Willi Oberbeck from Westphalia, Germany. When he set off through rain in the first stage of the 1938 Tour, from Paris to Caen, few knew who he was. He had ridden the Tour the previous year, but lasted only five stages. Maybe he had that in mind when he went off alone; maybe the rest had it in mind when they didn't chase.

Oberbeck ploughed on for hours, soaked and miserable. At Caen he had two minutes, and became only the third German to wear the yellow JERSEY. You would have expected his team to be delighted. Instead they abandoned him next day when he had a run of punctures. The German team was a collection of individuals interested in no one's chances but their own. Oberbeck, at the front one day, found himself alone at the back the next.

Not one member of the team stopped and SPECTATORS, officials and even riders were aghast at how he was left to wait for a MECHANIC. The result was that GERMANY lost their *maillot jaune* and came eighth in the team race. Oberbeck never rode the Tour again.

(*See* ÉMILE MASSON and KURT STÖPEL.)

Tour de France

1937 DNF
1938 DNF Stage win Paris—Caen, and
        Yellow Jersey

LUIS OCAÑA
b. Priego, Spain, Jun 9 1945, d. Mont-de-Marsan, France, May 19 1994

Few riders ever looked the equal of EDDY MERCKX. Most settled for coming second. But not Luis Ocaña, the little Spaniard who lived in south-west France; he cut Merckx down to size, only to be smashed in return.

Ocaña came to the 1971 Tour after winning the Tour of the Basque Country and the Tour of Catalonia. He had given Merckx a tough time in the Dauphiné Libéré before settling for second place, and he looked forward to lashing out again on many of the same climbs in the Tour. His campaign started on the stage from Grenoble through the Alps to ORCIÈRES-MER-LETTE, when he attacked after only 17km and took JOAQUIM AGOSTINHO, JOOP ZOETEMELK and GOSTA PETTERSSON with him. Pettersson tailed off on the Côte de Laffrey but the rest

built a lead of 3:10. And then Ocaña went off alone on the Col de Noyer after 74km.

Merckx had missed the move and begged the bunch to chase, saying it was in everyone's interest. But the peloton was enjoying his discomfort. The Belgian had given them too many hard rides for them not to revel in his suffering. If Merckx wanted to win the Tour, he'd get help only from his team-mates. His Molteni team threw itself into the fray. But while it made progress on the Zoetemelk group, it gained nothing on Ocaña, who had 5:25 on Merckx at the top of the Noyer. In fact, he was gaining on the flat as well as the climbs.

Ocaña finished almost nine minutes ahead of Merckx and took the yellow jersey. Merckx was not amused. The Tour moved on to the Pyrenees and he attacked repeatedly in appalling weather, Ocaña resisting and sometimes retaliating. They went together over the Col de Mente and began the descent. They hadn't done four kilometres when Merckx missed a left-hand bend, skidded in running water and crashed. Ocaña skidded behind him and ran into a low wall.

Both got up, Merckx replacing his chain and Ocaña taking a wheel from his MANAGER. The Bic team's service car was parked in the road and Zoetemelk, coming down behind, saw it only at the last moment as he raced down through the mist. He pulled out to avoid it and hit Ocaña instead, knocking him down. The Spaniard was lying on the road when Vicente Lopez-Carril and Agostinho also ran into him, hitting him in the kidneys. A helicopter took him to hospital at St-Gaudens, and Merckx, who by default became the new leader, declined to wear yellow next morning.

Two years later Ocaña won the Tour and six stages, finishing more than 15 minutes up on BERNARD THÉVENET, but it was a year Merckx didn't ride. It never became clear whether Ocaña was a flea who bit a bear, or the only man to have the match of Merckx.

He retired in 1977 and settled on a farm near Mont-de-Marsan, the French town to which his father had moved from Spain in 1945. But fortune was rarely with him, as his vines failed, he had two bad car crashes, one followed by a blood transfusion that went wrong. He slid into depression, developed hepatitis, and his wife Josiane left him. On May 19 1994 he shot himself at his home. There is a MEMORIAL to him at the site of the CRASH on the Col de Mente.

Winner

1968	National championship
1969	Midi Libre, Catalan Week, Tour Rioja
1970	Tour Spain, Dauphiné Libéré
1971	GP Nations, Tour Catalonia, Tour Basque Country, GP Lugano, Baracchi Trophy
1972	Dauphiné Libéré, National championship
1973	Tour de France, Dauphiné Libéré, Tour Basque Country, Catalan Week, Trophée Grimpeurs

Tour de France

1969	DNF	
1970	31st	Stage win Toulouse—St-Gaudens
1971	DNF	Stage wins Nevers—Puy-de-Dôme, Grenoble—Orcières-Merlette, and Yellow Jersey
1972	DNF	
1973	1st	Stage wins Divonne—Gaillard, Moûtiers—Les Orres, Perpignan—Thuir, Bourg-Madame—Luchon, Brive—Puy-de-Dôme, Versailles—Versailles, and Yellow Jersey
1975	DNF	
1976	14th	
1977	25th	

STAN OCKERS

b. Borgerhout, Belgium, Feb 3 1920, d. Antwerp, Belgium, Oct 1 1956

BELGIUM's stocky little Stan Ockers came second to FERDY KÜBLER in the 1950 Tour, and second to FAUSTO COPPI in 1952. Three years later he won the points competition. He never won the Tour itself, but he was a good single-day rider. He won the Flèche Wallonne in 1953 and 1955, and Liège-Bastogne-Liège in 1955, and he would have won Paris-Roubaix had he not declined to work against a fellow Belgian, RAYMOND IMPANIS.

His peak came with the world championship in 1955 at Frascati, near Rome, on a burning day which threatened to turn the event into a bore. There were 13 riders away with 80km to go, and the main field showed no inclination to chase. Ockers seized the moment, and bridged the eight minutes in one lap. He eased up, attacked again, and won alone to become WORLD CHAMPION.

Ockers held the hour record behind motorbikes at Antwerp TRACK, where he was always a draw. But he crashed behind a Derny motorbike on September 29 1956 and died soon afterwards. The track was filled for his memorial service.

His MEMORIAL, showing him riding out of a brick wall with a small flower garden beneath his wheel, stands at the summit of the Côte des Forges in Belgium. It marks his double win of the Flèche Wallonne and Liège-Bastogne-Liège in 1955.

Théo Mathy wrote in his history of Belgian cycling that Ockers and RIK VAN STEENBERGEN were cycling's equivalent of George and Lenny in John Steinbeck's novel, *Of Mice and Men*. George and Lenny were respectively a giant simpleton and his sidekick who repeatedly fell out but loved each other for the qualities the other lacked.

Winner

1941 GP Escaut
1946 GP Escaut
1948 Tour Belgium
1953 Flèche Wallonne
1955 World championship, Flèche Wallonne, Liège-Bastogne-Liège

Tour de France

1948 11th
1949 7th

1950	2nd	Stage win Lille—Rouen
1951	5th	
1952	2nd	
1954	6th	Stage win Bayonne—Pau
1955	8th	Points winner
1956	8th	Stage win Grenoble—St-Étienne, and Points winner

STUART O'GRADY
b. Adelaide, Australia, Aug 6 1973

Popular, round-faced 'Stuey' O'Grady was one of the Australian pursuit team which won the AMATEUR world championship at Hamar, Norway, in 1993. He became Australian amateur road champion the following year and travelled to Europe, where he won two stages in the Tour of the Italian Regions, and was the best YOUNG RIDER and best CLIMBER.

Winning a climbers' competition was out of character because O'Grady has made his name as a professional as a SPRINTER and TRACK rider. He won a world team pursuit gold at Bogota, COLOMBIA, in his first professional season in 1995, and came third in the individual event. He also won the fifth stage of the Circuit de la Sarthe that year, underlining his versatility.

He broke through at the Tour with a stage win in Grenoble in 1998 and then in late 1999 he was mugged after a meal with other riders at a restaurant in Toulouse. 'They hit me on the back of the head with a motor-drive from a windscreen wiper,' he said. 'I just about saw it coming but I didn't really know much about it.' It left him with a 5cm-long brain clot and two skull fractures. Team-mate Henk Vogels was also knocked unconscious.

O'Grady returned to Australia after treatment and tried racing. But his eyesight started faltering at the start of a race in Noosa Heads, Queensland, and months of partial blindness ensued. Then he lost feeling in his right side. He recovered slowly but completely, so much so that in 2001 he not only wore the Tour yellow JERSEY but only just missed the points title.

He took the race lead at mid-distance, lost it, then regained it on the rain-drenched stage to Pontarlier. That miserable day he got into a group of 14 which an apathetic bunch showed no willingness to chase. The group split, with ERIK DEKKER winning (35:54 ahead of the main field) and O'Grady coming fifth at 2:32. That gave him the jersey by 4:32, and an advantage of more than 35 minutes on the eventual winner, LANCE ARMSTRONG. O'Grady's lead was never going to last because the MOUNTAINS loomed, and climbing with professionals was a different prospect from taking on amateurs. But even so it wasn't bad for a man who months earlier hadn't been sure he'd walk again.

He focused instead on chasing the points competition. Only on the CHAMPS ELYSÉES did he lose it to ERIK ZABEL.

His friend JENS VOIGT calls him 'King of the Barbecues' and says, 'Stuart's an excellent rider, very professional in his job. But on the other hand he likes to mess around, laugh and joke, enjoy himself, have a good time. He's so open-hearted. He's someone who gives a lot. If you've got a problem, he'll set off immediately and do everything he can to help you. Stuart never does things by halves.'

Winner

1998   Tour Britain
1999   Tour Down Under, Haribo Classic
2000   Melbourne-Sorrento
2001   Tour Down Under

Tour de France

1997   109th
1998   54th   Stage win Valréas—Grenoble, and Yellow Jersey
1999   94th   Points leader
2000   DNF
2001   54th   Yellow Jersey and Points leader
2002   77th

ABRAHAM OLANO
b. Anoeta, Spain, Jan 22 1970

Spanish riders are suppose to be good CLIMBERS, poor descenders and appalling time trialists. Not Abraham Olano, who won the 1998 world TIME TRIAL championship but couldn't climb with the best. He set out to lose 15kg after turning professional and got down to 71kg, which made the MOUNTAINS easier although he was still no star. In fact, it wasn't that Olano couldn't climb, because in fact he came second in the 1995 Tour of SPAIN and won in 1998, the year he and other Spanish riders walked out of the Tour because of the FESTINA AFFAIR. He also came second in the Giro d'Italia. But he couldn't climb dependably.

Bad luck never seemed to leave him untouched. In 1992 his first team, CHCS, disappeared with money problems after only six weeks. In 1993 he crashed in the first week of the Tour and broke a collarbone. In 1994 he was named in a DOPING affair but emerged unscathed.

In 1995 he broke a collarbone again and couldn't ride the Tour. In 1996 he left the Mapei team after it had cut its budget. In 1997 he left the Vuelta early without saying why. In 1998 he crashed on the AUBISQUE in the Tour and subsequently left his Banesto team after being denied the team leadership. In 1999 he crashed again and cracked a rib. In 2001 he abandoned his attempt on the world hour record at San Sebastian after one test ride.

Olano's problem as a Spanish rider, like that of Italian riders since FAUSTO COPPI, has been SPAIN's longing for another MIGUEL INDURAIN. The fans turned against him when he couldn't fill this role, and his taciturn manner didn't help make amends. However, good luck and Indurain were on his side during the world championship in Colombia in 1995. As everyone watched Indurain, Olano attacked and rode to victory as his illustrious team-mate prevented a chase. Even a puncture in the final kilometres couldn't deny him the rainbow jersey.

Winner

1994	National championship, Tour Asturias
1995	World championship
1996	Tour Romandie, Tour Galicia
1997	GP Merckx, Bicyclette Basque
1998	World time-trial championship, Tour Spain, Tour Burgos, Tour Rioja, Bicyclette Basque, GP Merckx
1999	Tour Burgos
2000	Critérium International, Tirreno-Adriatico, Tour Valencia

Tour de France

1993	DNF	
1994	30th	
1996	9th	
1997	4th	Stage win Disneyland—Disneyland
1998	DNF	
1999	6th	
2000	34th	
2002	78th	

JEAN-PAUL OLLIVIER

Jean-Paul Ollivier is a much-respected commentator on French TV and a prolific author of cycling books. He was born in Concarneau, Brittany, and began reporting on races in 1961, every one of which he appears to remember. He made his first spoken radio report on his 20th birthday, May 22 1964, a year before covering his first Tour.

Ollivier moved from radio to television, where he provides background colour and on-the-spot reporting from a motorbike for the state channels France 2 and 3, as well as introducing a daily historical feature. He has covered cycling all his working life apart from one break as a political correspondent.

(*See* BROADCASTING for the history of Tour coverage; and *see* DANIEL MANGEAS for another remarkable memory man.)

BERT OOSTERBOSCH
b. Eindhoven, Holland, Jul 30 1957, d. Lekkerkerk, Holland, Aug 18 1989

Bert Oosterbosch was one of the best TIME TRIAL riders in the world, unmissable because of his carrot-coloured hair. The Dutch MANAGER Jan Gisbers liked to build teams around time trialists and took on Oosterbosch in 1978.

In 1979 he moved to the RALEIGH team to win the world pursuit championship, beating FRANCESCO MOSER on the Olympic TRACK at Amsterdam. He started three Tours but finished only in 1980, although he won three stages. Like many time trialists, he struggled over long distances and through MOUNTAINS.

Oosterbosch's professional career ended with a knee injury and meningitis in 1988, but he came back as an AMATEUR in July 1989. On August 13 he won his first amateur race, but five days later died at 32 of a heart attack. The circumstances remain a mystery but have been attributed to the blood-enhancer, EPO.

Winner

1980	Tour Luxembourg
1981	Four-days Dunkirk
1982	Tour Holland
1983	Étoile Bessèges, Tour America
1984	GP Harelbeke, Three-days De Panne

Tour de France

1980	36th	Stage win Flers—St-Mâlo
1982	DNF	
1983	DNF	Stage wins Châteaubriant—Nantes, La Rochelle—Bordeaux
1984	DNF	

HUBERT OPPERMAN
b. Rochester, Australia, May 29 1904, d. Melbourne, Australia, Apr 18 1996

Hubert Opperman, known as 'Oppy', was the great Australian who rode the Tour in 1928 because of a newspaper campaign mounted by the *Melbourne Herald*. Many years later the London *Daily Telegraph* wrote that he 'ranked alongside Don Bradman and the racehorse Phar Lap as an Australian sporting idol, but his fame at home proved less durable than theirs, perhaps because he went on to become a politician.'

Opperman, who was half English and half German, first rode a bike as a messenger boy with the post office, often working until 1am. He rode his first race at 15, and at 20 had become Australasian champion. The *Melbourne Herald* began its campaign in 1927 that he should ride the Tour with three Australians or New Zealanders and six Europeans. Their fare was to be paid by Dunlop, the tyre-maker.

The European part of the team was never engaged, and in the end Opperman, Harry Watson of New Zealand (described by RENÉ DE LATOUR as looking more like a priest than a bike rider) went with Percy Osborne, Frankie Thomas and Ernie Bainbridge to the VC de Levallois training camp run by the French Olympic trainer Paul Ruinart near Paris. There they prepared for the 1928 Tour by competing in the 320km Paris-Rennes race, where Opperman finished eighth to NICOLAS FRANTZ. Opperman then finished third of a three-man break in Paris-Brussels, after Frantz and the Belgian champion Georges Ronsse had attacked him repeatedly for miles.

It came as a shock to the Australians (and to others) that 15 stages of the 1928 Tour were to be team TIME TRIALS, none less than 119km and the longest 387km. The Australians were outclassed and outnumbered by rival 10-man teams. De Latour recalled, 'Even if I live to be 150 years old, I shall never forget the sight of Opperman being caught day after day by the various teams of 10 super-athletes, swapping their pace beautifully. The Australians would start together. Bainbridge would do his best to hang on, but the passing years had taken more of his speed and he would generally go off the back after 50 miles or so. Then if it was not Osborne it was Watson who would have to quit at the 100-miles mark. And almost daily, Oppy would be left alone for the last 50 miles.'

Opperman finished the 1928 Tour 18th at 8:34:25, Watson was 28th at 16:53:32, and Osbourne 38th at 22:01:49. Thomas and Bain-bridge abandoned on stages nine and fifteen respectively.

The ALCYON team generally started 10 minutes behind the Australians and would sweep up Opperman as they passed. Its MANAGER, Ludo Feuillet, was impressed by his doggedness and signed him. Opperman rewarded him by winning the 24-hour Bol d'Or race on the Buffalo TRACK in Paris, despite a sabotaged chain that snapped an hour after the start. The same thing happened to his spare bike. (*See* CHEATS for similar sawnthrough handlebars, loosened bearings and scattered nails.)

Opperman lost 17 laps in that race, but fought back to second place after 10 hours, and moved into the lead after 12 hours. He then made his first stop, having until then urinated on the move to the delight of the crowd. (*See* also GASTONE NENCINI and CHARLY GAUL.) He went on for another 79 minutes after the FINISH to break the 1,000km record as well.

He returned to France in 1931 and won the 1,186km Paris-Brest-Paris, which he rated his best win. He rode the Tour again that year but, weakened by dysentery, fell back from sixth to 12th place. He later came to BRITAIN where he broke the Land's End-John O'Groats record in 2 days 9hrs 1min; the 1,000-miles record in 3 days 1hr 52min; and London-York in 9hr 23min 00sec.

Opperman raced briefly after the war but retired in 1947 and went into politics. He became Australia's minister of transport and then minister of immigration, and later the High Commissioner to Malta. He was knighted in 1968, continued to cycle daily until he was 90. He died on his exercise bike in April 1996.

Winner

1924	National championship
1926	National championship
1927	National championship
1929	National championship
1931	Paris-Brest-Paris

Tour de France

1928	18th
1931	12th

ORANGE BRIGADE – *See* BRIGADE ORANGE

ORCIÈRES-MERLETTE

Orcières-Merlette in the Alps near Grenoble is 1,838m high and 14km long at an average gradient of 8.3 per cent. It will always be associated with the humiliation of EDDY MERCKX by LUIS OCAÑA in the 1971 Tour. (*See* Ocaña entry for more.) The little Spanish CLIMBER attacked after only 17km of the stage to Orcières, and not only dropped Merckx but, riding alone, gained considerable time on him despite a chase.

Ocaña took the yellow JERSEY at Orcières-Merlette only to crash in the Pyrenees and be taken to hospital. (And *see* JERSEYS for other riders who have left the race while leading.)

Ocaña won at Orcières-Merlette in 1971, LUCIEN VAN IMPE in 1972, PASCAL SIMON in 1982 and STEVEN ROOKS in a TIME TRIAL in 1989.

JAVIER OTXOA
b. Baracaldo, Spain, Aug 30 1974

Javier Otxoa won what *L'ÉQUIPE* called the 'Danté-esque', or infernal, stage from Dax to HAUTACAM in 2000, after a break that lasted 155km. The unknown Spaniard was riding only his second Tour, but got into an early break as the bunch winced under persistent glacial rain. He crossed the cols of Marie-Blanque, AUBISQUE and Soulor by himself as the others dropped away, and reached Hautacam, near Lourdes, to win only his second race as a professional. It won him the polka-dot JERSEY as best CLIMBER, although he lost it later to SANTIAGO BOTERO of COLOMBIA.

Behind him LANCE ARMSTRONG attacked JAN ULLRICH to set up his eventual overall win, which overshadowed Otxoa's success. He returned to the news the following year when he was badly injured in a training accident with his brother Ricardo after a car drove into them near Malaga. Ricardo died and Javier fell into a long coma with head and other injuries. There is a MEMORIAL where it happened. ERIK ZABEL placed his bouquet there after winning the points competition in the 2002 Ruta del Sol. Otxoa is slowly recovering and has talked about returning to cycling for the Paralymic Games in 2004.

Winner

2000 GP Villafranca de Ordizia

Tour de France

1999 86th
2000 13th Stage win Dax—Hautacam, and
             Mountains leader

PACERS

The enthusiasm that greeted the news of the first Tour de France in 1903 was also tinged with suspicion. Unlike other races, it appeared, there were to be no *entraîneurs*, or pacers, except for on the last stage. Competitors in other races sheltered behind relays of other riders, sometimes several pacers at a time, and eventually behind cars and motorbikes. SPECTATORS saw riders going as fast as they could, but in several ways the results were or could be falsified.

The quality of pacers depended on the MONEY available to pay them. And pacemakers were open to bribes not only from rivals but between themselves. Because of that, *L'AUTO* announced 'an end to the combines and bandits of every kind. Only muscles and energy will bring glory and fortune.' The remark was a dig at HENRI DESGRANGE's rival, Pierre Giffard, who employed pacers in Bordeaux-Paris, a race Desgrange had copied but failed to improve on.

Rule six in the 1903 Tour said, 'The race will be ridden without pacers or SOIGNEURS of any sort, nor with followers. However, pacing by bicycle will be allowed on the last stage, from Nantes to Paris. Any rider who uses any other form of pace, or trainer who uses another form of pace, will be thrown out of the race.'

While many were suspicious of pacers, critics doubted the Tour could be interesting without them. Others thought such superhuman effort impossible, and that riders would fall in exhaustion. Desgrange pointed out that 'doing away with pacers and soigneurs will lessen costs for the cycle industry and reduce the chance of CHEATING.' There would be 1000 'flying squad' judges on each stage, he said.

Desgrange's decision made for a better race, and spelled the end for pacemaking in most races, although it continued in Bordeaux-Paris until 1985. The winner of the 1903 Tour, MAURICE GARIN, who had been sceptical, congratulated Desgrange on his decision.

Pacemakers were abandoned for the whole of the 1908 Tour and never returned.

HIPPOLYTE PAGIE
b. Wervicq-Sud, France, Oct 21 1870, d. unknown

An official standing by Montélimar station on the second stage of the first Tour in 1903 was startled to see the Frenchman Hippolyte Pagie on the platform, sweaty and dust-streaked, holding his BIKE on his shoulder. Pagie was second to MAURICE GARIN, but had lost time in a CRASH 20km down the road at Loriol, and had become discouraged.

'I've had enough,' Pagie told the official. 'I'm quitting.'

'But you can't,' the other protested. 'You must press on.'

So Pagie agreed to ride 10km back towards Loriol, turn round, and ride back to Montélimar. In that way he repaid the 20km he owed the race. Pagie finished the stage and started again next day. But neither his injuries nor his morale had improved and he abandoned.

(And *see* ABDEL-KADER ZAAF for how that favour wasn't repeated after he fell asleep in mid-race in 1950; *see* LUCIEN PETIT-BRETON for an even more curious tale of trains and changed minds.)

Tour de France

1903	DNF

JOANNY PANEL
b. France, 1884

JOANNY PANEL is said to be the first rider to use derailleur GEARS in the Tour, having invented, according to cycling historian David Herlihy, a mechanism called the *Chemineau*, complete with indexed handlebar lever, ready for use in 1912. Panel used it to cross the Télégraphe, Allos and GALIBIER. But he didn't finish the Tour, and other riders, who considered gears suitable only for women and tourists, were persuaded it was unreliable.

Panel lived in St-Étienne, where the writer Paul de Vivie campaigned for gears under the pen-name Vélocio. De Vivie's MEMORIAL is at the top of the Col de la RÉPUBLIQUE outside the city, a climb that de Vivie made every day on the gears he championed.

Tour de France

1912	DNF
1913	DNF
1914	DNF

MARCO PANTANI
b. Cesena, Italy, Jan 13 1970

The most talented CLIMBER of the late 20th century, and also the most suspect, this troubled, jug-eared son of sandwich-shop owners initially made his name by winning the AMATEUR Giro d'Italia in 1992. Marco Pantani rode in that year's Olympic Games in Barcelona, and took a trial professional contract with the Carrera team. An unknown, he won two MOUNTAIN stages in the same weekend in the 1994 Giro. It was clear that a climber in the tradition of CHARLY GAUL and FEDERICO BAHAMONTES had arrived, a man who could ride his rivals off his wheel.

However, after winning two stages in the Tour in 1995 and finishing best young rider, disaster struck. Pantani was hit by a car during Milan-Turin in October 1995, and his lower left leg was broken in two places. He spent five months on crutches, and it seemed he would never walk again, let alone race. But the doctors were wrong. In 1997 he won two mountain stages of the Tour, including a second win at ALPE D'HUEZ, and came third overall.

Pantani started the Tour again on July 11 1998, faced by JAN ULLRICH on a course not considered ideal for climbers. Ullrich led, but Pantani came second and first in the two Pyrenean stages, then rode to a lone win at Les Deux Alpes to take the yellow JERSEY. He held on to win the Tour, the first Italian to do so since FELICE GIMONDI in 1965. The two embraced as Pantani headed for the press room. Pantani's team-mates dyed their hair yellow and Pantani, who was bald, dyed his goatee beard the same colour. The Italian president, Oscar Luigi Scalfaro, sent a message offering 'thanks of the Italian people for giving Italy this exceptional success'. Two thousand people in Cesenatico rode through the streets to celebrate their town's hero. A shop in Alessandria named a wine after him.

Then came a different disaster. In 1999 Pantani was thrown out of the Giro on DOPING charges as he was set to defend that title successfully. He had been discovered with too high a red blood cell count, the nearest doctors could come to detecting use of the blood-enhancing drug EPO. Subsequently, he and other Italians became embroiled in years of investigations by Italian police. The irony was that the 1998 Tour which Pantani won had been deeply tainted by the doping scandal known as the FESTINA AFFAIR. Yet he had passed through that unscathed.

But Pantani's career has never been the same. He rode the 2000 Tour and won on MONT VENTOUX, only to get into a row with LANCE ARMSTRONG about whether the American had let him cross the line first. Pantani said Armstrong had shown disrespect for his ability, Armstrong responded by being careful to refer to the Italian as '*Elefantino*', a hated nickname referring to Pantani's ears. Pantani's almost immediate response was to win a stage at Courchevel.

Pantani has since finished few other races and succeeded in still fewer. He became a recluse, and a short but brilliant career by a man as nervously brilliant on his BIKE as he was nervously inadequate off it seemed to be over. Because of his background he was not invited to the 2001 or 2002 Tours.

(And *see* BIANCHI.)

Winner

1998 Giro d'Italia, Tour de France
1999 Tour Murcia

Tour de France

1994	3rd	
1995	13th	Stage wins Aime—Alpe d'Huez, St-Orens—Guzet Neige
1997	3rd	Stage win St-Étienne—Alpe d'Huez, Courchevel—Morzine
1998	1st	Stage wins Luchon—Plateau de Beille, Grenoble—Les Deux Alpes, and Yellow Jersey
2000	DNF	Stage wins Carpentras—Mont Ventoux, Briançon—Courchevel

NAPOLÉON PAOLI

b. Campi Bisenzio, Italy, Feb 18 1892

The Frenchman Napoléon Paoli's contribution to the Tour was brief but entertaining. In the 1920 Tour he hit a donkey on the road to Bayonne, and ended up on its back as it galloped off the way he had come. Unable to get off, he clung to it until it damaged its leg and collapsed. Then he let go, ran back and carried on

racing, although with a sore stomach. But his relief lasted only a few moments. A rock fell from a cliff and hit him on the head. He struggled on until the TOURMALET where he gave up and fell asleep in a hut.

Paoli rode the Tour again in 1921, but still didn't finish, and never troubled the starter again.

(*See* CRASHES for other riders cursed with ill-fortune.)

Tour de France

1919	DNF
1920	DNF
1921	DNF

PARC DES PRINCES

The dingy Parc des Princes TRACK in western Paris (which was out in the country when it was built in 1897) marked the FINISH of the Tour from 1903 until 1967. It was demolished the day after ROGER PINGEON won the 1967 Tour there – half the seats had already been removed. The finish then moved to the PISTE MUNICIPALE. (*See* Piste Municipale entry and CHAMPS ELYSÉES for more.)

The Parc was a natural choice for the first Tour in 1903 – the actual finish was in VILLE D'AVRAY and the track appearance little more than a procession – because *L'AUTO*'s accountant, Victor Goddet, was its operator and HENRI DESGRANGE rode and promoted there.

The Parc des Princes proved so popular that in 1931 it was rebuilt to increase the seating from 20,000 to 50,000. Fashions changed, though; the gentle pink banking began to deteriorate, the crowds to dwindle, and in the end it was demolished. The site is now a concrete football and rugby stadium, home of the Paris St-Germain football team, opened in 1972.

GEORGES PASSERIEU

b. London, England, Nov 18 1885, d. Perray, France, May 5 1928

Born in London of French nationality, GEORGES PASSERIEU finished second to RENÉ POTTIER on the first stage in 1906 and, apart from a period after stage two when he relinquished second position to ÉMILE GEORGET and one day when Passerieu himself led the race, he held that place to the end.

More dramatic was the 1908 Tour, even though Passerieu came third this time rather than second. He won the opening stage from Paris to Roubaix, and was the only rider to manage the BALLON D'ALSACE and the Col de Porte without walking. He then won across more MOUNTAINS on the Metz—Belfort stage, and the 415km day from Brest to Caen, which he reached in 16 hours to beat the last man in by 23 hours.

Passerieu is credited with discovering PHILIPPE THYS and introducing him to PEUGEOT.

(And *see* DON KIRKHAM.)

Winner

1907 Paris-Roubaix, Paris-Tours

Tour de France

1906	2nd	Stage wins Nice—Marseille, Brest—Caen
1907	4th	Stage wins Grenoble—Nice, Caen—Paris
1908	3rd	Stage wins Paris—Roubaix, Lyon—Grenoble, Brest—Caen
1911	DNF	
1913	DNF	
1914	DNF	

PDM AFFAIR

On Monday July 15 1991, two members of the largely Dutch PDM (Philips Dupont Magnetics) team pulled out of the Tour. They were Nico Verhoeven and Uwe Raab, and both had ridden with a temperature. Then Jean-Paul van Poppel and MARTIN EARLEY were dropped soon after the race moved off towards Quimper the next day. They too retired, also with temperatures. Their German team-mate, Falk Boden, got to Quimper but outside the time limit.

That evening the team's doctor said that ERIK BREUKINK, RAUL ALCALA and SEAN KELLY had 'gritted their teeth today but if their fever doesn't improve in the night then I shall forbid them from starting from Quimper.' These riders then also abandoned, along with a further victim, Jos van Aert. At least one – Verhoeven – was kept in hospital.

Only riders were involved, and none of the staff. That ruled out food poisoning, because riders and officials had had the same meals. Explanations were hard to find. Word spread that doctors examining Verhoeven found nothing wrong except too few red blood corpuscles. JONATHAN BOYER, the team PR, said, 'Our riders received a glucose drip some evenings; it could be the infection came from that.' The team denied DOPING and the sport's governing body, the UCI, said nothing was proven.

Nine teams have walked out of the Tour. The first was ALCYON in 1907 after the MANAGER, Edmond Gentil, condemned as too lenient a penalty on ÉMILE GEORGET for changing a BIKE. The most recent was the mass abandonment in 1998 during the FESTINA AFFAIR.

(*See* also WIEL'S AFFAIR for another mysterious mass abandonment.)

CHARLES PÉLISSIER

b. Paris, France, Feb 20 1903, d. Paris, France, May 28 1959

Charles Pélissier was one of three brothers – a fourth died in the first world WAR – who delighted French cycling in the 1920s and 1930s. HENRI PÉLISSIER was the strongest (see his entry for more on the family), FRANCIS PÉLISSIER became a team manager, and the nattily-dressed Charles became, in 1930, one of the Tour's most spectacular stage-winners.

He took eight stages, including the last four, and finished seven times second and 18 times in the first three. To be precise, he won stages one, three, 10, 11, 18, 19, 20 and 21, came second on stages four, five, eight, 12, 15, 16 and 17, and third on stages two, six and seven. And yet he finished only ninth. Why? The answer was that French riders dominated cycling and that HENRI DESGRANGE had just introduced NATIONAL TEAMS to bring them together. The team was so strong that even MARCEL BIDOT wasn't selected, Desgrange saying that 'France needs first violins, not trombones.'

The strongest of the strong was ANDRÉ LEDUCQ and the team was so united that they chased for 70km after he crashed coming down the GALIBIER to make sure he won the sprint at ÉVIAN (*see* LEARCO GUERRA for fuller story). Leducq won the Tour by more than 14 minutes from Guerra and against such a margin Pélissier's stage wins could make little impression. He finished ninth at 1:04:37.

Winner:

1925   Paris-Arras
1926   National cyclo-cross championship
1927   National cyclo-cross championship
1928   Mont Faron
1933   Critérium As

Tour de France:

1929   28th   Stage win Évian—Belfort
1930   9th   Stage wins Paris—Caen, Dinan—Brest, Luchon—Perpignan, Perpignan—Montpellier, Belfort—Metz, Metz—Charleville, Charleville—Malo, Malo—Paris, and yellow jersey
1931   14th   Stage wins Vannes—Les Sables, Bayonne—Pau, Marseille—Cannes, Gap—Grenoble, Malo—Paris
1933   DNF
1934   DNF
1935   13th   Stage wins Lille—Charleville, Cannes—Marseille

FRANCIS PÉLISSIER

b. Paris, France, June 13 1894, d. Mantes-la-Jolie, France, Feb 22 1959

Francis Pélissier was the middle of three brothers (see also CHARLES PÉLISSIER and HENRI PÉLISSIER) who carved their name on French cycling. Francis was the weakest in the Tour, neither as pugnacious as Henri nor as good a sprinter as Charles. Of five Tours that he started, he finished only in 1923.

What earns him his place in history is his talent at spotting talent, in particular JACQUES ANQUETIL. He took the 19-year-old Norman into his La Perle team as an INDEPENDENT or semi-professional, precisely to win the 1953 Grand Prix des Nations TIME TRIAL. Anquetil obliged that year, and for another five years in a row, plus 1961, 1965 and 1966.

For all that his eye and technique earned him the NICKNAME of 'Sorcerer' he wasn't infallible. In 1954 he again fielded Anquetil for the Grand Prix des Nations but gave his attention to his fellow star HUGO KOBLET, who held the course record. Anquetil was upset, first because he found out only from the team mechanic and second because Pélissier's sorcery included the occasional illicit high-speed tow as he refilled his riders' food pockets from the seat of a car.

Anquetil never forgave Pélissier and not only won but bettered Koblet's record by 52 seconds. That evening he sent his winner's bouquet to Pélissier's wife, marked 'with deepest sympathies.'

Pélissier became the expert adviser for Bordeaux-Paris, the world's longest one-day race, which he himself had won in 1922 and 1924.

Winner:

1921   Paris-Tours, National championship
1922   Bordeaux-Paris
1923   National championship
1924   Tour Basque Country, Bordeaux-Paris, National championship
1926   Critérium As

Tour de France:

1919	DNF	Stage win Cherbourg—Brest
1920	DNF	
1923	23rd	
1924	DNF	
1925	DNF	
1927	DNF	Stage win Paris—Dieppe, and yellow jersey

HENRI PÉLISSIER

b. Paris, France, Jan 22 1889, d. Paris, France, May 1 1935

Henri Pélissier, together with his brothers Charles and Francis (a fourth brother, Jean, died at Argonne in the first world war) were the first to train for speed rather than distance – Henri rode speed sessions at dawn before training again in the afternoon. They were also the first to look after their diet and BIKES. A journalist once came upon Henri sand-papering his wooden rims. 'I can save 50gm,' he said, 'and on a moving part that's worth two kilos on the frame.'

The brothers neither drank alcohol during a race nor ate huge breakfasts. Until then riders trained endless daily distances, drank to numb the pain, and piled down food in the morning to ward off hunger. The result was that the START of races were sluggish, which was when the Pélissiers attacked.

All three brothers had good careers, Francis becoming a MANAGER and discovering JACQUES ANQUETIL. Henri was the best but also the most disagreeable. 'He treated every organiser and every factory [SPONSOR] as an enemy,' said Tour organiser HENRI DESGRANGE. He argued with Desgrange about the length of stages, around 360km in those days, insisting the future was with racehorses (riders like himself) rather than workhorses (Belgians). He could disagree about almost anything. And he died violently.

Henri Pélissier was a skinny semi-professional when LUCIEN PETIT-BRETON met him by chance in Paris in August 1911 and persuaded him to leave that afternoon for the Tour of Romany-Tuscany. He was so thin that friends called him 'Ficelle' (string). Pélissier crashed then, but went on to win Turin-Florence-Rome and the Tour of Lombardy. He won Lombardy in 1913 too, crashing at the FINISH with COSTANTE GIRARDENGO. Girardengo's fans set about him and he had to scramble up the judges' watchtower and wait for 80 policemen to force their way through the crowd to rescue him.

Pélissier came second to PHILIPPE THYS in his third Tour, in 1914, taking three stages. Then in 1923 he came first, at 34, after breaking away on the IZOARD. His win ended a run of domination by BELGIUM, and 25,000 SPECTATORS at the PARC DES PRINCES greeted him ecstatically. But he had a talent for upsetting people, once dismissing his rivals with, 'They are cart horses; I'm a thoroughbred.' Next day he punctured and the field galloped off like stallions, leaving him and Francis 30 minutes behind.

Desgrange called him 'a pigheadedly arrogant champion'. In 1920 Desgrange penalised him two minutes for leaving a flat tyre by the roadside, and Pélissier left the race in protest. In 1924 Henri, Francis and another rider abandoned at Coutances after Desgrange hadn't let him take off a jersey. They sulked in a café and spilled the beans about DOPING to ALBERT LONDRES. (*See* Londres entry for more.)

Pélissier's wife Léonie despaired of him, and shot herself in 1933. Henri took a lover, Camille 'Miette' Tharault, who was 20 years younger. They had lengthy rows. On May 1 1935 Pélissier cut her face with a knife. She pulled out the revolver with which Léonie had shot herself and pulled the trigger five times. At the trial she pleaded self-defence, and on May 26 1936 got a year's suspended jail sentence. It was the closest the court could come to acquittal.

Albert Baker d'Isy wrote in an obituary, 'He had few friendships because of his absolute opinions, and the way he expressed them cost him many friends . . . But they all bowed to the great quality of a champion they considered the greatest French rider since the [first world] war.'

The Pélissier brothers are remembered in a bas-relief bought by spectators at the PARC DES PRINCES and moved to the PISTE MUNICIPALE. (*See* LA SPORTIVE, STRIKES.)

Winner

1911	Tour Lombardy, Milan-Turin
1912	Milan-San Remo
1913	Tour Lombardy
1919	Bordeaux-Paris, Paris-Roubaix, National championship
1920	Paris-Brussels, Tour Lombardy, Circuit Battlefields
1921	Paris-Roubaix
1922	Paris-Tours
1923	Tour de France

Tour de France

1912	DNF	
1913	DNF	Stage win Cherbourg—Brest
1914	2nd	Stage wins Nice—Grenoble, Geneva—Belfort, Dunkirk—Paris
1919	DNF	Stage win Le Havre—Cherbourg
1920	DNF	Stage wins Cherbourg—Brest, Brest—Les Sables
1923	1st	Stage wins Cherbourg—Brest, Nice—Briançon, Briançon—Geneva, and Yellow Jersey
1924	DNF	
1925	DNF	

PELLOS

Sometimes a cartoonist finds a style which tells stories better than words. The French artist René Pellarin – 'Pellos' – drew frowning MOUNTAINS brandishing hammers at riders who dared to approach, wicked cobbles the shape of devils, and stars with extended noses, beetle eyebrows and deep cleft chins. His cruellest cartoons were the most sought after by his victims. JACQUES ANQUETIL had a gallery of Pellos cartoons the length of his stairs.

Pellos was born in Lyon in 1900, studied in Geneva, and started a satirical magazine when he was 16. He worked for several publications but particularly for *Miroir-Sprint* and *Miroir de Cyclisme*. He followed the first of 13 Tours in 1931, sometimes sitting in trees, caves or ditches to get the peace he needed. He died in 1988.

RONAN PENSEC
b. Douamenez, France, Jul 10 1963

Ronan Pensec – universally liked, and called '*Pinpin*' by everyone – made a name in his home region of Brittany, the heartland of French cycling, before winning the yellow JERSEY in 1990 after getting into a break with STEVE BAUER, CLAUDIO CHIAPPUCCI and Frans Maassen. Even though he had done nothing of importance before, the race was delighted to be led by him. He was never going to be a star, but nobody could have given more pleasure than Pensec with his floppy black hair, Jack-the-lad laughter, and much-vaunted love of Dire Straits and the Blues Brothers. GREG LEMOND said, 'I adore Ronan; he's so open and interested in everything.'

The 1990 race reached the MOUNTAINS and ROBERT MILLAR, his team's star CLIMBER, was deputed to look after Pensec. It even seemed for a while that he could cling to his lead all the way to Paris. It was not to be, but it took some beating as a fairy-tale possibility.

Pensec's wit and personality took him easily into a career as a television presenter in 1999. He explained the stories and history of the Tour, dressed in the style of the era he was explaining, campaigned for the things he liked, and protested at what he didn't, including EAR-PIECES.

Winner

1987	Étoile Bessèges
1988	GP Rennes, Route Sud
1992	GP Plouay

Tour de France

1986	6th
1988	7th
1989	58th

Tour de France (continued)

1990	20th	Yellow Jersey
1991	41st	
1992	52nd	
1993	47th	
1994	66th	

HENRI PÉPIN

b. France, Nov 18, 1864, d. Bordeaux,
France, 1914

The Baron Henri Pépin de Gontaud ... the very name has class. The story is that in spring 1907 this French nobleman told his valets to pace him round the Tour de France, staying at good hotels and eating at the best restaurants. He would pay them 4,000 francs, as much as the winner. The story has passed into legend.

Unfortunately it is only partly true. Pépin wasn't a baron, although he was rich enough not to work. The 'de Gontaud' wasn't aristocratic but merely his address: Gontaud is a village east of BORDEAUX. He didn't have valets, but he did employ two experienced riders as DOMESTIQUES – the expression was unknown then – and he and JEAN DARGASSIES and Henri Gauban, who had been caught the previous year taking a train (*see* CHEATS), joined the peloton of 112 at the Porte Bineau on July 8 1907.

Pépin was in no hurry, waving his boater and kissing the ladies. Eventually he told his helpers, 'Let us depart. But remember – we have all the time in the world.' They never separated. On the stage from Roubaix to Metz they took 12hr 20min longer than leader ÉMILE GEORGET and the judges were furious. The race was decided on points, so the judges had to hang on till everyone had got in.

At one stage the riders came across a figure in a ditch. 'My name is Jean-Marie Teychenne,' the wretch said. 'Like you, I am a *coursier*. But I have suffered the most terrible hunger. Leave me, I'm done for.'

'Nonsense,' Pépin shouted, and Dargassies and Gauban pulled him out. They set off again,

now a foursome, with Teychenne cleaned up and given a good meal at the next inn.

Pépin paid off his team between Lyon and Grenoble on stage five, and set off by train to Bordeaux. And so ended one of the most colourful incidents of Tour history. But Pépin was no dilettante. He rode seven stages in 1905, and set single and tandem records, as well as touring the world by BIKE.

The cover of *Le Cycle* in October 1894 showed a lean young man with intense eyes, a weak chin and a twizzled moustache. Studio pictures show him in the Oscar Wilde pose of 'gentlemen displaying their calves'. He didn't dirty his hands with MONEY. HENRI DESGRANGE wrote, 'Dear Mr Pépin, it is with the greatest pleasure that, according to the desire you expressed in your last letter, instead of sending you cash for the allowances owed to you, *L'Auto* will provide you with a medal to the same value.'

Pépin died 'of athleticism' aged 50 after riding the 1914 Tour, his third.

Tour de France

1905	DNF
1907	DNF
1914	DNF

LUCIEN PETIT-BRETON

b. Plessé, France, Oct 18 1882, d. Dec 20 1917

Only three riders have been known to ride the Tour under false names: Julien Lootens of BELGIUM who finished sixth in 1903 as 'Samson'; HENRI CORNET who won in 1904 (*see* entry for details); and Lucien Petit-Breton.

Lucien Mazan – his real name – was a dapper gent with a wide, greased moustache and carefully parted hair, the first rider to win the Tour a second time. His father, described as an optician and clock-mender, is supposed to have been a disappointed politician who fled from France to Argentina. There he lived and tested eyes or mended clocks in an introverted French quarter of Buenos Aires that followed all the big races back home and even organised some events itself.

M. Mazan forbade his 20-year-old son from racing. 'To him, to ride a bicycle was to bring dishonour on the family name,' Lucien said. 'So the first time I raced, without my parents' knowing of course, I was asked my name and I hesitated. I said "Breton . . . I'm a Breton" [meaning from Brittany]. But it turned out there was already someone in the race called Breton, so because I was younger they entered me as Petit-Breton.'

The tale of his first Tour in 1905 is extraordinary. The 1903 race had passed without incident, but the next year's Tour was marred by widespread cheating. (*See* 1904 AFFAIR.) Among the sabotage was the scattering of nails. This happened again in 1905 and organiser HENRI DESGRANGE wanted to cancel the race. He was finally dissuaded, but by then Petit-Breton, who had been stranded with no spare tyres, was so fed up that he headed for the station. There he bought a ticket for Paris. Getting out hours later, he happened on Robert Coquelle, a journalist, who said with some astonishment, 'I thought you were riding the Tour de France.'

Petit-Breton had had time to reflect and regret his decision. Coquelle said, 'Don't worry, I know Desgrange; he'll let you restart.' Petit-Breton turned back into the station and next morning stepped out of the Orient-Express at Nancy and rode to the START. Desgrange docked him 70 points, which put him last on the stage, but he finished the race and came fifth. (And *see* HIPPOLYTE PAGIE for another rider who continued after being found at a railway station.)

Petit-Breton won the Tour in 1907 – the same year he won the inaugural Milan-San Remo – and 1908. He set the world hour record at 41.110km in 1905, and won the new Tour of BELGIUM in 1908. He died as an army driver in the first world war when his car hit a vehicle approaching on the wrong side of the road. His son Yves was a MANAGER in the 1947 Tour.

(*See* ÉMILE GEORGET, HIPPOLYTE PAGIE, HENRI PÉLISSIER.)

Winner

1905	World hour record
1906	Paris-Tours
1907	Tour de France, Milan-San Remo
1908	Tour de France, Paris-Brussels, Tour Belgium

Tour de France

1905	5th	
1906	4th	
1907	1st	Stage wins Toulouse—Bayonne, Bordeaux—Nantes
1908	1st	Stage wins Roubaix—Metz, Nice—Nîmes, Toulouse—Bayonne, Bordeaux—Nantes, Caen—Paris
1910	DNF	
1911	DNF	
1912	DNF	
1913	DNF	
1914	DNF	

GOSTA PETTERSSON
b. Värgärda, Sweden, Nov 23 1940

Sweden's Gosta Pettersson, the first Scandinavian on the podium, looked set to light up cycling after he and his brothers Sture, Tomas and Erik won the world team TIME TRIAL championship in Uruguay in 1968 and in Czechoslovakia in 1969. They turned professional in ITALY and rarely left the country, although Gosta – the best of the four – finished third in the Tour in 1970. He also won the Giro in 1971. But the brothers' fame was short-lived and they vanished into history.

(*See* MAGNUS BACKSTEDT, LUIS OCAÑA.)

Winner

1970	Tour Romandie
1971	Giro d'Italia, Tour Appenines

Tour de France

1970	3rd
1971	DNF

PEUGEOT

The French car- and BIKE-maker has sponsored cycling through both divisions of the company. The bike factory has been in the Tour from the start, sponsoring LOUIS TROUSSELIER, the 1905 winner who gambled away all his prizes (see entry for details). PHILIPPE THYS was riding for Peugeot when he says he was given the first yellow JERSEY in 1913. Peugeot-sponsored riders won the Tour ten times from 1903 to 1983.

The firm began in the 18th century when Jean Pequignot Peugeot, who built water mills, opened a steelworks in Montbéliard with Jacques Maillard-Salins and his brothers Jean-Pierre and Jean-Frédéric. They made kitchenware, warehouse and hydraulic equipment, cars, motorbikes and bicycles. The trademark lion came in 1858, designed by Justin Blazer, a Montbéliard engraver. The first bicycle was made by Armand Peugeot in 1882.

In 1908 Peugeot riders pioneered group training in the winter sun of the south of FRANCE to prepare for Paris-Roubaix. Pascal Sergent, the race historian, says, 'They organised a training camp. Most people thought the idea was preposterous. On the other hand Cyril van Hauwaert and the ALCYON team remained faithful to their usual training over northern roads.' (It would be good to report that Peugeot won and proved Alcyon wrong; but in fact the winner was van Hauwaert.)

Peugeot in the 1950s had the WORLD CHAMPIONS STAN OCKERS and RIK VAN STEENBERGEN, in 1966 and 1967 there was TOM SIMPSON, the young EDDY MERCKX and FERDI BRACKE, and in the mid-1970s BERNARD THÉVENET. The firm also has a long association with British riders, including SEAN YATES and ROBERT MILLAR.

Its white jersey with a chequered black band – added to JERSEYS in 1963 – was familiar for decades until costs reduced Peugeot to a secondary role. The Peugeot team came to an end in 1986.

The Peugeot car factory became a Tour SPONSOR in 1954 when its Peugeot 203 convertibles replaced Jeeps.

(See BIANCHI, EUGÈNE CHRISTOPHE, GITANE, RALEIGH.)

RUDY PEVENAGE
b. Moerbeke, Belgium, Jun 15 1954

Rudy Pevenage of BELGIUM was one of JAN ULLRICH's bosses in the Deutsche Telekom team. But like many MANAGERS, he also has a record of his own.

The 1980 Tour started with three days in GERMANY, where BERNARD HINAULT made it plain he planned to win the Tour. The race then went into FRANCE and Belgium. All Belgians like to succeed in their own country, Pevenage no less than anyone else. He was a good sprinter but there were better. He also wasn't a good enough *rouleur* to get the yellow JERSEY in a lone break. Instead, he concentrated on intermediate sprints and collected enough BONUSES to take the lead in Liège.

No one expected him to keep it beyond the Belgian border. But Pevenage and his team clung to their lead for nine days. Not until the 14th day did Hinault take it back. And then he had to do it in a TIME TRIAL rather than by conventional attacks, which Pevenage had always managed to resist.

Pevenage came from Geraardsbergen, home of the Muur de Grammont climb in Belgian spring classics. But he was no CLIMBER and his chances of regaining the lead evaporated in the MOUNTAINS. Nevertheless, he reached Paris as best sprinter, thus achieving the biggest success of his career.

He became manager of the La William team when he retired and in 1994 joined Telekom. He joined Team Coast with Ullrich in 2003.

Winner

1980	GP Gippingen

Tour de France

1979	23rd	
1980	42nd	Stage win Frankfurt—Metz, and Yellow Jersey and Points winner
1981	75th	
1982	73rd	

PHOTO-FINISH

Until 1954 judges stood in a tower (called a *mirador*) and wrote the finishers' numbers onto pads. That changed in 1955 with photo-finish. The *mirador* is now called the *chrono-pole*. It's an elevated portable grey building with a round front. Two cameras placed face to face are linked to a photoelectric cell that triggers the shutter to a hundredth of a second as a rider passes. The picture is sent to a computer which can split tight finishes.

PHOTOGRAPHERS – *See* ROBERT CAPA, STRIKES

LECH PIASECKI
b. Poznan, Poland, Nov 13 1961

In 1987 the Tour started in Berlin, before the Wall had come down. The opening TIME TRIAL was won by Jelle Nijdam, but immediately behind him was a Pole, the moustachioed Lech Piasecki. A day later Piasecki became the first eastern European to wear the yellow JERSEY. He also won stages of the Giro d'Italia in 1986, 1988 and 1989.

Winner

1985   Peace Race
1986   Tour Romandie, Baracchi Trophy
1988   Baracchi Trophy
1989   Tour Friuli

Tour de France

1987   DNF   Yellow Jersey

JEFF PIERCE
b. San Diego, USA, Jul 20 1958

The 22-year career of AMERICA's Jeff Pierce peaked in the 1987 Tour when he won on the CHAMPS ELYSÉES. Altogether he rode the Tour four times, although always as a DOMESTIQUE. After leaving Europe he became the American

madison champion in 1995. After he retired he sold magazine advertising, and worked for the GT BIKE company, where he initiated a deal with the Belgian Lotto company to start a joint team for the 1999 Tour. In November 2001 he became vice-president of athletics at USA Cycling.

Tour de France

1986   80th
1987   88th   Stage win Créteil—Paris
1988   DNF
1989   86th

ROGER PINGEON
b. Hauteville, France, Aug 28 1940

The wonderfully hypochondriac Roger Pingeon, who bathed in diluted vinegar dosed with salt to rid himself of germs, was the winner of the 1967 Tour at the start of a two-year experiment with NATIONAL TEAMS.

Riding for FRANCE under MARCEL BIDOT, he was still unconsidered when he got into a break on the stage to Jambes. He then made the simple guess that the Belgians would want to win in their own country, so he jumped on when RIK VAN LOOY and BERNARD VAN DER KERCKHOVE made their move.

Before long they had six minutes. Then Pingeon committed the sin of attacking in the FEEDING AREA, taking advantage of other riders' lack of attention, and won alone to take the yellow JERSEY. Favourites such as JAN JANSSEN, RAYMOND POULIDOR and FELICE GIMONDI had missed the move and finished six minutes behind.

Janssen and LUCIEN AIMAR attacked Pingeon on the stage that ended at the top of the BALLON D'ALSACE, knocking Poulidor and Gimondi still further back. Gimondi and JULIO JIMENEZ tried again in the MOUNTAINS but Pingeon survived, his usual lack of self-confidence lessening the longer he wore the yellow JERSEY.

Pingeon's habitual uncertainty explains why he managed little else. He rarely believed in himself, always feared the worst, that he would puncture, that his GEARS would go into his wheel. Anything. He was a hypochondriac too, stuffing cotton wool into the keyholes of his hotel room to block out the light and then wearing eye shields. On rest days he stayed lying on his bed all day while others stretched their legs with some gentle kilometres. He rarely ate anything sweet on the rest day and never any meat.

He could, nevertheless, sometimes rise to the occasion. After all, few riders have won both the Tour de France and the Tour of SPAIN. But for Pingeon they were his only big wins. His all-consuming doubt wasted a huge talent.

(*See* PARC DES PRINCES.)

Winner

1967 Tour de France
1969 Tour Spain

Tour de France

1965	12th	
1966	8th	
1967	1st	Stage win Roubaix—Jambes, and Yellow Jersey
1968	5th	Stage wins Font Romeu—Albi, St-Étienne—Grenoble
1969	2nd	Stage win Thonon—Chamonix
1970	DNF	
1972	DNF	
1974	11th	

PISTE MUNICIPALE

The *'cipale*, as Parisians call the TRACK in the suburb of Vincennes, took over as the FINISH from the PARC DES PRINCES in 1968. The first winner there was JAN JANSSEN, who took his yellow JERSEY only in the closing TIME TRIAL. The last was EDDY MERCKX in 1974, after which the finish moved to the CHAMPS ELYSÉES.

Buildings at the Piste Municipale are named after JACQUES ANQUETIL, to whom there is a MEMORIAL at the end of the home straight. There is also a bas-relief in the driveway, commemorating HENRI PÉLISSIER and his brothers.

MIGUEL POBLET
b. Moncada, Spain Mar 18 1928

Miguel Poblet, a rare CLIMBER who could also sprint, became in 1955 the first Spaniard to wear the yellow JERSEY. His record includes 20 stages of the Giro; three stages each in the Tour de France and the Tour of Spain; Milan-San Remo in 1957 and 1959; and, by contrast, the Spanish TRACK madison championship in 1952 and the sprint championship in 1949, 1951, 1957, 1959, 1960, 1961 and 1962. Despite this impressive record his talents have gone largely unrecognised even in SPAIN. Maybe it was because his riding was workmanlike rather than spectacular. Angels are supposed to inspire, not just get on with the job.

RAPHAËL GÉMINIANI says Poblet was a victim of Spain's isolation from international cycling during the 1950s. Poblet's efforts to improve this situation were richly rewarded when he signed for an Italian businessman called Borghi, whose Ignis refrigerators led the Italian market. (*See* SPONSORS for Borghi's effect on the sport.) In 1959 Poblet won Milan-San Remo for the second time in three years. Borghi, who was already paying Poblet a bonus, went to the changing room where he found Poblet draped in a towel.

'Take this,' he said, handing him a key. Poblet went into the shower. When he came out, Borghi had left. Poblet walked out of the building and found a new Alfa Romeo outside. The key fitted.

Géminiani says, 'He never won as many races as his immense physical qualities justified. He was the equal of the great Belgian sprinters of the era and he could sometimes match the best climbers. This extremely gentle man more than modernised Spanish cycling.'

(*See* FEDERICO BAHAMONTES, JULIO JIMENEZ and MIGUEL INDURAIN for other Spanish riders.)

Winner

1952 Tour Catalonia
1955 Midi Libre
1957 Milan-San Remo, Milan-Turin

1959 Milan-San Remo
1960 Tour Catalonia

Tour de France

1955   26th Stage wins Dieppe—Dieppe,
              Tours—Paris, and Yellow Jersey
1956   DNF   Stage win Angers—La Rochelle
1957   DNF

PODIUMS

The word 'podium' is a shorthand way of describing those in the first three places and the winners of the subsidiary competitions such as those for MOUNTAINS and SPRINTERS. It refers usually to the final result but also less often at the end of stages. (*See* FINISH for more on where the podium is.)

The first podiums were in TRACK centres and more usually used for athletics races. The move to roadside finishes (see TRACK entry for why) led to primitive, crowded and seemingly not entirely stable constructions of scaffold and planks that lasted until recent times.

The modern Tour uses an inflatable grey podium like an oyster shell. Officials and dignitaries stand or sit in the wings, from where they are introduced to the day's winners by BERNARD HINAULT.

The podium is deflated soon after the post-race ceremony and re-erected at the next venue by the *BRIGADE ORANGE*. (*See* pages 292–294 for table of podium winners.)

WINNERS BY NATION	
France	36
Belgium	18
Italy	9
Spain	8
USA	7
Luxembourg	4
Holland	2
Switzerland	2
Denmark	1
Germany	1
Ireland	1

POLICE

The first dedicated police escort for the whole Tour was in 1933. Before then the roads were not closed to other traffic and local town police simply saw riders through tricky junctions and crowded city centres.

Since 1952 the job has been done by 33 motorcyclists and 11 car drivers from the Parisian Garde Républicaine, and around 20,000 policemen and gendarmes along the route. In France, the police operate in cities and are civilians; gendarmes have gold rather than silver buttons, are part of the army, and work in rural areas; the crop-haired riot police, the CRS, crack skulls anywhere and can be seen at the FINISH in Paris.

The 44 members of the Garde Républicaine chosen for the Tour are picked from those with at least two years' service who have escorted races such as Paris-Nice. Some, like Pierre Pothier, have been with the race for more than 30 years

Their role is to ensure the safety of the race and its fans, and every VILLAGE has a mobile police station to cope with crimes – usually thefts – within the Tour. French police who visited BRITAIN for stages at Plymouth in 1974, and Dover, Brighton and Portsmouth in 1994, were obliged to hand over their guns. SPECTATORS cheered every time a British policeman ordered a French colleague about.

MICHEL POLLENTIER
b. Diksmuide, Belgium, Feb 13 1951

Few riders have been so fascinating to watch as BELGIUM's Michel Pollentier (pronounced *Pollen-teer*), and few have hidden their talent so well with their poor riding style. JACQUES ANQUETIL said of one rider that he 'rode like a postman'. Pollentier was worse. He rode on the peak of his saddle, elbows out, body twisting, knees jutting. Style may have been lacking but the talent was genuine, and Pollentier won the Giro in 1977, the Dauphiné Libére in 1978 and the Tour of Flanders in 1980.

(*continued on page 295*)

PODIUMS

Year	Winner	Sponsor/team	Winning Team	King of the Mountains	Points winner
1903	Maurice Garin (F)	(a)			
1904	Henri Cornet (F)	(a)			
1905	Louis Trousselier (F)	Peugeot			
1906	René Pottier (F)	Peugeot			
1907	Lucien Petit-Breton (F)	Peugeot			
1908	Lucien Petit-Breton (F)	Peugeot			
1909	François Faber (Lux)	Alcyon			
1910	Octave Lapize (F)	Alcyon			
1911	Gustave Garrigou (F)	Alcyon			
1912	Odile Defraye (B)	Alcyon			
1913	Philippe Thys (B)	Peugeot			
1914	Philippe Thys (B)	Peugeot			
1919	Firmin Lambot (B)	La Sportive			
1920	Philippe Thys (B)	La Sportive			
1921	Léon Scieur (B)	La Sportive			
1922	Firmin Lambot (B)	Peugeot			
1923	Henri Pélissier (F)	Automoto			
1924	Ottavio Bottecchia (I)	Automoto			
1925	Ottavio Bottecchia (I)	Automoto			
1926	Lucien Buysse (B)	Automoto			
1927	Nicolas Frantz (Lux)	Alcyon			
1928	Nicolas Frantz (Lux)	Alcyon			
1929	Maurice Dewaele (B)	Alcyon			
1930	André Leducq (F)	France	France		
1931	Antonin Magne (F)	France	Belgium		
1932	André Leducq (F)	France	Italy		
1933	Georges Speicher (F)	France	France	Vicente Trueba (Spa)	
1934	Antonin Magne (F)	France	France	René Vietto (F)	
1935	Romain Maes (B)	Belgium	Belgium	Felicien Vervaecke (B)	
1936	Sylvère Maes (B)	Belgium	Belgium	Julien Berrendero (Spa)	
1937	Roger Lapébie (F)	France	France	Felicien Vervaecke (B)	

1938	Gino Bartali (I)	Italy	Gino Bartali (I)	Belgium	
1939	Sylvère Maes (B)	Belgium	Sylvère Maes (B)	Belgium	
1947	Jean Robic (F)	Ouest	Pierre Brambilla (F)	Italy	
1948	Gino Bartali (I)	Italy	Gino Bartali (I)	Belgium	
1949	Fausto Coppi (I)	Italy	Fausto Coppi (I)	Italy	
1950	Ferdy Kübler (Swi)	Switzerland	Louison Bobet (F)	Belgium	
1951	Hugo Koblet (Swi)	Switzerland	Raphaël Géminiani (F)	France	
1952	Fausto Coppi (I)	Italy	Fausto Coppi (I)	Italy	
1953	Louison Bobet (F)	France	Jesus Lorono (Spa)	Holland	Fritz Schaer (Swi)
1954	Louison Bobet (F)	France	Federico Bahamontes (Spa)	Switzerland	Ferdy Kübler (Swi)
1955	Louison Bobet (F)	France	Charly Gaul (Lux)	France	Stan Ockers (B)
1956	Roger Walkowiak (F)	Nord-Est-Centre	Charly Gaul (Lux)	Belgium	Stan Ockers (B)
1957	Jacques Anquetil (F)	France	Gastone Nencini (I)	France	Jean Forestier (F)
1958	Charly Gaul (Lux)	Holland-Luxembourg	Federico Bahamontes (Spa)	Belgium	Jean Graczyck (F)
1959	Federico Bahamontes (Spa)	Spain	Federico Bahamontes (Spa)	Belgium	André Darrigade (F)
1960	Gastone Nencini (I)	Italy	Imerio Massignan (I)	France	Jean Graczyck (F)
1961	Jacques Anquetil (F)	France	Imerio Massignan (I)	France	André Darrigade (F)
1962	Jacques Anquetil (F)	St-Raphaël	Federico Bahamontes (Spa)	St-Raphaël	Rudi Altig (Ger)
1963	Jacques Anquetil (F)	St-Raphaël	Federico Bahamontes (Spa)	St-Raphaël	Rik van Looy (I)
1964	Jacques Anquetil (F)	St-Raphaël	Federico Bahamontes (Spa)	Pelforth	Jan Janssen (H)
1965	Felice Gimondi (I)	Salvarini	Julio Jimenez (Spa)	Kas	Jan Janssen (H)
1966	Lucien Aimar (F)	Ford	Julio Jimenez (Spa)	Kas	Willy Planckaert (B)
1967	Roger Pingeon (F)	France	Julio Jimenez (Spa)	France	Jan Janssen (H)
1968	Jan Janssen (H)	Holland	Aurelio Gonzalez (S)	Spain	Franco Bitossi (I)
1969	Eddy Merckx (B)	Faema	Eddy Merckx (B)	Faema	Eddy Merckx (B)
1970	Eddy Merckx (B)	Faemino	Eddy Merckx (B)	Salvarini	Walter Godefroot (B)
1971	Eddy Merckx (B)	Molteni	Lucien van Impe (B)	Bic	Eddy Merckx (B)
1972	Eddy Merckx (B)	Molteni	Lucien van Impe (B)	GAN	Eddy Merckx (B)
1973	Luis Ocaña (S)	Bic	Pedro Torres (S)	Bic	Herman van Springel (B)
1974	Eddy Merckx (B)	Molteni	Domingo Perurena (S)	Kas	Patrick Sercu (B)
1975	Bernard Thévenet (F)	Peugeot	Lucien van Impe (B)	GAN	Rik van Linden (B)
1976	Lucien van Impe (B)	Gitane	Giancarlo Bellini (I)	Kas	Freddy Maertens (B)
1977	Bernard Thévenet (F)	Peugeot	Lucien van Impe (B)	Tl-Raleigh	Jacques Esclasson (F)
1978	Bernard Hinault (F)	Renault	Mariano Martinez (F)	Miko	Freddy Maertens (B)

Year	Winner	Sponsor/team	Winning Team	King of the Mountains	Points winner
1979	Bernard Hinault (F)	Renault	Renault	Giovanni Battaglin (I)	Bernard Hinault (F)
1980	Joop Zoetemelk (H)	TI - Raleigh	Miko	Raymond Martin (F)	Rudy Pevenage (B)
1981	Bernard Hinault (F)	Renault	Peugeot	Lucien van Impe (B)	Freddy Maerten (B)
1982	Bernard Hinault (F)	Renault	Co-op	Bernard Vallet (F)	Sean Kelly (Ire)
1983	Laurent Fignon (F)	Renault	TI-Raleigh	Lucien van Impe (B)	Sean Kelly (IRE)
1984	Laurent Fignon (F)	Renault	Renault (b)	Robert Millar (GB)	Frank Hoste (B)
			Panasonic (c)		
1985	Bernard Hinault (F)	La Vie Claire	La Vie Claire	Luis Herrera (Col)	Sean Kelly (Ire)
1986	Greg LeMond (US)	La Vie Claire	La Vie Claire	Bernard Hinault (F)	Eric Vanderaeden (B)
1987	Stephen Roche (Ire)	Carrera	Système U	Luis Herrera (Col)	Jean-Paul van Poppel (H)
1988	Pedro Delgado (Spa)	Reynolds	PDM	Steven Rooks (H)	Eddy Planckaert (B)
1989	Greg LeMond (US)	ADR	PDM	Gert-Jan Theunisse (H)	Sean Kelly (Ire)
1990	Greg LeMond (US)	Z	Z	Thierry Claveyrolat (F)	Olaf Ludwig (G)
1991	Miguel Indurain (Spa)	Banesto	Banesto	Claudio Chiappucci (I)	Djamolidine Abdoujaparov (Uz)
1992	Miguel Indurain (Spa)	Banesto	Carrera	Claudio Chiappucci (I)	Laurent Jalabert (F)
1993	Miguel Indurain (Spa)	Banesto	Carrera	Tony Rominger (Swi)	Djamolidine Abdoujaparov (Uz)
1994	Miguel Indurain (Spa)	Banesto	Festina	Richard Virenque (F)	Djamolidine Abdoujaparov (Uz)
1995	Miguel Indurain (Spa)	Banesto	ONCE	Richard Virenque (F)	Laurent Jalabert (F)
1996	Bjarne Riis (Den)	Deutsche Telekom	Festina	Richard Virenque (F)	Erik Zabel (Ger)
1997	Jan Ullrich (Ger)	Telekom	Telekom	Richard Virenque (F)	Erik Zabel (Ger)
1998	Marco Pantani (I)	Mercatone Uno	Cofidis	Christophe Rinero (F)	Erik Zabel (Ger)
1999	Lance Armstrong (US)	US Postal	Banesto	Richard Virenque (F)	Erik Zabel (Ger)
2000	Lance Armstrong (US)	US Postal	Kelme	Santiago Botero (Col)	Erik Zabel (Ger)
2001	Lance Armstrong (US)	US Postal	Kelme	Laurent Jalabert (F)	Erik Zabel (Ger)
2002	Lance Armstrong (US)	US Postal	ONCE	Laurent Jalabert (F)	Robbie McEwen (Aus)

(a) Riders' teams or sponsors not acknowledged in results
(b) Judged on time
(c) Judged on points

'The last of the real stone-hard characters of Flanders,' RIK VAN STEENBERGEN called him. Sadly his reputation is clouded by the events of 1978.

Pollentier – Tjelle to friends – had become *maillot jaune* by winning alone on ALPE D'HUEZ. He exchanged his polka-dot JERSEY for the yellow of leader. He should then have gone to the DOPING check. But there were rumours that he hadn't turned up two hours after the FINISH and that staff had gone looking for him.

When Pollentier finally got to the test caravan he was joined by José Nazabal and Antoine Gutierrez, two riders selected at random. Nazabal gave his sample but left the race that night. Gutierrez was next but had trouble getting himself ready. The doctor grew suspicious and pulled up his jersey to reveal a rubber bottle of pre-prepared urine and a tube. He then turned to Pollentier and found him similarly kitted up.

They were disqualified, suspended for two months – which cost Pollentier his CRITERIUM contracts – and fined the equivalent of about £5,000.

Pollentier stood on a balcony and announced he had taken something 'for his breathing', that he hadn't known whether or not it was allowed in FRANCE, and that he'd tricked the control to be sure. It turned out to be amphetamine, about which there was no doubt at all. Pollentier also said half the race was using 'products'. Pressed, he said, 'I'm not saying what they are using are drugs.'

He wrote to organisers FÉLIX LÉVITAN and JACQUES GODDET to say, 'The hardest thing to bear is the charge of sullying the Tour's standing. You know how I have committed myself to how I raced. That should have been the finest day of my career. Unhappily it will be the saddest. Please accept my sincere regret.'

He received 'thousands of letters, all very sympathetic, wishing me well and telling me to fight it and get back again'. There was even speculation that he had been set up because he was a threat to BERNARD HINAULT. FREDDY MAERTENS claimed Pollentier had been denounced from within his own camp. Writer Roger-Pierre Turine said, 'That day, believe me, Pollentier was sold in the way that slaves used to be sold.' The only certain thing is that he tried to trick the test.

After that, Pollentier dropped into mental gloom and sought treatment from a doctor in Ostend, under whose care he remained for a year. He had a brief revival and won the Tour of Flanders from FRANCESCO MOSER and JAN RAAS in 1980, but the flair had gone. He stopped racing on October 8 1984. 'I wasn't going so well. You know when you start as a racing cyclist it is not a career that lasts for ever. I was almost 34. You don't get to carry on much longer,' he said.

Pollentier – who learned English as a result of sharing hotel rooms with SEAN KELLY – lost money through unwise investments and went to work selling car tyres. He now helps run a club to bring on young talent.

Winner

1976	Tour Belgium, Montjuich, Baracchi Trophy
1977	Giro d'Italia, Tour Switzerland, National championship
1978	Dauphiné Libéré, Montjuich, National championship
1980	Tour Flanders, Flèche Brabançonne

Tour de France

1973	34th	
1974	7th	Stage win Orléans—Orléans
1975	23rd	Stage win Albi—Super-Lioran
1976	7th	Stage win Pau—Fleurance
1978	DNF	
1979	DNF	
1980	DNF	
1981	DNF	

HENK POPPE

b. Nijverdal, Holland, Jul 12 1952

Henk Poppe's only claim to fame is that he was the winner of the most unpopular Tour stage in decades, when in 1974 riders were flown from Brittany to Plymouth to race between roundabouts on an unopened bypass at Plympton.

Everyone but the organisers resented the long TRANSFER of cars, trucks and equipment by the ferry company which the stage was intended to publicise, and nothing of interest happened all day. HOLLAND's Poppe won the sprint, which few riders bothered to contest, and the race went home again. But Poppe never again made a mark, and in fact didn't even finish the Tour.

Tour de France

1974	DNF Stage win Plymouth—Plymouth

POST – *See* DYNAPOST

LUCIEN POTHIER
b. Cuy, France, Jan 15 1883, d. Apr 29 1957

Just 20 years old, Lucien Pothier was the surprise of the first Tour in 1903, when he came second to MAURICE GARIN. The margin of 2:49:45 between first and second was vast by modern standards – more than covered the first 121 riders in 2002 – but a pretty close-run thing when the 21st and last man came in at 64:07:22.

Pothier was therefore a man to be reckoned with in 1904, but he was disqualified along with Garin, Garin's brother César, and HIPPOLYTE AUCOUTURIER. Garin and Pothier persuaded GÉO LEFÈVRE, the chief official and reporter, to hand them food outside the FEEDING AREA. Lefèvre agreed to break the rules because Garin was in difficulties and he didn't want to risk the previous year's winner and runner-up dropping out through hunger.

Had that been all it would be easy to sympathise with the young Frenchman. But an inquiry established that Pothier had let his MANAGER pace him back to the race after a bad spell. (*See* 1904 AFFAIR.) He was banned for life but began racing again in 1907.

Tour de France

1903	2nd
1904	DNF
1907	DNF
1909	DNF
1910	28th
1911	20th

RENÉ POTTIER
b. Moret-sur-Loing, France, Jun 5 1879,
d. Levallois-Perret, France, Jan 25 1907

Demons always troubled René Pottier, an unsmiling man who said little and never joked. He was the Tour's first CLIMBER, winning the race in 1906 after taking four consecutive stage wins through the Vosges and the Alps. His dominance was such that he had an hour's lead on the stage from Grenoble to Nice, enough to stop at a bar for a jug of wine. He stayed there until the bunch caught him, rejoined the race, and won the stage.

In 1905 Pottier was first to climb the BALLON D'ALSACE, a MOUNTAIN that organiser HENRI DESGRANGE insisted no one could ride. Pottier rode all the way and next year even passed Desgrange's car on the same climb.

How many Tours he could have won we will never know. On January 25 1907 he was found hanging from a hook at the PEUGEOT clubhouse at Levallois-Perret. There was no suicide note, but his brother said he had died 'of sentimental reasons'. It emerged his wife had had an affair while he was away at the Tour. There is a MEMORIAL to him at the top of the Ballon d'Alsace climb.

Tour de France

1905	DNF	
1906	1st	Stage wins Douai—Nancy, Nancy—Dijon, Dijon—Grenoble, Grenoble—Nice, Caen—Paris

RAYMOND POULIDOR

b. Masbaraud-Mérignat, France, Apr 15 1936

The most popular rider since the WAR despite – or perhaps because of – never winning, FRANCE's Raymond Poulidor rode the Tour 14 times and finished in the first three on eight occasions. His NICKNAME, 'the Eternal Second', has stuck with him even though JOOP ZOETEMELK finished second six times to Poulidor's three.

Poulidor's problems were that he spent much of his career against the psychologically superior JACQUES ANQUETIL, and that he never believed in his own ability. But the contrast went beyond that. Anquetil, though he grew up on a farm, was portrayed as a city slicker. Poulidor, whose background was in fact no more rural, remained in the public perception the slow-talking country boy from the Limousin.

The image isn't entirely unfair. Poulidor hadn't even been on a train until he went off for national service in 1955, aged 19. By then Anquetil had already won an Olympic medal in Helsinki (in 1952) and, in winning the Grand Prix des Nations, had become the unofficial world TIME TRIAL champion while not yet a full professional. And Anquetil was more than a year younger.

The biggest clash between the two, and Poulidor's closest chance to beat Anquetil, was in 1964. The race reached the PUY-DE-DÔME on a day when neither man was at his best, Poulidor because he was on the wrong gear, Anquetil because he was struggling. The two rode shoulder to shoulder up the old volcano, even bumping shoulders as they struggled to demoralise each other. (See PUY-DE-DÔME for more.)

'I never again felt as bad on a bike,' Poulidor said. He finally managed to drop Anquetil just before the summit and crossed the line alone, although in third place. He couldn't see back down the climb from the FINISH and Anquetil took so long to come into the finish straight that he thought he had got off.

'For a moment I really thought I had finally won the Tour,' Poulidor said. Anquetil had been in the yellow JERSEY and Poulidor believed he

had done enough to get him out of it. He hadn't. The tussle came down to the closing TIME TRIAL, but only the romantic thought Poulidor could beat Anquetil at his speciality, let alone beat him by enough to win the Tour.

French newspapers, radio and television covered little else that day and the issue split France (just as GINO BARTALI and FAUSTO COPPI had also split ITALY) between Poulidor the humble countryman and Anquetil the smart-dressing slicker. (See Anquetil entry for more.) The division was so great that French politicians are still being asked whether they supported Anquetil or Poulidor in their youth. Their names have become political metaphors; Lionel Jospin, the prime minister until 2002, said, 'I was a big fan of Poulidor but it got on my nerves the way people celebrated the way he kept coming second. It went against my own winning instinct . . .' Thus Jospin effectively backed both sides and at the same time portrayed himself as a winner.

For a while Poulidor and Anquetil comunicated only through their wives, though their coolness was overstated and didn't last long. Paradoxically, the underdog factor meant that Poulidor's AGENT, Roger Piel, could get him a better deal than Anquetil in CRITERIUMS, a fact organisers asked him not to mention, or disguised by paying the surplus in cash.

Poulidor raced from the age of 16 to beyond his 40th birthday. ANTONIN MAGNE said, 'I know farms in the Limoges area where his picture hangs between Bernadette Soubirous [the 14-year-old saint who saw the Virgin Mary at Lourdes] and the picture of the family's late grandfather.'

He has only to pass for the crowd to cheer 'Poupou!' It's a nickname he accepts although he never liked it. It was coined by Émile Besson of L'Humanité in 1956 and allowed headlines like POUPOULARITE!

Poulidor finally followed the Tour in yellow in 2001, when he moved from the Maison du Café team to Crédit Lyonnais, SPONSOR of the maillot jaune, and worked in a yellow shirt. He rides a BIKE once or twice a week, although rarely for more than half an hour from St-Léonard-de-Noblat, the town of old houses and pleasant squares near Limoges where he grew up.

(*See* JOSÉ-MARIA ERRANDONEA, ADRI VAN DER POEL, ANDRÉ LEDUCQ, MEMORIALS.)

Winner

1961	Milan-San Remo, National championship
1963	GP Nations, Flèche Wallonne, GP Lugano
1964	Tour Spain, Critérium International
1965	Montjuich
1966	Dauphiné Libéré, Critérium International
1967	Montjuich
1968	Critérium International, Montjuich, Dauphiné Libéré
1969	Tour Haut-Var
1971	Critérium International, Catalan Week
1972	Paris-Nice, Critérium As, Critérium International
1973	Midi Libre, Paris-Nice

Tour de France

1962	3rd	Stage win Briançon—Aix-les-Bains
1963	8th	
1964	2nd	Stage win Toulouse—Luchon
1965	2nd	Stage wins Châteaulin—Châteaulin, Montpellier—Mont Ventoux
1966	3rd	Stage win Aubenas—Vals-les-Bains
1967	9th	Stage win Versailles—Paris
1968	DNF	
1969	3rd	
1970	7th	
1972	3rd	
1973	DNF	
1974	2nd	Stage win Seo-de-Urgel—St-Lary-Soulan
1975	19th	
1976	3rd	

POUR UN MAILLOT JAUNE – *See* FILMS

PRA-LOUP

Two stages have finished at the 1,630m Alpine ski station of Pra-Loup: in 1975, when it was won by BERNARD THÉVENET, and in 1980, when it was won by Jos de Schoenmaker. The Thévenet win was remarkable because he dropped EDDY MERCKX, changing a 58-second deficit to a 58-second lead, which set him up to win the Tour.

Pra-Loup climbs at a gradient of seven to eight per cent.

PRESENTATION

The Tour goes round the country generally alternating between clockwise and anticlockwise routes. The proportions of flat stages and MOUNTAINS, and the order in which they appear, as well as the STAGE TOWNS and TRANSFERS, are arranged with one eye on practicality and the other on commercial advantage. The SOCIÉTÉ DU TOUR DE FRANCE announces the route of the Tour after much rumour at a presentation in Paris in October. At the presentation stars past and present give opinions and make forecasts. The presentation for the 2003 Tour included all the Tour winners still alive, with the exception of ROGER PINGEON, who couldn't get there.

(*See ÉTAPE DU TOUR.*)

PRIZES

The first Tour cost 10 francs to enter and offered a total of 20,000 gold francs in prizes, with 3,000 francs going to the winner. It's never easy to work out values from so many decades and devaluations ago, but a workman in 1903 earned 25 centimes an hour, or 2½ francs for a 10-hour day. So the MONEY that MAURICE GARIN won represented more than nine years' pay for a manual labourer.

Paris—Lyon	1,500	700	350	200	100	100	50	50						
Lyon—Marseille	1,000	450	250	125	75	75	50	50						
Marseille—Toulouse	800	350	200	100	75	50	50	50						
Toulouse—Bordeaux	700	300	200	100	75	50	50	50						
Bordeaux—Nantes	1,200	500	250	125	100	75	75	75						
Nantes—Paris	3,000	2,000	1,200	800	500	250	200	100	50	50	50	50	50	15

There were also intermediate prizes, called *primes*, which judges were still sorting out after the race ended at VILLE D'AVRAY. The results were reissued several times before the winnings (in francs) were established as:

Maurice Garin	6,125
Lucien Pothier	2,450
Fernand Augereau	1,800
Rodolfo Muller	1,250
Léon Georget	900
Jean Fischer	795
Samson (Julien Lootens)	700
Hippolyte Pagie	700
Charles Laeser	700
Eugène Brange	600
Marcel Kerff	475
Alois Catteau	225

JEAN DARGASSIES, who finished 11th, seems not to have won anything. But to the rich it shall be given, so Garin was awarded 'a magnificent *objet d'art*' by *La Vie Claire*, and *Les Petites Annonces du Cycle et de l'Automobile* gave a 'medal of courage' to the Belgian, Marcel Kerff.

The price of bread is a standard in FRANCE because a baguette changes little in substance or demand. From that we can calculate that the first prize by 1990 was worth almost 21 times more than in 1903. But the pattern hasn't always been upwards. PHILIPPE THYS in 1920 won two and a half times more than EDDY MERCKX in 1970. In perceived value Thys's

prize may have been even greater because expectations were lower. FERDY KÜBLER in 1950 won less than SYLVÈRE MAES in 1939, and the value of first prize didn't change between 1950 and 1960. Its value had fallen by a quarter by 1970.

Things then moved towards the absurd. In 1976 the Tour began giving seaside apartments, sometimes but not always with extra money. The first such prizes, put up by the businessman Guy Merlin, were valued at 100,000 francs (£10,000). But things are worth nothing if you happen not to want them. And even if you do, the donor's estimation isn't necessarily realistic. All you can say is that LUCIEN VAN IMPE, BERNARD THÉVENET, BERNARD HINAULT, JOOP ZOETEMELK, LAURENT FIGNON, GREG LEMOND, STEPHEN ROCHE and PEDRO DELGADO would all be neighbours if they had moved into the flats they won. Hinault and Fignon won seven between them. Absurdity reached its peak in 1988 when Delgado won not only his place by the sea but a PEUGEOT 405, £50,000, and an '*objet d'art*'.

Today the Tour offers around 2,600,000 euros (£1,665,000). Stage winners collect 8,000 euros (£5,200), the second 5,000 euros, the third 3,000 euros, down to 80 euros (£50) for 30th. Each *prime* gives 800 euros to the first, 500 euros to the second, 300 euros for third. The toughest MOUNTAINS offer around 750 euros, the first rider on each lap on the CHAMPS ELYSÉES gets 1,600 euros, and the yellow and other JERSEYS pay 6,500 euros a day. At the end, the yellow jersey receives around 400,000 euros, the best sprinter and climber 25,000 euros, the first young rider and the most aggressive 16,000 euros each. The last man to Paris gets 400 euros.

(*See* DOMESTIQUES, LOUIS TROUSSELIER.)

TOUR DE FRANCE PRIZES (IN FRANCS)

Year	Prize total	Winner	Inflation index (the number of 250g baguettes the winner could buy)
1903	20,000	3,000	30,000
1904	21,000	5,000	
1905	25,000	4,000	
1906	25,000	5,000	
1907	25,000	4,000	
1908	30,000	4,000	
1909	25,000	5,000	
1910	25,000	5,000	
1911	30,000	5,000	
1912	32,500	5,000	
1913	39,900	5,000	
1914	45,000	5,000	45,452
1919	50,000	5,000	
1920	80,765	15,000	53,096
1921	80,000	15,000	
1922	80,000	10,000	
1923	100,000	10,000	
1924	100,000	10,000	
1925	99,000	15,000	
1926	109,000	15,000	
1927	100,000	12,000	
1928	100,000	12,000	
1929	150,000	10,000	
1930	606,000	12,000	22,324
1931	650,000	25,000	
1932	700,000	30,000	
1933	749,000	30,000	
1934	737,610	30,000	
1935	1,092,050	Not published	
1936	1,000,000	100,000	
1937	800,000	200,000	
1938	900,000	100,000	
1939	900,000	100,000	129,032
1947	4,580,000	500,000	
1948	7,000,000	600,000	
1949	12,000,000	1,000,000	

Year	Prize total	Winner	Inflation index (the number of 250g baguettes the winner could buy)
1950	14,000,000	1,000,000	112,992
1951	18,278,000	1,000,000	
1952	28,000,000	1,000,000	
1953	35,000,000	2,000,000	
1954	38,445,000	2,000,000	
1955	36,685,000	2,000,000	
1956	38,000,000	2,000,000	
1957·	40,000,000	2,000,000	
1958	40,000,000	2,000,000	
1959	41,710,000	2,000,000	

(N.B. 1960 saw the start of New Francs, each worth 100 times more than an old franc. Or, put another way, two zeros disappeared from the figure but the value stayed the same.)

Year	Prize total	Winner	Inflation index
1960	400,000	20,000	129,032
1961	500,000	20,000	
1962	583,425	20,000	
1963	550,000	20,000	
1964	543,200	20,000	
1965	414,275	20,000	
1966	424,700	20,000	
1967	541,300	20,000	
1968	574,850	20,000	
1969	600,000	20,000	
1970	605,525	20,000	34,780
1971	470,600	20,000	
1972	552,000	20,000	
1973	660,000	20,000	
1974	802,650	30,000	
1975	842,695	30,000	
1976	1,004,500	Apartment valued at 100,000	
1977	1,168,490	Apartment valued at 100,000	
1978	1,227,545	Apartment valued at 100,000	
1979	1,338,120	Apartment valued at 100,000	
1980	1,487,930	Apartment valued at 100,000	59,700
1981	2,324,000	30,000 and apartment valued at 100,000	
1982	2,207,220	30,000 and apartment valued at 100,000	

Year	Prize total	Winner	Inflation index (the number of 250g baguettes the winner could buy)
1983	2,304,260	40,000 and apartment valued at 100,000	
1984	2,561,450	40,000 and apartment valued at 120,000	
1985	3,003,050	40,000 and apartment valued at 120,000	
1986	4,500,680	180,000 and apartment valued at 120,000	
1987	6,284,700	180,000 and apartment valued at 120,000	
1988	7,567,250	500,000 and car valued at 118,000, apartment valued at 190,000, plus an '*objet d'art*' (total 1,300,000)	
1989	8,104,215	1,500,000	
1990	10,073,450	2,000,000	625,000
1991	9,017,850	2,000,000	
1992	10,162,950	2,000,000	
1993	11,000,000	2,000,000	564,120
1994	11,597,450	2,200,000	
1995	12,091,250	2,200,000	
1996	12,002,250	2,200,000	
1997	11,972,150	2,200,000	
1998	12,019,650	2,200,000	
1999	14,964,950	2,200,000	
2000	15,500,500	2,200,000	5,110
2001	16,470,750	2,200,000	

(France and most other West European countries switched to the euro in 2002. Prize values stayed the same.)

PROLOGUE

The prologue, a short TIME TRIAL run the day before the first long-distance stage, came to the Tour in 1967. It had first appeared in the Paris-Nice race as organiser Jean Leulliot's way of circumventing UCI RULES brought in to limit stage races after a succession of DOPING scandals. Leulliot held a time trial before the race and claimed it was to see who would wear the leader's JERSEY the following day, and therefore shouldn't count towards the total. The prologue became commonplace as a way of having a single leader on the first day rather than a mass of riders on the same time.

The first Tour prologue, at Angers, was won by José-Maria Errandonea of SPAIN. The prologue at Leiden, HOLLAND in 1978 – won by JAN RAAS – took place in a rainstorm, and there was chaos when half the field were told it wouldn't count. A row had broken out between local organisers and Tour organiser FÉLIX LÉVI-TAN over advertising banners for which, the Tour said, it hadn't been paid. An irate Raas won the next stage as well to ensure the yellow jersey was his.

Prologue specialists have included GERRIE KNETEMANN, THIERRY MARIE, Jean-Luc Vandenbroucke and the British rider CHRIS BOARDMAN. In 1988 the prologue was called the 'preface.' Riders start at one-minute intervals in an order decided by the organisers.

PUBLICATIONS

Eighteen sports papers circulated in 19th-century FRANCE, mixing sport, politics and opinion. The biggest, *Le Vélo*, lost advertisers when the editor, Pierre Giffard, who supported Alfred Dreyfus (falsely convicted in 1894 of passing secrets to the Germans), alienated one of his leading advertisers, the violently anti-Dreyfus Count de Dion. De Dion persuaded the businessmen Clément and Michelin to set up a new paper in direct opposition to *Le Vélo*, and appointed as editor Clément's publicity writer, HENRI DESGRANGE. Called *L'AUTO*, this appeared on October 16, 1900. (*See* entry for full story.)

Monthlies and weeklies also prospered during this period. *La Vie au Grand Air* devoted one issue to professional road cycling, and another in August 1914 covered all that year's Tour. *Miroir* opened in the rue d'Enghien in Paris in 1913. Containing little but sepia photos, it returned to sports coverage in 1920 after devoting itself to the war in 1914. It then changed to *Le Miroir des Sports* and appeared twice weekly during the Tour from 1924 and thrice weekly from 1934. Like *L'Auto*, it was closed after the liberation of France in 1944.

The superior *Match l'Intran* opened in 1927, closed in 1938, reappeared as a news magazine called *Match*, stopped during the Occupation, then restarted as *Paris-Match*. *Miroir-Sprint* was born in May 1946 from a Resistance magazine, *Le Jeune Combattant*, followed by a flurry of short-lived magazines which struggled, merged and struggled again. Among the most respected was *But et Club*.

The leading racing magazine in France now is *Vélo*, a monthly that is part of the *L'ÉQUIPE* group.

(*See* JACQUES AUGENDRE, PIERRE CHANY, RENÉ DE LATOUR, PELLOS, JOCK WADLEY.)

PUY-DE-DÔME

The Puy-de-Dôme, outside Clermont-Ferrand, is an old volcano and one of the steepest climbs in the Massif Central. The narrow road winds like a helter-skelter. It is a private road and only occasionally open to cyclists.

The climb's greatest day was July 12 1964, when JACQUES ANQUETIL and RAYMOND POULIDOR fought shoulder to shoulder for the yellow JERSEY, Anquetil on the mountain side, Poulidor nearer the ravine. Their rivalry had pushed newspapers to record sales and the police estimated the crowd on the mountain at 500,000.

Poulidor claimed he had wanted to check the climb, but when he had got there he had not been allowed beyond the barrier at the bottom. He had the wrong gears – 42 × 25 (3.58m) against the 42 × 26 (3.45m) that FEDERICO BAHAMONTES was using. His MANAGER, ANTONIN MAGNE, said, 'Raymond has lost the Tour because he lied to me [about his preparation for the climb].' Anquetil was simply riding badly. He let others break away during the day to deny the BONUS time to Poulidor.

The climb from Royat is five kilometres at a gradient of seven per cent, then a kilometre that looks flat but rises steadily, then five kilometres wavering either side of 13 per cent.

JAN RAAS

b. Heinkenszand, Holland, Nov 8 1952

Only three Dutchmen have won 10 stages of the Tour. JOOP ZOETEMELK and GERRIE KNETEMANN are two of the three and Jan Raas the other.

Raas, recognisable by his glasses and thinning hair, won the Dutch AMATEUR championship in 1974 and joined the emerging RALEIGH team. He could ride stage races and also classics, of which he won 14, including the Amstel Gold Race five times – four in a row from 1977. It became known as the Amstel Gold Raas. Raas could ride at crippling speed in the last kilometres and still produce a sprint.

In 1978 he won three Tour stages and wore the yellow JERSEY for a day – although he should have had two jerseys. The PROLOGUE in Leiden was a chaotic affair because not all the riders had been told that the danger caused by a sudden rain storm on cobbled streets meant the times wouldn't count. (See PROLOGUE for more.) Raas's MANAGER, Peter Post, hadn't told him the news for fear he would ease back.

It was the start of an eventful Tour. At Valence d'Agen riders went on STRIKE to protest at late nights and early starts, and the leader, MICHEL POLLENTIER, was caught defrauding the dope control at ALPE D'HUEZ.

Against that, the fact that Raas got no yellow jersey for winning at Leiden was little to shout about. And anyway he made up for it next morning by winning the stage to St-Willebrord, before the Tour crossed into BELGIUM. (See WIM VAN EST for St-Willebrord's most famous resident and Holland's first *maillot jaune*; and see also WOUT WAGTMANS.)

Raas's career ended with a CRASH on the descent of the Cipressa in Milan-San Remo in 1984. The back injury he received never got better and he stopped racing the following year. He works now as team MANAGER for the Dutch Rabobank squad.

Winner

1976	National championship
1977	Milan-San Remo, Amstel Gold
1978	Paris-Brussels, Paris-Tours, Amstel Gold
1979	World championship, Amstel Gold, Tour Flanders, GP Harelbeke, Tour Holland
1980	GP Harelbeke, Kuurne-Brussels-Kuurne, Amstel Gold
1981	Het Volk, Ghent-Wevelgem, Paris-Tours, Étoile Bessèges, GP Harelbeke
1982	Amstel Gold, Paris-Roubaix, A Travers Belgique
1983	Tour Flanders, Kuurne-Brussels-Kuurne, GP Marseillaise, National championship
1984	National championship

1976	83rd	
1977	DNF	Stage win Bordeaux—Limoges
1978	24th	Stage win Leiden—Leiden, Leiden—St Willebrord, Epernay—Senlis, and Yellow Jersey
1979	DNF	Stage win Neuville-de-Poitou—Angers
1980	DNF	Stage win Frankfurt—Wiesbaden, Beauvais—Rouen, St-Malo—Nantes
1982	DNF	Stage win Lille—Lille
1983	DNF	
1984	DNF	Stage win Nantes—Bordeaux

RADIO – *See* BROADCASTING

RADIO TOUR

The idea of a private radio service between Tour officials and the rest of the race convoy occurred to FÉLIX LÉVITAN in the 1950s, and became established over several years. It was arranged that Jacques Marchand, editor-in-chief of *L'ÉQUIPE*, should sit in organiser JACQUES GODDET's car behind the peloton, getting his information from the BLACKBOARD MAN.

Valve radio equipment of the time was unreliable, and the service was better known for breakdowns than bulletins. Goddet often found himself lagging behind the riders, officials and journalists he was supposed to inform. In the 1960s, rattle-proof transistors and more powerful transmitters improved matters.

The current organiser, JEAN-MARIE LEBLANC, was the voice of Radio Tour from 1982 to 1987. He recalls Goddet demanding, '*Animez, mon vieux, animez!*' ('Make it livelier!'), even if little was happening. Leblanc was followed by Philippe Bouvet. The current Monsieur Radio-Tour is John Lelangue. He hands the microphone to Leblanc as the race starts and lets him speak about the stage, safety, and outstanding incidents. Then Leblanc

introduces the day's guests before handing back to Lelangue, who sits beside the day-to-day organiser, Jean-François Pescheux.

Lelangue – which with a twist of grammar means 'the Tongue' – gives the news in French, Italian, Spanish and English. His station is also open to Leblanc at the head of the race and to the officials clearing a path several kilometres ahead.

Broadcasters use Radio Tour's bulletins to help their commentaries, and MANAGERS radio its details to riders' EARPIECES. The Tour organisation places televisions in team cars to keep managers abreast of the race, but pictures come mainly from the front of the race. Radio Tour by contrast gives a wider picture of riders abandoning, MOUNTAINS approaching, and other information.

RALEIGH

The French magazine *Vélo* named the Raleigh team (1976–1983) the greatest in history, citing two world road championships (GERRIE KNETEMANN in 1978, JAN RAAS in 1979), the 1980 Tour de France (JOOP ZOETEMELK), the Amstel Gold Race in 1978, 1979 and 1980, the Tour of Flanders in 1979, and Ghent-Wevelgem in 1980 as its greatest triumphs. Raleigh also collected 15 world championships, five World Cups, 77 major tour stages, the Giro d'Italia, 37 classics and 55 national championships. *Vélo* said that Raleigh 'imposed their astonishing collective force from the moment the team was created.... [MANAGER Peter Post] maintained great cohesion in a team rich with individual strengths.'

The company began in 1887 after a Nottingham doctor told the entrepreneur and traveller Frank Bowden that he should ride a bicycle for his health. Bowden walked through Raleigh Street, Nottingham, to buy one from Messrs Woodhead, Angois and Ellis. It impressed him so much that he bought the factory, which he moved to a four-storey building in Russell Street and called Raleigh Cycles after the road he'd entered three years earlier. In six years he had expanded his firm from three machines a day to the biggest BIKE factory in the world.

Raleigh peaked before the WAR and then went into a decline with the rest of the industry. It and the rival British Cycle Corporation, owned by Tube Investments, began buying failing factories, until in the end BCC bought Raleigh.

Raleigh had sponsored the world sprint champion Reg Harris, and after his retirement continued, at the suggestion of a Sheffield rider called George Shaw, to sponsor teams of semi-professionals such as ARTHUR METCALFE, who in 1967 and 1968 rode the Tour during his holiday from work.

Tube Investments supplied the money and ambition for an international team managed first in England by Shaw, and then in HOLLAND by Peter Post (riders shuttled across the Channel and North Sea). Discipline was so great that the abbreviation TI-R (for Tube Investments-Raleigh) earned it the name '*tirgruppe*' or 'firing squad' from riders. (*See* ALCYON for discipline that brought it the nickname 'the prison'.)

Costs became too much for Raleigh in 1983 and it withdrew from Continental sponsorship. The team was taken over by its co-sponsor, Panasonic. Raleigh's decline continued until it sold its bike-making machinery in Nottingham in 2000, and ended all bike production in Britain in 2002.

The company's bike collection can be found at Brooklands Motor Museum, south of London.

GASTON REBRY
b. Rollegem-Kapelle, Belgium, Jan 29 1905, d. Jul 3 1953

In 1931 the Belgian Gaston Rebry – 'the Bulldog' because of his squat, small size – lost the Tour as the result of an unsigned letter to ANTONIN MAGNE. The letter came from Rebry's own village, and warned Magne that Rebry and Jef Demuysère were planning to

attack on the penultimate stage to Malo-les-Bains. The Belgians made their move, but the Frenchmen were ready and Magne kept the yellow JERSEY. The writer of the letter, who indicated by his words that he must have known Rebry's mother, was never traced. (*See* ANTONIN MAGNE for the full story.)

Rebry was a tireless, aggressive rider but couldn't sprint, which meant he had to attack repeatedly to finish alone or in small groups. That was what he did to win Paris-Roubaix in 1931; in 1934 he won again after the first man across the line, ROGER LAPÉBIE, was disqualified for changing BIKES. In 1935 he won by 2:34 from ANDRÉ LEDUCQ, who had punctured in the last hour.

Rebry won the 1934 Tour of Flanders by 4:15 in 'very bad weather, much rain and wind,' according to *Het Nieuwsblad*. 'They rode like fools beneath a grey sky full of hail, snow and rain, fighting the roaring wind.'

Winner

1931	Paris-Roubaix
1934	Paris-Roubaix, Tour Flanders, Paris-Nice
1935	Paris-Roubaix

Tour de France

1927	DNF	
1928	12th	Stage win Cherbourg—Dinan
1929	10th	Stage win Nice—Grenoble, and Yellow Jersey
1931	4th	Stage win Charleville—Malo
1932	20th	Stage win Charleville—Malo
1933	14th	
1934	DNF	

RECORDS

The greatest number of Tour victories, five, is shared by JACQUES ANQUETIL, EDDY MERCKX, BERNARD HINAULT and MIGUEL INDURAIN. Only Indurain won in five successive years.

The first to lead the race from START to FINISH was OTTAVIO BOTTECCHIA in 1924. The greatest number of starts is by JOOP

ZOETEMELK, who finished all 16 he started. The fastest Tour was 2001, when LANCE ARMSTRONG averaged 40.276 km/h for 3,870km. The slowest was 24.056km/h by FIRMIN LAMBOT in 1919. The most time-consuming Tour was 1926, when LUCIEN BUYSSE took 238hr 44min 25sec.

Distances before 1928 were approximate, despite the apparent precision of quoted figures. The longest Tours, taking that into account, were 5,745km in 1926 and 5,560km in 1919; the shortest were 2,428km in 1903 and 1904. The 1919 Tour had fewest finishers, with just 11. Of years unaffected by WAR, the smallest field was 60 in both 1903 and 1905. The largest dropout rate was in 1919, when 84 per cent of riders abandoned.

The fastest stage other than a TIME TRIAL is 50.355kmh by MARIO CIPOLLINI for 194.5km from Laval to Blois in 1999. The fastest time trial is 54.545km/h over 24.5km from Versailles to Paris in 1989, by GREG LEMOND. The fastest PROLOGUE is 55.152km/h over 7.2km by CHRIS BOARDMAN at Lille in 1994. The fastest team time trial is 54.930km/h by Gewiss-Ballan over 67km from Mayenne to Alençon in 1995.

The longest lone break was by ALBERT BOURLON in 1947, 253km from Carcassonne to Luchon. The greatest winning margin by a single rider is 22:50 by JOSÉ-LUIS VIEJO in 1976 after 160km between Montgenèvre and Manosque.

Eddy Merckx is the record winner of stages, with 34 to Bernard Hinault's 28. Merckx also holds the record for the greatest number of yellow JERSEYS at 96.

The greatest winning margin overall between first and second place is 2hr 49min between MAURICE GARIN and LUCIEN POTHIER in 1903. The largest post-war margin is 28min 17sec between FAUSTO COPPI and STAN OCKERS in 1952. The smallest gap is eight seconds between GREG LEMOND and LAURENT FIGNON in 1989.

The oldest winner is FIRMIN LAMBOT in 1922, who was 36 and 4 months. The youngest was HENRI CORNET in 1904, who was 19 years 11 months and 20 days when the Tour started.

REGIONAL TEAMS

HENRI DESGRANGE's decision in 1930 to ban SPONSORS and organise his race in NATIONAL TEAMS proved popular with SPECTATORS because they could identify their nations' riders faster. (*See* NATIONAL TEAMS for details.) But it gave Desgrange problems because not enough countries had sufficient riders to put up a respectable team. The build-up to WAR also meant that ITALY and GERMANY rode intermittently, and they and SPAIN were missing from the 1939 Tour.

Desgrange filled his field with teams from the French regions. The first were North, Normandy, Midi, Provence, Côte d'Azur, Southeast, Alsace-Lorraine, Champagne and Ile-de-France.

Riders from regional teams who won the Tour were JEAN ROBIC (1947) and ROGER WALKOWIAK (1956).

Regional teams continued until the return to trade teams in 1962

RÉPUBLIQUE

The Col de la République, also known as the Col du Grand Bois, is a 1,161m climb on the edge of St-Étienne in the Massif Central. It rises 575m in 12.8km, and is a little easier from the St-Étienne side than from the other. It has featured in the Tour since 1903, when the first to cross was HIPPOLYTE AUCOUTURIER. In 1904 GÉO LEFÈVRE, the Tour's travelling judge and organiser, had to fire shots to disperse a mob at the summit trying to beat up some riders and let their favourites through in the darkness. (*See* 1904 AFFAIR.)

The writer Paul de Vivie (1853–1930) rode to the summit daily from St-Étienne to publicise derailleur GEARS, which were still regarded with suspicion (*see* JOANNY PANEL). He continued until he was killed by a tram while riding through the city. De Vivie wrote advice for long-distance riders under the pen-name Vélocio, and also coined the word *cyclotourisme*. There is a MEMORIAL to him at the summit, and a rue Paul de Vivie in the city.

St-Etienne was the heart of the BIKE industry until its decline in the 1960s.

BJARNE RIIS
b. Herning, Denmark, Apr 3 1964

Balding, solemn-faced Bjarne Riis seldom showed his warm side and was alternately lucid and abrupt at press conferences, answering sometimes with just a few words. But perhaps his actions spoke louder: on July 21 1996 he ended MIGUEL INDURAIN's hope of a record six Tours and became Denmark's first winner. (*See* ARNE JONSSON, ROLF SORENSEN and JESPER SKIBBY for other Danes; and *see* GOSTA PETERSSON for the first Scandinavian on the podium.)

Riis first rode a bike when his father Preben gave him one on his seventh birthday. He could ride it without fear of hills because Denmark, not known for its hills, is at its flattest around his home-town of Herning. He raced in Denmark but in 1985 moved to LUXEMBOURG on the advice of KIM ANDERSEN, when he was left out of the Olympic Games team for Los Angeles in 1984.

Riis turned professional in neighbouring BELGIUM, since neither Luxembourg nor Denmark had a professional team, but rode little except CRITERIUMS. In three seasons he won nothing, and was starting to despair, when he took the chance to join the Toshiba team in FRANCE in 1988. There he impressed LAURENT FIGNON during the Tour of the European Community, and switched teams to ride as the Frenchman's DOMESTIQUE. In 1989 he won a stage of the Giro.

The relationship broke up when both men moved to ITALY for different teams. Riis's freedom from his old boss gave him new power, and he came fifth in the 1993 Tour and third in 1995 riding for Aristan. In 1996 he won the shortened, snow-covered stage to SESTRIERE (*see* entry for details) to take the yellow JERSEY from EVGUENI BERZIN. He kept the jersey until reaching Paris.

His career faded after that. In 1997 he worked hard to help his Telekom team-mate Jan Ullrich win the Tour. In June 1998 he broke a wrist and elbow in the Tour of Switzerland, and stopped racing to become a MANAGER, notably of Denmark's first top-rank team CSC-Tiscali, led by LAURENT JALABERT until 2002. (*See* Jalabert entry for details.)

Winner

1992	National championship
1995	Tour Denmark, National championship
1996	Tour de France, Coppa Sabatini, National championship
1997	Amstel Gold

Tour de France

1989	95th	
1990	DNF	
1991	107th	
1993	5th	Stage win Peronne—Châlons-sur-Marne
1994	14th	Stage win Bagnères-de-Bigorre—Albi
1995	3rd	Yellow Jersey
1996	1st	Stage wins Monetier-les-Bains—Sestriere, Agen—Hautacam, and Yellow Jersey
1997	7th	
1998	11th	

ROGER RIVIÈRE
b. St-Étienne, France, Feb 23 1936, d. St Galmier, France, Apr 1 1976

As good on the TRACK as he was on the road, the Frenchman Roger Rivière took the world hour record in 1957 and could have won the Tour. A CRASH on the Col du Perjuret in 1960 denied him the chance.

Rivière was tall and talented. But he had two weaknesses: business sense (demonstrated by the failure of his bar, the Vigorelli, in St-Étienne) and DOPING. What the second was to cost him emerged in 1960.

He was then one of a team of 14 riding for FRANCE. He won the opening TIME TRIAL but had lost his yellow JERSEY to his team-mate HENRY ANGLADE by day six. It would have been normal to assume that Rivière would support Anglade, but French teams were often riven by rivalries and 1960 was no exception. Rivière was not alone in disliking Anglade, who was seen as being pompous and bossy (*see* Anglade entry for details), and far from supporting him he attacked on the stage to Lorient at a speed only a world-class pursuiter could manage, taking 14 minutes out of his leader in 112km.

Only HANS JUNKERMANN, JAN ADRI-AENSSENS and GASTONE NENCINI could stay with him. And if Rivière had dropped Nencini, he would probably not have suffered a terrible injury and might have won the Tour.

Rivière won that stage and Adriaenssens moved into yellow. That evening Rivière spent time with his wife and plotting his race. His decision was to follow Nencini, to hold him until the final TIME TRIAL, and then win the Tour. The problem was that Nencini also wanted to win and that he was a breathtakingly fast descender. Rivière's former team-mate RAPHAËL GÉMINIANI warned, 'The only reason to follow Nencini downhill is if you've got a death wish.'

On the stage to Avignon the day's main obstacle was the Perjuret. Nencini was fourth when he got to the top, with Rivière on his wheel. Together they started the descent, a run of zigzags with a gulf on both sides. Only one rider, Louis Rostollan, saw what happened next. He raised his hand to call the MANAGER, MARCEL BIDOT, but RADIO TOUR interpreted the gesture as signalling a puncture.

Rostollan was peering into the ravine when Bidot arrived, and he assumed Rostollan had dropped his wheel. But it was Rivière rather than a wheel that was lying on a grassy bank under trees. He had hit a parapet and fallen over the edge. He was lifted out and taken to hospital, his back broken. Journalist Antoine Blondin wrote, 'The emergency helicopter turned above us in the manner of a carrion crow.'

At first Rivière blamed oil on his brakes, which was angrily denied by his MECHANIC. Then doctors found him stuffed with Palfium,

a painkiller, and there were more tablets in his jersey. Rivière had been too numb to pull the brakes. Before long he confessed he was downing thousands of pills a year. He told a French paper, 'In 1958 I bettered the world hour record with the help of dope. I had to take stimulants for the heart and muscles. Five minutes before the start I had a big injection of amphetamine and solucamphor. During the attempt I had to take another five tablets because the injections would only work for 40 minutes.'

In Paris, Nencini gave his garland to Bidot and asked him to pass it to Rivière.

(*See* MEMORIALS.)

Winner

1957	World pursuit championship, World hour record, Mont Faron
1958	World pursuit championship, World hour record
1959	World pursuit championship, Mont Faron
1960	GP Alger

Tour de France

1959	4th	Stage win Blain—Nantes, Seurre—Dijon
1960	DNF	Stage win Brussels—Brussels, St-Malo—Lorient, Mont-de-Marsan—Pau

JEAN ROBIC

b. Condé-les-Vouziers, France, Jun 10 1921,
d. Villeparisis, Oct 6 1980

Little Jean Robic was a Mr Punch lookalike who in 1947 ignored the convention that the yellow JERSEY is never attacked on the last day. He became the first Tour winner never to have worn yellow.

Robic was only 1.61m and rode a 48cm frame but with 172mm cranks. His team-mate Éloi Tassin called him 'Biquet', a play on *Robic-quet*, which meant 'kid' or 'sonny.' But others disliked him, claiming he was stubborn, spiteful and foul-mouthed.

The story is that Robic went to the 1947 Tour not long after marrying his girlfriend

Raymonde, whose parents ran the *Au Rendez-vous des Bretons* bar near Montparnasse station in Paris. The day after they married he went out on a seven-hour BIKE ride, anxious not only to win the Tour for his new wife, as the sentimental story has it, but also to take revenge on the selectors who had left him out of the FRANCE team and put him into the Ouest REGIONAL TEAM instead.

In an era of instant phone connections it's hard to imagine a Tour where a rider would write a letter to his mother. But after winning on the fourth day, at Strasbourg, Robic wrote, 'I hope, as a follow-up, I can give you the final victory at the PARC DES PRINCES.'

The loser in the 1947 Tour was PIERRE BRAMBILLA, riding for a team of Italians living in France. On the final stage from Caen into Paris, Robic saw he was trapped in a group on the Bonsecours hill, going east out of Rouen, and attacked. Brambilla chased and got near, but Robic attacked once more. And then again. Another rider went away and Robic's chase led to a small breakaway. BRIEK SCHOTTE eventually won the stage but Robic won the Tour. Brambilla was reputedly so bitter that he buried his bike in his garden. (*See* Brambilla entry for accusations of bribery.)

In 1953 Robic again courted controversy when he was accused of throwing away a drinking bottle dangerously as he went down the TOURMALET. He denied it and claimed it would have been impossible to throw the bottle because it had been filled with 10kg of lead to add weight and thus speed up his descent. There is some doubt whether the story is true.

Robic's bad language and behaviour won him few friends. In 1959, when he finished outside the time limit at Châlon-sur-Saône and was eliminated, two days before Paris, JACQUES AUGENDRE said, 'Any other rider would have been let through.' It was 'his immoderate language,' according to Augendre, which 'gave rise to quite a few controversies and earned him very solid enemies.' The Tour kept in BRIAN ROBINSON, who was also outside the time limit because he was ill, but threw out Robic.

After cycling, Robic's life went to pieces. He opened a pizzeria in the Avenue du Maine in Montparnasse, but it failed along with his marriage. He wandered the streets, a bitter man looking for someone with whom to share a drink, someone who'd offer him a job. Eventually a friend employed him at his removals firm.

In 1980 Robic was returning from a reunion of old riders when he died in a car crash. He is buried in the Wissous cemetery in Paris, the city where he won a Resistance medal for carrying messages hidden in his bike during the Occupation.

Winner

1947   Tour de France
1950   Rome-Naples-Rome, World cyclo-cross championship
1952   Tour Haute-Savoie, Trophée Grimpeurs

Tour de France

1947	1st	Stage wins Luxembourg—Strasbourg, Lyon—Grenoble, Luchon—Pau, and Yellow Jersey
1948	16th	
1949	4th	Stage win Pau—Luchon
1950	12th	
1951	27th	
1952	5th	Stage win Aix-en-Provence—Avignon
1953	DNF	Stage win Cauterets—Luchon, and Yellow Jersey
1954	DNF	
1955	DNF	
1959	DNF	

BRIAN ROBINSON
b. Mirfield, England, Nov 3 1930

Brian Robinson was first Briton to finish the Tour, and the first to win a stage.

Robinson was 13 when he joined his first cycling club, in Huddersfield, and rode his first race at 18, a 25-mile hilly TIME TRIAL in 1hr 14min 50sec. His father wouldn't let him race when he was younger, and that inspired him to watch the Olympic road race at Windsor in 1948. 'I wanted to road race,' he said, 'which at the time was restricted to old wartime airfields and parks. I would ride to Sheffield or Birmingham and we would have to leave the park at 9.30am because the public wanted to use it.'

When the time came for him to do his two years' national service he ended up, deliberately, in a unit of cyclists. They were, he says with some irony, 'the finest bunch of soldiers any cyclist would want to see in his billet.'

In 1952 the army sent this unit to the Route de France, the AMATEUR Tour. He was fifth with three days to go, but then came the Pyrenees, and he slid to 40th. 'I never did get any prize MONEY,' he says. 'We were thrown in at the deep end. I had never seen MOUNTAINS like that before. It was a big learning session.'

Robinson signed next year as an INDEPENDENT (semi-professional) for a BIKE shop called Ellis-Briggs. Then he joined the HERCULES team to ride the Tour in 1955, finishing 29th, the first Briton to reach Paris. Hercules folded that year, and in the 1956 Tour Robinson rode for an International team, finishing 14th, his best place in five finishes. In 1957 he became the first Briton to ride for a major Continental team when he joined St-Raphaël. Within a few weeks he had his first win, in the GP de Nice, followed by third in Milan-San Remo. Unfortunately he broke his wrist on the Roubaix stage of the Tour and abandoned at the FINISH.

He won his first Tour stage in 1958, starting when he attacked after 50km of the 170km stage to Brest. With him went JEAN DOTTO and Arrigo Padovan. The big riders left them alone because none of them mattered to the overall result. Robinson and Padovan went into the uphill finish together. Padovan went left and Robinson came by on the right. Padovan twice pushed him into the crowd. Padovan won but the judges gave the victory to Robinson.

'I was elated because it meant I would be sure of a good contract for the following year,' he said.

JOCK WADLEY wrote, 'It would be criminal to pretend that this was an important stage of the Tour. It would not be unkind to Brian to say that this was, perhaps, the least important of all. The Alps were over; many riders were tired; it was the day before the TIME TRIAL, for which

the "heads" were reserving their strength. But a thousand cheers for Brian for his intelligence in picking such a day for his great effort.'

In 1959 Robinson was almost eliminated through stomach cramp on one stage, struggling in outside the limit with SHAY ELLIOTT, but he was allowed to continue even though Elliott wasn't. Robinson's MANAGER invoked a rule that no rider in the first ten could be thrown out. Robinson was still way back when he attacked on a quiet day between the Alps and a time trial. He went off alone on stage 14, led for 145km and won at Châlon-sur-Saône by 20:06, or about 11km.

His last big win was the Dauphiné Libéré in 1961, by more than six minutes. Next year he stopped racing, aged 32, and joined the family building business in Mirfield, West Yorkshire. Cycling businessman Ron Kitching, in whose shop Robinson had pored over French cycling magazines, said, 'Brian was a quiet lad, what you might call gentlemanly. He never seemed to be aggressive in any way. He was politeness itself. One might have got the impression that he would never be aggressive enough to be a success.'

Winner

1957	GP Nice
1961	Dauphiné Libéré

Tour de France

1955	29th	
1956	14th	
1957	DNF	
1958	DNF	Stage win St-Brieuc—Brest
1959	19th	Stage win Annecy—Châlon-sur-Saône
1960	26th	
1961	53rd	

STEPHEN ROCHE
b. Dublin, Ireland, Nov 28 1959

Ireland's Stephen Roche bought his first BIKE with the help of people in his village, Dundrum. And they helped him again when he wanted to give up welding machinery in a dairy

Stephen Roche *(continued)*

to go to FRANCE to turn professional. It was February 11 1980, and arrangements were less smooth when he got to Paris to look for the AC Boulogne-Billancourt, the club which had nurtured many English-speaking professionals. Roche found nobody to meet him at the airport, and when he went to the ACBB office at 10.30pm he discovered it was empty. He slept on the doorstep until members found him there at 4am.

Roche went on to win the AMATEUR Paris-Roubaix, and rode for IRELAND in the Olympic Games in 1980. In 1981 he turned pro for the PEUGEOT team and scored his first wins during the Tour of Corsica, Paris-Nice, and the Tour de l'Indre. His charm and choirboy looks disguised a toughness that brought him not only the first Tour win for IRELAND in 1987, but also the Giro d'Italia and world championship that same year.

The run-up to his Tour win in 1987 captures the erratic pattern of Roche's career. He had attracted attention by winning on the AUBISQUE in 1985 only to struggle the following year. He was repeatedly troubled with knee pain after a CRASH in the Paris six-day, and his season had ended with a hospital operation. The next year he came back with the Carrera team, winning the Tour of Valencia and the Tour of Romandie, and coming second to Moreno Argentin in Liège-Bastogne-Liège. 'I rode like an AMATEUR that day,' he lamented, 'getting caught in the last kilometre because Criquiélion and I were too busy watching each other; it was my greatest disappointment.'

He also won the 1987 Giro, but only after a rumpus in his team. Carrera was largely Italian, and the fans and most of the riders wanted Roberto Visentini to win. Roche held the leader's *maglia rosa* until he lost three minutes in the first TIME TRIAL. The Carrera MANAGER, David Boifava, then ordered Roche to wait when Visentini struggled in the mountains two days later. Roche hesitated, shouted 'No!', and pressed on. Visentini broke on the Sappada, losing eight minutes and the Giro.

From that moment on SPECTATORS shook their fists and spat as Roche passed. Even his team-mates gave cold stares. In the end Visentini cracked again, crashed, and pulled out. Roche won and ROBERT MILLAR, another ACBB prodigy, was second and King of the Mountains. Within weeks Roche had also won the Tour and the world championship.

The Irishman's assault on the Tour really started on the 19th stage to Villard-de-Lans, where Roche began challenging PEDRO DELGADO, the leading CLIMBER and the following year's winner. The Spaniard won, but Roche picked up enough time as the day ended to take the yellow JERSEY from French favourite JEAN-FRANÇOIS BERNARD.

The following day Delgado pushed Roche out of the lead at Alpe d'Huez, and then sought to deliver the final decisive blow the next day at La Plagne. Roche was attacked so hard that he lost 1:46 near the end of the final climb. But as Delgado slowed near the summit Roche thrashed himself and got within sight of Delgado, before collapsing over the line and being given oxygen. The decider came in the TIME TRIAL at Dijon. CLIMBERS are rarely good against the clock but Roche was also no likely winner. Nevertheless he came second to JEAN-FRANÇOIS BERNARD and, more importantly, did better than Delgado. He took a 40-second lead and kept it to Paris, home city of his wife Lydia.

Roche returned to Ireland to an ecstatic reception, and was made a citizen of honour of Dublin. But his career was repeatedly interrupted by health problems, with knee operations in April 1986, November 1986, November 1987 and January 1988. They cost him five of his 11 years as a professional. He says, 'I had so many operations that my left leg became unstable and wouldn't push straight on the pedal, which brought on a tendon problem.'

Roche rode the Tour 10 times, coming third in 1985 and ninth in 1992. He could have achieved more had his career not been interrupted by injury.

Today he is an amateur rally driver and works as a TV commentator. In 1999 he opened a hotel, Le Marina Baie des Anges at Antibes, where he runs training camps.

(See DOMESTIQUES, GREG LEMOND, BERNARD HINAULT, PAUL KIMMAGE.)

Winner

1981	Paris-Nice, Tour Corsica
1983	Tour Romandie, GP Wallonia, Paris-Bourges
1984	Tour Romandie
1985	Route Sud, Critérium International
1987	World championship, Tour de France, Giro d'Italia, Tour Romandie, Tour Valencia
1989	Tour Basque Country
1990	Four-days Dunkirk
1991	Critérium International

Tour de France

1983	13th	
1984	25th	
1985	3rd	Stage win Luz-St-Sauveur—Aubisque
1986	48th	
1987	1st	Stage win Saumur—Futuroscope, and Yellow Jersey
1989	DNF	
1990	44th	
1991	DNF	
1992	9th	Stage win St-Étienne—La Bourboule
1993	13th	

ANTONIN ROLLAND
b. Sainte-Euphémie, France, Sep 3 1924

Some riders are noisy, some just talk a lot, and some are quiet. Few were ever as quiet as the Frenchman Tonin Rolland. This DOMESTIQUE for LOUISON BOBET mixed quietness with shyness and barely spoke at all. Indeed he would have passed unnoticed had he not won the stage from Dieppe to Roubaix in 1955 and, to his surprise as much as everyone else's, held the yellow JERSEY for 12 days.

Nobody knows how far Rolland would have gone had he not developed a fever, cracked in the MOUNTAINS and lost the jersey. He eventually struggled on to fifth place, behind his team

leader Bobet. 'He could have become one of the great champions of FRANCE,' says JEAN-PAUL OLLIVIER, 'but quiet to the point of self-effacement, he never learned to acquire the bravery he needed.'

Winner

1950	Midi Libre, Circuit 6 Provinces
1956	Midi Libre

Tour de France

1949	45th	
1950	29th	
1952	21st	Stage win Vichy—Paris
1953	7th	
1954	19th	
1955	5th	Stage win Dieppe—Roubaix, and Yellow Jersey
1956	35th	
1957	39th	
1958	66th	
1960	59th	

TONY ROMINGER
b. Velje, Denmark, Mar 27 1961

Neither as colourful as FERDY KÜBLER nor as elegant as HUGO KOBLET, Tony Rominger spent much of his career in the shadow of GIANNI BUGNO in ITALY. Only later did he have confidence to shine in big tours, winning the Tour of SPAIN a record three times in succession and then the Giro d'Italia in 1995. In FRANCE he was one of few to challenge MIGUEL INDURAIN, although his record was spoiled by some big CRASHES – and two small ones after he changed his brake levers round and forgot which was the front and which the back.

One crash on the stage to Valence chipped his knee. 'No one realised it was broken, and it's never quite the same as the other knee,' he said. 'But at least I can tell when the weather is going to change.'

In 1994 he set the world hour record twice, with 53.832 on a 59x14 gear and 55.291km on 60x14. He also won the Tour of Lombardy alone twice, in 1989 and 1992, and in the 1993 Tour won the MOUNTAINS JERSEY and three stages, finishing second to Indurain. He retired after riding at Vall d'Uxo near Valencia, Spain, in November 1997.

Winner

1987 Tour Reggio Calabria
1988 Tour Emilia
1989 Tour Lombardy, Tirreno-Adriatico, Tour Mediterranean
1990 Tirreno-Adriatico
1991 GP Nations, Paris-Nice, Tour Romandie
1992 Tour Spain, Tour Lombardy, Tour Basque Country
1993 Tour Spain, Tour Basque Country
1994 Tour Spain, GP Nations, Paris-Nice, Tour Basque Country, GP Merckx, Montjuich
1995 Giro d'Italia, Tour Romandie
1996 Tour Burgos

Tour de France

1988	68th	
1990	57th	
1993	2nd	Stage wins Villard-de-Lans—Serre-Chevalier, Serre-Chevalier—Isola 2000, Brétigny-sur-Orge—Montlhéry, and Mountains winner
1994	DNF	
1995	8th	
1996	10th	
1997	DNF	

STEVEN ROOKS
b. Oterleek, Holland, Aug 7 1960

Steven Rooks (pronounced *Roaks*) is a lanky Dutchman who won Liège-Bastogne-Liège in 1983, his second year as a professional. His big season was 1988: he won on ALPE D'HUEZ after his compatriot and friend GERT-JAN THEUNISSE had sent him a telegram saying, 'You

can win it, you donkey,' and finished the Tour second to PEDRO DELGADO with the MOUNTAINS JERSEY on his shoulders. Customers at his favourite restaurant in Warmenhuisen in north-west HOLLAND celebrated by decorating it with the red polka-dots of the Mountains jersey.

Rooks won the mountain TIME TRIAL at ORCIÈRES-MERLETTE the following year. He and Theunisse made a killer pairing in the mountains, but both men's careers took a dive when they joined the TVM team, of which Rooks eventually became MANAGER. In January 2000 Rooks said on Dutch television that he had used testosterone and amphetamine throughout his 13-year career.

Winner

1983 Liège-Bastogne-Liège
1986 Amstel Gold, GP Wallonia, Ruta del Sol, Tour Luxembourg
1988 Championship Zurich
1991 National championship
1994 National championship

Tour de France

1983	DNF	
1985	25th	
1986	9th	
1987	DNF	
1988	2nd	Stage win Morzine—Alpe d'Huez, and Mountains winner
1989	7th	Stage win Gap—Orcières-Merlette
1990	33rd	
1991	26th	
1992	17th	
1993	DNF	
1994	DNF	

ROULEUR

A rouleur is a type of rider more easily recognised than described. The word is more easily understood in French, from which most cycling terms come, than in its English translation of 'driver' or 'roller'.

The word describes a rider who may not be gifted as a CLIMBER or SPRINTER but whose strength and speed on conventional stages is so great that his efforts can be decisive. It's possible to be a good rouleur without being a leader or a regular winner; SEAN YATES, for example, was an excellent rouleur who could charge along at the front of a group with such power that few riders could come by.

Climbers are rarely good rouleurs because they are too light; similarly, sprinters rarely try to be rouleurs because they save their energy for the FINISH. But when a rider like EDDY MERCKX can add strength as a sprinter and climber to his power as a rouleur, the effect is devastating. As indeed Merckx proved for a decade.

RULES

Like any event, there is no shortage of rules for the Tour de France. There are those of the sport itself, imposed by the UCI (Union Cycliste Internationale), and those of the Tour.

Riders compete in teams of equal size, usually nine or ten. Originally the choice of teams was the Tour's. Now most are decided by the UCI's ranking system. From 2003 places will go to the 10 best teams on the UCI classification at the end of the previous season, the teams of the winners of the previous year's Tour, Giro and Tour of Spain, and the team that wins the World Cup. In the case of any of those places being filled by the same team twice, remaining places will be given to the next best teams on the UCI ranking to bring the number of guaranteed selections to 14. The next four of the final eight places will go to the next four teams in the world rankings in February each year.

The remaining four places will be decided by the Tour selection committee, which in 2002 was JEAN-MARIE LEBLANC, his deputy Daniel Baal, Jean-Claude Hérault, Jean-François Pescheux, John Lelangue (the voice of RADIO TOUR), Laurent Bezault and Jean-Michel Monin.

The leader (yellow JERSEY) is the rider who takes least time to complete the course, includ-

ing any BONUS deductions offered for winning a stage or being first to reach a mountain summit. The MOUNTAINS (polka-dot jersey) winner is the rider who consistently finishes highest on climbs, each climb offering points according to its difficulty. The POINTS winner (green jersey) is the rider who places consistently highest each day, regardless of winning margin.

The time the points leader has taken throughout the race matters less than that he wins on as many days as possible. To him, the Tour is a succession of individual races rather than an accumulation. He may lose an hour in the mountains, but it barely matters provided he does well on the flatter days. The green jersey winner needs a fast finish, and the jersey is often called the sprinters' jersey because of that. It's points that count for a sprinter, not time.

Riders can cooperate with rivals from other teams, but can exchange wheels and BIKES only within a team. MECHANICS are allowed to repair or exchange bikes, but only behind the race and on the right-hand side of the road.

Riders are only allowed to take food in FEEDING AREAS or from their MANAGERS, except in the first 50km and last 20km. They may not accept food or drink from SPECTATORS, nor be pushed by them. They are not allowed to shelter behind cars or motorbikes, nor be pulled by them. They must follow the entire route, although the organisers can shorten, lengthen or cancel a stage.

Riders are not allowed to go through closed level crossings. If the race is split by a railway barrier, the leaders are held back until the chasers have got going again. Or the chasers are held back until the break has returned to its original lead.

Riders are not allowed to make commercial deals other than with their normal SPONSORS. They can give interviews after the race but not during it. Only managers can speak to reporters while the race is on, but they cannot do so in the last 20km. Managers must drive on the right and in the order of their teams in the team competition. They are not allowed to pass the race commissaire without permission.

Teams are allowed to communicate by radio but not by mobile phone. Riders must wear leaders' JERSEYS supplied by the race and use only official bottles.

Riders in a group are given the same time as the leader of that group provided there is no gap in the flow of riders. Each new group gets a fresh time. Riders are considered to have finished the stage if they puncture or CRASH in the last kilometre. They get the time of the group they occupied when they were forced to stop.

Riders asked to give dope tests must report to the DOPING test area within 35 minutes of the FINISH or of leaving the podium. They are chosen according to a formula decided by the UCI, the sport's governing body. If no announcement is made, the stage winner, over-all leader and three others at random are called. The samples go to the Châtenay-Malabry laboratory and results are announced within 24 hours. A rider who gives a positive test loses prizes won that day. If he is disqualified he loses all the money he has won in the whole race. The Tour's dope regulations are those of not only the UCI but of FRANCE.

Riders must get to the finish within a set percentage of the winner's time each day. Judges can disqualify riders after that but not if a group forms a substantial part of the total field. The limit varies with the difficulty of the stage. No rider can be eliminated in the PROLOGUE.

There are penalties and fines for offences such as not signing the start sheet, swearing, and obstructing another rider. Impeding another rider in a sprint usually results in being put to the back of the group.

SATELLITE POSITIONING

The established way of measuring gaps between break and bunch used to be for the official leading the race to announce a particular landmark such as a garage. Another official behind the bunch would time how long it took to reach that point, and the gap would be measured.

Things changed with satellite plotting, by which distances can be measured via a network of transmitters that send signals to satellites in space. The system was tested in the Classique des Alpes, and used at the Tour in 1998. Satellite plotting from motorbikes and cars can now fix the race to within a few metres. The result provides not only a good calculation of a break's advantage but also of the remaining distance of the stage. The figures are shown on TV coverage.

FRITZ SCHAER

b. Etzwilen, Switzerland, Mar 13 1926,
d. Sep 29 1997

The Tour celebrated 50 years in 1953 by establishing a green JERSEY to identify the rider with consistently best places each day. Fritz Schaer, a balding Swiss, was its first winner. He won the first two stages, at Metz and Liège, which put him in yellow. But when he lost the lead to ROGER HASSENFORDER on stage five, he swapped into his *maillot vert* instead. He never won another stage – he wasn't a specialist SPRINTER – but he came sixth overall.

Winner

| 1949 | Championship Zurich |
| 1950 | Championship Zurich |

Tour de France

1953	6th	Stage wins Strasbourg—Metz, Metz—Liège, and Yellow Jersey and Points winner
1954	3rd	
1956	DNF	

BRIEK SCHOTTE

b. Kanegem, Belgium, Sep 7 1919

Albéric Schotte – known as Briek from the last syllable of his first name – raced for 25 years, 20 of them as a professional from 1940 to 1959, and then worked another 30 years as MANAGER of the FLANDRIA team.

On his day and on the right course Schotte was unbeatable. He was an iron-hard lion of Flanders who rode until the rain washed off the mud that caked him, and then raced on again. His technique was to go to the front and challenge others to stay with him. Often they couldn't. If they could, he would outsprint them. He trained the same way. It might not have been scientific but it was devastatingly effective.

Poor climbing and time trialing limited his ability as a stage race rider, but he did come second to GINO BARTALI in the 1948 Tour, a race in which the Italian won seven stages. Only 44 of the 120 starters completed that Tour because of the weather.

Schotte's record includes the Tour of Flanders in 1942 and 1948 and the world championship in 1948 and 1950.

(*See* PIERRE BRAMBILLA, MEMORIALS, JEAN ROBIC.)

Winner

1942	Tour Flanders
1946	Paris-Brussels, Paris-Tours, Tour Luxembourg
1947	Paris-Tours
1948	World championship, Tour Flanders
1950	World championship, Ghent-Wevelgem
1952	Paris-Brussels
1953	A Travers Belgique
1955	Ghent-Wevelgem, A Travers Belgique, GP Escaut

Tour de France

1947	13th	Stage win Caen–Paris
1948	2nd	
1949	33rd	
1950	22nd	

LÉON SCIEUR

b. Florennes, Belgium, Mar 19 1888,
d. Oct 7 1969

Léon Scieur, a farmer's son from Florennes, near Charleroi in BELGIUM, rode his first Tour in 1913 having learned to ride a bike only two years earlier. His neighbour, FIRMIN LAMBOT, helped him train.

Scieur came fourth in the Tour in 1919 and 1920, and finally won in 1921 when he was 33. He took the yellow JERSEY on the second day and defended it so hard that reporters nicknamed him 'the Locomotive'. He powered on regardless of weather and wind, turning a low GEAR fast.

His compatriot Hector Heusghem attacked him when he punctured on the Col d'Allos – a climb to 2,250m – and Scieur was so angry at a breach of the era's unwritten rule that riders weren't challenged during mechanical trouble that he thrashed off in pursuit, passed all who had passed him, and caught Heusghem. Then he gave him a tongue-lashing, rode by, and won the stage at Grenoble. War broke out between them, and reporters arrived from everywhere for the fun. The dispute ended in truce, after which the race became dull.

Organiser HENRI DESGRANGE berated the rest of the riders for being too scared of him, but Scieur had his share of bad luck. He broke 11 spokes on the penultimate stage, from Metz to Dunkirk, and managed to get another wheel. But according to the RULES he could use it only if the judges agreed the original wheel was wrecked. There had been no judges to see the evidence, and repair was impossible. So he carried the damaged wheel on his back for 300km, and the sprocket left a mark on his spine for 15 years.

By then misery was no stranger to Scieur. In 1919 he punctured at least four times (some reports say six or more) on the stage from Le Havre to Cherbourg, and huddled in a doorway out of a storm to mend his tyres. Racing tyres had to be cut apart to reveal the air tube, then sewn back together with thick thread and a sailmaker's needle. He was watched by the woman who lived in the house and eventually, his fingers too cold to thread the needle, he asked her to help.

The chief official, Lucien Cazalis, was there to see his suffering was complete. 'It's forbidden to receive help,' he said. 'If *Madame* threads the needle, you'll be penalised.' (*See* ÉVIAN for Cazalis's role in race history.)

Scieur succeeded despite his shivering, but lost the race to FIRMIN LAMBOT by about the time he'd spent in that doorway.

Winner

1920	Liège-Bastogne-Liège
1921	Tour de France

Tour de France

1913	DNF	
1914	14th	
1919	4th	
1920	4th	Stage win Grenoble—Gex
1921	1st	Stage win Cherbourg—Brest, Nice—Grenoble, and Yellow Jersey
1922	DNF	
1923	DNF	
1924	DNF	

EDWARD SELS

b. Vorselaar, Belgium, Aug 27 1941

A British cycling magazine once portrayed Ward Sels as a giant, brainless Belgian who grunted 'Yes, boss' whenever RIK VAN LOOY told him to do anything. Bridge a gap, chase a break, lead a sprint – 'Yes, boss.'

Sels was a classic beefy SPRINTER, winning four stages in his debut Tour in 1964, when he also wore the yellow jersey. He never repeated that success but he did win seven stages in five rides from 1964 to 1970 and he could win a classic on his day. His record includes winning the Tour of Flanders in 1966, coming second in 1965, and coming fourth in Milan-San Remo in 1968.

He was eclipsed in the EDDY MERCKX era and retired after a series of CRASHES. 'All that falling off was doing me no good,' he said.

Winner

1964	National championship
1965	Paris-Brussels
1966	Tour Flanders
1967	GP Gippingen
1968	GP Escaut

Tour de France

1964	33rd	Stage wins Rennes—Lisieux, Toulon—Montpellier, Andorra—Toulouse, Bordeaux—Brive, and Yellow Jersey

Tour de France (continued)

1965	DNF	Stage win La Baule—La Rochelle
1966	38th	Stage win Caen—Angers, Orléans—Rambouillet
1968	DNF	
1970	DNF	

PATRICK SERCU

b. Roeselare, Belgium, Jun 27 1944

Albert Sercu, Patrick's father, came second for BELGIUM in the world professional road race in 1947, and was European madison champion in 1951, as well as collecting 23 CRITERIUM wins in 1945. So for his son it was in the genes: Patrick won the world AMATEUR sprint title in 1963, the Olympic kilometre gold in 1964, and the pro sprint title in 1967 and 1969. He set the indoor flying start kilometre record (1:01.23) in 1967, the standing start (1:07.35) in 1972, and the outdoor (1:02.46) in 1973. He turned professional in 1965 and won 59 championships.

That would have been enough. But Sercu, the '*Vlaamse Pijl*' or Flemish Arrow, also rode the Tour twice and won the points competition in 1974. He also came second in Het Volk in 1974 and 1975 and third in 1976. On top of that he won 88 six-day races. He retired in 1983 after 18 years as a pro, and in 1984 coached the Belgium Olympic team. He is now an AGENT and race director of the six-day at Ghent.

Winner

1972	Championship Flanders
1974	Circuit Flemish Ardennes
1975	Circuit Flemish Ardennes
1977	Kuurne-Brussels-Kuurne

Tour de France

1974	89th	Stage wins Morlaix—St-Malo, St-Malo—Caen, Chaumont—Besançon, and Points winner
1977	DNF	Stage wins Jaunay-Clan—Angers, Roubaix—Charleroi, Charleroi—Fribourg

SERVICE – *See* MECHANICS

SESTRIERE

The ski resort of Sestriere, west of Turin and halfway to Grenoble, was built in the 1930s for Giovanni Agnelli, boss of Fiat, so that he and his family could enjoy the snow. It's the highest resort in the area and is used by both Tour and Giro. Sestriere rarely fails to provide drama.

In 1952 FAUSTO COPPI won there by more than seven minutes; in 1992 CLAUDIO CHIAPPUCCI fought off MIGUEL INDURAIN; in 1996 the mountain provided the launch pad for BJARNE RIIS.

FÉLIX LÉVITAN wrote of Coppi in 1952 that he was 'the unchained warrior, the big cat on the trail of his prey, and because we were at his side on the motorbike, because we were scrutinising his face, because we could read it in his eyes, we would say that we saw there an animal glint, cruel, such as a tiger would have, leaping on his victim.'

Over the five cols from Bourg d'Oisans to Sestriere, Coppi rode away over the Croix-de-Fer, let himself to be caught on the descent, and moved on with the others to the Télégraphe. He rode away again 10 kilometres from the top of the GALIBIER and left the greatest – among them RAPHAËL GÉMINIANI, GINO BARTALI and STAN OCKERS – to do what they could. Coppi continued over the Col de Montgenèvre, soaked by rain, blown by mountain wind. Traffic jams began as Italian spectators tried to reach the FINISH. Police formed a cordon for his safety through the crowds. Coppi won the stage by more than seven minutes, and the Tour by half an hour. JACQUES GODDET had to double second PRIZE to keep the others interested.

As a prisoner-of-war in 1943 Coppi ate from the same plate as another prisoner called CHIAPPUCCI. In 1992 Chiappucci's son Claudio also won at Sestriere. Claudio Chiappucci went to the START at St-Gervais with a pulse meter, at that time considered high-tech. He attacked with 233km of the 254km to go, and rode the last 123km alone. MIGUEL INDURAIN finished 1:45 behind him, after chasing with GIANNI

BUGNO. Many were happy just to finish. (*See* Chiappucci entry for more.)

Riis's success came in odder circumstances. At 7am on Monday July 8 1996, the radio station France Inter had reported snow and the cancellation of the stage to Sestriere. JEAN-MARIE LEBLANC, waiting as snow built up around him in the Centre des Congrès in Val-d'Isère, decided to shorten the stage, skipping the ISÉRAN and starting at Monêtier-les-Bains.

The riders set off by bus, to the dismay of SPECTATORS who'd gone to the top of the Iséran regardless of the weather, and reckoned the riders should have done so as well. At 3.04pm the riders set off on a stage that had been 190km long and now measured just 46km. Over an hour and ten minutes to Sestriere, Riis attacked several times, became overall leader on the road and was still in yellow by Paris. Sestriere had again been the turning point.

OSCAR SEVILLA
b. Albacete, Spain, Sep 29 1976

Oscar 'El Niño' (the kid) Sevilla brought fresh air to the 2001 Tour with his youthful looks and spirited riding when he won the white JERSEY as best YOUNG RIDER. He was 24 but looked barely out of school. Sevilla stayed with the best CLIMBERS, in the top 10 on every MOUNTAIN stage except for a difficult 13th stage to Saint Lary Soulan His MANAGER, Vicente Belda, said, 'Sevilla is the next big star of Spanish cycling. He rides with a smile on his face. He was just born to be a climber.'

Sevilla comes from the hilly and very dry farming area of southern SPAIN where they make Manchego cheese. He turned professional in 1998 after Alvaro Pino, former director of KELME, saw him as an AMATEUR. Sevilla was only 21 but he accepted the offer. He won the hardest stage of the Tour of Romandie in 1999, where one pro said the youngster had been tearing the legs off the rest, and came 13th in his first Giro d'Italia. He lost the 2001 Vuelta in the final time trial on the last day, and missed the podium by one place in the equivalent stage in 2002.

2000   Trofeo Luis Ocaña
2001   Montjuich

Tour de France

2001   7th   White Jersey winner
2002   DNF

PASCAL SIMON

b. Mesnil-Saint-Loup, France, Sep 27 1956

In 1983 the Frenchman Pascal Simon won the yellow JERSEY at Luchon after he was in a group which got a lead on the stage that included the TOURMALET, Aspin and Peyresourde. ROBERT MILLAR won the stage, but Simon became *maillot jaune*. Next day he touched wheels and fell, breaking his shoulder, but insisted on carrying on. His team gathered round to keep him in the race.

Simon struggled on for six days with a huge bandage on his shoulder, still keeping his jersey. But the pain finally became too much on ALPE D'HUEZ and he climbed off, opening the way to victory to LAURENT FIGNON.

(*See* JERSEYS for other leaders who have abandoned.)

Winner

1980   Tour Haut-Var
1981   Tour Avenir
1984   Route Sud
1986   Tour Haut-Var

Tour de France

1980   28th
1982   20th   Stage win Manosque—Orcières-Merlette
1983   DNF   Yellow Jersey
1984   7th
1985   20th
1986   13th
1987   53rd
1988   17th
1989   13th
1990   35th
1991   57th

TOM SIMPSON

b. Doncaster, England, Nov 30 1937,
d. Mont Ventoux, France, Jul 13 1967

At a place on MONT VENTOUX, in the last few hundred metres of the approach to the summit from Bédoin, stands a large flat MEMORIAL set back from the road. It marks the spot where Tom Simpson died on July 13 1967. It is for his death, and the fact that he was found to be doped, that he is now most remembered. But he was also the first Briton to wear the yellow JERSEY (1962), and in SPAIN in 1965 he became BRITAIN's first professional world road race champion.

Simpson rode his last race in Britain in 1959 and moved to western FRANCE to ride as a professional. In that same race in 1959 was a Manchester rider called Harry Hall, who eight years later would try to save Simpson's life on Mont Ventoux.

Simpson's first classic win was the Tour of Flanders in 1961, although photos show runner-up Nino Defillipis has his brakes on before the line. In 1962 he wore the yellow jersey for a day, provoking the rare interest of the *Daily Express* and the headline 'Simpson pedals to glory'. In 1965 he became WORLD CHAMPION.

The race was at Lasarte, near San Sebastian. Simpson recalled, 'Coming up for just two laps to the finish, I attacked on the big climb near the village of Hernani. I was using 53x14 and I kept it in as we went up the climb. In a matter of yards I was clear, taking Altig with me. (*See* RUDI ALTIG.) I said to him, "Come on Rudi, remember the Baracchi!" We had been partners in the Baracchi Trophy event last year and he had shattered me. I was so dead that he practically pushed me over the last few miles.

'I must have made him think he could win. He just smiled and nodded and we got down to the work of keeping clear. I knew I could beat Altig and it was now merely a question of keeping the others at bay. Soon we were on the last lap and I was confident I was going to win. Going round the back of the circuit we came to a gentleman's agreement. We agreed to separate when we reached the "one kilometre to go" board and ride in side by side. So there we were, two gentlemen virtually fighting a duel over the last kilometre. I started my sprint a few hundred yards out and kept going as hard as I could. And I was over the line, grinning like a maniac, heart pounding and tears welling up in my eyes.

'I looked at my BIKE for the first time since it was swept away from me in a pandemonium of cheering and backslapping immediately after winning the championship. As I looked at the tyres I found that the rear one had a two-inch strip worn away, with strands of rubber hanging free, it was bulging at the side and was on the point of bursting at any moment.'

Simpson had a poor year in 1966 after breaking his leg skiing, and then he heard that 1967's Tour would be for NATIONAL TEAMS. That meant he could rely on a team that, although weaker, would be more loyal than his trade team of PEUGEOT, which he was then arguing with over MONEY. He was a tough rider, given to brave if eccentric lone attacks to overcome his relatively poor ability as a SPRINTER, and he could hold his own in the MOUNTAINS. He knew he needed a strong performance in the Tour to enable him to subsequently collect enough money to ride a couple more seasons and then retire. He could do that, alone if necessary, in British colours, but not with Peugeot. The set piece was scheduled for July 13 1967, and the stage that crossed Mont Ventoux on its way from Marseille to Carpentras.

Simpson wrote of an earlier ride over the mountain, 'It is like another world up there among the bare rocks and the glaring sun. The white rocks reflect the heat and the dust rises clinging to your arms, legs and face. I rode well up there doing about five miles to the gallon in perspiration. It was almost overwhelmingly hot up there and I think it was the only time that I have got off my bike and my pants have nearly fallen down. They were soaked and heavy with sweat which was running off me in streams and I had to wring out my socks because the sweat was running into my shoes.'

The bunch was still together at Bédoin at the foot of the mountain, except for a few who had crashed and been taken to hospital. RAYMOND POULIDOR and JULIO JIMENEZ led on the gentle rise to the main ascent. Only Poulidor could go with Jimenez when he attacked at the St-Estève hairpin. The two of them built a slight lead, and were closely followed after a while by a group including the yellow jersey, ROGER PINGEON, and Simpson, FELICE GIMONDI, JAN JANSSEN and LUCIEN AIMAR.

Jimenez attacked again, and he and Poulidor reached the Chalet Reynard alone. At that point the road turns left and leaves the hot shade for the stone of the last kilometres. By now Simpson had fallen back and riders were passing him. His MANAGER, Alec Taylor (a South London car-hire salesman), said, 'Sometimes this can be tactical but this time I thought not.' He was more worried that Simpson would take risks on the descent to make up the distance.

Just after the Chalet Reynard Simpson began 'riding like an amateur', said Harry Hall, the MECHANIC. 'He was zigzagging in the way amateurs do when they're in trouble.' And then he collapsed. Hall ran to him saying, 'That's it for you, Tom.' But Simpson insisted on going on, conscious enough to ask Hall to re-tighten his pedal straps, only to collapse again shortly afterwards.

The Tour doctor PIERRE DUMAS recalled, 'A policeman came and said, "Quick, there's been a *pépin* [a spot of bother]". We got there quickly but he'd already been put back on his bike and he'd fallen again and it looked bad. We spent more than an hour there with him: heart

massage, mouth-to-mouth. When I saw he was dead, I had him taken away in the helicopter.'

Simpson was taken to Avignon. FÉLIX LÉVITAN told reporters, 'Tom Simpson died at 17h 40 and burial permission has been refused.' The last words attributed to Simpson – 'Put me back on my bike' – were the invention of the *Cycling* reporter Sid Saltmarsh.

Few in BRITAIN saw the significance of the event. Doping was something foreigners did, and British riders copied only to match other people's cheating. In France, PIERRE CHANY remembered being with Dumas at the Hotel Noailles. 'It must have been 7am. He looked at the sky. The air was already tepid. We exchanged several words and he said something that I'll never forget: "The heat's going to be awful today: if the lads stick their noses in the *topette* [take drugs], we could have a death on our hands." The autopsy showed heart collapse from heat and overwork, and drugs in his blood. There were more in his jersey pockets. In a coded reference, JACQUES GODDET said, 'We often asked ourselves if this athlete, who at work often appeared in pain, had not committed some errors in the way he looked after himself.'

Five thousand are estimated to have been at the funeral at the twelfth-century All Saints church at Harworth, near Doncaster. Flags were said to have flown at half-mast for 15km. BRIAN ROBINSON, Reg Harris and JACQUES ANQUETIL's wife, Jeanine, were there. Only EDDY MERCKX represented contemporary Continental cycling, although there was a wreath from the Tour.

Cycling editors Alan Gayfer and Peter Bryan opened a MEMORIAL fund, originally for a stained-glass window at Harworth. 'Then we had the idea of a memorial on the spot,' said Gayfer. 'It fits in with a long-established tradition for riders who succeeded on the Continent.' A plaque added on the 30th anniversary says, 'There is no mountain too high. Your daughters Jane and Joanne, July 13 1997.'

Simpson's widow, Helen, whom he'd met in France, later married BARRY HOBAN, who won the next day's stage that became a tribute to Simpson. Simpson's daughters still live in Ghent, where Simpson and Helen moved. LUCIEN VAN IMPE opened a small Simpson museum in Harworth in 2001.

(*See* BENONI BEHEYT, SHAY ELLIOTT, SPRINTERS.)

Winner

1960	Tour Sud-Est
1961	Tour Flanders
1963	Bordeaux-Paris
1964	Milan-San Remo
1965	World championship, Tour Lombardy, London-Holyhead
1967	Paris-Nice, Manx Premier

Tour de France

1960	29th	
1961	DNF	
1962	6th	Yellow Jersey
1964	14th	
1965	DNF	
1966	DNF	
1967	DNF	

JESPER SKIBBY
b. Silkeborg, Denmark, Mar 21 1964

Jesper Skibby is the only Dane to have won stages in all three major Tours. (*See* ARNE JONSSON, BJARNE RIIS and ROLF SORENSEN for other Danes.) He was never a CLIMBER and yet his stage win in the 1996 TOUR OF SPAIN was in the MOUNTAINS. He also won two stages in the 1991 Tour of Spain. His Giro stage win was in 1989.

Skibby narrowly missed being run over in the Tour of Flanders on April 5 1987 when he fell on the steep and cobbled Koppenberg. An official in a BMW stopped as Skibby lay on the right of the road, then tried to squeeze by. Skibby's foot was still in his toe-clips as the car crushed his Colnago BIKE. Skibby was distressed but unhurt, but the climb was banned for several years.

Skibby was a light-hearted character who rode 11 Tours and finished eight, retiring in 2000. His father Willy was a rider and his sister Karina also raced, including the world championships.

Jesper Skibby *(continued)*

Winner

1994 Tour Holland
1998 Tour Flemish Ardennes

Tour de France

1987	29th
1989	41st
1990	DNF
1991	DNF
1992	56th
1993	53rd	Stage win Avranches—Evreux
1994	45th
1995	49th
1996	29th
1997	82nd
2000	DNF

SOCIÉTÉ DU TOUR DE FRANCE

The Société – French for company rather than 'society' – is the Tour's owner. It occupies a white office block in the rue Rouget de Lisle in Issy-les-Moulineaux in western Paris. (Claude Rouget de Lisle wrote the French national anthem in 1792.) 'Issy-the-watermills' sounds more pleasant than the industrial estate that it is today.

HENRI DESGRANGE had kept the Tour as the property of his newspaper, *L'AUTO*, during the early part of the 20th century. Its editor-in-chief, JACQUES GODDET, followed him as Tour organiser just before the WAR. Goddet started *L'ÉQUIPE* when *L'AUTO* was closed down with the Liberation of France in 1944, and took the Tour with him. It was run then by the Société du PARC DES PRINCES with Goddet at its head.

In 1962 an association began with *Le Parisien Libéré*, a daily newspaper with its own sports organisation, and Goddet signed a sponsorship contract with Emilion Amaury, its owner. Amaury made his editor, FÉLIX LÉVI-TAN, co-organiser. In May 1965 Amaury bought *L'ÉQUIPE* and in 1993 the Amaury Sports Organisation (ASO), led by Olympic skier Jean-Claude Killy, took over the Société du Tour de France.

ASO's divisions are the Société du Tour de France, the Thierry Sabine Organisation (which runs car rallies) and an athletics company. Amaury also publishes *L'Équipe, Le Parisien, Vélo* and some football magazines.

The Tour employs around 45 staff but administers 3,500, including the riders, 270 race staff, and more than a thousand journalists. It works with 13,000 POLICE along the route and with motorcyclists from the Garde Républicaine. The Tour's budget comes from SPONSORS (60 per cent), BROADCASTING rights (30 per cent) and contributions from stage towns. It is spent on organisation (50 per cent), PRIZES, hotels and TRANSFERS for riders (30 per cent) and 20 per cent on everything else.

The Société and *L'Équipe* have been in the rue Rouget de Lisle since August 1987. The bridge that had joined newspaper and Tour offices has now been removed, symbolic of the end of an era but irritating to reporters. The paper's name appears on race cars only as advertising.

The organisers meet the day after the final stage of each Tour and go through the race and comments made about it. Many then go on holiday. The route of the following year's Tour is known by then and rumours and tip-offs are rife enough for riders like LANCE ARMSTRONG to work out how to ride the main climbs. For everyone else the first hint comes with a glimpse along the route of Tour cars driven by two officials who meet mayors, police and other regional officials, and study the proposed route before announcing it at the PRESENTA-TION in late October.

The Société also runs or has run Paris-Nice, the Critérium International, Paris-Roubaix, Liège-Bastogne-Liège, Flèche Wallonne, Paris-Tours and the Grand Prix des Nations.

SOIGNEURS

The word means 'carers', and their jobs included massage, medical care, buttering sandwiches, carrying bags, and doing the washing. At first they were half-skilled quack doctors or svengalis, of whom the British manager and coach Choppy Warburton was the first to become famous in 1896. (*See* DOPING for more.) Warburton dressed in a long overcoat and a curly-brimmed hat, but the tradition was to wear rolled-up shirt sleeves, a wide belt and something that looked like a butcher's apron. Soigneurs in those times resembled wrestlers and flaunted their muscles and sausage-like fingers for the powerful massages they could give.

As the 20th century went on, many riders whose careers had finished became soigneurs. Like their predecessors they became legends for their 'magic hands', but it was often for rather more. A soigneur whose premises were raided in BELGIUM in the 1970s had more than 170,000 DOPING pills in his offices.

The Dutch soigneur Piet Liebregts told *De Stem* in south-west HOLLAND, 'It is really not the soigneurs who have made cycling so rotten. Until 1960 the riders knew almost nothing of doping. That was the secret of soigneurs, who held their tongues.'

Tour doctor PIERRE DUMAS said it was at about that time that both riders and soigneurs began going through medical catalogues to find drugs to make a rider more aggressive, painkillers to increase resistance, and then sleeping pills in the evening to bring them down from their hyper-stimulation. Soigneurs also traded on frequently crackpot medical and diet advice, with at least one insisting that his riders should eat cattle feed which, he said, would lie longer in the stomach and release its energy throughout the race. The era is full of tales of soigneurs warning riders off the most innocent of foods – ANTONIN MAGNE as a MANAGER denied his riders spinach – or insisting on the oddest of benefits. TOM SIMPSON was told to drink volumes of carrot juice 'to wash the drugs out of the system'.

The era of dope tests that followed Simpson's death in 1967, and particularly the increasing precision of tests from the 1980s, led soigneurs' medical duties to be transferred over the decade to qualified doctors. By the 1990s every respectable team had a doctor on its staff, and soigneurs were reduced to helping them. Evidence in the trial that followed the FESTINA AFFAIR in 1998 showed that the Festina team, at least, had a drug fund to which riders contributed, that the soigneur was involved in drug administration along with the doctor, and that the team manager had lost control of his riders to the medical team. (*See* FESTINA AFFAIR and WILLY VOET for more.)

Those revelations, especially the fund for systematic doping, brought the reputation of soigneurs to a new low. Men who in earlier decades would have been respected for their experience and 'magical' abilities were mocked as they passed in 1999 and 2000 by roadside crowds giving themselves imaginary injections.

Soigneurs now dislike the word and prefer to call themselves medical assistants or support staff – anything but soigneurs. But rat-catchers have never persuaded people that they are rodent sanitation operatives, and soigneurs look like remaining soigneurs for a long time yet.

(*See* MAURICE DEWAELE, PAUL DUBOC.)

ROLF SORENSEN
b. Copenhagen, Denmark, Apr 20 1965

In the 1991 Tour the team TIME TRIAL was an upset. It should have gone to the Dutch PDM team or to the ONCE team of SPAIN. It went instead to Ariostea, a largely Italian team with a Dane, Rolf Sorensen, as its best placed rider. That win put him in the yellow JERSEY, or '*den gule troj*' as he would have called it.

Sorensen was in his first Tour and rose to the occasion, defending his lead and reckoning he could hold it until the last time trial. Sadly he crashed in the last kilometres at Valenciennes and broke his collarbone. (*See* CRASHES for other upsets.)

Winner

1987   Tirreno-Adriatico
1989   Tour Etna, Coppa Bernocchi
1990   Paris-Tours, Sicilian Week
1992   Paris-Brussels, Tirreno-Adriatico

Winner (continued)

1993	GP Frankfurt, Liège-Bastogne-Liège, Milan-Turin, Coppa Bernocchi
1994	Paris-Brussels
1996	Tour Holland
1997	Tour Flanders
1998	Tour Holland
2000	Tour Denmark

Tour de France

1991	DNF	Yellow Jersey
1992	DNF	
1993	70th	
1994	19th	Stage win Castres—Montpellier
1996	28th	Stage win Le Puy-en-Velay—Superbesse
1997	68th	
2001	141st	

SPAIN

Spain has a thriving calendar and some of Europe's biggest teams, but only recently have Spanish riders come over the Pyrenees regularly for the Tour, and they still don't go in for northern classics such as Paris-Roubaix and the Tour of Flanders with much relish.

Spanish riders tend to be superb CLIMBERS. The first MOUNTAINS winner was VICENTE TRUEBA in 1933. The first to win the polka-dot jersey awarded to the Tour's best climber was another Spaniard, Jesus Loroño, in 1953. It was his compatriot and rival climber, FEDERICO BAHAMONTES, who in 1959 gave Spain its first Tour win. (*See* HENRY ANGLADE and JACQUES ANQUETIL for the incident that let this happen.) Bahamontes' six mountains victories are still a record, which he shares with LUCIEN VAN IMPE of BELGIUM. And van Impe's admiration for the Spaniard was such that he preferred not to win a seventh time.

There were no Spanish wins between Bahamontes and LUIS OCAÑA in 1973, although two Spaniards were on the podium in 1963: Bahamontes in second place and José Perez-Frances

in third. Ocaña was the only rider to seriously challenge EDDY MERCKX (*see* Ocaña entry for details) but his Tour record was damaged by a CRASH and his life cut short by suicide.

PEDRO DELGADO won in 1988, at a time when a rider who would turn out to be Spain's best ever, and the most successful of all Tour riders, was just getting into his career. This was MIGUEL INDURAIN, and he had such talent that he could rarely be beaten anywhere. Indurain was never as theatrical as the eccentrically brilliant Bahamontes, whose exploits included not only topping cols but stopping for an ice cream and throwing his bike into a ravine; nor was he as colourful as Ocaña, who outfought Merckx through the Alps. But he was hard to dislodge over the mountains and impossible to beat in long TIME TRIALS. In that respect, and in his detached air, he was like Anquetil. Both men won five Tours, and Indurain won his in succession (1991–1995), the only man to do so.

The Tour first visited Spain in 1906. The first Spanish team appeared in 1930. The only Tour to start in Spain was in 1992, setting out from San Sebastian.

SPECTACLE DU TOUR

For years the riders' rest at the end of each stage was potentially spoiled by open-air shows laid on at night in town centres by SPONSORS and radio stations. This is impossible now because the Tour is too big and spread across too wide an area each night. But in those days famous performers – in FRANCE anyway – and a lot of less well known ones would sing, while compères would organise competitions for SPECTATORS, and a good time was had by all. The biggest radio station on the circuit was Europe One, and its summer road shows inspired the BBC's Johnny Beerling to start the Radio One Roadshow.

The *Spectacle* was helped by the fact that Tour stages finished earlier then. Social life starts late in France, and there was time to watch the race, have a meal ('If you walked around town after dinner you often found the riders doing the same,' said Geoffrey Nicholson, who followed the race from 1965) and relax before going on to the show. The *Spectacle* is well featured in the FILM *Pour un Maillot Jaune*.

SPECTATORS

The Tour is a free show, and so many watch that it's said to produce a measurable dip in FRANCE's domestic production. But the link may be tenuous because the Tour is in July, the month when many French people go on holiday.

Among the most fanatical of fans are Yves Couvreur, a mechanic from Paris, who has followed almost 20 Tours, lately in an Iveco van with a huge flag in the colours of HOLLAND's Rabobank team; Lucien Blio from Geraardsbergen, BELGIUM, has followed more than 25, and always flies a tricolour carrying the lion emblem of Flanders (and a pun on the name Claude Criquielion, a Belgian star of the 1980s). 'The DEVIL', Didi Senff, also makes regular appearances. (*See* entry for other bizarre apparitions along the course.)

The START is the best place to see riders, although they stay behind barriers patrolled by POLICE. Watching from the roadside is a gamble. You could see a peloton stretched out in a line, or a break, or just an amble.

The best place to watch on a mountain is a bend two kilometres from the top. It's there that moves are made. Roads close three hours or more before the riders arrive, although police will sometimes let a BIKE through if the race CARAVAN isn't close. Cycling or walking as the caravan passes is illegal.

The most popular MOUNTAIN is ALPE D'HUEZ, where spectators camp for days. Next in the popularity stakes are the GALIBIER and TOURMALET. The Tourmalet gives spectacular views of approaching riders. However, the Galibier, Soulor and AUBISQUE are prone to bad weather, and MONT VENTOUX can also be cold.

Pushing riders on the climbs isn't well thought of and brings them penalties. 'Riders

aren't tom-toms,' says a warning. 'A tap on the back of a rider may seem innocent but it's wearing when it's repeated a million times before the top.' Running with the race is dangerous. Nor will riders appreciate being *arrosé* – sprinkled with water. A spectator who threw a bucket of water over JACQUES ANQUETIL on the Grand St-Bernard in 1966 was responsible for his pulling out at the bottom, frozen and unable to breathe. He left the race next morning.

It can take until midnight after a stage to get down from the mountain. Seasoned spectator Nev Chanin says the technique for leaving a col is to wait either three seconds or three hours. Crowds start making their way down before the last rider has passed. On high cols like the Tourmalet the police hold up traffic until jams and car parks have cleared lower down. They'll often let cyclists pass, but it can be a precarious ride.

French television shows at least half the stage. The best radio stations are France-Info (the news channel at around 105FM), France-Inter and Europe One. Near-continuous coverage is sometimes available on Europe One on long wave.

Arrive early at the FINISH. You won't see much live action because of the crowds and the speed, but you'll be able to see the race on a huge TV screen.

Fans have been known to get too involved in the action. They were blamed for a walkout by two Italian teams in 1950. GINO BARTALI was harassed on the Col d'Aspin and left the race.

Claims that Bartali was threatened by a man with a knife are dubious: the culprit seems to have had nothing more in his hand than a sandwich knife.

In 1975 a Frenchman punched EDDY MERCKX on the PUY-DE-DÔME. In 1997 Xavier Clément, a 30-year-old actor, did a streak behind the bunch on the CHAMPS ELYSÉES, and was fined for 'sexual exhibition'. Friends who had dared him to do it bought him lunch.

GEORGES SPEICHER

b. Paris, France Jun 8 1907, d. Jan 24 1978

Georges Speicher was a dilettante character, a regular at nightclubs. He came from the Ménilmontant area of Paris and had a long face, wavy hair and heavy eyelids. He turned professional the year before his first Tour in 1932. Until then he had been a swimmer and had learned to ride only to get a job as a messenger.

'I was 17 and I hadn't got a job,' he recalled. 'I read in the small ads that someone wanted a cyclist to make deliveries. The one problem was that I didn't know how to ride a bike. But I needed to make a living and so I turned up anyway. For the first few days I rode right up against the kerb, pedalling with one leg and scooting it with the other.'

He began racing the following year, turned professional in 1932, and won the Tour in 1933. His exploits brought *L'AUTO* record sales of 845,045. After his victory, selectors believed he would be too tired to ride the world championship as well as the Tour, and left him out. So Speicher went clubbing. But then a rider dropped out at the last hour, and the selectors had to scour the nightclubs of Paris to tell Speicher he had been chosen after all. Next morning he went to Montlhéry and became WORLD CHAMPION as well.

He was disqualified from the 1938 Tour for hanging on to a car. (*See* CHEATS and JACKY DURAND for proof that old tricks die hard.) He became a MANAGER after retirement and later drove the Tour's public relations car.

Winner

1933	Tour de France, World championship
1935	Paris-Angers, National championship, Paris-Rennes
1936	Paris-Roubaix
1937	National championship
1939	National championship

Tour de France

1932	10th	
1933	1st	Stage wins Grenoble—Gap, Gap—Digne, Cannes—Marseille, and Yellow Jersey
1934	11th	Stage wins Paris—Lille, Belfort—Évian, Évian—Aix-les-Bains, Marseille—Montpellier, Bordeaux—La Rochelle, and Yellow Jersey
1935	6th	Stage win Nîmes—Montpellier
1936	DNF	
1937	DNF	
1938	DNF	

SPONSORS

Most sports start as pastimes. Only later do people become good enough to make money. Cycling was the other way round. It was always a way to make money, and AMATEURS emerged only because they weren't good enough. It has also always been a sport for promoting commercial interests. In 1868 the Englishman James Moore was backed by the company that supplied his BIKE when he won the world's first race in the Parc de St-Cloud near Paris. The Compagnie Parisienne also organised the race. It was then linked to the first long place-to-place race, from Paris to Rouen in 1869, which Moore also won. Paris-Rouen was run by *Le Vélocipède Illustré* to promote the bicycle, but in reality to stimulate its sales.

Other bike factories soon saw the advantage. MAURICE GARIN, first winner of the Tour, was sponsored by LA FRANÇAISE, his rival HIPPOLYTE AUCOUTURIER by PEUGEOT. At first riders signed only for particular races. It was competition to keep the best riders that led to retainers, bonuses and permanent teams. Some, particularly ALCYON, became so powerful that they could dominate races by TACTICS. Those tactics – some illegal in the Tour – persuaded organiser HENRI DESGRANGE to ban sponsors in 1930 and run his race for NATIONAL TEAMS. He was angry that the Alcyon riders had contrived to help their leader MAURICE DEWAELE to win in 1929, even though other riders were stronger.

After the first world war there was a period when there so few riders and so little money that sponsors in FRANCE united to run a joint team, La Sportive, which won the Tour in 1919, 1920 and 1921. Not until the mid-twenties did full confidence return.

In the 1950s sponsors suffered again when post-war prosperity persuaded customers to buy cars rather than bikes. Bike firms could now no longer afford to sponsor teams. FIORENZO MAGNI turned for support to the company that made Nivea face-cream. GINO BARTALI did the same with chewing gum producers, Brooklyn. At first officials insisted that support from outside the sport was illegal. Bartali is said to have paid a fine before he could start the Mont Faron mountain TIME TRIAL in a jersey advertising a non-cycling company.

In fact, sponsorship from outside the sport wasn't new. From 1947 the football pools company ITP (International Totalisator Pools) had backed a semi-professional team in BRITAIN. This was managed by Percy Stallard, who brought road racing back to Britain during the war, and rode Stallard bikes with Simplex GEARS. Ken Russell, Les Plume, Mike Peers and Geoff Clark were among the riders, Clark winning the 1949 Brighton-Glasgow and Russell coming second in 1950. Riders in SPAIN also found outside backers. But both were too far from the heart of cycling for the sport's governing body, the UCI, to react.

The change came when RAPHAËL GÉMINIANI ordered bikes to be made under his own name at a factory in Montluçon, and then approached the Quinquina company. Quinquina saw the attraction of linking its St-Raphaël aperitif to a rider who shared its name. The result in 1962 was the St-Raphaël team led by JACQUES ANQUETIL, the first fully professional team with a main sponsor outside the industry.

This so-called *extra-sportif* sponsorship saved teams, but didn't bring in big money. Cycling was not suited to static television broadcasting, and sponsors were more interested in football. Even so, the Tour was angry about the new development, fearing commercial rivals and worried about losing advertising in its paper *L'ÉQUIPE*. Géminiani's team was banned from its first race, Milan-San Remo, but saved by sleight of hand. The UCI was against outside sponsorship but its president, Achille Joinard, favoured it. According to Géminiani, Joinard said, 'Go to the start with an ordinary JERSEY. Just before the off, take off the jerseys and wear your St-Raphaël shirts. I will send a telegram forbidding you from starting if you represent an *extra-sportif*. But I'll take care that the telegram arrives only after the race has started.'

The sport compromised by calling *extra-sportif* organisations not teams but 'groupes sportifs', and some had the initials *G.S.* on their jerseys. But the UCI insisted no *extra-sportif* could back a team without support from a bike company.

The biggest *extra-sportif* at this time was the refrigerator-maker Borghi, whose Ignis brand led the Italian market. Giovanni Borghi was so free with money that in 1959 he handed MIGUEL POBLET a bunch of car keys as he stood in a towel after winning Milan-San Remo. Poblet left the building and found an Alfa Romeo waiting for him outside.

Ignis' money completed what recession in the bike industry had started: it upped the stakes so much that bike firms could no longer compete. When critics accused Borghi of being keener on publicity than sport, he started another team – without advertising – and employed the WORLD CHAMPION, ERCOLE BALDINI, to show its credibility.

Borghi lost interest in 1962, and salaries tumbled as sponsors no longer had to compete. BRIAN ROBINSON only got a bike and jersey when he rode for La Perle, and the same at the Tour of Switzerland with HUGO KOBLET's Cila team. Only a handful of even the biggest teams were on wages. JULIO JIMENEZ said Spanish professionals of the sixties earned the equivalent of £15 per month and worked in the winter as truck drivers. The Flandria team including FREDDY MAERTENS, ROGER DE VLAEMINCK and MICHEL POLLENTIER in the mid-1970s cost just £750,000 a year. They were paid only 10 months a year.

Strange sponsors have included a 70-year-old Parisian nightclub dancer called Myriam De Kova, who advertised her legs on a pink jersey, and the Chris Barber Jazz Band in Britain. KELME is the doyen of sponsors, with more than 20 years in the bunch.

A number of sponsored teams have collapsed. Force Sud was nicknamed Farce Sud when bills brought it to an end in spring 1995. Le Groupement, which included LUC LEBLANC and ROBERT MILLAR, went under the same year, a week before the Tour after much negative publicity. The British company ANC fielded a Tour team in 1987 but vanished amid disputes over money the next year. Two other British teams also collapsed – Harrods in 1997 and Linda McCartney in January 2001 on the eve of its national presentation, when it emerged it had neither money nor even the advertised sponsorship.

Riders in the Santa Clara team in the mid-1990s turned up at their hotel during the Tour of SPAIN and found their bus impounded and all traces of their sponsoring team gone. Other sponsors have run out of money or not paid it. Freddy Maertens claims he is still owed wages from FLANDRIA. The UCI now insists sponsors register contracts and lodge a large percentage of their riders' wages with the ruling body.

(*See* CARAVAN, MONEY.)

> **Trivia note:** In 1958 the Aquila club in Portsmouth named itself VC St- Raphaël in honour of the team. The company gave the club tracksuits and a trophy. A Géminiani–St- Raphaël semi-professional team raced locally in 1959.

SPRINTERS

For most riders the Tour is sustained effort at less than maximum power. For sprinters their strength is – literally – ultimate power delivered for a handful of seconds. They are the knockout punch at the end of the stage, and DOMESTIQUES push up the speed in the last half-hour on the flatter stages to stop rival sprinters getting into good positions. The domestiques then sacrifice their own chance by swinging aside to let their team's sprinter make his last 200-metre lunge for the line, often at close to 60km/h.

Frenchman Jimmy Casper says, 'At 10km from the FINISH the teams involved in the sprint must set a rhythm. Then at one kilometre, perhaps even two, they have to really launch themselves forward and send out the riders who will force the final result. In the last 200–300m you have to position yourself in the slipstream created by the lead-out men and let your adrenaline start pumping. Once you're past the finish line, there is nothing better than victory. When you know you've made the wheels red hot, that you've worked to the point of falling over, you enjoy it. The exhilaration doesn't die down straight away.'

TOM SIMPSON portrayed the roughness of sprints when he said of the 1963 world championship, 'RIK VAN LOOY grabbed me by the jersey and just about brought me to a standstill. I managed to get going again, now in the middle of the bunch when, hell's bells! Dutchman JAN JANSSEN gave me a whacking great pull and just about stopped me completely. I should have gone up and given him a good thump round the earhole but what was the use? I did not see the finish for, by now, I was right at the back and, in fact, was placed 28th, last man in the sprint.'

Sprinters have their time in the Tour's first week, over flat roads. They rarely do well in MOUNTAINS, where their bulk puts them at a disadvantage.

Successful sprinters have included ANDRÉ DARRIGADE, FREDDY MAERTENS and RIK VAN LOOY. The most prolific recent sprinter is MARIO CIPOLLINI. The best modern sprinter to consistently finish the Tour is ERIK ZABEL.

1953	Fritz Schaer		1978	Freddy Maertens
1954	Ferdy Kübler		1979	Bernard Hinault
1955	Stan Ockers		1980	Rudy Pevenage
1956	Stan Ockers		1981	Freddy Maertens
1957	Jean Forestier		1982	Sean Kelly
1958	Jean Graczyk		1983	Sean Kelly
1959	André Darrigade		1984	Frank Hoste
1960	Jean Graczyk		1985	Sean Kelly
1961	André Darrigade		1986	Eric Vanderaerden
1962	Rudi Altig		1987	Jean-Paul van Poppel
1963	Rik van Looy		1988	Eddy Planckaert
1964	Jan Janssen		1989	Sean Kelly
1965	Jan Janssen		1990	Olaf Ludwig
1966	Willy Planckaert		1991	Djamolidine Abdoujaparov
1967	Jan Janssen		1992	Laurent Jalabert
1968	Franco Bitossi		1993	Djamolidine Abdoujaparov
1969	Eddy Merckx		1994	Djamolidine Abdoujaparov
1970	Walter Godefroot		1995	Laurent Jalabert
1971	Eddy Merckx		1996	Erik Zabel
1972	Eddy Merckx		1997	Erik Zabel
1973	Herman van Springel		1998	Erik Zabel
1974	Patrick Sercu		1999	Erik Zabel
1975	Rik van Linden		2000	Erik Zabel
1976	Freddy Maertens		2001	Erik Zabel
1977	Jacques Esclassan		2002	Robbie McEwen

Speeds and styles have risen as GEARS have grown higher. Sprinters have their own competition in the Tour, the leader wearing a green jersey first awarded in 1953.

The Tour's original organiser HENRI DESGRANGE hated bunched finishes. He considered riders hadn't tried hard enough or the course had been too easy if the bunch came in together.

(*See* CARAVAN, CLUB DU TOUR, SPONSORS.)

JEAN STABLINSKI
b. Thun-St-Amand, France, May 21 1932

Edward Stablewski's name was too difficult for French journalists to manage when he rode as a Polish AMATEUR, so they inadvertently changed it to Stablinski. Somehow he also became Jean, and in 1948 changed from the Polish nationality of his parents, who had emigrated to northern France, to become French. Jean Stablinski, the future French international, had been created.

He rode his first race in 1948 in swimming trunks and ordinary shoes, coming 15th, but he was disqualified for being too young. Next year he rode into BELGIUM and won his first race as a junior.

As a professional Stablinski was a great all-rounder. From 1960 to 1964 he won the French championship every year but one, 1961, when RAYMOND POULIDOR won with Stablinski second. In 1962 he became WORLD CHAMPION at Salo with the connivance of Ireland's SHAY ELLIOTT and a SPECTATOR. Elliott was away alone, but Stablinski rode up to him with Jos Hoevenaars. Elliott let him have the championship by not chasing when Stablinski attacked. Stablinski punctured just before the line and finished on a bike borrowed from a spectator. It is perhaps not a coincidence that

Jean Stablinski (*continued*)

Elliott later married Stablinski's sister. (*See* Elliott entry for more.)

Stablinski spent most of his life riding for JACQUES ANQUETIL, through the Helyett, St-Raphaël, Ford and Bic teams. Then Anquetil wrote about him unkindly in a newspaper – he later insisted the paper had changed his words – and the two men fell out. Stablinski joined Poulidor's Mercier team.

RAPHAËL GÉMINIANI was unstinting in his praise of Stablinski: 'Young riders would sometimes complain to me that they weren't CLIMBERS or SPRINTERS. And I always told them to name a French rider who wasn't one of the ten best climbers, who wasn't one of the ten best *rouleurs* nor one of the ten best sprinters, but nevertheless had some of the world's biggest races on his record. And they can never tell me. Well, the answer is Jean Stablinski.

'His talent was his brain. He was the craftiest rider, a tactician without equal. He'd attack over and over again. The first three times the others would match him because he'd attack within himself. And then the fourth time he'd attack flat out and the rest would be demoralised, realising they'd chased him three times for nothing.

'He could ride well for himself but alongside Jacques Anquetil he was superb, whether it was the Tour, the Giro or the Tour of SPAIN. He was like a guard dog, always at the head of the bunch to get into breaks and work for his teammates.

'Jean Stablinski was one of the greats of cycling. It was a shame he never got the coverage that he deserved so that more people knew of his intelligence. There's not been a rider like him for a long time.'

He became a MANAGER when he retired and signed LUCIEN VAN IMPE (*see* entry for details). He still turns up at events, and has a *cyclosportif* event named after him. He still rides regularly, although deliberately without a bottle. 'I take a few euros instead,' he says, 'and that way I have to go into a café for a drink and I get to chat to people and it reminds me that there's more to cycling than racing.'

(*See* JEAN GRACZYK for another Pole who became a Frenchman.)

Winner

1954	Paris-Bourges
1956	Tour Sud-Est
1957	GP Fourmies, Tour Oise
1958	Tour Spain
1960	National championship
1962	World championship, National championship
1963	Paris-Brussels, National championship
1964	National championship
1965	GP Gippingen, GP Frankfurt, Paris-Luxembourg, Tour Belgium
1966	Amstel Gold, GP Isbergues

Tour de France

1954	DNF	
1955	35th	
1957	43rd	Stage win Cannes—Marseille
1958	68th	
1959	DNF	
1961	42nd	Stage win Belfort—Châlon-sur-Saône
1962	30th	Stage win Luchon—Carcassonne
1963	DNF	
1964	35th	Stage win Clermont-Ferrand—Orléans
1966	61st	
1967	81st	Stage win Bordeaux—Limoges
1968	DNF	

STAGES

Each individual race within the Tour is an *étape*, or stage. The time each rider takes is totalled through the three weeks, sometimes with BONUSES for wins or other successes, and the overall result decides the WINNER, who's simply the rider who's taken the least time to complete the route.

There was originally no limit to the length of stages, and some started in late evening, went on all night and finished the following day. The first stage was 467km from Paris to Lyon. It began at 3.16pm and finished next day. Riding through the night became less common as officials tried to overcome CHEATS who flourished in the darkness, and the sometimes violent intervention of SPECTATORS (*see* 1904 AFFAIR). DISTANCES remained lengthy, though, and several days' rest were needed between each.

The longest ever day was 482km from Les Sables d'Olonne to Bayonne in 1924. ALBERT LONDRES recorded, 'No one feels like racing. They cross the Vendée, the Gironde and the Landes as though someone they hate is tugging them by the ear. This isn't cycling. They're riding so slowly that it's no longer a bike race. It's more like one of those trick-cycling exhibitions in the olden days. In short, from Les Sables to BORDEAUX, they were sick to the teeth of it.'

However, before 1928 distances were only approximate, despite the apparent precision of the figures. The longest post-war stage was 359km from Clermont-Ferrand to Fontainebleau in 1967.

Single days have sometimes been split into two or more stages, which is unpopular with riders. So-called third-stages – three races in a single day – were tried from 1936. These were run as miniature stage races and their results combined into one. The number and length of stages is now limited by international RULES to suppress DOPING. The record number of wins is 34 by EDDY MERCKX.

How and why the Tour goes to some towns and not to others is a mixture of geography, chance and MONEY. The original organiser HENRI DESGRANGE followed the French boundary, making it the circuit that the word *tour* means in French. The only commercial interest for stage towns on that 1903 Tour came from GÉO LEFÈVRE's suggestion that hotelkeepers could give riders cheap meals in return for publicity. The Tour depended on train connections, since that was how officials travelled.

Changing to NATIONAL TEAMS in 1930 meant that Desgrange had to pay riders' costs himself, and he began charging towns for the trade and publicity the race would bring in. The Tour took a more commercial turn with the arrival of FÉLIX LÉVITAN as organiser in

1962. Lévitan arranged for stage finishes to occur at publicity-conscious ski centres and seaside developments.

In 1988 the Tour came under JEAN-MARIE LEBLANC's control and found a healthier balance, although the organisation is still aware of the value a stage brings a town. The number of towns can be increased by holding the FINISH in one and the START in another. The Tour doesn't publish accounts (and is said to pay a fine every year as a result). But an inquiry in November 1995 established that hosting the start of the Tour could cost £607,500 in FRANCE and £870,000 abroad. Hosting both the start and finish – a *ville-étape* – cost £68,500. Those amounts are likely to have increased since. A *ville-étape* is expected to recoup £123,000 in immediate benefits and continuing publicity.

The Tour has more finishes in rich areas than in underpopulated, poor ones. BORDEAUX has legendary status as a gateway to the Pyrenees. Other towns have been less content. In 1987 the mayor of Valence d'Agen spent a year preparing for the biggest day his little town of 8,000 had known – only for the bunch to walk across the line on STRIKE. The Tour finished in Marseille every year from 1927 to the WAR and then almost every year until 1971. That was the year that EDDY MERCKX went at such skittling speed that the race was over long before the mayor, Gaston Deferre, got there. Most riders had gone for their shower. Deferre was so angry that he banned the Tour and it didn't come back until 1989, after he had died.

The 2003 Tour, the centenary, will be routed to include all the stage towns of 1903.

STAGES

(Team names in stage results refer to winners of team time trial stages)

Stage towns		Year	Winner
Agen	4	1951	Koblet
		1980	start
		1996	start
		2000	start
Aime (La Plagne)	4	1984	start
		1987	start
		1995	start
		2002	start

Stage towns		Year	Winner
Aix-en-Provence	6	1913	Garrigou
		1920	Heusghem
		1952	Rémy
		1956	Thomin
		1961	van Aerde
		1962	Daems
Aix-les-Bains	22	1931	Bulla
		1932	Leducq
		1933	Guerra
		1934	Speicher
		1935	Vietto
		1936	Meulenberg
		1937	Deloor
		1938	Kint
		1948	Bartali
		1951	Ruiz
		1954	Dotto
		1958	Gaul
		1960	Graczyk
		1962	Poulidor
		1965	Jimenez
		1972	Guimard
		1974	Merckx
		1989	LeMond
		1991	Konyshev
		1996	Boogerd
		1998	cancelled
		2001	Ivanov
Albertville	1	1998	Ullrich
Albi	9	1953	Darrigade
		1955	De Groot
		1959	Graf
		1968	Pingeon
		1971	Merckx
		1975	Knetemann
		1991	start
		1994	Riis
		1999	Commesso
Alençon	4	1984	Hoste
		1991	Indurain
		1995	Gewiss-Ballan team
		2002	Zabel
Alès	2	1957	De Filippis
		1991	Argentin
Alfortville	1	1983	start
Alpe d'Huez	21	1952	Coppi
		1976	Zoetemelk
		1977	Kuiper
		1978	Kuiper
		1979	Agostinho, Zoetemelk

Stage towns		Year	Winner
		1981	Winnen
		1982	Breu
		1983	Winnen
		1984	Herrera
		1986	Hinault
		1987	Echave
		1988	Rooks
		1989	Theunisse
		1990	Bugno
		1991	Bugno
		1992	Hampsten
		1994	Conti
		1995	Pantani
		1997	Pantani
		1999	Guerini
		2001	Armstrong
		2003	......
Altkirch	1	1977	start
Amiens	10	1932	Leducq
		1962	Altig
		1964	Darrigade
		1967	Basso
		1970	Spruyt
		1971	Leman
		1975	De Witte
		1979	start
		1993	Bruyneel
		1999	Cipollini
Amsterdam	1	1954	start (Tour)
Ancenis	1	1988	Panasonic team
Andorra	3	1964	Jimenez
		1993	Rincon
		1997	Ullrich
Angers	17	1936	Maye
		1950	Lauredi
		1951	Koblet
		1954	De Bruyne
		1956	Fantini
		1960	Battistini
		1963	De Breuker, Anquetil
		1966	Sels
		1967	Errandonea
		1970	Zilioli, Faemino team
		1972	Merckx
		1976	Maertens
		1977	Sercu, Fiat team
		1979	Raas
Angoulême	1	1975	Moser
Annecy	2	1939	van Schendel
		1959	Graf

Stage towns		Year	Winner
Antibes	2	1961	Carlesi
		1962	Altig
Antwerp	2	1954	W. Wagtmans
		2001	Wauters
Aoste	2	1949	Coppi
		1959	Baldini
			(at St-Vincent-
			d'Aoste)
Arbois	1	1963	start
Arcachon	1	1938	Rossi
Arcs-et-Senans	1	1996	start
Argelès-sur-Mer	1	1973	Hoban
Argelès-Gazost	1	1996	start
Argentan	1	1991	van Poppel
Arlon	1	1968	start
Armentières	1	1964	Abdoujaparov
Arpachon	1	1999	start
Arras	1	1991	start
Aubagne	2	1969	Gimondi
		1973	Wright
Aubenas	1	1966	De Roo
Aubisque	1	1985	Roche
Auch	3	1975	Merckx
		1976	Bracke
		1977	Villemiane
Aulnay-sous-Bois	2	1981	Wijnands
		1982	Willems
Aurillac	6	1959	Anglade
		1963	van Looy
		1968	Bitossi
		1975	start
		1983	Lubberding
		1985	Chozas
Autrans	1	1985	start
Autun	1	1998	Backstedt
Auxerre	6	1965	Wright
		1968	Leman
		1972	Rini Wagtmans
		1979	Knetemann
		1980	start
		1981	start
Avesnes-sur-Helpe	1	1999	start
Avignon	7	1951	L. Bobet
		1952	Robic
		1955	L. Bobet
		1960	van Geneugden
		1974	start
		1987	van Poppel
		2000	start
Avoriaz	6	1975	Lopez-Carril
		1977	van Impe

Stage towns		Year	Winner
		1979	Hinault
		1983	van Impe
		1985	Herrera
		1994	Ugrumov
Avranches	3	1990	start
		1993	GB-MG team
		2002	McGee
Ax-les-Thermes	6	1933	Aerts
		1934	R. Lapébie
		1937	Canardo
		1955	Pezzi
		1957	Bourles
		1965	Reybroeck
Bagnères-de-Bigorre	9	1952	Géminiani
		1959	M. Janssens
		1963	Anquetil
		1965	Jimenez
		1970	start
		1974	start
		1994	start
		2000	start
		2003	start
Bagnoles de l'Orne	3	1968	Desvages
		1977	start
		2002	start
Ballon d'Alsace	4	1967	Aimar
		1969	Merckx
		1972	Thévenet
		1979	Villemiane
Barcelona	3	1957	Privat, Anquetil
		1965	Perez Frances
Barcelonnette	1	1975	start
Bar-le-Duc	1	2001	Crédit Agricole
			team
Basle	3	1971	Leman
		1982	Hinault, start
Bastide d'Armagnac	1	1989	start
Bastogne	1	1976	start
Bayonne	32	1906	Dortignacq
		1907	Petit-Breton
		1908	Petit-Breton
		1909	Menager
		1910	Lapize
		1911	Brocco
		1912	Mottiat
		1913	van Lerberghe
		1914	Egg
		1919	Alavoine
		1920	Lambot
		1921	Mottiat
		1922	Alavoine

Stage towns		Year	Winner
		1923	Jacquinot
		1924	Huysse
		1925	Bottecchia
		1926	Frantz
		1927	Verhaegen
		1929	Moineau
		1931	Loncke
		1938	Servadei, Rossi
		1954	Bauvin
		1956	De Bruyne
		1959	Queheille
		1962	Vannitsen
		1964	Anquetil
		1966	Karstens
		1968	Bellone
		1972	Duyndam
		1986	start
		1987	start
		2003	.....
Bazas	1	2002	start
Beaulieu	1	1976	start
Beauraing	1	1982	start
Beauvais	1	1980	TI-Raleigh team
Belfort	29	1907	Georget
		1908	Faber
		1909	Faber
		1910	Georget
		1911	Faber
		1912	Christophe
		1913	M. Buysse
		1914	H. Pélissier
		1927	Geldhof
		1928	Leducq
		1929	C. Pélissier
		1930	Bonduel
		1931	Di Paco
		1932	Leducq
		1933	Aerts
		1934	R. Lapébie
		1935	Aerts
		1936	Archambaud
		1937	Bautz
		1938	Masson
		1961	J. Planckaert
		1967	start
		1969	start
		1970	start
		1973	start
		1978	Demeyer
		1979	start
		1988	start

Stage towns		Year	Winner
		2000	start
Bergerac	2	1961	start
		1994	Indurain
Beringen	1	1981	start
Berlin	3	1987	start (Tour)
			Nijdam,
			Verhoeven,
			Carrera team
Besançon	16	1905	Aucouturier
		1938	Kint
		1947	Kübler
		1954	Teisseire
		1957	P. Baffi
		1958	Darrigade
		1960	Graf
		1963	Anquetil
		1964	H. Nijdam
		1968	Huysmans
		1974	Sercu
		1977	J-P.
			Danguillaume
		1981	start
		1988	van Poppel
		1990	Ludwig
		1996	Blijlevens
Besse	1	1996	start
Besse-en-Chandesse	1	1978	start
Bethune	1	1984	van den Haute
Béziers	5	1938	F. Vervaecke
		1939	Archambaud
		1953	Lauredi
		1958	P. Baffi
		2002	D. Millar
Biarritz	2	1948	Bobet
		1978	Lasa
Blagnac	6	1984	Poisson
		1986	Ruttimann
		1987	Golz
		1988	start
		1989	Hermans
		1990	start
Blain	1	1959	start
Blois	3	1971	start
		1992	Indurain
		1999	Cipollini
Bobigny	1	1984	start
Bondy	1	1984	start
Bonneval	2	1939	Jaminet
		1999	start
Bordeaux	78	1903	Laeser
		1904	Beaugendre

Stage towns		Year	Winner
		1905	Trousselier
		1906	Trousselier
		1907	Garrigou
		1908	Paulmier
		1909	Faber
		1910	Paul
		1925	Bottecchia
		1926	van Dam
		1927	Benoit
		1928	Fontan
		1929	Frantz
		1930	Aerts
		1931	Hamerlinck
		1932	Leducq
		1933	Aerts
		1934	Meini
		1935	Moineau
		1936	Le Greves
		1937	Chocque
		1938	Meulenberg
		1939	Passat
		1947	Tacca
		1948	Rémy
		1949	G. Lapébie
		1950	Pasotti
		1952	Dekkers
		1953	Nolten
		1954	Faanhof
		1955	W. Wagtmans
		1956	Hassenforder
		1957	P. Baffi
		1958	Padovan
		1959	Dejouhannet
		1960	van Geneugden
		1961	van Geneugden
		1962	Bailetti
		1963	van Looy
		1964	Darrigade
		1965	De Roo
		1966	Willy Planckaert
		1967	Basso
		1968	Godefroot
		1969	Hoban
		1970	Wolfshohl, Merckx
		1971	Merckx
		1972	Godefroot, Merckx
		1973	Godefroot, Agostinho

Stage towns		Year	Winner
		1974	Campaner, Merckx
		1975	Hoban
		1976	Karstens
		1977	Esclassan, Thurau
		1978	Maertens
		1979	TI-Raleigh team
		1980	Priem
		1981	Freuler
		1982	Villemiane
		1983	Oosterbosch
		1984	Raas
		1985	Vanderaerden
		1986	Dhaenens
		1987	Phinney
		1988	van Poppel
		1989	De Wilde
		1990	Bugno
		1992	Harmeling
		1993	Abdoujaparov
		1995	Zabel
		1996	Moncassin
		1997	Zabel
		1999	Steels
		2003	......
Bornem	1	1976	Kuiper
Boulougne-Billancourt	1	1986	start (Tour), Marie
Boulogne-sur-Mer	3	1949	Callens
		1994	van Poppel
		2001	Zabel
Bourg-d'Oisans	16	1952	start
		1966	Otano
		1976	start
		1979	start
		1981	start
		1983	start
		1987	start
		1984	start
		1989	start
		1991	start
		1992	start
		1994	start
		1995	start
		1997	start
		1999	start
		2003	start
Bourg-en-Bresse	1	2002	Hushovd
Bourges	1	1973	start
Bourg-Madame	3	1937	Meulenberg

Stage towns		Year	Winner
		1973	start
		1976	start
Bourgoin-Jallieu	1	1962	start
Bourg-St-Maurice	2	1939	S. Maes
		1996	start
Brasschaat	1	1954	W. Wagtmans
Brest	28	1906	Trousselier
		1907	Garrigou
		1908	Faber
		1909	Garrigou
		1910	Garrigou
		1911	Godivier
		1912	Heusghem
		1913	H. Pélissier
		1914	Engel
		1919	F. Pélissier
		1920	H. Pélissier
		1921	Scieur
		1922	Jacquinot
		1923	H. Pélissier
		1924	Beekman
		1925	Mottiat
		1926	van Dam
		1927	Leducq
		1928	Verhaegen
		1929	Delannoy
		1930	C. Pélissier
		1931	Battesini
		1929	Cloarec
		1952	start (Tour)
		1954	Forlini
		1958	Robinson
		1962	Cazala
		1974	start (Tour), Merckx
Bretigny-sur-Orge	2	1990	start
		1993	start
Briançon	31	1922	Thys
		1923	H. Pélissier
		1924	Brunero
		1925	Aymo
		1926	Aymo
		1927	J. Vervaecke
		1936	Goasmat
		1937	Weckerling
		1938	Bartali
		1939	S. Maes
		1947	Camellini
		1948	Bartali
		1949	Bartali
		1950	Bobet

Stage towns		Year	Winner
		1951	Coppi
		1953	Bobet
		1954	Bobet
		1955	Gaul
		1957	Nencini
		1958	Bahamontes
		1960	Battistini
		1962	Daems
		1964	Bahamontes
		1965	Galera
		1966	Jimenez
		1967	Gimondi
		1969	van Springel
		1972	Merckx
		1986	start
		1989	Richard
		2000	Botero
Brighton	1	1994	Cabello
Brive	8	1951	Ruiz
		1964	Sels
		1969	Hoban
		1973	Tollet
		1987	start
		1996	start
		1998	Cipollini
		2001	start
Bron	1	1991	start
Brussels	11	1947	Vietto
		1949	Lambrecht
		1958	start (Tour)
		1960	Schepens, Rivière
		1962	start
		1978	Walter Planckaert
		1979	Maas, Hinault
		1981	Maertens
		1992	Jalabert
Caen	34	1905	Dortignacq
		1906	Passerieu
		1907	Georget
		1908	Passerieu
		1909	Duboc
		1910	Lapize
		1927	H. Martin
		1928	Frantz
		1929	Dossche
		1930	C. Pélissier
		1931	Hamerlinck
		1932	Aerts
		1933	Le Grevès

Stage towns		Year	Winner
		1969	Leman
		2003	.....
Chassieu	1	1991	Ariostea team
Châteaubriant	1	1983	start
Châteaulin	4	1958	Gaul
		1965	van Espen, Poulidor
		1982	Hoste
Château roux	1	1998	Cipollini
Château-Thierry	1	2002	ONCE team
Châtel	1	1975	van Impe
Châtellerault	1	1955	start
Chaumeil	1	1987	Gayant
Chaumont	1	1974	Guimard
Cherbourg	17	1911	Garrigou
		1912	Alavoine
		1913	Masselis
		1914	Rossius
		1919	H. Pélissier
		1920	Thys
		1921	Bellenger
		1922	Bellenger
		1923	Bottecchia
		1924	Bellenger
		1925	Bellenger
		1926	Benoit
		1927	van de Casteele
		1928	Leducq
		1929	Leducq
		1968	Bontempi
		1994	start
Chôlet	2	1936	F. Vervaecke
		1998	Blijlevens
Ciney	1	1970	start
Clermont-Ferrand	10	1951	Géminiani
		1959	Le Dissez
		1964	start
		1967	start
		1969	start
		1971	start
		1973	start
		1983	start
		1986	start
		1988	start
Cluses	2	1994	Ugrumov
		2002	start
Colmar	6	1931	Leducq
		1949	Géminiani
		1955	Hassenforder
		1957	Hassenforder
		1997	Stephens

Stage towns		Year	Winner
		2001	Jalabert
Cologne	1	1965	start (Tour)
Colomiers	2	1972	Huysmans
		1974	Genet
Commercy	1	2001	start
Compiègne	2	1980	J-L Gauthier
		1981	start
Concarneau	1	1982	Verschuere
Corbeil-Essonnes	1	2001	start
Cork	1	1998	Svorada
Corrèze	1	1998	Ullrich
Cosne-sur-Loire	1	1986	start
Courchevel	2	1997	Virenque
		2000	Pantani
Crans-Montana	1	1984	Fignon
Creteil	3	1969	Spruyt
		1983	Pirard
		1987	start
Damazan	1	1980	start
Dax	5	1951	van Est
		1958	van Geneugden
		1965	start
		2000	Bettini
		2003	start
Deauville	1	1979	van Vliet
Dieppe	9	1927	F. Pélissier
		1928	Magne
		1929	Leducq
		1953	Voorting
		1955	Poblet, Holland team
		1960	De Filippis
		1966	Planckaert
		1974	De Witte
Digne	10	1993	Speicher
		1934	Vietto
		1935	Vietto
		1936	Level
		1937	R. Lapébie
		1938	Gianello
		1939	Cloarec
		1947	Vietto
		1967	Samyn
		1969	Merckx
Dijon	17	1906	Pottier
		1926	van de Casteele
		1939	Archambaud
		1950	Sciardis
		1951	Derijcke
		1958	Gaul
		1959	Rivière

Stage towns	Year	Winner
	1977	Knetemann, Thévenet
	1979	Parsani, Hinault
	1983	Leleu, Fignon
	1987	Clère, Bernard
	1991	De Wilde
	1997	Traversoni
Dinan 6	1927	Le Drogo
	1928	Rebry
	1929	Taverne
	1930	Guerra
	1931	Bulla
	1995	start
Dinant 1	1971	start
Dinard 6	1948	Rossello
	1950	Corrieri
	1962	start
	1968	Dumont
	1989	start
	1993	Abdoujaparov
Disneyland 2	1994	start
	1997	Olano
Divonne-les-Bains 7	1967	Reybroeck
	1969	Diaz, Merckx
	1970	Merckx, Merckx
	1973	Danguillaume
	1976	Esclassan
Dôle 2	1939	Neuens
	1992	start
Domaine-du-Rouret 1	1984	F. De Wolf
Douai 1	1906	start
Dover 1	1994	start
Draguignan 1	2000	Garcia-Acosta
Dublin 2	1998	start (Tour), Boardman, Steels
Dunkirk 18	1911	Garrigou
	1912	Crupelandt
	1913	M. Buysse
	1914	Faber
	1919	Lambot
	1920	Goethals
	1921	Goethals
	1922	Sellier
	1923	Goethals
	1924	Bellenger
	1925	Martin
	1926	van Slembroeck
	1927	Leducq
	1958	Voorting
	1960	Privat

Stage towns	Year	Winner
	1966	Karstens
	1995	Blijlevens
	2001	start (Tour), Moreau
Embrun 1	1973	start
Enniscorthy 1	1998	start
Épernay 3	1963	Pauwels
	1978	start
	2002	start
Epinal 4	1954	F. Mahé
	1985	Ducrot
	1987	Lavainne
	1990	Alcala
Epinay-sur-Senart 1	1987	van Poppel
Esch-sur-Alzette 1	1968	Grosskost
Euralille 1	1994	Lille
Eurotunnel 1	1994	GB-MG team
Évian 15	1925	H. Martin
	1926	start (Tour), van Dam
	1927	Verhaegen
	1928	Moineau
	1929	J. Vervaecke
	1930	Leducq
	1931	Demuysère
	1932	Di Paco
	1933	Louyet
	1934	Speicher Le Greves
	1935	Di Paco
	1936	Le Grevès
	1979	Demeyer
	2000	start
Evreux 4	1978	start
	1986	Ruiz-Cabestany
	1988	Da Silva
	1993	Skibby
Evry 1	2001	Zabel
Fécamp 1	1995	start
Felsberg 1	1970	A. Vasseur
Figeac 1	1978	start
Flers 1	1980	start
Fleurance 7	1973	David
	1975	Smit
	1976	Pollentier
	1977	start (Tour), Thurau
	1979	start (Tour), Knetemann
	1982	start
	1983	Clère

Stage towns		Year	Winner
Foix	1	2001	start
Fontaine	1	1990	start
Fontaine-au-Pire	2	1982	stage cancelled
		1983	Co-op-Mercier team
Fontainebleau	1	1967	Lemeteyer
Fontenay-sous-Bois	4	1980	Kelly
		1981	van der Velde
		1982	start
		1983	start (Tour), Vanderaerden
Font-Romeu	3	1968	start (Font-Romeu-Pyrenees 2000)
		1973	van Impe
		1976	Delisle
Forest	6	1964	van de Kerckhove, Kas team
		1968	E. de Vlaeminck, Belgium team
		1970	Merckx, Gonzales-Linares
Forges-les-Eaux	2	1997	Cipollini
		2002	start
Fougères	1	1985	La Vie Claire team
Francorchamps	2	1980	Hinault
		1989	Alcala
Frankfurt	2	1980	start (Tour), Hinault, TI-Raleigh team
Freiburg	4	1964	Derboven
		1971	Karstens
		1977	Sercu
		2000	Commesso
Fribourg	1	1997	Mengin
Frontignan-la-Peyrade	1	1998	start
Futuroscope	10	1977	start
(and Jaunay-Clan)		1986	Sarrapio
		1987	Roche
		1989	Pelier
		1990	start (Tour) Marie, Maassen, Panasonic team
		1994	Svorada
		1999	Mondini, Armstrong
		2000	start (Tour), D. Millar

Stage towns		Year	Winner
Gaillac	1	2003	start
Gallard	2	1973	Ocaña
		1974	Merckx
Gap	19	1931	Demuysère
		1932	Leducq
		1933	Speicher
		1934	Martano
		1935	Aerts
		1950	Géminiani
		1951	Baeyens
		1953	W. Wagtmans
		1956	Forestier
		1958	Nencini
		1960	van Aerde
		1965	Fezzardi
		1970	Mori
		1986	Bernard
		1989	start, Jelle Nijdam
		1991	Lietti
		1996	Zabel
		2003	.....
Geneva	10	1913	M. Buysse
		1914	Garrigou
		1919	Barthélémy
		1921	Goethals
		1922	Masson
		1923	H. Pélissier
		1935	Archambaud
		1937	Amberg
		1951	Koblet
		1990	Ghirotto
Gex	2	1920	Scieur
		1924	Frantz
Ghent	2	1951	Diederich
		1958	Darrigade
Gourette	1	1971	Labourdette
Grand-Bornand	2	1995	start
		1999	start
Granon	1	1986	Chozas
Granville	1	1957	Darrigade
Grenoble	38	1905	Trousselier
		1906	Pottier
		1907	Georget
		1908	Passerieu
		1909	Faber
		1910	Lapize
		1911	Georget
		1912	Christophe
		1913	Faber
		1914	H. Pélissier

Stage towns		Year	Winner
		1919	Barthélémy
		1920	Heusghem
		1921	Scieur
		1928	Magne
		1929	Rebry
		1930	Guerra
		1931	C. Pélissier
		1932	R. Lapébie
		1933	Guerra
		1934	Vietto
		1935	Camusso
		1936	Middelkamp
		1937	Bartali
		1947	Robic
		1954	L. Lazaridès
		1956	Gaul
		1959	Gaul
		1961	Gaul
		1963	Bahamontes
		1968	Pingeon
		1970	Merckx
		1971	Thévenet
		1978	start
		1984	Vichot
		1988	start
		1998	O'Grady
		2001	start
Guzet-Neige	3	1984	R. Millar
		1988	Ghirotto
		1995	Pantani
Harelbeke	2	1974	L. Molineris, Molteni team
Hasselt	1	1981	Maertens
Hautacam *(see* Lourdes)			
Hendaye	3	1928	Dewaele
		1930	Merviel
		1996	Voskamp
Herentals	2	1962	Darrigade, Flandria team
Huy	2	1995	start
		2001	start
Hyères	1	1964	Janssen
Isle d'Abeau	1	1989	Fidanza
Isola 2000	1	1993	Rominger
Issoire	1	1983	start, Le Bigaut
Ivrea	1	1966	start
Jaca	1	1991	Mottet
Jambes	4	1963	van Looy, Pelforth team
		1967	Pingeon, Belgium team

Stage towns		Year	Winner
Jaunay-Clan *(see* Futuroscope)			
Joinville	1	2003	.....
Jonzac	1	1999	start
Karlsruhe	1	1987	start
Koblenz	1	1992	Nevens
La Baule	3	1965	Reybroeck
		1972	van Linden
		1988	start (Tour), Weinmann team, Bontempi
La Bourboule	1	1992	Roche
Lacanau	1	1976	Maertens
La Châtre	2	1997	Vasseur
		1998	start
La Chaux-de-Fonds	1	1998	start
Lac de Madine	2	1993	Indurain
		1996	Saugrain
La Défense	1	1992	start
La Ferté-sous-Jouarre	1	2003	start
La Grande Motte	2	1969	Reybroeck
		1972	Teirlinck
La Guerche	1	1951	start
La Haye Fouassière	1	1988	start
La Mongie	2	1970	Thévenet
		2002	Armstrong
Lanester	2	1985	Matthys
		2002	start
Langon	3	1975	start
		1976	Maertens
		1984	start
Lannemezan	2	1999	start
		2002	start
Lannion	1	1995	Baldato
Lans-en-Vercors	1	1985	Parra
Laon	1	1938	Servadei
La Plagne	4	1984	Fignon
		1987	Fignon
		1995	Zülle
		2002	Boogerd
Laplume	1	1980	Zoetemelk
La Rochelle	20	1905	Aucouturier
		1911	Duboc
		1912	Alavoine
		1913	M. Buysse
		1914	Egg
		1933	Aerts
		1934	Speicher
		1935	Leducq
		1936	S. Maes
		1937	R. Lapébie
		1938	Meulenberg

Stage towns		Year	Winner
		1939	Storme
		1948	Pras
		1949	Coppi
		1956	Poblet
		1959	Hassenforder
		1962	Anquetil
		1965	Sels
		1970	Guimard
		1983	start
La Roche-sur-Yon	5	1934	Le Grevès
		1935	Le Grevès
		1936	Kint
		1937	R. Lapébie
		1938	Meulenberg
La Ruchère	1	1984	Fignon
Laruns	1	1985	start
La Tour du Pin	1	1983	start
Lausanne	5	1948	Bartali
		1949	Rossello
		1952	Diggelmann
		1978	Knetemann
		2000	Dekker
Laval	1	1999	Steels
Lavalanet	1	2002	start
Lavaur	1	2001	Verbrugghe
Le Blanc	1	1997	start
Le Creusot	1	1998	Ullrich
Le Havre	19	1911	Duboc
		1912	Borgarello
		1913	Michelotto
		1914	Thys
		1919	Rossius
		1920	Mottiat
		1921	Mottiat
		1922	Jacquinot
		1923	Jacquinot
		1924	Bottecchia
		1925	Bottecchia
		1926	Sellier
		1927	Dewaele
		1955	start (Tour)
		1962	van den Bergen
		1979	TI-Raleigh team
		1983	Demierre
		1991	Marie
		1995	Cipollini
Leiden	1	1978	start (Tour), Raas
Le Mans	7	1952	Rosseel
		1953	van Geneugden
		1975	Esclassan
		1981	R. Martens

Stage towns		Year	Winner
		1983	Gaigne
		1984	Fignon
		1988	van Poppel
Le Perreux	1	1979	start
Le Pleynet	1	1981	Hinault
Le Puy-en-Velay	3	1954	Forlini
		1990	start (Tour), Indurain
		1996	Richard
Le Puy du Fou	3	1993	start (Tour) Indurain
		1997	Minali
		1999	start (Tour), Armstrong
Les Arcs	1	1996	Leblanc
Les Deux Alpes	2	1998	Pantani
		2002	Armstrong
Les Échelles	1	1984	start
Les Essarts (*see* Rouen)			
Les Ménuires	1	1979	van Impe
Les Orres	1	1973	Ocaña
Les Sables d'Olonne	16	1919	Alavoine
		1920	H. Pélissier
		1921	Mottiat
		1922	Thys
		1923	Dejonghe
		1924	Goethals
		1925	Frantz
		1926	Frantz
		1927	Decorte
		1928	Frantz
		1929	P. Le Drogo
		1930	Leducq
		1931	C. Pélissier
		1947	Tassin
		1949	Deledda
		1993	Cipollini
Le Touquet	2	1971	Simonetti
		1976	Maertens
Le Tréport	2	1951	Meunier
		1958	Bauvin
Levallois-Perret	1	1986	start
Lezignan-Corbières	1	1980	start
Libourne	3	1957	Anquetil
		1969	start
		1992	Panasonic team
Liège	9	1948	Bartali
		1950	Leoni
		1953	Schaer
		1956	Darrigade
		1965	van Looy, Ford team

Stage towns		Year	Winner
		1980	Lubberding
		1989	start
		1995	Bruyneel
Liévin	2	1986	Phinney
		1988	J. Nijdam
Lille	16	1906	Georget
		1933	Archambaud
		1934	Speicher
		1935	R. Maes
		1936	Egli
		1937	Majerus
		1938	Neuville
		1947	Kübler
		1950	Pasotti
		1953	Bobet
		1954	Bobet
		1956	De Bruyne
		1960	start (Tour)
		1980	Hinault
		1982	Raas
		1994	start (Tour),
			Boardman
Limoges	12	1951	Rosseel
		1952	Vivier
		1960	De Filippis
		1963	Janssen
		1967	Stablinski
		1970	start (Tour),
			Merckx
		1977	Raas
		1985	Lammerts
		1988	Bugno
		1990	Bontempi
		1995	Armstrong
		2000	Agnolutto
Lisieux	2	1964	Sels
		1970	Godefroot
Lodève	2	1974	start
		2002	start
Longwy	5	1911	Masselis
		1912	Defraye
		1913	Faber
		1914	Faber
		1982	Willems
Lons-le-Saunier	2	1937	Puppo
		1963	Brands
Lorient	9	1939	Louviot
		1956	De Bruyne
		1960	Rivière
		1968	A. Gonzales
		1977	Santambrogio

Stage towns		Year	Winner
		1982	start
		1985	start
		1998	Heppner
		2002	Botero
Loudenvielle	2	1997	Brochard
		2003	.....
Loudun	1	2000	Steels
Lourdes (inc Hautacam)	5	1948	Bartali
		1990	start
		1994	Leblanc
		1996	Riis
		2000	Otxoa
Louvain	1	1976	TI-Raleigh team
Louvroil	1	1984	M. Madiot
Luchon	49	1910	Lapize
		1911	Duboc
		1912	Defraye
		1913	Thys
		1914	Lambot
		1919	Barthélémy
		1920	Lambot
		1921	Heusghem
		1922	Alavoine
		1923	Alavoine
		1924	Bottecchia
		1925	Benoît
		1926	L. Buysse
		1927	Frantz
		1928	Fontan
		1929	Cardona
		1930	Binda
		1931	A. Magne
		1932	Pesenti
		1933	Louyet
		1934	Vignoli
		1935	S. Maes
		1936	Ducazeaux
		1937	Meulenberg
		1938	F. Vervaecke
		1947	Bourlon
		1949	Robic
		1951	Koblet
		1953	Robic
		1954	Bauvin
		1956	Schmitz
		1958	Bahamontes
		1960	Gimmi
		1961	start
		1962	start
		1963	Ignolin
		1964	Poulidor

Stage towns		Year	Winner
		1966	Mugnaini
		1967	Manzaneque
		1969	Delisle
		1971	Fuente
		1972	Merckx
		1973	Ocaña
		1979	Bittinger
		1980	R. Martin
		1983	R. Millar
		1989	start
		1997	start
		1998	Massi
Luçon	2	1962	Minieri
		1993	start
Lugny	1	1991	start
Lunéville	1	1964	start
Luxembourg	7	1947	Ronconi
		1989	start (Tour), Breukink, Da Silva, Système-U team
		1992	Indurain
		2002	start (Tour), Armstrong, Bertogliati
Luz-Ardiden	7	1985	Delgado
		1987	Lauritzen
		1988	Cubino
		1990	Indurain
		1994	Virenque
		2001	Laiseka
		2003	......
Luz St-Sauveur	1	1985	start
Lyon	16	1903	Garin
		1904	Frédérick
		1907	Cadolle
		1908	Faber
		1909	Faber
		1910	Faber
		1947	Teisseire
		1950	Kübler
		1953	Meunier
		1954	Forestier
		1956	Bover
		1962	Anquetil
		1965	van Looy
		1991	start (Tour), Marie, Abdoujaparov
		2003	......
Maastricht	1	1969	Stevens

Stage towns		Year	Winner
Machecoul	1	1988	Bauer
Mâcon	3	1991	Ekimov, Indurain
		2002	Armstrong
Malbuisson	1	1984	Abdoujaparov
Malo-les-Bains	5	1928	Dewaele
		1929	Dewaele
		1930	C. Pélissier
		1931	Rebry
		1932	Rebry
Manosque	2	1976	Viejo
		1982	start
Marche-en-Famenne	1	1971	Genet
Marennes	1	1997	Blijlevens
Marseille	32	1903	Aucouturier
		1904	Faure
		1906	Passerieu
		1911	Crupelandt
		1912	Defraye
		1914	Lapize
		1919	Alavoine
		1927	Dewaele
		1928	Leducq
		1929	Leducq
		1930	A. Magne
		1931	Bulla
		1932	Orecchia
		1933	Speicher
		1934	R. Lapébie
		1935	C. Pélissier
		1936	Le Greves
		1937	Danneels
		1938	Bartali
		1939	Galateau
		1947	Fachleitner
		1948	Impanis
		1949	Goldschmit
		1951	Magni
		1953	Quentin
		1955	L. Lazarides
		1957	Stablinski
		1967	Riotte
		1971	Armani
		1989	Barteau
		1993	Roscioli
		2003	....
Martigues	3	1980	Vallet
		1981	van der Velde
		1982	Hinault
Maubeuge	1	1999	Cipollini
Mayenne	1	1995	start

Stage towns		Year	Winner
		1965	Durante
		1966	start
		1970	R. Wagtmans
		1973	start
		1974	Hoban
		1980	L. Peeters
		1989	Tebaldi
		1993	Ludwig
		1994	Sorensen
Montpont-Menesterol	2	1985	start
		1995	start
Montrieul-sous-Bois	1	1984	start (Tour)
Mont St-Michel	1	1990	Museeuw
Morcenx	1	1977	start
Morlaix	1	1974	start
Morzine	16	1977	start
		1977	Wellens
		1978	Seznec
		1979	start
		1980	Martinez
		1981	Alban
		1982	Winnen
		1983	Michaud
		1984	Arroyo
		1987	Chozas
		1988	Parra
		1991	Claveyrolat
		1994	start
		1997	Pantani
		2000	Virenque
		2003	.....
Mourenx	3	1969	Merckx
		1970	Raymond
		1999	start
Mouscron	1	1982	Knetemann
Moutiers	2	1973	start
		1994	start
Mulhouse	14	1925	Frantz
		1926	J. Buysse
		1948	van Dijck
		1952	Géminiani
		1959	start (Tour)
		1969	Agostinho
		1970	Frey
		1971	start (Tour), Molteni team, van Vlierberghe
		1973	Godefroot
		1976	Maertens
		1981	Hinault
		1992	Fignon

Stage towns		Year	Winner
		2000	Armstrong
Namur	3	1952	Diederich
		1955	Bobet
		1959	Favero
Nancy	15	1905	Trousselier
		1906	Pottier
		1949	Coppi
		1952	Coppi
		1954	Bobet
		1962	start (Tour)
		1966	start (Tour)
		1969	start (Tour)
		1971	R. Wagtmans
		1973	Zoetemelk
		1976	Parecchini
		1978	Hinault
		1982	Anderson
		1988	Wijnants
		1995	Golz
Nanterre	2	1986	start
		1992	P. de Clercq
Nantes	29	1903	Garin
		1904	Dortignacq
		1906	Trousselier
		1907	Petit-Breton
		1908	Petit-Breton
		1909	Trousselier
		1910	Trousselier
		1932	Stöpel
		1934	A. Magne
		1935	Aerts
		1938	Schulte
		1939	Fournier
		1948	G. Lapébie
		1953	Isotti
		1957	start (Tour)
		1959	Rivière
		1968	Bitossi
		1974	Vianen
		1980	Raas
		1981	Wijnands
		1982	Mutter
		1983	Oosterbosch
		1984	Jules
		1986	E. Planckaert, Hinault
		1988	start
		1990	Argentin
		2000	Steels
		2003	.....

Stage towns		Year	Winner
Narbonne	7	1935	Le Greves
		1936	Le Greves
		1937	Camusso
		1938	A. van Schendel
		1939	Jaminet
		1955	Caput
		2003	start
Narbonne-Plage	1	1981	Maertens
Nay	1	1981	start
Nemours	1	1988	start
Neufchâtel	1	1998	Steels
Neufchâtel-en-Bray	2	1985	start
		1988	start
Neuville-de-Poitou	1	1979	start
Nevers	4	1962	Bruni
		1971	Leman
		1986	Bontempi
		2003	.....
Nice	35	1906	Pottier
		1907	Passerieu
		1908	Dortignacq
		1909	Faber
		1910	Maitron
		1911	Faber
		1912	Lapize
		1913	Lambot
		1914	Rossius
		1919	Barthélémy
		1920	Thys
		1921	Lambot
		1922	Thys
		1923	Alavoine
		1924	Thys
		1925	L. Buysse
		1926	Frantz
		1927	Frantz
		1928	Frantz
		1929	B. Faure
		1930	Peglion
		1931	Gestri
		1932	Camusso
		1933	Cornez
		1934	Le Greves
		1935	Aerts
		1936	Maye
		1937	F. Vervaecke
		1947	Camellini
		1950	Kübler
		1973	Lopez-Carril
		1975	start
		1981	start (Tour),

Stage towns		Year	Winner
			Hinault,
			Maertens, TI-
			Raleigh team
Nîmes	14	1905	Trousselier
		1907	Georget
		1908	Petit-Breton
		1909	E. Paul
		1910	Faber
		1925	Beeckman
		1935	Bergamashi
		1936	Le Greves
		1937	Antoine
		1949	Idée
		1950	Molines
		1953	Quennehen
		1958	Darrigade
		1986	Hoste
Niort	1	1950	Magni
Nogent-sur-Marne	2	1979	Hinault
		1983	start
Nogent-sur-Oise	2	1992	start
		1996	Zabel
Noisy-le-Sec	1	1984	Hinault
Oléron	1	1983	Magrini
Oloron-Ste-Marie	1	1977	start
Orange	1	1974	Spruyt
Orchies	1	1982	start
Orcières-Merlette	4	1971	Ocaña
		1972	van Impe
		1982	P. Simon
		1989	Rooks
Orléans	7	1964	Stablinski
		1966	Beuffeuil
		1974	Merckx,
			Pollentier
		1985	start
		1987	start
		2001	start
Orthez	1	1993	start
Palaiseau	1	1996	start
Pamplona	1	1996	Dufaux
Pantin	1	1984	start
Paris Parc des Princes	53	1904	Dortignacq
		1905	Dortignacq
		1906	Pottier
		1907	Passerieu
		1908	Petit-Breton
		1909	Alavoine
		1910	Azzini
		1911	Godivier
		1912	Alavoine

Stage towns		Year	Winner
		1913	M. Buysse
		1914	H. Pélissier
		1919	Alavoine
		1920	Rossius
		1921	Goethals
		1922	Thys
		1923	Goethals
		1924	Bottecchia
		1925	Bottecchia
		1926	Dossche
		1927	Leducq
		1928	Frantz
		1929	Frantz
		1930	C. Pélissier
		1931	C. Pélissier
		1932	Leducq
		1933	Guerra
		1934	S. Maes
		1935	R. Maes
		1936	Mersch
		1937	Vissers
		1938	A. Magne =
			Leducq
		1939	Kint
		1947	Schotte
		1948	Corrieri
		1949	van Steenbergen
		1950	Baffert
		1951	Deledda
		1952	Rolland
		1953	Magni
		1954	Varnajo
		1955	Poblet
		1956	Nencini
		1957	Darrigade
		1958	P. Baffi
		1959	J. Groussard
		1960	Graczyk
		1961	Cazala
		1962	Benedetti
		1963	van Looy
		1964	Anquetil
		1965	Gimondi
		1966	Altig
		1967	Poulidor
Paris stage town	1	1951	Lévèque
Paris start		1903–1925,	
		1927–1950,	
		1963, 2003*	

(*prologue from Stade-de-France to Montgeron,
stage one from Montgeron to Meaux)

Stage towns		Year	Winner
Paris Piste Municipale	7	1968	Janssen
		1969	Merckx
		1970	Merckx
		1971	Merckx
		1972	Teirlinck
		1973	Thévenet
		1974	Merckx
Paris Champs-Elysées	31	1975	Godefroot
		1976	Maertens,
			Karstens
		1977	Thurau, Meslet
		1978	Knetemann
		1979	Hinault
		1980	Verschuere
		1981	Maertens
		1982	Hinault
		1983	Glaus
		1984	Vanderaerden
		1985	R. Matthys
		1986	Bontempi
		1987	Pierce
		1988	van Poppel
		1989	LeMond
		1990	Museeuw
		1991	Konyshev
		1992	Ludwig
		1993	Abdoujaparov
		1994	Seigneur
		1995	Abdoujaparov
		1996	Baldato
		1997	Minali
		1998	Steels
		1999	McEwen
		2000	Zanini
		2001	Svorada
		2002	McEwen
		2003	.....
Pau	58	1930	Binda
		1931	C. Pélissier
		1932	Ronsse
		1933	Guerra
		1934	Vietto
		1935	Morelli
		1936	S. Maes
		1937	Berrendero
		1938	Middelkamp
		1939	Litschi
		1947	Robic
		1949	Magni
		1950	Dussault
		1952	Coppi

Stage towns		Year	Winner
		1953	Magni
		1954	Ockers
		1955	Brankart
		1956	De Filippis
		1957	Nencini
		1958	Bergaud
		1960	Rivière
		1961	Pauwels
		1962	Pauwels
		1963	Cerami
		1964	Bahamontes
		1966	De Pra
		1967	Mastrotto
		1968	van Rijckeghem
		1971	van Springel
		1972	Hézard
		1973	Torres
		1974	Danguillaume
		1975	Gimondi
		1976	Panizza
		1977	Thurau
		1978	Lubberding
		1979	Hinault
		1980	Knetemann
		1981	Hinault
		1982	Kelly
		1983	Chevallier
		1984	Vanderaerden
		1985	R. Simon
		1986	Delgado
		1987	Breukink
		1988	van der Poel
		1989	Earley
		1990	Konyshev
		1991	start
		1992	Murguialday
		1993	Chiappucci
		1995	no result
			(Casartelli's
			death)
		1997	Zabel
		1998	van Bon
		1999	Etxebarria
		2001	start
		2002	Halgand
		2003	start
Périgueux	2	1961	Anquetil
		1994	start
Peronne	1	1993	start
Perpignan	36	1910	Paulmier
		1911	Duboc

Stage towns		Year	Winner
		1912	Borgarello
		1913	M. Buysse
		1914	Alavoine
		1919	Alavoine
		1920	Rossius
		1921	Mottiat
		1922	Alavoine
		1923	Alavoine
		1924	Bottecchia
		1925	Frantz
		1926	L. Buysse
		1927	van Slembroeck
		1928	Leducq
		1929	Demuysère
		1930	C. Pélissier
		1931	Di Paco
		1932	Bonduel
		1933	Leducq
		1934	R. Lapébie
		1935	Archambaud
		1936	S. Maes
		1937	Meulenberg
		1938	Frechaut
		1950	Blomme
		1952	Decaux
		1957	Hassenforder
		1961	Pauwels
		1964	De Roo
		1965	Janssen
		1973	start
		1993	Lino
		1997	Desbiens
		2001	start
Perros-Guirec	1	1995	start
Peyrehorade	1	1964	start
Pforzheim	1	1987	Frison
Piau-Engaly	1	1999	Escartin
Plâteau de Beille	2	1998	Pantani
		2002	Armstrong
Plâteau de Bonascre	2	2001	Cardenas
		2003	.....
Plouay	2	1998	start
		2002	Kroon
Plumelec	3	1982	TI-Raleigh team
		1985	start (Tour),
			Hinault
		1997	Zabel
Plymouth	1	1974	Poppe
Poitiers	7	1955	Forestier
		1971	Danguillaume
		1978	Kelly

Stage towns		Year	Winner
		1986	start
		1987	start
		1990	start
		1994	start
Pontarlier	6	1927	A. Benoit
		1928	P. Magne
		1960	start
		1972	Teirlinck
		1985	Pedersen
		2001	Dekker
Pont-Audemer	1	1985	Solleveld
Pontchâteau	1	1988	start
Pont-l'Évêque	1	1962	start
Pontoise	2	1961	start
		1984	(Cergy-Pontoise) P. Ferreira
Pornic	1	2003	start
Pornichet	1	1972	start
Port Barcarès	1	1976	start
Portsmouth	1	1994	Minali
Pouilly-en-Auxois	1	1975	start
Pra-Loup	2	1975	Thévenet
		1980	Deschoenmaecker
Prapoutel	1	1980	Loos
Privas	1	1966	start
Puy-de-Dôme	13	1952	Coppi
		1959	Bahamontes
		1964	Jimenez
		1967	Gimondi
		1969	Matignon
		1971	Ocaña
		1973	Ocaña
		1975	van Impe
		1976	Zoetemelk
		1978	Zoetemelk
		1983	Arroyo
		1986	Maechler
		1988	Weltz
Puy-du-Fou (*see* Le Puy-du-Fou)			
Pyrenées 2000 (*see* Font Romeu)			
Quimper	4	1958	start
		1962	start
		1965	start
		1991	Anderson
Rambouillet	1	1966	Sels
Régnié-Durette	1	2002	start
Reims	10	1938	Galateau
		1949	Dussault
		1951	G. Rossi

Stage towns		Year	Winner
		1956	start (Tour)
		1963	start
		1973	Guimard
		1985	Castaing
		1988	Tebaldi
		1991	Abdoujaparov
		2002	McEwen
Renazé	1	1987	van der Poel
Rennes	14	1905	Trousselier
		1933	Aerts
		1937	Chocque
		1939	Tassin
		1951	Muller
		1952	van Steenbergen
		1959	Graczyk
		1963	Bailetti
		1964	start (Tour)
		1970	Basso
		1977	Thaler
		1989	LeMond
		1991	Ribeiro
		1994	Bortolami
Revard	2	1965	Gimondi
		1972	Guimard
Revel	7	1966	Altig
		1969	Agostinho, Merckx
		1971	start
		1990	Mottet
		1995	Outschakov
		2000	Dekker
Rochefort	1	1979	start
Rochefort-sur-Mer	3	1935	Le Greves
		1980	start
		1981	start
Rochetaillée	1	1982	start
Rodez	1	1984	Menthéour
Roquefort	1	1983	Andersen
Roscoff	1	1998	start
Rotterdam	1	1973	Teirlinck
Roubaix	25	1907	Trousselier
		1908	Passerieu
		1909	van Houwaert
		1910	Crupelandt
		1948	B. Gauthier
		1952	P. Molineris
		1955	Rolland
		1957	Janssens
		1959	Cazala
		1961	Darrigade
		1963	Elliott

Stage towns	Year	Winner
	1965	van de Kerkhove
	1967	Reybroeck
	1968	Godefroot
	1969	start (Tour), Altig
	1971	P. Guerra
	1973	Verstraeten
	1975	van Linden
	1977	Danguillaume
	1979	Delcroix
	1981	Willems
	1983	R. Matthys
	1985	Manders
	1992	start
	1994	start
Rouen	18 1949	Teisseire
	1950	Ockers
	1952	Lauredi
	1954	Dussault, Swiss team
	1956	Padovan, Gaul
	1957	Anquetil
	1959	Bruni
	1961	start (Tour)
	1963	Melckenbeeck
	1965	Gimondi
	1968	Chappe
	1970	Godefroot
	1977	Den Hertog
	1980	Raas
	1990	Solleveld
	1997	start (Tour), Boardman
	2002	Kirsipuu
Royan	7 1937	Bautz
	1938	F. Vervaecke
	1939	Pagès
	1958	P. Baffi
	1966	van Vlierberghe
	1968	van Rijckeghem
	1972	Guimard
Ruelle	1 1988	start
Ruffec	1 1970	start
Rungis	1 1971	start
Sablé	1 1975	start
St-Amand-les-Eaux	1 1978	Esclassan
St-Amand-Montrond	1 2001	Armstrong
St-Brevin	1 1958	start
St-Brieuc	9 1938	Majerus
	1947	Impanis

Stage towns	Year	Winner
	1950	Kübler
	1954	Kübler
	1958	van Geneugden
	1965	Sorgeloos
	1972	Guimard
	1979	J. Jacobs
	1995	start (Tour), Durand
St-Denis	1 1984	Hoste
St-Dier d'Auvergne	1 1978	start
St-Dizier	1 2003	.....
St-Émilion	2 1978	start
	1996	Ullrich
St-Étienne	22 1950	Géminiani
	1953	Bobet
	1956	Ockers
	1959	Bruni
	1961	Forestier
	1963	Ignolin
	1966	Bracke
	1968	Genet
	1971	Godefroot
	1977	no winner (Agostinho disqualified)
	1978	Hinault
	1980	Kelly, Zoetemelk
	1983	Laurent
	1985	Herrera
	1986	Gorospe, Hinault
	1990	Chozas
	1992	Chioccioli
	1995	Sciandri
	1997	Ullrich
	1999	Dierckxsens
St-Flour	1 1999	Etxebarria
St-Galmier	1 1999	start
St-Gaudens	11 1950	Bartali
	1955	Gaul
	1957	De Filippis
	1959	Darrigade
	1962	Cazala
	1968	Pintens
	1970	Ocaña
	1976	Teirlinck
	1981	start
	1991	start
	1999	Konyshev
St-Germain-en-Laye	2 1978	start, Thaler

Stage towns		Year	Winner
St-Gervais-Mont Blanc	2	1990	(Le Bettex)
			Claveyrolat
		1992	Jaermann
St-Gilles-Croix-de-Vie	2	1974	start
		1975	start
St-Girons	4	1984	start
		1988	start
		1995	start
		2003	start
St-Herblain	1	1991	Mottet
St-Hilaire-du-Harcouët	2	1979	start
		1986	L. Peeters
St-Jean-de-Monts	5	1972	Gualazzini,
			Molteni team
		1975	Smit, Merckx
		1976	start (Tour,
			Merlin-Plage),
			Maertens
St-Julien-en-Genevoix	1	1987	start
St-Lary-Soulan	8	1974	Poulidor
		1975	Zoetemelk
		1976	van Impe
		1978	M. Martinez
		1981	van Impe
		1982	Breu
		1993	Jaskula
		2001	Armstrong
St-Malo	7	1949	Kübler
		1956	Morvan
		1960	Darrigade
		1962	Daems
		1967	Godefroot
		1974	Sercu
		1980	Oosterbosch
St-Martin-de-Landelles	1	2002	start
St-Maixent-L'École	1	2003	.....
St-Nazaire	4	1958	Darrigade
		1962	Zilverberg
		1999	Steels
		2000	ONCE team
St-Niklaas	2	1973	Catieau, Maes
			team
St-Omer	1	2001	start
St-Orens-de-Gameville	1	1995	start
St-Pol-de-Léon, Roscoff	1	1974	Gualazzini
St-Priest	5	1979	Thurau
		1981	Willems,
			Hinault
		1982	van
			Houwelingen,
			Hinault

Stage towns		Year	Winner
St-Quentin	1	1938	F. Vervaecke
St-Quentin-en-Yvelines	1	1986	Système-U team
St-Raphaël	1	1939	Neuens
St-Trivier	1	1977	start
St-Valery-en-Caux	1	1997	start
St-Willebrord	1	1978	Raas
Ste-Foy-la-Grande	3	1973	start
		1976	start
		1978	Hinault
Ste-Geneviève-des-Bois	1	1995	start
Saintes	3	1936	Meulenberg
		1937	Braeckeveld,
			Wengler
		1982	start
Salies-de-Béarn	1	1939	Kint
Sallanches	2	1968	Hoban
		2003	start
San Remo	1	1948	Sciardis
San Sebastian	3	1949	Caput
		1992	start (Tour),
			Indurain,
			Arnould
Santenay	1	1988	Martinez-Oliver
Sarran	1	2001	Voigt
Saarbrücken	3	1985	start
		1990	start
		2002	Freire
Sarrelouis	1	1970	start
Saumur	1	1987	start
Sauternes	1	1997	start
Savines-le-Lac	1	1974	start
Sceaux	1	1986	Verschuere
Scheveningen	1	1973	start (Tour),
			Zoetemelk
Sedan	1	2003	start
Seignosse-le-Penon	1	1977	Delépine
Senlis	2	1975	van Linden
		1978	Raas
Sens	1	1982	start
Séo-de-Urgel	2	1968	van Springel
		1974	Merckx
Seraing	2	1995	Indurain
		2001	Zabel
Serre-Chevalier	4	1974	Lopez-Carril
		1975	Thévenet
		1980	start
		1993	Rominger
Sestriere	4	1952	Coppi
		1992	Chiappucci
		1996	Riis
		1999	Armstrong

Stage towns		Year	Winner
Sète	2	1966	Vandenberghe
		1967	Hoban
Seurre	1	1959	start
's Hertogenbosch	2	1996	start (Tour), Zülle, Moncassin
Shupfart-Mohlin	1	1982	L. Peeters
Soissons	3	1983	start
		1996	start
		2002	start
Spa	1	1962	Altig
Strasbourg	22	1919	Lucotti
		1920	Thys
		1921	Barthélémy
		1922	Masson
		1923	J. Muller
		1924	Frantz
		1927	Decorte
		1928	Mauclair
		1929	Leducq
		1932	Loncke
		1938	Fréchaut, Masson = Weckerling
		1947	Robic
		1948	Lambrecht
		1953	start (Tour)
		1961	Bergaud
		1967	Wright
		1971	Merckx
		1985	Hinault
		1987	Sergeant
		1988	J. Simon
		1992	van Poppel
		2001	Kirsipuu
Stuttgart	1	1987	Da Silva
Superbagnères	6	1961	Massignan
		1962	Bahamontes
		1971	Fuente
		1979	Hinault
		1986	LeMond
		1989	R. Millar
Super-Besse	2	1978	Wellens
		1996	Sorensen
Super-Lioran	1	1975	Pollentier
Tarascon-sur-Ariège	1	1998	start
Tarbes	10	1933	Aerts
		1934	A. Magne
		1951	Biagioni
		1975	start
		1978	start
		1987	start

Stage towns		Year	Winner
		1988	start
		1993	start
		1995	start
		2001	start
Thionville	1	1999	Cipollini
Thonon-les-Bains	9	1955	Hinsen
		1957	Anquetil
		1960	Manzaneque
		1964	Janssen
		1969	Dancelli
		1970	Basso
		1975	start
		1977	Quilfen
		1981	Kelly
Thuir	1	1973	Ocaña
Toulon	11	1905	Aucouturier
		1921	Lucotti
		1922	Thys
		1923	L. Buysse
		1924	Mottiat
		1925	L. Buysse
		1926	Frantz
		1927	A. Magne
		1937	Meulenberg
		1950	Dos Reis
		1964	Anquetil
Toulouse	25	1903	Aucouturier
		1904	Cornet
		1905	Dortignacq
		1906	Trousselier
		1907	Georget
		1908	Faber
		1909	Alavoine
		1939	Vissers
		1948	Bartali
		1949	van Steenbergen
		1952	Rosseel
		1954	De Bruyne
		1955	van Steenbergen
		1956	De Filippis
		1958	Darrigade
		1960	Graczyk
		1961	Carlesi
		1963	Darrigade
		1964	Sels
		1967	Wolfshohl
		1970	van Vlierberghe
		1978	Esclassan
		1985	Vichot
		1989	start
		2003	.....

Stage towns		Year	Winner
Tourmalet	1	1974	Danguillaume
Tournai	2	1966	Reybroeck,
			Televizier team
Tours	6	1955	Brankart
		1957	Darrigade
		1961	Darrigade
		1970	Basso
		1992	T. Marie
		2000	van Bon
Trelissac	1	1994	Hamburger
Trets	1	1980	start
Trouville	1	1948	Bartali
Troyes	7	1939	Le Greves
		1954	De Bruyne
		1960	Beuffeuil
		1963	De Breucker
		1987	Dominguez
		2000	Zabel
		2003	start
Tulle	2	1976	Mathis
		1996	Abdoujaparov
Turin	4	1956	De Filippis
		1961	Ignolin
		1966	Bitossi
		1996	start
Vaison-la-Romaine	1	2002	start
Val-d'Isère	2	1963	Manzaneque
		1996	Berzin
Valence	1	1996	C. Gonzalez
Valence-d'Agen	2	1978	stage cancelled
			(strike)
		1982	Knetemann
Valenciennes	4	1970	R. De Vlaeminck
		1983	start
		1984	Renault-Elf team
		1991	J. Nijdam
Valkenberg	1	1992	Delion
Valloire	2	1972	Merckx
		1975	start
Val-Louron	1	1991	Chiappucci
Valréas	3	1987	start
		1994	start
		1998	start
Vals-les-Bains	1	1966	Poulidor
Val-Thorens	1	1994	N. Rodriguez
Vannes	11	1925	Frantz
		1927	van Slembroeck
		1928	M. Bidot
		1929	van Slembroeck
		1930	Taverne
		1931	Godinat

Stage towns		Year	Winner
		1947	Tarchini
		1954	Vivier
		1985	start
		1993	Nelissen
		2000	start
Vassivière (Auphelle)	3	1985	LeMond
		1990	Breukink
		1995	Indurain
Ventoux	7	1958	Gaul
		1965	Poulidor
		1970	Merckx
		1972	Thévenet
		1987	Bernard
		2000	Pantani
		2002	Virenque
Verdun	2	1993	Armstrong
		2001	Jalabert
Versailles	16	1958	Gainche
		1961	Darrigade,
			Anquetil
		1964	Beheyt
		1965	Karstens
		1967	Bingelli
		1970	Danguillaume
		1971	Krekels
		1972	Bruyere, Merckx
		1973	Hoban, Ocaña
		1975	Rottiers
		1976	Maertens
		1977	Knetemann
		1989	start
Verviers	1	1976	Lasa
Vesoul	1	1972	start
Veurey-Voroise	1	1981	start
Vichy	1	1952	Magni
Villard-de-Lans	7	1985	Vanderaerden
		1986	start
		1987	Delgado
		1988	Delgado
		1989	Fignon
		1990	Breukink
		1993	start
Ville d'Avray	2	1903	Garin
		2003	start
Villefranche-sur-Saône	2	1984	Hoste, Fignon
Villeneuve-sur-Lot	2	1996	Podenzana
		2000	Dekker
Villers-sur-Mer	1	1986	van der Velde
Villeurbanne	1	1991	start
Villié-Morgon	1	1984	start
Vire	5	1935	Le Greves

START

The start is where to see the riders, but you won't get into the TOUR VILLAGE, where they congregate, without a pass. You should write to the SOCIÉTÉ DU TOUR DE FRANCE at the start of the year to request a pass for a specific day. But riders will come out from their hotels, sometimes by BIKE, for *le signature*, the signing-on routine outside on the road to the commentary of DANIEL MANGEAS. Get there an hour and a half before *le départ*.

Once you could get close to riders, but now they usually stay behind barriers patrolled by POLICE, although early arrivals have a chance of an autograph and a handshake. L'ÉQUIPE lists riders left in the race and their numbers.

The CARAVAN moves away an hour before the riders. With them go journalists and officials who want to reach the FINISH before the riders. They follow a route signposted hours earlier.

The *départ fictif* (neutralised section) takes up the first kilometres as riders, officials and police negotiate city streets without racing. The official start, the *départ réel*, is marked by a *panneau* or banner. *Vélo, Procycling* and other magazines in BRITAIN give the route with intermediate towns and road numbers. *Vélo* gives the arrangements. To find out what's going on, initiative and guesswork make up for a lack of fluent French.

The first start in 1903 was in MONTGERON. The first starter was Georges Abran. A flag was used for the first Tours but in 1905 a starter's pistol was introduced. All Tours began in or near Paris until ÉVIAN had the start in 1926. In 1923 the start was moved from the Porte Maillot in Paris to Eaubonne, without telling the crowds at Porte Maillot, who had hoped to combine a local celebration with a sight of the riders.

TOM STEELS

b. Sint-Gillis-Waas, Belgium, Sep 2 1971

SPRINTERS are sometimes said to be half-mad, and Steels puts on a convincing show of this. The greater the rough house, the more he thrives. At Marennes in 1997 he pulled out his bottle at close on 70km/h and hurled it at Frédéric Moncassin, who had displeased him. He was thrown out of the race, which calmed him down in future. It also prompted a Dutch fan to transpose his name as he wrote it across the road later in the race. *Stom Tells* it said. 'Stom' is Dutch for stupid.

Steels began as a BMX rider and won five national championships. The balance and nerve that tight tracks demanded gave him his sprinter's power. In 1989 he turned to the TRACK and won silver in the 1,000m TIME TRIAL at the world championships, turning professional in 1994. Moving to the road, he won Het Volk, Ghent-Wevelgem and two stages of the Tour of SPAIN, as well as coming second in Paris-Roubaix.

His Tour career includes four stage wins in 1998, three in 1999, two in 2000 but none in 2001 because of glandular fever. An apparent

Tom Steels *(continued)*

reoccurence of the same complaint forced him out of the 2002 race during the first week. His fastest timed finish was 76km/h when he beat ERIK ZABEL at Neufchâtel in 1998.

Winner

1996	Ghent-Wevelgem, Het Volk
1997	National championship
1998	A Travers Belgique, National championship
1999	Ghent-Wevelgem
2002	National championship

Tour de France

1997	DNF	
1998	85th	Stage wins Dublin—Dublin, Tarascon-sur-Ariège—Cap d'Agde, Aix-les-Bains—Neufchâtel-en-Bray, Melun—Paris, and Points leader
1999	104th	Stage wins Challons—St-Nazaire, Nantes—Laval, Mourenx—Bordeaux
2000	DNF	Stage wins Futuroscope—Loudun, Loudun—Nantes, and Points leader
2001	DNF	
2002	DNF	

ALEX STIEDA
b. Belleville, Canada, Apr 13 1961

Alex Stieda, a 25-year-old from Vancouver, Canada, was the only foreigner in the American 7-Eleven team in 1986. He was the first North American to wear the yellow JERSEY, in the stage from Nanterre to Sceaux, won by Pol Verschuere. He held it for a day.

(*See* STEVE BAUER, CHARLIE HOLLAND.)

Tour de France

1986	120th	Yellow Jersey

KURT STÖPEL
b. Berlin, Germany, Mar 12 1908, d. Jun 24 1997

Chosen as a SPRINTER for the NATIONAL TEAM in 1932 after coming fifth in the Giro d'Italia, Kurt Stöpel was the first German on the Tour podium, and first to wear the yellow JERSEY. But on the face of it he seemed to have won the 300km stage from Caen to Nantes by sabotaging his team-mate, Oskar Thierbach. Thierbach and three others looked like staying away until the FINISH, but he was a poor sprinter and Stöpel set off in chase with three others.

All eight riders came together for the FINISH, where Stöpel came off the wheel of the Belgian Frans Bonduel and beat the favourite, ANDRÉ LEDUCQ. The BONUS was four minutes, which put him in yellow. Next day he was dropped six times in the heat of a 387km stage from Nantes to BORDEAUX, and finally finished 13 minutes down, not helped by six punctures, and no German MECHANIC to help either him or the two team-mates who waited for him. He did finish the Tour, though, coming second. It would be another 64 years before JAN ULLRICH did as well.

Stöpel's record includes fourth place in the 1930 world road championship and eighth in the 1933 Giro.

(*See* WILLI OBERBECK for the German *maillot jaune* abandoned by his team.)

Winner

1934	National championship

Tour de France

1931	16th	
1932	2nd	Stage win Caen—Nantes, and Yellow Jersey
1933	10th	
1934	22nd	
1935	DNF	

STRIKES

Put men under great stress in rotten working conditions and strikes are inevitable. The first strike in the Tour was in 1905, on the first day. Saboteurs had scattered 125kg of nails and only one rider survived without puncturing. Others struggled on after numerous punctures, or caught the train to get to the FINISH. HENRI DESGRANGE wanted to eliminate all but the 15 who finished within the time limit, but the strike persuaded him to accept anybody who reached the FINISH however late, although he docked them points.

In 1920 half the race pulled out at Les Sables d'Olonne on the Atlantic coast to protest at Desgrange's dictatorial management. In the Tour paper L'AUTO he responded, 'These riders are provided with beds, fed and paid, and all they're asked to do is repay it all with physical work.'

In 1921 HENRI PÉLISSIER refused to ride because he didn't like the standard *musette*, or food bag. He and his brother Francis set up a riders' union after the ALBERT LONDRES affair over jerseys in 1924. (*See* Londres entry for Pélissier's protest and confession.) The union's first job, with Henri as chairman, was to fight off Desgrange's idea that every rider in 1925 should have the same food, both type and quantity. This was the wildest idea in his plan to put all riders on equal footing, and he had proposed it for Paris-Tours. The union decided to strike. That changed Desgrange's mind, but it didn't mean the union was a success. Pélissier had too many enemies, not only among fellow Frenchmen but also the influential Belgians whom he needed to create a union of true strength. He was also in no position to negotiate with organisers and SPONSORS because he was barely on speaking terms with many of them.

Some riders ignored Pélissier because he was Pélissier, others didn't want to get involved, others gave in to pressure from teams. The union collapsed.

The most entertaining strike was on July 28 1950, a day so hot that the only action came when riders passed streams and filled their bot-tles or rinsed their faces. Then the road turned down by the bay at Ste-Maxime, across from St-Tropez. APO LAZARIDES shouted that he was stopping for a dip and 61 others followed, some not getting off their bikes before plunging into the Mediterranean. The organisers were furious.

In 1966 riders struck after officials demanded a dope test from RAYMOND POULI-DOR, the only rider they could find in his hotel after word of a POLICE raid had slipped out. Other riders were challenged elsewhere. The riders left BORDEAUX next morning, but stopped in La House after five kilometres, and walked. They claimed their liberty had been offended and demanded that PIERRE DUMAS, the Tour doctor, should also take a test. Next day they held a go-slow. Weeks later the organiser FÉLIX LÉVITAN reacted by announcing he was tired of SPONSORS (whom he suspected were behind the strike) and would go back to NATIONAL TEAMS.

In 1978 the bunch climbed off in Valence d'Agen to complain at their hours. There were five TRANSFERS that year. On the day of the Valence d'Agen stage, the riders had been called at 4.30am even though some hadn't reached their hotels until 9pm or their beds before midnight, after meals and massage. They were to race from Tarbes to Valence d'Agen in the morning and from there to Toulouse in the afternoon, 254km in all. They rode to Valence d'Agen at 15km/h while JACQUES GODDET begged them to race first and argue afterwards. Then he threatened to withhold PRIZES. This did little to lighten the mood, so he agreed to pay if they would race the last 30km. The riders were still not impressed and the bunch got off in the centre of town. 'You treat us like animals, not athletes,' they protested.

The front row included FREDDY MAERTENS, MICHEL POLLENTIER and BERNARD HINAULT. The mayor of Valence d'Agen pleaded with them not to spoil the town's big day and Hin-ault, called to the front because he was national champion, promised they would ride a CRI-TERIUM in the town for nothing. The stage was cancelled and Goddet dismissed protests with, 'It's necessary to keep the inhuman side to the

Tour; excess is necessary.' But split stages – separate races in morning and afternoon – disappeared from the Tour agenda.

In 1988 riders refused to ride for 10 minutes after a DOPING row around PEDRO DELGADO, whom they supported because probenicid, the offending drug, wasn't yet on the banned list of the UCI, the sport's governing body. (*See* Delgado entry for explanation.)

And in 1991 riders struck for 40 minutes after Urs Zimmerman was disqualified for driving from Nantes to Pau rather than taking the arranged TRANSFER by plane. He said he disliked flying, and was reinstated. The last rider's strike was in 1998 when they sat in the road after POLICE raids during the FESTINA AFFAIR.

The Tour has also provided a stage for outside protests. Strikers from the steelmaker Usinor put barricades across the road to block the team TIME TRIAL at Denain in 1982. They had nothing against the race but had hit on a novel way to make sure their complaints reached an international audience.

Sheep farmers came close to doing the same in 1990. The Union Paysanne (farmers' union) was protesting at eastern European imports which, they said, threatened their livelihoods. There were demonstrations on the first stage, and then the presentation of a live lamb decked out in ribbons to the last team in the team time trial that formed the second stage. Fabio Parra accepted it for KELME but opinion was divided as to whether the gesture was an apology for roadside protests or a hint of more.

The organisers decided it was a hint of more. Word arrived that farmers gathering in the village of St-Gemme, near France's biggest abattoir, had felled four trees and lined them up by the roadside. Agricultural types were playing *pétanque* beside them. Smoke was drifting across the road from burning tyres. Banners accusing President François Mitterrand of ruining the rural economy were on display.

The Tour took the hint and JEAN-MARIE LEBLANC halted the race 10km before St-Gemme. Maps were spread to work out a detour. Legend says that at this point a local 16-year-old called Michael arrived on a moped to lead the race through country lanes behind the waiting protesters. As the British reporter Geoffrey Nicholson pointed out, 'It seems unlikely that the race *direction* [management] and the gendarmerie . . . couldn't have found their own way but . . . the press know a good legend in the making when they see one.' The race was neutralised for 25km before setting off again.

Journalists, too, have gone on strike. Flat stages against the wind and bunch sprints produced by blocking TACTICS made the 1968 Tour a bore. Reporters began grumbling. Lévitan accused them on TV of being blasé and watching 'with tired eyes'. Next day they went on strike from Bordeaux to Labouheyre and put on dark glasses to jeer at him. Some waved banners warning, 'Riders! Tired eyes are watching you.'

BROADCASTING officials acted in 1967 when the respected commentator Robert Chapatte was excluded from television in a row. Unhappy with his stand-in, they transmitted French TV to the sound of Belgian TV's commentators. In 1987 photographers went on strike on the stage to Dijon to complain that cars carrying Tour guests were getting in their way.

In 1992, Basque independence protesters set fire to journalists' cars, including one belonging to Britain's Channel Four, a fact it reported with wonderment and resentment. In 1999 the race was stopped by firemen and pelted with stink bombs by hooligans.

> ***Trivia note:*** In 1986 Bernard Hinault grew so vexed at a strike that halted Paris-Nice that he slugged the nearest communard. The others, impressed, parted to let the race pass.

TACTICS

In most years the aim of the race has been to get to Paris in less time than anyone else. Each rider's time is totalled as the Tour goes on, BONUSES are deducted and penalties added, and the result decides a rider's placing and PRIZES.

However, from 1905 until 1912 Tours were decided on points. HENRI DESGRANGE insisted riders should repair their own BIKES but recognised the time that would take. In practice, riders were spaced over many hours, so a repair often cost a rider time rather than his place on the road. Desgrange reasoned that judging the race on time alone put too great a penalty on unlucky riders, and he made the change for Tour number three in 1905.

But the points system only substituted one problem for another. Now there was no pressure on riders to get to the FINISH urgently – so long as nobody passed them, they would get the same number of points. That meant judges sometimes had to wait hours for the riders to come in (see HENRI PÉPIN). Riders at the front realised they no longer had to attack (see ODILE DEFRAYE and EUGÈNE CHRISTOPHE). Finishing an hour ahead or a second ahead made no difference; half a wheel would be as good. Desgrange changed his mind (see Christophe's entry for the incident that provoked it) and since 1913 riders have been judged on time.

At first the change made little difference. Riders were no longer as scattered as before, but races remained trials of attrition. Like marathon runners, the best set a pace and challenged the rest to follow. The pace got faster, though, with increased fitness, better roads and better tactics, so riders stayed more grouped to gain from each other's slipstream.

The slipstream may seem small but it is a great help. The most important law in cycle racing is that it is easier to ride behind another rider than in front of him – up to 40 per cent easier. Desgrange didn't want riders to share the pace in this way because he wanted a race between individuals on equal terms. Competitors knew the advantage, of course, and were free to use it in other races, but not in the Tour. Pictures of early Tours in which riders are scattered across the road display not an ignorance of tactics but an awareness that a photographer was about.

The decision of Desgrange's successor JACQUES GODDET to allow GEARS from 1937 raised the winner's speed to 31.77km/h from an average 30.00km/h over the previous five years. As speeds went up, so DOMESTIQUES were employed to ride, protecting their leader, bridging gaps for him, and pacing him back to the race when he punctured. That remains the system to this day. All riders would like to win the Tour, but few are capable, and still fewer are employed to do so.

For most of the day the Tour rides in one group, known as the *peloton* from the French word for a herd. Small groups or individuals may go ahead early on the off-chance of succeeding – and they have: ALBERT BOURLON of FRANCE rode 253km alone to win the Carcassonne-Luchon stage in 1947, THIERRY MARIE of France rode alone for 234km of Arras-Le Havre in 1991, and José Perez-Frances of SPAIN rode 223km from Ax-les-Thermes to Barcelona in 1965. But the opening hours of a stage are normally just a wearing-down process for the last hour.

One of two things will then happen. Either a breakaway will succeed or the peloton will near the line complete and the day will be decided by SPRINTERS. Most teams have riders employed for their power in a finish. The last half-hour can get hellishly fast (*see* Jimmy Casper's comments in sprinters entry) as each team tries to make the race so fast that rival teams can't get their own sprinters forward and so no one can attack from the bunch late on. Get your man to the last 200 metres a few metres ahead of the opposition and he stands a better chance of winning.

That is the domestiques' job. One by one they will pull aside when they're exhausted until just one man remains ahead of the sprinter. This tail-end Charlie is the lead-out man, called the *poisson pilote* (pilot fish) in cyclists' French. Often good enough to be a winner himself, he will barge through the surviving riders to get his star to the front with 100 metres to go. Then he too pulls to one side to let the big sprinter battle it out for the line.

The same happens when a breakaway group remains clear to the line, although they are rarely specialist sprinters and never dedicated lead-out men. Breakaway riders will share the pacemaking with rivals to their common advantage. Better to help each other than be swallowed up by chasers.

Things change in the last kilometres. A team with more riders will take turns attacking to wear out their rivals. Poor sprinters will attack early to wear out better sprinters or to surprise them.

(*See* NATIONAL TEAMS for why tactics were sometimes distorted by riders conscious that their employment was more important than their patriotism.)

ANDREI TCHMIL
b. Khabarovsk, USSR, Jan 22 1963

Stony-faced Andrei Tchmil was born Russian in 1963 and spent his childhood in Odessa before going to a sports school in Gorki. Russian in those days meant Soviet Union and it was *CCCP*, the Cyrillic form of USSR, that topped his licence from 1981 to 1991. Tchmil had a licence from Russia itself after the USSR split – because that's where Gorki is – and from 1993 to 1994 a licence from Moldova where he started racing, in Kichinov. Moldova had no cycling federation for the 1993 world championship, so Tchmil rode in a white jersey.

In 1994 he rode the world championship for Ukraine, the country where Odessa is and where his wife Helena comes from. He kept that licence until 1997. Then he became a Belgian in 1998, although he still raced on a Ukrainian licence. He had already moved to Roubaix in FRANCE, the scene of his most famous win.

In 1994 he finished alone in Paris-Roubaix, becoming the first eastern European to win a classic, beating Johan Museeuw in what was billed as the hardest Roubaix for decades due to appalling weather conditions. He finished only two Tours, but maybe there had already been enough excitement in his life. He rode his last race in Belgium in May 2002.

Winner

1991	Paris-Bourges, National championship
1994	GP Plouay, GP Harelbeke, Paris-Roubaix
1995	Tour Limousin
1996	Veenendaal-Veenendaal
1997	Paris-Tours, A Travers Belgique
1998	Kuurne-Brussels-Kuurne, Trofeo Luis Puig
1999	Milan-San Remo, World Cup

Winner *(continued)*

2000	Tour Flanders, Coppa Sabatini, Kuurne-Brussels-Kuurne
2001	GP Harelbekè, Milan-Vignola

Tour de France

1994	DNF
1995	71st
1996	77th
1997	DNF
1998	DNF

TELEVISION – *See* BROADCASTING

GERT-JAN THEUNISSE
b. Oss, Holland, Jan 14 1963

HOLLAND has produced many good CLIMBERS for such a flat country. Gert-Jan Theunisse (pronounced *Tuh-nissuh*) was one of them but his career was as much criticised as admired. In the 1988 Tour he came second behind STEVEN ROOKS on the ALPE D'HUEZ, and then won there himself the following year. Then DOPING scandals in the Flèche Wallonne and the Tour undid him, and in 1990 he had the unusual experience of finding riders going on STRIKE at the Tour because he had not been thrown out. They believed he should have been banned for a second offence in two years, but he got a suspended sentence because of a technical error in the way he was told the results. The Tour organisers protested they were powerless to overrule the sport's governing body, the UCI, but the riders, far from supporting one of their own, demanded a meeting with the UCI.

The UCI accepted that Theunisse had been caught using drugs twice in two years, but BELGIUM, the country whose licence he held because he lived there, officially knew only of the first offence. Belgian federation officials had read of the other one in the papers but they hadn't received a formal letter. So Theunisse stayed in the race. The UCI said it would discuss the affair at the world championships in Japan, but by then FRANCE was upset at being

blamed for not telling Belgium about Theunisse's previous history, and rounded on the UCI.

Frustrated, it asked Belgium to accept what it already knew, that Theunisse was guilty. Theunisse insisted his body produced unusually large amounts of testosterone naturally, but he was asked to prove it and that – plus a fine of 5,000 Swiss francs – ended the matter.

Theunisse came back in the Tour of LUXEMBOURG in 1991, winning the first stage and the race overall. In the Tour itself he was less successful. He came 13th in 1991 and 1992, but his career dwindled with injuries and illnesses, including a saddle cyst. He retired in 1995 and became MANAGER of the mountain-biker Bart Brentjens.

(*See* STEVEN ROOKS for the 'donkey' telegram of encouragement.)

Winner

1988	San Sebastian Classic
1989	Tour Asturias
1991	Tour Luxembourg, Tour Mining Valleys

Tour de France

1987	48th	
1988	11th	
1989	4th	Stage win Briançon—Alpe d'Huez, and Mountains winner
1991	13th	
1992	13th	
1994	DNF	

BERNARD THÉVENET
b. Saint-Julien-de-Civry, France, Jan 10 1948

The Frenchman Bernard ('Nanard') Thévenet began racing in 1963, won the Burgundy youth championship in 1965 and 1966, and the national amateur championship in 1968, and then turned professional for PEUGEOT in 1970. He might have missed his first Tour in that year had his mother not thought to ring the friend with whom he had arranged to go training. Would he pass on a message? Gaston Plaud, Thévenet's MANAGER, had called to say that

FERDI BRACKE and GERBEN KARSTENS were ill, and that Thévenet, 22 years old and newly professional, was to ride.

Thévenet was in a break of five on the TOURMALET when Plaud told him to attack. He pushed on through the rain to the FINISH at the ski station of La Mongie and crossed the line freewheeling, his right arm in the air. The following year he won at Grenoble and then, in 1972, on MONT VENTOUX and the BALLON D'ALSACE. In 1973 he won two more stages and finished second overall.

Thévenet's real impact came in 1975 when EDDY MERCKX repeatedly attacked to tire the CLIMBERS before the MOUNTAINS. Thévenet was his closest rival. Merckx decided to see him off in the first stage in the Alps, from Nice to PRA-LOUP, and attacked at the top of the Col d'Allos. He hurtled down the other side faster than Thévenet dared and began the climb to Pra-Loup with almost two minutes on the chase. Halfway up, Thévenet passed him – still on the big ring – and after several attacks left Merckx behind him. By the roadside, a woman in a bikini held up a poster. 'Merckx is beaten,' it said. 'The Bastille has fallen.' Thévenet finished almost three minutes up on the five-time winner in Paris.

Journalists were delighted to find Thévenet's family came from Le Guidon (The Handlebars). Anyone who had ever passed him in the street was interviewed and accorded celebrity. It was also a sign that Merckx could be cracked.

In 1977 Thévenet won again. But by 1981 his career was over, and he blamed this on systematic DOPING by his team. He had ridden 11 Tours, won nine stages, and ridden the world championship eight times. RAPHAËL GÉMINIANI said, 'You can talk of Bernard Thévenet the nice guy, the gentle man, the brave man, and it's true he's got all those qualities. But he's also a grand champion. He was good whatever the race.'

Thévenet became a team MANAGER and then a journalist, and finally joined French television. He lives near Grenoble and his accent and odd vocal stresses help make the summer for many a TV Tour-follower. Unkinder cartoonists portray him as the Spock character from *Star Trek*.

In 2002 he became a Chevalier de la Légion d'Honneur, French equivalent of a knight.

Winner

1972	Tour Romandie
1973	National championship
1974	Tour Catalonia, Critérium International
1975	Tour de France, Dauphiné Libéré
1976	Dauphiné Libéré
1977	Tour de France, Montjuich

Tour de France

1970	35th	Stage win St-Gaudens—La Mongie
1971	4th	Stage win St-Étienne—Grenoble
1972	9th	Stage wins Carnon—Mont Ventoux, Pontarlier—Ballon d'Alsace
1973	2nd	Stage wins Gaillard—Méribel, Versailles—Paris
1974	DNF	
1975	1st	Stage wins Nice—Pra-Loup, Barcelonnette—Serre-Chevalier, and Yellow Jersey
1976	DNF	
1977	1st	Stage win Dijon—Dijon, and Yellow Jersey
1978	DNF	
1980	17th	
1981	37th	

DIETRICH THURAU
b. Frankfurt, West Germany, Nov 9 1954

Dietrich Thurau looked like an angel. His golden hair and light tan were perfectly set off by the yellow JERSEY he won in the PROLOGUE at Fleurance in 1977. He was riding his first Tour and two days later found himself more than two minutes behind HENNIE KUIPER, BERNARD THÉVENET and JOOP ZOETEMELK on the road. And then one of those things happened that 22-year-old professionals can only dream of: EDDY MERCKX rode up to him in the

Pyrenees and asked for a hand chasing the break.

Thurau felt outclassed but could hardly refuse. They closed the gap on the AUBISQUE and Thurau won the stage. Everyone expected him to lose his jersey in the TIME TRIAL at BORDEAUX, where Merckx had to take only eight seconds. Maybe the Belgian was too confident; perhaps Thurau was inspired. Far from losing eight seconds, he picked up almost a minute.

The Tour went into GERMANY and had a rest day. If Thurau slept, he was lucky. His hotel was circled by shouting fans. The strain began to tell. He did badly in the next time trial and his hopes came tumbling on ALPE D'HUEZ. In one long, painful ride he lost 12 minutes. He finished fifth, but still won best YOUNG RIDER.

His career didn't last. In the 1979 Tour he finished three-quarters of an hour down. He rode again intermittently but in 1985 was disqualified for hitting an official. He found guest appearances and supermarket openings paid as much as races, but took less trouble, and rode mainly six-days on the TRACK before retiring.

Winner

1975 Tour Oise, GP Fourmies, National championship
1976 National championship
1977 GP Gippingen, GP Harelbeke, Ruta Sol
1978 GP Escaut, Etoile Bessèges, Championship Zurich
1979 Liège-Bastogne-Liège, Ruta Sol, Tour Germany

Tour de France

1977	5th	Stage wins Fleurance—Fleurance, Auch—Pau, Bordeaux—Bordeaux, Morzine—Chamonix, Versailles—Paris, and Yellow Jersey
1979	10th	Stage win Bourg d'Oisans—St-Priest
1980	DNF	
1982	DNF	
1985	DNF	
1987	DNF	

PHILIPPE THYS
b. Anderlecht, Belgium, Oct 8 1890,
d. Jan 16 1971

Who was the first rider to wear the yellow JERSEY? Legend says EUGÈNE CHRISTOPHE but even the Tour history doesn't dismiss the Belgian Philippe Thys's claim that he wore one in 1913, six years before Christophe.

Thys – pronounced *Tayce* – came from Anderlecht in Brussels, and was first to win three Tours (1913, 1914 and 1920). When he was 67 he told the magazine *Champions et Vedettes* that HENRI DESGRANGE had asked him to wear a distinctive colour as race leader, but that he had declined because he didn't want to be more visible to rivals.

'Several stages later it was my manager at PEUGEOT, the unforgettable Alphonse Baugé, who urged me to give in. The yellow jersey would be an advertisement for the company and, that being the argument, I was obliged to concede. So a yellow jersey was bought in the first shop we came to. It was just the right size, although we had to cut a slightly larger hole for my head to go through.'

The details become even more convincing when he says of the following year that 'I won the first stage and was beaten by a tyre by Bossus in the second. On the following day the *maillot jaune* passed to ÉMILE GEORGET after a CRASH.'

The Tour history says Thys was 'a valorous rider . . . well known for his intelligence,' and his memories 'seem free from all suspicion'. But it adds that 'no newspaper mentions a yellow jersey before the WAR [and] being at a loss for witnesses, we can't solve this enigma.'

Thys's first win in 1913 came after a battle with LUCIEN PETIT-BRETON that went on throughout the Tour. The 1914 race came only a week before Germany declared war on France. Thys won despite asking a BIKE shop to change a damaged wheel on the last but one stage. The owner warned he'd be docked time, but Thys reasoned that he'd lose even more making the repair himself and told him to go ahead. He was docked half an hour but the gamble worked.

Belgium became a non-combatant in the war, which meant Thys survived when other stars didn't. (*See* FRANÇOIS FABER and OCTAVE LAPIZE.) He should have come back with a fitness that his French rivals would have lacked. Instead, he was so fat and slow in 1919 that his team-mate Jean Rossius thought it worth suffering a 30-minute penalty to help him through the opening stage. Thys was for going home, and before long he did. That autumn Desgrange accused him of growing smug, keener on his reputation than winning races. 'You have become *un petit bourgeois* who's lost his love for his bike and wasted a huge talent,' he chided.

Thys was hurt. He trained ferociously and even cut his hair short to reduce wind resistance. For a while the effort seemed wasted when he broke a collarbone in Milan-San Remo, although he still rode the remaining 50km. But come the Tour, he won four stages and never finished outside the first five on any day. He won the Tour by 57 minutes, and Belgians took the first seven places, winning 12 of the 15 stages. Thys finished at the PARC DES PRINCES to the sound of *La Brabançonne*, the Belgian anthem, and had to walk across the line among crowds who had spilled onto the TRACK to greet him. In 1922 Thys won five stages but didn't finish in the top ten.

He was an austere man who rarely wasted effort, and rarely acted on impulse. He finished the Tour at the weight – 69kg – at which he started. He was 29 when he won his final Tour.

Winner

1913	Tour de France
1914	Tour de France, Paris-Menin
1917	Paris-Tours, Tour Lombardy
1920	Tour de France
1921	Critérium As

Tour de France

1912	6th	
1913	1st	Stage win Bayonne—Luchon
1914	1st	Stage win Paris—Le Havre

Tour de France (continued)

1919	DNF	
1920	1st	Stage wins Le Havre—Cherbourg, Aix-en-Provence—Nice, Gex—Strasbourg, Strasbourg—Metz, and Yellow Jersey
1921	DNF	
1922	14th	Stage win Brest—Les Sables, Perpignan—Toulon, Toulon—Nice, Nice—Briançon, Dunkirk—Paris
1923	DNF	
1924	11th	Stage win Toulon—Nice
1925	DNF	

TIME LIMITS – *See* GRUPPETTO

TIME TRIALS

The first individual time trial was 80km from La Roche-sur-Yon to Nantes in 1934, won by ANTONIN MAGNE. The first mountain time trial was over the ISÉRAN from Bonneval to Bourg-St-Maurice in 1939, and was won by SYLVÈRE MAES. The time trial starting ramp – enabling a flying START from an elevated platform – was introduced at Cologne in 1965.

The start order in time trials is the reverse of the result sheet, with the exception of the PROLOGUE, where the starting order is decided by the organisers.

In the Tours of 1927 and 1928 HENRI DESGRANGE with his drive for novelty decided to turn the flat stages of the Tour into team time trials. Teams set off on staggered starts on 16 days, but the formula never proved successful with either riders or SPECTATORS, and favoured bigger and stronger teams. What rich teams like ALCYON gained on the flat couldn't be overturned in the MOUNTAINS. The system gave LUXEMBOURG'S NICOLAS FRANTZ his win in 1928. (*See* also HUBERT OPPERMAN.)

In the modern Tour, team time trials appear most years. 'There is no rule,' says JEAN-MARIE LEBLANC, 'except it must be before the sixth day of the race and link two towns 50–60km apart on a course that's easy to negotiate.'

(*See* ROGER LÉVÈQUE.)

TOUR DE L'AVENIR

The 'Tour of the Future' was created in 1961 by FÉLIX LÉVITAN and JACQUES GODDET for AMATEURS and INDEPENDENTS (semi-professionals) in NATIONAL TEAMS. Riders from both sides of the Iron Curtain had competed in the Peace Race but the Tour de'Avenir was the first race of that international standard in the west. It preceded the professional Tour on a shorter course, and produced several riders who went on to win the Tour as pros, notably FELICE GIMONDI (1964), JOOP ZOETEMELK (1969), GREG LEMOND (1982) and MIGUEL INDURAIN (1986). The leader wore a yellow JERSEY with two white bands.

The race has changed its name several times, notably to the Tour of the European Community from 1987 to 1990.

1961	Guido De Rosso (Italy)
1962	Antonio Gomez del Moral (Spain)
1963	André Zimmerman (France)
1964	Felice Gimondi (Italy)
1965	Mariano Diaz (Spain)
1966	Mino Denti (Italy)
1967	Christian Robini (France)
1968	Jean-Pierre Boulard (France)
1969	Joop Zoetemelk (Holland)
1970	—
1971	Régis Ovion (France)
1972	Fedor Den Hertog (Holland)
1973	Gianbattista Baronchelli (Italy)
1974	Enrique Martinez-Heredia (Spain)
1975	—
1976	Sven-Ake Nilsson (Sweden)
1977	Eddy Schepers (Belgium)
1978	Sergei Soukhoroutchenkov (USSR)
1979	Sergei Soukhoroutchenkov (USSR)
1980	Alfonso Florez (Colombia)
1981	Pascal Simon (France)
1982	Greg LeMond (USA)
1983	Olaf Ludwig (East Germany)
1984	Charly Mottet (France)
1985	Martin Ramirez (Colombia)
1986	Miguel Indurain (Spain)
1987	Marc Madiot (France)
1988	Laurent Fignon (France)
1989	Pascal Lino (France)
1990	Johan Bruyneel (Belgium)
1991	—
1992	Hervé Garel (France)
1993	Thomas Davy (France)
1994	Angel-Luis Casero (Spain)
1995	Emmanuel Magnien (France)
1996	David Etxebarria (Spain)
1997	Laurent Roux (France)
1998	Christophe Rinero (France)
1999	Unai Osa (Spain)
2000	Iker Flores (Spain)
2001	Denis Menchov (Russia)
2002	Evgeni Petrov (Russia)

TOUR VILLAGE

The Tour Village, introduced in 1988, is a collection of sponsored stands set up at each START to make a fuss of guests, former riders, SPONSORS, journalists and anyone else who can get in. Access is by pass from the SOCIÉTÉ DU TOUR DE FRANCE.

The Village has coffee, soft drinks and sandwich stalls, all free, a relaxation area for riders and anyone else, a hairdresser, newspaper stands and anything else that sponsors and the host town arrange. The Village is the place to meet regular visitors such as EDDY MERCKX and RAYMOND POULIDOR.

The *BRIGADE ORANGE* starts demolishing the Village 10 minutes after riders leave.

(And *see* POLICE.)

TOURISTE-ROUTIER

Until 1938 you could almost just turn up and ride the Tour. It was more complicated than that, of course, but provided you found your own accommodation and caused the organisation no trouble, you could take part and win what you could. You were a touriste-routier.

RENÉ DE LATOUR said, 'Some of the more experienced men booked their rooms by post.

But the majority just trusted to luck. Sometimes it was hours before they got fixed up. There may have been many at the start of the Tour but not so many at the FINISH. Many of the retirements came in the MOUNTAINS with the riders absolutely dead. Others were not short of form but they were short of money and they couldn't pay their hotel bills. They had no alternative but to pack up at the point nearest their region – and cycle back home.'

Touriste-routiers included men like JULES DELOFFRE, who performed acrobatic tricks each day and went round the crowd for centimes. Then he'd balance a suitcase on his bars and find a hotel. Others spent their nights in barns.

Deloffre finished seven times between 1908 and 1921 and only twice outside the first two dozen. The bike shop owner, Henri Touzard, rode seven times so he could hang his bike in his window for publicity. In 1930 Max Bulla of Austria wore the yellow JERSEY.

Even respected names like SYLVÈRE MAES and the first king of the MOUNTAINS, VICENTE TRUEBA, rode sometimes as individuals. The star touriste-routier, though, was BENOIT FAURE, a climber so tiny that he was called 'the Mouse'. (*See* Faure entry for more.)

HENRI DESGRANGE put them into ad hoc teams after he introduced NATIONAL TEAMS in 1930 and they gradually disappeared.

(*See* KISSO KAWAMURO.)

TOURMALET

Tourmalet means 'bad route' in patois. It is the highest pass in the Pyrenees and the most visited MOUNTAIN in the Tour itineraries, although only one stage, won by JEAN-PIERRE DANGUILLAUME in 1974, has finished at the top. However, two have finished at La Mongie, the highest village on the mountain. BERNARD THÉVENET won there in 1970 and LANCE ARMSTRONG in 2002.

The Ste-Marie side starts as a drag from Bagnères-Bigorre, running up a valley through the village of Campan (a place where villagers traditionally put life-sized dolls on verandas or by bus stops). It turns right at the foot of the Col d'Aspin in Ste-Marie-de-Campan, where EUGÈNE CHRISTOPHE mended his forks in the forge (*see* Christophe entry for details), and there the steep section begins. It rises 1,258m in 16.5km at an average gradient of 7.6 per cent.

The other side, from Luz-St Sauveur, climbs 1,405m in 18.8km, at an average gradient of 7.5 per cent.

A café and shop stand at the top, together with MEMORIALS to OCTAVE LAPIZE and JACQUES GODDET. The café has a display of old bikes, including one in which pedalling forwards gives a high gear and backwards a low one.

The Tourmalet is often ridden with the Col de Soulor, the AUBISQUE and the climb to LUZ-ARDIDEN. In 1922 the Tourmalet was abandoned because of snow.

TRACKS

The habit of ending stages at a vélodrome died out in the 1970s because of the danger of the peloton arriving while the leaders – who had to ride a lap and a half – were trying to sprint on the same section of track. There was also no room for the CARAVAN.

The most used track was BORDEAUX (see entry for details). Before moving to the CHAMPS ELYSÉES in 1975, the Tour used to finish at the tracks of the PARC DES PRINCES and then of the PISTE MUNICIPALE.

In the race's first years, HENRI DESGRANGE had to ban riders from making track appearances on rest days. He had expected them to be exhausted but they quickly found a way to cash in on the fame of the new race.

TRANSFERS

The race doesn't always start in the same town that the previous day's stage finished. Consequently, riders then have to be transferred from one place to the next. The first transfer was in 1906, when riders travelled from Lille to Douai. It wasn't repeated until 1955, when the transfer was from Poitiers to Châtellerault. The first rail transfer was from BORDEAUX to Mont-de-Marsan in 1960. The first air transfer was Clermont-Ferrand to Nice in 1975. The first sea transfer was to Plymouth, BRITAIN, in 1974 (riders went by plane, everybody else by ferry). The first transfer through the Channel Tunnel was in 1994 to mark the 50th anniversary of D-day.

(And *see* STRIKES.)

LOUIS TROUSSELIER

b. Levallois-Perret, France, Jun 29 1881,
d. Apr 24 1939

In 1905, 24-year-old Louis ('Trou-Trou') Trousselier took unofficial leave from the 101st Regiment where he was a conscript, and won five stages against strong opposition from HIPPOLYTE AUCOUTURIER and Jean-Baptiste Dortignacq, who each won three stages. By BORDEAUX Trousselier was unbeatable, so far ahead on points that no one could pass him. Which was just as well because he'd come to the race with just 24 hours' leave, and it took victory to placate his officers back at the barracks.

Trousselier's PRIZES came to 6,950 francs, including 4,000 for winning. PEUGEOT, which had made his BIKE, paid him a bonus. And he had already pocketed cheques for the first of the races he would ride after finishing the Tour in Paris. In all, he had 25,000 francs. Today that would be about £2,500. Not a huge sum now, but in 1905 it represented many years' wages for a working man. And what did Trousselier do?

'That same night,' said Georges Berretrot, a track announcer, 'he shut himself away in one of the cabins at the Buffalo track with two colleagues. They sat round a massage table, and the dice [other reports say cards] rolled all night and much of the following morning. By the time Trousselier left the cabin, he didn't have a sou in his pocket. He'd lost everything he'd suffered to win on the road. He'd had the joy of winning the Tour de France and he'd been delighted to win. And to his credit, he accepted his losses without a grumble and had only one thought – to get back on his bike and win some money all over again.'

Trousselier rode like he lived, with abandon. In 1909 he took his feet off the pedals on the Col de Porte, balanced them on his fork crown, and sailed down the MOUNTAIN with flailing pedals. It wasn't his only trick. He was a master of what he called the dinner-sprint, a trick he pulled at Melun, Fontainebleau and Rombouillet.

He and two or three friends would enter the most expensive restaurant in town and order the most expensive meal. As they ate it they made a point of arguing, sometimes with heated voices, about which of them was the best rider. The *patron* would come over and ask if all was well. Trousselier would explain the row and ask for the man's help. Would he suggest a landmark a kilometre down the road and set the riders off in a race there and back? The losers would pay for the meal. Time and again the *patron* would agree . . . and time and again the riders disappeared leaving the unpaid bill behind them.

He retired to run the family flower business on the Boulevard Haussman in Paris. In 1934 he told *Match* (later *Paris-Match*), 'The Tour today is nothing like what we rode or even the Tours of the after-war years. Equipment is better, the roads – above all those in the mountains – are nothing like the quagmires we sometimes had to ride through for hundreds of kilometres. It's not the same job. These days the Tour is a succession of little races.

'The ideal formula should be changed. What would bring back the suffering of the old riders would be an individual formula. Every rider for himself. No stars depending on their DOMESTIQUES. No good riders condemned to defending someone else's yellow JERSEY just because he's not in the lead. For me, what I find moving is a Tour where you see a rider well ahead during several stages only to lose precious time on repairs and seeing the others pass in front of his nose.'

(*See* CRITERIUMS, ODILE DEFRAYE, MONEY.)

Winner

1905 Tour de France, Paris-Roubaix
1908 Bordeaux-Paris, Liège-Bastogne-Liège

Tour de France

1905	1st	Stage wins Paris—Nancy, Besançon—Grenoble, Toulon—Nîmes, Toulouse—Bordeaux, La Rochelle—Rennes
1906	3rd	Stage wins Marseille—Toulouse, Bayonne—Bordeaux, Bordeaux—Nantes, Nantes—Brest
1907	DNF	Stage wins Paris—Roubaix, Roubaix—Metz
1909	8th	Stage win Bordeaux—Nantes
1910	DNF	Stage win Bordeaux—Nantes
1911	DNF	
1913	11th	
1914	38th	

VICENTE TRUEBA

b. Torrelavega, Spain, Oct 16 1905,
d. Nov 10 1986

On unmade roads where riders picked a way between rubble and wound round rocks, Vicente Trueba of SPAIN became the Tour's first King of the MOUNTAINS in 1933. There was no JERSEY, though. HENRI DESGRANGE had concocted the category to recognise the public's affection and esteem for the little men of the hills, but he hadn't thought to identify them. That didn't happen until 1953 with Jesus Loroño.

Trueba was riding his third Tour but was largely unknown, along with his brother José. Vicente came into his own in 1933, bouncing on the pedals and earning the NICKNAME 'the Flea of Torrelavega'. He led over the GALIBIER, Lauteret and TÉLÉGRAPHE in the Alps, and then over the ASPIN, AUBISQUE and Peyresourde in the Pyrenees. And in the Vosges he did the same on the BALLON D'ALSACE.

Like many climbers, though, he was as bad going down as he was good at going up. He lost all he had gained – more than 12 minutes sometimes, almost a minute a kilometre – and had to open the gap again on the next climb. It meant he never won a stage, mountain finishes not coming until 1952.

Tour de France

1930	24th	
1932	27th	
1933	6th	Mountains winner
1934	10th	
1935	DNF	

JAN ULLRICH
b. Rostock, East Germany, Dec 2 1973

In 1987 when the Tour started in Berlin, East Germany's Jan Ullrich was 13 and at school. This was just a kilometre away from the START but he couldn't watch because the Berlin Wall was between him and the start. The fall of the Wall in 1990 released a lot of talent. Ullrich remembers, 'I was a student at the sports school. The following day was Saturday and we could just drive across the old border. I bought a pair of socks. It was exhilarating to buy whatever you wanted.'

Ullrich – whose first ambitions had been running and football – had gone to races in his mother's Trabant. (His father Werner left home when Ullrich was three and Jan has never forgiven him.) He remembers wearing 10-year-old jerseys in his first big race in 1991, 'which didn't stop me coming third'.

He won the world AMATEUR championship in Oslo at 19 in 1993, the year that LANCE ARMSTRONG won the professional race. His early hero was OLAF LUDWIG, whom he'd watched winning the Olympic road race in Seoul, so Ullrich's joy was complete when he emulated his hero by winning the newly pro-am Olympic title at Sydney in 2000.

Ullrich was the surprise of 1996 when he came second in his first Tour after working for his team-mate BJARNE RIIS. He followed it by winning in 1997, and then coming second in

1998 after MARCO PANTANI took nine minutes out of him on the GALIBIER.

Ullrich's misfortune has been to run up against Armstrong, a rider who can match the German's strength on the flat but with a climbing technique Ullrich can't match. Ullrich prefers a fast but steady ascent which denies others the chance to come by; Armstrong is more classic as a climber, varying his speed and opening gaps.

'Armstrong is more fluid than I am,' Ullrich says. 'His pedalling rate is higher than mine and he can economise a bit by riding a lower gear. But I've never wanted to imitate him. I've got the ability and if I trained the right way, I could do it. But in a race I prefer to feel the pedals, which stimulates me.'

Ullrich still has comparative youth on his side, but a problem mastering his weight. He became known for ballooning up during the off-season and plodding round at the back of races as he tried to shed fat. Journalists who once wrote of the fab now spoke of the flab. Ullrich, sheltered from criticism in East Germany and regarded in Germany as a saint, had difficulty taking the criticism. He has never been a man to speak easily, being accustomed, in the words of his MANAGER RUDY PEVENAGE, to taking rather than giving orders.

He persevered, at one time trying a banana diet in which he ate four in the morning and ten at night. ('Not advised for anyone with a fragile liver.') His weight came back down, only for a greater problem to strike, a persistent knee injury which forced him out of the 2002 race. Ullrich began to despair, and said in spring 2002 that he would no longer ride the Tour, but his manager, WALTER GODEFROOT, asked, 'How do we know his knee injury has not been caused by his lack of professionalism?'

The hidden meaning of the question became clear when a night of partying on May 1 2002 ended with Ullrich driving his Porsche into a row of bikes in a rack. He was three times over the alcohol limit. On June 12 an out-of-season drugs test found he had taken amphetamine at a night club, and he was fined and suspended.

Ullrich's AGENT, Wolfgang Strohband, said his rider had grown frustrated and depressed when his knee hadn't responded to surgery. By the end of the year he appeared to have come out of the worst, and a newly slim, fit-looking Ullrich turned up at the Tour PRESENTATION in Paris to say that he would after all be riding the Tour in 2003, although not for the Telekom team he has ridden for since turning pro.

Ullrich lives at Merdingen, a village of 2,500 in the Black Forest, where his girlfriend Gaby grew up and worked as a policewoman. They built their own home there, 500 metres from her parents' house.

(*See* HENNIE KUIPER, JENS VOIGT, MONEY, ERIK ZABEL.)

Winner

1997	Tour de France, HEW Cup
1999	World time trial championship
2000	Olympic road title, Coppa Agostini
2001	World time trial championship, National championship, Tour Emilia

Tour de France

1996	2nd	Stage win Bordeaux—St Emilion
1997	1st	Stage wins Luchon—Andorra, St-Étienne—St-Étienne, and Yellow Jersey
1998	2nd	Stage wins Meyrignac L'Église—Corrèze, Vizille—Albertville, Montceau-les-Mines—Le Creusot, and Yellow Jersey
2000	2nd	
2001	2nd	

WIM VAN EST

b. Fijnaart, Holland, Mar 25 1923

Wim ('Iron Will') van Est is one of the sport's great anecdote tellers, a barrel-shaped man as ready to laugh now as he was at the height of his career. In 1951 he became HOLLAND's first yellow JERSEY – a lead he lost in a bizarre CRASH, about which he laughs of course.

He began racing in 1947 after watching a race in his village, St-Willebrord, marvelling that they didn't go any faster. (*See* JAN RAAS for a Tour finish in the village.) He began in races that had a coal-delivery lorry as *VOITURE BALAI*, and he attacked so hard and often that before long it was full of those who had given up, which annoyed them because they got coated in soot.

He rode his first Tour in 1951. Twelve days into the race he outsprinted a small group on a cinder track at Dax and won his first stage. The next stage went over the TOURMALET and AUBISQUE to Tarbes. Van Est wasn't a CLIMBER so he went away early to get enough time to finish the climbs and defend his jersey.

He was about to catch STAN OCKERS and FAUSTO COPPI on the Aubisque when he reached a slippery bend. 'It was wet from the snow,' he said. 'And there were sharp stones on the road that the cars had kicked up and my front wheel hit them and I went over.' He fell 20 metres down the mountainside, rolling until he landed on the one ledge that could stop him falling into the ravine.

'A metre left or right and I'd have dropped on to solid stone, six or seven hundred metres down. My ankles were all hurt, my elbows were *kapot*. I was bruised and shaken up and I didn't know where I was, but nothing was broken. I just lay there. And the other riders were going by, I could see. And then right at the top I could make out my team-mate, Gerrit Peeters, looking down at me.

'"You looked just like a buttercup down there," he told me afterwards, with the yellow jersey on, you know.'

The MANAGER, Kees Pellenaars, threw a rope. (*See* HOLLAND, DOPING and JO DE ROO for more on Pellenaars.) But it was too short, and so he tied on the only thing he had – the team's spare tyres. 'They got 40 tubulars, knotted them together, tied them to the tow rope and threw it down to me. It was all the tyres that Pellenaars had for the team. By the time they'd pulled me up, they were stretched and wouldn't stay on the wheels any more. One of the journalists gave me a flask of cognac and I was saying, "I want to go on, I want to go on." But I couldn't. Pellenaars stopped the whole team. "We'll be back next year," he said. It was good publicity. I got home and the whole neighbourhood was out to greet me.'

A newspaper advertisement showed van Est offering his watch to the camera. 'My heart nearly stopped on the mountain but not my Pontiac [watch],' it said.

Van Est retired and worked for the Dutch railways for 18 years. In July 2001, the 50th anniversary of the fall, a marketing company put a MEMORIAL on the Aubisque. Director Karel Hubert said, 'There, in that ravine, is the beginning of Dutch Tour history.'

Winner

1950	Bordeaux-Paris
1952	Tour Holland, Bordeaux-Paris
1953	Tour Flanders
1954	Tour Holland
1956	National championship
1957	National championship
1961	Bordeaux-Paris

Tour de France

1951	DNF	Stage win Agen—Dax, and Yellow Jersey
1952	17th	
1953	13th	Stage win Marseille—Monaco
1954	16th	Stage win Rouen—Caen
1955	15th	
1957	8th	
1958	46th	
1960	39th	
1961	DNF	

LUCIEN VAN IMPE

b. Mere, Belgium, Oct 20 1946

LANCE ARMSTRONG has been criticised for being interested in little more than the Tour. It's an attitude the cherubic Belgian Lucien van Impe beat him to by 30 years. But van Impe wasn't interested even in winning the Tour. He based his year on the MOUNTAINS prize. He seemed as surprised as anyone else when he won the whole Tour in 1976.

Baby-faced with a bubble perm, van Impe looked too lethargic to stir coffee let alone his legs. He was different from most CLIMBERS in having big legs beneath a small body. He could also sprint.

His career began in 1969 when FEDERICO BAHAMONTES, his childhood hero, told JEAN STABLINSKI he should consider van Impe for his Sonolor-Lejeune team. Van Impe had been riding the AMATEUR Tour of Navarra and had already won 100 races. His father drove him to Stablinski's house at Valenciennes, then to Brussels to sign for a professional licence. That week he started the Tour de France, his second race as a professional.

'I owe a lot to Bahamontes,' he said, 'so much that when I'd won the King of the MOUNTAINS six times, as he had, I didn't try to win it again. I could've won it 10 times.'

That hesitation coloured his career. 'He never takes risks,' MANAGER CYRILLE GUIMARD said. 'He behaves in the peloton as he does in life: like a child.'

Van Impe rode every Tour bar two from 1969 to 1985 and finished them all. Ten times he finished in the top 10. He was always there, a joy to watch and a pleasure to talk to, but never a contender. Then in 1976 it was as though everyone had ganged up to force him to win. EDDY MERCKX wasn't riding, and BERNARD THÉVENET was a shadow of the man he'd been. That left JOOP ZOETEMELK, another regular participant who rarely looked like winning, but the Dutchman wasn't as good a climber as van Impe. Zoetemelk took the stages at ALPE D'HUEZ and Montgenèvre, but van Impe had his say where it mattered.

Or he did some of the time. He and Guimard disagreed on TACTICS. The accepted version seems to be that van Impe wanted to trick Zoetemelk into attacking and wearing himself out by feigning tiredness on the 14th stage from St-Gaudens to St-Lary-Soulan. Guimard says he wanted van Impe to attack long and hard, and kept sending team-mates up to tell him so. Van Impe snapped that if Guimard wanted to debate it then he should come up and give orders himself. He did. And van Impe attacked.

He rode off, caught the break, beat Zoetemelk by three minutes, and put 45 of the 93 riders outside the time limit. Peter Post, manager of the RALEIGH team, had to ask on their behalf that they should be reinstated or the Tour would be only half the size. Zoetemelk had seen his hopes of winning the Tour slide away with every turn of van Impe's pedals.

Crossing 22 cols alone, and winning six mountains titles in the Tour and the mountains title in the 1983 Giro, suggests he was capable of much more. But the mountains were his love and were really all that interested him.

(*See* TOM SIMPSON for how van Impe opened the museum at Harworth.)

Winner

| 1976 | Trophée Grimpeurs |
| 1983 | National championship |

Tour de France

1969	12th	
1970	6th	
1971	3rd	Mountains winner
1972	4th	Stage win Carpentras—Orcières-Merlette, and Mountains winner
1973	5th	Stage win Thuir—Pyrenees 2000
1974	18th	
1975	3rd	Stage wins Aurillac—Puy-de-Dôme, Morzine—Châtel, and Mountains winner
1976	1st	Stage win St-Gaudens—St-Lary-Soulan, and Yellow Jersey
1977	3rd	Stage win Morzine—Avoriaz, and Mountains winner
1978	9th	
1979	11th	Stage win Morzine—Les Ménuires
1980	16th	
1981	2nd	Stage win St-Gaudens—St-Lary-Soulan, and Mountains winner
1983	4th	Stage win Morzine—Avoriaz, and Mountains winner
1985	27th	

RIK VAN LOOY

b. Grobbendonk, Belgium, Dec 20 1933

Known as 'the Emperor of Herentals' because of the town in which he still lives, Rik van Looy was the great Belgian rider before EDDY

MERCKX. He had a fearsome sprint and exerted great control over his team. 'Tactics in van Looy's teams were simple: you had to ride for van Looy,' said VIN DENSON. These qualities brought him every single-day classic, including Paris-Roubaix three times. He raced as a professional from the age of 19 to 36, winning the world championship in 1960 and 1961, and twice coming second.

Van Looy came into cycling through working on a newspaper round which helped pay for a second-hand racing BIKE. He was lapped five times in his first race and swore never to race again, but despite that early setback went on to win the national amateur championship in 1952 and 1953, and turned professional. This put him into immediate conflict with the established star, RIK VAN STEENBERGEN.

'I had to fight to dominate van Steenbergen,' van Looy said, 'When you're at the top, you fight to stay there. You don't give way easily. I was the same when EDDY MERCKX was coming up. It is for the newcomer to prove himself.'

That attitude, hard, bossy and uncompromising, brought him around 500 victories (the reported number varies), including every classic, two world championships, five Tour stages, six stages of the Giro, and 18 stages of the Tour of SPAIN. He never won the Tour itself because he was too bulky to be a good CLIMBER. Even so, he won the MOUNTAINS prize in the 1960 Giro and the green JERSEY in the 1963 Tour.

He stopped racing on August 22 1970, a decision he took in his Mercedes on the way from Valkenswaard in HOLLAND. 'I was tired of riding against snot-noses who, even if you took them all together, hadn't managed a fraction of what I'd achieved,' he said. 'And yet sometimes I'd hear them say, "Oh, we gave that old geezer a hard time today." They knew what I'd achieved and how difficult it was to do it. And these little riders thought they could laugh at me.'

He missed the break in his last race but won the bunch sprint to come eighth. There were no farewell performances. 'I stopped racing on instinct,' he said. 'I told my wife as we were driving and I don't think she believed it, but it was true and I don't regret it.'

Rik van Looy *(continued)*

He managed the IJsboerke team in Belgium, and in 1974 became technical director of the Flemish Bike School near his home.

(*See* BENONI BEHEYT for the straying hand that cost van Looy a third world championship and Beheyt his career.)

Winner

1956	Tour Holland, Ghent-Wevelgem, Paris-Brussels
1957	Tour Holland, Ghent-Wevelgem
1958	Milan-San Remo, Paris-Brussels, National championship
1959	Paris-Tours, Tour Flanders, Tour Lombardy
1960	World championship
1961	World championship, Tour Belgium, Liège-Bastogne-Liège, Paris-Roubaix, Critérium As
1962	Ghent-Wevelgem, Paris-Roubaix, Tour Flanders
1963	National championship
1964	GP Harelbeke, Paris-Luxembourg
1965	Paris-Roubaix, GP Harelbeke
1966	GP Harelbeke
1967	Paris-Tours
1968	Flèche Wallonne
1969	GP Harelbeke

Tour de France

1962	DNF	
1963	10th	Stage wins Reims—Jambes, Limoges—Bordeaux, Toulouse—Aurillac, Troyes—Paris, and Points winner
1964	DNF	
1965	31st	Stage wins Cologne—Liège, Mont Revard—Lyon, and Yellow Jersey
1966	DNF	
1967	DNF	
1969	DNF	Stage win Charleville—Nancy

GUSTAF VAN SLEMBROUCK
b. Ostend, Belgium, Mar 25 1902, d. Jul 7 1968

Crazy name, crazy guy. Staf van Slembrouck, an easygoing, laughing Belgian of the 1920s, would often take a moment during the Tour to light a cigarette and puff as he rode. It made him popular with SPECTATORS and photographers, and he played up to it.

He was even more popular after a CRASH in the Tour of Flanders. As the race moved at speed in single file along a cycle path, van Slembrouck crashed to the ground. A cow grazing at the roadside had reversed into him. With his hope of winning gone he advanced towards the cow with his bottle – and milked it.

Tour de France

1926	DNF	Stage win Metz—Dunkirk, and Yellow Jersey
1927	14th	Stage wins Brest—Vannes, Luchon—Perpignan
1929	DNF	Stage win Brest—Vannes

HERMAN VAN SPRINGEL
b. Ranst, Belgium, Aug 14 1943

In the 1968 Tour Herman van Springel had only the TIME TRIAL to negotiate to keep his yellow JERSEY and win in PARIS. Then JAN JANSSEN came from obscurity, having never led the race, to deny him his victory. (*See* Janssen and FERDI BRACKE for more.) He partly compensated for this in the 1973 Tour by winning the points competition.

Van Springel is one of BELGIUM's most overlooked riders, overshadowed by flashier and more prolific performers like EDDY MERCKX and FREDDY MAERTENS. But he won the Super Prestige Pernod, forerunner of the World Cup, in 1968, coming second in 1970 and third in 1969. He also came second to GOSTA PETTERSSON in the Giro in 1971, and second to VITTORIO ADORNI in the world championship of 1968. His most remarkable record was 10 podium places between 1967 and 1981 in Bordeaux-Paris, seven times as winner.

Van Springel had a long, mournful face like an undertaker searching for a coffin. He was never happier than when he could just sit and pedal, on and on and very fast.

Winner

1966	Ghent-Wevelgem
1968	Tour Lombardy, Het Volk
1969	GP Nations, Paris-Tours
1970	Bordeaux-Paris, GP Nations, Flèche Brabançonne
1971	Championship Zurich, National championship
1974	Bordeaux-Paris, Flèche Brabançonne, GP Harelbeke
1975	Bordeaux-Paris
1976	GP Wallonia
1977	Bordeaux-Paris
1978	Bordeaux-Paris
1980	Bordeaux-Paris
1981	Bordeaux-Paris

Tour de France

1966	6th	
1967	24th	Stage win Jambes—Metz
1968	2nd	Stage win St-Gaudens—Seo de Urgel, and Yellow Jersey
1969	18th	Stage wins Chamonix—Briançon, Clermont-Ferrand—Montargis
1970	DNF	
1971	14th	Stage win Gourette—Pau
1973	6th	Yellow Jersey and Points winner
1974	10th	
1975	31st	
1976	DNF	

RIK VAN STEENBERGEN

b. Arendonk, Belgium, Sep 9 1924

The 24-year career of the remarkable Belgian, Rik van Steenbergen, did not end until he was 42, in December 1966. He won three world road championships (1949, 1956, 1957) and came third in 1946. In all, he won 1,314 events on the track, and his 40 six-days wins were a record for almost 20 years. Around 25,000

turned up for his farewell race at the Sportpaleis in Antwerp.

Van Steenbergen began racing before the WAR. 'My parents didn't like the idea. Luckily I went well from the start. Everything was allowed in those days, and as a young lad I won a couple of races against grown men. I was bringing money home with my prizes. That got me permission from my parents to carry on.'

He turned professional at the end of 1942 and in 1943 became Belgian champion and, six years later, WORLD CHAMPION in Denmark.

'Those were good days. They had a class to them. When the WAR was over, I went straight to Mercier. I started on 5,000 Belgian francs a month plus equipment and by the time I left Mercier was on 100,000 a month. That was a lot then.'

He went over to PEUGEOT because LOUISON BOBET had joined Mercier and was threatening his leadership, and it was for Peugeot that he became world champion in Waregem in 1957. That was, he said, the most beautiful championship he ever rode, unlike his first attempt on the world championship in 1946:

'I had bad luck in my first world championship, at Zürich. Just as ever, there was no agreement between the Belgian riders who they were going to ride for. Since nothing had been settled I thought, "Right, I'll take my chance." On the last lap MARCEL KINT attacked, the best rider in the world in those days, and took 25 seconds. Then I went and on my wheel I had the Swiss, Knecht. I couldn't get him off.

'I had to pull out everything, to get up to Kint. I swung over for the other guy, but he wouldn't come through. One kilometre from the line, I finally got up to Kint. At that moment, the guy on my wheel jumped away. I couldn't react, nor would Kint. We were beaten, the two best riders in the world. Here in BELGIUM, they were convinced we had sold out to Knecht. It got so bad that my MANAGER, van Buggenhout, said, "Stay away for 14 days, keep out of Belgium." It was a great scandal. Never in 22 years have I sold a world championship.' Then there was pressure on the Belgian federation that van Steenbergen shouldn't be picked any more.

Rik van Steenbergen *(continued)*

'Well, against my personal taste, I decided to ride the Tour de France in 1949, just to win a stage and get my place back in the world championship team. I won the last stage – 300km to Paris in the PARC DES PRINCES. That was the breakthrough. It was settled and I was picked for the world's.'

By 1958 he was 35. The younger RIK VAN LOOY had enrolled the best Belgian riders so van Steenbergen switched to six-days. From these he said he collected half the five or six million francs that came his way each year in contracts and PRIZES.

Van Steenbergen had a reputation for looking after his money. RENÉ DE LATOUR said, 'I hear that he likes to play around with stocks and shares and that one friend in particular gives him valuable tips in return for tickets to vélodromes. But, the cynics say these are free tickets given to Rik by the management.' An organiser at Herne Hill TRACK in London was surprised to find van Steenbergen demanding his contract money as soon as he arrived. He had to raid the turnstiles and empty his own wallet.

Van Steenbergen had a difficult retirement. 'The mistake I made was not to get another job straight away. For 12 years I just sat and did nothing. I had no spirit left. I think I rode a year or two too long. If I had stopped a bit earlier I would have had more character to do something else.

'My first wife left. I started going out drinking, having fun, falling in with bad friends . . . . That was in 1966 to 1970. Then in 1970 I started pulling myself straight. I had been living here alone and a man by himself – well you know what I mean. You go out visiting. I met Doreen in 1970. She was working here in BELGIUM and since then we have been going to England, to Wigan where she comes from, every Christmas.'

Van Steenbergen lives at Zoersel in a black-and-white vaguely Spanish house with a tower and pool. Pictures on his wall include him in his red Solo jersey – the first non-cycling sponsor Belgium had – and a near-lifesize picture of him in a rainbow jersey. A professional race is run in his name every year.

Winner

1943	National championship
1944	Tour Flanders
1945	National championship
1946	Tour Flanders
1948	Paris-Roubaix, Critérium As
1949	World championship, Flèche Wallonne
1950	Paris-Brussels
1952	Paris-Roubaix, Critérium As
1954	Milan-San Remo, National championship
1955	Critérium As
1956	World championship
1957	World championship, Critérium As
1958	Flèche Wallonne, Critérium As

Tour de France

1949	29th	Stage wins Luchon—Toulouse, Nancy—Paris
1952	DNF	Stage win Brest—Rennes, and Yellow Jersey
1955	55th	Stage win Ax-les-Thermes—Toulouse

CÉDRIC VASSEUR
b. Haezebroucke, France, Aug 18 1970

In the 1997 Tour the stage from Chantonnay to La Châtre had barely started when the Frenchman Cédric Vasseur made a tentative attack. The bunch showed little interest and he pushed on. Vasseur stayed away for 147km, getting a lead of 17:45 with 100km to go, and taking the yellow JERSEY.

He held it for another 1,000km, defending it into the Pyrenees where, exhausted, he nevertheless managed to attack. Vasseur eventually lost the jersey to Jan Ullrich, but won a reputation.

Vasseur's father Alain also won in a lone break, to Felsberg in 1970 before finishing 40th.

Tour de France

1996	69th
1997	40th Stage win Chantonnay—La Châtre, and Yellow Jersey
1998	24th
1999	83rd
2000	52nd
2002	55th

MICHEL VERMEULIN
b. Montreuil, France, Sep 6 1934

On his first Tour in 1959, Parisian Michel Vermeulin secured the yellow JERSEY by getting into the right breaks despite lacking the talent to start them. Almost unknown, he won hearts by cocking a snook at the stars, leaving them for 11 minutes in the stage to Roubaix.

If you're going to have the jersey anywhere, then the most romantic place other than Paris is the MOUNTAINS. And there it was that Vermeulin's boyhood dream came true. Like also-rans before him, leading the Tour gave him confidence. He was with the leaders over the TOURMALET and kept his jersey. He kept it again next day, and the day after that had the astonishing audacity to break away with the Swiss Rolf Graf. Audacity, because leaders rarely need to attack, and astonishing because nobody reacted.

JOCK WADLEY wrote, 'Never in the history of the Tour had a *maillot jaune* brought off so audacious a move – and with his 30-second time BONUS for second place Vermeulin increased his lead.'

The jersey finally vanished in a hard stage in the Cevennes, but by then he'd lived his ambition.

Winner

1960	GP Fourmies

Tour de France

1959	20th	Yellow Jersey
1960	30th	
1962	DNF	

JOSÉ-LUIS VIEJO
b. Azuqueca, Spain, Nov 2 1949

The longest lone break in the Tour's post-war history belongs to ALBERT BOURLON. But the greatest winning margin in a stage is 22:50 by José-Luis Viejo in the Montgenèvre-Manosque stage of 1976. He won after a 160km break. Viejo's overall record includes fifth place in the Tour of SPAIN in 1977.

Tour de France

1973	DNF	
1975	25th	
1976	31st	Stage win Montgenèvre—Manosque
1979	DNF	

RENÉ VIETTO
b. Rocheville, France, Feb 17 1914, d. Jan 1 1988

A slight, brush-haired and rarely happy man, René Vietto had been a lift boy in various hotels in Cannes. He and his mother lived in Rocheville in the hills behind the town. Vietto was lightly built, and the daily ride from Rocheville and back made him a good CLIMBER. He began winning races. In 1932 he met ALFREDO BINDA, a guest at his hotel, and went training with him. The advice the Italian gave led him to become one of greatest riders never to win the Tour.

The leader of the French team in 1934 was ANTONIN MAGNE, who had won in 1931. But the revelation of the Tour was Vietto. He won a stage in the Alps at Grenoble, then at Digne, and finally alone in Cannes. For a while it looked as if he would win the Tour. But when Magne crashed on a bend on the Col de Puymorens, Vietto had to hand over his front wheel to save Magne's yellow JERSEY. Vietto was left to wait for the service lorry.

Next day, from Ax-les-Thermes to Luchon, he led over the Col de Porte and Col d'Aspet when Magne crashed again. Vietto dropped back, waiting to pace him back. But Magne didn't appear so Vietto turned and rode 500m down the MOUNTAIN to find Magne in a ditch, holding his wheel. Again Vietto sacrificed his chances and sobbed by the roadside as he lost half an hour. A popular photo depicts Vietto on the wall, one foot on the ground, the other drawn up to his chest. His bike, number 38, has its rear wheel on the verge and its empty front forks on top of the wall. Vietto is looking down the hill with an air of distress. It suggests he was alone in his misery but for the photographer. In fact there was a small crowd, but editing has removed them to increase the drama.

The world turned on Magne for abusing a father-son relationship, and the legend grew that Vietto would have won but for what happened. But Vietto knew where he had really lost the Tour – not in the mountains but on the flat. He took to training on flat roads on big GEARS to improve his ability as a *rouleur*. He succeeded but only by worsening his power as a climber.

It looked as if Vietto would never win. In 1935 he took a stage but was held up by crashes. In 1936 he was only 22, but his knee was injured and his morale ruined when he lost his money to a swindler. He didn't ride in the 1937 and 1938 Tours. In 1939 his knee, which had been kept going only by nightly injections, gave way over the AUBISQUE, ASPIN, and TOURMALET. SYLVÈRE MAES pulled away on the IZOARD and Vietto finished half an hour down. He managed only the second rung of the podium in Paris. A month later the world was at WAR.

In the 1947 Tour Vietto was 33 with three knee operations behind him. He won the

yellow jersey by riding alone for 130km between Lille and Brussels, lost it after five days, then regained it in the Alps at Digne. Only three days separated him from Paris and his first victory. But the first of those days was a TIME TRIAL, 139km from Vannes to St-Brieuc. He ordered a yellow jersey in silk, only to be told he'd be docked 10 seconds if he wore it. Vietto threw the jersey at the official's feet. He called the organisers liars and cheats, all on live radio. He packed his case and put it in his hotel. An official carried it out. Vietto put it back. Again the official sneaked off with it, again Vietto hauled it back.

In a fairytale, Vietto would have won. But he finished third, losing 15 minutes to RAYMOND IMPANIS. By Paris, Vietto had slipped to fifth. Years later, a television programme reminded him of that time trial. 'It was like watching a man commit suicide,' someone said. 'Monsieur,' Vietto replied, 'I have had suicidal tendencies since I was seven years old.'

He was a professional from 1932 to 1952, champion of FRANCE in 1941, winner of Paris-Nice in 1935, second in the 1939 Tour, and fifth in 1934, taking four stages and the mountains prize. He went on to manage the Helyett team in the 1950s with much bossing but little success. He said of his team in the Giro, 'I have never attended such a long funeral; it was 5,000km long and my team followed the whole way. They call themselves racers but they were more like mourners.'

Vietto made a fortune from CRITERIUM appearances after giving his wheel to Magne, and earned more than if he had won the Tour. But his business adviser lost the lot and Vietto retired to run a pig farm near his boyhood home and grew cranky. He had few visitors and welcomed barely any. He did, though, meet GREG LEMOND and BERNARD HINAULT at the end of the Tour in 1986, and spoke a few words about the value of self-sacrifice. His MEMORIAL is at the top of the Col de Braus near Nice, in a design similar to TOM SIMPSON'S.

(And *see* APO LAZARIDES for one of cycling's most bizarre tales of influence and unnecessary surgery.)

VILLE D'AVRAY

The first Tour started and finished outside Paris, with the START at MONTGERON and the FINISH outside the Restaurant Père Auto at Ville d'Avray south-west of the capital. Of that occasion GÉO LEFÈVRE wrote, 'a human sea of crowds invades the road. The forces of public order try to push them to the right and the left. An impossible struggle.

'They're coming!'

'Look out!'

'There they are!'

'The waves of the human sea come crashing down. No human force can stop them and the riders have to do what they can. No point in wondering which one has just ridden by. Each second, the crowd becomes denser. There are people everywhere, at the windows, on roofs, in trees, on BIKES, cars and horses: deep in the crowd GARIN passes under the banner ten sec-

onds in front of Augereau and Samson [real name Julien Lootens]. It's 2.09pm and the emotion is at its peak and the cheers are a fantastic roar. The crowd is all waving hats and umbrellas.'

From there riders had only to ride to the PARC DES PRINCES for a lap of honour. Mounted POLICE had to form an escort as an estimated 2,000 rode along with them, 'yelling to the utmost of their lungs'. Spectators jumped over the railings at the TRACK and invaded the bankings and infield.

The commotion meant judges had to reissue their results several times.

RICHARD VIRENQUE
b. Casablanca, Morocco, Nov 19 1969

Richard ('Rico') Virenque is the controversial darling of FRANCE, especially middle-aged women. He is a CLIMBER, not history's best but always a contender. His fans admire his panache, his detractors say he picks up too many points on small climbs and gets beaten on the great ones. He won the Tour's MOUNTAINS competition in 1994, 1995, 1996, 1997 and 1999, but few other important races. His strength is multi-day events and specifically the Tour.

His weak spots are his personality, which can be brash and thoughtless, and his involvement in the FESTINA SCANDAL of 1998. (*See* Festina entry for details.) Virenque was no more guilty than other riders, but they confessed whereas he wept on television and published a book insisting he was innocent. It was that lack of honesty as much as the cheating that prompted the Swiss federation (Virenque is French but lived near Geneva) to suspend him for nine months. Afterwards no French teams, and few others, would consider him.

There is a side to Virenque that is boyish and soft. He talks appealingly of the time his family moved to France from Casablanca when he was nine. He remembers fishing in the sea with his brother Lionel and sister Nathalie when he should have been at school. 'I soon realised that

I didn't have the intellectual ability to be anything but a racing cyclist,' he told the Festina inquiry.

But this is the man whose reaction to WILLY VOET's arrest in 1998 was, 'But how am I going to do it without my products?' So said the MANAGER, Bruno Roussel. The TV programme *Les Guignols d'Info* – France's equivalent of *Spitting Image* – portrayed Virenque as a crying and gibbering moron with hypodermics in his head.

Virenque insisted on his innocence at an inquiry in Lille, but then gave up. '*Oui, je me suis dopé,*' he said. He could have been jailed. His wife Stéphanie said he spent day after day crying. He agreed to move back to FRANCE.

Virenque once demanded the equivalent of £1,250,000 a year, a great deal for a man who, says Philippe Brunel of *L'ÉQUIPE*, is 'high in the opinion polls, arrogant towards his rivals, but a champion who doesn't win.'

Too many teams, too many riders, remember his thoughtless public criticism of them. MARCO PANTANI refused to be pictured with him. 'I'm the best climber in the world,' he scoffed. 'Virenque merely wears the climber's JERSEY.' But he still received 589 letters during the 2000 Tour, more than any other rider, and his fan club has 5,000 members.

In 2002 he won alone on MONT VENTOUX for his best Tour stage win.

Winner

1994	Trophée Grimpeurs
1996	Tour Piedmont
1997	GP Marseillaise
2001	Paris-Tours

Tour de France

1992	25th	Yellow Jersey
1993	19th	
1994	5th	Stage win Hautacam—Luz-Ardiden, and Mountains winner
1995	9th	Stage win St-Girons—Cauteret, and Mountains winner
1996	3rd	Mountains winner

Tour de France (continued)

1997	2nd	Stage win Bourg d'Oisans—Courchevel, and Mountains winner
1998	DNF	
1999	8th	Mountains winner
2000	6th	
2002	16th	Stage win Lodève—Mont Ventoux

WILLY VOET

Voet (pronounced *foot*) was the SOIGNEUR at the centre of the FESTINA AFFAIR in 1998. His arrest with a carload of drugs set off the Tour's biggest DOPING scandal.

Voet was an AMATEUR rider who began as a soigneur in 1972. He moved from BELGIUM to FRANCE to work with Fagor, a Franco-Spanish team, then with RMO. That was where he met Bruno Roussel, who became MANAGER of Festina.

'To start, my job was to give massage, prepare food bags, water bottles and all that. Those were the days of amphetamines and corticoids. There were no team doctors. The soigneurs did everything. Today by contrast, you can't work without a doctor. It's become too complicated. For 30 years the word "doping" never passed my lips: even today it's difficult for me to say, "so-and-so was doped." It's uncomfortable. I've had to learn to use the word. The word we use is "prepared".'

Voet's book, *Breaking the Chain*, was written after his arrest and trial. It explains how riders cheated controls, and claims drugs were so commonplace that even managers and mechanics took them casually while following races. One rider – named in the French but not the British edition – was caught after cheating the control with a MECHANIC's urine only to find the mechanic had been helping himself to the team's stocks of drugs.

He remained unemployed for years after the Festina affair and was declared *persona non grata* at the Tour.

(*See* RICHARD VIRENQUE.)

VOITURE BALAI

The *voiture balai* (broom wagon) – a truck or car to sweep up riders who have abandoned or dropped too far behind – was introduced in 1910 when the Tour first went into the MOUNTAINS. Riders had branded the Pyrenees 'the circle of death', and even HENRI DESGRANGE worried at what he had done – so much so that he stayed at home rather than be associated with possible disaster. The fear turned out partly justified because only 41 of 110 starters reached Paris. (The highest drop-out rate since the war was in 1948, when all but 44 of the 120 starters climbed off.)

The *balai* used to have an old-fashioned broom strapped to its roof, pointing up the road. This vanished in 1992 when the Tour decided it wanted a modern image, although rumour says there's a broom inside to satisfy tradition. It follows the last rider on the road, although stars rarely use it, preferring their team cars. The riders are taken to their hotel and a motorcyclist takes their *dossards*, the numbers on their backs, to the FINISH. Anyone else has merely to touch the broom wagon for his number to be torn off. Their name will be on RADIO TOUR before they've sat down.

Sometimes minnows inside the *balai* have been astonished at the company they attract. FEDERICO BAHAMONTES climbed into the *balai* in 1965 in his blue Margnat-Paloma tracksuit – the moment is caught in the FILM *Pour un Maillot Jaune*.

Jean-Christophe Dauman, the *voiture balai* driver, said in 2002, 'I'm right at the back of the race. Only a van to collect the bikes is behind me. Some of the riders prefer to finish the race in their team cars. The rest get into the *voiture balai*. A commissaire takes their number, the bike goes into the van, and then we set off again. Some riders want to talk straightaway but most just sit very quietly, drinking and eating fruit and maybe cake to help them recover. And then after 20 minutes they start talking, about the race, about how hard it was, the steepness of the climbs, that sort of thing. And sometimes they just cry.'

JOCK WADLEY

John Borland Wadley, or 'J.B.', or Jock Wadley, was the British journalist who founded *Sporting Cyclist* and introduced thousands to Continental racing when little was heard of it in BRITAIN in the 1950s and 1960s.

Wadley's enthusiasm was fired when he was 14. He and a friend took a wrong turning and ended up on a farm track one night in March 1929. The friend, Alf Kettle, said it was 'just like the Tour de France', and Wadley wanted to know more.

He joined *The Bicycle* soon after it started in February 1936, cycling round Europe and calling on riders or watching races. One article described how he saw a BIKE outside a café, found it belonged to HUGO KOBLET, and went inside to eavesdrop.

Wadley left *The Bicycle* after two years and joined the PR department of HERCULES Cycles, from where he was conscripted at the outbreak of war. After the war, he was one of three press officers for the sport's governing body, the Union Cycliste Internationale, at the London Olympics in 1948. He rejoined *The Bicycle*, became its editor and stayed until it closed in 1955. In winter 1955 he founded *Coureur*, which in May 1957 became the monthly *Sporting Cyclist*. Its star reporter was RENÉ DE LATOUR.

Sporting Cyclist lasted 11 years and 131 issues, and was followed a month later by *International Cycle Sport*, which ran until issue 199 in December 1984. Wadley edited it until September 1971, when his contract wasn't renewed for reasons which were never clear.

The cycling wholesaler Ron Kitching, who put Wadley in touch with the printers who founded *International Cycle Sport*, said, 'I don't think Jock ever really worked as such, he just put down in words what his thoughts were. Jock was a real gentleman but he did tend to wander off. We were sponsoring the Tour of the North [race] and *ICS* was one of the SPONSORS. He turned up on his bike, just pottering about. He seemed more interested in riding his bike than covering the race. Which was his downfall, really.' (*See* ANDRÉ LEDUCQ for how he and Kitching sang *On Ilkley Moor B'at 'at* together in a Parisian nightclub.)

Wadley followed the Tour from 1955 to 1972 and was given the *Médaille de la Reconnaissance du Tour* by JACQUES GODDET and FÉLIX LÉVITAN at Carpentras in 1970. He died in March 1981.

On July 13 that year seven friends rode to the Torrent des Sept Laux on the Col du Glandon in the Alps to scatter Wadley's ashes while a policeman stood guard. Mary Wadley had asked that his ashes be scattered on the route of the Tour, and the Glandon was significant to him because he had crossed it on his 59th birthday in 1973.

RINI WAGTMANS
b. St-Willebrord, Holland, Dec 26 1946

Rini Wagtmans, known as *Kuifje* (Tufty) because of a white patch in his hair, was WOUT WAGTMANS' cousin. He spent much of his career as a DOMESTIQUE, particularly to EDDY MERCKX, and would have won more than CRITERIUMS if he had been given a free hand in the classics. Nevertheless he wore the yellow JERSEY in the 1971 Tour and won three stages. He also came fifth in the 1970 Tour and sixth in 1969, as well as third in the 1969 Tour of SPAIN. He was well known as a fast descender.

In 1969 he sprinted away in the neutralised section before the official START in Clermont-Ferrand. LUCIEN AIMAR set off in pursuit and the whole group raced off on his heels, marvelling how the Dutchman could have got so much of a lead so quickly that he was out of their sight. The truth was that Wagtmans had hidden in a side-street and was planning to join in at the back when the last rider passed. In fact the race passed in such a panic that he was forced to chase after it.

Wagtmans stopped racing in 1973 because of a heart problem, and ran a clothing company in his village of St-Willebrord. He helped organise the village club to run raffles and other events to pay for a stage finish there in 1978. The stage was won by JAN RAAS. (*See* Raas entry for the curious circumstances that led to

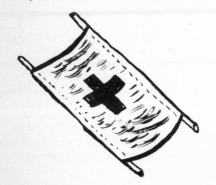

it.) The white patch in his hair, by the way, has almost disappeared; it is all grey these days.

(*See* JOOP ZOETEMELK for Wagtmans's comments.)

Tour de France

1969	6th	
1970	5th	Stage win Carpentras—Montpellier
1971	16th	Stage win Strasbourg—Nancy, and Yellow Jersey
1972	54th	Stage win Vesoul—Auxerre

WOUT WAGTMANS
b. St-Willebrord, Holland, Nov 10 1929, d. Aug 15 1994

Wout Wagtmans came from the village of St-Willebrord that produced RINI WAGTMANS and WIM VAN EST. His win in the 1952 Tour of Romandie was the first Dutch success in a foreign stage race. He led from beginning to end. In 1953 he was the first Dutchman to wear the green JERSEY.

He could have won in 1956 had he not cracked in the Alps. 'I wore the yellow jersey for 13 days and I was one of the favourites to win. Then on the stage from Turin to Grenoble, it all went wrong and I finished the day 30th and lost the jersey. ROGER WALKOWIAK won the Tour. I still don't understand what happened that day. I was so close to winning and that should give you wings. But not me.'

The best story about him comes from Wim van Est. 'We were riding the Dutch club championship and we'd got an eight-minute lead. Five hundred metres before the line he saw a little children's bike and he got on it and pedalled across the line on that. The judges didn't get the joke and they disqualified us. But how we laughed.'

Wagtmans became national MANAGER in 1967.

Winner

1952 Tour Romandie
1955 GP Zurich

Tour de France

1950	DNF	
1951	DNF	
1952	25th	
1953	5th	Stage wins Monaco—Gap, St-Étienne—Montluçon, and Points leader
1954	DNF	Stage win Amsterdam—Brasschaat, and Yellow Jersey
1955	19th	Stage win Pau—Bordeaux, and Yellow Jersey
1956	6th	Yellow Jersey
1957	DNF	
1961	DNF	

ROGER WALKOWIAK

b. Montluçon, France, Mar 2 1927

Former Tour organiser JACQUES GODDET and TV commentator JEAN-PAUL OLLIVIER both claim the Frenchman Roger Walkowiak as their favourite rider. Yet he was unknown before winning the Tour in 1956, and his success afterwards was so slight that he went back to factory work.

Walkowiak, a Frenchman of Polish parents, was picked at the last moment in 1956 for a REGIONAL TEAM called North-East-Centre. The original choice, Gilbert Bauvin, had been elevated to the NATIONAL TEAM. It was the first Tour where no previous winner was riding. Just days before the race started in Reims JACQUES ANQUETIL, the rising hope, was breaking FAUSTO COPPI's hour record.

Walkowiak (*Vull-koh-vee-uck*) got into a break of 31 between Lorient and Angers that won by 13 minutes, then took his chance in the Alps by following CHARLY GAUL. It spelled the undoing for the Dutchman WOUT WAGTMANS (*see* entry for why). Walkowiak clung on against expectations and won in Paris by a minute over Bauvin. Moreover, he won at record speed and was the second rider, after FIRMIN LAMBOT, to win without taking a stage.

Not everyone was impressed. 'The applause from spectators [at the PARC DES PRINCES]

sounded like a lamentation,' Goddet wrote. Walkowiak rode all the post-Tour CRITERIUMS but won none. By 1958 he had moved from winner to almost *LANTERNE ROUGE* (last man). He raced two more years, won a stage of the Tour of SPAIN in 1957, then realised his peak had gone after 17 small wins and one very big one.

He bought a bar but became disillusioned when even customers said he should never have won. He began to think so too and refused to discuss his career. He went back to his lathe at a car factory in Montluçon and now lives in retirement, persuaded at last that he won legitimately.

Un Tour à la Walko has come to mean a win by an unforeseen rider.

Winner

1956 Tour de France

Tour de France

1951	57th	
1953	47th	
1955	DNF	
1956	1st	Yellow Jersey
1957	DNF	
1958	75th	

WAR

The first world war brought racing to an end in most areas. The main exceptions were HOLLAND, which stayed neutral, and ITALY, which stayed out of the conflict until 1915, running the Tour of Lombardy and Tour of Piedmont, and cancelling Milan-San Remo just twice. In FRANCE, Paris-Tours ran in 1917 and 1918.

The first world war took a toll of stars, including Émile Engel, who won a Tour stage in 1914, Émile Friol, a world TRACK champion, and the Tour WINNERS OCTAVE LAPIZE, LUCIEN PETIT-BRETON and FRANÇOIS FABER. The Tour held a three-minute silence on June 29 1919 when it restarted.

France ran a Circuit of the Battlefields in honour of the dead in 1918. It was won by

Stage		Winner
1	Paris—Le Mans	Guy Lapébie
2	Le Mans—Poitiers	Frans Bonduel
3a	Poitiers—Limoges	Georges Guillier
3b	Limoges—Clermont-Ferrand	Louis Caput
4	Clermont-Ferrand—St-Étienne	François Neuville
5a	St-Étienne—Lyon	F. van de Weghe
5b	Lyon—Dijon	Albert Goutal
6	Dijon—Paris	Raymond Louviot

Charles Deruyter, although cheating was so rife that nobody knows if he rode the whole way. It was followed in 1919 by Paris-Roubaix, a journey into shell-blasted towns and countryside of northern France that created the phrase 'the Hell of the North'. It was won by HENRI PÉLISSIER.

There was no Tour in the first war because HENRI DESGRANGE had urged his readers to bayonet Germans 'without mercy'. Desgrange's successor JACQUES GODDET resisted pressure to run the Tour between 1939 and 1945, when German policy was to encourage normal life. 'It is something of which I feel very proud,' he said.

France was divided between occupied and non-occupied zones, each nominally independent. Travel between the two was impossible until 1942, when Germany occupied the whole country. In September 1942 *La France Socialiste* organised a six-stage Circuit de France starting and finishing in Paris via Le Mans, Poitiers, Limoges, St-Étienne and Dijon. Organisation was chaotic and the race's socialist leanings were tainted by a reception with Pierre Laval, the Vichy prime minister later shot as a traitor. It was won by the Belgian François Neuville at 36km/h.

L'AUTO still refused to run a Tour de France but responded with a Grand Prix du Tour de France, a points competition starting with Paris-Roubaix and ending with the GP de l'Industrie. It was abandoned in 1944 when *L'Auto* was closed. It did, though, keep the yellow JERSEY alive, the first wartime holder being Jo Goutourbe.

L'ÉQUIPE, which replaced *L'Auto*, had to start anew. Goddet recalled, 'Henri Desgrange was dead, Lucien Cazalis his right-hand man was dead, the usual *commissaire général* was out of service; the three people who had conceived, constructed and operated the Tour had all disappeared at the same time along with all the dossiers, equipment and paperwork built up between 1903 and 1939.'

L'Équipe experimented with a race from Monaco to Paris in 1946 and then set about the rebirth of the Tour.

'All we could do, with our friends from *Le Parisien Libéré*,' wrote Goddet, 'was build a brand new Tour in a modern style. But in the same way that old historic sites are restored in style, in a way that matches the region to which they belong, we carefully kept the character of the new Tour, keeping its spirit. Events hadn't altered the essential character. To the contrary, in fact. The grandeur and dignity of this peaceful international tournament came at just the right moment to calm nerves and bring new hope.'

Parisians had been reduced in the war to eating rats and dogs, and rationing was still widespread. Splashing out on a circus like the Tour was in dubious taste. But in the end the government decided it would be good for morale. It allowed the organisers generous rations for the time, but riders such as JEAN ROBIC still used their rural connections to get better food.

Goddet wrote, 'This Tour sends a message of joy and confidence, a moving, inspiring, astonishing picture of heroic adventure from which hatred is absent.' Riders were told to enter by telegram to avoid a post office strike, and to make sure their passports were valid.

(*See* JEAN-PIERRE DANGUILLAUME, ANDRÉ LEDUCQ, ROGER LÉVÈQUE.)

THE WIEL'S AFFAIR

In the 1962 Tour, the stage from Luchon to Carcassonne set off 10 minutes late because the German HANS JUNKERMANN decided he would start that day's race after all. Junkermann, of the Belgian Wiel's-Groene Leeuw team, had been ill most of the night. He was eighth overall and, as a team leader, was important to the race. The Tour granted him time to get ready and the 116 riders bowled away.

They didn't ride fast. Carcassonne is a medieval hilltop town between Toulouse and the Mediterranean and the weather can be hot, so there was no point in haring away. Nevertheless Junkermann was soon at the back, and after 50km he lost contact on the first hill and collapsed. And there he sat, his bike by his side, onlookers around him.

'Bad fish at the hotel,' he complained. 'I was sick from it all night.'

An extraordinary number of riders seemed to have dined on fish. Eleven others left the race that day, including the former leader WILLY SCHROEDER, the 1960 winner GASTONE NENCINI, and the 1966 yellow JERSEY, KARL-HEINZ KUNDE. They or their handlers also blamed fish.

Hoteliers like the Tour. It fills beds and sells food. But they don't like being blamed for poisoning a sizable proportion of the field. They were quick to show there had been no fish on

the menu. JACQUES GODDET said he suspected DOPING but nothing was ever proved.

The papers had fun with the incident for days while MANAGERS reacted angrily to the way it was reported. Riders threatened to STRIKE for 15 minutes but they were dissuaded by Jean Bobet. The event is portrayed in *Vive le Tour* by the independent producer Louis Malle (*see* FILMS for more; *see* also PDM AFFAIR for another mysterious mass retirement.)

WINNERS (*see* PODIUMS for full list of winners since 1903)

WORLD CHAMPION

World champions wear a white JERSEY with striped bands around the middle. The stripes are called rainbow bands and the jersey a rainbow jersey, or *maillot arc-en-ciel*, but the bands are the colours of the Olympic flag. One at least is in the flag of every nation.

World champions are chosen in a one-day race run in a different country each year by the Union Cycliste Internationale, the governing body based in Switzerland. The jerseys differ slightly for road, TRACK, cyclo-cross and other championships. They can be worn only in the type of event for which they were won. That means only the road champion wears his jersey in the Tour, except in TIME TRIALS where the time trial champion may ride in rainbow bands. Current and former champions wear rainbow cuffs and neck edges.

World champions aren't known for their success in the Tour. Oscar Freire's stage win at Saarbrucken in 2002 was the first by a world champion for 21 years. The previous winner as world champion was BERNARD HINAULT in 1981.

MICHAEL WRIGHT
b. Bishop's Stortford, England, Mar 25 1941

Fair-haired Michael Wright was famous as the English Tourman who couldn't speak English. His stage win at Auxerre in 1965 was the second

by a Briton after BRIAN ROBINSON, and he rode for BRITAIN in the Tours of 1967 and 1968. But he couldn't speak to his team-mates because he had left Bishop's Stortford as a child to live in BELGIUM. Poor English didn't end his affection for Britain, though, and he rode with a Union Jack on his sleeves.

Wright was mainly a CRITERIUM rider and spent his career in minor teams. He rode twice in Britain, in the Corona GP at Crystal Palace, London, in 1965, and in the Vaux GP which he won in 1967. He retired in 1976 after 14 years as a professional. His record includes fifth place in the 1969 Tour of SPAIN.

Winner

1967	Vaux GP

Tour de France

1964	56th	
1965	24th	Stage win Lyon—Auxerre
1967	DNF	Stage win Metz—Strasbourg
1968	28th	
1969	71st	
1972	55th	
1973	57th	Stage win Nice—Aubagne
1974	57th	

SEAN YATES

b. Ewell, England, May 18 1960

Sean Yates – *See-yunn Yat-tezz* to the French – spent much of his career as a powerful DOMESTIQUE who could close gaps at frightening speed. But he occasionally had his day of glory, enough to wear the yellow JERSEY in 1994 and win the Tour of BELGIUM in 1989.

Yates left BRITAIN to join the ACBB club in Paris after riding the 1980 Olympics as a TRACK pursuiter, but he made a poor start as a road professional. His luck changed in 1987 when he won a stage of the Nissan Classic alone, and thus collected the confidence he needed. When the Tour came to BRITAIN in 1994, the year he took the yellow jersey at Rennes, Yates was allowed to head it through his home of Forest Row, Sussex. He retired in 1996 and later managed the McCartney professional team, which ended in 2001 when the money ran out. In 2003 he joined the Danish CSC team as a team manager.

Winner

1989 GP Merckx, Tour Belgium
1992 National championship

Tour de France

1984	91st	
1985	122nd	
1986	112th	
1987	DNF	
1988	59th	Stage win Liévin—Wasquehal
1989	45th	
1990	119th	
1991	DNF	
1992	83rd	
1993	88th	
1994	71st	Yellow Jersey
1995	DNF	

YOUNG RIDER CATEGORY

The under-23 category began in 1975, when it was won by FRANCESCO MOSER. The leader wears a white JERSEY, although this token of success has been missing some years, and particularly after 1989. LAURENT FIGNON was the first under-23 to win the Tour, in 1983. Few WINNERS of the white jerseys have been as embarrassed as JAN ULLRICH, whose mother climbed on the rostrum to kiss and hug him. He is now never portrayed in cartoons in *Vélo* without Mama Ullrich.

UNDER-23 WINNERS

Date	Winner	Date	Winner
1975	Francesco Moser	1989	Fabrice Philippot
1976	Enrique Martinez Heredia	1990	Gilles Delion
1977	Didi Thurau	1991	Alvaro Meija
1978	Henk Lubberding	1992	Eddy Bouwmans
1979	Jean-René Bernaudeau	1993	Antonio Martin
1980	Johan van der Velde	1994	Marco Pantani
1981	Peter Winnen	1995	Marco Pantani
1982	Phil Anderson	1996	Jan Ullrich
1983	Laurent Fignon	1997	Jan Ullrich
1984	Greg LeMond	1998	Jan Ullrich
1985	Fabio Parra	1999	Benoît Salmon
1986	Andy Hampsten	2000	Francesco Mancebo
1987	Raul Alcala	2001	Oscar Sevilla
1988	Erik Breukink	2002	Ivan Basso

ABDEL-KHADER ZAAF
b. Chabli, Algeria, Jan 28 1917, d. Algeria,
Sep 22 1986

The Algerian Abdel-Khader Zaaf will be for-
ever known as the man who raced the wrong
way. On July 28 1950 the Tour was going from
Perpignan to Nîmes on an extremely hot day.
Nobody wanted to race except Zaaf and
MARCEL MOLINES, another rider in the North
Africa team.

They set off with 200km to go and got
enough lead to make Zaaf leader on the road.
He might well have won and become the Tour's
first African yellow JERSEY because in the end
Molines did stay away to win the stage. Zaaf,
however, began zigzagging with 15km to go
and an official tugged him off his BIKE. Zaaf
tried again, wobbled more, and eventually fell
asleep under a tree.

In time he came round, stared in panic at the
crowd around him, got back on his bike and set
off in the wrong direction. SPECTATORS called
an ambulance and Zaaf was taken away. Legend
says he was drunk, because a spectator had
revived him with wine, and this had gone to
Zaaf's head as a Muslim is supposed never to
drink alcohol.

The story is delightful but raises doubts.
How much wine could a groggy man drink?
How much wine would a devout Muslim drink
before refusing it? And, given that few people

like wine at their first taste, how much would he
have tolerated? And how much does it take to
make a man so dizzy that he'd ride off the
wrong way in the Tour de France? Further
doubt comes from his recollection that 'after
the Tour everyone wanted to drink a glass of
wine with me. I couldn't refuse but I drank far
too much.' Zaaf had either speedily renounced
Islam or he was improbably talking of lemon-
ade while others drank wine. Less charitable
reports mention DOPING, dehydration and
confusion.

Zaaf asked if he could ride the missing distance before the next day's stage, but the
authorities refused and he was out. The incident made him a celebrity and his fee in CRI-
TERIUMS rose sharply.

When the novelty passed Zaaf vanished and
became another legend of the Tour. And then
in 1982 a fan recognised an old man shuffling
through a train station in Paris. It was Zaaf. It
seemed that in Algeria an argument over
papers had led to his being shot in the leg by a
soldier. His injury was left untreated and then
he was thrown into jail on suspicion of smuggling. He went two years without trial, losing
almost all he owned. Diabetes had damaged his
sight and he had come to Paris for an operation. Fans sent telegrams, flowers and presents.
Zaaf died in Algeria four years later.

(*See* ALI NEFATTI, HIPPOLYTE PAGIE.)

1948	DNF
1950	DNF
1951	66th
1952	DNF

ERIK ZABEL

b. Berlin, East Germany, Jul 7 1970

The likeable Erik Zabel is one of the sport's fastest finishers. He holds the RECORD for green (points) JERSEYS, often called sprinters' jerseys.

Zabel came up through a sports school in East GERMANY after starting cycling at 10. He turned professional for 1993 and the following year won the SPRINTERS' classic, Paris-Tours. He didn't finish that year's Tour but in 1995 won two stages. In 1998 and 1999 he won the points competition without winning a stage.

In 2001 he was forced to scrap right up to the CHAMPS ELYSÉES with STUART O'GRADY. He said, 'That was the most emotional of my six green jerseys. That doesn't mean I've forgotten my first green Jersey win in the Tour, in 1996 when I took the jersey at Gap and kept it to Paris. That was something as well. But 2001, that demanded a lot of energy, a lot of pressure, a lot of investment, and it all hung on a handful of points and stayed uncertain right up until the last sprint on the Champs Elysées.'

He is a good CLIMBER for a sprinter, a popular, smiling man who takes his son Rik on the podium. His father Detlef was a prominent East German roadman in the 1960s.

Zabel keeps every JERSEY in a cabinet in his house in Unna, near Dortmund, which has an underground garage. It's 'just like a bike shop, full of bits and pieces he's bought from bike shops round the world,' says MECHANIC Jean-Marc Vandenberghe.

Winner

1994	Paris-Tours, Haribo Classic
1997	Trofeo Luis Puig, Milan-San Remo, GP Escaut, Ruta Sol
1998	Milan-San Remo, National championship

Winner (continued)

1999	GP Frankfurt
2000	Trofeo Luis Puig, Amstel Gold, Milan-San Remo, World Cup
2001	HEW Cup, Trofeo Luis Puig, Milan-San Remo
2002	GP Frankfurt

Tour de France

1994	DNF	
1995	90th	Stage wins Dunkirk—Charleroi, Pau—Bordeaux
1996	82nd	Stage wins Wasquehal—Nogent-sur-Oise, Turin—Gap, and Points winner
1997	66th	Stage wins Vire—Plumelec, Marennes—Bordeaux, Sauternes—Pau, and Points winner
1998	62nd	Yellow Jersey, and Points winner
1999	89th	Points winner
2000	61st	Stage win Belfort—Troyes, and Points winner
2001	96th	Stage wins St-Omer—Boulogne, Antwerp—Seraing, Orléans—Évry, and Points winner
2002	82nd	Stage win Forges-les-Eaux—Alençon, and Yellow Jersey and Points leader

JOOP ZOETEMELK

b. Rijpwetering, Holland, Dec 3 1946

Tot up placings in the Tour – 10 points for a win down to one for 10th – and Gerardus 'Joop' Zoetemelk comes out top. And yet he won just once, in 1980, and then only after a sore knee had eliminated BERNARD HINAULT. Winning that way did little to improve the reputation of the fair-haired Dutchman with the pale complexion. 'Why does Joop Zoetemelk never have a sun tan?' the jokers asked. 'Because he always rides in the shadow of EDDY MERCKX.' The message was that Zoetemelk was more a wheel-sucker than a man prepared to make the most of his talents. And yet, say his supporters, how would you ride if you had the bad luck to have a career which spanned Merckx, Hinault, GREG LEMOND, BERNARD THÉVENET and LUIS OCAÑA?

Zoetemelk was a regional speed-skating champion before he turned to cycling. He showed immediate success as an AMATEUR, winning the Tour of Yugoslavia, three stages and the mountain class of the Tour of Austria, an Olympic gold at Mexico in the 100km team TIME TRIAL, and the TOUR DE L'AVENIR in 1969. He turned pro in 1970 for BRIEK SCHOTTE's Mars team, and came second to Merckx in that year's Tour.

In 1980 he won the Tour, but without cheers ringing in his ears. That year was the so-called 'Battle of Bernard's Knee', when litres of ink were spent on discussing the tendinitis which gave Hinault the problem. Could he win despite it? Would he pull out because of it? The answers: no and yes. That put Zoetemelk in yellow at 33. But he won to less than total acclaim. Offended, Zoetemelk said, 'Surely winning the Tour de France is a question of health and robustness? If Hinault doesn't have that health and robustness and I have, that makes me a valid winner.'

The Dutch chartered 350 coaches to the CHAMPS ELYSÉES to see him win, along with thousands who drove or came by train or plane. Some say there were 25,000.

RINI WAGTMANS says, 'Joop Zoetemelk is the best rider that the Netherlands has ever known.

There has never been a better one. But he could not give instructions. He was treated and helped with respect. But when Zoetemelk won the Tour, the instructions had to come from GERRIE KNETEMANN and JAN RAAS.'

Zoetemelk rode 16 Tours and finished them all, coming second five times, finishing in the top ten for a dozen years, spending 22 days in yellow, and winning 10 stages. But a near-fatal CRASH into a British car left unattended at the FINISH of the Midi Libre in Valras-Plage in 1973 nearly stopped all that. He cracked his head and was taken to hospital in Béziers, and wasn't expected to live, let alone to race again. Nine months later he won Paris-Nice, only to come close to death once more from meningitis. He never fully recovered and the head injury still affects his sense of taste.

Zoetemelk speaks poor English but good French, so good that he married Françoise Duchaussoy, daughter of Tour executive Jacques Duchaussoy, and moved to Germiny-l'Evêque. There he opened a 40-room hotel called Le Richemont at Meaux, on the Marne. In 1985 he became the oldest WORLD CHAMPION in history at 38.

(*See* RALEIGH.)

Winner

1971 National championship
1972 Trophée Grimpeurs
1973 Tour Haut-Var, National championship
1974 Paris-Nice, Tour Romandie, Catalan Week
1975 Tour Holland, Paris-Nice, GP Isbergues
1976 Flèche Wallonne
1977 Paris-Tours, GP Isbergues
1978 Paris-Camembert, GP Lugano
1979 Tour Spain, Paris-Tours, Paris-Nice, Critérium As, Trophée Grimpeurs, Critérium International, Tour Haut-Var
1980 Tour de France, Critérium As
1981 Montjuich
1982 Montjuich
1983 Tour Haut-Var
1985 World championship, Tirreno-Adriatico
1987 Amstel Gold

1970	2nd	
1971	2nd	Yellow Jersey
1972	5th	
1973	4th	Stage wins Scheveningen—Scheveningen, Reims—Nancy, and Yellow Jersey
1975	4th	Stage win Pau—St-Lary-Soulan
1976	2nd	Stage wins Divonne—Alpe d'Huez, Bourg d'Oisans—Mongenèvre, Tulle—Puy-de-Dôme
1977	8th	
1978	2nd	Stage win Besse—Puy-de-Dôme, and Yellow Jersey
1979	2nd	Stage win Alpe d'Huez—Alpe d'Huez, and Yellow Jersey
1980	1st	Stage wins Damazan—Laplume, St-Étienne—St-Étienne, and Yellow Jersey
1981	4th	
1982	2nd	
1983	23rd	
1984	30th	
1985	12th	
1986	24th	

THE 1904 AFFAIR

HENRI DESGRANGE felt pleased with himself after 1903. He had been dubious about GÉO LEFÈVRE's idea of mounting a race around FRANCE, and made a point of staying away from an event he feared would be a disaster. But now he had the stunt of a lifetime, the paper *L'AUTO* and his job as editor of it were secure. There was no doubt there would be a second race.

As it turned out, 1904 was the Tour that was to have been the last. Desgrange wrote, 'The Tour de France is finished and the second edition will, I fear, also be the last. It has died of its success, of the blind passions that it unleashed, the abuse and dirty suspicions . . . We will therefore leave it to others to take the chance of taking on an adventure on the scale of the Tour de France.'

The winner of the 1903 Tour, MAURICE GARIN, had been banned for two years for taking short cuts and hanging on to cars; Pierre Chevallier, LUCIEN POTHIER and a rider known only as Chaput were thrown out for life – Pothier for taking a train; and a rider called Prévost was banned for a year.

Garin had won 1903 easily, his rival HIPPOLYTE AUCOUTURIER pulling out with stomach complaints. In 1904 he survived despite more CRASHES and punctures than seemed normal. And he always seemed the victim rather than the instigator, ending up under heaps of riders. Some suspected others were being paid to put him out of the race.

Garin used his influence to insist that Lefèvre should hand him food, which was against the RULES. Lefèvre was young and in awe of riders, who teased him repeatedly. He would have been aware that Aucouturier was in trouble and the last thing he wanted to report was that the other favourite had left the race through hunger or after a row.

The illegal feeding angered other riders, but things were already out of hand. A rider called Chevallier was repeatedly left for dead in the darkness, and yet each time he got back to the race. The suspicion was that he was taking a tow or even a ride from his MANAGER, who was following the race illegally by car. Others were also cheating, sometimes by tying a line to a car with a cork on the other end, which the rider gripped between his teeth to maintain the image of pedalling.

Word of all this spread to SPECTATORS. Fans on the Col de la RÉPUBLIQUE were upset that Garin's illegal food routine, and his assumed complicity in various kinds of cheating, were doing down their local man, Antoine Fauré. They swelled out onto the road in the night and set about Garin and an Italian, Giovanni Gerbi. The mob broke Gerbi's fingers and he had to abandon. Violence turned into a riot which ended only when Lefèvre fired his gun. The mob turned out again the next day, looking now not for cheats but for the officials who had intervened.

The next to cheat was Ferdinand Payan, who was spotted using pacers. A spectator threw a stone, and another fight started. Garin was struck in the face, Pothier on the arm, and Aucouturier waded into the crowd with his arms flailing. Lefèvre was in the middle of it all. This time it was his colleague Jean Miral who fired a gun.

A report from Nîmes on July 16 said, 'Payan is responsible for the trouble at Nîmes and we have the proof . . . . He led the band of apaches who scattered broken glass and nails.' A picture in *La Vie Claire* on July 28 showed cyclists picking up nails scattered beneath the aqueduct at Buc.

After that events became more peaceful, perhaps because the night stages were over and chances to cheat lessened. But national officials were already writing reports. Garin's illegal food cost him disqualification, which seemed tough considering Desgrange had already fined him 500 francs.

Perhaps there was more in the reports than just that. It seems extraordinary even in a less sensitive time that the penalties should be so harsh. The UVF (Union Vélocipédique Française) never explained these decisions, nor did they clearly set out what the riders were said to have done. It left outsiders to look at 'rules 6, 7, 8, 9, 11 and 12' which it said had been broken. Rules six and seven forbade pacers and following cars; the others governed conduct of riders and the race, riding behind or behind pulled by a car, riding anything but a bicycle, using short cuts, changing numbers, illegal feeding, and so on.

Desgrange claimed the UVF had no right to punish riders whom his judges had already penalised. The UVF, on the other hand, insisted that although Desgrange was organiser and judge, only the UVF could discipline riders. What Desgrange did was up to him but the UVF had the ultimate right to impose sanctions. That being so, it wouldn't recognise the result.

The UVF couldn't have been wholly confident because it waited until November before announcing its verdict. No doubt it feared a revolt if it pronounced sentence while emotions were running high. The winner was named eventually as HENRI CORNET, who wasn't entirely clean himself as he too had been warned during the race.

Desgrange, as we have seen, said the Tour was over, finished, killed by 'blind passions'. But nobody was likely to give up a stunt like that and Desgrange, of all people, was never going to think of a better one.

Acknowledgements

Material in this book has been drawn largely from my own computer and cuttings files, with additional research in France, Belgium and Holland. I have relied particularly on the files of the Tour de France and on *L'Équipe, Vélo* and *Libération* in France, *Het Volk* in Belgium, various sources in Holland, and on *Procycling* in London, as well as books published in France, Belgium, Holland and the USA.

Memories and recollections were collected in conversations with, among others, Pierre Ballester, Derek Buttle, Vin Denson, Jan Derksen, Tony Doyle, William Fotheringham, Jacques Goddet, Laurent Jalabert, Jan Janssen, Ferdy Kübler, Hennie Kuiper, Arthur Metcalfe, Peter Nye, Gerald O'Donovan, Jean-Paul Ollivier, Michel Pollentier, Peter Post, Brian Robinson, Stephen Roche, Wim van Est, Rik van Looy, Rik van Steenbergen, Rini Wagtmans and the gravediggers of Lens, to whom I'm grateful for their time.

I'm indebted to the knowledge and enthusiasm of Owen Mulholland in California, to Peter Cossins of *Procycling* for his fact-checking and to Rachel Cugnoni at Yellow Jersey, without whose whip-cracking this book would never have attained the shape it has and may never have appeared at all.